OPERATION KE

ROGER LETOURNEAU
DENNIS LETOURNEAU

OPERATION KE

THE CACTUS AIR FORCE AND THE JAPANESE WITHDRAWAL FROM GUADALCANAL

Naval Institute Press • Annapolis, Maryland

This book has been brought to publication with the generous assistance of Marguerite and Gerry Lenfest.

Naval Institute Press
291 Wood Road
Annapolis, MD 21402

© 2012 by Roger Letourneau and Dennis Letourneau
All rights reserved. No part of this book may be reproduced or utilized in any form or by any means, electronic or mechanical, including photocopying and recording, or by any information storage and retrieval system, without permission in writing from the publisher.

First Naval Institute Press paperback edition published in 2023.
ISBN: 978-1-68247-137-1 (paperback)
ISBN: 978-1-61251-179-5 (eBook)

The Library of Congress has cataloged the hardcover edition as follows:
Letourneau, Roger.
  Operation KE : the Cactus Air Force and the Japanese withdrawal from Guadalcanal / Roger Letourneau and Dennis Letourneau.
   p. cm.
  Includes bibliographical references and index.
  ISBN 978-1-59114-446-5 (hardcover : alk. paper)—ISBN 978-1-61251-179-5 (ebook) 1. Operation KE, 1943. 2. Guadalcanal, Battle of, Solomon Islands, 1942–1943. 3. World War, 1939–1945—Aerial operations. 4. Allied Air Forces in the Solomons. 5. United States. Army Air Forces. Air Force, 13th. I. Letourneau, Dennis. II. Title.
  D767.98.L47 2012
  940.54'265933—dc23

2012026505

∞ Print editions meet the requirements of ANSI/NISO z39.48-1992 (Permanence of Paper).

Printed in the United States of America.

9 8 7 6 5 4 3 2 1

Sometimes during the course of researching historical subjects there occur rare moments when one can reach out and touch the past. In our case, the past came to life when we were given the opportunity and privilege of meeting and interacting with some of the veterans who actually took part in the events we describe. We are honored to dedicate this story to the following airmen, ground crew, and seamen who participated in the events described herein and with whom we had the pleasure of working:

Tom Classen: 72nd BS(H)
Joe Conrad: VMSB-131
Jeff DeBlanc: VMF-112
Basil Debnekoff: 23rd BS(H)
Jim Feliton: VMF-112
John Irwin: VMO-251
Jack Maas: VMF-112
Allan McCartney: VMO-251, VMF-214
Barney McShane: VMSB-131
Ryoji Ohara: 204th Kokutai
Martin Roush: VMSB-131
Harland Van Ness: VP-44
Pat Weiland: VMO-251
Leighton Wood: *PT-124*

Miracles are ceased; and therefore we must needs admit the means how things are perfected.
—William Shakespeare, *Henry V*

CONTENTS

List of Maps and Diagrams   xi
List of Terms, Acronyms, and Abbreviations   xiii
Acknowledgments   xix

Introduction   1

CHAPTER 1   The Genesis of Operation KE-GO   5

CHAPTER 2   Japanese Aircraft and Air-Combat Doctrine   11

CHAPTER 3   American Aircraft and Air-Combat Doctrine   25

CHAPTER 4   Of Pilots and Preparedness   43

CHAPTER 5   Pregame Warm-Ups: Munda and Vila   55

CHAPTER 6   Bombarding the Phoenix   77

CHAPTER 7   Kickoff!   101

CHAPTER 8   Blitzing the Quarterbacks   122

CHAPTER 9   Turnovers   141

CHAPTER 10   Pass Interception   161

CHAPTER 11   General Patch's End Run   175

CHAPTER 12   The Great Escape Begins   192

CHAPTER 13   Night Action and Daytime Pursuit   207

CHAPTER 14	ComAirSol's Vendetta	220
CHAPTER 15	The Half-Time Show	228
CHAPTER 16	The Final Touchdown	247
CHAPTER 17	Of Men and Machines	258
CHAPTER 18	Good Luck or Good Management?	271

	Notes	295
	Bibliography	345
	Index	361

MAPS AND DIAGRAMS

DIAGRAM 1	Freehand drawing of Munda airstrip as it appeared in early January 1943	58
DIAGRAM 2	Freehand drawing of Vila-Stanmore base and airstrip	59
MAP 1	Tokyo Express KE Supply Run Outbound, 11 January 1943	104
MAP 2	Tokyo Express KE Reinforcement Run Outbound, 15 January 1943	111
MAP 3	Tokyo Express KE Reinforcement Run Outbound, 15 January 1943	116
MAP 4	Tokyo Express Russells Garrison Run Inbound, 28 January 1943	144
MAP 5	1st Tokyo Express Evacuation Run Inbound, 1 February 1943	199
MAP 6	1st Tokyo Express Evacuation Run Outbound, 2 February 1943	214
MAP 7	2nd Tokyo Express Evacuation Run Inbound, 4 February 1943	230
MAP 8	2nd Tokyo Express Evacuation Run Inbound, 4 February 1943	237
MAP 9	3rd Tokyo Express Evacuation Run Inbound, 7 February 1943	251

TERMS, ACRONYMS, AND ABBREVIATIONS

AA	antiaircraft
AEM2c	aviation electrician's mate second class
Airman2c	airman second class
AirSols	air forces, Solomons (joint service command)
AK	freighter, cargo ship
AMM3c	aviation machinist's mate third class
Anzac	Australia–New Zealand Army Corps; generic term for joint Australia–New Zealand military units per se
AP	transport
APD	assault purpose destroyer
ARM3c	aviation radioman third class
armor piercing	type of bomb or shell designed to penetrate an outer protective shield and explode within; primarily used against warships, tanks, and heavy fortifications
avgas	aviation gasoline
bandit	enemy aircraft
BG(H)	USAAF bombardment group (heavy), as in 5th BG(H)
BG(M)	USAAF bombardment group (medium), as in 70th BG(M)
Black Cat	USN's Consolidated Catalina flying boat (PBY-5A), used for night patrol
bogey	unidentified aircraft, usually used to describe an unknown radar plot
BS(H)	USAAF bombardment squadron (heavy), as in 394th BS(H)
BS(M)	USAAF bombardment squadron (medium), as in 69th BS(M)
CA	heavy cruiser

CAP	combat air patrol
CAVU	ceiling and visibility unlimited
chutai	JNAF unit equivalent to a USAAF flight or USMC/USN division, usually containing two to three *shotai*, or six to nine aircraft; JAAF unit equivalent to an Allied squadron, containing three to five *shotai*, or nine to fifteen aircraft
CIC	combat information center of a warship, containing electronic surveillance gear used to track surface, subsurface, and airborne units within its range
CinC	commander in chief
CinCPac	commander in chief, Pacific
CL	light cruiser
ComAirSols	commander, air forces, Solomons
ComAirSoPac	commander, air forces, South Pacific
ComGenSoPac	commanding general, South Pacific
ComSoPac	commander, South Pacific
CPO	chief petty officer
CV	aircraft carrier
Dai Hachi Homen Gun	IJA 8th Area Army
Dai Nippon Teikoku Kaigun	IJN; Imperial Japanese Navy
Dai Nippon Teikoku Rikugun	IJA; Imperial Japanese Army
daihatsu	motorized Japanese barge
daisy cutter	bomb or shell designed to destroy through fragmentation of its thick skin of soft metal; primarily an antipersonnel weapon
daitai	JNAF land-based unit equivalent to an Allied squadron, comprising two to three JNAF *chutai*, or twelve to twenty-seven aircraft
DF	to locate by radio direction finding
division	two sections of USMC/USN aircraft; roughly equivalent to a JNAF *chutai*

DSIO	deputy supervising intelligence officer manning coastwatcher HQ on Guadalcanal
Dumbo	generic euphemism for USN amphibious rescue aircraft
element	a unit of two USAAF aircraft; equivalent to a JAAF *shotai*
fish	torpedo
flak	generic term for AA fire
flight	two elements of USAAF aircraft; roughly equivalent to a JNAF *chutai*
general purpose, (GP)	bomb or shell designed to destroy by both concussion (shock wave) and fragmentation; used against shipping, artillery batteries, parked aircraft or vehicles, supply dumps, runways, buildings, and other ground installations
HF	high-frequency radio band
hiko sentai, *sentai*	JAAF air group or, less correctly, an "air regiment," equivalent to an Allied air wing; usually comprising 27 to 36 aircraft; can go up to 45 aircraft
hiko shidan, *shidan*	JAAF "air division," comprising two to three *hikodan*, or 160 to 260 or more aircraft
hikodan	JAAF "air brigade," equivalent to a British or Commonwealth air group, comprising four *hiko sentai*, or 80 to 130 aircraft
hikokitai	JNAF carrier air group, equivalent to an Allied wing, comprising three hikotai or squadrons, or 36 to 81 aircraft
hikotai	JNAF carrier-based air unit equivalent to an Allied squadron, comprising 12 to 27 aircraft
HQ	headquarters
IFF	identification friend or foe; electronic aircraft recognition system
Immelmans	airplane pulls up into a climbing turn, rolls over, and emerges flying in the opposite direction
imperial GHQ	Japanese imperial general headquarters
incendiary	bomb or shell designed to destroy by setting a flammable target on fire

JAAF	Imperial Japanese Army Air Force
JNAF	Imperial Japanese Navy Air Force
knots	aircraft speed in nautical miles per hour (1 nautical mile = 6,075 feet)
koku kantai	JNAF land-based air fleet, equivalent to an Allied air fleet, comprising three or four *koku sentai*, or 162 to 324 or more aircraft
koku sentai	JNAF air flotilla, equivalent to an Allied air group, comprising two or more *kokutai*, or 54 to 72 or more aircraft
kokutai	JNAF land-based air group equivalent to an Allied wing, comprising three *daitai* or squadrons, or 27 to 36 aircraft
LA	leading airman, JNAF; also referred to in some texts as LS for leading seaman
LCT	landing craft, tank
LF	low-frequency radio band
Love, L	Guadalcanal time, as in @1200L, meaning "at 1200 hours Love"; versus "Tokyo time" used by the Japanese, which was two hours slower, thus here 1000 hours
Lufbury circle	flying circles laced with slow rolls to monitor all surrounding airspace
Mae West	life vest
MAG	USMC air group; e.g., MAG-14
Marston matting	perforated steel matting used for rapid construction of temporary runways and landing strips
maru	adjunct applied to names of Japanese merchant ships, e.g., the *Toa Maru 2*
MF	medium-frequency radio band
MG	USMC gunner
mile	used herein means a nautical mile (6,075 feet), versus a statute mile (5,280 feet)
MoMM1c	motor machinist's mate first class
Nanto Homen Kantai	IJN Southeast Area Fleet
NAP1c, 3c	IJN air pilot, first class, third class
paint scraper	a bomb that explodes next to a ship's hull

pancake	originally a wheels-up landing, herein it means any landing without delay or due to urgency
PBY	amphibian; can take off and land on water and on land; also called Catalina
pitot tube	airborne device for measuring wind speed, located near the wingtip on the leading edge
PO	petty officer
PO1c, 2c	petty officer first class, second class, JNAF, IJN
POW	prisoner of war
PT boat	USN motor torpedo boat
R and R	rest and relaxation
R Homen Koku Butai	IJN rear area air force
R4D	USN version of the USAAF's Douglas DC3 transport
Recon	Cactus Fighter Command's fighter controller unit, aka Cactus Recon
Rengo Kantai	IJN combined fleet
rikusentai	Japanese naval infantry, roughly comparable to Marines, but not specifically trained in amphibious warfare
RNZAF	Royal New Zealand Air Force
SBD	USN Douglas Dauntless dive-bomber
section	A unit of two USMC/USN aircraft; equivalent to a JNAF *shotai*
seppuku	hara-kiri, or ritual suicide
shotai	JAAF/JNAF air unit equivalent to an Allied element or section, comprising three aircraft in late 1942/early 1943
six	an enemy plane on one's tail, attacking from astern, or from behind
Slot	nickname for the New Georgia Sound, also called the Groove, the Chute, and Broadway; stretches from Bougainville to Guadalcanal
snafu	situation normal, all f—d up
Split-S	aircraft rolls into a steep curving dive to emerge flying in the opposite direction
Strike Command	Cactus Bomber Command, aka Cactus Strike Command
tail-end Charlie	the last aircraft in a formation

Tally-ho!	code for enemy aircraft sighted
tarfu	Totally and royally f—d up
TBF	USN Grumman Avenger torpedo bomber
TF	USN task force
TG	USN task group
Tokyo Express	generic term for Japanese convoys operating in the Slot
Torpedo Junction	expanse of water between Vella Lavella and Choiseul; Vella Gulf
VF	USN fighter squadron
VGS	USN escort carrier scouting squadron
VMF	USMC fighter squadron
VMGR	USMC aerial refueler transport squadron
VMO	USMC observation squadron
VMSB	USMC scout bombing squadron
VP	USN patrol squadron
VPB	USN patrol bombing squadron
wilco	will comply
WO	warrant officer

ACKNOWLEDGMENTS

Among the more recent monographs and articles dealing with the Solomon Islands campaign that we read, only two treat Operation KE-GO—the Japanese evacuation operation—in any detail: Richard B. Frank's *Guadalcanal: The Definitive Account of the Landmark Battle* and Russell S. Crenshaw Jr.'s *South Pacific Destroyer: The Battle for the Solomons from Savo Island to Vella Gulf*. Of the two, Frank's version is the more comprehensive, examining as it does the land, sea, and air aspects of Operation KE-GO in a fully dedicated chapter. Of necessity, this account treats only the more important air engagements in summary fashion in the interest of presenting the overall story from the multiservice perspectives of both the Americans and the Japanese. We have relied primarily upon these two works, supplemented by many others, to flesh out the overall background of the Solomons campaign against which the Guadalcanal-related air and sea actions we describe in depth were fought.

A major reference source for setting the stage in the three background chapters and for the two concluding chapters was Eric M. Bergerud's *Fire in the Sky: The Air War in the South Pacific*. While we had written several comprehensive drafts of these chapters before consulting this seminal treatise, we were gratified to see that our observations and arguments, for the most part, were confirmed by Mr. Bergerud, who had examined the entire South Pacific theater using a broader time frame and based his conclusions largely on different documentary source material. We were able to strengthen these chapters with information drawn from his excellent work.

We relied primarily on war diaries and combat reports to put together the narratives of events as accurately as possible—straight from the horse's mouth, so to speak. Where possible we fleshed out these accounts with other primary and secondary sources to provide the fullest possible description of these happenings.

The research that eventually culminated in the publication of this manuscript began after our return from a trip to the Solomon Islands in 1999; the bulk of it was undertaken between 2000 and 2005. Barry Zerby of the U.S. National Archives diligently located pertinent records. Mark Evans of the Naval Historical Center (since renamed Naval History and Heritage Command) of the U.S. Navy provided guidance and information on the available U.S. Navy records.

In truth, this manuscript would never have been complete without the selfless contributions over the past twelve years of many individuals whose passion for the subject drove them to go the distance for us in locating and unraveling military sources from both sides of the conflict. Allan Alsleben, Rick Dunn, Minoru Kamada, Jim Lansdale, Allyn Nevitt, Luca Ruffato, Henry Sakaida, Justin Taylan, and Ryan Toews provided a wealth of Japanese data and offered stimulating interpretive opinions. Jiro Yoshida and Koji Takaki kindly contributed their translation expertise, as did Junko Postma, who was instrumental in unlocking the information in the Japanese war diaries. Ewan Stevenson graciously shared his extensive research and correspondence on the subject. Our gratitude also goes out to John Cook (44th FS veteran), Charles Darby, George Dooley (VMSB-131 veteran), Doug Drumheller, Peter Flahaven, Bruce Gamble, John Innes, Lt. Col. (Ret.) Greg Johnson, Danny and Kerrie Kennedy of Dive Gizo, Ragnar Ragnarsson, William Sabel, Lt. Col. Douglas Stumpf (VMGR-234), Richard Watson (VPB-44 veteran), and the Operation KE veterans and their families who shared their recollections and supplied various supporting documents, ranging from logbooks and diaries to photographs.

Finally, an expression of gratitude from both husband and son to Bonnie Letourneau—an accomplished graphic designer who not only Photoshopped the photos used in this book, but also drew the maps and prepared the diagrams for publication.

Roger and Dennis Letourneau

INTRODUCTION

Many are those who have marveled at the rescue by Japanese destroyers of some 10,600 exhausted and emaciated soldiers from certain annihilation or capture on Guadalcanal in early 1943. Some regard the feat as nothing short of a miracle, given that American theater commanders were prepared to contest any imminent enemy activity in the Eastern Solomons. Once the Japanese set in motion Operation KE-GO (or, simply, Operation KE), its six Tokyo Express runs were detected en route and attacked by vigilant U.S. air and naval forces. Yet these missions were successfully carried out although at an acknowledged cost to Dai Nippon Teikoku Kaigun of one destroyer lost and three others damaged. (Actually, some seventeen destroyers were damaged, and double that if counting those that were hit on more than one occasion.) The Japanese also recorded losing around seventy aircraft in KE-related combat. Even then, the Dai Nippon Teikoku Kaigun and Dai Nippon Teikoku Rikugun had braced themselves to pay a far heavier price.

That an evacuation was contemplated at all seems uncharacteristic of the Japanese military. As the war progressed, the U.S. Navy's tightening grip over the Central Pacific successively cut off defending Japanese island garrisons from the rest of the empire. Since reinforcement or withdrawal was no longer possible, and surrender was not an option, death in battle was deemed preferable, guaranteeing resistance to the last man. Conversely, the fight for Guadalcanal was not a last-ditch effort in the same vein, given the possibility of withdrawal from an untenable situation.

Initially, the Eastern Solomons comprised the outermost defensive shield for Rabaul—the heart of Japan's military presence in the South Pacific. However, once the Japanese realized that U.S. troops on Guadalcanal could not be dislodged and were actually assuming the offensive, Lt. Gen. Hitoshi

Imamura, the Dai Hachi Homen Gun's commander, sought to redeploy the remaining 12,000 men of the Japanese 17th Army to the Central Solomons. This revised strategy was to stop the Allied advance up the Solomons in the New Georgia group. Given the pitiful physical condition and lack of wherewithal of these troops, both he and Adm. Jinichi Kusaka, who commanded both the Nanto Homen Kantai and the 11th Koku Kantai, believed they could do little to the Americans if they were left to fight to the death on Guadalcanal; these men could better serve the emperor at another time in another place. So, before the window of opportunity slammed shut, imperial GHQ gave the 17th Army a reprieve at the eleventh hour.

Operation KE marked several departures from the features that had characterized the Guadalcanal campaign till then.

First, though the Imperial Japanese Navy (IJN) sent a potent task force deep into no-man's-land, the provocation did not bring about a major clash with the U.S. Navy. After an attempt to ambush Adm. Nobutake Kondo's Advance Force was thwarted by Japanese air power, the U.S. Navy was content to hold sizable task forces in the wings, waiting for any further escalation that might open a window of opportunity for a full-fledged fleet action. This "sitzkrieg" posture aptly suited the IJN goal of evacuating the 17th Army with as little interference as possible.

Second, in a theater where naval warfare was characterized by major surface actions and air–sea battles dominated by aircraft carriers, all airborne antishipping and base-suppression sorties mounted during Operation KE were flown exclusively by land-based air power, operating entirely from insular airfields—the "unsinkable" aircraft carriers. KE-related seaborne actions involved only light cruisers, destroyers, and motor torpedo boats.

Third, several *kokutai* of the Dai Nippon Teikoku Kaigun Kokutai and the Dai Nippon Teikoku Rikugun were assembled into an air armada to do battle with a significantly reinforced, though marginally less numerous, Cactus Air Force for the first time in the Guadalcanal campaign.

Fourth, while both sides still flew lengthy missions between the Western and Eastern Solomons as they strove to neutralize each other's main air bases, taxing the limit of aircraft ranges and aircrew endurance, the air-combat zone shifted toward the Central Solomons—within comfortable range of major Japanese airbases in Bougainville, virtually on the doorstep of a new forward airstrip in the New Georgia group, and close to a seaplane base on nearby Santa Ysabel. Henceforth, the Japanese could benefit from shorter operating ranges and better utilize their new airstrip at Munda Point. Together, these advantages presented an unprecedented opportunity to protect Operation KE's Tokyo Express runs by holding American air power temporarily at bay.

Notwithstanding suggestions of the miraculous, when the air–sea engagements surrounding the Japanese withdrawal are analyzed objectively, the course of events suggests that the Fates had less influence on the success of the Guadalcanal evacuation than did military professionalism. The Japanese developed a reasonably sound strategy that not only profited from the closer proximity of the prospective combat zone, but also exploited tactically the strengths and limitations of the tools and methods of war then employed in the South Pacific.

Admittedly, records left by Allied and Japanese airmen regarding their respective roles in intercepting or defending the historic Tokyo Express runs of 10–11, 14–15, and 28–29 January, as well as 1–2, 4–5, and 7–8 February, are incomplete—understandably so. These often terse and fragmentary accounts are the impressions of men reacting to a kaleidoscope of fleeting images in the heat of air combat. Those accounts of the web of ancillary actions woven around Operation KE are frequently found to be no less wanting. Opposing combatants were almost always at variance with one another regarding what actually transpired.

For example, victories claimed by pilots on one side were invariably greater than the losses acknowledged by the other side. Was a given plane destroyed? Shot down? Probably shot down? Damaged? In the absence of gun cameras, individual judgment calls on the part of participating airmen prevailed, and errors abounded on both sides.

Aircraft misidentification was another anomaly. When it arrived in the Solomons, the JAAF Ki-43 Hayabusa fighter was universally mistaken for a new variant of the JNAF's A6M Zero. Conversely, Japanese pilots often confused Bell's P-39 Airacobra with Curtis' P-40 Warhawk, and Grumman's TBF Avenger was sometimes mixed up at long distance with Grumman's similarly silhouetted F4F Wildcat. Although the Zero was painted either grey (carrier based) or green (landn based) with a black cowl, observations by U.S. airmen included orange, dune colored, tan, dirty brown, yellow lacquered with a red cowl, and mustard yellow with a rusty-red cowl—usually when describing the Hamps of the 204th Kokutai. Sunlight reflecting off the peculiar light-grey shade of this unit's planes at different times of the day probably accounts for this nonexistent spectrum of hues.

This having been said, when integrated with other historical records plus a host of secondary treatises, these incomplete and oft-times inaccurate observations—as set down in the combat action reports and war diaries of participating American and Japanese air and naval units—still provide fresh insight into the hitherto fragmented story of the Cactus Air Force and its achievements between mid-December 1942 and mid-February 1943. Distilled from a synthesis of these sources, the following account fleshes out a glaring gap in the historical record by chronicling the air war that was fought over Operation KE—one of World War II's "great escapes."

CHAPTER 1
THE GENESIS OF OPERATION KE-GO

The Solomon Islands were an obscure British colonial backwater until the dramatic sweep of Japanese military might through Southeast Asia and the western reaches of the Pacific unwittingly propelled this malarial archipelago to center stage. Even when a series of calamitous defeats beset them after Pearl Harbor, the Allies brooked no thoughts of acquiescing to Japanese imperialism; a counteroffensive aimed at dismantling the new Southeast Asia Co-prosperity Sphere was inevitable, but who would have guessed it was destined to begin on Guadalcanal?

Adm. Isoroku Yamamoto, the architect of the attack on Pearl Harbor, remained convinced that Hawaii was the main threat to Japan's newly won empire—an unshakable conviction that spawned his overwrought Operation MI-GO, designed to draw Hawaiian-based U.S. carriers into a decisive naval action by invading Midway Island. Having crippled the U.S. Navy's surface fleet at Pearl Harbor, Yamamoto believed that destruction of these flattops would leave Hawaii under a perceived threat of invasion and provide Japan with the leverage it needed to force the Americans to accept a truce based on the geopolitical status quo. Admiral Yamamoto duly led his Rengo Kantai to Midway, where a fateful clash on 4 June 1942 saw U.S. naval air power sink four Japanese fleet carriers in exchange for the loss of the *Yorktown*.

For its part, the Imperial Japanese Navy general staff regarded Australia as the greater threat to Japan because it constituted a strategic base from which the Allies could interdict the flow of natural resources—especially oil from Borneo and the Dutch East Indies. In January 1942 the Japanese established major South Pacific bases at the captured Australian outposts of Rabaul and Kavieng in the Bismarck Archipelago to protect this fragile lifeline. They went on to occupy Bougainville on the edge of the Western

Solomons, thereby moving swiftly to sever the seaborne lifeline between Australia and the United States.

In addition, Japan's plan to secure New Guinea went awry at the Battle of the Coral Sea. Despite the destruction of the U.S. fleet carrier *Lexington* and heavy damage to her sister *Yorktown*, which more than offset the loss of the light carrier *Shoho* and serious damage to the fleet carrier *Shokaku*, Japanese air groups were badly ravaged for the first time. Deprived of adequate air cover, the Port Moresby invasion fleet had to turn back. The forfeiture of four more carriers and most of their aircrews at Midway compelled the Japanese to attempt, unsuccessfully, the capture of Port Moresby via a land-based assault across the rugged, inhospitable Owen Stanley mountain range.

As a prelude to their Coral Sea operation, the Japanese leaped from Bougainville to clear across the Solomons to seize the modest Australian seaplane base and naval anchorage at Tulagi Harbor in the Florida Islands on 3 May 1942. This move represented the next step toward the seizure of major island groups between New Caledonia and Samoa in Japan's bid to seal off Australia.

Adm. Ernest King, chief of U.S. Naval Operations, convinced the Allied combined chiefs of staff that a Japanese presence in the Solomons seriously menaced the "island continent." To counter this threat the Americans received the blessing of their British and French allies to fortify Samoa and occupy Fiji, the New Hebrides, and New Caledonia. Admiral King and Gen. George Marshall then agreed to restore Allied control over the Eastern Solomons. First, the Americans would move into the nearby Santa Cruz Islands; second, they would retake the Tulagi anchorage and seaplane base. Both sides were now poised for an unanticipated clash in the Solomon Islands.

At this juncture Japanese troops from Tulagi landed on Guadalcanal near Lunga Point on 8 June 1942 and began to build a wharf. Coastwatcher Martin Clemens soon reported that large-scale grass burning was in progress on Lunga Plain to create what looked to be an airstrip. On 4 July U.S. intelligence intercepted enemy messages regarding plans to move a large force of troops to Guadalcanal; Japanese transports began to land engineers, pioneers, laborers, and light construction equipment at Lunga Point two days later. Within two weeks a B-17 reconnaissance flight confirmed that construction of an airstrip was in progress.

From Guadalcanal, Japanese long-range bombers could interdict Allied shipping along the sea-lanes to Australia and stymie any Allied effort to advance upon Japan's Rabaul bastion through the South Pacific. A joint directive issued by Admiral King and General Marshall on 2 July 1942 cancelled the USN's upcoming Santa Cruz operation. Instead, Adm. Chester Nimitz was ordered to galvanize his amphibious forces for a major thrust in the Eastern Solomons. Thus was Operation Watchtower conceived as the first phase of a full-scale Allied offensive aimed at removing the threat to Australia and neutralizing Rabaul.

After a week of concentrated air bombardment by B-17Es of the USAAF's 11th BG(H), followed by a naval barrage on D-day, the first waves of U.S. Marines went ashore unopposed at Guadalcanal and under fire at Tulagi and the adjacent islets of Gavutu-Tanambogo on 7 August 1942—exactly eight months after Pearl Harbor and one day after the Japanese had completed their new airstrip for fighter operations.

Armed with poor intelligence, the Japanese seriously underestimated the strength of the defensive perimeter established by the 1st Marine Division around the captured airstrip. They launched their intended recapture of newly named Henderson Field with an ill-planned counterattack by an understrength battalion of elite troops that was repulsed with staggering losses. Then they concocted a series of complex land–sea–air counterstrokes that misfired because Guadalcanal's nearly impenetrable rainforest prevented the 17th Army from coordinating its attacks with supporting naval bombardments and air raids. In contrast, Brig. Gen. Archer Vandegrift's Marines remained on the defensive. Benefitting from interior lines of communication, they whittled down their aggressive and overconfident foe while building up their own strength for an eventual offensive to sweep the Japanese off the island.

Both sides lost heavily in ships, planes, and men in several naval and air–sea battles that accompanied the struggle on Guadalcanal, but the U.S. Navy was able to replace its losses more readily than could its adversary. Japanese naval air and surface-fleet strength grew steadily weaker; by the end of 1942 Japan could no longer sustain its aggressive posture in the Solomons. Inevitably, American land, sea, and air forces went on the offensive.

Under Vandegrift's successor, Maj. Gen. Alexander Patch, GIs and Marines drove the 17th Army back while carrier and land-based air power, supported by several task forces, choked off the enemy's supply lines from Rabaul. Wracked by disease, starvation, and battle fatigue, bereft of arms, ammunition, food, and medical supplies, and short of reinforcements to replace losses from combat and illness, Lt. Gen. Harukichi Hyakutake's valiant soldiers could do little more than fight a stubborn rearguard action as they slowly retreated westward along Guadalcanal's north coast.

Watching the fortunes of General Hyakutake's troops deteriorate over months of successive defeats after having fed some 30,000 men into the meat grinder, the Imperial Japanese Army general staff waxed acutely sensitive to incessant prodding from the IJN for the IJA to recapture Henderson Field. Japanese army leaders reacted by criticizing the navy's inability to keep the emperor's soldiers adequately supplied and reinforced and went on to chastise the IJN for its failure to choke off the steady buildup of American military might on Guadalcanal.

The JNAF now counted on its newly formed 11th Koku Kantai to wrest control of the air over the Eastern Solomons as the prelude to a new ground offensive; visiting staff officers found the JNAF's land-based *kokutai* in Rabaul and Bougainville at substantially less than full strength, however. Vice Adm. Jinichi Kusaka had already felt compelled to divert some of his naval air power to bolster the New Guinea campaign. Reluctantly, it was decided that JAAF units would have to reinforce land-based naval air power in the Solomons. Even then, war games at Rabaul predicted that Guadalcanal-bound convoys of *maru* would never reach the 17th Army unless the Japanese firmly dominated the airspace above the Slot—something they had yet to do.

Lt. Gen. Hitoshi Imamura had managed to concentrate some 50,000 troops at Rabaul by mid-December 1942. However, after seven out of eleven transports loaded with reinforcements had failed to reach Guadalcanal a month earlier, he was at a loss about how to get even some of these men to General Hyakutake without subjecting them to punishing U.S. air attacks. Frustrated, he reassigned these soldiers to bolster the flagging Japanese campaign in New Guinea; control of this expansive island now surpassed the retention of Guadalcanal as the highest defense priority in the Southeast Area.

Lacking sufficient air cover, the IJN by the end of November was reduced to supplying and reinforcing the Guadalcanal garrison by destroyers, submarines, and air drops alone. Interdiction of Rear Adm. Raizo Tanaka's Guadalcanal Reinforcement Unit by American planes and PT boats escalated between late-November and mid-December 1942, culminating in the loss of Tanaka's flagship, the new AA destroyer *Teruzuki*, and the serious wounding of the admiral himself. Hospitalized in Rabaul, the despondent Tanaka rashly issued a memorandum urging the abandonment of Guadalcanal. Such blatant defeatism was still anathema to imperial GHQ; Admiral Tanaka was summarily banished from the bridge of a warship and posted on shore, where he languished until the war's end. Rear Adm. Tomiji Koyanagi was appointed to replace him.

Several army delegations from imperial GHQ graphically described the deteriorating condition of the 17th Army in late 1942, expressing grave doubts about its ability to mount yet another offensive. The last fact-finding mission returned to Japan in December with Rabaul's unvarnished conclusion that time had run out to muster enough resources to turn the tide. The question now was whether to abandon or rescue the remaining 12,000 troops.

Navy planners at imperial GHQ doubted the 17th Army could be evacuated without prohibitive losses in naval surface and air units. Embittered army counterparts charged the navy with flinching at the eleventh hour, insisting that Admiral Yamamoto commit his destroyer flotillas to the primary transport role in lieu of pledging barges and collapsible boats, which the army regarded as little more than a token gesture. A skeptical Yamamoto surmised that perhaps one-third of General Hyakutake's troops could be saved at the cost of half the destroyers involved; under mounting pressure he had little choice but to accede reluctantly to the evacuation, however.

A recommendation to extricate the remnants of the 17th Army from the "Island of Death" received the tacit approval of imperial GHQ toward the end of December and the official sanction of Emperor Hirohito on 4 January 1943. Operation KE-GO (or KE) was jointly finalized by the Nanto Homen Kantai, the Dai Hachi Homen Gun, and the Rengo Kantai on 9 January. Nanto Homen Kantai issued its detailed operations plan for KE on 16 January. At last armed with this document, Admiral Kusaka hastened to cooperate with General Imamura to implement the evacuation plan.

Twenty-two destroyers, including replacements, were ultimately assigned to carry out Operation KE; all had previously served with the Guadalcanal

Reinforcement Unit. Admiral Kusaka placed them under the command of Rear Adm. Shintaro Hashimoto on 26 January. Nanto Homen Kantai also earmarked the two heavy cruisers *Chokai* and *Kumano*, plus the light cruiser *Sendai*, for retention at Kavieng in New Ireland should the Tokyo Express require support from heavier naval firepower, and removed itself to Faisi from Rabaul on 29 January to oversee the evacuation phase of Operation KE.

The approved plan called for Admiral Hashimoto's destroyer flotilla to retrieve the 17th Army in three runs spaced over a two-week period, ending no later than 10 February. Landing barges and collapsible boats would be brought in to load the destroyers. The evacuees would be taken to the Shortlands for processing and reassignment.

As they invariably did throughout the war, Japanese planners concocted geographically dispersed, diversionary initiatives to mask the real intention of Operation KE from American intelligence. Moreover, at the beginning of January they changed their ciphers. No longer able to read Japanese codes in depth, U.S. theater commanders were kept on pins and needles by snippets of intelligence reporting (1) increased convoy activity between Truk and New Guinea and Rabaul and between Rabaul and the Solomons; (2) sizable troop and materiel movements to Rabaul; (3) a concentration of Japanese capital warships at Truk; (4) the reinforcement of JNAF Kokutai in Rabaul and Bougainville; and (5) the construction of airstrips in the New Georgia group.

American intelligence had interpreted such developments correctly up till the waning days of 1942; the Japanese military had indeed been preparing for a new offensive in the South Pacific. When this initiative was scrapped and replaced by preparations for the Guadalcanal evacuation operation, the activity associated with the change merely served to perpetuate Allied belief that the perceived buildup was proceeding apace. Ironically, discovery of an upcoming operation called KE-GO in conjunction with these redirected preparations served to reinforce Allied convictions that a renewed offensive in the Solomons was in the offing, thereby successfully masking the true Japanese intent to pull out of Guadalcanal.

CHAPTER 2
JAPANESE AIRCRAFT AND AIR-COMBAT DOCTRINE

Four JNAF fighter *kokutai* of the 11th Koku Kantai, which had been somewhat beefed up to support both the New Guinea campaign and a renewed Guadalcanal offensive, were now ordered to establish air superiority over the Slot by annihilating U.S. fighter squadrons as a prelude to Operation KE. A *hikokitai* of scarce carrier-based pilots and planes was detached to lend support to the IJN's land-based *kokutai*.

All of these JNAF fighter wings flew the legendary Zero. Guadalcanal's fighter pilots dueled with three variants of this formidable Mitsubishi adversary: the A6M2 Model 21, initially referred to as a Nagoya Zero (a reference to Mitsubishi's Nagoya aircraft plant), and later assigned the code name Zeke; the A6M3 Model 32, at first called a Mark II Zero, and later codenamed Hamp; and the A6M3 Model 22, also referred to as a Nagoya Zero and a Zeke.

The 204th Kokutai carried a mixed establishment of sixty Model 21 Zekes and Model 32 Hamps, whereas the 252nd, 253rd, and 582nd Kokutai each had an authorized strength of forty-eight Zeros. The 252nd and 253rd operated a mix of Model 21 Zekes and Model 32 Hamps; the 582nd operated the Model 22 Zeke and the Model 32 Hamp exclusively.

Designed to play a chiefly offensive role, the Zero reached a top speed of nearly three hundred knots. It exhibited maximum agility in medium-speed combat below 25,000 feet, where no Allied fighter could turn inside it. The A6M's cruising range was phenomenal even without an external drop tank; an auxiliary tank readily allowed it to fly down the Slot from faraway Rabaul to do battle over Guadalcanal. The standard killing power of all three variants resided in a pair of wing-mounted 20-mm cannons supplemented by two cowl-mounted 7.7-mm machine guns.

The fastest and most maneuverable variant was the Model 32 Hamp. Arriving in the South Pacific in September 1942, it incorporated a more-powerful prime mover than the Model 21 Zeke, and its wingtips were squared or clipped to increase its speed. Possessing an operational ceiling higher than the Zeke's, it could also dive and climb faster, and it rolled better at high speeds. On the down side, the Hamp's aerobatic agility fell off slightly due to its extra weight and modified wingtips. Its larger, turbo-supercharged aeroengine left less room for fuel, thereby limiting its range to three-quarters' of the Zeke's. Initially, the Hamp played a defensive role until the construction of airfields in southern Bougainville enabled it to fly into the Eastern Solomons with enough fuel reserve for extended combat—especially if fitted with a drop tank.

The Model 22 Zeke had the stronger aeroengine, smaller fuel capacity, and shorter range of the Model 32 Hamp, but its overall performance resembled more that of the Model 21 Zeke.

As for the JAAF's 6th Hiko Shidan, the success of its proposed offensive against Guadalcanal depended on whether escorting Nakajima Ki-43 Hayabusa fighters of the crack 12th Hikodan could shoot down American interceptors in large numbers. The Hayabusa—code name Oscar—was the JAAF's frontline fighter. Powered by the same aeroengine as the JNAF's Zero, the smaller and lighter army fighter could climb faster and higher. Its extendable butterfly combat flaps enabled the Oscar to even turn inside a Zero in simulated combat and perform complex aerobatics with ease. Otherwise, the ultralight Oscar found itself outclassed in diving and zooming. Moreover, the Oscar attained a maximum speed under 270 knots and had an inferior cruising range that could be extended, however, by carrying up to two auxiliary fuel tanks, enabling it to reach Guadalcanal from Bougainville with a sufficient reserve for limited combat.

Like the inferior fighters that the Oscar had bested in China, the latest version of the Ki-43 was still woefully underarmed at the time of Operation KE, sporting only a single 7.7-mm machine gun mated to a 12.7-mm machine cannon. But these cowl-mounted weapons were highly accurate over long distances. In the hands of a skilled pilot, the sharp-cornering Oscar was still a dangerous adversary for any Allied fighter pilot foolish enough to tackle one in a close-in dogfight.

The Oscar made its debut in the Solomons with Operation KE; hence, the newcomer was unfamiliar to Guadalcanal's aviators. Though it was smaller, the Ki-43 closely resembled the Model 21 and Model 22 Zekes in both appearance and performance. Not surprisingly, when they did encounter the nimble Nakajima fighter, American pilots consistently identified it as a variant of its Mitsubishi cousin.

Veteran Zero and Oscar pilots were favored to emerge victorious from any dogfight fought on their terms, even if opposing pilots were of comparable competence. "I think an Army P-39 pilot chased one of them [a Zero] around Baraku Island one day—around and around and around and he never did get to shoot the Jap," marveled Maj. Joe Renner, CO of VMO-251. "The Jap planes are very maneuverable—jinking and flying up the coves and jumping over the coconut trees and down the other side—the P-39 just couldn't get on him."

An aggressive samurai ethos, coupled to the superior maneuverability of Japanese fighters, largely molded Tokyo's air-combat doctrine; the fighter pilot's tactical lexicon was founded on offensive tactics that had been forged in China. Japanese pilots preferred to engage Chiang Kai-shek's obsolescent air force in large battles fought at medium speeds to exploit the superior dexterity of their aircraft. In these engagements, the so-called Chungking method prevailed: that is, Japanese pilots were cautioned to engage the enemy only under favorable conditions, such as numerical superiority, surprise, altitude advantage, or an up-sun position.

Until 1943 the basic Japanese air-combat unit remained the *shotai*—an element or section of three aircraft flying in a vee formation not dissimilar to the British vic. The vees quickly dissolved upon initial contact, each *shotai* often reforming into line-astern, with the two wingmen trailing the *shotai* leader in a loose string before breaking up into one-on-one duels.

The *shotai* rarely flew in a rigid triangle when in a combat zone. The *shotai* leader maintained a straight, level course while his two wingmen flew well back, executing a mixed horizontal and vertical weaving pattern to protect his and each other's tails. Thus, large Japanese formations appeared bereft of structure or discipline, with planes diving, zooming, and even looping. But this apparent raggedness was misleading: each extended *shotai* functioned like a Venus flytrap. If one of its members was bounced by an Allied fighter, the other two would either turn inward to envelop the attacker in a pincer or break outward to fall back on his tail.

In the Solomons, however, the Japanese ran into combat-wise American pilots who adopted the German two-man *rotte* system for mutual protection and who refused to mix it up in their less-agile ships, thereby forcing the Japanese to modify their tactics. By early 1943 the growing influx of less-skilled aviators led both the JNAF and JAAF to replace dogfighting with a new offensive concept: hit-and-run attacks in three-man *shotai*, delivered by executing high, diving passes followed by steep, zooming pullouts. Moreover, Japanese veterans readily improved their own defensive tactics; they continued to practice weaving, but now learned to stick together as units in their *shotai*. They also began to use other maneuvers for mutual protection, such as Lufbury circles laced with slow rolls to monitor all surrounding airspace.

Lt. Zenjiro Miyano, the 204th Kokutai's brilliant tactician, came to favor the U.S. two-man element or section over the Japanese three-man *shotai*. During Operation KE, the 204th's *chutai* sometimes showed up in multiples of two planes, rather than three, or multiples of two plus a *shotai* of three, implying that the unit was already experimenting with the *rotte* system. Adoption of the tactically superior *rotte* may also help explain the proliferation of aces and near-aces in this particular *kokutai*.

Since Imperial Japanese Navy and Imperial Japanese Army fighters were lightly armed, accurate aerial gunnery was crucial. The better Zero pilots learned to find the range of their quarry with their 7.7-mm machine guns before opening up with their 20-mm cannon. Frequently, the cowl-mounted 7.7s were so accurately trained on the enemy's cockpit that their fire killed or wounded the pilot outright.

Highly disciplined pilot training tended to engender a certain tactical rigidity, but, however limited or predictable their repertoire of maneuvers, veteran Japanese fighter pilots could execute their maneuvers with consummate skill. They proved to be worthy adversaries, never to be underestimated. On the other hand, less-experienced pilots could be quickly overwhelmed by task overload, especially if their leader happened to fall at the outset of an air battle. Not yet tactically competent or capable of instinctive decision making under fire, novices became easy prey. This situation was worsened in the JNAF by a habit of familiarizing only *daitai* and *chutai* leaders with the tactical details of a given mission. Junior pilots were expected to follow their leaders' signals in flight.

Moreover, since all Japanese fighters were constructed to save weight, they featured neither armor protection for the pilot's seat nor self-sealing fuel tanks, rendering them vulnerable to the heavy gun batteries of Allied fighters. Tactical mistakes all too often proved instantly fatal until pilot-seat armor and self-sealing fuel tanks were installed to give pilots some reprieve.

Japanese fighter pilots regarded their aircraft as high-performance weapons that became extensions of themselves in intensely personalized, one-on-one, aerial duels. But Allied pilots learned to avoid this kind of combat, relying on quite different tactics that exploited the qualities of their better-armed and sturdier fighters. Consequently, though they could collectively field more aircraft than the Americans on the eve of Operation KE, JNAF and JAAF airmen were saddled with less-robust planes and flawed doctrinal baggage. Ill equipped to persevere through a renewed slugfest of attrition, they faced the more daunting challenge.

The Faisi-based R Homen Koku Butai was formed on 5 September 1942. Its float fighters, though agile when flown well, were adequate performers at best, achieving only moderate success against most U.S. fighters.

The Nakajima A6M2-N Rufe was designed as an amphibious version of the Mitsubishi A6M2 Zeke, sporting identical firepower. Because of its pontoons, however, its maximum speed fell below 250 knots, and its overall performance suffered. Nevertheless, it could still cruise as far as Guadalcanal from seaplane tenders operating furtively in the Slot or from the 802nd and 958th Kokutai's shared anchorage and ramp-equipped servicing facility at Nila, on Poporang Island. Also, Rufes could stage through an advance seaplane base at Rekata Bay from which they could easily raid Henderson Field and its satellites. However, in deference to the plane's comparative vulnerability, the IJN limited most of its Rufes to defensive patrols over Bougainville and its environs from November 1942 on. Even then, despite the inferior performance of their float fighters, Rufe pilots seldom hesitated to take on U.S. fighters.

Not only did the floatplanes of the R Homen Koku Butai share CAP duties over Guadalcanal-bound convoys with Zeros, but also, beginning

2 January 1943, they assumed this role exclusively during nocturnal hours. Most adaptable was the Mitsubishi F1M2 float biplane. Slower than regular fighters at two hundred knots, the two-seat Pete was lightly armed, featuring just two forward-firing 7.7-mm machine guns and one similar rear-mounted weapon. But it was highly maneuverable like all biplanes, and with a range of four hundred miles carrying two 133-pound bombs, it proved ideal for harassing PT boats, destroyers, and corvettes at night with strafing and bombing attacks. The Aichi E13A Jake patrol floatplane was also used for nocturnal CAP duty. This long-range, three-seat monoplane could carry 551 pounds of bombs or depth charges. Maximum speed, however, was only two hundred knots, and it was poorly armed, sporting a single, rear-firing 7.7-mm machine gun.

The floatplanes assigned from the 958th Kokutai or the seaplane tenders *Kamikawa Maru*, *Kunikawa Maru*, and *Sanyo Maru* to fly nocturnal CAP over a Guadalcanal-bound convoy would usually proceed from their Poporang seaplane base to the forward staging base at Rekata Bay, where they would be refueled to await the convoy. When the Tokyo Express arrived in the Central Solomons at twilight, up to four floatplanes would take over the covering screen, escorting the ships to Guadalcanal and back to the Central Solomons. Some floatplanes were eventually based at Rekata, which was completed in August 1942 to incorporate large fuel and ammo dumps, in addition to a modest maintenance facility.

The IJN committed a dive-bomber and two twin-engine level bombers to carry out the bomber offensive planned for KE.

The Aichi D3A—code name Val—was still the frontline JNAF dive-bomber in early 1943. Fitted with a spatted, fixed landing gear, the D3A2 reached a surprising 250 knots and could fly nearly nine hundred miles with a full bomb load of 805 pounds. Standard armament was a pair of wing-mounted 7.7-mm machine guns and a rear-firing 7.7-mm gun. When flown by an experienced crew, the Val proved to be a stable and accurate bombing platform.

Three JNAF medium-bomber *kokutai* were assigned to launch daylight attacks on Henderson Field and its satellite strips during the last week of January to help achieve command of the air. A program of nocturnal harassment raids was also scheduled between mid-January and mid-February to disrupt the Canal's air operations.

The Mitsubishi-built G4M Betty—dubbed a Mitsubishi 01 and a Mitsubishi T-97 by Guadalcanal airmen—was designed as a fast, long-range, torpedo bomber for the JNAF, but was quickly pressed into service as a medium land-attack bomber. With a maximum speed of around 250 knots, the Betty was armed with four 20-mm cannons plus two 7.7-mm machine guns. Lack of adequate crew and fuel-tank protection earned the aircraft an unflattering reputation for catching fire under attack; originally called the "flying cigar," G4M aircrews morbidly rechristened it the "flying lighter" and the "Type 01 lighter."

The G4M's Achilles' heel was its small bomb capacity. Prior to the provision of staging bases in Bougainville, the round-trip from Vunakanau Field in Rabaul—call sign MU—to Guadalcanal limited the Betty's payload to one 551-pound bomb plus two 133-pound bombs. Even after Buka, Kahili, and Kara came on line as staging fields, permitting maximum payloads of three to four 551-pound bombs or fifteen 133-pound bombs per aircraft, this marginally heavier punch still failed to disrupt the operations of the Canal's airfields, especially since high attrition rates prevented Betty *kokutai* from amassing enough bombers to strike a knockout blow. In truth, beneath the rhetoric the Betty raids planned for Operation KE were little more than decoy missions—feints to lure Guadalcanal's fighters up so they could be destroyed by large swarms of escorting Zeros.

Also designed as an attack bomber, the Mitsubishi G3M Nell predated the Betty. This twin-engine aircraft normally carried around 1,323 pounds of bombs or a single aerial torpedo. The Nell reached a maximum speed of two hundred knots and could cruise up to 2,700 miles. But its light armament featured only one 20-mm cannon plus four 7.7-mm machine guns and, like the Betty, the Nell lacked adequate aircrew and fuel-tank protection. The IJN added a limited number of Nells to its Southeast Area roster in early 1942 to support its Betty *kokutai*. The last major mission flown by the G3M in the Solomons was a torpedo attack against an American task force, delivered by the 701st Kokutai during Operation KE.

For its part, the JAAF committed its twin-engine Kawasaki Ki-48 Lily to assist overworked JNAF bomber units in winning mastery of the air over the Slot. Originally designed to fulfill the JAAF's need for a fast, light bomber similar to the successful Russian Tupolev, the Ki-48 turned out to be pedestrian at best. Though it could fly at 260 knots and had a cruising range of 1,300 miles, it had only three 7.7-mm machine guns for protection and carried a negligible bomb load of 1,160 pounds. The Lily performed adequately as a low-level, hit-and-run bomber only at night or under local air superiority, due to its vulnerability to enemy fighter attack. In Operation KE the Lily, like its IJN counterparts, was to act as bait to draw American fighters into combat.

During the Guadalcanal campaign, the long-range eye of the Japanese was the Mitsubishi Ki-46 reconnaissance plane, supplemented by bombers and flying boats. The twin-engine, two-seat Dinah was designed to fly at altitudes up to 34,400 feet, where, with a top speed of nearly 350 knots, it had little trouble evading Allied interceptors. The Dinah was armed with a single rear-firing 7.7-mm machine gun to save weight. Although it was built for the JAAF, this highly successful reconnaissance aircraft was also used by JNAF fighter units. With authorized establishments that included eight reconnaissance planes each, the Japanese navy's 204th, 252nd, and 253rd Kokutai regularly flew Dinah missions over the Slot.

Used for long-range reconnaissance, attack, and rescue missions, the H6K Mavis and the H8K Emily were four-engine flying boats built by Kawanishi for the JNAF. The H6K5's maximum speed reached two hundred knots, and it could cruise up to 3,660 nautical miles. Crewed by nine men, it could carry two torpedoes or up to 2,205 pounds of bombs. The Mavis was defended by four 7.7-mm machine guns in bow, beam, and dorsal positions, and a 20-mm cannon in the tail. Ten men flew the newer H8K2 Emily, whose speed reached nearly 250 knots. With a range of 3,900 miles, it could deliver two torpedoes or a bomb load of 4,410 pounds. Defensive armament consisted in part of three 7.7-mm machine guns in ventral and aft-window positions; five 20-mm cannon fired from power-operated bow, dorsal, and tail turrets; plus two beam blisters. The 851st Kokutai, headquartered at Faisi with moorings along Shortland's shoreline, handled most of the IJN's flying boats during Operation KE; the 802nd Kokutai operated at least one additional *shotai*.

The total number of operable land-based aircraft under both Southeast Area IJN and Southeast Area IJA command is difficult to estimate, but likely added up to a conservative 413 planes. Of these, it was the JNAF component that really spearheaded the air support for KE.

Lt. Mitsugu Kofukuda led an advance detachment of eighteen 6th Kokutai Zeros to Rabaul—call sign YO—on 21 August 1942 where they were joined by the CO, Capt. Chisato Morita, in addition to twenty-six other veterans. Captain Morita then brought the entire unit down to Bougainville after Kahili airfield (also known as Buin airfield)—call sign TSU—was completed on 8 October. Five more distinguished fliers joined the 6th Kokutai after the unit became the 204th Kokutai on 1 November. By the time Operation KE began, the 204th boasted at least eight ace-quality pilots, including Lieutenant Miyano, WO Hatsuo Hidaka, PO1c Yukiharu Ozeki, PO1c Kiyoshi Shimizu, LA Shoichi Sugita, LA Masaaki Shimakawa, LA Ryoji Ohara, and LA Kenji Yanagiya. Ohara would achieve fame as the "killer of Rabaul," with forty-eight victories. Sugita would ultimately claim more than one hundred twenty victories, but his confirmed tally was closer to a still-impressive seventy.

The 252nd Kokutai under Lt. Motonari Suho transferred its Zeros to Kahili on 9 November and stayed there until 16 January. The 252nd briefly moved back to Rabaul until 25 January, when they advanced to Ballale to defend the Buin-Faisi area against U.S. air raids. Under orders to transfer to Truk on 1 February, the unit's move was postponed until after Operation KE. In addition to Suho, with the 252nd flew WO Bunkichi Nakajima, PO1c Kaneyoshi Muto, PO2c Tomezo Yamamoto, and PO2c Isamu Miyazaki—all aces or future aces.

A contingent of Zeros from the Kavieng-based 253rd Kokutai joined the 204th and 252nd at Kahili in November. Cdr. Yoshito Kobayashi brought with him future aces PO1c Minoru Honda and PO1c Shigeru Shibukawa. The remaining 253rd *daitai* left Kavieng on 28 January, pausing at Buka to fly one mission on 30 January before advancing permanently to Kahili the next day.

The 582nd Kokutai first flew out of Rabaul in August 1942 as the 2nd Kokutai; then it operated from the newly completed Buka airfield—call sign RE—after 8 September. The unit was renumbered the 582nd Kokutai on 1 November and departed for Lae, New Guinea, under the command of Lt. Cdr.

Fumito Inoue seven days later. With the CO went WO Kasuo Tsunoda and PO1c Kiichi Nagano. Nagano would become the 582nd's top ace. They were joined by future aces WO Kanichi Kashimura, CPO Kiyoshi Sekiya, and PO1c Yoshio Nakamura. The entire *kokutai* was moved to Kahili airfield at the end of January 1943 to support Operation KE.

After the Battle of the Eastern Solomons in October 1942, the carrier *Zuikaku* retired to Kure naval base for repairs and for replenishment of her air group before sailing with smaller sister *Zuiho* for Truk on 17 January 1943. There a *hikotai* of Zero pilots was assembled on 24 January and placed under administrative command of the *Zuikaku* for temporary shore duty at the behest of the architects of Operation KE. A modest levy of twenty-nine fighter pilots from the *Zuikaku* and other carriers duly reported to Rabaul, including WO Katsuma Shigemi, CPO Maseo Sasakibara, and PO1c Masaichi Kondo—whose individual prowess in air combat ranked uniformly high.

These veteran IJN air units and distinguished aviators, including no fewer than twenty-three aces and future aces, collectively brought considerable experience and expertise to Operation KE.

One can use the 252nd Kokutai as a rough yardstick to determine the operable aircraft of JNAF units versus their authorized establishments. Capt. Yoshitane Yanagisawa brought the 252nd into Rabaul on 9 November at just over half strength with twenty-six Zeros—twenty-one Hamps and five Model 21 Zekes—that is, at 55 percent of its full complement. Applying this 55 percent ratio to the aircraft of all four JNAF mixed Zero *kokutai* yields a very conservative estimate of 112 operable fighters based in Bougainville in early January versus a total authorized strength of approximately 204 land-based IJN fighters.

On 29 January, with the help of *Zuiho*, the carrier *Zuikaku* ferried a fighter *hikotai* of twenty-two Zeros, plus twenty-five replacement Zeros for the 11th Koku Kantai, partway between Truk and Rabaul. The *Zuikaku*'s Lieutenant Notomi and twenty-eight other carrier pilots, together with pilots from the *Zuiho*, then flew these planes the rest of the way. Only pausing at Rabaul for servicing, the *Zuikaku* fighter *hikotai*'s pilots and planes hastened to Kahili airfield. All forty-seven Zeros were made combat ready before the transfer from Truk took place.

The R Homen Koku Buntai inherited fifty-two float fighters and float patrol planes gathered from three seaplane tenders and a seaplane carrier. The force had dwindled to thirty-nine aircraft of all types by October, but was replenished by twelve Petes transferred from seaplane tender *Kunikawa Maru* in early December. With the delivery by the *Kunikawa Maru* of a dozen Petes on 16 January, the 958th Kokutai became the main F1M2 unit, splitting its planes between Poporang, Rabaul, Kavieng, and Rekata Bay. Six new Rufes for the recently reconstituted 802nd Kokutai were also delivered to Poporang, the 802nd's CO, Lt. (jg) Takao Yokoyama, having just arrived there via flying boat with eight pilots. Although this *kokutai* also inherited the remaining A6M2-Ns of the disbanded 14th Kokutai, it had shrunk to a single float fighter and two pilots by 16 December 1942. Replacements beefed up this unit to at least nine planes by 5 January 1943.

The *Sanyo Maru* offloaded five Jakes and five Petes before departing the Shortlands for Truk on 9 January to repair torpedo and air raid damage. Sister *Kamikawa Maru* brought her floatplanes to the Shortlands on 29 January, remaining there with *Kunikawa Maru* throughout KE's evacuation phase. The former operated seven Jakes and three Petes, the latter a dozen Petes. Their aircraft and the *Sanyo Maru*'s were combined into a single unit: the 11th Seaplane Tender Division.

By the end of January 1943, the R Homen Koku Butai's roster included some sixty float fighters and patrol planes. With the seaplane tenders on hand to provide maintenance, possibly two-thirds, or forty, were available on average in early January to support Operation KE.

The Vals of the much-battered 954th Kokutai were replaced at Rabaul by the ten Vals of the 956th Kokutai on 10 November 1942. By mid-January the 956th's dive-bombers had been replaced by the twenty-four Vals of the 582nd Kokutai, of which about thirteen aircraft were operational if one applies the 55 percent ratio. One *chutai* of its Vals advanced to Kahili for Operation KE. On 29 January a *hikotai* of seventeen rejuvenated Vals was ferried from Truk to Rabaul via the carrier *Zuiho* as part of the detached *Zuikaku hikokitai*. Thus, some thirty operable Vals were available to support the crucial evacuation phase of Operation KE.

Having been active in the theater for some time, the three JNAF land-based bomber units—the 701st, 705th, and 751st Kokutai—likewise operated closer to 55 percent, or forty-five of their allotted establishment of seventy-five Bettys and Nells, based at Rabaul and Buka.

Long-range U.S. reconnaissance flights flown in late January and early February reported at various times two large flying boats moored at Rekata Bay with another five four-engine flying boats at the main anchorage off Shortland Island. All told, an estimated dozen Kawanishis probably flew from Rabaul, Kavieng, Faisi, and Rekata Bay during Operation KE. The three JNAF fighter *kokutai* equipped to fly reconnaissance missions probably operated an average seven of their allotted twelve Dinahs.

Turning to the JAAF, the 76th Independent Chutai, operating perhaps a dozen Dinah reconnaissance aircraft, was placed under command of the Japanese 17th Army in September 1942. Arriving at Rabaul in early October 1943, the 76th was the first JAAF unit to serve in the Southeast Area.

Approximately 117 Oscar fighters of the 12th Hikodan were transferred from Surabaya to Rabaul between mid-December 1942 and mid-January 1943. Before departing for Rabaul, both its 1st and 11th Sentai were brought to above-normal strength with used aircraft from Truk that had served with other units. Since the recycled JAAF planes were given at least a tune-up and remedial maintenance before reassignment to the 1st and 11th Sentai, some one hundred reliable Oscars would have been available to these two units for duty in the Solomons, though some of their *chutai* had to undertake assignments over the Bismarck Archipelago and New Guinea as well.

Of the JAAF fighter units assigned to Operation KE, the 11th Sentai was the first to arrive at Vunakanau Field, transferring in on 18 December with fifty-eight Ki-43s. The 11th's total combat and operational losses over New Guinea and the Bismarck Archipelago to mid-January came to twenty-six fighters, with seven pilots listed as KIA. Fortunately, these planes were replaced by another thirty fighters flown in from Truk. The 11th advanced a *chutai* to Buka on 21 January. During the next ten days, these fifteen Oscars, reinforced by others from Rabaul, fought the JAAF's first air combat in the Solomons, emerging from these operations with claims of four fighters and two transports shot down, plus two bombers destroyed on the ground, for a loss of two Oscars. The 11th was later ordered to detach a *chutai* of Oscars to Munda airstrip on New Georgia to reinforce JNAF fighter CAPs assigned to escort Operation KE convoys; consequently, the entire 3rd Chutai wound up at Munda during the last week of January.

The 1st Sentai followed the 11th to Rabaul with fifty-nine Oscars officially joining its sister wing at Vunakanau on 9 January. With the 11th flying out of and staging through Buka and the 1st leapfrogging to the recently completed fighter strip on Ballale Island in the Shortlands, both *sentai* could share in CAP duties over Admiral Hashimoto's Tokyo Express. In mid-January the 1st was the first *sentai* to supply a *chutai* of fighters for Munda's new airstrip; its 1st Chutai Oscars remained there until relieved by the 11th's 3rd Chutai at month's end.

Several *chutai* of Lily bombers from the 45th Sentai were also assigned to KE, bringing with them from Truk to Bougainville between eighteen and twenty-three planes, of which, applying the 55 percent ratio previously discussed, at least a baker's dozen were in service, again for shared operations out of Rabaul.

In total, around 125 JAAF aircraft of all types were poised to take part in Operation KE. At least five JAAF fighter aces fought in the Solomons during Operation KE. WO Masatoshi Masuzawa and WO Nauharu Shiromoto of the 1st Sentai were joined by Lt. Hironojo Shishimoto, SSgt. Takao Takahashi, and Sgt. Kenji Kato of the 11th Sentai. Ace lieutenants Tomoari Hasrgawa and Haruo Takagaki also flew with the 11th Sentai and may have participated in Operation KE.

Gen. Douglas MacArthur's reports, based on Japanese sources, specify 212 IJN and 100 IJA planes assigned to Operation KE for a total of 312 aircraft, most of which were fighters. Subtracting the attrition due to combat, operational accidents, and just plain wear and tear from authorized strength, the air arms of the Dai Hachi Homen Gun and the Nanto Homen Kantai probably fielded, respectively, at least 125 and 288 operable fighters, bombers, and reconnaissance aircraft, plus the twenty-five replacement Zeros, on the eve of KE. Since the Rabaul- and Kavieng-based Bettys, Nells, Vals, floatplanes, and flying boats had to be shared with operations in the Bismarck Archipelago and New Guinea, the number of planes available for Operation KE at any one time hovered between Macarthur's 312 and our 413.

The JAAF had accumulated a reserve of seventy Oscar fighters at Truk by March 1943, thirteen of which were new. Some may have already been available during Operation KE.

Adm. Isoroku Yamamoto retained at Truk the fleet carrier *Zuikaku*, plus the two super-battleships *Yamato* and *Musashi*, with the cruisers *Atago* and *Nagara* in support. To provide direct support for Operation KE, Adm. Nobutake Kondo initially had at his disposal the light carriers *Junyo* and *Zuiho*, the two older battleships *Haruna* and *Kongo*, as well as the light cruiser *Jintsu*, and a dozen destroyers. Immediately accessible to Admiral Hashimoto were the heavy cruisers *Chokai* and *Kumano*, which were poised at Kavieng Harbor in New Ireland along with the light cruiser *Sendai*.

Assuming their air groups were topped up before they were dispatched to Truk, among them the three carriers operated 155 Zeros, Vals, and Kates. Since *Junyo* and *Zuiho* were to sail with Admiral Kondo's Advance Force, their air groups were not likely emasculated to put together the Zero and Val *hikokitai* sent to Rabaul to support Operation KE.

Both Kondo's Advance Force and Yamamoto's Rengo Kantai were better prepared for a traditional surface action than an air–sea action in the event the U.S. Pacific Fleet should decide to contest the evacuation operation. Always pursuing his decisive battle with the U.S. Navy, Yamamoto was by now probably resigned to a surface fleet action should the moment of truth materialize. Unfortunately, with the IJN's carrier-based air arm still rebuilding, apart from the modest composite Zero and Val *hikokitai* reluctantly detached from Truk under command of the carrier *Zuikaku*, Rengo Kantai could not furnish any larger-scale air support to those land-based JNAF and JAAF units supplying the umbrella for Operation KE.

CHAPTER 3
AMERICAN AIRCRAFT AND AIR-COMBAT DOCTRINE

Of some 276 U.S. Navy and U.S. Marine Corps planes spread around airfields across the South Pacific, eighty-one were based at Guadalcanal—radio call sign Cactus. Sixty-five of these were operational according to an estimate of 28 January that likely included nine Wildcats flown in that same day by VMF-112 pilots returning for a second tour of duty. Lt. Jack Maas brought another VMF-112 F4F from Espiritu Santo—radio call sign Button—the next day, in time to replace one of two Wildcats demolished in a dreadful midair collision over Henderson Field. For its part, as of 22 January the Army air corps fielded around 92 planes out of an establishment of 272, including transports.

Regarding Marine fighter squadrons, VMO-251 had been feeding its pilots and planes into Guadalcanal for a month or more. VMF-122 had been rotated out, but its F4Fs and ground echelon were ordered to remain behind. VMF-123 arrived in R4D transports for its first tour of duty on 3 February, likely inheriting Wildcats from VMF-121, whose pilots had recently left on furlough. VMF-121's ground echelon also stayed behind.

Cactus' meager USMC fighter force was considerably beefed up in early February with USN fighters on loan from a fleet of auxiliary carriers. The normal fighter complement of a *Bogue*-class carrier's scouting squadron was twenty-four F4Fs, or twelve if the allotted nine TBF torpedo bombers were on board. Inadequately armored and armed, with flight decks too confined to handle aircraft rapidly and too slow for use as light fleet carriers, a trio of these baby flattops was assigned in the autumn of 1942 to ferry replacement aircraft across the Pacific. Thirty-four F4Fs from these three carriers were sent ashore as the main event of Operation KE got under way. Joining them were the seventeen F4Fs of the *Enterprise*'s VF-72, thereby upping the Canal's operable USMC/USN fighters by 51 for a total of 116 Wildcats. The arrival of these fighters made the job of eradicating the fighter arm of the Cactus Air Force that much more difficult for the Japanese.

Not the most aesthetic specimen of aeronautical architecture, the chunky Grumman F4F-4 Wildcat emerged as the only Navy/Marine fighter that had a remote chance of keeping up with a Zero. The Grumman boasted a sturdy airframe designed for carrier duty that could absorb unheard-of punishment. Featuring a radial motor with horsepower equivalent to the Zero's, it could match the latter's speed but only under 29,000 feet, where it fought best. A maximum range of nearly 850 miles allowed the Wildcat to cruise to the Central Solomons and back without a drop tank. Pilot armor plating and self-sealing fuel tanks made it heavier than Japanese fighters, resulting in inferior acceleration, climb rate, and maneuverability, but these protective features were deemed indispensable. The Wildcat's trump card was its ability to change directions quickly at high speed, ducking enemy fire by outrolling and outdiving any Japanese opponent.

Brig. Gen. Claire Chennault's Flying Tigers had demonstrated that when handled properly, any heavy but powerful fighter like the Curtiss P-40B Warhawk could rack up an impressive kill ratio against more nimble Japanese aircraft. Warned of an oncoming air raid, his P-40 pilots would climb into the sun and bounce Japanese planes in elements of two: a leader and his wingman. Each pair would dive at high speed through a Japanese formation, fire at a selected target, and climb back up-sun from the enemy to repeat the maneuver. The P-40 could easily outdistance lighter Japanese fighters in a fast dive since pursuing Zeros could not roll out at high speed due to poor aileron control and had a tough time breaking to the right because of opposing engine torque.

Enterprising Wildcat pilots charged with defending the Henderson Field complex were not slow to catch on, but F4Fs needed upwards of thirty minutes to reach 30,000 feet. Frequently, raiders would sneak in under cover of bad weather before being spotted; they also flew low to avoid Cactus' search radar, and skirted islands with known coastwatcher outposts, only climbing to bombing altitude to make their runs. Scrambled at the last minute, Henderson's fighters often found themselves climbing beneath attacking bombers, or worse, bounced from above by Zeros.

At Coral Sea and Midway, USN fighter pilots not only confirmed the lessons learned in China, but also devised their own tactics to foil the fabled Mitsubishi fighters. Particularly successful was a weaving pattern executed by sections of fighters wherein a section leader and his wingman protected one another's tail by crisscrossing diagonally in front of each other. This maneuver was dubbed the Thach weave, after its inventor Lt. Cdr. John "Jimmy" Thach. His technique aptly lent itself to formation tactics with groups of fighters crisscrossing diagonally over slower-flying light bombers. Though effective, the Thach weave involved continuous maneuvering that required pilots to remain alert, which proved both exhausting and stressful on long missions.

Enter Maj. Harold "Indian Joe" Bauer (later lieutenant colonel), a master tactician and one of the most aggressive ace pilots ever to sit behind the gunsight of a fighter. Major Bauer put his Wildcat pilots through a rigorous training program that featured offense as the best form of defense. Bauer saw to it that VMF-212 learned to execute both beam and high-side passes followed by rapid dispersal via a dive, as per Chennault's doctrine.

The CO also stressed the advantages of the overhead pass. The F4F pilot approached his quarry head-on from above, then, rolling over to the inverted position, he executed a curving dive toward his enemy. This technique gave him several advantages: first, diving from the inverted position exerted positive G forces on the pilot and allowed an unobstructed view of the target throughout the entire maneuver; second, the closing speed of the two aircraft shrank significantly as the pilot passed through his arc, coming down from above and behind to take up a position astern of his opponent. This offered a better chance to follow any evasive maneuver the enemy might attempt.

Above all, Major Bauer taught his pilots to stay face to face with the agile Zeros, avoiding dogfights by attacking head-on. To attain this position, his pilots mastered scissoring, which involved a modified version of the Thach weave. If a section leader came under attack, he turned toward his wingman, drawing his attacker with him. The wingman banked sharply to face his section leader and line up the attacker for a head-on pass. Or the leader could initiate a scissor by executing a diving turn toward his wingman. The latter turned toward him, crossed astern, and reversed course to fall on the attacking plane's six, forcing the enemy pilot to break off. If the wingman were bounced, the roles reversed.

Taking advantage of the Wildcat's ruggedness, pilot, and fuel-tank protection, and its ability to roll into a high-speed turn, Bauer was willing to risk catching a few arrows from the Zero's guns if he could, in turn, bring his six fifties to bear on the enemy's more-fragile "paper tiger." Superior gunnery skills and heavier firepower could destroy one's opponent before the enemy's tighter turns gave him a firing advantage. Bauer considered these the ultimate scissoring tactics.

But no combat-wise Wildcat pilot expected to roost on a Zero's tail for more than a second or two before his opponent pulled the lithe Mitsubishi up into a tight loop or zoomed into a climbing turn to fall back on the F4F. At this point Chennault's P-40 pilot would have flipped his heavy fighter over, dropping like a stone in the opposite direction from the Zero's pullout. USN and USMC pilots discovered during the carrier battles of the Central Pacific that a fast dive sprinkled with rolls worked equally well as an evasive tactic for the F4F.

However, escaping via a corkscrew dive did not shoot down enemy planes. If a Zero slid in on one's tail, an alternate, tried-and-proven tactic espoused by Bauer and others was to hit the brakes. Abrupt, rapid deceleration by throttling back, dropping flaps, and skidding often caused the surprised enemy to overshoot, briefly opening a window of opportunity for the Wildcat pilot. Pushing the throttle open and triggering the six fifties at close range often brought the contest to a victorious end.

Together with Bauer, gifted fighter alumni like majors John Smith and Len Davis and captains Joe Foss and Marion Carl, honed Cactus' lexicon of maneuvers to a fine art. Augmented over time by their refinements, Bauer's system was working well for experienced Marine and Navy fliers when Operation KE debuted.

Unfortunately, the less-agile Airacobras and Warhawks flown by U.S. Army (USA) pilots pretty much limited them to Chennault's hit-and-run tactics, though P-39 and P-40 aviators did employ weaving and scissoring at lower altitudes, where their fighters performed better.

Clearly outclassed by the Zero, Bell's P-39 Airacobra and its P-400 export variant were the only USAAF fighters on Guadalcanal until the P-38 Lightning arrived in mid-November 1942. The P-39D flown by the 12th, 68th, and 70th FSs could fly at more than three hundred knots at lower altitudes—faster than its adversaries. But it lacked a turbo-supercharger, severely limiting its ability to climb and fight above 17,000 feet. The optimal combat altitude of the P-400 variant was further reduced to 12,000 feet by a British-designed, high-pressure oxygen system that could not be recharged by Cactus' apparatus, thereby preventing the pilot from flying on oxygen. The K and L models of the P-39 that arrived in the late autumn of 1942 performed marginally better.

Lighter than other American fighters, the Airacobra experienced some difficulty trying to outdistance a Zero in a dive. Instead, Cobra pilots learned to duck into the nearest cloud bank, make a climbing turn on instruments, and, with any luck, emerge above their foe to execute a surprise pass before being jumped again.

On the plus side, the Cobra was solidly constructed, sporting pilot and fuel-tank protection. When mated to large tires, its tricycle landing gear permitted takeoffs and landings on mud-clogged runways that often grounded other Cactus fighters. The Bell fighter also was well armed—in theory. The P-39D's in-line motor was mounted behind the cockpit to accommodate a bulky, nose-mounted, 37-mm cannon that fired through the spinner. A pair of cowl-mounted .50-caliber machine guns flanked the cannon; four wing-mounted .30-caliber machine guns rounded out the P-39's arsenal. While the trajectories of the different-caliber machine guns were not dissimilar, that of the 37-mm differed markedly from the other two, making it hard to find a bore-sight range at which the three streams of fire could converge. Consequently, Cobra pilots seldom fired their jam-prone cannon. The P-400 sported a more-reliable and more-compatible 20-mm cannon.

Bell's fighter could only cruise five hundred miles, but a drop tank ensured enough avgas to take it to the Central Solomons and back. Notwithstanding, in September 1942 a dozen of the 67th FS's P-400s were reassigned exclusively to local patrol, search, and attack roles against ground and seaborne targets. There the P-400s found their niche as fighter-bombers: they proved impressively stable in high-speed dives, exhibited a high degree of bombing and strafing accuracy, and could evade AA fire better than could the Dauntless SBD.

As the 67th's P-400 inventory eroded, the unit reequipped with sixteen P-39s during October and November 1942. The P-39s of the 68th FS were recruited for ground support; the sister squadron frequently shared this duty with the 67th. The 70th FS arrived in mid-December to begin its tour with twenty Airacobras. Most of the pilots of the 67th FS returned to the Canal from Christmas leave on 29 December to begin a third tour. Though the 12th FS participated briefly in Operation KE's preliminaries, most of the squadron's pilots had rotated out to Efate, New Caledonia—call sign Roses—during KE's critical evacuation phase. Their twenty P-39Ds were left behind at Cactus, along with a few remaining pilots who flew with sister squadrons. Thus, an estimated total of fifty serviceable Airacobras were on hand at the end of January 1943.

Only a growing shortage of superior fighters compelled the Cactus Air Force to press its Airacobras into air combat after 23 December, undertaking reconnaissance and local patrol roles or flying as low-altitude escorts on air strikes. Although they remained administratively distinct, all Cactus P-39 squadrons were sharing their Cobras by the end of 1942. They became collectively known as the 347th Detachment's "Cactus Flight" and the "Jagdstaffel" because their pilots commonly flew missions together.

The Curtiss Warhawk was blessed with pilot armor, fuel-tank protection, superior roll rate, and superior diving speed. The P-40E could exceed three hundred knots at medium altitudes—faster than the Zero. But, not possessed of a turbo-supercharger, the Hawk was cursed with a slow climb rate, though markedly faster than that of the P-39. Its ability to withstand punishment under fire was matched by the havoc wreaked upon frail Japanese planes by the P-40's six .50-caliber machine guns. Heavier even than a Wildcat, no P-40 could turn into an attacker at the medium speeds Zero pilots preferred for close combat. Its ace in the hole was to make a fast pass, rolling into a high-speed dive to escape trouble.

Lt. Allen Webb of the 68th FS remarked of the P-40F, perhaps a tad overoptimistically, "This type of plane . . . proved very good as a long range escort at any altitude up to 30,000 feet, with the very best performance at 25,000 feet."

The 68th FS assumed fighter status after the arrival of its first nine of twelve P-40Fs on 23 December. Using its remaining P-39s in a ground-support role, the 68th initially employed its P-40s to cover the lower-flying Cobras. However, Cactus P-40Fs could cruise 850 miles when fitted with drop tanks, giving them sufficient range to undertake an extended fighter sweep into the Central Solomons as well as an escort or reconnaissance run up to Bougainville.

Before long, the 68th FS began to fly long-range reconnaissance patrols in addition to medium- or high-cover escort missions on B-17 raids. Hitherto, the 339th FS's P-38s were the only USAAF fighters capable of escorting the heavy bombers into the Western Solomons and beyond. However, the Lightning's inferior performance at lower altitudes restricted it to top cover; fortunately, this dovetailed with the preferred operating altitudes of the high-flying Fortresses. With the Warhawks along to act as medium cover and, in particular, to provide forward firepower to deter the much-favored head-on attacks by Japanese interceptors, the Forts could now cruise more safely at the lower altitudes needed for better bombing accuracy. Capt. Stan Palmer of the 68th FS summed it up thus: "The P-40F proved to be a satisfactory airplane for medium cover in conjunction with the P-38 as high cover."

However, by the end of January most of the remaining pilots of the 68th had been sent to the rear area on the customary two-week furlough and consequently missed most of Operation KE. Reporting in on 20 January, the 44th FS put up twenty-five P-40s of its own that it pooled and operated with those of the absentee 68th pilots.

The Lockheed P-38 Lightning was something else again. When this bimotor, twin-boom fighter made its debut at Cactus on 12 November 1942, the newly formed 339th FS became the first twin-engine fighter unit to see action in the South Pacific. The first eight P-38Gs were ferried in by Maj. Dale Brannon, the 339th's new CO, and his cadre of pilots. Paradoxically, Friday the thirteenth saw eight P-38Fs ferried in from the the U.S. 5th Air force. Veterans of New Guinea, they were followed by four more P-38Gs from Tontouta—call sign White Poppy—the next day. The 339th received between twenty and twenty-four Lightnings in all; due to fuel shortages, however, the eight P-38Fs on loan from the 5th Air Force were returned before Operation KE began. Six P-38Gs became operational or combat casualties during December and January. Another G was badly damaged in an accident on New Year's Eve, but might not have been written off. On 27 January ComGenSoPac radioed General Mulcahy, ComAirSols, that four P-38s were scheduled for delivery to Cactus in two days' time, to be followed by another dozen on 5 February, but none actually arrived before Operation KE was over.

Capable of 350 knots, the Lightning was fast—very fast. But the restrictive effect of its weight on maneuverability was undeniable; of the four Cactus fighters, the P-38 proved least able to cope with Zeros and Oscars at lower speeds and altitudes. The Lightning could not break quickly to either side with its two counterrotating props, though it could roll fairly well at high speed—especially if pilots advanced the throttle of the outboard engine while cutting back that of the inboard engine. The P-38's salvation was its ability to dive and climb; it could fall away from opposing Japanese fighters with ease, relying on its powerful engines to climb back into the fight. Boasting an operational ceiling of 39,000 feet, the Lockheed fighter invariably flew top cover on escort missions from 18 November onward.

The P-38 could cruise an adequate eight hundred miles at two hundred knots with a single auxiliary tank. It put out enough power to handle two 310-gallon drop tanks—a feature that would make it the interceptor of choice to ambush Adm. Isoroku Yamamoto and his retinue over distant Bougainville in April 1943. The P-38, like the P-39, was designed with a tricycle landing gear and large tires that gave it a tremendous advantage over other American fighters whenever rain turned Cactus' fighter strips into quagmires. Even the Cobra occasionally bogged down as mud, splashing over its wing surfaces, accumulated during a takeoff roll; the Lightning experienced less buildup because its wings were mounted higher off the ground.

Ruggedly built to take punishment, with pilot and fuel tanks protected, the Lockheed fighter packed a nose full of trouble—a 20-mm cannon flanked by four .50-caliber machine guns. These parallel-firing, nose-mounted guns were on target up to a remarkable distance of one thousand yards, making the Lightning especially lethal at long range. Simply put, the Lightning was a fast, high-flying, long-range fighter—a compatible escort mate for both the B-17 and the later B-24.

The unique flight characteristics of the P-38 required radically different combat tactics. Capt. John "Mitch" Mitchell, who as a major and ace pilot, was destined to lead the Yamamoto ambush mission, took over the 339th FS on 25 November. As the new Lightning squadron gained combat experience, Captain Mitchell, on the advice of his predecessor, Maj. Dale Brannon, began to hammer out a modus operandi for engaging Japanese fighters.

The gargantuan Lockheeds turned too slowly to stay with Japanese fighters or practice the Thach weave. Instead, Mitchell devised a circular formation of three or four flights spread over a mile, each flight consisting of a pair of two-plane elements flying in a loose finger-four formation. He reckoned that sixteen Lightnings in four flights constituted an optimal configuration for mutual defense if enough planes were in service.

After he took over, Captain Mitchell preached his version of Colonel Bauer's tactical doctrine, advocating head-on confrontation with Japanese fighters. Lightning pilots were taught to maintain group integrity when furnishing high cover for B-17s; the order to break up was only given to intercept Japanese fighters at high altitude. Mitchell further stressed the critical necessity of maintaining their two-plane integrity once opposing flights melded into one another. The trick was to not get sucked into a one-on-one with the supple Zeros. If a Zeke or Hamp got on one's tail, one relied on the sturdy Lightning to withstand the enemy's fire until one could dive out of range or until a wingman brushed him off. When pursuing enemy fighters, the 339th's pilots were instructed to bank under a tight-turning opponent, then catch up to him in a shallow high-speed climb.

Because the core veterans of the 339th had been culled from the 67th and its sister squadrons in the 347th FG, a warm rapport flourished between them and the 339th. Mitchell was not above giving air time in his Lightnings to senior pilots of these units, whose growing familiarity with the P-38 made them ideal potential replacements.

On 27 January a message from ComSoPac to CinCPac reported an actual roster of 150 USAAF fighters belonging to the newly formed 347th Fighter Group, of which 107 were in service—up from 69 operable fighters on 22 January. Adding the 65 Marine Wildcats, total operable fighter strength accessible to the Cactus Air Force climbed to 172 aircraft by the end of January

1943. The 51 Navy F4Fs detached at the beginning of February upped the net available total to some 223 fighters just as the evacuation phase of Operation KE was getting under way.

Generally, the Cactus fighter pilot regarded his aircraft as a gunnery platform in which he could survive behind protective armor, surrounded by a sturdy airframe, until he could train formidable firepower on an enemy plane. Coupled to rugged, American fighter-design principles, such a practical attitude aptly suited the campaign of attrition into which the contest for Guadalcanal had quickly devolved. Subscribing to the combat savvy of Bauer and other ace pilots, at least eighteen USMC, fifteen USAAF, and three USN fighter aces and future aces participated in Operation KE.

As for light-bomber units at Cactus, only two squadrons of dive-bombers and one torpedo-bomber squadron were available at the end of January to oppose the evacuation phase of Operation KE.

VMSB-234 had been stationed at Espiritu Santo since the New Year; there its ground echelon feverishly repaired planes for the unit's Cactus detachment. VMSB-233 was in the midst of its tour of duty when January dawned and could operate only twelve to fourteen SBD-4 Dauntlesses. To offset attrition, the squadron ferried ten SBD-4s to Cactus—its total inventory on the Canal as of 28 January. VMSB-142 operated its twenty SBD-3s from Cactus during the preliminary phase of Operation KE, but rotated out in the third week of January.

On 31 January General Mulcahy urgently requested replacements for eleven Cactus SBDs that had to be sidelined for four days of overdue maintenance. This left between eleven and thirteen operable dive-bombers on the eve of KE's main event. The pilots of VMSB-132—technically on furlough—responded within three days, ferrying eighteen Dauntlesses from Button. Two Cactus SBDs crashed in separate accidents in the interim. Thus, between them VMSB-233 and 234 mustered about twenty-nine operable aircraft at the end of the month. VMSB-144 relieved VMSB-233 on 5 February, flying in twenty-two SBD-4s just as Operation KE was winding down.

Although it was an accurate dive-bombing platform, by early 1943 the Douglas Dauntless was already obsolescent. It could fly reasonably fast at a maximum of 240 knots, but it could only climb to altitude at 125 knots and cruise at 150 knots with a 1,000-pound bomb, and then for only four hundred miles. The presence of Douglas dive-bombers in a strike force necessitated escorting fighters to practice an exaggerated version of the Thach weave with throttles cut back to keep pace with the sluggish dive-bombers.

The standard bomb load comprised one 500-pounder plus two 100-pounders to extend range and time over the target. Even then, SBDs could not tarry on missions into the Central Solomons; the Dauntlesses invariably bombed first when in the company of Grumman Avengers.

Accurate dive-bombing was facilitated by a set of perforated flaps that acted as brakes to stabilize the aircraft. Forward firepower consisted of a pair of cowl-mounted .50-caliber machine guns. The SBD-3 featured one rear-firing .30-caliber machine gun; twin thirties were mounted in the SBD-4's rear cockpit after experience revealed its predecessor to be undergunned.

The Grumman TBF Avenger was designed as a torpedo bomber, but it performed equally well as a level bomber and a glide bomber. Its versatility even extended to depth charging and mine laying. The TBF-1 could carry up to 2,000 pounds of bombs usually configured as four 500-pounders. With this load, or carrying a torpedo, it could cruise for one thousand miles or more. Its maximum speed hovered around 240 knots. Defensive firepower consisted of one cowl-mounted .50-caliber machine gun firing forward in addition to two .30-caliber machine guns firing to the rear: one mounted topside in a turret, the other sighted through a ventral port at the radio operator's post behind the bomb bay. Later models sported twin thirties in their turrets.

VMSB-131 operated the only Avengers flying out of Cactus at the outset of Operation KE. The squadron brought the first six Marine TBF-1s to the South Pacific on 12 November 1942, followed by another six a few days later. Lieutenant Aggerbeck flew a single TBF to Cactus on 3 January; three more left Button on 18 January behind an R4D guide plane. VMSB-131's roster boasted at least twelve planes the next day. Another three replacement aircraft flew in on 22 January from the carrier *Copahee*, upping the total to fifteen planes. However, by 2 February attrition had whittled the squadron down to only three operable aircraft. Fortuitously, the *Altamaha*, *Copahee*, and *Nassau* detached three small TBF squadrons to Henderson Field along with their F4Fs. Arriving at Cactus on 3 February behind a chaperoning

PBY, the twenty-seven Avengers commanded by Lt. Cdr. Charles Brunton linked up with the remnants of VMSB-131.

Saddled with a limited supply of stubby aerial torpedoes, between 3 December and 19 January VMSB-131's combat activities were hamstrung by Cactus Operations, which would not permit its TBFs to fly "unless the ships coming down the groove [sic] were cruisers or larger." Twelve Avengers finally flew a search-and-destroy mission on 19 January, but hampered by foul weather over the Slot, they could not find their targets: a "cruiser and seven destroyers." Toward month's end, VMSB-131 at long last received permission to arm its planes with 500-pound bombs as well as torpedoes—in time to cooperate with the new USN TBF squadron on joint missions.

Records suggest that four light-bomber squadrons probably operated around fifty serviceable aircraft on the eve of Operation KE; by 3 February that number had dwindled to around thirty-five aircraft belonging to three squadrons, taking into account previous losses offset by the replacements noted above. Operation KE was in full swing by then.

When the USAAF's 13th Air Force was formed in mid-January 1943, it inherited from the 7th Air Force the 5th BG(H) and the 11th BG(H), both of which flew B-17Es in the Solomons.

The Boeing B-17E could cruise comfortably from Espiritu Santo in the New Hebrides to Guadalcanal, drop six thousand pounds of bombs on the Japanese airfield under construction, and fly back. Some B-17s could be fitted with one or two auxiliary tanks mounted in the bomb bay to extend their range from Espiritu Santo to northern Bougainville. These could be jettisoned, but the tradeoff was a reduced bomb load of four thousand pounds or less.

Although the B-17 was dubbed the Flying Fortress, losses inflicted by heavily armed Luftwaffe interceptors on unescorted Forts over Europe proved shockingly heavy. But in the Solomons B-17s routinely flew without fighter escort against the less-lethal Zeros until mid-November 1943, mainly because the only Army fighter then operating out of Cactus—the Bell Airacobra—was unsuited for high-altitude escort duty. When the longer-range, higher-flying Lightnings made their appearance on 12 November, they began to escort B-17 strikes up the Slot. The first B-17Gs, with their distinctive chin turrets armed with twin fifties arrived at about the same time to augment forward-directed firepower. The 68th FS's P-40Fs began flying medium cover near the end of December; they were joined by the newly arrived Hawks of the 44th FS a month later.

Together, the eight squadrons of the two heavy bombardment groups should have marshaled seventy-two B-17Es—a sizable force for the South Pacific. The 11th BG arrived in the theater with thirty-five aircraft, but its attrition rate was high. The 11th lost seventeen aircraft between 31 July and 15 October 1942—twelve of them to operational causes, two to the overnight naval bombardment of Henderson Field on 13–14 October—leaving eighteen flyable aircraft. The 5th BG showed up after mid-September with few aircraft of its own. Neither its 23rd or 31st BS(H)s were operating any aircraft as late as December 1942. The 394th BS(H) flew nine aged Forts transferred to the South Pacific from New Guinea after the 19th BG(H) rotated out. The 72nd BS(H) fielded nine more, which were placed on loan to the 11th BG.

Losses to the end of December reached twenty-three B-17s. By 5 January the combined inventory of the 5th and 11th BGs totaled around twenty-nine aircraft, including eleven Forts recently returned from temporary duty at Port Moresby. Fifteen remained at Cactus (twelve for strikes and three for patrols); the rest were assigned to Button. A return dated 22 January listed a mere thirteen operational Forts in the South Pacific. Counting replacement aircraft, the two air groups struggled to muster only thirty-six B-17s at Button and Cactus combined by 27 January.

The 11th BG had been active over the Solomons ever since the 26th BS(H) had arrived at the start of the campaign. Initially, the group's squadrons flew six to eight solo reconnaissance sorties daily out of Espiritu Santo, fanning out over the Slot and the Coral Sea. The two B-17s assigned to overfly the Slot as far as the Japanese Buka and Bonis airfield complex at the northern tip of Bougainville—1,500 miles one way—flew photoreconnaissance missions, staging through Henderson Field to refuel.

Strike missions were sparse due to the chronic shortage of aircraft. B-17 groups rarely sent up more than nine bombers on any given mission in late 1942, pooling the aircraft of several squadrons to muster that many. In fact, until Maj. Don Ridings brought in the 5th BG's first squadron on 23 September, the 11th could spare only a standby strike force of six B-17s at Button, supported in an emergency by another six at Roses. Air strikes were sent out against targets of opportunity by day, concentrating on warships and merchant shipping. Those few raids that ventured as far as Bougainville returned via Henderson Field to top up fuel tanks. During the crisis occasioned by the Japanese offensive of mid-November 1942, Espiritu Santo rallied to send up between fourteen and seventeen B-17s against Japanese task forces.

After Col. Brooke Allen, the CO, reached the South Pacific in October with the other three squadrons of the 5th BG, enemy airfields, seaplane bases, and harbors from the New Georgia group to northern Bougainville were targeted around the clock. Cactus B-17 solo and multiaircraft nocturnal raids went far beyond the scope of Japanese Maytag Mike sorties; enemy airfields as far away as Buka and Bonis were sprinkled with mixed loads of daisy cutters and 100-pound general-purpose bombs. Even with extra fuel on board, each Fort carried between six and eight 500-pound armor-piercing bombs on antishipping strikes to the Shortland–Tonolei harbor complex.

Although American strategists longed to consolidate Henderson Field and its satellite airstrips into their key bomber base for the air campaign in the Solomons, the 11th BG could not actually base any B-17s at Cactus due to a shortage of aviation fuel, poor field conditions, inadequate ground-servicing facilities, and enemy air and naval bombardments. Only when American land forces went on the offensive in the New Year were a minimum of fifteen B-17s permanently deployed to Henderson Field.

To rectify the ground-support deficiency, an advance party of the 31st BS arrived at Cactus on 3 December to prepare a base camp and begin servicing heavy bombers. By 17 January the rest of the squadron's ground echelon had moved in to service all B-17s staging through or operating out of Cactus. Three days earlier a dozen 31st BS Forts flew from Button to Cactus, followed by five more from the 26th BS on the 22nd. The 26th's bombers appear to have remained until 5 February, but took no part on their own in the action against Operation KE. The 72nd rotated in on 29 January with seven planes to bolster the ranks of the forward echelon. The 42nd BS(H) continued to operate out of Button for the duration of KE, staging through Henderson Field. Four of its B-17s advanced to Cactus toward the end of January to undertake expanded reconnaissance sorties up the Slot as far as Buka Passage.

The Martin B-26 Marauder was roughly the equivalent of the Japanese Betty—a medium attack bomber. Introduced into the Pacific theater in April

1942, the Marauder was preceded by an unsavory reputation for operational accidents in the hands of inexperienced or careless pilots. Undoubtedly, its relatively short wingspan, high wing loading, and 110-knot landing speed made it a tricky and unforgiving airplane to handle. But the B-26B serving in the South Pacific was fast, reaching 250 knots. And this twin-engine bomber could carry nearly as many bombs as the four-engine B-17, cruising 1,150 miles with a 3,000-pound bomb load. A standard general-purpose bomb load consisted of four 500-pounders plus twenty 100-pounders; these were usually dropped at altitudes between 10,000 and 15,000 feet. The B-26 eventually boasted no fewer than eleven fifties for defense, outgunning even the early B-17.

The 13th Air Force carried the two medium-bomber squadrons of the 38th BG in its establishment: the 69th BS(M) and the 70th BS(M). Their Marauders began operating out of Cactus on New Year's Eve. ComSoPac's return for 27 January listed seventeen B-26s in the theater after a month of combat, ten of which were operable as of 22 January. The 70th BS flew out of Cactus until, regrettably, it was withdrawn from combat on 4 February at the height of the struggle against KE's Tokyo Express. After refitting at Efate, the 69th operated its remaining B-26s out of Espiritu Santo, staging through Cactus on missions up the Slot. On 7 February it transferred its Marauders, and some recently acquired B-25 Mitchells, back to Henderson Field, replacing the 70th's well-worn aircraft. The controversial B-26 was phased out of the South Pacific theater altogether when KE ended, to be replaced by the less rugged but more forgiving B-25.

Three long-range Allied patrol aircraft operated during Operation KE: the Consolidated Catalina PBY flying boat and amphibian, the Lockheed Hudson medium patrol bomber, and the Consolidated B-24 Liberator bomber and its Navy PB4Y-1 patrol variant.

Looking like an aeronautical designer's nightmare, the gangly PBY is regarded as the most successful amphibian of all time. Designed in the 1930s, it so exceeded its performance specs as a patrol plane that it was officially redesignated by the USN as a patrol bomber capable of handling bombs, depth charges, and torpedoes. This versatile aircraft excelled not only in reconnaissance and bombing roles, but also in antisubmarine, air–sea rescue, and transport work. It operated deep in Japanese territory during the Guadalcanal campaign, taking advantage of its amphibious capability to evacuate downed fliers as well as to transport men, equipment, and supplies for the Allied coastwatcher network. Equipped with radar and a radio-altimeter, the PBY-5A Black Cat variant achieved special distinction for its sterling work as a nocturnal ferret, attack bomber, and artillery spotter for naval bombardments.

The PBY-5A reached 170 knots and could cruise 2,200 nautical miles. Strongly built and with a crew of seven or eight, it routinely handled up to four thousand pounds of bombs, four 650-pound depth charges, or two aerial torpedoes. Standard defensive armament consisted of two .50-caliber and three .30-caliber machine guns. When harassed by enemy float fighters at night, its best defenses were to duck in and out of cloud cover or, using its radio-altimeter to maintain accurate height, skim the sea to blend in with its dark surface. The USN operated fifty-four PBYs in the South Pacific on the eve of Operation KE.

Flown in the Solomons by the RNZAF's No. 3 Squadron, the MkIII Hudson emerged as an ersatz military adaptation of the Lockheed 14 transport and the successful Electra airliner. Crewed by four or five men, the Hudson found its niche as a long-range patrol bomber when fitted with extra fuel tanks. The MkIII reached a maximum speed of 222 knots and could cruise for 1,877 nautical miles. For defense it sported a pair of nose-mounted, forward-firing .303-caliber machine guns. Other .303s were mounted in left and right beam positions and in a retractable ventral ball turret. Twin .303s also fired from a dorsal-mounted power turret. The Hudson could carry 1,600 pounds of bombs or four depth charges.

No. 3 Squadron RNZAF began operating out of Cactus on 23 November 1942 with the arrival at Henderson of the first six of its twelve Hudsons. The squadron's primary role was twofold: first, it flew round-the-clock reconnaissance missions along the approaches to the Canal—especially up the Slot as far as northern Bougainville; second, it carried out low-level search sorties along the coastlines of those islands suspected of harboring staging bases for troops and materiel destined for the Japanese 17th Army. After mid-November these roles distilled to tracking the Tokyo Express and interdicting any barge traffic island hopping along the Slot. To the extent that the ground echelon kept their Lockheeds in the air, the New Zealanders also relieved those light bombers and B-17s hitherto pressed into reconnaissance duties, thus releasing these aircraft to fly more of the tactical and strategic bombing missions for which they were intended.

Designated the B-24 by the USAAF and the PB4Y-1 by the U.S. Navy, the British-dubbed Liberator replaced the B-17 as the key Allied heavy bomber in the Pacific. The B-24 debuted in the South Pacific near the end of Operation KE with the dispatch from Hawaii of the 307th BG(H) on 4 February. Already operational, radar-equipped PB4Y-1s saw action in the Solomons during KE as long-range reconnaissance aircraft; it is in this role that one encounters them.

The Liberator was fitted with a long, narrow wing mounted across the top of its fuselage; this permitted a bomb capacity of up to eight thousand pounds. Its four radial engines propelled it to a top speed of 250 knots. The B-24 could cruise for almost 1,800 nautical miles with a crew of eight and a full bomb load; that is, it could carry more bombs and take them farther than could the B-17. Its defensive punch comprised four turrets: nose, dorsal, ventral (ball), and tail—each mounting twin fifties.

The high wing loading of the aircraft's specially designed teardrop airfoil made for difficult handling, but the addition of extensible Fowler flaps, coupled to a tricycle landing gear, enabled shorter takeoff distances, making the B-24/PB4Y-1 ideal for operation on the South Pacific's short and often muddy airfields. Certain weakness in its wing design rendered the Liberator somewhat vulnerable to heavily armed Luftwaffe interceptors over Europe, but it found its niche in the Pacific theater, where it proved more resilient against relatively undergunned Japanese fighters. In response to a growing demand for B-17s in Europe, the Forts were phased out in the Pacific beginning in early 1943, to be replaced with B-24s and PB4Y-1s. Around eighteen B-24s of all subtypes were in the South Pacific at the time of Operation KE.

The estimated number of fighters, bombers, and reconnaissance aircraft under command of the Cactus Air Force and 13th Air Force prior to the start of Operation KE on 10 January 1943 reached some 445 aircraft. In reality, operable aircraft totaled around 315, of which some 210 were Cactus-based. These figures compare well against the authorized establishment figure of 425 discounted by an arbitrary average of 25 percent (due to better maintenance than that given Japanese aircraft) for a theoretical 320 operable aircraft. Naturally, in-service aircraft decreased rapidly due to accelerated wear and tear, combat losses, and operational accidents as Operation KE played itself out. A USN/USMC aircraft return report for 17 February 1943 lists only one hundred fighters and light bombers left in the Solomons after KE. For the same reasons, USAAF planes had likely been whittled down by a similar proportion.

Besides another 147 USN and USMC planes supposedly en route to the South Pacific, the fleet carriers *Enterprise* and *Saratoga*, together with six escort carriers, boasted a floating air reserve of around 340 Navy fighters and light bombers. But in the wake of onerous carrier losses in the Solomons, Admiral Nimitz was reluctant to commit Admiral Halsey's flattops unless a clear and present danger threatened the American position on Guadalcanal. Nimitz was watching for the actual launch of a renewed land offensive actively supported by those major units of the Japanese Rengo Kantai that were known to be congregating at Truk. To counter this threat, Admiral Halsey could call upon three modern battleships, plus thirteen cruisers and forty-five destroyers; this put the USN roughly at par with the Dai Nippon Teikoku Kaigun in any surface action. But ComSoPac's real tactical advantage rested in his naval air power, which though significantly weakened, remained stronger than its Japanese counterpart.

CHAPTER 4
OF PILOTS AND PREPAREDNESS

Ironically, having spearheaded the formation of the League of Nations to resolve international disputes, America proceeded to isolate itself from European affairs after World War I. Eager to return to normalcy, the United States rapidly disarmed in the face of the rampant militarism welling up in Fascist Italy and Nazi Germany during the 1920s and early 1930s. As a result, the U.S. Army and U.S. Navy air arms together could field but eight fighter squadrons as late as 1934.

However, America's acquisition of the Philippines and pursuit of commercial interests in the Orient aroused imperial Japan's suspicions and then its animosity. Increased saber rattling from across the Pacific during the 1930s soon encouraged the Army and Navy to extend pilot and aircrew training to enlisted men, college and university reservists, and youths in their late teens. Despite this modest expansion, before the outbreak of war with Japan, America's cadre of military airmen formed little more than a nucleus of the air armada needed to defeat the Axis.

All branches of military aviation desperately accelerated their training programs upon the sudden outbreak of hostilities. Entrance standards were lowered, and course syllabuses were pruned back. Such expedients produced decidedly mixed results. Maj. Dick Baker, who served on Guadalcanal with VMF-123 around the time of Operation KE, later noted, "Several pilots came directly from flight training school and had less than 50 hours in F4Fs before Cactus." Major Baker estimated that fighter pilots needed three hundred hours at flight school in combat-type trainers, and another one hundred hours in the Wildcat, before they were ready to fly combat in the Solomons. VMSB-141, a Marine SBD squadron, arrived at Cactus at the beginning of October 1942 virtually unprepared. Casualties were high and successes few.

Learning on the job proved to be too much: the rigors of combat burned out its poorly trained crews by mid-November. A flight surgeon had the squadron's entire air echelon summarily removed from combat after a mere six weeks.

Converting auxiliary units to fighter squadrons was another expedient used to create more fighter pilots. Upon taking over VMO-251 at Espiritu Santo on 10 December 1942, Maj. Joe Renner inherited two experienced fighter pilots in addition to Maj. Bill "Soupy" Campbell, his executive officer. The squadron's other aviators had already been siphoned to Guadalcanal to bolster undermanned Marine fighter units. In short order Major Renner took delivery of Lt. Allan "Hank" McCartney and five other SBD pilots who had amassed an average 220 hours' flying time but had never flown combat. Joining them were fourteen SBC-4 pilots from VMO-151—another scout observation squadron. Renner was given just twenty-five days to retrain these men before VMO-251 transferred to Cactus.

The resulting ersatz course began with an hour spent flying familiarization solos in the available photoreconnaissance F4F-3Ps plus some F4F-4s on loan from the carrier *Hornet*. Then there followed two hours of flying in sections and divisions to learn the basics of fighter formations. Next, Major Renner's pilots spent an hour in gunnery practice, followed by air combat training. They flew in two teams of four aircraft each to practice scissoring as well as Maj. Joe Bauer's preferred attack tactics. Novices learned to revolve about the same airspace once engaged; they were instructed not to get baited by lone enemy fighters and sucked into a trap. Instead, they were to "swing back into the middle of the merry-go-round" and "look for a Zero on some other Grumman's tail." Continued Renner, "If you can summon up the courage . . . to quit worrying about the guy peppering . . . you from behind and go after the Zero peppering your wingman . . . gradually the Zeros all disappear from the fight." If section leaders and wingmen became separated, pilots were advised to join up on the nearest friendly fighter for mutual protection.

Since U.S. fighters per se were more maneuverable at higher speeds, neophytes were instructed to keep their speed up in the combat area. When attacking Val dive-bombers, Major Renner's drill was to close from behind low enough for the Val's own horizontal stabilizer and elevator to obstruct the rear gunner's view. This maneuver offered the F4F pilot a no-deflection shot into the vulnerable underbelly of the enemy plane. If the pilot stalked the Pete biplane the same way, it also became duck soup.

Not surprisingly, Major Renner's ex-SBD pilots had never flown above 15,000 feet. Learning to fly on oxygen at high altitudes, where one usually ran into Zeros, was an absolute prerequisite for fighter pilots. Training dives were made on tow targets flying at altitudes starting at 8,000 feet and on up to 16,000 feet. Next, pilots bounced each other in simulated combat, pushing over from 26,000 feet to attack their quarry at 22,000 feet. Pilots thereby grew accustomed to flying their heavy Wildcats in rarified air.

Having thus received between forty-five and fifty hours of condensed combat training in F4Fs, Lieutenant McCartney and his fellow pilots joined on the wing of a Navy R4D transport for the four-hour flight to Guadalcanal on 11 January 1943.

USAAF aviators were no better prepared for combat. When they arrived in the South Pacific in early 1942, the 70th FS's pilots knew next to nothing about dueling with Japanese fighters in their Bell Airacobras. Ironically, in Fiji they logged some four hundred hours of combat training, based on the USAAF's standard fighter doctrine, only to be bested in mock combat by the carrier *Saratoga*'s air group. The more maneuverable F4Fs made passable clones of Japanese fighters in the hands of the Navy fliers who selflessly spent two weeks teaching the 70th's pilots the value of fighting in pairs and scissoring.

Capt. Dale Brannon's 67th FS underwent a similar catharsis during the spring of 1942 at Tontouta Field in New Caledonia. Only two—Brannon and Lt. John Thompson—out of twenty-nine pilots were checked out in the P-39/P-400; the others had logged fewer than thirty-five hours in fighters per se. Once these pilots learned to fly the Airacobra, the CO appealed to the closest fighter squadron—VMF 212, stationed at Efate in the New Hebrides—for a few tow targets to permit aerial gunnery practice. Instead, Major Bauer arranged to give Captain Brannon a real helping hand. For a solid month, Bauer's Marine pilots instructed their Army pupils in the fine art of deflection shooting as well as executing overhead and high-side passes.

To supplement firing at tow targets, the ingenious 67th invented shadow gunnery. Flying above and parallel to the calm lagoons between the island's shoreline and its fringing reef, a plane cast a perfect silhouette on the surface of the water. Other fighters could make shallow runs at the shadow to practice deflection shooting. Waterspouts thrown up by the attacker's slugs recorded the results instantly and accurately, enabling pilots to correct their fire as they went.

Fortunately, the investment in rear-area bases like Tontouta furnished convenient training facilities, and the furlough system provided both the seasoned instructors and the time to break in new pilots or tutor old hands transitioning to a new fighter. For example, when the first Lightnings arrived in the South Pacific in October 1942, Major Brannon and six other pilots who had logged one hundred or more hours of two-engine time were on hand at Tontouta to familiarize ten exceptionally gifted, veteran Airacobra pilots with the new fighter. Brannon's group splintered from the 67th FS to form the highly competent core of the new 339th FS, whose timely training in P-38s enabled it to hit the ground running upon its arrival at Cactus.

Even so, upon being furloughed from Cactus on the eve of Operation KE, Lt. Paul Hansen of the 68th FS was still inclined to recommend more practical instruction: "Pilots should be trained to combat in pairs before going up there and should have more gunnery and escort practice."

Things were no different for the Japanese. The IJN air fleet that devastated the U.S. Pacific Fleet at Pearl Harbor was manned by the best-trained aircrews in the world. Prewar naval flight cadets—initially recruited exclusively from among naval academy cadets—endured three to five years' rigorous preflight and flight training. At least two-fifths failed to achieve the exacting standards of excellence and were routinely washed out of aircrew programs. At the end of the 1920s, aircrew training was offered to serving NCOs and, subsequently, to teenage civilians who joined as enlisted men. But passing standards would be relaxed only in response to wartime exigencies.

As of 1937 the survivors of these grueling training regimens proceeded to accumulate valuable combat experience in the proving grounds of China. By the time they faced Allied pilots after Pearl Harbor, most Japanese naval aviators of the 11th Koku Kantai had logged an average six hundred hours or more, much of it air time in the cockpit of the Zero—reputedly the hottest fighter in the Pacific.

Maj. W. H. McCarroll, the 347th Fighter Group's flight surgeon, rode as an observer in a B-17 on an antishipping strike over Bougainville during Operation KE. Afterward he described the skill and prowess of the fifteen 204th Kokutai pilots who engaged his Fort in a vicious running fight:

> The Zero's normal frontal attack was to fly straight and level into the front of the B-17, then execute a half-roll on the same level. Sometimes the enemy would climb and at others, he would dive. One flew in upside down and came about 10 feet above the bomber in a slight dive, firing down. Another one came in toward the nose, pulled straight up into a loop, came back over upside-down firing.

Inevitably, a year of grueling air combat whittled down these skilled fighter pilots faster than the rate of replacements flowing from reserves and training programs. The proportion of JNAF pilots with at least five hundred hours' flying time had dwindled to a mere 15 percent by January 1943. IJN flight schools continued to set unrealistic entry standards; after Pearl Harbor they were still graduating too few fliers to keep up with the attrition rate, though courses had at least been shortened. Consequently, valuable veterans tended to be kept in combat indefinitely, resulting in predictably high losses. The 204th Kokutai was a case in point: after it arrived at Kahili in August 1942, this unit lost two ace commanders and three other aces in less than a year.

An acute shortage of pilots by the beginning of 1943 resulted in abbreviated training programs that were erroneously limited to teaching dogfighting tactics that exploited the superior agility of the Zero—long after Allied airmen had ceased to be enticed into one-on-one duels. Replacement fighter pilots now reached the South Pacific with only one hundred hours of air time, mostly in obsolescent A5M Claude fighters; some had no experience whatsoever in Zeros. These individuals tended to execute their limited tactical repertoires with less skill and predictably fared poorly against better-trained Allied pilots.

Unlike the Americans, the Japanese provided scant opportunity for veterans to train newcomers in rear areas. Infrequently, JNAF replacements were sent to the airbase at Kavieng for a brief period of practical training during which a scarce cadre of veterans gave them a crash course in combating the prevalent American aircraft operating in the Solomons. Alternately, novice pilots proceeded directly to the combat zone, where they were given on-the-job lessons and initially were assigned to the easier missions. These measures proved to be an unsatisfactory stop-gap solution at best, but they were better than nothing.

The skies over Southeast Asia also proved a highly instructive aerial laboratory for JAAF fighter pilots before 7 December 1941. Many entered World War II with five hundred to six hundred hours' flying time and continued to fly in the China–Burma–India theater where, apart from the Flying Tigers, they dueled with opponents who were inferior to Allied pilots facing the JNAF in the Pacific. Consequently, veteran JAAF pilots had accumulated little experience in operational flying over open water or insular topography when their *sentai* arrived in the South Pacific in December 1942 and January 1943, and they had not gone up against USN planes and pilots. Knowledge of unfamiliar terrain and enemy aircraft could only be garnered on the job, but travel up the learning curve at the controls of relatively fragile and lightly armed fighters cost them dearly.

JAAF pilots posted to Rabaul initially flew most of their missions over New Guinea and the Bismarck Archipelago. Combat with tough USAAF and Anzac airmen had already begun to decimate the ranks of the 1st and 11th Sentai even before they were deployed to the Solomons in support of the JNAF.

Novice Japanese army pilots—also reporting from attenuated flight-school programs—were even less prepared for combat in the South Pacific. At least one JAAF unit—the 11th Sentai—reorganized its *chutai* to preserve some measure of fighting excellence. Replacements reporting to the 11th Sentai were placed in the 3rd Chutai with a few well-skilled aviators as mentors. The 1st Chutai contained nearly all the best pilots; the 2nd Chutai, too, contained mostly veterans supplemented with some of the more-experienced younger pilots. Thus, one *chutai* always remained fully geared for combat with another nearly as capable. The 3rd Chutai became de facto an in-theater training unit where on-the-job instruction was carried out; consequently, it was assigned less-demanding tasks whenever possible. Presumably, as its pilots became more competent they either transferred to the other two *chutai* or took over the senior positions in the 3rd. However, one cannot help but wonder about the survival rate of the green pilots in the 11th Sentai's 3rd Chutai when subjected to combat with better-trained opponents flying sturdier aircraft.

Not every candidate for pilot's wings meshed with the job, no matter how much training he received. Notwithstanding the candidates who washed out or were killed in Stateside training accidents, the winnowing process remained imperfect. Every fledgling U.S. aviator who arrived at Cactus was an unknown quantity until he actually sampled the rigors and terrors of aerial combat. Those who fought the air war over the Solomons were little more than youths; most were college students in their early twenties who found themselves suddenly immersed in a shooting war amidst the hostile environment of the Solomons. Living conditions were appalling; air combat was callously cruel and not for the squeamish. One had to *want* to be there.

Once embroiled in combat, any naïve sense of self-confidence new arrivals may have harbored was rapidly eroded by a nagging feeling of ill preparedness and inadequacy. Sagging morale was fueled by the misconception that pilots would be relieved from combat after a four-week tour. When newcomers realized they would be rotated through combat tours indefinitely, they became obsessed with the odds against their survival that swelled with every mission. The more aggressive among them responded positively to on-the-job training by experienced colleagues, learning how to survive until they matured into combat veterans.

Others soon realized that they lacked the stomach to mete out or risk suffering violent death in the air and asked to be taken out of combat. But, for every pilot who openly admitted he was too afraid to fight, there were two others who could neither confront their fears nor admit to their failings as warriors. VMO-251's Major Renner reckoned that fully 10 percent of fighter pilots in the theater were what he sardonically called "giggle girls."

These individuals used all manner of ploys to duck combat missions, including regularly reporting on sick parade with questionable symptoms of malaria or other illnesses. During a scramble, some waved a "thumbs down" from the cockpit of a functional plane, indicating it was not running properly. Others hopped into aircraft that had been sidelined for repairs. A few even knowingly climbed on board write-offs—wrecked hulks scattered about the field. By the time these individuals had corrected their "mistakes," it was conveniently too late to take off. Whenever a giggle girl did manage to get airborne, he predictably requested permission to turn back due to some trumped-up mechanical malfunction.

The policy dealing with these lackluster performers ordained they be whisked back to the States without fanfare and given training assignments. Naturally, the stalwarts who stayed on the Canal to fight felt abandoned by an indifferent and seemingly unjust code of military ethics that appeared to reward failure rather than success with repatriation.

To preempt epidemics of unearned Stateside postings, Major Renner recommended that those pilots who ducked missions with the excuse that they needed more training be retained in the combat zone. If they failed to improve with further instruction, they were to forfeit their wings and be reassigned to ground duties. Should they prove inept in these capacities, they should be summarily washed out of the armed forces. Predictably, higher authorities balked at such strong medicine.

USAAF policy toward those who asked to be grounded, whether they were ducking their flying duties or genuinely suffering from combat fatigue, was simply to ground them. Here, too, this policy naturally generated cynicism, lowering the morale among those who were left to assume more than their fair share of the combat burden.

The inhospitable environment took an exacting toll. Recurring attacks of malarial fever, chills, and delirium were the number one culprits. Attacks varied so widely in severity that men did not always seek treatment. When they did, flight surgeons were mandated to get these individuals back to their duties without delay. Consequently, those pilots and airmen suffering from bouts of malaria were regularly flying combat missions—occasionally in a state of semidelirium. Suppressants, such as quinine and its synthetic substitute, Atabrine, were not available in quantity; at any rate, many refused to take them in order to avoid real and perceived side effects.

Other tropical illnesses—dengue and dysentery, in particular—cut a wide swath through the ranks of all Cactus personnel. The mental stress occasioned by continuous combat and operational flying helped erode the immune systems of even the hardiest souls, rendering them more prone to disease. Only an estimated 130 out of 200 Cactus fighter pilots were deemed medically fit to fly when Operation KE began.

The Japanese homeland is situated in a temperate climatic region not dissimilar to those of its Occidental opponents. The South Pacific was no less foreign to the Japanese, and they proved equally susceptible to its hostile environment. They also recognized malaria as the "Great Enemy," but utterly failed to cope with this disease, thereby compounding the attrition rate of pilots and aircrew—a rate that far surpassed the number of U.S. airmen rendered hors de combat by malaria. Though Japan had no counterpart to Atabrine, it did control Java, the world's major supplier of quinine, but wartime demand far outpaced production.

Cactus airmen were kept in the air as long as their temperatures remained below a certain threshold, but Japanese pilots routinely flew while suffering from severe malarial symptoms and aftereffects. Harsh training that instilled an unflinching duty to accept hardship stoically and adapt to any adverse situation kept them in the air; inevitably, combat efficiency suffered with dire consequences. For example, the 204th Kokutai lost two of its ace pilots to malaria in early 1943.

Although debilitating interservice and interunit rivalry sometimes ran rampant within the Japanese military establishment, the relationship between the JNAF and the JAAF during Operation KE seemed to be a cooperative one. The Cactus Air Force, was beset with its share of internal friction. A composite command from the outset, Cactus experienced clashes, not only between sister squadrons within the same branch, but also among its USN, USMC, and USA components.

Upon taking command on 23 December 1942, Brig. Gen. Francis Mulcahy inherited a heterogeneous outfit that comprised the bomber and fighter squadrons of three services spread around three separate airfields. Among the subordinates reporting to him were three commanders: one for Strike Command, another for Fighter Command, and one for Bomber Command.

On 1 February, with the first Tokyo Express evacuation run setting sail for Guadalcanal, Lt. Col. Edward Pugh—at the time the CO of MAG-12—

arrived at Cactus at the behest of General Mulcahy to take over as fighter commander, to whom all fighter squadron COs reported, regardless of service. The timing was undeniably awkward for the fighter CO to break into his new job; the Japanese were not about to permit him the luxury of a learning curve. That Colonel Pugh may not have had the time to establish fully his authority amidst the frenetic action surrounding Operation KE is evinced by the comments of Major Renner:

> If the squadron commander of the Army or Navy or Marines didn't like the way a plan was outlined, he nevertheless agreed to it and went out on the mission—but then did as he pleased. When on returning from the mission he was reminded of his failure to follow planned procedure, he always had a reason for it; something had happened, or the situation had changed, and he thought it best to do it this other way.

The evidence also mildly suggests that General Mulcahy, his fighter commander, and his strike commander may not have been granted sufficient authority or autonomy to mold their respective organizations as they saw fit. Marine fighter squadrons were commanded by Marines who reported to General Mulcahy through Colonel Pugh—both Marines. But the Army and Navy squadrons on detached duty answered to commanders within their own branches as well as to the local Marine commanders. Thus, to some degree Mulcahy's hands and those of his direct subordinate, Colonel Pugh, were tied when it came to such issues as awards and disciplinary actions. A similar situation undoubtedly prevailed within Strike Command after the Navy TBF squadron deployed to Cactus.

With the formation of a separate 13th Air Force within the USAAF on 13 January 1943, the issue of command in the Solomons became even more complex. Initially headquartered at Noumea in the New Hebrides, then at Espiritu Santo, the 13th Air Force was commanded by Maj. Gen. Nathan Twining. His two principal subordinates were Brig. Gen. Dean Strother, leading 13th Fighter Command, and Col. Harlan McCormick, heading 13th Bomber Command. The 13th's fighter and bomber squadrons reported to these three individuals in all administrative matters; operational command, however, was given to General Mulcahy's Cactus-based fighter and bomber commanders, but these Army units were spread over a large area: from Guadalcanal through Espiritu Santo and New Caledonia to Fiji. This arrangement inevitably caused similar planning, coordination, and disciplinary problems—only on a more-complex scale due to geographic separation of the units.

Major Renner's summary comment about the Cactus Air Force's flawed chain of command is revealing: "I don't believe we'll ever have a satisfactory unified command until the man who is in command of the combined forces has the power of writing fitness reports for the officers serving under him, of making recommendations for decorations for everybody under him and of being able to give a court martial to anybody under him." Renner's conclusion poignantly suggests that General Mulcahy had a somewhat less-than-firm grip on the forces under his command as long as the Cactus Air Force remained saddled with a fragmentation of authority.

The question of authority based on rank and seniority posed potential problems at the squadron level. Maj. Dick Baker, commanding VMF-123, purposefully selected his division leaders from among his most fit and experienced aviators. Normally the senior officers would qualify on both counts, but when this was not the case Major Baker did not hesitate to appoint those junior men he believed were better qualified in terms of flying skill and judgment. However, some of the other units assigned command positions according to rank and seniority, giving leadership responsibilities to individuals who were not always best suited to shoulder them under combat conditions.

It would not be unreasonable to conclude that both the Japanese and American land-based air groups in the Solomons on the eve of Operation KE suffered from a paucity of adequately trained fighter pilots and bomber aircrews. Both sides lost additional manpower to tropical diseases, whose debilitating effects lowered the fighting efficiency of those airmen still fit to fly.

Morale problems further threatened to attenuate the performance of newer, partially trained American and Japanese airmen. Japanese training was far more psychologically and physically demanding than American training, however, weeding out most of the faint hearts before they got to the war zones. An inculcated devotion to duty and regard for death in battle as the ultimate honor imparted to the remainder a certain stoic resignation, if not an unflinching willingness to embrace death. The closest counterpart in the psyche of most American airmen was a kind of cynical fatalism wherein they considered themselves already dead, thereby pushing the fear of death into the back of their minds.

A command structure in the Cactus Air Force that often incorporated parallel reporting channels to two different military branches could potentially weaken control over air operations. At the squadron level, seniority policies did not always guarantee that leadership positions went to the best men, resulting in a lowering of a unit's fighting efficiency.

For better or worse, on the eve of Operation KE the two opposing air arms were thus imperfectly arrayed to wrestle for control of the air over the Slot.

CHAPTER 5
PREGAME WARM-UPS: MUNDA AND VILA

By early September 1942 JNAF fighter CAPs escorting Tokyo Express convoys out of Rabaul operated to, or staged through, the captured Australian airstrip at Buka on the north coast of Bougainville. Situated some 130 nautical miles closer to Guadalcanal than Rabaul, Buka was rapidly expanded by the Japanese into a bustling airfield from which Zeros furnished CAPs for the still lengthy but less onerous leg to Guadalcanal. A patrolling B-17 counted some forty bombers and fighters dispersed around the field on 2 September.

Large convoys sailing from Bougainville's Tonolei–Shortland harbor complex to the Central Solomons after 20 October were escorted by fighters dispatched from Kahili airfield, built on the south coast of Bougainville. Called Buin airfield by the Japanese, Kahili was typically hacked out of a prewar coconut plantation, but its above-standard 4,700-foot runway was surfaced with a mixture of crushed coral and tar. Later, Kara, built to the north of Kahili, was used as a backup fighter strip. Covering aircraft based at Kahili often departed *after* the Tokyo Express convoys, catching up to the convoys farther down the Slot before they got into range of the Cactus Air Force. This drill conserved fuel and extended gas-consuming dwell time overhead when it was most needed.

Some 517 British prisoners from Singapore labored to complete a defensive fighter strip on Ballale in the nearby Shortlands in early January 1943, at the cost of their lives.

These installations acted as advance bomber and escort-fighter bases as well, further reducing the distance to Guadalcanal by an average ninety-five miles. Long-range A6M2 Zekes still flew the Rabaul-Kahili leg, but now the shorter-range A6M3 Hamps and Zekes—and later, JAAF Oscars—could safely escort air strikes into the Eastern Solomons, thereby upping by one-third the Japanese fighter availability over Guadalcanal. The smaller airstrip at Bonis—across Buka Passage from Buka—and other primitive airstrips farther down the east coast of Bougainville at Tenekau and Kieta were available for emergency use only.

Smaller convoys or individual ships usually merited a CAP provided by Pete or Jake floatplanes out of the seaplane base on Poporang Island. The floatplanes would overfly a convoy in relays down into the Central Solomons. Since all Tokyo Express convoys headed down the Slot out of Rabaul, Faisi, or Buin were timed to arrive at their destinations around sunset, the last day shift would turn over escort duties to other Petes or Jakes. Early next morning, floatplanes or fighters would fly back down the Slot in relays to rejoin the returning convoy for the trip back to Bougainville. Spelled off by the first day shift, floatplane crews would return to the seaplane base at Rekata Bay to refuel and rest, then either push on to Poporang or linger in the Central Solomons, where they would carry out local reconnaissance patrols while awaiting another nocturnal CAP assignment. Assuming nighttime CAP duties in early January 1943, the F1M2 Pete, in particular, quickly excelled in its nocturnal fighter-bomber role.

At first the Japanese did not perceive a pressing need for intermediate airstrips in the Central Solomons, given their belief that the reconquest of Guadalcanal would require only a short campaign. But aircraft losses climbed alarmingly once the struggle for Henderson Field devolved into a prolonged slugfest of attrition. Rabaul and its satellite fields lost at least 507 planes between early August and late December 1942. The barge-staging base and auxiliary seaplane base at Gizo Island—one of only two seaplane facilities in the New Georgia group—was bombed out of existence by the Cactus Air Force during October. The JNAF realized—some critics say too late—that a disproportionate number of damaged or fuel-starved aircraft, especially those flying all the way to Guadalcanal from Rabaul during August and early September, were simply not making it back, being forced to ditch en route somewhere in the Slot.

Ergo, the destroyer *Hakaze* hove to off Munda Point at the southwestern tip of New Georgia on 11 November 1942 and disgorged three companies of the 6th Sasebo Rikusentai. Once on shore these Japanese "marines" occupied Lambeti plantation and the nearby Methodist mission on Kokengolo Hill. They then proceeded to scour the outlying areas for Anzac coastwatcher outposts and to round up any locals who were suspected collaborators with, or members of, the British native constabulary. A shallow but tight security zone was thrown up to cordon off the environs of Munda Point. Transports returned to unload a survey team, a rifle battalion, building materials, rudimentary construction equipment, and two pioneer battalions.

The surveyors tested the soil's ability to support an airstrip and then laid out a runway and taxiways while the troops constructed a defensive perimeter around the area. Eschewing the help of native labor, the construction crews began to clear the undergrowth and cut the coconut palms flush with the ground. In an ingenious job of camouflage, they wired the fronds of the trees together along the long, narrow alley of the proposed runway. They then severed the crowns and felled the trunks, leaving selected trees standing as anchors for the wires that kept the tops of their absentee neighbors in place. Working mostly at night beneath this verdant camouflage, the crews graded the runway, spreading a crushed coral surface out from four different points along its axis. At this stage, Cactus reconnaissance photos finally laid bare the Japanese ruse.

Allied suspicions about an airfield in the making had been aroused as early as 1 December, when coastwatchers radioed Cactus that enemy barges, working down past Vella Lavella from Bougainville, were loaded with cement and other heavy construction materials. Lt. Henry Josslyn and Lt. John Keenan correctly guessed that these materials were earmarked for an airstrip. From the outset, natives loyal to the ex-British colonial regime reported the landings and subsequent goings-on at Munda to chief coastwatcher Maj. Donald Kennedy, ensconced at Segi, on New Georgia. Major Kennedy, in turn, alerted Cactus. Reconnaissance flights were immediately dispatched to Munda. On 5 December photo interpreters on Guadalcanal noticed that the isolated white pockets of packed coral visible beneath the palm trees were not only the same width, but they were being extended toward one another in a straight line in the general direction of the prevailing wind. The jig was up! Cactus launched its first bombing raid on Munda the next day.

Coastwatcher HQ now ordered Lt. Dick Horton to set up an observation outpost overlooking the fledging Munda-Lambeti base. Flying in to Segi by PBY, Horton set up shop temporarily in a secluded ravine next to Morovo Lagoon. Then he and Sgt. Harry Wickham, an NCO in the local British native constabulary who was intimately familiar with the area, scouted the coastline by canoe to within five miles of Munda Point. They found no location commanding an unobstructed view of the point, but observed enough activity to confirm that an airfield was taking shape despite Cactus air strikes.

The Japanese began to knock down the remaining overhead cover within days of the photo-interpretation unit's discovery, revealing an all-weather runway some forty-four feet wide and nearly eleven hundred feet long. They also dismantled the camouflage over the taxiways, which were flanked by revetments for upwards of thirty fighters built in the shelter of the remaining palms. Quickly finishing the revetments, workers started to lengthen the runway eastward to accommodate bombers. Japanese fighters and bombers made successful test landings on the new field on 15 December. Munda airstrip brought the Japanese another 105 nautical miles closer to Guadalcanal (see diagram 1).

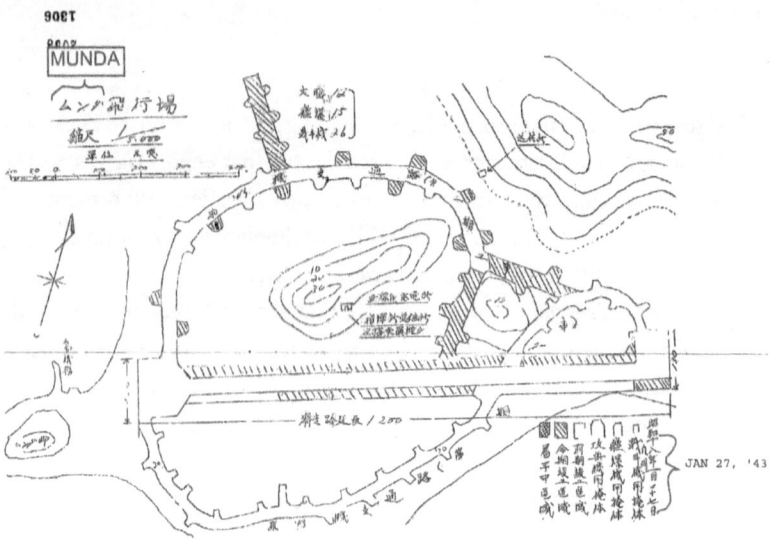

Freehand drawing of Munda airstrip as it appeared in early January 1943.

The opening of Munda airstrip was followed in the New Year by the breaking of ground for a satellite field at the Vila-Stanmore plantations, on nearby Kolombangara Island. Not even bothering to disguise this new endeavor, the Japanese simply hacked the runway out of the immense coconut groves that sprawled across the island's southeastern peninsula. Here, too, they built connecting taxiways to wood-buttressed, earthen revetments hidden beneath adjacent stands of coconut palms (see diagram 2).

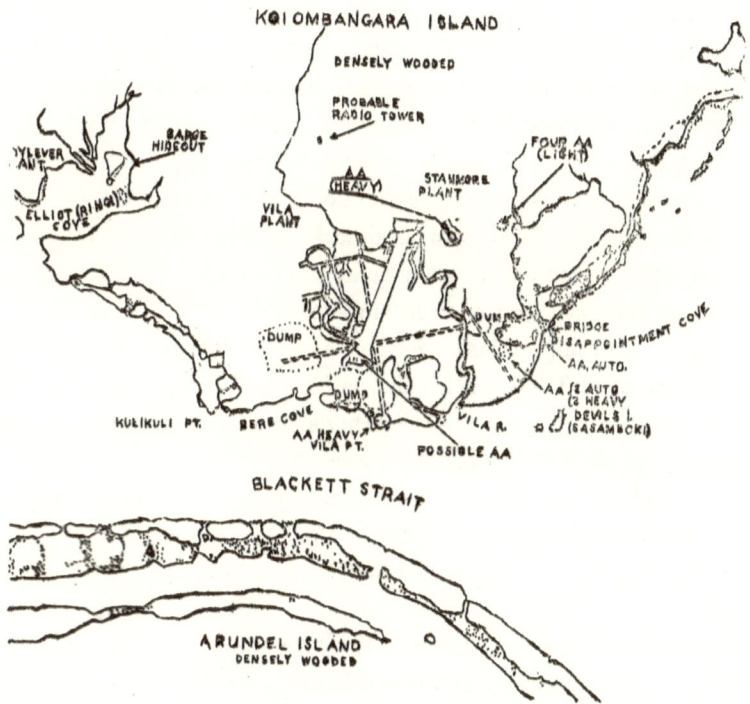

Freehand drawing of Vila-Stanmore base and airstrip. Copies were given to pilots on airstrikes for marking appraoch, direction, bomb hits, targets strafed, and so on.

Paradoxically, both fields had been planned as elements of the new Japanese offensive, but were developed just as imperial GHQ prepared to abandon the contest for Guadalcanal. However, given the anticipated Allied advance up the Solomons, both Munda and Vila were now deemed essential as frontline bases for the air defense of Fortress Rabaul, acting as staging and emergency strips for ongoing missions into the Slot.

With the Cactus Air Force growing stronger as the Guadalcanal campaign dragged on, Rabaul elected to establish an observation post along the mountain front overlooking the Henderson airfield complex, which included Henderson Field plus the two fighter strips: Fighter One and Fighter Two. Its purpose was to report on Cactus air traffic—and especially on fighter sorties. Although these radio reports were intended to impart some tactical leverage to Japanese strike forces en route to the Canal, they proved more useful to Rabaul's overall command of air operations in the Solomons—both offensive and defensive.

Emulating the Cactus Air Force, the Japanese began to develop a whole network of observation posts like those at Visu Visu and Vera Vera on New Georgia, supplemented by radio-equipped launches and small schooners, *maru*, and subs, to protect their new bases from surprise air attack. But native guerrillas loyal to the Allies took out some of these outposts or reported their locations, whereupon Cactus sent out air strikes to destroy them. Occasionally, despite ingenious camouflaging, Cactus airmen themselves spotted a floating vedette. At 1800 on 7 January seven patrolling Wildcats led by Capt. Joe Foss spotted a radio-equipped Japanese schooner nestled under a camouflage net against a steep bluff at Kalokale Point. In Foss' own words, "We riddled the schooner at the waterline and returned to the field just as darkness fell. Next day only a mast was sticking out of the water." Notwithstanding such setbacks, intercepted Japanese radio traffic revealed that most Allied movements by air or sea throughout the Slot were being reported to Rabaul by March 1943.

At 0800 on 23 December 1942 the JNAF's 252nd Kokutai flew twenty Zeros out of Rabaul in one *chutai* of fifteen plus a separate *chutai* of five. Landing at Munda in the company of nine escorting 204th Kokutai Zeros at around 1045, Lt. Motonari Suho and his pilots taxied over to revetment areas to disperse their planes. A harbinger of the next few days' unpleasantness arrived at 1210 in the form of a USMC welcoming committee that swooped down, targeting the west end of the runway and the adjacent AA positions along the shoreline.

Maj. Don Yost—the new CO of a reconstituted VMF-121—who had just stepped off an R4D transport that morning with his cadre of pilots, found himself climbing into the cockpit of an F4F to lead a division of Marine Corps Wildcats up the Slot. Capt. Joe McGlothlin of VMO-251 followed with another. They arrived over the new airstrip with a dozen Dauntlesses in tow to find some fifteen Zeros already airborne and aggressive. The F4F escort moved to fend them off while the SBDs went in to bomb the field. In the ensuing air battle Major Yost claimed a pair of Zeros, Captain McGlothlin was credited with another, Lt. Irwin Carter and Lt. Ben Wisner of VMF-121 claimed one apiece. The SBDs put in for two Zeros destroyed on the ground. Japanese pilots returned the compliment by air conditioning the Grumman flown by VMO-251's Lt. Blaine Baesler and shooting down Capt. Dave Andre of VMF-121.

Captain Andre pulled off a successful water landing in Roviana Lagoon and made it to an isolated islet, where he went into temporary hiding. Alerted by the coastwatcher network, local natives quickly tracked him down. Somewhat apprehensive as to where the loyalties of his rescuers lay, the downed pilot was relieved to be taken in by a friendly village. There he waited in safety until Major Yost returned on 31 January with a VMF-121 division, flying escort for a PBY.

A USAAF welcome wagon in the form of five B-17s, escorted by five P-39s from the 12th FS and four P-38s from the 339th, showed up over Munda at 1222 to find the hornet's nest thoroughly stirred up by the first raid. Unfortunately, a sixth Fort and two Cobras had to abort the mission due to mechanical problems. Then Lieutenant Orick of the 12th got lost en route, having possibly become disoriented while threading his way through extensive heavy cumulus.

Assistant coastwatcher Harry Wickham had by now crossed over to Rendova, where he eventually found an excellent observation post on a high ledge in the island's uplands. From there he had an unobstructed view of Munda airstrip. It was he who observed six Zeros that had likely just touched down after the first raid take off again for a second interception. Shortly after, the heavy bombers unloaded their payloads on the airstrip amidst heavy flak. Eight 500-pounders, and eighty-six 100-pounders, tumbled from open bomb bays. Damage claims included a fuel bowser and at least two grounded Zeros. One of the Mitsubishi pilots broke through the fighter screen and made a run on a Fort, but was pursued and driven off by a Cobra. It was likely this P-39 that had a tire blown out and an elevator damaged by flak in the process.

Through the haze of coral dust, Sergeant Wickham saw three of the six Zeros touch back down at Munda. Maj. Paul Bechtel's Cobra pilots put in for three planes destroyed, which for once jibed with Wickham's reports to Horton. U.S. claims totaled ten Zeros shot down for the entire day's two actions, but the JNAF recorded only one airborne fighter, flown by PO2c Takeo Matsubayashi, lost. Another four were damaged with two pilots wounded. Nineteen Zeros were still extant but seven had admittedly been damaged on the ground; this tends to confirm the seven aircraft the Marine pilots saw burning on the field when they left immediately prior to the USAAF raid. In return, of the day's twenty-four estimated attacking planes, the 252nd's pilots put in for three SBDs, four "Grummans," and a P-38 shot down, plus four SBDs and two "Grummans" as probables. Exaggerated claims all around!

Munda got another taste of Cactus' version of Maytag Mike harassment raids that night. A solitary B-17 droned to and fro overhead between 0245 and 0510, dropping flares and dispensing twenty 100-pound bombs at appropriate intervals to keep everyone awake. Indeed, B-17s and PBYs had been staging nightly visitations over Munda almost continuously from the moment the nascent airstrip had been discovered.

Two more airborne Zeros fell from the sky the next day, and six more were damaged in air combat. Ens. Yaichiro Fukunishi and LA Kazufusa Harano were killed and three more pilots wounded, one seriously. Some of these planes may have been minor casualties from the previous day's raid that had been patched in time to go up again.

Major Yost led a division of F4Fs with Lt. Ken Kirk of VMO-251 as his wingman. Along with Maj. Paul Bechtel's eight 12th FS Airacobras, the Wildcats flew cover for twelve Dauntlesses, of which three had to abort. Arriving over Munda at 0800, the Cactus strike force ran into a dozen Zeros lying in wait at 12,000 feet while others hastily attempted to get off the ground. Again, these Zeros had only been lightly damaged or not hit at all the previous day.

Strangely, while the four Grummans proceeded to intercept enemy fighters in their taxiing and takeoff patterns, the inferior Cobras engaged the airborne ones. Major Bechtel's P-39s slid in behind them from out of the sun.

Squinting against the glare, the Japanese *chutai* leader apparently mistook the Cobras for another flight of Zeros attempting to join up and cruised on accommodatingly. Bechtel closed in for his first kill, trembling with anticipation but with enough presence of mind to ignore his untrustworthy 37-mm cannon. Triggering his fifties and thirties, he fired short at the tail-end Charlie. Quickly he adjusted his aim and poured a long burst of machine-gun fire into the unsuspecting Zero, which fell off and caught fire.

The jubilant CO of the 12th FS climbed up behind the next Mitsubishi, opening fire long enough to claim a probable. Suddenly realizing they were under attack, the remaining Zeros scattered in climbing turns with the P-39s in questionable pursuit—sans turbo-superchargers. A Zero quickly pulled around onto the tail of Bechtel's slower-turning Cobra. When his number two, 2nd Lt. Everett Anglin, called the Zeke out, Bechtel reversed his climbing turn to the right. The enemy fighter closed in with guns winking. Red-hot tracers were zipping all around him when Bechtel's straining fighter finally stalled and fell off into a right-hand spin. While his flight leader plummeted earthward, Lieutenant Anglin moved in to splash the Zero.

Major Bechtel recovered from his spin over Rendova. Counting his blessings, he now proceeded to join up on a fighter that turned out to be yet another Zero. The enemy pilot politely gave him elbow room as he crept up on his quarry's right flank—another case of mistaken identity. The Cobra's machine guns rattled. The Zero slowed, then dropped off lazily to the right. Another pilot saw the Zero burst into flames. Major Bechtel's first two kills were probably the easiest ones he ever got.

In their strafing spree, the Marines claimed eight of the scrambling enemy fighters, with Major Yost accounting for four, Captain Kirk three, and MG Ed Zielinski one. The SBDs put in for two Zeros shot down and four more destroyed amidst the gaggle piled up at the east end of the runway, but some of the latter may have been double-claimed with the F4Fs. In addition to Major Bechtel's two victories and Lieutenant Anglin's one, Captain Lanphier claimed a fourth airborne Zero. P-39 pilots also claimed two probables. The overclaiming totaled eighteen Zeros destroyed plus the probables! The Japanese regarded the two aircraft lost and six damaged in the air, and the five shot up on the ground, as a serious blow. Two pilots were dead and three more were wounded, one seriously. In turn, the 252nd Kokutai modestly claimed an SBD and an F4F shot down.

A reconnaissance flight passed over Munda at 1000 to photograph the results. Photos revealed fifteen planes dispersed around the field. Nine were in revetments, and another six that appeared to be wrecked lined the runway. Not only did the runway appear to be usable, but several hundred feet of coconut trees had been cleared at its eastern end in preparation for the new extension to accommodate bombers.

Eight SBDs, escorted by Major Viccellio's six P-39s and Lieutenant Colonel McNeese's seven P-38s, hit Munda for the second time that day at high noon. No enemy opposition was encountered in the air as the Dauntlesses dove in. Japanese ground crews were probably still refueling, rearming, and repairing. A quartet each of 500-pounders and 100-pounders rained down. One hit the water, seven potholed the runway. The remainder fell "on or near gun emplacements." A PB4Y-1 on a photoreconnaissance flight an hour later recorded twenty Zeros (condition unspecified) on the disheveled field, plus two airborne Zeros that chose to stay aloof.

A late-afternoon antishipping strike, searching the New Georgia group for a transport and a pair of escorting destroyers, failed to locate its prospective targets due to worsening weather. Coincidentally, the nine SBDs stumbled upon thirteen *daihatsu,* loaded with troops and supplies, plying Blanche Channel, off Munda. A quartet each of F4Fs and P-40s waited in vain for Japanese fighters to come up while nine SBDs went after the helpless barges. Only four of the sluggish enemy craft reached shore intact, with "very few personnel" escaping the carnage wrought by the bombing and strafing. One Cactus plane then buzzed the airstrip at fifty feet, uncontested by Munda's surprised AA gunners. The pilot reported that the runway had been "chewed up," with the wrecked aircraft now cleared to one side. The two days' losses had proven onerous for the JNAF; three replacement Zeros flown into Munda later that day made for small compensation.

A pair of long-range searches by B-17s and RNZAF Hudsons hustled up the Slot every day as far as Bougainville; Cactus also dispatched fighters on daily reconnaissance flights. Starting at 0600 a trio of Baker search, Dog search, and Easy search left the Canal to patrol the New Georgia group, Santa Ysabel, Choiseul, and the Shortlands, the fighters overflying the major enemy bases and installations in those areas. The Russell Islands were also given the once-over along the way. Strike Command relied heavily on the intelligence gathered by these and other probes.

Twenty-six December was a day for chance meetings. Easy search's two P-39s were jumped by four "Zeros" over Munda at 0930. Surprisingly, the assailants turned out to be four 582nd Kokutai dive-bombers out of Buin on daily reconnaissance patrol to Munda. Incredibly, the Val pilots gave chase, but Major Viccellio and Captain Rivers chose not to give them the opportunity to commit mass seppuku, leaving them far behind above the southeastern tip of New Georgia. Within the hour, a pair of 339th FS P-38s on a reconnaissance mission ran into a Val southeast of New Georgia—probably one of the same four encountered earlier. But Captain Shaw and Lieutenant Jacobson entertained no qualms about attacking a sitting duck and made two passes, damaging the dive-bomber before it escaped into a cloud bank with a wounded crewman. Nine 252nd Kokutai Zeros were also aloft, patrolling the New Georgia group; they sighted the Lightnings in the distance, but no exchange took place.

What started out as a bombing mission turned into another fighter sweep when fifteen SBDs failed to rendezvous with eight VMF-121 Wildcats and eight 12th FS Airacobras. After orbiting over Savo Island for twenty minutes, Capt. Hunter Reinburg and Capt. Phil White shoved off for Munda with their F4F divisions, accompanied by the Cobra flight.

Arriving in the Central Solomons around 1500, the Cactus pilots found New Georgia shrouded by heavy cloud cover, but they persevered. Reinburg found a hole in the clouds and led his pilots through, emerging over the airstrip to find two Zeros preparing to take off and another dozen on the ground. PO2c Bunkichi Nakajima, a future sixteen-kill ace, and LA Magoichi Kosaka had apparently just flown in from Rabaul—the last of five replacements. They may have been taxiing in when the raiders arrived. Swinging around, they gunned their planes down the runway and scrambled back up. As the Mitsubichis cleared, the Wildcats and Cobras strafed the field with great enthusiasm, destroying two Zeros. They also set fire to seven or eight more and a fuel or ammo dump and took out a gun emplacement.

The two airborne Zero pilots initially eschewed combat until they had gained sufficient altitude to favor a bounce. By the time they reached an advantageous position, the raiders had reformed and were leaving. Nakajima and Kosaka proceeded to shadow the F4Fs until Reinburg's divisions—

low on fuel and almost out of ammo—decided to bluff. Unexpectedly, they scissored, turning into the two stalkers. In their haste to scatter, the surprised Zero pilots dove dangerously close to the water. U.S. pilots claim that one Zero caught a wing and cartwheeled, but 252nd Kokutai records show both Nakajima and Kosaka returning safely to Munda.

For Munda's garrison there was no respite. Three 98th BS(H) Forts showed up on their way back from an antishipping strike over the Tonolei-Shortland harbor complex. Only one B-17 had managed to bomb through the poor weather, claiming a hit and several near misses on an unidentified ship off Buin, possibly the 451-ton *Izumi Maru*, which was recorded sunk by air attack that day. Pausing over Munda, the other two Forts proceeded to unload twenty 500-pounders on the airstrip and surrounding area, once again setting off several fires.

The Japanese barge base at Wickham anchorage, nestled between Vangunu and Gatukai Islands, also hosted an unwelcome visit by a Cactus strike force on 26 January. The small freighters *Takashima Maru* and *Iwami Maru*, ineffectively disguised with palm fronds, were unloading cargo to be transshipped via barge to submarines supplying the 17th Army. Baker search's P-39 pilot discovered them at 1015 after temporarily shaking off four covering Zeros.

As a result, the two ships came under attack by seven SBDs at 1410 hours. The dive-bombers wasted no time going in while Maj. Don Yost's Wildcat division from VMF-121 circled above in the company of a flight of 339th FS Lightnings. Planting bombs on both ships, the Dauntless pilots quickly sank the larger *Iwami Maru*, estimated at 3,200 tons displacement, but it actually displaced 773 tons.

Surprisingly, despite their earlier presence in the vicinity none of the known nine airworthy Zeros from Munda showed up to defend the merchantmen before the fighter sweep and B-17 raid on the airstrip further whittled their number. A second Cactus strike force sent to finish off the remaining cargo ship was turned back by worsening weather. One of its P-40 escorts had to ditch; the pilot was rescued. Major Kennedy later reported from nearby Segi that the stricken 494-ton *Takashima Maru* lingered on the surface until 2200 hours.

Utterly frustrated, Rabaul threw in the towel, ordering the Munda detachment to withdraw its remaining operable fighters, but not before Cactus raiders had struck again the next day. Capt. Pat Weiland of VMO-251 took off at 0730 from Fighter Two with Lt. Harvey "Fateye" Gardner of VMF-121 on his wing. A second section comprising Lt. Roy Spurlock of VMO-251 and Lt. Alex "Sandy" Hearn of VMF-121 formed up on Weiland's right. With them flew Lt. Irwin Carter's division of VMF-121 F4Fs. The two Wildcat divisions were to conduct a fighter sweep in advance of a bombing mission.

Capt. Dave Shaw's eight P-39s from the 12th FS and Capt. Tom Lanphier's four P-38s from the 339th followed the Marines with three SBDs in tow. Protected by two 339th FS wingmen, Lt. Col. George McNeese, ramrod of the 347th Fighter Group, tagged along to observe the proceedings from the gondola of a Lightning.

Arriving over Munda the Marine Corps pilots found a *shotai* of Zeros already airborne and proceeded to engage them. Leading his Wildcats toward the airstrip, Weiland spotted the three Zeros after they had scrambled to escape the impending attack. As the A6Ms climbed slightly below and perpendicular to his line of flight, the F4F leader dove in.

The enemy *shotai* leader, Lt. Yuzo Tsukamoto, immediately turned to meet him. Reacting to a short burst of gunfire from Weiland's F4F, the veteran of the attack on Pearl Harbor snapped his Zero into a diving turn to the right. Instinctively, the Marine stood his Wildcat on its left wing to follow, but, mindful of his enemy's superior agility, he checked his dive. Unable to lure his adversary into a dogfight, Weiland's wily antagonist reversed course and again shot up past the F4F, which was now executing a shallow dive to the left. Weiland checked his dive, pulling up steeply as the Mitsubishi flipped into a left wingover and fell off.

This time, when the inverted Zero pilot dangled his tail invitingly, Weiland obliged, yanking his stick into his lap. Before Tsukamoto realized it, the Wildcat was rising steeply toward his left flank. With his airspeed declining alarmingly, Weiland managed to close to one hundred yards before triggering a long burst into his opponent. No longer able to sustain its climb, the straining Grumman fell off and dropped. Weiland recovered from his stall in time to observe the vanquished Zero plunge earthward in an inverted spin to splash off Munda Point.

A parachute wafted down over the airstrip, but the victor did not interfere with its descent. Lieutenant Tsukamoto landed safely, injuring himself slightly when he touched down—a mere inconvenience compared to being shot up in his chute. Having descended to 12,000 feet for a better look at the action, Colonel McNeese, Capt. John Mitchell, and Lt. Wally Dinn caught sight of the chute but, not daring to take their P-38s any lower, passed up the notion to strafe the enemy pilot.

Weiland, Spurlock, and Hearn each claimed one of the three Zeros. After airborne opposition melted away, the escorting fighters braved intense AA fire to strafe six more A6Ms parked under coconut trees. The three SBDs each dropped a 500-pound plus 100-pound bomb combo that shredded a Zero and left three fires raging: two in supply dumps north of the runway, and another in a revetment containing a fuel dump.

All told, between four and six Zeros had made it into the air. The Americans collectively claimed a dozen planes destroyed in the air and on the ground. Veteran LA Chuichiro Hata was lost in air combat. Ens. Toshiyuki Sueda conceded that after knocking down two P-39s, his own plane was seriously damaged, and he was forced to make an "emergency landing" at Munda. For the record, no Cactus planes, P-39s or otherwise, were lost.

Of the six Zeros that according to the Japanese actually remained intact after this last raid, only three were fit to fly back to Bougainville. On 28 December a trio of Mitsubishi Nells was dispatched from Vunakanau with an escort of nine Zeros to deadhead the surplus 252nd fighter pilots back from Munda to Buin. To rub salt into the wound, two 70th FS P-39s on a Cactus reconnaissance mission intercepted the Mitsubishis as Munda Point hove into view.

After nosing around Wickham anchorage, Easy search had climbed back up to 11,000 feet when Lt. Rex Barber and Lt. Bill Daggitt observed an estimated nine Hamps in two string formations of five and four "doing slow rolls and loops over clouds." Dropping down to nine thousand feet, the Cactus pilots flew over to reconnoiter Munda beneath the cover of a "thunderhead." Munda's gunners did not open up, evidently regarding the two P-39s as part of their own airborne formation. While circling the field, Barber sighted a Nell bomber flying westward off shore. Reaching Munda Point, the G3M reversed course to begin its final approach.

With Lieutenant Daggitt on his wing to keep an eye on the unsuspecting escort, Lieutenant Barber sneaked back and dove on this lead Nell. Intent on getting his first kill, Barber suddenly became aware that something was inducing a lot of drag. Then it dawned on him: he had forgotten to jettison his near-empty belly tank. Releasing the tank, the mortified pilot depressed the trigger on his control column. The drop tank plummeted seaward, angling toward the enemy plane as the P-39D's nose and wing guns ignited in pulsating flashes. A spate of slugs ripped into the Mitsubishi, flaming the port engine and wounding several crewmen.

While his dorsal gunner continued to fire at the P-39, Lt. (jg) Keizo Kondo coaxed his faltering bomber around to his right in a wide arc. Exhibiting considerable skill, he ditched on Munda Point's fringing reef just 1,800 feet off shore. The crew made good their escape before the Nell slipped beneath the surface to settle on the reef in three fathoms of water. It sits there yet, a passive host to a thriving colony of marine life.

Pulling out, Barber noticed a second Nell abort its approach, swing over the water, and roar away. Munda's batteries were throwing up a "terrific" umbrella of AA fire by now, so the P-39 pilots climbed into the cloud cover, making good their escape before the escorting Zeros could react. The two remaining Nells soon returned. Quickly loading up, they left Munda at 1250, touching down at Rabaul at 1430 without further incident.

Witnessing Barber's attack from across Blanche Channel, assistant coastwatcher Wickham gaped in amazement at an American fighter apparently dive-bombing a Japanese bomber! When word got back to Cactus via coastwatcher Horton, it undoubtedly took some time for Barber to live down this perceived feat amidst much heckling from fellow airmen. Lieutenant Barber became an ace, and has been unofficially credited with the destruction of Adm. Isoroku Yamamoto's Betty.

Seven Wildcats from VMF-121 and VMO-251 joined seven Cobras and four 339th FS Lightnings later that day for a fighter sweep to Munda. Encountering no airborne opposition but lots of AA fire, Major Bechtel's P-39s and the F4Fs under Capt. Harry Coleman and Lieutenant Railsback strafed the field. Knocking out an AA gun, they set three Zeros and a possible avgas dump alight.

Another pair of Japanese cargo ships, offloading at Wickham anchorage, bore the brunt of two Cactus air strikes the next day, 29 December. First discovered by two reconnaissance P-38s despite some elaborate camouflaging with palm fronds, their presence was confirmed by Easy search's P-39s. Before long, Major Yost's ten F4Fs and Major Bechtel's seven P-39s escorted a dozen SBDs to the targets, acquiring them at 0950 hours. The Dauntlesses swooped in to drop four of their 500-pounders next to the ships. A near miss ten feet off her stern started one of the tramps to settle. Strafing runs by the fighters set both the *Azusa Maru* and the other coastal freighter on fire. Again, no Japanese fighters showed up to interrupt the proceedings.

However, nine 204th Kokutai Hamps on standing patrol over New Georgia fell upon Captain Grey's PB4Y-1 at 1130 as he flew a photoreconnaissance mission between Munda and nearby Ramada Bay. The Liberator's gunners claimed two of the clipped-wing Zeros; no A6Ms were lost, although three took hits. In return, Japanese pilots raked their quarry with 3,113 rounds of cannon and machine-gun fire, wounding Grey and copilot Lieutenant Builes as well as Radioman Schaub. The big patrol bomber managed to survive the onslaught, and made a beeline for Cactus.

Capt. Phil White and Capt. Harry Allen arrived at Wickham anchorage with their VMF-121 divisions at 1305, escorting a second strike force. Once again the CAP prepared to defend against enemy interceptors while another dozen SBDs, in the company of Major Viccellio's eight bomb-laden P-39s, attacked the unprotected ships with impunity. The dive-bombers scored four direct hits. Only six 500-pound bombs out of eight dropped by the Cobras exploded, but two were bull's eyes. All these hits, plus two near misses and copious strafing, left both vessels "blazing and exploding."

Two or three Zeros were actually observed flying low over the water nearby, but their pilots were likely disabused of any impulse to intercept the SBDs by the superior Cactus fighter cover. Shipboard AA gunners offered ineffective opposition. Exhibiting unbridled optimism, the SBD pilots claimed a "light cruiser" and a "cargo ship" sunk. The Japanese acknowledged the loss of the coastal freighter *Azusa Maru* in the waters around Wickham. Her colleague's fate is unknown, though both appeared to be anchored over a submerged reef that supposedly hindered their sinkings—at least temporarily.

On 30 December Capt. Pat Weiland's VMO-251 division was aloft with Capt. Hunter Reinburg's VMF-121 F4Fs en route to New Georgia in search of a brawl. With them flew another four bomb-carrying P-39s on yet a third visit to Wickham anchorage. The covering Wildcats watched for enemy interceptors while Capt. Tom Lanphier's Cobras bombed five well-camouflaged barges, there being no sign of the two cargo ships damaged the previous day.

Lt. Robert Petit went in too low; when his bomb detonated, shrapnel tore a hole in the underside of his plane. Lesson learned, the hard way. Reforming, the Army pilots observed that all the barges were burning. The formation then winged its way along Blanche Channel to Munda. Again nothing beyond AA fire greeted the Cactus airmen as they made three lazy circuits around the airstrip before departing empty-handed to sweep around northern New Georgia.

Over the next few weeks U.S. forays into the Central Solomons continued unabated—and uncontested—by the JNAF; the Munda-based Zero threat had been neutralized for the time being. But, despite the lack of Japanese opposition, Cactus was slow to realize that the facility had been abandoned as a permanent fighter strip.

B-26s from the 69th BS(M) arrived at Cactus at 1205 on New Year's Eve. Picking up four P-38s, four P-39s, and Capt. Phil White's division of VMF-121 Wildcats, they were on their way by 1630 to help the Japanese ground echelon at Munda ring out the Old Year with yet another pyrotechnic demonstration on the pockmarked airstrip. One P-39 was forced down at sea on the way up, but the pilot made it on shore in the Russell Islands to await rescue. Six 500-pounders plummeted down along with forty-two 100-pounders on what appeared to be an empty airfield. Heavy but ineffectual 75-mm flak from some eight gun positions blossomed all around the raiders.

The mission was marred at its outset when an Airacobra pilot misaligned his plane for takeoff from Fighter Two, rolling down the runway at enough of an angle to clip the left wing of a taxiing Lightning that was crowding the flight path. The impact spun the P-38 around, minus the outer part of its wing, and it ploughed into a nearby structure, shearing off its nose wheel. The P-39 pilot wasted no time getting out when his plane skidded to a halt on its belly before igniting.

Such setbacks did nothing to deter nine B-26s from returning to Munda the following morning at 0700 to usher in the New Year under the protection of four P-39s, four P-40s, and three P-38s. More than five tons of bombs further cratered the airfield and adjacent bivouac areas, starting fires that were still burning vigorously when a Cactus recon aircraft visited the airstrip at 1205 hours. Only two planes were seen on the field. Intense AA fire again failed to claim any of the attackers.

Six Marauders and nine SBDs raided Munda at 0820 the next day. The dive-bombers unloaded twenty-eight 500-pounders and seventeen 100-pounders on taxiways and AA positions, knocking out six of the latter. The B-26s followed suit. Eight escorting Wildcats and four Hawks met no airborne opposition, though Major Bechtel's six Cobra pilots sighted "four square wing tip Zeros about 15 miles north of field about 1 mile above." They "made no attempt to attack (could have been F4Fs)." Forewarned just in time, the Hamps barely scrambled out of the way. As for the possible F4F sighting, the Marines were strafing Rekata Bay that day.

Smarting at having been given the bum's rush out of Munda by the Cactus Air Force, the JNAF doubtless sought an opportunity to administer some payback. With the moon almost gone, the vehicle for revenge was a 2 January supply run to Guadalcanal by ten destroyers of Rear Adm. Tomiji Koyanagi's Reinforcement Unit. Two *chutai* of Zeros from the crack 204th Kokutai were to supply the fighter CAP in relays, along with four to six *Sanyo Maru* Petes. When the Tokyo Express arrived within range of Cactus' light bombers that day, the second 204th *Chutai* was on hand, spoiling for a fight.

According to the acerbic Cdr. Yasumi Toyami, then chief of staff of Rabaul-based Destroyer Squadron 2, "We are more a freighter convoy than a fighting squadron." Indeed, his frustration reflected the handicaps inherent in the modus operandi of the fabled Tokyo Express, handicaps that sometimes go unappreciated by students of the Guadalcanal campaign. In a transport role, each destroyer carried one hundred or more drums of supplies lashed to one another in strings on its deck. These were to be jettisoned over the side within three hundred yards of the shoreline, whence troops would attempt to drag them ashore. Consequently, ammunition and torpedoes had to be cut drastically to accommodate the drums, and deck space was cramped, thereby gravely reducing the ship's fighting capabilities. Small wonder these destroyers were under strict orders to flee if confronted by U.S. warships.

Sighted the previous morning as they entered the western entrance to the Shortland-Tonolei harbor complex, and erroneously reported at 0910 as four battleships or heavy cruisers and six destroyers, Admiral Koyanagi's supply convoy left the next day, retracing its path into the Solomon Sea before turning south under the first umbrella of six Zeros from the 204th Kokutai. Between 1415 and 1426 the Reinforcement Unit was unintentionally intercepted twenty-seven miles west of the Treasury Islands—still well out from the Solomons.

Five B-17s from the 431st BS, on their way to plaster Bougainville in the company of five P-38s at 1345, could not pass up the tempting target presented by the seemingly unprotected Tokyo Express as it steamed southwest. Unloading forty-five 100-pound bombs over the scattering columns, the Forts scored four near misses in an attempt to rearrange the deck architecture of several destroyers. Seeing the well-defended Forts bombing ineffectively from a high altitude, the Zero and Pete CAPs made no move to challenge their fifty machine guns. With his impromptu attack, the B-17 flight leader had alerted Cactus to the presence of the destroyer convoy speeding in its direction.

Not surprisingly, four P-40s that took off too late missed their rendezvous with the Forts over Vella Lavella and returned to Cactus. Capt. Dave Shaw of the 339th also had to abort his mission due to a leaking belly tank. This incident proved to be the harbinger of a fatal belly tank problem that would befall Shaw's P-38 a mere three days later.

Coincidentally, on 2 January Cactus airmen exhibited some laxity in their strike routine, unwittingly playing right into the hands of enemy fighter pilots. A strike force was already taking off when the two P-39s of Easy search found Admiral Koyanagi's destroyers at 1705, by now cruising in the vicinity of Nusa Simbo Island, some thirty miles west of Rendova. The 204th Kokutai's second CAP arrived on station barely ten minutes after the reported sighting.

As they left Guadalcanal, the rendezvous drill between VMSB-233's nine dive-bombers and their twelve escorting fighters was sloppily effected. The formation never really tightened up; strung-out groups of SBDs, F4Fs, and P-38s showed up over the convoy west of Rendova at 1805 hours. They were promptly bounced from above by Lt. Zenjiro Miyano's Zeros. Among the attackers was LA Shoichi Sugita, one of the JNAF's hottest Zero pilots.

The Wildcat division put up by VMF-121 was so aggressively harassed at first that it hardly had an opportunity to retaliate, leading Marine pilots to believe they had been jumped by some fifteen attackers. Capt. Irwin Carter traded fire with two Zeros in rapid succession; he was credited with shooting them both down before gunning his badly shot-up Grumman into a cloud bank. Capt. Jack Foeller was hit in the shoulder and his ship heavily damaged before he also managed to duck into some clouds. Lt. Youell "Joe" Crum and Lt. Bob "Pete" Peterson failed to escape the onslaught; both were posted MIA. Doubtless, one of them went down before the hammering guns of the deadly Sugita, who claimed one victory.

The destroyers were moving in two columns of five ships each. VMSB-233 concentrated on the first three ships in the port column, claiming direct hits on the second and third destroyers. P-38 pilots also observed what looked like two hits. In reality, the dive-bombers managed to shake up the *Suzukaze* with a near miss, the concussion alone inflicting sufficient hull damage to force her to turn back in the company of a sister vessel—a single glimmer of good news. As the SBDs rendezvoused after their bombing runs, MG Clyde Stamp's plane was jumped by four Zeros that made five runs on him as he tried to join up. Stamps' rear gunner, SSgt. Warren Sanders, managed to fire back at the A6Ms making the last two passes, catching the Zero executing the fifth pass. According to the SBD crew, it "burst into flames and fell off toward the sea."

The free-for-all netted some dramatic claims by the 204th: no fewer than seven Wildcats shot down and three SBDs damaged. In reality only two F4Fs failed to return, and only one SBD took hits. Though Cactus airmen put in for three Zeros, none was lost, but two of the seven that put in at Munda after the fight were slightly damaged. These apparently stayed overnight for servicing and emergency repairs. The five Lightnings, flying top cover, never intervened, nor did any Petes, if they were still flying CAP.

To complete the snafu, four P-39s scheduled to accompany the strike force missed the rendezvous entirely. Flying toward the New Georgia group on their own in the hopes of finding and rejoining the raiders, they sighted four Zeros near Munda, but nothing came of the encounter.

This was one time the pilots of the 204th Kokutai taught the Cactus Air Force a poignant lesson regarding the need for vigilance, coordination, and formation discipline on an air strike that the enemy was expected to contest.

Admiral Koyanagi's remaining destroyers were last seen turning toward Munda, probably electing to steam through Blanche Channel while the exhausted fighter CAP put into the nearby airstrip in relays to assess combat damage, rearm, and refuel. Emerging from between New Georgia and Rendova, the Reinforcement Unit passed to the south of the Russell Islands to arrive off Guadalcanal after dark where, despite the admiral's elaborate routing to elude air attacks, he promptly ran into waiting motor torpedo boats.

PT boats had debuted in the Solomons in late 1942, encountering an unsuspecting Tokyo Express for the first time on the night of 7–8 December. Eight of the little wooden-hull craft had bored in and launched their fish, but had failed to score any hits against the eleven destroyers and destroyer-transports of Rear Adm. Raizo Tanaka's flotilla. However, their attacks so unnerved the admiral that he aborted his supply run, putting about for Bougainville.

But things were different on 2 January; three relays of single Jake floatplanes from the *Sanyo Maru*, flying out of Rekata, took over CAP duties at twilight. Patrolling over a starlit seascape, the on-station Jake easily picked up the wakes of the eleven PT boats and proceeded to disrupt their attacks with four bombing runs mingled with simulated passes. Because of this harassment, none of the eighteen torpedoes fired at the Japanese ships found their mark or, if some did, they failed to explode. The transport destroyers went about disgorging their drums of supplies off Cape Esperance before withdrawing without mishap. From this night on, the Mitsubishi F1M2 Pete and Aichi E13A Jake inherited the nocturnal stewardship of the Tokyo Express.

While Admiral Koyanagi's destroyers prepared to weigh anchor, over the darkened reaches of New Georgia a pair of Black Cats were going about their usual harassment of Munda. They dropped flares at precisely 2300 before going on to loose forty-five 100-pound bombs on the airstrip over the next four hours. Another pair of PBY-5As returned the following night at 2400 with the Navy spotters assigned to direct an upcoming bombardment on board. Dropping flares followed by four 500-pounders and batches of 100-pounders, they scored six hits that started several fires. Irritated Japanese gunners put up weak flak barrages, and a solitary Zero scrambled in vain to overtake one of the Cats. Three floatplanes out of Rekata Bay were apparently patrolling in the vicinity, but did not interfere before the raiders withdrew at 0200 hours.

A half-dozen B-26s, accompanied by eight P-39s, hit the airstrip again at 1220 on 3 January. Fifteen 500-pound bombs churned up the real estate while nineteen fragmentation clusters sprayed shrapnel all about. The most murderous AA fire yet encountered put finis to one Marauder, whose seven crewmen were forced to bail out off Rendova. All made it on shore to await rescue.

Cactus' light bombers had a go at Munda the following day. Twelve SBDs, accompanied by sixteen P-39s and P-40s, dropped more than eight tons of ordnance on AA positions, taxiways, and the main runway, but only a lone wrecked plane was on hand to weather the pounding.

By now Cactus air raids had become a way of life, but Munda's woes were about to be compounded by a new wrinkle. Indignant at the failure of the Cactus Air Force's efforts to dissuade the persistent Japanese from developing the airstrip, Admiral Halsey turned to the Long Toms of the U.S. Navy to convince them. A timely naval bombardment of Munda would also help mask the arrival at Guadalcanal of an important U.S. supply and reinforcement convoy. Rear Adm. Waldon Ainsworth's Task Force (TF) AFIRM duly received orders to undertake the operation.

CHAPTER 6
BOMBARDING THE PHOENIX

On 4 January Rear Admiral Ainsworth sortied with Task Force (TF) AFIRM divided into two task groups. His Task Group (TG) AFIRM was to conduct a cordite fugue, featuring the cruisers *Nashville, St. Louis*, and *Helena*, accompanied by a light percussion section consisting of the destroyers *Fletcher* and *O'Bannon*. Four more cruisers and three destroyers, composing TG TARE, steamed in support. Four divisions of VMF-121 Wildcats led by Maj. Don Yost covered the bombardment force until twilight. To the west, several Cactus patrol planes were searching all the approaches to the New Georgia group as far away as Bougainville and the Shortlands. A *chutai* of six Zeros from the 204th Kokutai out of Kahili reported sighting a B-17, then a P-38, but failed to intercept either. Unmolested, the snoopers came across no telltale movements of Japanese warships.

Preceded by a pair of PBY-5As from VP-12, each carrying a Navy gunnery officer, the armada proceeded up the Solomon Sea through the gathering darkness. Southwest of the Russell Islands, Ainsworth's support ships turned back at 2000 to stand by off Guadalcanal.

One of the Black Cats picked up a weak surface blip off the western tip of Rendova on its radar and reported its position to the task group commander. After a short pause the flagship radioed back, "Wilco. Wilco. Wilco," indicating the "spook" was a friendly vessel. The PBYs continued their search for hostile surface forces, ranging to the west and north of Munda for seventy-five miles before turning back. Arriving over Munda at 0030, the Catalinas executed the prescribed drill of the previous two nights, dropping four flares followed by eight 500-pound bombs on the unsuspecting Japanese, who by this time regarded such nighttime harassment as déja vu.

With zero hour approaching, one PBY turned north for a mile or so and began to fly an elliptical circuit parallel to Munda Point, while the other PBY continued to make dry runs across the field. Churning past the radar blip—the submarine *Greyback* that had been stationed off Banyetta Point to mark the outer limit of shoals protruding from Rendova—TG AFIRM rounded Rendova and headed toward Munda Point. At 2330 each cruiser launched its scout plane to help guide the warships away from dangerous waters during the shelling and to guard against Japanese ship movements. The task group slowed to eighteen knots as it came up to Munda-Lambeti.

Above, the "Relief Spotter" switched on its IFF set before making another pass. Reaching the center point of the airstrip, it radioed, "Mark. Mark. Mark." Inside the *Nashville*'s dimly lit CIC, the bearing and range of the Cat was at first difficult to extrapolate from the radar screen and the ship's IFF transceiver because the PBY's position was masked by radar waves bouncing off the high terrain behind it. But the fire-control radar got a fix on Beresford Island; the center of Munda airstrip was approximated using this reference point. Drawing abeam of Munda Point, her main battery trained to starboard, the flagship opened fire. Circling overhead north of the field, the "Spotting Plane" radioed corrections to her first salvo. Then there came, "No change."

With one Black Cat shifting to pinpoint the centers of successive target areas and the Navy observer on board the other calling the fall of shot, all ships opened fire. Munda airstrip and Lambeti plantation erupted in fountains of brilliant explosions shortly after 0100 hours. Three thousand 6-inch and nearly 1,500 5-inch shells rained down within fifty minutes, plastering the target from the tip of Munda Point to the bivouac area on Lambeti plantation. However, the damage caused by the bombardment looked far worse than it really was. The shelling demolished some buildings; three fires burned at the apex of the point, and another flared south of the runway. The surrounding palm groves were thinned out somewhat, but the shelling "did not do much damage," and the well-massaged runway was made operable within eighteen hours.

Nonetheless, Rabaul was infuriated by such an audacious incursion into Japanese-controlled waters. While TG AFIRM receded into the night behind its vanguard of screening Black Cats, a retaliatory air strike, comprising four Vals from the 582nd Kokutai plus a Val *chutai* from the 956th Kokutai, lifted out of Kahili in determined pursuit. Fourteen Zeros from the 204th Kokutai provided the fighter escort. The strike force persisted down the Solomon Sea, at length catching up to Admiral Ainsworth about a dozen miles south of Guadalcanal's Cape Hunter. Ainsworth's bombardment and support groups had already rejoined into TF AFIRM when the Japanese swooped in without warning.

Captains Greg Loesch and Bill Marontate, leading two divisions of VMF-121 Wildcats, had picked up the returning task group at sunrise, relieving the tired Black Cat crews. Loesch's division included Bill "B" Freeman, Frank "Skeezix" Presley, and newcomer Jack Gifford. The F4Fs were well into their four-hour shift, patrolling over the reassembled task force at ten thousand feet, most with their IFF sets turned off, when Captain Loesch observed AA fire at 0940 hours.

With the fighter CAP cruising overhead and a PBY flying by, the appearance of a formation approaching from the direction of Cactus had caused no immediate alarm among the ships. The *Nashville*, *St. Louis*, and *Helena* were getting set to recover their seaplanes, which had flown on to Tulagi after flying CAP over TG AFIRM while it shelled Munda. Further adding to the confusion, the *Honolulu* was just wrapping up a simulated air-attack drill with her seaplanes.

Of course, the first two Vals chose the *Honolulu* as their target. With her guns belatedly clearing for action, she lunged into evasive maneuvers, managing to squeak past a pair of near hits. Next in line, the Kiwi cruiser *Achilles* took a direct hit on her number 3 turret; the 551-pound bomb shattered the structure, killing eleven men and wounding at least eight others.

The Wildcat CAP peeled off and dove on "eight to ten" busy Vals. Friend and foe whirled around amidst an indiscriminating AA barrage. Grummans flamed the fourth Val before it could release on the *Columbia*, but all four 582nd Vals managed to drop their 551-pound bombs before the F4Fs got in among them.

After expending most of their ammunition, the Cactus pilots reformed, subsequently claiming four "certain" dive-bombers and three probables. Captain Marontate was credited with two Vals; Captain Loesch and Lieutenant Presley were credited with one each. Captain Loesch, Lieutenant

Freeman, and Lieutenant Gifford were also awarded credit for a probable apiece. By the same token, the cruisers *Louisville*, *St. Louis*, and *Helena* each claimed a Val shot down by AA fire.

The 582nd listed one Val shot down, another missing, and the other two damaged. The two returning Val aircrews claimed a pair of F4Fs destroyed. Of the six 956th dive-bombers, three were presumably lost with the rest damaged; records for this *kokutai* covering January 1943 are not available, however.

As for the VMF-121 pilots, they should have checked their own sixes more carefully. The fourteen "mustard-yellow" Hamps with "rusty-red" noses pounced somewhat tardily on the Wildcats, precipitating a brief but ferocious dogfight. By now low on both fuel and ammo, the Marines attempted to break away. Diving down to one thousand feet, they reformed into their respective divisions—line abreast in two finger-four formations—and headed for the barn.

Resolved to make the Americans fight, the 204th's Hamps reformed to chase after the fleeing Grummans, pursuing them to within sight of Henderson Field. Finally catching up, the Japanese pilots executed high-side passes in *shotai* of three or four planes. The two Marine divisions turned up into their attackers to disperse them with gunfire, but after a few bursts everyone ran dry. However, the F4F pilots succeeded in bluffing their tormentors by continuous scissoring, confronting the Hamps head-on whenever they attempted a firing pass.

Upon entering friendly airspace, VMF-121's harried Marines were at last rescued by the local air patrol, which intercepted and drove off all but one of the Mitsubishi fighters. VMF-121 reported that this lone damaged and smoking Hamp glided toward the east to crash in flames within sight of the Cactus airfield complex. The 204th, however, recorded no losses, with but a single Zero hit by enemy fire. Conversely, the *kokutai*'s pilots put in for five Wildcats destroyed plus one probable. No losses were reported by VMF-121.

A relief CAP from VMF-121, commanded by Capt. Hunter Reinburg, took over late in the afternoon. Darkness closed in accompanied by worsening weather as the task force continued along the south coast of the Canal. The CAP broke off to return to Cactus, but Lt. Irwin Carter and wingman MG Joe Moravec became separated from the flight. Alone, disoriented, and running out of fuel, they flew on into the night and were swallowed up without a trace by the storm front.

Notwithstanding the naval bombardment, ComAirSols was directed to continue both his antishipping and base-suppression campaigns, concentrating on Munda. Photos taken on 5 January showed the airstrip's runway and taxiways in a badly damaged state after the shelling by TGF AFIRM. Eight planes—probably wrecks—were sitting on the field. Nine B-26s from the 69th BS were back that same day at 1040 hours. Four tons of high explosives and seventy-one daisy cutters added to the havoc created by the shelling and previous raids. Surprisingly, no flak greeted the raiders, but three "Nagoya Zeros" showed up briefly to give chase—a half-hearted pursuit at best.

Cactus B-26s were again over Munda at 0730 on 7 January, dropping fifty 100-pound bombs that took out a pair of AA guns, damaged a bomber, and started a fire. Pictures taken later revealed that resurfacing of the runway was in progress, and damaged revetments had been rebuilt. After five more Cactus raids, mostly by B-26s, 16 January found the Japanese constructing a new taxiway and dispersal area. Another pair of air strikes went in that same day. On 22 January a reconnaissance plane noticed that new machine-gun nests were sprinkled around the airstrip. Cactus strike forces rounded out the mayhem next day by raiding Munda no fewer than four times in preparation for another sortie by TF AFIRM. A follow-up reconnaissance run reported on 24 January that construction of the runway extension was progressing unabated.

By 25 January Munda boasted the completion of the new taxiway, fifty-three new blast shelters, and ten new 75-mm AA positions. Vila-Stanmore was socked in that morning, so four P-39s and four P-40s, escorting Marine SBDs, had to abort. Five B-26s and three P-38s also diverted from Vila, but persevered to bomb Munda through thinner overcast. Bomber crews claimed they demolished the wharf at Repi Repi and scored hits on the "strip and taxi area." Escorting pilots believed that poor visibility over the target prevented the 70th BS(M) Marauders from unloading their seventy-one 100-pounders accurately. No enemy planes were encountered, though a *chutai* of JAAF Oscars was now stationed there.

Escorted by seven 44th FS Warhawks plus twelve VMO-251 Wildcats, five VMSB-233 and seven VMSB-142 Dauntlesses bombed AA positions, plane revetments, and other installations at Munda at 1800 on the morrow. Optimistic Japanese AA gunners ranged in on the CAP, flying at 18,000 feet.

When the dive-bombers went in, the AA gunners hastily adjusted their fire, putting up a heavy barrage between eight hundred and eight thousand feet. VMSB-142's pilots scored hits on two 75-mm guns on the beach northwest of the runway, destroyed part of a wharf, and demolished a large tin barn on Munda Point. Flak hit Lieutenant Finch in the right wing as he dove, sending his plane into a spin. He managed to release his bomb, recovering in time to rejoin the formation over Blanche Channel, somewhat shaken by the close call. VMSB-233's SBD pilots smugly reported, "All bombs fell in the target area and created considerable damage among the installations."

Six 70th BS B-26s from Henderson paid another unfriendly visit to Munda at 1740 on 27 January. Eight P-39s from the 70th FS flew above the medium bombers in two flights at 12,000 and 15,000 feet, respectively, since it was rather pointless for the Airacobras to fly much higher. The P-39s came together over Munda to patrol at 10,000 feet while the Marauders went in at 8,000 feet. Lots of flak greeted the attackers—much of it fired by 75-mm guns located in a clearing near revetments beyond the east end of the runway.

The first element of three B-26s bombed an area north of the runway; the second element unloaded on the northeast portion of the field. A mix of 500-pounders and 100-pounders churned up the real estate. Overall, escort pilots observed the bombing to be good, though one Marauder dumped its bombs in the water. Fires broke out here and there. A big one flared up in an avgas dump after the first three sticks fell into a revetment area north of the runway, virtually wiping out Munda's avgas supply that had already been depleted earlier by the 11th Sentai's Oscars. Consequently, Munda's resident twenty-seven Oscars, which were not in evidence during the raid, were recalled to Rabaul temporarily until five hundred drums of fuel had arrived from Vila by barge.

Bad weather forced five B-26s and a dozen P-39s to abort a raid on Munda on 28 January, but the Marauders were back over New Georgia early the next morning. A flight of nine B-26s made a run below 12,000 feet through heavy flak to deliver four tons of bombs on the airstrip. Flying at 15,000 feet amidst lighter flak, Capt. Jim Robinson's eleven escorting P-39 pilots from the 70th FS watched three sticks of bombs plow into the water south of the field. Another two chewed up the woods just to the north. Apart from intense fire thrown up by 75-mm guns positioned at the northeast end of the strip near the Lambeti wharf, little activity was observed, and no enemy aircraft showed up.

Although the JAAF based Oscars at Munda from 18 January on, the lack of Japanese air opposition throughout most of these raids probably reflected a directive from Rabaul to both IJA and IJN air arms that they conserve their aircraft for CAP protection over the Tokyo Express. Besides, experience showed that damage to Munda's runway and taxiways could usually be repaired in less than a day after a raid, resulting in little disruption of air operations; rather than risk losing aircraft in a brawl with Cactus raiders, once alerted, any fighters on the field likely scrambled out of harm's way if they could.

Just prior to TG AFIRM's bombardment, the Japanese learned from a disaffected Solomon Islander that coastwatcher Harry Wickham had crossed over to Rendova. On 5 January Dick Horton joined Wickham in their new outpost. Linking this "enemy base" with the shelling, the frustrated Japanese decided to eradicate it from the air; a landing party would then come ashore to flush out these spying interlopers. Convinced that the coastwatchers' "landing area" was near some old plantation structures that could serve as a handy observation post, Munda requested a surprise air attack for 5 January. Newly ensconced in the uplands, Horton observed through his pilfered enemy binoculars a *shotai* of 582nd Kokutai Vals divebomb the "enemy buildings," which to the embarrassment of the Japanese and to Horton's amusement remained standing after the smoke and dust had cleared. Following up on 8 and 9 January, the 204th Kokutai ran a pair of back-to-back fighter sweeps to Rendova, presumably to strafe targets of opportunity, such as suspected hideouts. But the Zero pilots found nothing to shoot up. Troops landed on 12 January and searched the coastal plain, but did not probe the upper reaches of the labyrinthine rainforest before returning to Munda on 15 January. The Japanese eventually came back to establish permanent outposts along Rendova's coast in early February intending to harass the coastwatchers and "suppress" their activities.

The Cactus Air Force did not neglect the R Homen Koku Butai's seaplane base at Rekata Bay. The 69th BS(M) rang in the New Year with a visit to Rekata in the company of VMF-121 and VMO-251 Wildcats. The Marauders unloaded on the seaplane base first; Capt. Hunter Reinburg and Capt. Pat Weiland then led their divisions on a fighter sweep over the area, strafing everything in sight. Nine floatplanes were airborne in the vicinity, having probably scrambled out of the way upon being forewarned of the raid by a lookout post down the Slot.

Eight 69th B-26s headed for Rekata the next day, escorted by seven P-39s and a division of F4Fs. A pair of Cobras had to be detached en route to escort an ailing Marauder back to Cactus. Fox search had sighted five floatplanes moored there that morning, two of which appeared to be operational; this report likely led to the attack. But the Marauders dropped wide, most bombs falling harmlessly offshore. Three Cobras then shot up four Petes, and bivouac areas and supply dumps, starting a few fires.

On 7 January another B-26 strike force aborted its mission to Munda amidst bad weather and hit Rekata instead at 1545 hours. With a dozen Cobras escorting, six 69th BS Marauders streaked in under a low ceiling to drop seventy-two 100-pound bombs from a mere six hundred feet. Rekata's AA gunners gave thanks and then opened up with everything in their arsenal. Captain Behling's lead ship was hit square in the cockpit. "Krejan" jerked up into a near-vertical attitude and stalled. Falling off on one wing, the Marauder spun down in flames and disintegrated in a violent explosion as it hit the water.

The remaining bombers roared in through an awesome flak barrage to drop their bombs. A large blaze broke out, and shrapnel damaged two of six floatplanes moored along the shore. However, the results hardly merited the havoc wreaked overhead. Captain Lingamfelter, who had led the second flight, did not even attempt to land upon limping back to Cactus, so badly shot up was his plane. He ordered his crew to bail out over Henderson. Last to leave the doomed B-26, his legs got tangled in his chute. He was but five hundred feet from the ground when the canopy at last deployed.

Captain Long coaxed his ship back on one engine without electrical and hydraulic support. Flak had holed and ripped every surface of his aircraft, but he made a safe landing. Lt. Howbert's Marauder bore fifty-two holes, and came in with a damaged landing gear that luckily held. Thirty-seven scars adorned Lieutenant Field's ship. Although AA fire had punched a hole in an oil reservoir, his plane touched down before leakage could cause the engines to seize up.

Losses totaled two aircraft and one crew. Another Marauder was transformed into a hangar queen, and one crewman was injured; the future of a fourth bomber was doubtful. It was a staggering setback for the 69th BS.

A Cactus patrol plane reported only two floatplanes on the beach the following day; when 347th FG P-40s and P-38s strafed the seaplane base on 9 January, however, they left no fewer than seven floatplanes near the beach in various states of disrepair.

Two raids went into Rekata four days later. Eight P-39s and five P-38s observed six B-26s unload four tons of bombs on supply dumps and a bivouac area in Suavana plantation's coconut groves at 1500 hours. Three hours later a fighter sweep strafed the seaplane base for good measure. Neither the ten F4Fs nor four P-40s nor the B-26 strike force encountered any airborne opposition.

Four 958th Kokutai Petes flew down in pairs from Poporang the next morning at 0540 to patrol over the destroyer *Mochizuki* and the minelayer *Tsugaru*, which were transporting troops to Rekata. At 0920 Lt. George Topoll and Lt. Harvey Dunbar, patrolling in their P-39s, encountered the pair of Petes flown by Lt. Kinotsudu Miyawaki and LA Yoshito Kawamoto. After a "Tally-ho!," Lieutenant Dunbar made a high-side pass on a Pete flying four thousand feet below, scoring some hits, but the pilot eluded him by sharp vertical zigzagging.

Alerted by Dunbar, Lieutenant Topoll searched for the second Pete, which he soon spotted nearby, skimming over the water at three hundred feet. He executed a high-side pass on the floatplane's left flank and poured machine-gun fire into its cowl and fuselage. The rear gunner returned fire until the damaged F1M2 veered to the right and appeared to crash into a grove on Papatura Fa Island. The pilot managed to hedgehop around the trees, through clearings, to safety.

Climbing back up over Papatura Ite Island, Lieutenant Topoll came face to face with the first Pete, which had returned and was now closing head-on. Both pilots opened fire but failed to score before the agile biplane dipped beneath the P-39 and zoomed into a tight, climbing turn to fall on Topoll's tail. Topoll poured on the coal and pulled out of range. Dunbar, too, broke off and soon rendezvoused with Topoll. The Cobra pilots emerged from the short dogfight claiming one F1M2 shot down. The 958th suffered two Petes damaged. Their crews expended 210 rounds of 7.7-mm ammo but failed to get a hit in return. The third Pete, cruising some five miles distant, was too far away to engage; if the fourth was still airborne, the Cobra pilots never ran into it.

Five P-38s from the 339th FS left Cactus at 1340 on 26 January, flying a fighter sweep to the western end of Choiseul under CAVU weather conditions. There they ran into a front that had the Shortlands totally socked in. Unable to attack shipping in the Shortland-Tonolei harbor complex, Capt. John Mitchell took his flight over to Rekata Bay. Seeing no enemy planes or ships below, the pilots released their ordnance at one thousand feet on shore facilities with pitiful results. Bombs on three of the Lightnings failed to drop, swaying in their shackles and tearing up the braces; bombs from the other two Lockheeds apparently did not explode. A snafu mission if ever there was one.

The stepped-up activity of the Tokyo Express prompted the 13th Air Force to redouble its antishipping strikes against the Tonolei-Shortland harbor complex in the New Year.

Of the five B-17 raids scheduled for Buin-Faisi during the first week of January, the one on the afternoon of 5 January proved particularly instructive. JNAF float Zero units from the Aleutians to New Guinea had been claiming victories over the P-38 Lightning ever since the fighter had been introduced into the Pacific theater. The upcoming encounter further illustrated the vulnerability of the big twin-boom fighter in low-altitude combat—even to slower, outgunned, but highly agile Pete biplanes.

The last two operable Rufes of the 802nd Kokutai joined up with six 204th Kokutai Zeros, in addition to some Petes from the 11th Seaplane Tender Division, over the Buin-Faisi area to await five B-17s, escorted by six P-38s from the 339th FS. U.S. combat reports estimated the strike force encountered twenty-five "float biplanes and Zeros." The Lightnings flew in two elements of three planes above and behind the bombers. After the Forts made their run on a "cruiser," the 11th's Rufes and Petes, in the company of the 204th's Zeros, quickly moved in.

One Rufe, piloted by Leading Airman Matsuyama, pounced on Lt. Ron Hilken at the outset. A Pete quickly joined in. Before they were driven off by Lt. Besby Holmes and Lt. Emmett Norris, they had set Hilken's right engine on fire. He was last seen going down toward Vella Lavella. Matsuyama also shot out Lt. Wally Dinn's left engine with 20-mm fire, sending Dinn spinning into the water one final, fatal time.

Experiencing trouble with his oxygen mask, Capt. Bob Hubbell conned his P-38 to a lower altitude, followed by wingman Norris. A Zeke made a firing pass on Norris and missed. Two more moved in, but were driven off by Lieutenant Holmes, who was attempting to rejoin when three Petes slid in behind Lieutenant Norris. Hastily diving, Norris came back up to stalk his stalkers. He fired a full deflection shot into one of the Petes before attacking another. This Japanese pilot turned up to meet him head-on as he dove. He fired into the biplane's nacelle and fuselage, then watched it pass by, trailing smoke.

Meanwhile, Captain Hubbell turned into six Petes closing on his right quarter, whereupon the floatplanes dove past without firing, zooming away to reposition for another pass. Hubbell and Norris joined up and then climbed to the rescue of Capt. John Mitchell's element which had likely come under attack by the same group of Petes. A wild melee ensued before the ultra-agile F1M2s again scattered. Next, Hubbell dove on a Zeke that easily escaped by executing a chandelle. Climbing, he shot into a Rufe piloted by Airman 2nd Class Ohshima who had already made two passes on Lieutenant Holmes, claiming a probable. Captain Mitchell also fired into Ohshima's Rufe. When his float Zero caught fire, Ohshima bailed out. Parachuting to safety, he was rescued by a Pete that landed on the water to retrieve him.

Raked by Hubbell's fire from cockpit to tail, another Pete started smoking as one of its airmen panicked and bailed out. Yet another F1M2 slithered away from his attack. Diving under a Rufe, he pulled up beneath it, but the float Zero executed a wingover before he could open fire.

Lieutenant Holmes made several head-on passes on Petes. When the nimble biplanes turned to give their rear gunners a go, Holmes took deflection shots as they presented their fuselages to his guns. He flamed one, shooting off one of its wing floats, but missed another.

The six 204th Kokutai pilots emerged unmaimed from their brief combat with, according to their estimate, five B-17s and seven P-38s, claiming one Lightning shot down, one probable, and one damaged. The only real losses were the two P-38s shot down by the floatplanes. On the Cactus side, Captain Hubbell claimed a Rufe, and Captain Mitchell and Lieutenant Holmes each put in for a Pete. Besides this, his first victory, Holmes claimed two probables, and Lieutenant Norris claimed another. This low score against such plentiful, ostensibly inferior opposition reflects the lackluster performance of the Lightning when fighting out of its element against more-maneuverable opponents.

Reconnaissance flights had been monitoring the steady buildup of air power at the new Japanese fighter strip on Ballale Island throughout January. Unescorted B-17s raided Buin-Faisi's airfields, bombing both Kahili and Ballale as the sun sank toward the horizon on 17 January. Kahili's revetments and runways swallowed six 2,000-pounders and sixteen 500-pounders between 1940 and 2020, starting two large fires. Three *shotai* of five "Mitsubishi type 97s" that were flying nearby elected not to interfere. Ten minutes later, four Forts sprinkled thirty-two 500-pound bombs on Ballale's runway and revetments, again starting a large fire. This time, fifteen "single-engine land planes" approached one of the Forts, but it escaped undamaged. Since no JNAF bombers or fighters were up over the area that evening, these vague descriptions suggest a twilight flight of JAAF Lilys and Oscars in the area.

Nine B-17s, escorted by seven P-40s and six P-38s, made a bombing run over Shortland Harbor at 1345 on 18 January. The Forts claimed two hits on a freighter anchored amongst another dozen merchantmen and warships. As the formation turned away, an escorted float Zero, towing a target sleeve, was spotted low over Poporang, headed for a deserted part of the anchorage. Seven other airborne Rufes from the 802nd Kokutai slated for aerial attack drill had not yet appeared when Capt. Stan Palmer's flight of three P-40s bounced the two float fighters.

Handicapped by the target sleeve, PO2c Keiji Tsunami could only dive for the deck. The heavier Hawks quickly caught up and shot up his Rufe, whereupon Tsunami hit the silk. LA Jinichi Minesawa turned to give battle and was seen to get on the tail of a P-40. Flames spurted out of the Hawk, and it was thought to have gone down, but this was not the case. The P-40s overwhelmed Minesawa and killed him in his chute when he bailed out. By then the other Rufes had arrived on the scene. Inexplicably, these usually gutsy pilots chose not to engage what they thought were six P-39s.

Captain Palmer scored hits on one of the Rufes, but it was Capt. Bob Hubbell and his wingman, Lieutenant Webb, who claimed both Nakajima fighters after the short dogfight.

Meanwhile, Palmer returned to take up his position slightly below the B-17s only to find several gunners firing at him. Wagging his wings to expose the U.S. ensignia, he was dumfounded when the Forts cut loose again. "Someone in the B-17s quit shooting at the P-40s!" he exclaimed over the radio as .50-caliber slugs tore into his nacelle. He veered under the bomber formation and made for Vella Lavella. When his engine quit five minutes later, Palmer bailed out. The formation circled briefly over his one-man dinghy while one of the bombers swooped down to drop a water canteen and two D ration bars.

"There were no suspicious moves on my part," insisted Captain Palmer after his rescue, adding, "in parallel flight the U.S. stars on wing and fuselage were plainly visible." White stars on a blue field failed to save Captain Hubbell and Lt. Lloyd Huff from being hosed as they, too, flew within range of itchy trigger fingers. Though neither Warhawk was hit, radio operator Corporal Schaeffer reported with satisfaction that the B-17s had shot down two enemy fighters.

The 204th Kokutai scrambled nine Zeros out of Kahili. They succeeded in making an intercept, judging by the paltry 776 rounds of ammo expended by the Japanese, but the exchange was short and inconclusive, with neither side scoring. Despite U.S. claims for four Rufes, all but the two that fought the Warhawks made it back intact. One of the downed pilots survived, having fired 2,820 rounds to claim a pair of "P-39s."

A PBY landed to rescue Captain Palmer the next day. As the Dumbo taxied over, one of the escorting P-40s made an unexpected forced landing nearby courtesy of motor gremlins. Lt. Joe Lynch joined his 68th FS colleague for the ride back to Cactus.

On 19 January at around 1630 a modest strike force of seven B-17s and six P-38s hit Shortland Harbor. The raiders were met by an equally modest force of seven Zeros from the 204th Kokutai, whose pilots used up 1,213 rounds of ammo claiming to have bagged two Lightnings and damaged a Fort. Capt. John Mitchell's P-38 flight actually suffered no losses nor did it make any claims. A pair of Vals from the 582nd Kokutai stumbled onto the air battle, but wisely ignored it, landing at Kahili.

The fighter cover was again thin when nine B-17s showed up over Shortland Harbor at 0815 on 20 January. The four P-40s and five P-38s soon had their hands full, defending against a mix of seventeen 204th Kokutai Zekes and Hamps, led by Lt. (jg) Takeshi Morisaki, plus nine Petes from the Shortland-based seaplane tenders. Two *shotai* of F1M2s attempted simultaneous frontal and side passes at the Hawks. Capt. Bob Hubbell and Lt. John Smith turned into the first two head-on, then split into separate dogfights, shooting both down. Eight other Petes joined the remaining four in swarming the P-40s. Captain Hubbell sprayed one in the center of its fuselage, and it went down in a roll. Another fell away after absorbing a fusillade from Lt. Bob Kennedy. Lt. Fred Ploetz flamed a third floatplane before his Warhawk took hits in its wing, fuselage, and cockpit. Shrapnel fragments lacerated his arm as he dove out of the line of fire.

As yet unmolested, the Forts proceeded to bomb the shipping in the harbor, but registered no hits. Flying high cover, the Lightnings spotted two *shotai* of Zeros that had reached 23,000 feet in a scramble to intercept the bombers. When the big Lockheeds turned to meet them, the Mitsubishis peeled off, retreating behind a cloud bank. The P-38s climbed back above the B-17, and had barely resumed their covering role when the Zeros pounced from out of the clouds.

With the high cover now engaged, more Zeros—mistakenly identified as float Zeros in one combat report—fell among the Forts that "were pretty well shot up," four of them absorbing hits. This initiative again demonstrates the exceptional élan of the 204th Kokutai's pilots.

Lt. Emmett Norris' P-38 started down with a smoking engine and an A6M on its tail. Norris never recovered, splashing in near Vella Lavella. Capt. Dave Shaw led wingmen lieutenants Murray Shubin and Holmes in a near-vertical dive on the culprit. Raked by the combined fire of three P-38s, the pilot hit the silk as his shattered plane fell away. Lieutenant Holmes fired into another Zero, but failed to bag it.

Lt. Fred Purnell, who had traded in his P-40 for a P-38 for this mission, found himself separated from Lieutenant Norris after evading the enemy's first pass. Climbing through a cloud layer, he stumbled upon four Zekes of another *chutai*, whose pilots had yet to commit. Purnell now made a shallow diving turn to the right to reposition for a bounce, hoping he had not been seen. Zooming back up, he was startled to find himself facing the *chutai*'s other two Zekes head-on! Purnell squeezed the trigger, and one A6M spiraled out of sight as he passed by. Not knowing where the other A6Ms were, he broke off, found Captain Shaw, and joined up. Together, they climbed to 15,000 feet in a loose element to catch up with the bombers. But one of Purnell's recent playmates decided to follow and bushwhack him. He spotted the stalking Zeke as it closed in, so he accelerated out of range, rejoining Shaw once more. The pair then caught up to a lone wayward Zero. A concentrated burst from Shaw sawed off its tail section; the remaining half spun earthward in a blaze.

On the return leg, nine Petes were again seen between the Shortlands and Choiseul, one thousand feet above, closing hard from ahead in "string formation" to attack the P-40s. The Hawk pilots, tired and low on ammo, put their ships into power dives and "managed to escape" by outrunning their pursuers.

The Lightnings claimed three enemy fighters destroyed; the Hawks put in for another two. WO Hatsuo Hidaka of the 204th Kokutai went missing, but survived; he was back in the air by 23 January. Another Zero was damaged. Altogether, the nine escorting Cactus fighters had run into some forty-five Japanese aircraft, engaging thirty-four, among them the aces of the 204th who claimed a pair of P-40s destroyed. Afterwards, Lt. Bob Kennedy and Lt. Lloyd Huff protested against sending to Bougainville small fighter escorts that risked being overwhelmed by superior forces. They believed that a minimum of three flights each of P-40s and P-38s were needed to escort bombers.

On 26 January six Forts from the 26th and 431st BSs paid an afternoon visit to the burgeoning Ballale airstrip, whose planes, ironically, had been assigned the specific task of intercepting Allied raids into the Western Solomons. Fifty-six 500-pound bombs whistled down, fifty-four of them churning up the airfield. A "shower" of Japanese AA fire failed to claim any of the heavies. One B-17 had to abort due to an oxygen malfunction. The heavies of the 13th Air Force rounded out the month with another raid against Kahili airfield on 29 January.

Work began on the Japanese auxiliary airstrip at Vila-Stanmore on 8 January with the arrival of the torpedo boat *Otori*, escorting a transport full of construction personnel. The 6,705-ton *Kaku Maru* finished unloading her cargo at 0214 on 18 January and stole away into the night. Next to dock, the 6,777-ton cargo ship *Yamashima Maru*, escorted by the torpedo boat *Hiyodori*, unloaded AA units on 16 January. On her return trip she was attacked and damaged from the air. The following evening the *Giyu Maru* and her escort called in at Vila under cover of 958th Kokutai Petes to unload two hundred barrels of foodstuffs and twenty barges. Plagued by intermittent Cactus bombing forays, the construction of Vila airstrip inched steadily forward nevertheless. Photos taken on 22 January revealed that the facility was nearing completion. The field was reported to be "almost completely cut out of [the] coconut grove with taxiways well under way." Ergo, Admiral Halsey directed the virtuosos of the Munda concert to orchestrate an encore performance for the Japanese audience at Vila-Stanmore on 23 January.

Although three weeks had passed since TG AFIRM had shelled Munda, a precedent had been established. The Japanese had grown more vigilant, especially with Operation KE's timetable now set. Anticipating increased air opposition to a second base-suppression sortie, ComSoPac took extra measures to protect the Vila bombardment force by disrupting enemy air operations over the New Georgia group.

To furnish the Vila bombardment force with maximum fighter protection during daylight hours, as well as to carry out a two-day base-suppression campaign against Munda airstrip, Vice Adm. Aubrey Fitch arranged for the carrier *Saratoga*'s air group to be sent ashore between 1200 on 22 January and 0300 on 24 January. Its primary duty was to protect Cactus and Ringbolt—the Tulagi base—from enemy air or naval attack. Cactus also was authorized to cover TF AFIRM with fighters from the *Sara*. Accordingly, starting at 0830 on 23 January, twenty-four F4Fs, twenty-five SBDs, and seventeen TBFs touched down on the Canal. Forty-five minutes later, eight USN Wildcats were back in the air to beef up the CAP over Admiral Ainsworth's task force. They were relieved at 1225 by another octet that was, in turn, spelled off by the last eight Navy F4Fs at 1530 hours.

In compliance with ComAirSol's orders, Cactus' bomber fleet—now amply protected by its own fighters—delivered four air strikes against Munda during 23 January. First, six B-26s arrived at high noon in the company of twelve P-39s. The Marauders sprinkled 8,400 pounds of explosives around the field. Eight Marine SBDs showed up on the heels of the Army raiders. Five 1,000-pounders threw up clouds of debris as they slammed into Munda. Another ton of smaller bombs rounded out the second delivery. Barely two hours elapsed before eight B-17s dropped by, escorted by twelve

F4Fs and a dozen P-39s. The heavies further cratered the area with another 8,400 pounds of bombs. Finally, six B-26s returned to Munda at 1730 to sow yet another eighty-four 100-pound bombs.

Several airborne Zeros were spotted throughout the day, but none braved running the gauntlets of escorting fighters to get at the bombers. Reeling under the incessant pounding, the shell-shocked Japanese must have shaken their fists skyward in utter frustration.

Meanwhile, TF AFIRM sortied on 22 January for its encore in the New Georgia group. This time, Admiral Ainsworth brought with him the cruisers *Nashville* and *Helena*, in addition to the destroyers *DeHaven*, *Nicholas*, *O'Bannon*, and *Radford*; he also brought along the cruisers *Honolulu* and *St. Louis* with three destroyers for support. The admiral's flotilla had hardly started out when it was discovered, likely by a sub, 230 miles southeast of Guadalcanal. Had Ainsworth known that Rabaul thought he was headed for Munda again, he would have grinned.

Coastwatchers on Choiseul reported the *Toa Maru 2* steaming down the Slot southeast of the Shortlands with her escort, *Oshio*, at 1350 on 23 January. She was on her way to embark personnel from the 4th Engineer Detachment who had just completed the major work on Vila airstrip. Following Admiral Fitch's directive, a dozen VMSB-233 SBDs and four VMSB-131 TBFs flew to the intercept, escorted by an estimated twenty Wildcats from VMO-251. By late afternoon the transport was steaming in mid-channel abeam of central Choiseul while Admiral Ainsworth's force approached from the opposite direction. Directly overhead orbited two 958th Kokutai Petes, flown by Lt. (jg) Kyoshi Suzuki and PO2c Fumio Ogawa, while slightly in advance flew the rest of the CAP: nine Zeros from the 204th Kokutai. Such hefty aerial cover reflected her important mission.

The Zero *chutai* ran up against the Cactus strike force at 1815 hours. Seeing the combat break out, the F1M2s wasted no time, speeding ahead to join in the action. A sharp firefight ensued while the light bombers proceeded to attack the ships amidst heavy flak. Lieutenant Frazer led the SBDs in registering a near hit on the *Toa Maru 2*. Several near misses followed. TSgt. Ralph Ackerman dove into concentrated 20-mm fire; just as he released his bomb at two thousand feet, his Dauntless was hit. Ackerman could not pull out in time and plunged into the sea. While the fighter pilots dueled, the Petes assaulted the light bombers. One 958th F1M2 went after Sergeant Olson's SBD, trading 1,000 rounds of 7.7-mm for 180 rounds of .30-caliber from Olson's gunner, Pfc. C. Tapp. The Marines prevailed, flaming the Pete. Although it made a forced landing and was later seen still burning as it rode the swell, this floatplane managed to make it back to Poporang, its crew claiming the SBD as a probable. The other two Petes returned intact, the second one having been struck but once.

When the fighters called it quits, the 204th listed two Zeros lost—Lt. (jg) Kiyoharu Shibuya was shot down and PO2c Sakuichi Fukuda was missing. A third Zero was damaged, but the pilot, Petty Officer Fukuda, bailed out. He was fished from the water by local natives, who asked the coastwatcher network what they should do with their captive. Lieutenant Horton informed Lieutenant Keenan the next day that the prisoner "was now pushing up daisies" courtesy of the Solomon Islanders. No love lost here.

Maj. Joe Renner, Lieutenant Irwin, and Lt. Glen Loban were each credited with a Zero. However, Lieutenant Irwin and Lt. Phil Leeds were both shot down; Leeds was rescued, but Irwin was last seen under attack by several Zeros. The 204th pilots claimed four VMO-251 F4Fs destroyed and one probable.

VMSB-131's mission board starkly stated, "Drops made without success." While VMSB-233's crews estimated they had damaged both the transport and her escort, in reality they scored hits on neither. The *Toa Maru 2*, her journey now delayed by the air strike, pushed on to Vila oblivious to the approaching U.S. task force.

Admiral Ainsworth advanced up the Solomon Sea under cover of a large fighter CAP provided by the *Saratoga*'s air group. A Japanese long-range patrol bomber bumped into TF AFIRM southwest of Guadalcanal at around 1030 on 23 January. Japanese watchdogs locked on, intermittently shadowing the task force until nightfall. Once alerted, Rabaul's ground echelon hurried to ready the Bettys of the 705th Kokutai for a nocturnal torpedo attack. Originally scheduled for midevening, the takeoff was put back due to ensuing delays as daylight ebbed.

The *Sara*'s CAP left at 1840 hours. Within five minutes, one of a pair of Bettys from the 705th Kokutai, flown by CPO Sandai Toyota, cast its silhouette against the twilight. Admiral Ainsworth remained nonplussed. Turning west briefly at 1900, he pretended he was making for Munda again. An hour later, with darkness closing in, the admiral left his support group, which turned back to take up a position south of Guadalcanal. He then headed north into New Georgia Sound. Three Black Cats now droned overhead in place of the fighter CAP. Rabaul's air strike was close to takeoff when nightfall and a rainsquall enabled Ainsworth to give Chief Petty Officer Toyota the slip. Veering to port, he crept up the Slot while his three PBYs flew on ahead to conduct a radar sweep.

Suddenly, according to U.S. observers, "three planes" showed up. They cruised overhead through unsettled skies, challenging the *O'Bannon* several times with the recognition signal "uncle" in Morse before departing an hour later, just prior to TG AFIRM's turn into Kula Gulf. What had at first been reported as Catalinas was "definitely identified as Mitsubishi twin-engine bombers," implying that one or more Bettys had found the task force once more. A *shotai* of *Kunikawa Maru* floatplanes that had taken off at 2230 also arrived over Kula Gulf to search through a brooding overcast. They finally ran down Admiral Ainsworth's elusive warships at 0014, staying overhead until 0130 hours.

Clearing the tip of New Georgia, TG AFIRM steamed in file behind the *Nicholas* across Kula Gulf toward the coast of Kolombangara. Reaching Vila-Stanmore, the warships swung about while the returning Black Cats positioned themselves over the sprawling Japanese base. With "Spotter One" directing the fire of the Nashville, "Spotter Two" calling the fall of shot for the *Helena* and the four destroyers, and "Spotter Three" facilitating fixes on the target area, the curtain went up at 0200 on percussion-appreciation night at Vila-Stanmore. After the *Nashville*'s first salvos flashed into the night, the main batteries of the six vessels lobbed two thousand rounds of 6-inch shells, intermingled with 1,500 rounds of 5-inch shells, into various grid quadrants for a solid half-hour.

The *Toa Maru 2* was still anchored in either Buki or Bambari Harbors when the first salvos from TG AFIRM slammed into Vila-Stanmore. Her captain and crew shook off their initial surprise and hastily weighed anchor in a flurry of frenzied activity. Overhead, the *Nashville*'s Black Cat interrupted its routine to report "an unidentified vessel attempting to escape through Blackett Strait." Ordered to take the transport under fire, the *Helena* could not pinpoint her either visually or by radar nor could the *DeHaven*, though she was nearest to the two harbors. Thus, still leading a charmed life, the *Toa Maru 2* narrowly escaped both the earlier air attack and the bombardment.

When Admiral Ainsworth ordered the cease-fire, five conflagrations were blazing in supply dumps, and a haze of acrid cordite fumes drifted over the badly scarred airstrip. At 0250 Spotter One unloaded two 500-pound bombs and six "mortar shells" on the enemy base for good measure, starting "additional fires." Vila reported that nearly all the supplies for its ground echelon in addition to those destined for the 45th Sentai were destroyed; only one hundred drums of food and five hundred fuel drums consigned to Munda survived. The 45th Sentai's Lily bombers had been scheduled to stage through Vila airstrip on their upcoming Cactus raids, but now had to be diverted to Ballale and Munda.

At some point between TF AFIRM's entrance into Kula Gulf and its retirement, an 851st Kokutai Emily, patrolling the Munda Area, blew the whistle on Admiral Ainsworth.

Now aware that Vila-Stanmore was the target, the 705th Kokutai sent eighteen Bettys armed with torpedoes winging down from Rabaul in three *chutai* of six bombers each, leaving at staggered intervals after midnight to widen the timeframe for at least one *chutai* to find and attack the task group. Meanwhile, after the Petes left, a pair of Jakes from the *Kamikawa Maru* found the U.S. warships as they withdrew through New Georgia Sound under the providence of intermittent rainsqualls. The third Black Cat, radar-equipped and acting as vanguard, reported "enemy planes in the air at all times," likely referring to the shadowing Jakes that had begun to drop flares and float lights to mark the position and course of their quarry. One popped out of the clouds near the *Helena* shortly after 0400 only to be promptly chased off by her AA batteries.

The solid ping of a submarine had appeared on the *Radford*'s sonar not ten minutes earlier. It was the *I-9*, which had been diverted from its supply runs to Guadalcanal to stalk and sink Admiral Ainsworth's warships. As the enemy sub maneuvered into position, TG AFIRM ran into a succession of squalls. The sonar contact became intermittent; then it disappeared altogether.

Two of the 705th Kokutai's *chutai* failed to find the task group. One used up so much avgas trying that it had to pause at Buka to refuel before pushing on for Vunakanau. After searching for hours, the Bettys of the other put in at Buin to top up before striking out to resume their search.

The third and only Betty *chutai* to make contact finally showed up at 0434 near the position last reported by the Jake at 0400 hours. The American ships promptly picked up the bombers on their radars. Having found their quarry, at least two Bettys made runs on the ships through the overcast. As they started to close, the *Helena* was ordered to track the nearest bandit. She "opened up sporadically at several promising contacts," her radar-directed fire unknowingly scoring a near miss that punched five shrapnel holes in one of the attacking Bettys. The pair launched their torpedoes amidst the flak, but both fish ran wide. Frustrated, the attackers broke off at 0441 hours. A few minutes before, radar-directed, main-battery fire from the *Radford* splashed an unidentified plane at four thousand yards. Since all the G4Ms made it back to Vunakanau, the victim that "burst through the overcast and crashed into the sea" must have been one of the floatplanes.

While Admiral Ainsworth was shelling Vila-Stanmore, Maytag Mike raiders from the 751st Kokutai were taking turns romping over Tulagi and the Lunga perimeter. But despite the moody weather and the 751st's efforts to incapacitate Cactus' airfields, at first light the *Saratoga*'s air group took off to leave its calling card at Vila. Twenty SBDs, seventeen TBFs, and twenty F4Fs attacked through the hazy pall to drop some twenty-five tons of bombs on the hapless base, destroying dock facilities and silencing the only two AA guns that dared challenge them. Satisfied with the results of their raid, the USN air group returned to the *Sara* at 1500 that afternoon.

Pictures taken at 0945 reveal the following damage: Stanmore plantation buildings destroyed, Vila plantation pier destroyed, six AA positions knocked out, and the entire area "well worked over." Five men perished in the blazing cauldron, and twenty more were wounded.

Sunrise on 24 January also brought to a reassembled TF AFIRM a fighter CAP of six 339th FS Lightnings and four 68th FS Hawks that relieved the Black Cat at 0620 hours. Then eight Wildcats, nine Cobras, and seven P-40s successively took their turns over Admiral Ainsworth's ships. The last relay arrived on station at 1745, the seven F4Fs and Four P-40s remaining until sunset. Cactus fighters continued to fly CAP all the next day. A final relay of eight P-39s covered the task force from 1700 to 1915, but the Japanese had yet to mount another follow-up air strike.

The next day, it was business as usual at Vila-Stanmore. Two freighters, a transport, and a tanker dropped anchor off shore. The destroyer *Isokaze* brought in a freighter, the subchaser *Ch-26* arrived with the 7,189-ton *Noshiro Maru*, which disembarked more garrison troops and picked up the remainder of the 4th Engineer Detachment. Twelve SBDs, six TBFs, eight F4Fs, and six P-38s took off from Cactus at 1615 to intercept the tanker, but were forced to abort near New Georgia by heavy weather. The destroyer *Arashio* arrived from Rabaul the following day, shepherding a freighter loaded with coastal defense artillery and antiaircraft guns. A Cactus reconnaissance run of 27 January reported only three days after TG AFIRM's shelling that "Vila plantation looks better."

On 28 January a dozen 70th FS P-39s under Captain Nichols took off at 1535, picking up five B-26s out of Henderson on their way to bomb Vila-Stanmore. Overcast conditions did not prevent the 70th BS Marauders from making their runs. One stick of bombs struck the water, then worked its way over a taxi strip just to the west of the runway. Two other sticks began to burst about three hundred feet immediately west and north of the runway, then both walked across it, starting a large fire in a clearing some five hundred feet to the north. A smaller fire flared up immediately west of the runway about halfway down. One 75-mm AA gun was observed energetically throwing up inaccurately aimed flak from a clearing across the Vila River about one thousand feet northeast of the runway. A tedious trek through the rainforest will take one to see this 75-mm dual-purpose gun. It and a nearby mate are still there, rusting away in their revetments, attended by several stacks of neatly piled ammunition.

While the Marauders were visiting their wrath upon Munda on the morning of 29 January, a pair of P-40s from the 44th FS, piloted by Capt. Ken Taylor and Lt. Bob Westbrook, flew Baker search to nearby Kolombangara. Peering down through scattered cumulus as they circled the airstrip, the pilots found that the palm trees still obstructed good observation despite the leveling effects of the bombardment. Then Vila's 75-mm AA guns opened up. The flak quickly ranged in between 8,000 and 11,000 feet, though it burst some 1,700 feet behind the two snoopers. Unruffled by the barrage, Taylor and Westbrook observed that bomb damage to the runway caused by the previous day's B-26 raid had been filled in. The taxiways were now developed though no planes were parked on the field. They also saw a campfire north of the field, indicating a bivouac area. They concluded that the "field looks good."

Responding to this report, Cactus mounted another strike against Vila-Stanmore that very afternoon. Ten P-39s from the 67th and 70th FSs took off behind Captain Nichols at 1235 to escort a flight of SBDs from VMSB-234. Cruising up the Slot at 15,000 feet under clear to hazy skies sprinkled with cumulus, the strike force gave the Russell Islands a wide berth to avoid detection by the Japanese garrison there. Over Vila, the Dauntlesses had to dive through stinging flak to deliver their payloads. Bombs were seen to hit around three hundred feet west of the runway in what might have been the bivouac area. Two AA positions near the north end of the field—one some three hundred feet to the east and one another six hundred feet beyond that—threw up an intensive barrage that may have distracted some of the SBD pilots while they were making their runs. That evening, the torpedo boat *Hiyodori* dropped anchor off Vila-Stanmore alongside yet another *maru* that disgorged more troops to swell the burgeoning garrison that now more than doubled that of New Georgia.

To support Kolombangara's role as the key defensive bulwark in the New Georgia group, the Japanese had intended to develop Vila into a major fighter and bomber airbase for the JAAF. However, this concept was abandoned after the U.S. naval bombardment, along with the plan to stage Lilys through Vila on airstrikes against Cactus. Just as well, since Vila's soil proved inadequate to support runways in continuous use by medium bombers fully loaded with ordnance.

However, the soil did contain enough nutrients to help diversify the local economy; Vila's extensive taxiways and plane revetments were cultivated and sown with a variety of seeds introduced by Lt. Bill Sabel, U.S. Army Engineers, in 1944. Sabel's commanding general asked him to plant an extensive vegetable garden in the denuded coconut groves leveled by the Japanese for the airstrip in order to supply the base hospital at Munda with fresh produce. The project proved successful, and natives still grow watermelons in abundance on nearby Ranonga Island.

When the Allies crossed over from New Georgia to Kolombangara in the fall of 1943, they found three partially destroyed Hamps parked in U-shaped revetments around Vila's abandoned airstrip. Remnants of these Zeros were still in evidence as late as 1999, when the writers visited Vila-Stanmore—a testimonial to Vila's continued use as an auxiliary strip to Munda. After the war it was repaired for use by the light planes of logging companies that harvested Kolombangara's rainforest over the next four decades.

CHAPTER 7

KICKOFF!

The first destroyer run of Operation KE left Faisi for Guadalcanal on 10 January 1943, carrying supplies for the Japanese 17th Army plus twenty-three-days' rations for a rearguard contingent scheduled to arrive at Guadalcanal on 15 January. The flagship *Naganami* fell out with engine trouble at the last minute, so Adm. Tomiji Koyanagi had to transfer his flag to the *Kuroshio*. Shrouded by rainy weather, the *Arashi*, *Arashio*, *Makinami*, and *Oshio*, escorted by the flagship plus the *Hatsukaze*, *Kawakaze*, and *Tokitsukaze*, steamed undetected down the Slot under several six-Zero CAPs provided by the 204th Kokutai. Coastwatcher Donald Kennedy reported the convoy's passage past the eastern end of New Georgia at 1600—too late for Cactus to mount an air strike. The last CAP completed its shift without incident, putting into Munda at 1940 to sojourn overnight with orders to fly cover for the returning destroyers with six other 204th Zeros at 0600 the next morning.

Lt. Cdr. Alan Calvert barely had time to put together another PT-boat ambush out of Tulagi. Five motor torpedo boats were quickly made ready to join the four on patrol in Iron Bottom Sound. Lieutenant Curley's PBY-5A took off from Henderson at 2330 to find the Japanese destroyers and direct the PTs to the attack. Lt. Rollin Westholm's *PT-112* and Lt. Charles Tilden's *PT-43* were patrolling together between Tassafaronga and Doma Cove when the Black Cat raised them by radio at 0015, alerting them and two other PTs to a column of three Japanese screening destroyers probing into Iron Bottom Sound. A fourth enemy picket had just turned about when the Cat picked it up on its radar near Savo, misidentifying it as a "light cruiser."

The PBY patiently vectored the two PTs toward the three remaining destroyers over the next thirty minutes. Closing to within four hundred yards, the *PT-43* launched its first pair of torpedoes at the lead vessel. A bright flash pierced the darkness when powder in the port tube ignited. The *Hatsukaze* and *Tokitsukaze* immediately opened fire on their attacker. Their second salvo hit the *PT-43*, killing one crewman and blowing two others overboard. The badly mauled torpedo boat managed to escape, but Lieutenant Tilden had to abandon her. An enemy destroyer passed close aboard the wreckage, raking the area with random machine-gun fire; miraculously, no one in the water was hit. Wallowing in the swell, the *PT-43* drifted with the tide, at length grounding on the Japanese-occupied coast. Enemy soldiers tried to pull her on to the shore, but the RNZN corvette *Kiwi* arrived to destroy her with gunfire.

The destroyers next caught Lieutenant Westholm's *PT-112* in a cross fire. Two rounds struck the speeding boat, but not before she got her four fish away at the third destroyer. A blaze in the PT's engine room was soon out of control, and Westholm's crew abandoned ship. All survived: two seamen were later treated for shrapnel wounds, and one suffered burns. Meanwhile, eyeing the flashes of guns and explosions, Lieutenant Faulkner had conned the *PT-40* toward the commotion; now guided by the Black Cat's reports, Faulkner closed to deliver an attack on the second destroyer.

An explosion rocked the *Hatsukaze* when a torpedo bored into her port side, detonating beneath her wardroom. Either the *PT-112* or *PT-40* had scored a hit. Eight men died, and twenty-three were wounded by the blast. The *Hatsukaze* was forced to withdraw behind a smoke screen hastily put up by her colleagues. Driven off by flak at 0115, the Cat lost contact as the dense smoke spread from Cape Esperance toward Doma Reef. After slowing down to assess damage and permit emergency repairs, the *Hatsukaze* got under way again, managing to turn between sixteen and eighteen knots as she headed back up the Slot accompanied by the *Kawakaze* and *Tokitsukaze* and another destroyer.

Focusing now on his "light cruiser," Lieutenant Curley began to make low-level runs at intervals, dropping "smoke lights" ahead of the target to mark its course. A third pass at 350 feet was met with bright flickers erupting from the dark silhouette below. Curley pulled his pokey amphibian into a sharp banking turn; the tracers from the destroyer's "broadside" flashed harmlessly astern. Though the Japanese later claimed to have shot down a PBY, their retaliatory gesture not only missed—it failed to deter Curley, who clung to his "cruiser" like glue.

When more PT boats approached, the Cat again moved in, circling over its quarry at five hundred feet. Desperate to be rid of this nettlesome stalker, the destroyer switched on her searchlights and opened up with her secondary batteries. Caught momentarily in a bright beam, the PBY dove out of the illumination as tracers arced up toward it. After an hour's patient vectoring by the persistent VP-12 Catalina, six other PTs finally made contact with the destroyer, which had begun to turn in tight defensive circles with random zigzags. Despite decanting some dozen torpedoes, Lieutenant Curley's patient efforts went unrewarded; not a single detonation lit up the night.

Meanwhile, the transport destroyers cruised slowly along the darkened coast, dumping hundreds of supply drums overboard. Once the unloading was complete, Admiral Koyanagi made haste to get his remaining ships out of range of Cactus' light bombers, leaving the *Hatsukaze* and her escorts to follow.

Lieutenant Curley landed at Henderson to refuel and was again probing the Slot when he spotted another smoke screen off the Russell Islands at 0300 hours. Approaching the haze, he came across his "light cruiser" again, heading up New Georgia Sound at a brisk pace, apparently undamaged. The Black Cat had probably overtaken the *Hatsukaze* and her escorts, moving within the protective envelope of smoke. The odds on a successful night attack in such circumstances—even on the partially visible vanguard vessel—bordered on nil, so Curley called it quits and turned away.

A Hudson bomber picked up the four destroyers 115 miles from Guadalcanal at 0630 and proceeded to shadow them. The CAP from Munda, consisting of a dozen Zeros, arrived over the convoy at 0650, but one *chutai* pulled out after ten minutes. Still anticipating the inevitable air strike, Kahili sent a further eight Zeros from the 204th; these arrived at 0745 to relieve their cohorts. The other original *chutai* duly left at 0800—just thirty minutes before the long-awaited Cactus air strike showed up. The Japanese had steamed at twenty-five knots to a point opposite Choiseul by the time the Cactus strike force ran into the octet of Hamps, patrolling in mid-channel between Santa Ysabel and New Georgia—well to the southeast of the destroyers. A revealing U.S. intelligence report on the raid explains the delay:

On the morning of Jan. 11th it was planned to send out 12 SBD's [sic] and 12 F4F's [sic] at 0500 to attack the Cactus Express on its way out. Planes were assigned but were very difficult to find because of the complete blackout. All engines had been turned up at 0430 and cut after warming up. When the fighter pilots finally got to their planes, only three of the 12 would fire because of condensation. There was difficulty in taxiing to the runway because of the wide dispersal and the muddy condition of the taxiways [at Fighter One]. When all fighters finally got off they were 45 minutes late in reaching the rendezvous. Meanwhile, the SBD's [sic] had burned up so much gas that the leader decided to return, refuel and start over again.

The dozen SBDs from VMSB-233, accompanied by three divisions of VMF-121 F4Fs led by Maj. Bill Campbell, Capt. Hunter Reinburg, and Lt. Herb Long, finally headed up the Slot at 0730, only to run into the 204th Kokutai's bushwhackers. The Marines were immediately bounced by ace aviator LA Masaaki Shimakawa and seven other Hamp pilots who dove out of the sun (see map 1). Those escort pilots who spotted the enemy *chutai*'s descent could not give a "Tally-ho!" because some of the SBD crews were tying up the airwaves. Impulsively, several Wildcat sections broke formation to meet the oncoming A6Ms.

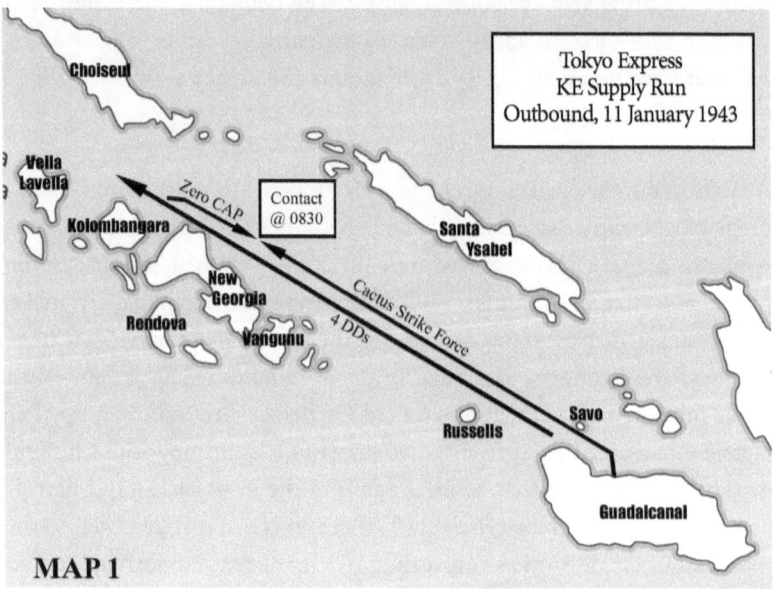

MAP 1

Fearful that another flock of Zeros might be waiting to pounce on the dive-bombers once the Wildcats accepted combat, the F4F leader tried to recall his errant pilots. Major Campbell need not have worried about the SBDs: evidently spoiling for a fight, the clipped-wing Mitsubishis ignored the Dauntlesses, falling pell-mell among the Wildcats. One 204th *shotai* slid in behind a section of F4Fs. Eyeing their predicament, Lieutenant Long banked around to lead his division to the rescue. Before he could intervene, the three Hamps overwhelmed Lt. Joe Cannon, who was flying with a newly designed but flawed belly tank that had failed to release. Hit by incendiaries, the center-mounted forty-two-gallon tank burst into flames that quickly engulfed Cannon's plane as it spiraled into the sea.

Captain Reinburg managed to score hits on the cowl of a Zero before losing track of it in the melee, but he claimed the next Zero he attacked as a sure kill. His was the only success, however.

Group integrity went out the window with the departure of Lieutenant Long's division. VMF-121's pilots found themselves being chased all over the sky by the aggressive Japanese, who gave their opponents little chance to catch their breath. So relentless were the attacking 204th pilots that some desperate leathernecks formed a Lufbury circle to ward off their assailants; other Wildcats hastily joined in. The Hamps then began to execute diving attacks on the rear quadrants of the circling F4Fs, darting in to fire short bursts before zooming away to set up for another pass.

The spirit of Joe Bauer must have been riding in MG Ed Zielinski's cockpit that day. Throwing away the book, Zielinski gunned his Wildcat into the Lufbury circle. Flying against the direction of rotation, he confronted head-on those Hamps that attempted firing passes. This unorthodox tactic took the enemy by surprise; after facing Zielinski, who claimed two Zeros destroyed, the Japanese broke off their attacks.

The besieged Wildcat pilots seized this opportunity to escape. Reforming into ad hoc sections, the F4Fs rallied to charge back into the fray. Capt. John McMahon emerged with claims for three Hamps, Capt. Frank Pierce put in for two A6Ms and a probable, Lt. Elton Mueller put in for a pair of Hamps, and Lieutenant Long claimed a "Zeke" before the combat petered out with planes running low on fuel and ammo. Besides his kill, Captain Reinberg put in for three probables.

Both sides overclaimed outrageously. VMF-121 reported from nine to fourteen Zeros destroyed out of the sixteen to twenty-four they estimated had engaged them; this tally was later reduced to four Zeros and four probables. CPO Sueji Itsukaichi was the only Zero pilot lost out of the eight involved, but three other Zeros took hits. The 204th Kokutai pilots put in for eleven out of twelve Wildcats plus three probables. Actually, only Joe Cannon's F4F went down.

After the escorting Grummans reformed, VMSB-233 persisted a ways up the Slot amidst unsettled weather in search of the four destroyers, but the *Hatsukaze* and her escorts were long gone.

Some observant Japanese pilot had evidently kept track of MG Zielinski. Making his solitary way back to Cactus, the intrepid maverick glanced over his shoulder to find a lone Hamp parked on his wing. Having gotten the Marine's undivided attention, the Japanese pilot dove ahead, looped, and came out on the F4F's tail but did not open fire. Instead, before the startled Zielinski could take evasive action, the Zero pilot repeated the maneuver as if trying to taunt him. Zielinski obligingly triggered his fifties when the Zero pilot pulled ahead to perform his second loop. To his surprise, the Wildcat's guns remained silent. Enemy tracers had started the F4F's gun-control system smoldering during Zielinski's altercations around the Lufbury circle.

The frustrated leatherneck sat helpless as the Hamp came back down on his six to linger briefly before peeling away. Having toyed with his opponent—as a haughty master does to humiliate an upstart pupil—he was content with a gesture of dominance: getting into killing position, then sparing his enemy's life. No neophyte would have played this dangerous game; the man in the Hamp's cockpit was a master, perhaps none other than LA Masaaki Shimakawa.

After the air battle, six surviving 204th Hamps paused at Munda between 0945 and 1110 before proceeding to Kahili, followed later by MG Zielinski's phantom tormentor.

A second Cactus strike force attempted to find the Japanese destroyers without success. "On the way home the bombers unloaded on Munda Airfield," recalled Captain Foss, who led the escort. "There was no air opposition but a lot of anti-aircraft."

Cactus raiders again went into Munda at 1030 on 14 January after a fruitless search for a lone Japanese destroyer spotted earlier. Five of the six Dauntlesses dropped nearly two tons of bombs, taking out the bomber and two Zeros parked on the airstrip. The sixth SBD failed to release its ordnance. Spoiling for a fight, Captain Foss and ten other escorting Wildcat pilots eyed a few airborne planes in the distance, assuming they were Zeros that were "too timid to argue with us."

General Hyakutake had been wrestling with the three alternatives left open to him by the ongoing deterioration of his 17th Army. His options were brutally simple: muster a final mega-banzai attack against advancing U.S. troops, dig in for a last-ditch defense to the death, or conduct a fighting withdrawal toward Cape Esperance. Lt. Col. Kumao Imoto, an 8th Area Army staff officer, carried the solution to General Hyakutake's dilemma on board a Tokyo Express destroyer ferrying him to Kamimbo Bay. IJA Directive 184 ordered the 17th Army to withdraw behind successive rearguard positions: first, at the Matanikau River; second, at the Manala River; third, west of Tassafaronga; fourth, in the vicinity of Kamimbo.

Discounting the Japanese 17th Army's ability to conduct a sufficiently stubborn rearguard action to ensure its own escape, imperial GHQ authorized a contingent of fresh troops for this express purpose. Besides Colonel Imoto and his small retinue, sailing with the Tokyo Express on 14 January were the three rifle companies and one machine-gun company of the newly formed Yano Battalion, totaling 750 men. In support were some one hundred men and a battery of 75-mm cannons of the 8th Mountain-gun Company, 38th Howitzer Regiment. Although Maj. Keiji Yano was an expert in delaying tactics, most of his men were partially trained reservists—a perplexing choice of manpower for such an exacting task. Privately, Colonel Imoto held out little hope for their survival against the battle-hardened American Marines and GIs awaiting them on Guadalcanal, but Yano's troops were to prove him wrong.

Consisting of the transports *Arashi*, *Hamakaze*, *Isokaze*, *Tanikaze*, and *Urakaze* guarded by the *Akizuki*, *Kuroshio*, *Maikaze*, and *Tokitsukaze*, the destroyer convoy plowed doggedly through dirty weather toward the Eastern Solomons during the afternoon of 14 January, its progress shrouded by thick overcast and rain. When the day began to ebb, the six-Zero CAP from the 204th Kokutai took its leave, landing at Munda's freshly repaired airstrip at 1940 for an overnight sojourn. Scheduled to take off at 0600 on the morrow, the Zero *chutai* was assigned to fly CAP over the returning destroyers until 0650 hours.

Two VP-12 Catalinas were up on patrol that night. One Black Cat, cruising in the vicinity of Vangunu Island, made radar contact at 2250 hours. Then a visual sighting erroneously revealed five destroyers and "three transports" heading toward Guadalcanal. Regardless, Rear Adm. Susumu Kimura, who had replaced a newly promoted Admiral Koyanagi as commander of these destroyers, had been found out. The PBY-5A captain continued to shadow the Reinforcement Unit, following the Tokyo Express to the vicinity of Savo Island.

Even before the first Cat made contact in the bad weather, the second Cat sighted the flagship *Akizuki*, transport destroyers *Arashi* and *Urakaze*, plus two other destroyers about sixteen miles northeast of the Russell Islands. Acquiring the five ships some four to six miles ahead by radar, the Catalina pilot closed to visual contact. As he approached, he scanned the troubled sky for signs of enemy floatplanes, ready to dive down and blend into the sea where he could skim safely over its surface using his radio-altimeter.

Once Cactus got wind of the approaching Japanese ships, there remained only enough time to prepare another torpedo-boat ambush. Lieutenant Commander Calvert decided to picket thirteen boats along the Guadalcanal coast between Kamimbo and Doma Coves. The PTs boldly sallied forth in the closing darkness to take up their stations, but the stormy weather severely limited visibility. Since the meddlesome PT boats had engaged the Tokyo Express on its two previous runs, the Japanese assumed they would show up again. Accordingly, four Jake floatplanes—two each from the *Sanyo Maru* and *Kamikawa Maru*—were enlisted to search for the PTs.

On station since 2000, the first two Jakes were relieved at 2335 by the next pair of poorly armed floatplanes that could do nothing should opposing aircraft appear. Unhindered, the second Black Cat proceeded to glide toward its quarry. About to come under air attack, the five destroyers lunged ahead at flank speed. According to Admiral Kimura, by the time "two planes" made a bombing run on them at 0038, his ships were "in position to westward of Savo Island." The amphibian's crew dropped four 500-pounders on a single target, claiming two near misses, in addition to a hit that started a fire. What they likely mistook for a hit and subsequent fire were gouts of flames spurting from the ship's funnels as it knifed flat out through the restless sea, rolling from side to side. However, Kimura does mention "reduced speed" after the attack in connection with the transport destroyer *Urakaze*, which might infer a severe shake-up by the three detonations.

Unable to ward off the Black Cats, the Jakes turned their attention to a pair of motor torpedo boats. They proceeded to drop up to eight 133-pound bombs, holding the PTs momentarily at bay. But that night Lady Luck smiled on these two PT commanders. Lt. (jg) Les Gamble's *PT-45* and Lt. (jg) John Claggett's *PT-37* were dodging the E13As when lightning chanced to silhouette the five destroyers entering Iron Bottom Sound between Savo Island and Cape Esperance. With nothing to lose except the vexatious floatplanes, both boats charged in at 0048—a mere ten minutes after the Black Cat had completed its bombing run.

After launching their fish, the two PTs found themselves to the west of Savo. Coming about, they tried to retire at high speed past the Japanese. Tall spouts tracked the little boats until they zigzagged out of range. Gamble eventually made it to Tulagi. Claggett almost made it to Tulagi, but hung his *PT-37* up on a reef off Florida Island in a blinding downpour. A USN tug had to pull his stranded command free the next morning.

Having survived their ordeal, the skippers of the *PT-45* and *PT-37* believed they had scored direct hits on a destroyer and a "light cruiser"—that is, on the larger, single-stack *Akizuki* and a *Kagero*-class colleague. Here, too, flashes of light in the direction of the enemy were misconstrued as explosions from hits. Indeed, the first Black Cat, hovering over the area amidst pelting rain, had already picked up two separate ships "on fire" off Cape Esperance at 0030—nearly ten minutes before the second Cat's attack and a full twenty minutes prior to the assault by the PT boats. Clearly, when the other PBY-5A had begun to close in, the five destroyers initiated their high-speed evasive maneuvering with its telltale flickering of flames amidst the smoke belching from their funnels.

The rest of Commander Claggett's PTs made contact with the Tokyo Express, but no further hits were scored. Other than his oblique reference to the *Urakaze*, Admiral Kimura made no mention of any destroyers actually struck by bombs or torpedoes; his partially translated radiogram simply states, "The other ships were engaged by enemy PT boats between 0048 and 0130 and drove them off."

Arriving off Cape Esperance on the heels of the air and surface attacks, the transport destroyers dropped anchor between 0100 and 0150, whereupon they proceeded to unload Major Yano's rear guard and its equipment, as well as some badly needed supplies. The second pair of Jakes pulled out for Rekata Bay at 0145, having harassed the PT boats until they finally withdrew. Meanwhile, that night's edition of Maytag Mike swept across Henderson Field on three separate occasions to keep the Cactus Air Force in its muddy slit trenches and dugouts while the Tokyo Express put its troops, equipment, and supplies on shore. According to Capt. Joe Foss who watched one of the raids from a hilltop overlooking Henderson, "It was the first multiple plane attack since November." Death's icy hand fingered six members of the ground echelon during the bombing.

As night wore on, the first Black Cat attempted to shadow what it thought was the pair of "burning" destroyers it had spotted at 0030 hours. Two destroyers had evidently stolen a march on their colleagues—most likely the damaged *Urakaze* and an escort. She had probably been unloaded first so she could withdraw without delay. The pair was now steaming back up the Slot at a moderate twenty knots. Focusing on the intermittent flashes still issuing from their funnels due to earlier overexertion, the PBY crew continued to misinterpret these as flames from deck fires. After sixty-five miles the Cat lost them in the stormy weather but persisted up the Slot for another thirty-five miles in an unsuccessful attempt to reestablish contact. Instead, the PBY wound up cruising over the Japanese seaplane base at Rekata Bay for a half hour, sighting a pair of enemy planes—probably the last two Jakes returning from their CAP mission to stage through Rekata for fuel before pushing on to Bougainville at 0400 hours.

Their cargos finally unloaded, the rest of Admiral Kimura's transport destroyers hastened to weigh anchor and depart with their screen for the Shortlands. First light brought with it a Hudson patrol bomber, combing the unsettled waters of the Slot for the retiring convoy. The New Zealanders spotted a reassembled flotilla at 0630, still steaming at an estimated twenty knots about twenty miles off Vangunu Island. The transport division had evidently caught up to the *Urakaze* and her escort overnight.

The Hudson radioed back its sighting, whereupon fifteen VMSB-142 Dauntlesses took wing from Henderson to rendezvous with twelve Marine Wildcats and six Army Cobras. Clearing Savo Island, the strike force set out after the Japanese. The Tokyo Express was 140 miles distant from Henderson when the formation caught up to it abeam of the westernmost cape of New Georgia at 0735 hours (see map 2).

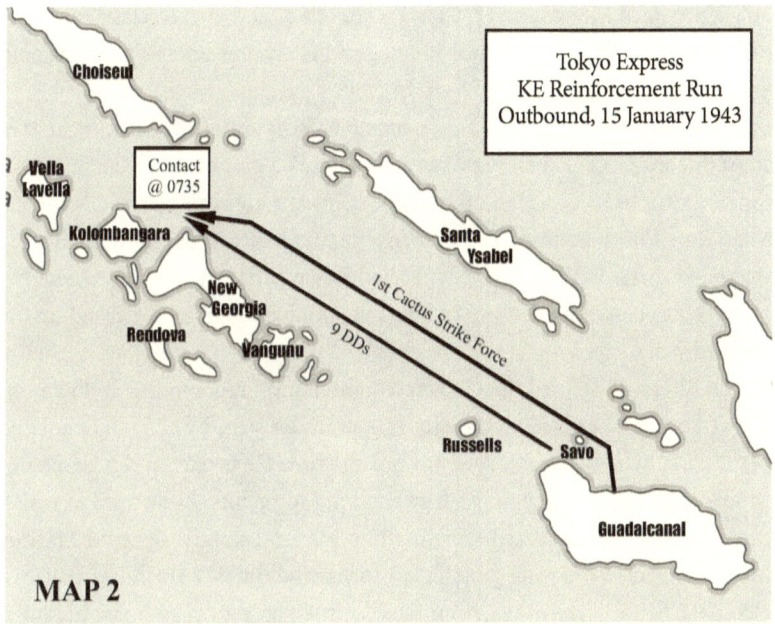

MAP 2

Major Richards, the SBD leader, signaled his divisions to form up for an attack as flak erupted around them. Below, the three columns of ships began to disperse, their guns winking and flashing. High above the light bombers, two VMF-121 divisions under Capt. Hunter Reinburg and Lt. Herb Long, along with Maj. Joe Renner's VMO-251 division, tangled with an estimated twenty to twenty-four "Zeros," more specifically, clipped-wing "02 fighters." The planes were in fact a mix of nine Hamps and Zekes from the 204th Kokutai, plus a dozen or more 6th Shidan Oscars belonging to the 1st or 11th Sentai. Recently transferred to Rabaul, the JAAF fighters probably staged through Buka or Ballale to take up their CAP duties. A six-Zero *chutai* from the 252nd Kokutai arrived in the vicinity at 0710 but for some reason did no take part in the combat.

Captain Reinburg turned into the enemy leader and opened fire, scoring hits on the Japanese fighter, which streaked past him and disappeared. Reinburg next squared off against a full *shotai* of fighters. The combat drifted over Kula Gulf toward Vella Lavella before he broke off, claiming one "Zero" victory plus two probables. Squadron mate Lt. Herb Long also engaged enemy fighters off Vella, claiming a pair of Zeros shot down. Sparring over the gulf, Capt. Jack Moore and Lt. Glen Loban of VMO-251 each claimed a pair of victories. Fellow pilots Major Renner and Lt. Walter Baran put in for one apiece.

Lt. Elton Mueller of VMF-121 sent pieces flying off a "Zeke" near the coast of New Georgia before proceeding to stalk a pair of "02s." Catching up to them over the Slot near Santa Ysabel, he put in for both planes destroyed. Maj. Tom Pierce claimed three enemy fighters before being jumped and wounded. After bailing out, he splashed down safely in the Slot, where he managed to elude the denizens of the deep long enough to be picked up by a friendly destroyer.

Lt. Bill Lundin lined up a Japanese fighter and fired, sending it down off New Georgia. Then, seeing Captain Moore under siege by a *shotai* of enemy planes, Lieutenant Lundin sped toward the fray. He broke up the attack on Moore, but his F4F grew sluggish after taking some hits. As he tried to withdraw, Lundin was bounced. Turning into his attacker, the intrepid Marine hit the trigger. When his guns failed to fire, he quickly surmised that his electrical firing system had been damaged. Unable to dive away, his only recourse was to dodge his opponent's line of fire until he got the chance to dust him off. But there was no eluding this persistent enemy pilot who kept pivoting around to zoom back for another firing pass. Each time, the harried Lundin took evasive action, desperately trying to shake off his persecutor. Luckily, the Japanese pilot's guns finally ran dry, whereupon he broke off, having scored but a single hit on the elusive F4F. Judging by this account, the enemy fighter was a lightly armed Oscar.

Congratulating himself on still being in one piece, Lieutenant Lundin set a course for Cactus, but came up short when his faltering Wildcat gave up the ghost between Savo Island and Cape Esperance after its tanks ran dry. Lundin abandoned his plane, parachuting into Iron Bottom Sound—deep in shark country. Bobbing around in his Mae West, he survived a strafing run by a Japanese scout plane and some unwelcome interest from an inquisitive squalus before finally being rescued by a friendly patrol boat the next day.

Captain Moore also went down before the guns of the relentless Japanese despite Lieutenant Lundin's valiant effort on his behalf. A spate of slugs slammed into his F4F's cowling; the oil pressure fell off, and the engine seized up. Moore managed a dead-stick water landing, only to float aimlessly around the Slot in his inflatable dinghy for four days before making landfall on Santa Ysabel. The local coastwatcher had him back at Cactus by month's end.

Guarded by the 12th FS's Cobras, the SBDs braved intense flak as Lieutenants Allen and Clarke each proceeded to plant a direct hit on a *Kagero*-class destroyer. Ten near misses in all were observed next to an "older" destroyer and three "*Terutsuki*" destroyers, but the *Akizuki*—the only ship of that class present—was not damaged. The *Hamakaze*, *Isokaze*, and *Urakaze* all sustained "minor damage" from this attack; the *Arashi* and *Tanikaze* suffered more. Both had hull damage, and the *Arashi*'s rudder was jammed by a near miss. According to the departing attackers, she glided to a stop and was left dead in the water about twelve miles north-northwest of Kolombangara at 0750 hours. A reconnaissance plane later reported two destroyers stopped with another three circling around them; the *Maikaze* had evidently come alongside to assist the *Arashi* and may already have been rigging up a towline.

Lieutenant Wiggins' SBD was hit by flak during his dive. After dropping a paint scraper on the second destroyer in the port column, he leveled out and then force-landed in the water off the mouth of Morovo Lagoon, suffering head lacerations when he pitched forward into the bombsight assembly. He and his gunner hurried to launch their dinghy before the plane went under, and they were subsequently picked up by a PBY. Besides Lieutenant Wiggins, another SBD ditched, having either sustained battle damage or run out of fuel.

Capt. Cyril Nichols and Lt. Roger Ames of the 12th FS claimed two Zero probables, but two Cobra pilots were shot down while gamely defending the dive-bombers. The 204th Kokutai claimed five U.S. planes shot down plus four probables. The 6th Shidan's claims and losses are not known. All told, three F4Fs, two P-39s, and two SBDs were lost, for a total of seven aircraft.

One U.S. source claimed eight "Oscars" destroyed; coincidentally, VMF-121 put in for eight "Zeros" shot down. VMO-251 added another six, but the 204th posted a mere three Zeros missing; another four were damaged, however. The three pilots lost in the morning's combat were Lt. (jg) Tatenoshin Tanoue, LA Shoichi Fujisada, and LA Yutaka Kimoto. The six survivors paused at Munda for twenty minutes to catch their breath and assess damage. With only two of their Zeros left unscathed, these remaining 204th pilots pulled out for Bougainville at 0835 hours.

Under the scrutiny of the patrolling Hudson, Admiral Kimura placed the *Arashi* in the care of his flagship, *Akizuki*, and screening destroyers, *Kuroshio*, *Maikaze*, and *Tokitsukaze*. He sent the four damaged transports—the *Hamakaze*, *Isokaze*, *Tanikaze*, and *Urakaze*—on ahead to Bougainville, apparently sans fighter CAP. In truth, no fighter cover was needed: by the time another air strike of light bombers made it up the Slot from Cactus, the abbreviated convoy would have progressed beyond its striking range. As for long-range bombers, they would first come across the near-crippled *Arashi* and her escorts farther down the Slot and attack them, which is precisely what happened. Unchallenged from the sky, the transport destroyers glided into Faisi around midday.

Meanwhile, reconnaissance "3V40," the B-17 assigned to search "H" sector, ranged up the Slot toward Zero-infested southern Bougainville, guarded by eight P-38s. From 0910 to 1010 the flight played cat and mouse with six 252nd Kokutai Zeros between Munda and the Shortlands; Lt. Yuzo Tsukamoto's Zeros were flying CAP over the small freighter *Giyu Maru* when Tsukamoto committed his *chutai* to the intercept. According to the Zero pilots, their hit-and-run attacks netted three Lightnings destroyed plus one probable. However, when six 204th Kokutai Zeros scrambled out of Kahili after the B-17 at 0940, it reportedly still had at least seven P-38s in tow. Another 204th *chutai*, on its way to fly CAP over the five straggling destroyers, sighted the B-17 at 1000, but missed its escort. Five Petes, returning to the *Kunikawa Maru* at 1020 after flying CAP over the same destroyers, reported a B-17, escorted by five Lightnings and some Airacobras.

Unfazed by all this attention, the Fort cruised above the Buin-Faisi area, sending three reports to Cactus between 1001 and 1010 that described ship and aircraft locations in the sprawling Tonolei-Shortland harbor complex. Fifteen minutes later, a pair of 958th Kokutai Petes, also flying CAP over the damaged destroyers, spotted the Fort and its full escort of eight P-38s as it headed back down the Slot with four unidentified Zeros nearby, looking to cut out a straggler.

Baker search was also active. Its sole P-39 ran into two F1M2 floatplanes out of the seaplane base at Rekata Bay at 0900 and proceeded to attack them. Flying unscarred through 210 rounds of 7.7-mm return fire, the Cobra chewed into both Petes before breaking off to resume its reconnaissance duties.

After the first Cactus air strike, the 6th Shidan's tired Oscar pilots had evidently resumed CAP duties over the damaged destroyers, possibly availing themselves of nearby Munda to refuel and rearm their depleted and damaged Ki-43s in relays. Nevertheless, an urgent call went out to the 11th Koku Kantai at 0740 and another at 0800 for JNAF fighter cover. The Oscars were relieved by two Petes from the 958th Kokutai around 1000; a 204th Zero *chutai* joined the floatplanes at 1015 hours. The F1M2s stayed on station until 1130, the A6Ms remaining overhead until 1230 hours. Another Zero *chutai* from the 204th arrived at 1300, putting in an uneventful shift that ended at 1510 hours.

In the interim, the five destroyers got under way again, making nine knots with *Arashi* in tow behind *Maikaze*. However, after finally managing to free her rudder at 1245, *Arashi* was able to proceed independently at a reduced twenty knots. A report reached Cactus at 1435 that Admiral Kimura's five stragglers were approaching Bougainville. With the flotilla nearing the Shortlands, an umbrella of ten to thirteen Petes arrived between 1405 and 1515 to relieve the Zeros: three from the 958th Kokutai and seven to ten from the 11th Seaplane Tender Division. Although these inadequate F1M2s had been charged with CAP duty, the threat posed by long-range B-17s or B-26s was serious enough for the 252nd Kokutai to dispatch two six-Zero *chutai*, including one that was escorting a flying boat down from Rabaul, to provide additional cover. Providentially, the 252nd's CAP arrived overhead minutes before a Cactus air strike showed up.

B-17Es of the 72nd BS had indeed arrived at Henderson the previous day, managing to escape the wrath of marauding Bettys overnight. Ground crews toiled into the next afternoon to service the four-engine behemoths and load ordnance into their spacious bomb bays. Finally, seven Boeings lumbered down Henderson's runway and lifted off. They were joined by four P-39s flying low cover, four P-40s from the 68th FS flying medium cover, and six P-38s from the 339th FS providing high cover.

The torpedo boat *Hiyodori*, heading down the Slot with a merchantman, sighted the formation ten miles off the coast of Choiseul. Her radio warning pierced the airwaves at 1538 hours. The destroyers were in the homestretch when the Cactus strike force caught up to them several minutes later in mid-channel about fifty miles northwest of New Georgia (see map 3).

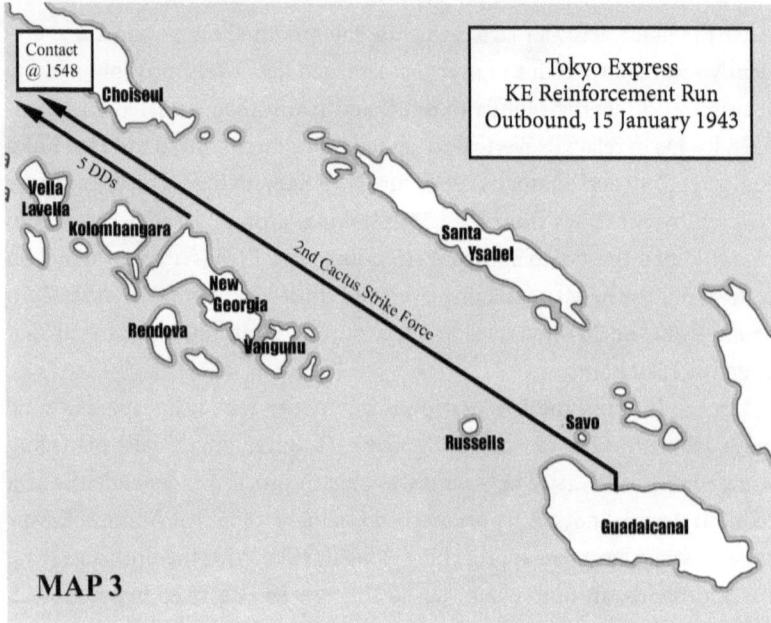

MAP 3

With their three 7.7-mm machine guns, the slow-flying Petes were far more vulnerable than the B-17s they proposed to attack, yet these biplanes did not hesitate to push over when the Forts and their escorts showed up over the Japanese destroyers. One four-plane *shotai* started a head-on pass at the B-17s. Lt. Lloyd Huff led the P-40s down to intercept them, his flight claiming all four on its first pass. The Airacobras and Warhawks then broke up into elements, swarming the Japanese CAP. The Cactus pilots purportedly bagged all the remaining Petes within minutes. Meanwhile, the Forts proceeded to unload seventy-two 500-pound bombs on the destroyers, claiming several hits, but they characteristically failed to score with these high-altitude runs on moving targets.

P-39 pilots claimed four Petes in the air combat: Captain Rivers a pair, and Lt. Darrell Cosart and Lt. Phil Hendrix one each. The P-40 pilots put in for nine more. Lt. Lloyd Huff claimed a hat trick; lieutenants Bob Kennedy, Marty Smith, and Allen Webb each accounted for two more. Only five Petes were lost, but others had undoubtedly been damaged. Shortly after the raiders left, the *Tokitsukaze* and *Kuroshio* were detached to pick up two F1M2 crewmen who had radioed for rescue before ditching in the Slot about twelve miles off Choiseul opposite Vella Lavella.

The two *chutai* from the 252nd Kokutai also joined in the interception, identifying the raiders as nine B-17s, escorted by P-38s and P-39s. Between 1530 and 1600, shots were traded in an on-and-off exchange; the 252nd's few hit-and-run attacks against the formidable firepower arrayed against it proved a desultory exercise. Each side had yet to score when the Zeros broke off, the Rabaul *chutai* having fired a paltry twenty rounds of 20-mm and four hundred rounds of 7.7-mm ammo. Cactus airmen dismissed the incident as contact but no combat with a pair of Zeros.

With the action over and the raiders gone, five Petes—four from the *Kunikawa Maru* and one from the *Kamikawa Maru*—arrived overhead at 1715 to shepherd the destroyers on their final leg into the Shortlands. The exhausted convoy finally dropped anchor at 1820 hours.

Cactus mounted a third air strike later that afternoon. Capt. Joe Foss took off at the head of seven VMF-121 Wildcats to escort a dozen Dauntlesses to "bomb enemy surface craft reported dead in the water off Vella Lavella Island, due to the first bombing attack of the SBD's [sic]." Also escorting were eight Airacobras of the 12th FS, acting as low cover. Maj. Greg Loesch had to abort on the way out because of engine trouble. By the time the rest of the strike force headed up the Slot, Admiral Kimura's first four destroyers had reached Faisi. Still en route, his flagship *Akizuki*, together with the *Arashi* and their three escorts, had safely weathered the B-17 attack and were nearly home.

At 1455, however, an Allied patrol bomber reported a cargo ship—the 6,777-ton *Yamashimo Maru*—plying rough seas about fifteen miles southeast of the Shortlands, escorted by the torpedo boat *Hiyodori*. She was Vila-bound to deliver 120 men and their AA unit for base defense.

Another transport, as yet unnoticed, was somewhat more heavily protected. The lone Jake that watched over the 878-ton *Giyu Maru* between 1610 and 1830 on 14 January as she beat her way past southern Bougainville gave way next day to a series of six-Zero *chutai* from the 204th and 252nd Kokutai, supported by Petes from the 958th Kokutai and the *Sanyo Maru*. Thus amply protected, she arrived safely in the New Georgia group where she unloaded her high-priority cargo. When she finished, *Giyu Maru* quietly made her way back to Bougainville in ballast under a modest CAP of floatplanes, arriving at Buin on 16 January at 1400 hours.

The *Yamashimo Maru* was less fortunate. Two successive pairs of Petes from the Shortland-based seaplane tenders watched over her between 1150 and 1630 hours. Passing the damaged destroyers going in the opposite direction, she reached the New Georgia group under a 204th Kokutai CAP of four Zeros that had come on station at 1445 hours. A Jake from *Kamikawa Maru* also cruised overhead briefly between 1600 and 1640 hours.

The Cactus search plane was subsequently surprised by "nine Zeros" off the south coast of Choiseul at 1605, but escaped into nearby cloud cover. Reforming, the 204th's CAP whiled away the rest of an uneventful shift before pulling out at 1735 hours. Apparently, the second pair of Petes was also in on the action, expending all their ammo on a "B-17" before heading back at 1630, having been relieved by the *Kunikawa Maru* F1M2 ten minutes earlier. Another *chutai* of four Zeros from the ace-studded 204th Kokutai that had arrived behind Lt. Zenjiro Miyano at 1645 now took over. The ships were some ten miles off the northern tip of Kolombangara when the Cactus strike force stumbled upon them not ten minutes later.

No sooner had they appeared than the would-be attackers were bounced by "a swarm of new square-wing Zeros," according to Captain Foss. Surprisingly, the interceptors comprised a mix of six Zeros and Hamps belonging to the 252nd Kokutai, whose pilots, in turn, estimated they were attacking sixteen Cactus aircraft. This same *chutai* had earlier brushed up against the B-17 raiders shortly after it arrived on station over the destroyers, garnering no results one way or the other. Now flying CAP over the anchored *Giyu Maru*, it had spotted the Cactus strike force preparing to attack the nearby *Yamashimo Maru* and sped northward to intercept the oncoming raiders before they could reach the convoy.

The firefight that followed began at 1740 and lasted at least ten minutes. Seeing a *shotai* of defenders move in to attack the dive-bombers, the P-39 pilots hurried to cut them off, but were themselves jumped by the second *shotai*. Above, Capt. Frank Pierce and Capt. Bill Marontate peeled off with their F4F divisions. Diving into the fray, Captain Pierce claimed a hat trick in the ensuing altercation.

Captain Foss held his division back on a hunch; sure enough, he eventually spotted a second group of Zeros, most likely the 204th CAP, jockeying for position. With the Cactus strike force now under attack but still closing in, Lieutenant Miyano finally committed his *shotai* to the intercept at 1810 hours. The Grummans peeled off to engage the approaching Zeros, and the opposing flights melted into each other. Foss got off a short burst into a fighter that was closing with another F4F; the Zero was on him so quickly, however, that it passed by before he could see the results. Glancing around, he saw the receding plane "burst into flames and spin down."

Meanwhile, Lt. Oscar Bate locked onto an enemy fighter and purportedly dispatched it before coming under attack by a *shotai*. Hounded by the three Zeros, Bate wound up heading toward none other than Captain Foss, who instinctively sized up Bate's predicament. As Foss banked to intercept Bate's pursuers, one of the closing fighters dove directly in front of him, its pilot intent on bagging Bate. Foss opened up at point-blank range, and the enemy plane blew up in his face.

Bate's Grumman dove past, hell-bent for leather with a Zero still glued to its tail. Foss fired, but again the Japanese plane closed so swiftly that he didn't see any results before it had flown by. Swiveling around, he caught sight of the A6M as it burst into flames and spun out of sight.

Bate was five hundred feet below Foss' right by now with another "red-cowled" Zero sliding in behind him. The "yellow-lacquered" A6M opened up on Bate, but Foss sent a short burst across the Mitsubishi's nose to distract its pilot. The enemy flier honked his steed around then zoomed up toward the Marine ace. Curving into each other, both adversaries opened fire but scored no hits, their tracers skimming over their respective canopies. As they whizzed by, they exchanged glances before scissoring for another go-around.

The talented Zero pilot zoomed up again. Guns blazing, he dove at the climbing Wildcat head-on. Just as he was about to pass the Grumman, he attempted to turn to the right—too soon. Foss skidded for a shallow deflection shot and fired a short burst that walked into his foe's wing-root and cockpit area. The Japanese fighter continued its diving turn as if nothing had happened. After dropping three thousand feet or so, the enemy pilot circled to starboard before beginning another climb. Foss was on the verge of diving on him when other Zeros appeared. As he turned toward some nearby cloud cover, he saw his recent opponent pass by about one hundred yards distant. All of a sudden, smoke puffed out, and the A6M began to smolder. Flames licked back from its left wing tank as the burning plane winged over and spiraled toward the ocean. The pilot failed to bail out.

Lieutenant Miyano's A6Ms continued to harass the Cactus raiders for a quarter of an hour, prompting the U.S. pilots to believe they had encountered at least a dozen Zeros in a single, prolonged engagement. While the escorting fighters were entangled with the Zeros, the Pete stole a piece of the action. Its pilot fastened onto Lieutenant Brushert and "almost [ran] him down." The F1M2 managed to expend all its 7.7-mm ammo before breaking off. Both Brushert and his rear gunner returned fire, observing the floatplane begin to trail smoke as it retreated into a cloud. However, the smoke trail may have been nothing more than a prolonged spurt of oily exhaust fumes as the pilot gunned his engine to make his escape.

The *Hiyodori* radioed at 1822 that she was engaging VMSB-142's SBDs. Some dozen Zeros hovered nearby, yet Major Richard's crews somehow went in unmolested. Lieutenant Hood and Lieutenant Henderson both scored hits on the *Yamashimo Maru*. She also shuddered from four "very near misses" and five near misses. Someone dropped a near hit on the *Hiyodori*, badly injuring one crewman and slightly wounding four others. The escort reported at 1825 and again at 1915 that she had "engaged about eighteen Grummans and fighters," shooting down "four medium sized attack planes."

VMSB-142 claimed it left the *Yamashimo Maru* burning and "dead" in the water. Although damaged, the transport got under way again with the lone Pete, its ammo depleted, still flying CAP. Reaching Vila after nightfall, the *maru* unloaded her cargo and then returned back to the Shortlands. She arrived at Faisi early the next day, alternately escorted by Jakes and a *chutai* of five Petes from the Shortland-based seaplane tenders. From there the *Yamashimo Maru* was ordered to Rabaul to effect emergency repairs before steaming back to Kure naval yard via Truk.

The returning F4Fs arrived at Cactus circa 1935 in the midst of a Maytag Mike raid, courtesy of a 751st Kokutai Betty, but all managed to land safely. Eventually emerging from his protective cloud, Captain Foss bumped into Lieutenant Bate, who joined up for the trip home through rain-swept darkness. They also touched down at Cactus amidst the eruptions of Maytag Mike's bombs.

As the SBDs began to touch down at 2015, another Betty joined the landing circle over Henderson Field, dropping bombs among the taxiing dive-bombers, but no one was hit.

When Captain Marontate failed to make the postcombat rendezvous, his fellow pilots feared the worst. The thirteen-kill ace had been seen by Lieutenant Bate and Lieutenant Presley to vanquish another Zero. Lt. Roger Haberman caught a glimpse of the ace's Wildcat still in the fight, but lost track of him. Then Captain Foss espied an F4F wafting slowly seaward in a flat spin at a 45-degree angle, its left wing sheared off. Recalling the doomed Wildcat, he surmised that his colleague must have collided with a Japanese fighter. Later, an SBD gunner said he saw Marontate bail out. If his was one of the six chutes seen descending amongst the Japanese ships, he might have been picked up, but was either executed or died in prison.

Neither the dive-bombers nor the Cobras lost any aircraft. While the 252nd Kokutai recorded no victories for the second time, only expending three hundred rounds of ammo during both air battles, neither did it incur any casualties. The 204th Kokutai claimed two "Grummans" shot down plus one probable; in return, the F4F pilots claimed six kills and a probable. Only Lieutenant Miyano's damaged 204th Zero returned to Buin. His wingman, PO2c Makoto Terao, either ditched or bailed out; he was rescued, but did not fly for some time, so he must have been seriously wounded. WO Saji Kanda, the 2nd *shotai* leader, also survived; he was back in the air four days later. However, his wingman, LA Seikichi Sakai, was killed. Both Miyano and Kanda were destined to die in combat together over Guadalcanal on 16 June 1943.

Captain Foss finally managed to tie Eddie Rickenbacker's World War I record; his day's claims upped his tally to twenty-six victories. Lieutenant Bate, too, eventually matured into an ace.

CHAPTER 8
BLITZING THE QUARTERBACKS

The air war in the Solomons shifted into high gear on 25 January with the sortie of the first massed daylight raid against the Henderson Field complex since the previous autumn. Early that morning Chief Petty Officer Kizaki of the 204th Kokutai flew a Dinah reconnaissance plane down the Slot, reporting favorable weather conditions all the way to Guadalcanal. Eighteen 705th Kokutai Bettys rose from Rabaul at midmorning to rendezvous with fifty-four Zeros gathered from three *kokutai*. The bombing mission was actually a feint to mask a fighter sweep. This tactic had been introduced on 29 September 1942 to entice ComAirSol's fighter pilots into combat, but on that occasion its success had been befuddled by the premature withdrawal of the bomber contingent as the formation passed over the Central Solomons. Anzac coastwatchers had observed the split and reported it to Cactus.

The coastwatcher command center had relocated to a spacious and better-protected dugout several hundred yards north of Henderson Field by October 1942. From there messages from the network could be quickly passed on to General Mulcahy's intelligence and operations staffs. Now, as the enemy formation passed over northern Bougainville, it was picked up by Lt. John "Jack" Read, the coastwatcher at Buka Passage, who was ensconced 2,500 feet up in the highlands at Pora Pora, monitoring the goings-on at Buka and Bonis airfields. Lieutenant Read promptly radioed the particulars of the strike force to the DSIO on Guadalcanal. By then only seventeen bombers remained, the Betty flown by PO2c Eiichi Shimako having had to drop out at 1050 due to engine trouble.

Since the Bettys were to act as decoys, they probably carried no bombs, so they could fly the entire trip at a faster cruising speed that permitted the

Rabaul-based escort of eighteen Zeros from each of the 252nd, 253rd, and 582nd Kokutai to fly more efficiently as well. With drop tanks these fifty-four escorting fighters did not need to top up fuel to maximize combat time over Guadalcanal.

As the small air armada approached the Buin area, Lt. Cdr. Mitsugu Kofukuda of the 204th Kokutai got ready to lead another twenty-two Zekes and Hamps from Kahili into the air. Flying with their *daitai* leader were Lt. Zenjiro Miyano, Lieutenant (junior grade) Morisaki and CPO Hatsuo Hidaka. Excellent pilots, both Miyano and Hidaka were destined to achieve ace status. Kofukuda's *daitai* lifted out of Kahili, joining up with the Guadalcanal-bound formation as it passed overhead under the watchful eye of coastwatcher Paul Mason, ensconced on Malabita Hill.

Flying down the Slot through deteriorating weather, the eighteen fighters of the 582nd Kokutai went astray, but tried to make their own way to Guadalcanal. After some three hours' flying through massive cloud banks, their destination still eluded them, so this *daitai* aborted and returned to Rabaul. The remaining formation was finally picked up by search radar at 1313, its progress henceforth being tracked by Cactus fighter controllers.

Already aloft on patrol, Lt. Herb Peters' VMO-251 Wildcats were vectored to the bogeys. The four Marine Corps F4Fs were the first to intercept the enemy. When the Japanese spotted the oncoming Grummans near Savo Island at 1320, the raid abruptly metamorphosed into a fighter sweep with the about-face of the bomber contingent. Having drawn Cactus fighters up, the Betty pilots considered their decoy duty done and made for a billowing cloud formation over Tulagi. From there the 1st and 2nd Chutai went their separate ways, the 1st flying directly to Vunakanau, the 2nd stopping at Buin to pick up personnel. Flying above the overcast on his way back with the 2nd Chutai, CPO Mitsuo Toyota suddenly dropped out of formation at 1415. Shortly, his Betty disappeared—a casualty of some technical malfunction.

Flying over the Lunga area, Lieutenant Peters' division had spotted the "flight of approximately 30 enemy fighters, both Nagoya and Mark II Zeros . . . in loose formation at altitudes from 18,000 to 25,000 feet in the vicinity of Savo Island." Climbing above this Japanese *daitai*, the Marines proceeded to utilize their height advantage and the hazy overcast to make individual overhead passes on stragglers from the 253rd Kokutai. Zooming back up into the cloud cover after hit-and-run attacks, Peters was credited with knocking down two Zeros plus two probables; Maj. Ray Vroome claimed a Zero and a probable. Lt. Henry "Hank" Sabatier claimed another Zero before avgas shortage forced the F4Fs to pancake. VMO-251 also put in for three Zeros damaged. The 253rd Kokutai's airmen claimed one "Grumman" shot down, but the fourth leatherneck pilot, Lt. Hank McCartney, emerged unscathed, though he remained scoreless.

Capt. Joe Foss was airborne with eight VMF-121 Wildcats barely six minutes after receiving the order to scramble at 1245, but failed to join up with the VMO-251 division as it darted in and out of the clouds. Climbing to a ceiling of 18,000 feet, he did catch sight of a dozen enemy fighters near Savo Island, "playing around, doing nip-ups and chasing each other." Far from playing around, these seemingly undisciplined Zero pilots were almost surely executing their vertical and horizontal scissoring tactics for mutual defense.

Foss initially headed over to engage these two *chutai*, then began to wonder what they were doing there exposed at a relatively low altitude. It was at that point he noticed the break in the overcast ahead. Cautiously leading his flight up into the edge of the hole, he observed another thirty or so Zekes and Hamps stacked loosely between 18,000 and 25,000 feet above Savo Island. Apparently, after the exchange with VMO-251's patrol, the remaining fifteen Zeros of the 253rd's *daitai* joined forces with the twenty-two Zeros of the 204th's *daitai* to egg on and ambush any other Cactus fighters that showed up.

Beyond the hole, another estimated twenty-four enemy fighters orbited between Cape Esperance and the Russell Islands. Captain Foss and his pilots mistook them for "dive-bombers ... apparently waiting for the Zeros to clear away the opposition before coming in." Orbiting farther out were apparently more enemy planes. Though he partially misidentified the types and strength of the bandits, Foss rightly guessed that the Japanese were setting up for a one-two punch: Lt. Motonari Suho's eighteen-Zero *daitai* of the 252nd Kokutai was being deliberately held back to sneak in unopposed and work over Henderson Field and its fighter strips, strafing all the planes it could on the ground.

His force outnumbered, Foss tried to keep all the Japanese formations at bay by forming a Lufbury circle between them and the Henderson airfield complex. Even as he radioed for more support, another seven VMF-121 F4Fs were already roaring into the sky behind Capt. Greg Loesch. Once airborne, however, these reinforcements failed to make direct contact with the Japanese formation amidst the evolving storm front. Instead, they joined up on Foss' fighters.

The Marine Corps ace continued to lead his expanded Wildcat formation in a cat-and-mouse game over Savo. Six of the twelve low-flying Zeros now peeled away, dropping to between one thousand and two thousand feet. With their brethren cavorting enticingly below, a *shotai* of Zeros would drop down briefly through the haze to monitor the circling F4Fs in order to position their colleagues for a bounce on the Marines' six. But Foss kept his sorely tempted pilots in tight formation slightly beneath the ceiling, circling around the fringe of the hole. Try as they might, the *chutai* of low-flying Japanese pilots could not bait the Marines into going down after them.

Had Foss permitted piecemeal section attacks on these tempting targets, he would have been sucked into a general engagement—just the cue the 252nd's *daitai* would have been waiting for to head in unmolested and shoot up Henderson and its satellites. The standoff continued with neither side choosing to come to grips. Foss greatly respected the Zero and forever cautioned his pilots not to tangle with one unless they possessed an advantage, such as height or surprise—preferably both. In refraining from swallowing the bait, Captain Foss exhibited the self-discipline that tempered the natural eagerness of the best fighter pilots, enabling them to become the top aces.

The 339th FS scrambled six Lightnings at 1330 hours. Climbing westward, they were the first ones to spot the eighteen retreating Betty bombers over Savo Island as the latter turned toward Tulagi. Pursuit was pointless. Reaching 17,500 feet, the P-38s split into three pairs, and these elements proceeded to cruise at equidistant points around the outer edge of Foss' Lufbury circle.

Unexpectedly, four of the six Zeros that had been acting as bait climbed back up into the clouds. The other two also sped upward, darting between the F4Fs and one of the P-38 elements. They had finally grown tired of this waiting game that seemed to be going nowhere. One of the two A6M pilots rose to within range of Captain Foss while the other made an about-face, heading up past Captain Loesch. The P-38s, meanwhile, had begun to close in. Suddenly, one of the unsuspecting Zeros streaked up right in front of the closest approaching P-38 element—so close that it went by the USA pilots before they could react. Wagging his wings to see them better, the enemy aviator was unaware of a second P-38 element coming up on him.

Covered by Lt. Besby Holmes, Lt. Ray Bezner turned into the left side of the Mitsubishi. The surprised Zero pilot executed a left turn to meet this new threat head-on butthen changed his mind. Swinging right, he exposed the underside of his plane to Lieutenant Bezner's guns. Bezner opened up at point-blank range with his 20-mm cannon and four fifties. Momentarily caught in this deadly fusillade, the Japanese fighter rolled over and began to smolder. As flames erupted, the Zero dropped to two thousand feet, leveled off for an instant, then flipped over to spiral toward the sea.

The downed pilot's teammate dove in on Lieutenant Bezner, who gunned his heavy twin-boom fighter into a shallow turn to lead the Zero toward the Grummans. But it was Lieutenant Holmes' P-38 that scissored onto the Mitsubishi's tail. The A6M absorbed a full-deflection shot in its cowl. Banking to the right in a zoom, the desperate Japanese pilot attempted to run back for cover, but Holmes clung to his tail, guns blazing in a single long burst. When they emerged again, the enemy fighter had begun to smoke as it nosed down into a long glide. Another element of P-38s spotted the rest of the original twelve exposed bandits as they, too, climbed for the cloud cover.

Eight Marine Wildcats, led by Maj. Don Yost, CO of VMF-121, had also scrambled out of Fighter Two, as had a flight of U.S. Army Airacobras. Neither group managed to intercept the enemy, nor did Maj. Kermit Tyler's six Army Warhawks, which had been held on alert until 1400 before being sent up. With Cactus reinforcements drawing nearer to the hole in the clouds, the Japanese—by then growing short of avgas and patience—wisely elected to pull out. It was all over by 1410 hours.

By now the weather was taking a rapid turn for the worse as the treacherous storm front settled over the Slot. Bucking the turbulence, many returning planes from the 204th and 253rd Kokutai—some damaged, most low on fuel—began to pancake wherever they could. By 1715 all twenty-four 204th Zeros had made it as far as Buin.

Buka took in the lion's share of the 253rd, with only a scattered few of its fighters reaching Rabaul directly. In the day's action the 253rd lost PO1c Shin Iwamoto and PO1c Tsugio Fukutome. WO Mitsunori Nakajima ditched on the return trip due to engine trouble, but he survived, ending up as a POW. The remaining fifteen Zeros from the 253rd apparently put in at Munda to refuel before pushing on to Rabaul, with several pausing at Buka en route.

The 252nd Kokutai saw no action, having spent its time and fuel circling over Savo, waiting in vain for the word to either strafe Cactus' airfields or join in the air combat. Without radios, and with hand and lamp signals hampered by the bad weather, Lieutenant Suho's *daitai* may not even have realized at what point the 204th and 253rd Zeros had pulled out. When he finally did decide to turn back, his planes were already being buffeted by the brunt of the tempest.

For his part, with all six of his Zeros having sustained some damage in the maelstrom, Lt. Koichi Yoshida decided to ditch his 2nd Chutai on a reef in the relatively calm waters of the only harbor still under Japanese control. Five pilots made safe water landings; the sixth elected to carry on, somehow eventually reaching Ballale. A Cactus patrol plane, searching the Guadalcanal coastline the next day, counted four downed "Zeros" in the shallows of Coughlan Harbor. The fifth may have missed the reef and put down in deeper water. All five pilots survived and were likely evacuated with the Japanese 17th Army.

Two other 252nd Kokutai pilots were forced down by the weather, one damaged Zero pancaking at Munda—possibly the 3rd Chutai's LA Shiro Tsukahara. The 1st Chutai's LA Takesaburo Ikeda ditched and was lost. The remaining eleven Zeros of the 252nd's *daitai* made it back to Ballale.

Cactus sounded "All Clear" at 1502 hours. The P-40s fell in with the six P-38s and followed them back to Fighter Two. As an extra precaution against any enterprising Zero pilots who may have thought to double back and pluck an easy kill from among the landing planes, the Grummans and Cobras continued to patrol over Cactus' airfields in lazy circles until everyone else had landed. The Lightnings touched down amidst deteriorating flying conditions at 1530 without incident, followed by the other units.

Twenty-eight F4Fs, six P-38s, six P-40s, and eight P-39s had been sent aloft, but only Captain Foss' and Captain Loesch's Wildcats, and the Lightnings actually made contact. In the second combat, the Lightnings claimed two Zeros in addition to three more damaged. Though the 204th Kokutai reported no losses, one Zero returned heavily damaged, probably Lieutenant Holmes' victim. In this second exchange, the 204th claimed a pair of F4Fs shot down; the 253rd claimed two P-38s.

Though the Japanese did not specifically mention any strafing of Cactus airfields, some 253rd Zeros may have dropped down to Henderson and its satellites to deliver a surprise flurry of low-level runs, for they also claimed a P-39 and a B-25 as probables. However, the records of U.S. squadrons and ground echelons do not mention any such attack or report any losses among the parked aircraft.

Twenty-six January turned out to be a day for rescues. Two days earlier, an American-style dinghy had been sighted by an RNZAF Hudson near the entrance to Manning Strait, between Choiseul and Santa Ysabel. While the Japanese Dinah was reconnoitering Guadalcanal in advance of the following day's JNAF air strike, a pair of P-40s from the 68th FS flew toward Choiseul on a search mission. Reaching the southeastern tip of Choiseul, Captain Hubbell's Hawk suddenly began to run rough. He and Lieutenant Smith turned back, but not before sighting "signs of life raft." Lt. Larry McKulla and Lt. Bill Fiedler of the 70th FS duly arrived in the vicinity of Choiseul in their P-39Ds at 0730 on 26 January. McKulla dropped to five hundred feet to renew the search while Fiedler hovered at 2,500 feet.

The Cobra pilots were approaching Rob Roy Island at about 0850 with McKulla still flying on the deck. Keeping watch above him, Lieutenant Fiedler spotted a "Kawanishi Type 97 4-Engine Flying Boat" rising over the bay west of the island at two thousand feet with a "Mark II Zero" escort.

Having spotted the downed Japanese airman, the Mavis had landed off shore and taxied in. The crew beckoned the pilot to swim out, but when he saw sharks cruising nearby, he refused. Evidently, the escorting Hamp pilot saw them too, for he tried to disperse them by strafing the area. When impatient crewmen ventured to the outer edge of the Mavis' long wing and threw him a "buoy" tied to a lifeline, the stranded flier was persuaded to make his way out to it only after emptying his sidearm at the menacing fins scything through the blue-green water.

Upon seeing the big Kawanishi climbing after its takeoff, Fiedler radioed a warning to his element leader, but received no answer. Pulling back on his stick, he coaxed his straining fighter up to four thousand feet just as the Mavis and Hamp emerged from the bay. Fiedler kicked his Cobra over and executed a high-side pass on the Mavis' right flank, unaware of five more 252nd Kokutai fighters circling above. The H6K's waist and tail gunners returned his fire as he let fly at the huge flying boat. Certain he had scored several hits, Fiedler pulled out in time to see McKulla zoom up to make a firing pass from below. As he climbed past the Kawanishi in his pullout, McKulla was jumped by Lt. Yuzo Tsukamoto's Zeros that dove to the intercept after Fiedler's initial attack.

Lieutenant Fiedler was making a climbing turn back up to four thousand feet when he was startled by the unexpected sight of his leader's burning Airacobra as it flashed by him with a pair of Hamps glued to its tail, followed by three others. Fiedler immediately dove to McKulla's rescue. Lining up one of the two Mitsubishis for a deflection shot, he sent a number of rounds into its fuselage. The enemy fighter spurted smoke, prompting Fiedler to claim it blew up—a premature call since all the Hamps made it back to base. Having recovered with a left turn, Fiedler spotted McKulla's P-39 in a shallow dive, heading toward the water with its landing gear down. The cockpit doors flew off the doomed Cobra as it plowed in near Wagina Island. Its wheels knifed into the surface, flipping the plane over onto its back. The fuselage quickly settled, disappearing beneath the swell.

The Zeros were now converging on Fiedler, so he paused only long enough to make a single pass over Wagina. He caught sight of an uninflated dinghy floating near the spot where the P-39 had gone under, but there was no sign of Lieutenant McKulla. Pulling out, Fiedler glanced over his shoulder at the Hamps closing in. He rammed the throttle wide open and dove for the deck. With the Zeros singeing his tail feathers, the desperate Cobra pilot hedgehopped his way over Santa Ysabel. At length managing to outdistance his slower pursuers, Fiedler breathed a sigh of relief when, halfway down Ysabel, the Japanese finally broke off the chase. Exhausted, he landed at Fighter Two at 0955 hours.

Though the 252nd pilots correctly claimed McKulla as a victory, they also claimed Fiedler as a probable; Fiedler, however, emerged unscathed. As for McKulla, he survived his ditching; the submarine *Grouper* rescued him from Ringi Island on 10 February. The Mavis fared worse: McKulla's attack not only wounded a crewman fatally—it severely holed the underside of its hull. Radio operator Sochio Hirayama noted that the big flying boat soon became waterlogged after mooring in Shortland Harbor.

At around 1000 that morning six Hamps from the 204th Kokutai, led by WO Hayato Noda, were also escorting a Kawanishi flying boat, this one searching the south coast of New Georgia for "an emergency landed plane"—a Zero that had ditched on the return flight from Guadalcanal the previous day. Unexpectedly, the formation crossed paths with a Cactus PBY on a rescue mission, flying along Blanche Channel at two thousand feet. Perhaps as a gesture of live and let live, the escorting Zeros passed by the vulnerable Dumbo. Coastwatcher Donald Kennedy watched as the Japanese flight then probed the recesses of Wickham anchorage. A Zero was spotted awash on a reef, its pilot on shore nearby. Lt. Dick Horton again sighted the Kawanishi and its escort as they flew back over Rendova a bit later, having evidently picked up the stranded airman.

The JAAF's 6th Shidan had its first go at Henderson on 27 January. The previous day, thirty-three 11th Sentai Oscars out of Rabaul arrived at Buka for an overnight stay, joining the unit's resident fifteen-plane *chutai*. Another thirty-six Ki-43s from the 1st Sentai, plus three from the 12th Hikodan's Rabaul HQ, sojourned at Ballale. So did nine 45th Sentai Lilys and two Dinahs from the 76th Independent Chutai. The original plan had been to stage at least the Lilys through Vila airstrip, but this option was scrapped on 25 January in the wake of TG AFIRM's bombardment.

Between 0310 and 0425 on 27 January no fewer than fourteen Bettys from the 751st Kokutai blitzed Henderson Field. All told, the 751st planted 151 133-pound bombs within and without the U.S. perimeter and sprayed it with 9,060 rounds of machine-gun fire for good measure. But American AA gunners exacted their revenge, hitting eight bombers, one of them fatally. This heavy raid was undoubtedly laid on by the JNAF as an extra initiative to prepare the way for the massive JAAF air strike scheduled to hit Cactus later that morning.

At 0810 hours the thirty-three Oscars from Buka took off for Ballale to join up with the Oscars and Lilys that had spent the night there. Forty-five minutes later the combined strike force of some seventy-eight aircraft started down the Slot behind Dinah scouts. Evidently spotting only the bombers and their low cover, coastwatchers reported the passage of an estimated thirty "Zeros" escorting ten "Mitsubishi bombers." The 11th Sentai's *chutai* leader apparently ran into some mechanical difficulty over Kolombangara and had to abort the mission.

Warned in time, a mixed bag of twelve Wildcats, six Lightnings, and ten Warhawks were airborne, waiting to intercept the Japanese when they arrived over Iron Bottom Sound at 1045 hours. To a man, not only the coastwatchers, but also the Cactus pilots from no fewer than six squadrons, again mistook the Oscars for a Zero variant—a gross case of mistaken identity.

Capt. Hunter Reinburg had been preparing to scramble a division of four VMF-121 Wildcats when he discovered that the F4F he had chosen was sans radio. With no time to waste, Reinburg decided to make do and took off anyway. On the climb toward Savo Island to reach 20,000 feet, he instructed his wingman by hand signals to take over as flight leader. Lt. Elton Mueller acknowledged. Shortly after, Reinburg caught sight of the "Zero" low escort, but he could not radio a "Tally-ho!" Meanwhile, Lieutenant Mueller had been ordered back by Cactus Recon to cover Henderson Field against the oncoming raiders. Seeing Mueller turning the flight around, Reinburg signaled that he was retaking command. He then banked to the right to attack the 1st Sentai formation—alone! Mueller and the others had obviously missed Reinburg's attack signal.

Selecting his first customer, Captain Reinburg gunned his F4F head-on from above. In the grand Bauer tradition, he executed an overhead pass on the Nakajima. Despite some swift maneuvering by the enemy flier, Reinburg adjusted his aim while in his inverted dive and shot his quarry down. Emerging victorious, Reinberg saw another Japanese fighter climbing toward him about three thousand feet below. He pushed over and dove toward his would-be assailant. Guns blazing, the two pilots closed and passed each other at high speed with inconclusive results. Now Reinburg's momentum brought him within range of yet another hostile fighter; he centered it in his gunsight and quickly flamed it.

The Japanese low cover began to swarm around the single F4F, which had now reached the bombers heading for Henderson Field. But Reinberg decided to settle for his two kills and broke off. Diving away toward Fighter Two, he proceeded to land while the Lilys prepared to attack the nearby bomber field. Puzzled at Reinburg's disappearance, the other three

VMF-121 pilots had remained aloft over the Lunga perimeter for a time. Seeing no action, they eventually touched down safely.

Upon returning from an early morning patrol, Capt. Mike Yunck's four VMF-112 Wildcats scrambled out of Fighter Two at 0950. Climbing to 20,000 feet to intercept "enemy dive-bombers over Cape Esperance," they, too, were unable to make contact. Lt. Joe Lynch of VMF-112 managed to get off Fighter Two's tarmac at 1020 with a flight of three VMO-251 F4Fs led by Capt. Jim Anderson. These Wildcat pilots *did* intercept what they thought were "enemy zero [sic] type fighters and dive-bombers over Esperance." At Captain Anderson's signal, his wingman crossed behind him, taking up a position in right echelon between the leader and the one-man second section. Anderson's division then peeled off to the left to bounce the Oscars flying low cover.

Lieutenant Lynch had just outfought and claimed a "Zero" when, to his surprise, his F4F coughed and quit. Breaking off, he tried to make it back to his home field but ran out of sky short of the strip. Settling for a water landing, Lynch set his plane down in shallows west of Fighter Two. Boats from Lunga Point effected his rescue, returning him to base none the worse for his experience, save for bruises and cuts about the face. Evidently, the excited pilot had grabbed a Wildcat that had just come in off morning patrol and had not yet been refueled. Lynch had given the instrument panel a cursory glance in his haste to get airborne, misreading the fuel gauge levels.

A warning crackled over Cactus Recon's USA channel that enemy fighters were approaching Guadalcanal while a flight of bombers orbited over the Russell Islands. Six Lightnings from the 339th FS scrambled on the tails of the USMC Wildcats at 0955 hours. Capt. John Mitchell's flight climbed toward the Russells, vainly searching for the Lilys in the vicinity where they had been reported. Sweeping around at 30,000 feet, Mitchell's flight sighted "between twenty and thirty Nagoya Zero Fighters" to the southwest of Henderson Field at 20,000 feet. The 11th Sentai planes were arrayed in a "loose string formation doing loops and rolls." Cactus pilots interpreted these sloppy antics as a ruse to entice them into combat, but the Japanese were simply performing their embellished defensive drills.

Far below, ten Warhawks from the 44th and 68th FSs that had taken off twenty minutes after the Lightnings were slowly climbing in two separate flights of four planes, trailed by a two-plane element. Upon seeing the Cactus newcomers rising from the east some 15,000 feet below, the 11th's pilots pushed over to bounce this vulnerable quarry. In turn, Mitchell's P-38s sliced downward to deliver a bounce of their own.

Though the Oscars dove more slowly, they held a low-altitude advantage, and their lead *shotai* fell upon the first flight of P-40s before the P-38s could intervene. The climbing Hawks tried to turn into their attackers or disperse into power dives, but two were immediately shot down. Bailing out, both Capt. Hubbell and Lieutenant Mosely were temporarily swallowed up by the dense enemy-occupied rainforest south of Henderson Field. Lt. Paul Hansen recalled, "We went into the center of about 30 Zeros and after our first pass on a Zero, I never saw another Army plane until I peeled out of the mess." An enemy fighter obligingly peeled out with him and proceeded to rake Lieutenant Hansen's P-40. Hansen fell away wounded, nursing his badly damaged ship as far as Henderson Field, where he force landed on the bomber strip, totaling his airplane.

By now, the plunging Lightnings had caught up to the enemy's rear *shotai*. To avoid the diving passes of the P-38s, the Japanese half-rolled their lithe Oscars to dive out of the line of fire. But several honked their planes into tight turns, butterfly flaps extended, presenting the P-38s with fleeting targets. One Japanese pilot swung around, closing on Captain Mitchell from the right in a high-side pass. Mitchell managed to turn his bulky ship into his attacker in time to fire. A lethal concentration of .50-caliber and 20-mm slugs flashed all over the Ki-43's cockpit and surrounding fuselage. The Oscar dropped way down to three thousand feet, where it recovered momentarily before rolling over to crash into the trees near Cape Esperance. The P-38 attack scattered a portion of the enemy fighters, thereby bringing some relief to the beleaguered P-40s.

Meanwhile, the second flight of four P-40s circled the field behind Major Tyler, their Allisons laboring to pull them up higher. The Warhawk pilots were pointed south at 8,000 feet when they observed eleven enemy fighters headed in the opposite direction some 11,000 feet above them. The latter had obviously seen them too; in no time, a *shotai* of three planes peeled off to make a high-side pass. The Americans briefly tried to scissor in a Thach weave, but their heavy ships moved too slowly in a climb so they gave it up, diving to 6,000 feet in an attempt to gain some speed. Following them down, the Nakajima pilots proceeded to execute high left-frontal passes on the lead element of Warhawks.

As Major Tyler and his wingman, Lt. Elmer "Doc" Wheadon, easily turned into their assailants, both sides opened fire. The opposing knights screamed past one another but, according to the action report, "final results were not observed." This was not entirely correct: Lieutenant Wheadon's P-40 emerged from the joust looking like a rivet gun had pounded it. One of the Oscar pilots must have skidded to the left for a better firing angle from which to rake Wheadon's Hawk. No fewer than sixty-nine hits from accurate, cowl-mounted guns had scarred the right side of the Curtiss' fuselage from propeller to aft of the radio compartment, as well as chewing into its rudder and left aileron. Miraculously, Wheadon emerged unscathed, but promptly removed himself and the remnants of his plane from the combat area, pancaking at Fighter Two. Undaunted, he commandeered another plane and took off to rejoin the fray.

The nine Lilys that had been circling over the nearby Russell Islands waiting for the fighters to clear the way now moved in. Unlike the JNAF Bettys on 25 January, the bomb-laden Kawasakis flew eastward, hugging the coast to escape detection by Cactus' radar. Unwilling to risk penetrating the air battle above in order to climb to bombing altitude, their crews opted to streak in low over the Matanikau River, bombing and strafing their way across Fighter Two to the edge of Henderson Field before scurrying back up the Slot. The 45th Sentai subsequently submitted an unsubstantiated claim for nine U.S. planes destroyed on the ground.

While the Lilys stole away, a full-fledged donnybrook broke out over Henderson Field between the 44th's Warhawks and the 1st Sentai's low CAP. The P-40s were quickly overwhelmed, even after Captain Anderson's division of Marine Corps F4Fs dove down to lend a hand. Captain Anderson, Lieutenant McCartney, and the two other Wildcat pilots engaged in a scissoring contest with the agile Ki-43s as each side maneuvered to get into firing position. Otherwise, the air combat was classic Chennault. The lithe Japanese fighters maneuvered to get on the tails of the cumbersome P-40s. The Hawks, in turn, pushed over in violent aileron rolls to plunge earthward in inverted dives. Once clear of danger, the Hawk pilots clawed their way back up to pounce on unsuspecting Oscars. Capt. Ken Taylor put his ship through these tactics no fewer than four times, driving attackers off the tails of beleaguered P-40 colleagues. One of the Oscars he raked from behind fell away smoking.

One Japanese pilot bored in after Lt. Bob Westbrook. Feeling the attacker's slugs rattle into his P-40, Westbrook shoved everything into the corner. His inverted Curtiss plunged into a G-pulling dive, carrying him safely out of range. After zooming out, the young eager beaver banked around Henderson in a climbing turn. Returning to the fracas, he spotted a *shotai* of Ki-43s off to his right and turned into his unsuspecting quarry. Firing into the nose of an Oscar, he watched it burst into flames. The other two quickly scattered.

Curiously, Lieutenant Westbrook's victim was the only one to catch fire. When they triggered their six fifties, the Hawk pilots were confronted by a mystifying phenomenon: every P-40 pilot managed to get a piece of a Nakajima at some point, several scoring numerous hits. Captain Taylor alone fired ten times into various adversaries, placing well-aimed bursts into three targets. None caught fire. Another Oscar took hits in its cowl as the pilot made a head-on pass at a P-40, but no flames could be seen when he passed under the Hawk. Given the flammable nature of fuel lines and unprotected Japanese fuel tanks, all this was baffling in the extreme.

Not till they landed did the pilots of the 44th find out why. Upon examining some of the magazines, it was discovered that their ammunition belts contained a very low ratio of incendiary rounds. A number of these P-40s had just arrived from Roses, where they had been armed. Armorers at Roses had belted machine-gun rounds in the following sequence: five armor piercing, three ball, two tracer, and a single incendiary.

It was almost 1100 when the raiders began to withdraw. The 11th Sentai's 3rd Chutai, acting as rear guard, was still dueling with the 339th FS's Lightnings in a running fight that traced a web of white contrails ranging over Cape Esperance toward the Russell Islands. Exploiting the high-flying capability of their P-38s, the U.S. Army pilots proceeded to make high-side passes on the Oscars. Butterfly flaps extended, the Ki-43s cornered violently to evade their attackers. Lt. Ray Bezner caught one Japanese pilot doing a half-roll and shot up his adversary's Oscar, forcing him to bail out. Lt. Besby Holmes got in a perfect no-deflection shot. Streams of lead punched into the Ki-43's canopy and wings. Rolling over lazily, the Nakajima fighter disappeared below.

But Japanese airmen were not unaware of the heavy Lockheed's low-level handicap. Reflecting on his experience fighting the P-38, PO Takeo Tanimizu remembered how lethargic it was at low altitudes. Themselves realizing this, Lightning pilots learned to pass up any perceived opportunity to dogfight with Japanese fighters at lower altitudes. Of course, low-level engagements grew harder to avoid as the locus of combat invariably inched downward.

Meeting it for the first time in the Solomons and New Guinea, Japanese fighter pilots like Petty Officer Tanimizu quickly caught on to the Lightning's diving hit-and-run tactics. The more aggressive among them learned to counter with a fast, zooming turn as the P-38 pulled out of its bounce. Tanimizu observed that the Lightning's tail booms proved especially vulnerable to cannon fire from a Zero. CPO Saburo Saito recalled that 20-mm rounds, when exploding in the P-38's wing root, would sometimes cause the wing to shear off.

As the air battle moved beyond Cape Esperance, Japanese fighters cunningly drew some of the Lightnings down toward sea level. When the P-38s dove on them, the Oscars turned away sharply, forcing the Lightnings to pull out steeply. To recover safely from a low-altitude diving attack, P-38 pilots had to ease up on their speed, resulting in a slower pullout. How dangerous a game this became for the heavy P-38s was about to be tragically illustrated.

Capt. Bill Shaw was still flying with a drop tank that he had tried unsuccessfully to jettison before engaging the Ki-43s. Deciding to fight anyway, Shaw dove on a bandit flying just above the water well beyond Savo. After making a firing pass, he started to pull out, whereupon the crafty JAAF pilot ambushed him. As the Lightning slowly climbed away, its climb rate further hampered by the drop tank, the enemy pilot easily zoomed up and closed in. When he hosed the exposed underside of the sluggish P-38, 7.7-mm and 12.7-mm fire hit the tank, igniting the volatile fumes within. Shaw's Lightning exploded in a debris-strewn fireball.

Unable to intervene in time, a vengeful Captain Mitchell got onto the tail of this particular Japanese pilot and torched the Oscar with a single short burst. The flaming Ki-43 crashed into the sea—Mitchell's sixth victory. Shaw's wingman, Lieutenant McDaniel, had followed him down. He was last seen disappearing into low cloud cover, so some Oscar pilot must have ambushed him, too.

The two P-40s at the bottom of the heap, piloted by Lt. Fred Purnell and Lt. Dale Tarbet, climbed above Henderson Field after the second flight of Warhawks. Passing through 3,000 feet, Purnell and his wingman noticed "about 20 Zeros circling at various levels from 10,000 to 20,000 feet south of the field"—probably the same Nakajima high-flying CAP seen and subsequently attacked by the P-38s. Monitoring the sky around them as they continued their corkscrew climb, the P-40 pilots drifted northwest. By the time they reached 17,500 feet, the combat had begun to ebb. They could see the pursuing P-38s making passes at the 11th Sentai's rear guard as the sprawling gaggle of combatants spread out toward Kokumbona at 15,000 feet.

Noticing six or seven enemy planes flying apart from the main group, the two air corps pilots closed in to stalk a straggler. Purnell turned across his target with his trigger depressed; the six fifties tattooed the enemy fighter from cockpit to tail as it passed through Purnell's converging fire. Tarbet was already making an overhead pass on another Oscar. This one turned, arcing downward to disintegrate upon impacting the jungle near Aruligo.

Reforming, the pair climbed back up to 15,000 feet. They then spotted another lone Ki-43 below and bounced it. The enemy pilot hit the silk and was promptly shot up by the P-40s while his damaged aircraft flew on into a cloud.

Paradoxically, shooting the parachutist was the type of callous act for which Allied propagandists berated the Japanese at every opportunity. With few exceptions, those Japanese pilots who adhered to the code of Bushido neither offered nor expected quarter. Moreover, they appear to have made an esoteric distinction between a victory and a kill, considering the act complete only if both pilot and plane were destroyed, hence the proclivity to gun down Allied airmen in their chutes. (They themselves were instructed to use their parachutes only over friendly territory to avoid any risk of capture and were issued suicide pistols for the same purpose.) Many Americans, like Purnell and Tarbet, interpreted chute strafing as morally unethical and righteously responded in kind; others condemned it, but could not bring themselves to exact revenge. Capt. Pat Weiland, for one, never told anyone (apart from the writers) that when an enemy pilot he shot down bailed out over Munda, Weiland decided not to shoot him. Concerned that his decision not to strafe his foe would be dimly regarded by his more vengeful colleagues, Weiland prudently kept quiet about the incident.

Thus did the air war over the Solomons bring out the basest brutality on both sides, even though, tout au contraire, Allied and Japanese airmen alike by this time had come to respect the courage, tenacity, and professional skill demonstrated by many of their opponents.

Climbing once again to 15,000 feet, lieutenants Purnell and Tarbet shadowed two more Oscars that were heading northwest some two thousand feet below. The Japanese pilots were not long in finding them; both unexpectedly turned to the left, one zooming around to come up under the Warhawks, the other turning tight to fall back on Purnell's tail. Tarbet dropped into an overhead pass on the closest fighter below him, firing a burst before diving through. Purnell flipped over into a power dive, making for parts unknown. Having eluded their quarry-become-hunters, the serendipity-prone P-40 drivers leveled off just above yet another lone enemy fighter. After Purnell had made a high frontal pass, this one caught fire and splashed into the water.

Eventually leaving the persistent Lightnings behind, the JAAF raiders reformed as they droned back up the Slot. A number of 11th Sentai Oscars took their leave near Munda, landing to refuel before resuming the long haul back to Rabaul. A flurry of activity descended over Munda at high noon, when fifteen fighters winged in from the east. Five Oscars touched down immediately, while four drifted westward and another six circled overhead. After servicing, one Oscar took off again at 1300 to rejoin its ten airborne colleagues. The formation then flew on a brief sweep eastward to ensure no Cactus fighters were following. Fifteen minutes later another Oscar flew after them. Possibly damaged, the remaining three took off at 1320, heading directly for Rabaul.

The four remaining P-38s of the 339th landed at Fighter Two around 1120, claiming three "Zeros" destroyed plus one probable. A pair of Lightnings was confirmed as having gone down in low-altitude combat. All seven of the remaining Warhawks were down by 1215 hours. Two of their number had been shot down; the damaged ships flown by lieutenants Hansen and Wheadon were written off upon their return, but the P-40 pilots claimed four "Zeros" destroyed and at least three more damaged or probably destroyed. Lieutenant Westbrook submitted his claim for his first "Zero" with particular satisfaction. A natural fighter pilot, he went on to become a lieutenant colonel and ranking ace of the 13th Air Force before himself being shot down by flak on 22 November 1944 while strafing shipping in Makassar Strait in the Dutch East Indies.

Apart from Lieutenant Lynch, who ditched his Wildcat when its tanks ran dry, the other eleven Marine Corps pilots also made it back. In addition to Reinburg's two kills and Lynch's single victory, they submitted claims for two "Zeros" confirmed and one probable.

All told, claims by Cactus pilots totaled twelve planes destroyed plus four probables. As for actual Japanese losses, the 1st Sentai's fighter inventory emerged from the melee lighter by a half-dozen Oscars. Among the pilots who were shot down were Capt. Tatsuji Yamashita, Lt. Ichiro Sumi, Sgt. Haruo Sato, and Sgt. Mesara Koda. Another pilot ditched his Oscar off Gatukai Island in the New Georgia group at 1120 hours. Five more Ki-43s made it into Ballale, all of them damaged. The 14th Field Air Repair Depot pronounced four as salvable, but wrote off the fifth.

The JAAF claimed six Cactus fighters destroyed in return. Actual American losses were four fighters shot down and four written off. Unlike the engagement of 25 January, wherein the Cactus Air Force claimed six Zeros with no loss to itself, neither side really emerged victorious from the slugging match of 27 January.

Nevertheless, it would appear that at least seven Lilys continued to fly in and out of Munda over the next few days, possibly ferrying in bombs to stockpile for another raid on Cactus initially scheduled for 30 January.

Logically, it was advantageous in terms of fuel consumption and extended air time to load ordnance at Munda on the morning of a raid rather than in Bougainville. Moreover, if the Lilys were required to spend one or more nights at Munda, parking them on the airstrip with full bomb loads was an invitation to disaster in the likely event of a Cactus air strike.

So far, the Japanese air-supremacy campaign had proven inconclusive; the Cactus Air Force was giving as good as it got. Only two noteworthy raids had been undertaken to lure the Canal's fighters into combat. USA and USMC fighter pilots had proven more than willing to oblige, but JNAF and JAAF pilots had conspicuously failed to shoot them down en masse. The impact of the JNAF raid had been especially enfeebled by bad weather. Overall, not only did American fliers claim large numbers of Japanese aircraft destroyed and damaged, but the Cactus Air Force continued to bomb Munda and Vila airstrips and to keep up its attacks on enemy shipping in the Slot.

Frustrated by this stalemate, the IJN entertained second thoughts about continuing Operation KE. When one of several U.S. task forces was discovered southeast of Guadalcanal, steaming toward the Central Solomons, another large daylight raid against Guadalcanal's airfields, scheduled for 29 January, was unceremoniously scrubbed. Instead, the JNAF proceeded to track TF GEORGE while rearming its twin-engine bombers with torpedoes for an air–sea action.

Irrespective of this potential threat from the U.S. Navy, the IJA was now firmly committed to evacuation and flatly insisted that its retreating troops be rescued without any further shirking on the part of the IJN before American land forces caught up to them.

CHAPTER 9
TURNOVERS

Both CinCPac and ComSoPac remained convinced that the Japanese were mounting another thrust to retake Guadalcanal. In spite of a change in Japanese ciphers that took effect on 1 January, U.S. intelligence analysts managed to piece together disturbing indications of renewed Japanese air and naval activity in the Slot, enemy shipping and troop concentrations at Rabaul and Truk, and an upcoming operation called "KE." Rear Adm. Aubrey Fitch, ComAirSoPac, consequently ordered the Cactus Air Force, supported by the newly created 13th Air Force, to redouble its efforts to sink all Japanese shipping found in the Slot as a preemptive measure.

After being delayed by the 6th Shidan's raid on Guadalcanal during the morning of 27 January, which forced airborne Avengers from VMSB-131 to scurry away to the east temporarily, a Cactus strike force intercepted Japanese shipping at Torpedo Junction off the northern tip of Kolombangara at 1740 hours. Flying some 230 miles up the Slot, ten SBDs and six TBFs fell upon the transport *Mikage Maru*, carrying ammunition and various supplies as well as troops of the 6th Kure Special Naval Landing Force. The subchaser *Ch-17*, steaming one mile distant, was escorting her. The pair had left Faisi that morning, headed down the Slot on a course of 115 degrees under the protection of four successive relays of Petes from seaplane tender *Kamikawa Maru*. The last pair of F1M2s was still on station overhead when the strike force appeared.

Captain Williamson led the SBDs in first. Weak flak drifted up, tracking them as they dove from ten thousand feet. Despite her desperate but lame efforts to turn and zigzag, the dive-bombers scored three hits on *Mikage Maru*, sending up a column of black smoke. First to dive was Captain Schlendering, whose salvo overshot the transport by thirty yards. Three other Dauntlesses attacked in rapid succession: Lieutenant Brown's ordnance hit her port side amidships, Lieutenant O'Sullivan scored a direct hit midway between her stack and bow, and Lieutenant Cook claimed a sure hit. Lieutenants Mitchell, Hacker, and Woodley followed Captain Williamson down on the swerving escort. Lieutenant Woodley's bombs failed to release; the other three pilots registered near misses. After the attack, the "corvette" was observed to be emitting white smoke—possibly steam escaping from pipes ruptured by the concussion from a near hit.

Capt. Bill Hayter then led the TBFs in a torpedo attack. Although several good runs were made between 250 feet and 150 feet off the deck, and the fish were released at only 800 yards, any torpedo that found its mark failed to detonate.

At their debriefing the dive-bomber crews waxed confident they had sunk the transport, but both ships remained afloat. Troops pitched in to help the *Mikage Maru*'s crew get the fire under control before she resumed her voyage, finally dropping anchor at Vila around 2120 hours.

The two floatplanes valiantly attempted to attack the light bombers. One was shot down at 1808 by Capt. Hank Sabatier, who led the nine covering F4Fs of VMO-251. Two minutes later the other Pete scored hits in the nacelle of Capt. Jim Maguire's Avenger, but turret gunner Cpl. Joe Blotnick also scored, puncturing a fuel tank and hitting the Pete's pilot. His plane leaking avgas, the Pete's wounded pilot broke off. An F4F briefly gave chase to the damaged floatplane, but it managed to get away. Four P-40s from the 44th and 68th FSs felt no need to intervene. The U.S. planes reformed to cruise back to Cactus at 150 knots. Though saddled with a rough-running engine, Captain Maguire managed to coax his TBF home. Interestingly, the *Kamikawa Maru*'s war diary records the return of both Petes, having expended 1,950 rounds of ammunition between them.

A fretful Rear Adm. Shintaro Hashimoto pondered the experiences of Operation KE's first and second sorties: the supply run of 10–11 January and the reinforcement run of 14–15 January. The convoys of both Rear Admiral Koyanagi and Rear Admiral Kimura had been well covered by JAAF Oscars and JNAF Zeros and floatplanes. Significantly, no destroyers had been sunk, but among them Cactus PT boats, PBYs, and light bombers had pushed through to inflict significant damage to three destroyers and lesser damage to three others—more than half the ships involved. The unshakable feeling that the Americans could still marshal sufficient naval and air power to oppose future destroyer runs must have gnawed at Hashimoto's confidence.

Although Rear Admiral Kimura had been considered for the job, Hashimoto was given command of the Tokyo Express after Kimura was injured when the U.S. sub *Nautilus* torpedoed his flagship *Akizuki* on 19 January. It was with mixed feelings that the new commander prepared to sortie six destroyers on 28 January to garrison the Russell Islands as a prelude to the first evacuation run.

Should the upcoming evacuation of the Japanese 17th Army by destroyer to the proposed recuperation camp in the Shortlands prove unfeasible due to U.S. naval and air intervention, Operation KE called for a more modest alternative: a portion or all of the troops would be withdrawn by landing barges to the Russell Islands, just over the western horizon from Guadalcanal; thence they would be transferred in stages back up the Slot to the Central Solomons and, ultimately, to Bougainville. To prepare for this contingency, the preliminaries to KE entered a third phase on 28 January with the aforementioned sortie of the *Kawakaze*, *Tanikaze*, and *Urakaze* transporting 328 soldiers to secure temporary control over Baisen Island. Escorting the destroyer transports were the *Kuroshio* and *Shirayuki* and the flagship *Tokitsukaze*.

On 28 January a coastwatcher alerted Cactus at 0830 to a freighter and a tanker leaving Faisi with subchaser *Ch-17*, headed down the Slot. Coastwatchers on Choiseul reported at 1405 that the six destroyers bound for the Russell Islands were leaving Faisi at high speed. The Tokyo Express was again sighted an hour later as it approached Vella Lavella. By this time six TBFs from VMSB-131 and twelve SBDs—seven from VMSB-233 and five from VMSB-142—were on their way up the Slot. They were accompanied by seven F4F Wildcats from VMF-112, plus a USA escort of six P-40 Warhawks and two P-38 Lightnings. Two of the TBFs developed engine trouble en route and aborted, leaving twenty-seven aircraft in the strike force.

Flying high cover in the frigid gondola of "Oriole," Lt. Murray "Jim" Shubin ran into a cloud ceiling that bottomed out between 16,000 and 24,000 feet. He and Lt. Julius "Jake" Jacobson gunned their Lightnings up to 27,000 feet to escape the overcast; in so doing, they lost contact with the formation about halfway up the New Georgia coast, thereby missing the action.

Arriving over Kula Gulf at around 1530 under CAVU weather conditions, the remaining Cactus pilots spotted the freighter, the tanker, and their lone escort steaming at an estimated ten knots off the northeast coast of Vella Lavella. Having been redirected by Cactus Recon at 1430 to attack the merchantmen, the dive-bomber leader, Lieutenant Wiggins, quickly pushed over. Capt. Arthur "Art" Molvik's torpedo bombers were to concentrate on the Tokyo Express, which was spotted some dozen miles to the northwest. Molvik scanned the SBD attack developing below him in the distance and, concluding that the dive-bomber pilots had things well in hand, banked away to intercept his primary target—the Tokyo Express destroyers (see map 4).

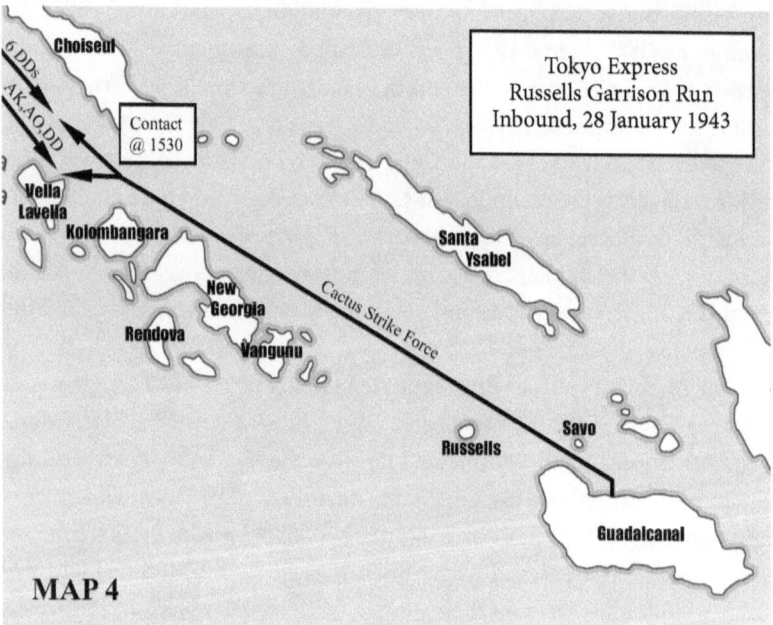

MAP 4

The SBDs had barely begun their attack when four Zeros came out of broken cloud cover from the south. They were part of a nine-plane CAP from the 582nd Kokutai assigned to protect the destroyers. Seeing a fracas developing over the merchant convoy but failing to spot the two *Kamikawa Maru* Petes flying CAP overhead, these pilots readily abandoned their post and sped to the rescue. Luckily, the Cactus fighter escort elected to remain with the dive-bombers.

The 44th's P-40s were stacked between 16,000 and 17,000 feet when the four Zeros jumped Lt. H. "Mat" Matson. Lieutenant Matson evaded his attackers and, along with Lt. Mike Carter, went after a Zero that had latched on to the tail of an SBD. Capt. Bob Fraser and Lt. John Moran of VMF-112 also dove after the same Zero. Matson fired into the Mitsubishi and saw it start down, but then lost track of it. The two Marines later confirmed Matson's hits. However, the 582nd reported no planes damaged; conversely, it claimed three "P-39s" destroyed. Intimidated by the heavy U.S. fighter escort, the two Petes held back.

VMSB-233 dove in from 11,000 feet, releasing four and one-half tons of bombs at heights of between 2,000 and 800 feet. All three enemy vessels made 45-degree lunges to port, unleashing a light barrage of AA fire. Lieutenant White loosed a 1,000-pounder that "nicked" the port side of the tanker's bow, starting a fire. His colleagues went after the merchantman. Lieutenant Etheridge's 1,000-pounder registered a paint scraper off the latter's port bow, causing smoke to rise from the area. Lieutenant Otteson planted one of his 100-pounders on her starboard side just aft of amidships. Lieutenant Weber's 1,000-pound missile threw up a column of water between the subchaser and the damaged transport. Shrapnel from his near miss killed ten seamen and wounded another thirty on board *Ch-17*. Twisting like an agitated snake, the subchaser managed to evade Lieutenant Bachtel's 1,000-pound bomb by fifty yards.

Lieutenant Wiggins, leading VMSB-142, made a stern attack on the transport. As she slowed, one of his three bombs hit her starboard beam. Lieutenant Fitzpatrick's 1,000-pounder threw up a geyser in front of her bow. He strafed her for good measure on his pullout. As Lieutenant Stock released, the transport swung to port again, and his 1,000-pound bomb splashed off her starboard quarter. A 40-mm slug punched through Lieutenant McGukin's left wing, throwing him off target before he could release his bomb; he was unable to try again. Lieutenant Milby missed the transport's stern with two 100-pound bombs, but was unable to release his 500-pounder.

The SBD and P-40 pilots claimed they left both the transport and the tanker smoking and dead in the water with the former in sinking condition. Captain Nissen's reconnaissance Fort subsequently passed over the area and observed "burning Jap tanker and destroyer near Vella Lavella." The "tanker" on fire was probably the transport. Since his vessel was in better shape, the tanker's captain was undoubtedly anxious to exit Torpedo Junction and had left without further ado to finish his journey solo.

The remaining five enemy fighters covering the destroyer flotilla were spotted at 17,000 feet, but they chose not to challenge the P-40s that tried to go after them—for a very good reason. On their way over the Zeros had unknowingly passed over the Avengers heading in the opposite direction five thousand feet below them. When a flak barrage erupted over their now-unprotected destroyers, betraying the torpedo bombers to the absentee Zeros, these five Mitsubishi pilots had not yet engaged the SBDs and their escort. They were either recalled, if their leader had a radio, or saw for themselves that the destroyers entrusted to their care were under attack. Streaking back with throttles wide open, the A6Ms returned too late to break up VMSB-131's torpedo attack.

As the Avenger pilots approached, they saw that their quarry was arrayed in two columns of three vessels, unprotected by Japanese air cover. Immediately after spying the oncoming Cactus aircraft, the enemy vessels lunged into evasive, 60-degree turns with slight zigzags and opened up a "terrific" AA fire. The TBFs prepared to engage, breaking off to set up for individual torpedo runs. Leveling off at altitudes from three hundred to two hundred feet, they slowed to between 180 and 215 knots for the run in. Six torpedoes were dropped at about nine hundred yards from selected targets with gunners strafing the ships as the TBFs sped by on their pullouts. MTSgt. George Nasif claimed a hit on the second destroyer in the left column, "resulting in serious damage and subsequent sinking." The damaged vessel appeared to be settling, so the next destroyer in line pulled up alongside. Lieutenants Charlton "Bud" Main and Barney McShane claimed probable hits on the second destroyer in the right column. Fearful of climbing out through the murderous flak barrage, McShane hugged the deck, crossing the two columns of swerving destroyers at masthead level.

From afar, Capt. A. L. Johnson's P-40 pilots observed a single explosion that threw up a high waterspout. The Japanese acknowledged damage to one destroyer, causing seventeen casualties, but she did not turn back, let alone sink. The remaining six pilots all missed. Emerging from the flak unscathed, the torpedo bombers formed up and departed in the intervening moments before the Zeros arrived, leaving the enemy destroyers to regroup before pushing on resolutely toward the Russells.

The Tokyo Express was subsequently spotted and reported as "two light cruisers" and "four destroyers" by Captain Nissen of the 26th BS. The ships had resumed their journey down the Slot with their nine-Zero CAP, leaving the burning transport and its escort to fend for themselves. Fifteen Zeros from the 204th Kokutai relieved the combat-worn 582nd fighters at 1800 hours. If ace Lt. Zenjiro Miyano's *chutai* had run into the Cactus strike force, the outcome might have been different. Behind Lieutenant Miyano flew Lt. (jg) Takeshi Morisaki, WO Hatsuo Hidaka, and LA Ryoji Ohara; PO2c Masaaki Shimakawa flew on Warrant Officer Hidaka's wing; all were ace-quality pilots. With dusk creeping over the horizon, this 204th CAP pulled out at 1855 after an uneventful shift.

Any Cactus strike force trying to chase the Tokyo Express back up the Slot the next morning would have returned empty-handed; the destroyer convoy headed back to the Shortlands through open seas to the south of the Solomons. Anzac coastwatchers did not spot it until 0911, proceeding due north some twenty-seven miles off the southwest coast of Vella Lavella.

An Allied observer team had gone ashore in the Russells the previous October. Landing on Pavuvu Island, the coastwatchers had cut a pathway to high ground and established a makeshift observation post before several weeks of probing revealed that the islands were empty of Japanese, whereupon they abandoned the project. Cactus having now been made aware that the Japanese may have landed in the Russell Islands, four P-39s took wing at 0800 on 30 January to escort a Black Cat ferrying a coastwatcher to the area. Once on shore Lt. "Robbie" Robinson likely availed himself of these existing facilities. That same evening, he began earning his pay with a report confirming that four "sampans" had offloaded an estimated four hundred garrison troops, ferrying them to Baisen Island at around 1400 on 28 January—ready information he had probably garnered from local islanders shortly after landing.

Convinced that the Japanese were mounting another large-scale offensive to retake Henderson Field and its satellites, Admirals Nimitz and Halsey at first prepared to meet this perceived threat by committing practically the entire naval force at their disposal in the South Pacific.

TF GEORGE, comprising six cruisers, a pair of escort carriers, and a destroyer screen, proceeded from Efate on 28 January to rendezvous the next day off Cape Hunter on the southwest coast of Guadalcanal with the four destroyers of the Tulagi-based Cactus Strike Force. Halsey had intended that the combined force should then proceed westward through the Solomon Sea roughly parallel to the Slot, ready to intercept enemy warships or the reinforcement convoys believed to be building up at Rabaul and in the Shortlands. In so doing, TF GEORGE would also act as a shield between the enemy and a long-awaited American convoy of four transports, escorted by four destroyers, that was to begin offloading in Lunga Roads that day.

Fearful that he would not make the rendezvous on time, Rear Adm. Richard Giffin, TF GEORGE's commander, detached his two slow-moving "geep" carriers at 1500, ordering them to retire southeastward temporarily. This allowed him to churn toward Cape Hunter at twenty-four knots while fighters from the *Chenango* and *Suwanee* could continue to cover the task force until sunset.

Elsewhere, the four cruisers and supporting destroyers of TF AFIRM were to proceed to the edge of the Coral Sea, rendezvousing with the three battleships and four destroyers of TF LOVE ONE along the way. Also headed for a mutual rendezvous, and then for the Coral Sea, were two carrier task forces: the *Saratoga*'s TF ROGER and the *Enterprise*'s TF SUGAR. There the combined carrier, battle wagon and cruiser forces would lie in wait to ambush Admiral Kondo's task force, should Admiral Yamamoto order Kondo to sortie from Truk toward the Solomons in support of the anticipated reinforcement operation.

Knowing that TF GEORGE was steaming up the Solomon Sea, the 751st Kokutai advanced at least one *chutai* of Bettys from Buka to Ballale to facilitate long-range search missions. Its reconnaissance G4Ms picked up TF GEORGE shortly after dawn on 29 January and shadowed it throughout the day.

Baker search was deep in the Central Solomons around 0800 on 29 January, its two Warhawks probing through hazy skies. In the distance Maj. Kermit Tyler and his wingman, Lt. "Doc" Wheadon, momentarily picked up two of the 751st Kokutai Bettys from Ballale that were on their way down to survey the interesting American naval activity southeast of Guadalcanal. Between 0935 and 1040 these Bettys cased TF GEORGE thoroughly, reporting ship types and numbers.

As the day wore on, south of Guadalcanal the American transports and their destroyer escort briefly came within sight of Admiral Giffen's task force still working its way toward the rendezvous point. Operators at the Cactus Crystal Ball—the Canal's tiny radio intercept station—monitored a succession of transmissions from the Japanese reconnaissance aircraft shadowing Admiral Giffen's force. A final 751st Kokutai Betty finished its reconnaissance run as daylight ebbed, spending an hour over TF GEORGE before breaking contact at 1800 to put in at Munda for the night.

Although shipboard search radar had picked up bogeys all day, the radio silence imprudently imposed throughout the task force at the time prevented the fighter control director on board the cruiser *Chicago* from vectoring the CAP to intercept and identify the planes. In any case, whether or not they displayed IFF, the planes were thought to be friendly, given the close proximity of the ships to Guadalcanal. On their own initiative, suspicious CAP fighters chased after elusive Japanese reconnaissance aircraft whenever they sighted one, but came up empty-handed.

By early evening further radio intercepts had revealed to the Crystal Ball that enemy strike forces were on the way. As daylight faded into twilight, the radar screens of the task force began to display an intermittent assortment of blips—some friendly, a few not so friendly.

Sixteen Bettys from the 705th Kokutai, stationed at Rabaul's Vunakanau airbase, were the first to arrive over the American warships that had by now approached to within sixty-six miles of Guadalcanal. The Japanese bombers had the good fortune to come upon the task force just before dusk—a mere ten minutes after the fighter CAP provided by the two detached escort carriers and the Cactus Air Force had pulled out for the night.

In his haste to join up with the Cactus Striking Force, Admiral Giffen had elected to steam without zigzagging. Instead, as a precaution against submarines—three to ten of which were thought to be operating in the Eastern Solomons—he relied on his convoy-escort experience in the North Atlantic, positioning his cruisers in two columns behind a half-circle of vanguard destroyers. This configuration, however, left the rear and flanks of his ships exposed to air attack.

Realizing this at first glance, Lieutenant Commander Nakamura decided to forgo an attack out of the western twilight; instead, he led his bombers around to the east of TF GEORGE. All sixteen Bettys then closed from behind to make simultaneous runs in two separate groups, thereby splitting up defending AA fire. Despite the protective advantage of dim lighting and the absence of U.S. fighter cover, they either failed to score a single hit, or those torpedoes that found their mark were duds. Pilot Bunzaburo Imamura's G4M was struck by AA fire during his low-level attack. The flaming bomber plowed into the sea aft of the *Chicago*, taking Imamura and his veteran crew to their deaths. Three other Bettys were hit by flak, killing one crewman and injuring another.

A follow-up strike by fifteen Nells of the 701st Kokutai, also out of Vunakanau, arrived over Admiral Giffen's task force within twenty minutes, but by now in near-total darkness. Aided by flares dropped from an assisting reconnaissance plane, Lt. Cdr. Joji Higai's Nells managed to hit three ships, but only the torpedo that struck the *Chicago* actually exploded, crippling her. Two Nells took fatal hits within moments of each other, one at 1943 and the other two minutes later. Trailing flames, Commander Higai's G3M crossed the *Chicago*'s bow and splashed in a fireball off her port quarter.

During the night, Coastwatchers Keenan and Josslyn heard a succession of returning Betty and Nell bombers that had overflown Vella late that evening on their way to intercept TF GEORGE. All remaining 705th Bettys, both intact and damaged, plus ten Nells, were now straggling back to Vunakanau. Three other Nells had absorbed incapacitating hits: two had to stage back to Rabaul via Buka, and a third made it as far as Buin, where emergency repairs were made before it could push on to Vunakanau. All three were safely back by sunrise.

A trio of SBDs from VMSB-233 took off from Henderson Field at 0300 on 30 January, vanishing into the gloom of the western sky. Lieutenants Cummings, Cook, and Thompson had volunteered for a high-risk, "special attack" mission: an unescorted, hit-and-run strike on Munda. They were probably gambling that some of the Japanese bombers returning from their strike on TF GEORGE might have set down at Munda for the night. Chances were they could be caught before daybreak by a surprise raid. Grinding up the Slot with their heavy bombs, hampered by the thick overcast of a lingering weather front, the stalwart aircrews arrived within twenty-five miles of Munda to find the area totally socked in. The flight leader searched in vain for a hole through the soup before reluctantly turning back for Cactus with little fuel to spare.

Four 69th BS B-26s did strike Munda on 30 January, bombing the airfield and surrounding AA positions in the first of two raids. Launched at 0830, this mission ran into rainsqualls over the eastern end of New Georgia, but the mediums, escorted by Captain Graves' seven P-39s from the 70th FS, persevered to arrive over Munda Point just under a 14,000-foot ceiling of cumulus. With a vigorous flak barrage blossoming around them—most of it coming from 75-mm guns situated west of the runway this time—the Marauders made their runs, dropping four tons of bombs. The sticks erupted a hundred feet to the south of the runway, beginning about midway, and walked parallel to it in an eastward direction to just beyond the north taxi strips.

The morning wore on under a brightening sky. From Vella, lieutenants Keenan and Josslyn spotted several lone aircraft passing overhead up and down the Slot. The 204th Kokutai's Lieutenant Hoshiza and his observer flew over, headed for Guadalcanal on a Dinah reconnaissance mission. Another sighting was no doubt the reconnaissance plane that had attempted to shadow TF GEORGE overnight and was now on its way back. A third was surely the IJN flying boat—either a Mavis or an Emily—on its way toward Rennell Island to take up its vigil over the U.S. task force.

Baker search left Cactus in the forenoon of 30 January as the enemy flying boat droned down the Slot. Taking off at 0925, Capt. Albert Johnson and Lt. Jack Bade of the 44th FS climbed into the west. Reaching 1,500 feet, they spotted what they thought was a Japanese four-engine "bomber" west of the Russell Islands. It was going toward Guadalcanal at 10,000 feet. Captain Johnson immediately tried to raise Cactus Recon, but got no answer.

Veteran Pat Weiland—then a captain in VMO-251—reminisced amusingly of Cactus fighter controllers: "In compliance in answering questions from the air, Recon had stereotyped answers." According to Captain Weiland, some responses—like, "Wait. Wait." or "Repeat. Repeat." and "There is no dope"—became "the card words of the day." On one occasion, a pilot who had become frustrated trying to contact Cactus Recon finally blurted out, "Recon, shit or get off the pot!" Recon's answer? "Repeat. Repeat."

Unfortunately, in the case of Baker search, radio malfunction had serious repercussions this day. What the 44th pilots sighted and evidently failed to communicate was the Japanese flying boat that would eventually stumble upon the damaged cruiser *Chicago* and her escorts. Forewarned by coastwatchers, if not by Baker search, Cactus should have scrambled fighters to intercept and knock down this aerial ferret before it found the wounded cruiser. Arriving unmolested on station southeast of Guadalcanal around noon, the enemy flying boat briefly reconnoitered the torpedoed *Chicago*, which was creeping along at four knots under tow by the U.S. Navy tug *Navajo*. The snooper also noted the cruiser's six-destroyer entourage before being driven off by ten *Enterprise* Wildcats that were flying CAP over the little flotilla. Unfortunately, the flying boat's cursory observations sufficed to merit the dispatch of a force of Bettys to deliver yet another attack aimed at putting an end to the crippled *Chicago*. Eleven bombers duly sortied out of Buka airfield at 1230 hours.

Meanwhile, the Warhawk pilots of Baker search flew through broken cloud cover between 1,500 and 8,000 feet right up to New Georgia. They came up against solid overcast at 13,000 feet over Vila. Due in part to this dense cloud cover that was rolling through the Solomons, the afternoon of 30 January would be marked by two more missed opportunities to intercept Japanese air strikes.

A scouting mission from the 44th FS took off at 1230, led by Lieutenant Morrisey. Preceding a second strike force of four B-26s, two B-17s, and seven P-39s up the Slot, the four P-40s found Vila still socked in by heavy overcast. Crossing over to Munda, they found its airstrip pretty much socked in as well. There they decided to circle while awaiting the oncoming raiders.

Lieutenant Johnson's seven P-39s from the 67th and 70th FSs left Cactus fifteen minutes after Lieutenant Morrisey's P-40s. With foul weather closing in, the P-39s joined up with the bombers, following the P-40s up the

Slot amidst a thin but solid overcast layered between 13,000 and 13,500 feet. Also flying with them was an escort of F4Fs from VMO-251. As the raiders approached the New Georgia group, they ran into scattered thunderheads that stretched from southern Kolombangara to southeastern New Georgia.

Trying to skirt these huge pockets of turbulence, the first flight of four Airacobras became separated from the bombers. As they continued to pick their way around towers of cumulonimbus, the Cobra pilots reckoned they were not far from the target area. Convinced that Munda was already on the verge of being bombed by now, they were content to turn about. Flying some distance southeast of Munda at around 1400, they suddenly caught a distant glimpse of "eleven or twelve" Japanese bombers, cruising at around ten thousand feet. Lieutenant Johnson judged the formation to be about one hundred miles out from the Canal, proceeding on an estimated heading of 110 degrees. Though not the ideal fighter with which to take on the speedy G4M at higher altitudes, the Bell P-39 performed optimally at the altitude flown by these Bettys. However, the exasperated Cobra pilots could not maintain unbroken contact long enough to close with the bombers as they flitted through thick cloud banks. Then the enemy vanished—swallowed up for good by the overcast.

Whether Lieutenant Johnson reported the sighting to Cactus Recon is not clear, but Cactus received a message at 1445 that eleven twin-engine bombers had been spotted bearing 268 degrees from the Canal, 130 miles out on an estimated heading of 150 degrees. Guadalcanal relayed the word twenty minutes later, from either the P-39s or a coastwatcher, to both TF GEORGE and the *Chicago* that an enemy raid had been sighted south of New Georgia, bound for Rennell Island.

Minus the four errant Airacobras, the Cactus strike force arrived over Munda at 1345, just beneath the cloud ceiling. With the remaining P-39s one thousand feet above them and the F4Fs higher still, the B-26s and B-17s bombed from 12,000 feet. Twenty-five 500-pounders and thirty-six 100-pounders rained down on the target. Three sticks landed in the water, some hit the west end of the field, several more cratered the lower east end. All in all, it was a desultory performance, marred in part by the bad weather.

To make matters worse, heavy-caliber AA fire quickly bracketed the formation, bursting from one thousand feet above to one thousand feet below, apparently hitting a B-17 fatally. Over on Vella Lavella, Keenan heard what he thought were sounds of heavy bombing coming from the direction of Munda. But it was only two days later that the DSIO at coastwatcher HQ advised his Vella outpost that a Fort had gone down over Munda Point and to watch out for its crew.

The return trip, flown amidst worsening weather, found the pilots trying to maintain position without drifting into the planes around them—a tedious and stressful ordeal. According to Lt. Bob Bryson, two fighters, flown by Lt. Wayne Christian and Lt. Glen Loban, entered the landing pattern over Fighter Two at the same time and collided. Both fighters went down off shore with neither pilot having time to bail out. VMO-251 listed them as MIA since their bodies were apparently never recovered. Lt. Hank McCartney and the rest of the F4F escort pilots were safely back at Cactus by 1500 hours.

At about the time the Japanese flying boat previously spotted by the pilots of Baker search arrived over the *Chicago*, a lone 751st Kokutai Betty left Ballale to reconnoiter ahead of the main bomber force that sortied from Buka ten minutes later. Guided by information garnered from the snooping Mavis or Emily, the vanguard Betty came across the plodding *Chicago* about thirty miles east of Rennell at 1450—not long after Admiral Giffen had withdrawn the bulk of TF GEORGE farther to the southeast. Four F4Fs from the CAP moved in to chase after the retreating bomber. The G4M soon radioed that it had come under attack by three fighters; a last message at 1555 said it had been hit. The Wildcats finally splashed it some forty miles away.

Belatedly, the *Enterprise*, whose air group had been assigned to protect the cripple, prepared to launch another ten Wildcats. The carrier's air-group commander vectored the half-dozen F4Fs still flying cover in the vicinity of the *Chicago* to intercept the incoming strike force. Before Lt. Cdr. James Flatley's fighters could reposition themselves to intervene, the torpedo-laden Bettys of the 751st Kokutai came upon the limping cruiser and her escorts thirty-five miles south of Guadalcanal's "Kaliula [read Koloula] Pt."

The Bettys flew amidst banks of brooding cumulus past the *Chicago* at 1606; they briefly scouted the well-protected fleet carrier forty miles farther on then, wheeling around, deployed to launch their torpedoes at the *Chicago*. The F4F CAP strove to intercept them as they went into their final runs at the cruiser's starboard side. The destroyer *LaVellette* drew abreast in a valorous but vain attempt to mask the *Chicago* from the onslaught, while the tow-tug *Navajo* tried to turn the cruiser bow-on to the onrushing planes.

As the bombers skimmed in over the water, the guns of the two warships, in conjunction with the dozen defending Wildcats, managed to splash seven Bettys and damage three others. But nine bombers successfully dropped their torpedoes. One fish ripped into the *LaVellette* amidships, inflicting considerable damage to her forward engine and fire rooms. One struck the *Chicago* at 1624, followed by three others in rapid succession. The doomed cruiser quickly took on a heavy list. Rolling over to starboard about twenty minutes later, she plunged by the stern to the bottom of the Solomon Sea about thirty miles northeast of Rennell Island, taking with her sixty-two men and leaving another 1,049 in the water.

Only four of the eleven attacking planes survived. Of these, two made it directly back to Buka together, both of them struggling up the Slot on one engine. The third Betty—badly shot up and with a wounded crewman—limped into Munda, escorted by a colleague from the same *shotai* that also had been damaged. Seeing the pair approach from the east against a darkening sky, Munda's AA gunners mistook them for a pair of Cactus harassment raiders and opened fire. As the bombers veered away, Oscars scrambled to investigate. Upon being identified as friendlies, the orbiting Bettys were cleared to land. After servicing, the escorting G4M took off for Buka, reaching its home base at 1900 hours.

Another 751st Betty, flown by CPO Fukuo Houga, left Buka at 1330 hours. Finding TF AFIRM at 1657, Houga continued to shadow the ships until 1800, when he broke off and headed for Munda, landing there at 1935 hours.

Not ten minutes after the ill-fated reconnaissance Betty found the *Chicago*, Capt. Jim Robinson led four P-39s from Cactus to search for the Japanese reconnaissance aircraft that was shadowing the damaged cruiser, likely in response to TF GEORGE's plea for more protective cover over the vulnerable cripple. Crossing over Guadalcanal on a course of 162 degrees, the flight covered a hundred miles of empty ocean, its search plagued by a front of rainsqualls that limited visibility to three miles. Frustrated, the Cobras swung around to a heading of 300 degrees—*away* from the battle unfolding over the horizon to the southeast. Ironically, while the patrol unknowingly receded into the northwest, the eleven Bettys were at that very moment delivering their attacks on the *Chicago*. Some fifteen minutes after she slipped beneath the waves, the pilots of Captain Robinson's search mission landed at Cactus to report that they "saw nothing of enemy aircraft or our cruiser."

Tragically, despite the discovery by Baker search of a Japanese flying boat sent to shadow the lame *Chicago*, as well as an actual sighting by Cactus Airacobras of the Betty strike force sent to finish her off, neither the U.S. Navy nor the Cactus Air Force was able to prevent the 11th Koku Kantai from inflicting the coup de grâce. If Captain Robinson's search planes or the quartet of Cobra pilots wandering southeast of the New Georgia group or the *Enterprise*'s fighter CAP, had managed to intercept the swift Bettys of the 751st Kokutai in time to deter them from launching their torpedoes at the stricken *Chicago*, the battle of Rennell Island might not have ended so disastrously for the USN. Another tantalizing case of "What if?" that marks wartime happenstance.

Under cover of darkness the first elements of the Japanese 38th Division furtively pulled out of their positions on 20 January and withdrew westward through a rear guard furnished by the Yano Battalion and Sendai Division. General Hyakutake's ragged 17th Army had at last begun its odyssey to Cape Esperance and salvation. To the east, flashes lit the sky over Henderson Field as Japanese bombers hurtled overhead for seven hours. With Japanese troops now on the move, the JNAF stepped up its nocturnal harassment of Henderson Field and its satellites in an ongoing campaign to disrupt Cactus' air operations. But the 751st Kokutai found itself spread too thin, having to run nocturnal base-suppression sorties over both Guadalcanal and Port Moresby, so the 701st and 705th Kokutai were called upon to lend a hand.

The 705th Kokutai made only one appearance over Cactus—on 21 January, but it left a memorable calling card. Between 2045 and 0357, six two-plane *shotai* dropped eight 551-pound and eighty-six 133-pound bombs plus its pièce de resistance: a pair of 1,764-pound blockbusters. Some seven hours of random strafing used up 8,710 rounds of ammo. Small wonder VMF-122's war diarist recorded, "No sleep!"

Ten Nells from the 701st did the honors the following evening. Starting at 2130 they unloaded three and one-half tons of mixed ordnance. At 0425 the last pair of G3Ms loosed two 551-pound bombs and a spread of twelve 133-pound missiles, at least one of which fell on VMF-122's bivouac area, catching Sergeant Myers back in his cot. The blast shredded his tent, killing him instantly. Some 5,270 rounds of random machine-gun fire rounded out the night's delivery. Three other ground crewmen were killed and two wounded. Bomb fragments peppered a PBY-5A and a B-26; a store of spare radio parts near Fighter Two was also damaged.

Braving foul weather, fifteen Bettys of the 751st Kokutai took off from Kavieng late in the afternoon of 23 January. Three G4Ms apparently strayed and got lost; after jettisoning their bombs, they eventually returned to base. Arriving over Cactus at 2205, two three-plane *shotai* successively dropped sixty or more 133-pound bombs, causing slight damage. Another *shotai* paused briefly at Munda before reaching the Florida Islands; there the three Bettys dumped thirty missiles on the Tulagi anchorage. The last three Bettys hit a nearby target, possibly the PT-boat base at Purvis Bay. The raiders collectively sprayed some 6,060 rounds of ammo during their bombing sprees.

The 751st lost a Betty on the way back. Forced down by the weather, the returning G4M from the first *shotai* radioed at 2305 that it was ditching some fifteen miles off Vangunu Island. All seven crewmen made landfall on Mbulo Island at the eastern end of the New Georgia group. There they waited anxiously on the coast by the mouth of a small creek until a flying boat, escorted by a dozen 253rd Kokutai Zeros, landed offshore on 27 January to pick them up.

Fourteen 751st Bettys again paid their disrespects to Cactus on the night of 26–27 January. Between 0310 and 0323 two three-plane *shotai* each dumped thirty-six 133-pound bombs, most falling outside the Lunga perimeter south of Fighter One. Their last salvo hit near Cactus' search radar. At around 0415, with the inhabitants of the Lunga perimeter settling back in, eight Bettys roared in to dispense another eighty 133-pound bombs over the next hour. The search radar came close to being hit again, but the MAG-14 bivouac area was less fortunate: flying shrapnel wounded two men. Among them the fourteen raiders poured some 9,060 machine-gun rounds into the area, but Cactus' AA gunners exacted a fearful revenge. No fewer than eight Bettys were hit: five took multiple hits, one of them disappearing into the night; it was later posted missing.

Late on 27 January five Oscars prepared to escort a Lily bomber out of Munda on the JAAF's first nocturnal harassment mission to Cactus; the mission was scrubbed, however, probably for lack of avgas after Munda's fuel dump was destroyed by an earlier Cactus air strike.

These nocturnal raids had been highly disruptive, hence the determination of the 339th FS's new CO to greet the next one in the air. Officially, night interceptions were frowned upon at Cactus, but, according to the 5th Air Force and 751st Kokutai, a *shotai* of Bettys en route to harass Port Moresby on the night of 27 January was jumped by a pair of P-38s at 0340 hours. The antagonists traded shots by moonlight; although one A4M was hit, overall results were inconclusive. However, if knowledge of this nocturnal intercept was picked up by Cactus, it may have helped pave the way for Capt. John Mitchell to go up with special permission to ambush 28–29 January's edition of Washing Machine Charlie.

Taking off from Fighter Two shortly before dawn, Mitchell climbed straightway to medium altitude, where he expected to find Charlie when the bomber returned on its next pass. But, unknown to him, some seven Lilys from the 45th Sentai had been taking turns stalking Henderson's airfields most of the night, peppering them with high explosives and incendiaries.

Making the most of the unobstructed view from the P-38's gondola, Mitchell scanned the cloud cover as a band of soft light crept up over the eastern horizon. There would be time for only one more attack by the enemy bomber, for it was almost 0630 hours. Cactus' search radar picked up a large blip; ground controllers vectored Mitchell toward the bandit. Then he saw it: the dark silhouette of a large aircraft coming in high above Lunga Roads for a run on the shipping riding at anchor there. Arming his guns, Mitchell closed in for the kill.

Far below, another sinister shadow was sneaking out of the south, skimming over the jungles and ridges bordering Fighter Two. "Reville [sic] was pretty unusual this morning," remarked Capt. Bob Fraser, diarist of VMF-112. "A T-97 Bomber flew high over the field at 0630 and while everyone was watching it another T-97 popped over the hill at the south side of the field and from about 300 feet bombed and strafed the field." The bombs did little more than crater the area. Random 7.7-mm machine-gun fire sprayed the bivouac of the ground echelon, hitting Corporal Marteness of VMO-251 in the foot. Lieutenants Percy, Raber, Stack, and Seifert of VMF-112 were sitting in their cockpits on strip alert, waiting for an order to scramble, when the dark hulk of the lumbering bomber roared by right over their heads, "adding to their pilot fatigue considerably." AA fire tracked the Lily as it crossed over the coastline and began to climb away. Suddenly, the bomber seemed to falter and nose over toward the water, but it was not seen to crash. A 29 January entry in Munda's war diary vaguely states, "Army Air Force returned." This terse comment raises some speculation regarding the fate of this particular Lily.

Not so the fate of its comrade. Putting "Mitch's Squitch" into a shallow dive, Mitchell caught the unsuspecting Lily from behind, only opening fire as it salvoed its bombs on the ships. Below, men watched the staccato flickering of the Lightning's guns and tracked the tracers as they arced into the silhouette of the bomber. Flames spurted out, and the interloper "went down in a large beautiful ball of flame over Sealark Channel."

The 45th Sentai had intended to repeat the exercise the following two nights, but was thwarted by adverse weather and a change in plans, not to mention the loss of a Lily. Including the cancelled raid of the previous evening, this was the only harassment raid of four planned by the JAAF to be carried out amidst the dozens flown by the JNAF. Ironically unprotected this night by a fighter escort similar to the one that had been laid on for 27 January, the raid was fated to run into Cactus' only ambush.

Charlie's Cactus-based, nocturnal counterparts were having a decidedly better time of it. Between 2200 and 2315 on 28 January a duo of Black Cats treated Vila airstrip to a pair of flares, followed by a quartet of 500-pound bombs. They sprinkled a smorgasbord of high explosives, incendiaries, and daisy cutters on Munda airstrip beginning at 2315 hours. Munda's sleep-starved inhabitants again scrambled for shelter an hour later when the two PBYs returned to serve up a second helping, raining down four more high-explosive, incendiary, and fragmentation bombs.

For their part, the Japanese were pulling out all the stops to throw the proverbial monkey wrench into the Cactus Air Force and the 13th Air Force. At 0140 on 20 January a long-range Kawanishi flying boat flew over Button, deep in Allied territory, dropping at least eight 133-pound bombs between Bomber Two and Segond Channel. The stroke of midnight on 22 January ushered in another Emily that spread up to twenty more bombs around Bomber One. The western tip of Aore Island hosted eight missiles between 0030 and 0100 on 27 January. Though practically no damage resulted, these raids were designed to disrupt the flow of replacement aircraft from Espiritu Santo to Guadalcanal in an attempt to further weaken Cactus' air arm.

The rising crescendo in the Slot left little doubt that all this activity was the prelude to something big about to take place in the Solomons. On 31 January Admiral Kondo's powerful task force left Truk on its decoy mission. It was soon discovered steaming northwest of the Solomons on an easterly course. In light of recent events, U.S. theater commanders interpreted this as the possible beginning of the anticipated Japanese offensive on Guadalcanal. Kondo's sortie signaled just the opposite for the Japanese—the beginning of Operation KE's evacuation phase.

CHAPTER 10
PASS INTERCEPTION

At 1715 on 30 January coastwatcher John Keenan spotted eleven large aircraft over Vella Lavella, headed southeast in the company of eight smaller planes. Forty-five minutes later Dick Horton on nearby Rendova confirmed that this formation of "transports or cargo planes" had landed at Munda. Surprisingly, this was not a follow-up JNAF strike force on its way to attack TF GEORGE; neither were the planes transports. These eleven unfamiliar aircraft were Lily bombers staging into Munda for an upcoming JAAF raid on Cactus the next morning. The eight Oscars with them were likely 1st Sentai Ki-43s assigned to help escort these bombers on their upcoming raid against Guadalcanal.

A radiogram sent at 1427 on 30 January from the 11th Koku Kantai outlining the JAAF raid scheduled to leave Munda at 1100 the next morning was intercepted by U.S. intelligence. Two bomb-laden B-17s flew solo missions to the New Georgia group in the wee hours of 31 January, ostensibly to catch the newly arrived Japanese planes on the ground. The first Fort lifted off from Henderson into the darkness to overfly Munda at bombing altitude at around 0215 hours. Finding the airstrip too obscured to permit any bombing accuracy, the crew flew over to their secondary target, Vila-Stanmore. Dropping eight 500-pound bombs and six 100-pound bombs, they claimed a possible hit on an ammunition dump before retiring at 0245 hours.

The second Fort reached Munda at 0505 to find the airstrip still socked in. This crew also elected to cruise over to Vila. Making their bombing run under somewhat clearer skies, they were greeted by heavy, accurate flak thrown up by thoroughly aroused gunners. An identical ordnance mix whistled down, and the plane commander set a course for Cactus at 0545 hours.

A pair of B-17s—one each from the 42nd and 23rd BSs(H)—took off from Henderson between 0500 and 0530 on their daily reconnaissance missions up the Slot. The 42nd BS Fort headed on a northwesterly course of 304 degrees for 310 miles, whence it would turn right to fly a dogleg to azimuth 310 degrees and return the 310 miles to Cactus on the reciprocal heading. Riding in the 23rd's plane, radio operator Basil Debnekoff flew an adjacent, wedge-shaped search pattern between 310 degrees and 316 degrees out four hundred miles and back reporting the mission as "uneventful."

But the first Fort came across fifteen destroyers and an estimated three cruisers at 1115 hours. The convoy was steaming at a leisurely twenty knots just south of Bougainville on its way to Shortland Harbor. Unknown to the B-17 crew, Admiral Hashimoto's destroyers were gathering for the next phase of Operation KE. The search plane also observed a total of thirty-one warships and merchantmen in the spacious anchorage of the Shortland-Tonolei harbor complex; four floatplanes were moored off the Poporang seaplane base. As the Fort cruised through the New Georgia group on its return flight, Vella's coastwatchers observed it pass over at 1150 hours.

Taking wing from Cactus behind the pair of daily reconnaissance Forts, the two Lightnings of Baker search also headed up the Slot. Capt. John Mitchell and Lt. Besby Holmes of the 339th FS noted on the way up that the overcast over Munda had lifted to eight thousand feet. They then proceeded to snoop around the Shortland-Tonolei harbor complex under clearing skies. Captain Mitchell confirmed the abundance of shipping noted earlier by the bomber crew, reporting, "Tonolei-Shortlands area 21 ships total—some AP, AK, DD, CL." In the forenoon, the P-38s reconnoitered the New Georgia group again on their return from Bougainville as coastwatcher John Keenan observed them "skulking about." But weather conditions had failed to improve; Munda remained under 60 percent low cloud cover when they flew over at 16,000 feet. Mitchell later reported, "Couldn't see anything."

Cactus Recon ordered a fighter sweep out of Guadalcanal around noon of 31 January consisting of Lt. Gil Percy and Lt. Addison Raber from VMF-112 plus three more F4F pilots from VMO-251. Joining them was a contingent of eight P-39s from the 67th FS, four P-40s from the 44th, and two P-38s from the 339th. This cosmopolitan force headed up the Slot under an overcast ceiling that had by now lifted to between 18,000 and 20,000 feet, with visibility unobstructed to fifty miles. Its mission was to reconnoiter the airstrips at Munda and Vila and engage the enemy planes reportedly operating in the area. Hopefully, they would catch numerous Japanese planes still parked in their revetments.

The Cactus fighters arrived over Vila amidst lingering cloud cover. Apart from a hot reception put up by the base's 75-mm and 40-mm AA batteries, little activity could be observed on the airstrip through the partial overcast. Flying over the field circa 1400, Captain Nichols' P-39s reluctantly went down to 8,000 feet to test the strength of enemy flak—a decidedly unpleasant task ordered by Cactus of pilots on routine reconnaissance missions. Japanese gunners found the Cobras' altitude, putting up an intense barrage that trailed harmlessly behind the fighters. Major Tyler's P-40s, flying cover at around 19,000 feet, and the P-38s flown by Lieutenants Jacobson and Richardson at 21,000 feet, drew light but accurate attention as well. Harboring no planes, Vila airstrip looked to be inoperative at the moment. After leaving Kolombangara, the fighter sweep cruised over to New Georgia.

What was thought to be a lone "Nagoya type Zero" was spotted at 1415, flying at 13,000 feet just east of Munda. Sporting bright mottled-green uppers, a grey underside and "square" wing tips, the shiny "land type Zero" tried unsuccessfully to lure the American fighters into the range of Munda's AA guns. The many flak batteries sprinkled around the field were still in business despite their having been targeted by the previous day's B-17 raid. Finally seizing an opportunity, one element of P-39s executed an overhead pass on this poorly identified Japanese fighter. The aerobatic enemy plane easily spiraled away, flitting tantalizingly in and out of the thick cloud cover but refusing combat. Lieutenants Percy and Raber of VMF-112 also chased after an "enemy Nagoya type Zero" or "type 20 painted brilliant green and grey" that took cover among the clouds.

These descriptions of "Zeros" suspiciously point to the fighters sojourning at Munda—specifically, several *shotai* of the 1st Sentai's 3rd Chutai, led by Capt. Yoshihiko Kanaya. When the Cactus raid came in, Captain Kanaya tried to scramble his Oscars but, for reasons soon to be made clear, only WO Naoharu Shiromoto made it off the ground before the raiders showed up.

The Lily bombers that had landed the previous evening were highly vulnerable to air attack, as was the lone reconnaissance Betty. With the raid on Cactus delayed until the morrow, the safety of the Lilys became a prime concern once Munda was alerted to the inbound hostiles. That they at least had enough time to take off suggests that the Cactus fighter sweep had been spotted some distance down the Slot by an alert warning net. Since they were unencumbered by bombers, however, the raiders were moving fast; after the lumbering Lilys scrambled, there was barely time for one of Munda's fighters to follow them up before the Cactus raiders swooped over.

In an account dripping with drama and not a little braggadocio, Shiromoto said he engaged twenty P-38s, shot down two of them, and caused another pair to collide while chasing him. Neither of the two P-38 pilots present reported engaging enemy fighters. In reality, his is probably the Ki-43 that taunted the P-39s and F4Fs. Distracted by Warrant Officer Shiromoto's brazen antics, the U.S. pilots merely gave Munda a cursory once-over at altitude, missing a rare opportunity to catch a field brimming with parked Oscars. Through the partial overcast, the airstrip far below appeared barren of aircraft and in doubtful shape. Apparently satisfied and unwilling to brave Munda's flak, the Americans moved on. Having thus provided a valuable if not intentional diversion, the brassy and boastful Shiromoto took his Oscar back down.

An air collision between a pair of SBDs that occurred the next day over Munda is probably the basis for his concocting a supposed collision between two P-38s—a fanciful recollection that even found its way into Japanese official reports.

Meanwhile, rather than circle in the general vicinity for an indefinite period, the Lily bombers apparently made for Kahili or Kara since these fields were about an hour's flying time away. They would thereby not be left hanging around in the air with the risk of running out of fuel in the event runway repairs took an unduly long time to effect. Okayed by radio to return, the Ki-48s made their way back to Munda later that afternoon.

Coastwatcher John Keenan monitored the progress of the Lilys as they roared across Vella Gulf at 1730, mistaking the strange twin-engine aircraft for a flight of "nine transport planes bound for Vila." Though numerically incorrect, his observation may not have been entirely erroneous. The Lilys would not have been bombed up until the morning of their Guadalcanal strike for fear of being caught on the ground full of ordnance by a Cactus air raid. Consequently, the empty bombers likely availed themselves of the opportunity to ferry in loads of supplies for Munda. Plowing through the cloud cover building above Kolombangara's crater, the Ki-48s emerged northwest of Vila and began to let down for Munda airstrip as the day ebbed.

Grasping every opportunity to weaken the anticipated Japanese offensive he believed was about to be unleashed in the Eastern Solomons, ComAirSoPac exhorted the Cactus Air Force to sink all enemy shipping that could be found plying the Slot within striking range of its aircraft. On 31 January coastwatchers from Choiseul spotted an unprotected and unescorted merchantman off Faisi as it started down the Slot at 0745 with cargo destined for the New Georgia group. A patrolling PBY intercepted the freighter at 1435 as it entered the top of Vella Gulf, dropping two 500-pound bombs and a pair of depth charges. The ordnance barely missed the *maru*, which weaved as though it were "out of control."

The 6,732-ton transport *Toa Maru 2* was reported by coastwatchers tracing the same route a few hours later with two DD escorts. A small CAP of floatplanes cruised leisurely overhead. Inexplicably, as far as CAPs go, these floatplanes and their predecessors proved rather marginal given that Rear Adm. Minoru Ota and his staff, in addition to two small battalions of *rikusentai* from the 8th Combined Special Naval Landing Force, occupied the *Toa Maru 2*'s passenger quarters. Indeed, fearing that the small convoy might be detected amidst the intensive Cactus air activity over the New Georgia group that day, Combined Fleet radioed a request to Buin at 1645 for Zeros to beef up the transport's CAP. Thus, the convoy commander was most likely aware that an airborne attack on a transport had recently taken place right in his path—an incident that bore an ominous portent.

Weighing anchor in the forenoon of 31 January, the *Toa Maru 2* moved south past Shortland Harbor. Subchaser *Ch-30*—based at Faisi—steamed out to join her and the torpedo boat *Hiyodori*, as the new flagship. Three successive pairs of Petes from the 958th Kokutai covered the convoy from 1000 to 1630, overlapped at midday by F1M2s from the *Kamikawa Maru* and *Kunikawa Maru*.

The convoy was observed leaving the Shortlands by coastwatchers on Choiseul. Lt. Nick Waddell duly radioed the coastwatcher DSIO on the Canal at 1445, noting the ships' passage with two 958th Kokutai Petes overhead. At 1530 the transport and her escorts were reported heading southeast off the north coast of Vella Lavella by local coastwatchers who guessed that they were headed for Vila-Stanmore via Vella Gulf and Blackett Strait.

Cactus Strike Command was already hastening to scramble its light bombers and fighters in a race against the waning sun. Off Lunga Point, twenty-one orbiting SBDs and TBFs started up the Slot. Eight F4Fs and six P-39s joined up as the formation passed Savo Island. Thus assembled, the thirty-five-plane strike force rose past rugged Cape Esperance, settling down to a pace of 150 knots after the slower-climbing dive-bombers reached their cruising altitude. The planes had barely progressed up the Slot when a pair each of Wildcats and Avengers turned back with various mechanical malfunctions. The remaining thirty-one aircraft continued up the Slot in pursuit of the ebbing light.

Catching sight of the *Toa Maru 2* convoy at 1800, steaming eight miles off the southeast coast of Vella Lavella, the strike force was on top of the ships in no time. As the planes approached, the transport and her escorts threw up an especially vigorous AA barrage. A *shotai* of slower, outnumbered, and outgunned F1M2s from the *Sanyo Maru* was in its second hour of CAP duty when the Cactus raiders showed up. The three Petes could do little more than veer off toward the sun to avoid the fighter escort, all the while looking for an opportunity to pick off some of the light bombers that might stray when coming out of their bombing and torpedo runs.

While her escorts turned sharply to port, the *Toa Maru 2* began an evasive turn to starboard. The dive-bombers from VMSB-233 and VMSB-234 plunged into the flak, releasing seven 1,000-pounders, three 500-pounders, and six 100-pounders. A P-39 escort pilot observed a possible direct hit on the transport—perhaps Lieutenant Mitchell's 1,000-pounder that had appeared to hit her port side amidships. Also observing the action, VMSB-131's aircrews confirmed the lone bomb hit.

Individual dive-bombers joined up on their leader at about one thousand feet as they recovered from their runs. The maneuver presented a perfect opportunity for the *shotai* of Petes. Heading east-southeast in line-astern, two of them began to close in from out of the sun for a six o'clock bounce. The third Pete may have trailed at a distance in bushwhacking position, prepared to pick off any cripples.

An excited radio call from the gathering SBDs brought Lt. Jim Secrest's medium cover of two F4Fs and Lt. Jeff DeBlanc's low-cover section to the rescue. DeBlanc's section came in too fast on its first pass, overleading the slower biplanes. The two Wildcats pulled through, recovering in a tight turn while the Petes broke off and fled southward. DeBlanc hit them both on his second pass. Flames began to lick back from the trailing Pete, which fell off in a slow spiral while the F4F's guns riveted the lead floatplane from below. Fatally hit, it climbed lazily to the right then nosed over and disintegrated in a searing flash. Upon observing the F4Fs flame his two comrades in rapid succession, the third F1M2 pilot apparently lingered on the edge of the combat area.

Lieutenant Secrest and his wingman arrived as DeBlanc put finis to the second Pete. Irked by the disappointing performance of the SBDs, Secrest took Lt. Joe Lynch down for a strafing run on the ships as the Avengers prepared to go in. DeBlanc then peeled off, followed by Staff Sergeant Feliton, for a "deck-clearing" run on the rear gun platform of the *Toa Maru 2*. Some VMSB-131 crews witnessed the strafing attacks, noting that a fire broke out on the subchaser. After their runs Secrest led Lynch upward in a turn to port to cover the seven TBFs that had already started their attack.

Three of the portly but versatile Avengers of VMSB-131 were armed with torpedoes; the other four carried a quartet of 500-pound bombs apiece. Concentrating on their main target, the three torpedo-carrying Avengers peeled off, diving for the deck in a loose string to begin their attacks. At 1804, as Lt. Bud Main completed his torpedo run at the transport's port quarter and clawed for altitude, aircrews spotted a single column of brown-tinged water spouting up alongside the *Toa Maru 2*'s bow. Boring in from starboard, Lt. Marty Roush and Lieutenant Hayter dropped two fish in succession at about the same time, each claiming a hit on that side.

Lt. Joe Conrad had already drifted down on the *Toa Maru 2* in a steep glide to release his four-bomb salvo. A Wildcat pilot—probably Lieutenant Lynch—glimpsed the flash of a bomb exploding just aft of amidships as he was streaking past her to strafe the subchaser.

Lt. Joe Warren took MTSgt. George Nasif down toward the main source of the flak—the *Hiyodori*. Both section leader and wingman claimed hits on the meddlesome torpedo boat. VMSB-233 reported, the "DD suffered several explosions after direct hits" and "was smoking and burning." The P-39 pilots also reported "one probable hit" on the smaller escort, *Ch-30*, but Lieutenant Dean reported that none of his bombs had struck home. The probable may have been a near miss.

Cactus torpedo bombers were still delivering their attack when a warning pierced the airwaves: "Zeros!" It was Lt. Tom Hughes, flying top cover on the wing of Lt. Jack Maas. Hughes had spotted a flight of Japanese fighters closing from the southwest. The "Zeros" actually were nine mottled-green Oscars, sporting the yellow lightning-bolt emblem of the 11th Sentai's 3rd Chutai.

The sun was low on the horizon when a message from a Japanese observation station—likely the one at Ramada Island, or the thirty-man outpost at Lever Harbor—warned Munda that a group of inbound hostiles had passed overhead, apparently headed toward the top of Kula Gulf—in the general direction of the approaching *Toa Maru 2* convoy. Having scrambled to escape being caught on the ground by the earlier Cactus fighter sweep, the visiting *chutai* of Lily bombers had coincidentally returned and was now in the midst of landing. Ground crews were still directing the last of the eleven bombers along taxiways to revetment areas, effectively stymieing any attempt to scramble Munda's fighters.

Providentially, to the northwest of Vella Lavella Lt. Toshio Kimura was leading eight other Nakajima Ki-43 fighters from their home base at Buka to Munda. Capt. Juro Fujita, CO of the 3rd Chutai, seems to have flown down on 29 January with ten other Oscar pilots to familiarize himself with the airstrip and arrange for his unit to relieve the Oscars of the 1st Sentai in support of Operation KE. Unlike the JNAF's Zero *kokutai*, most JAAF Oscar units had kept their radios. If the 3rd Chutai was still radio-equipped, when the observation post reported the hostiles passing overhead, Fujita would have advised Munda to raise Kimura, find his current position, and warn him of the enemy formation heading across the top of Kula Gulf.

Judging by subsequent events, if and when he received the message, Lieutenant Kimura's three *shotai* were sweeping around the western side of Vella Lavella, already letting down through five thousand feet in preparation for a landing at Munda. As the Nakajimas skirted the northern half of the island, Mount Tambisala, with its 2,600-foot summit typically wrapped in a thick column of cumulus at that time of day, would have obscured the air–sea action unfolding on the far side. Only when they pulled abreast of the lower reaches of the island would the JAAF pilots have clearly seen ragged puffs of flak bursting off their port quarter in the direction of the junction between Kula and Vella Gulfs.

However he found out about the convoy's predicament, the 3rd Chutai's exec closed to the intercept, his attention fixed on the action taking place over the *Toa Maru 2* and her escorts. The last of the TBF pilots were by now expending their ordnance on the Japanese convoy; others were regrouping before heading off to rejoin the SBDs. The Dauntlesses, reforming to the southeast of the scattered ships under cover of the P-39s, failed to register against the somber surface of the darkening gulf, as did the Wildcat fighters striving to regain altitude after their strafing runs.

Flying above the SBDs, the USAAF pilots gave no hint of joining the upcoming fray. Likely monitoring the common frequency shared with the F4Fs, they may not have heard Lieutenant Hughes' radio warning. Heading away with most of the light bombers in tow, they may not even have noticed the approaching Oscars. If they did see the Nakajima fighters, they chose to remain at altitude above the main formation to guard the Dauntlesses and Avengers against any Japanese attackers that might get past the screening Wildcats. Indeed, this may have been prudent on their part, given their prior role as almost exclusively a ground support unit throughout most of the Guadalcanal campaign—a role that left them short on air-combat experience flying obsolescent fighters.

After strafing the ships, lieutenants Secrest and Lynch were still climbing over the combat area between the last attacking TBFs and the reforming SBDs when they spotted the bandits above their four o'clock position at about five thousand feet. Also climbing farther back, Lieutenant DeBlanc spotted the nine trim Nakajima fighters, mistaking them for Zeros in the waning light as they swung left through his one o'clock. Feliton picked them up seconds later as they passed abeam of the F4Fs.

Still in vee formation, their attention riveted on the last of the TBFs buzzing around the convoy, Kimura's pilots found themselves closing with unfamiliar USMC aircraft for the first time, having encountered only USAAF planes over New Guinea and the Bismarcks. Indeed, Lieutenant Kimura subsequently reported that his three *shotai* had engaged a *dozen* Wildcats, mistaking the larger but similarly silhouetted and painted Avengers in the far distance as F4Fs. In fact, there were twelve Grumman F4Fs and TBFs involved, confirming Kimura's numerical estimate.

DeBlanc climbed up beneath the oncoming Oscars, opening fire a mere five hundred feet below the unsuspecting Lieutenant Kimura. When DeBlanc's bullets chewed into Kimura's tail assembly, the Ki-43 snapped up, flipped to port, and tumbled out of view. Kimura's wingmen immediately split up. His number two—the veteran ace SSgt. Takao Takahashi—instinctively snapped his plane into a gut-wrenching left turn and opened his throttle. The other wingman had started up in a banking turn to the right when DeBlanc came around onto his six, fired, and blew his fighter apart.

Curving back toward Lieutenant DeBlanc's section, Staff Sergeant Takahashi rushed down in a stern attack. Luckily, DeBlanc glanced rearward. Upon spying the lone Oscar, he honked his Grumman around to the right to meet the attack head-on. Behind and to the left, Feliton put his Wildcat into a tight right turn, cutting across DeBlanc's tail in a textbook Bauer scissor. Emerging ahead and to the right of DeBlanc, Staff Sergeant Feliton inadvertently became the Oscar pilot's prime target.

Feliton was astonished to see the Oscar's cowl-mounted guns winking at "an impossible distance." He was even more surprised when a spate of 12.7-mm and 7.7-mm slugs rattled into the nacelle of his Wildcat's engine, striking an oil line or reservoir. Dense smoke poured back from the cowl. As his fighter started to lose altitude, he set his windmilling prop to coarse pitch to extend the glide. DeBlanc glanced briefly at his wingman's stricken F4F as it crossed in front of him and fell away toward Kolombangara.

Arriving too late to help Feliton, Secrest opened fire on Takahashi from behind, but his six fifties merely coughed a few times. No more ammo! Realizing that the armorers at Fighter Two had probably neglected to top up his magazines, Secrest impulsively closed in on the dappled-green Oscar. Shocked at the sudden sight of Secrest boring in on his tail while DeBlanc veered toward his nose, Takahashi jerked his Ki-43 into a split-S to escape his lethal predicament. Secrest sheared off, convinced that Takahashi had hit the water before recovering from his diving turn.

Another *shotai* leader—possibly Sergeant Major Miyamoto—led his two wingmen down in a loose trail formation to intercept DeBlanc, who was now alone. Lieutenants Maas and Hughes dropped down and probably intercepted the rearmost wingman in this *shotai*, for DeBlanc and Feliton both caught a glimpse of an Oscar plummeting seaward, all aflame, its pilot having bailed out. Feliton himself hit the silk just seconds before his burning plane crashed into the jungle near Ropa Point. Pilot and parachute landed high in the jungle canopy. Trapped at the apex of a tall banyan tree, Feliton anxiously watched the dogfight raging nearby over the gulf, hoping that his sprawling white chute would not attract a strafing enemy fighter.

Miyamoto and his remaining wingman closed in on DeBlanc from above at two o'clock. DeBlanc turned once more into the enemy to give battle, knowing that his gas-guzzling Wildcat would likely run dry before he made it back to Cactus. With Japanese slugs already punching holes in his slowly climbing Grumman, he opened fire. Hits flashed on the lead Ki-43; its cowl burst into flames, and it disintegrated in a fiery ball.

Recovering from the shock of his leader's violent explosion, the surviving wingman zoomed by. He pulled his Ki-43 up into a tight turn, then screamed back down on the Grumman in a high-side run as DeBlanc tried to bank his sluggish plane around to the right. The Japanese fighter swung in behind DeBlanc's shoulder just as the Wildcat fell off into a dive. DeBlanc hit the brakes. The fast-diving enemy pilot sailed past his decelerating plane, fishtailing his Oscar to cut his speed. DeBlanc boosted power, pulled up the F4F's nose, and bagged his adversary with a short burst before the latter had a chance to maneuver evasively.

The dogfight raged across the upper reaches of Vella Gulf as the combatants converged piecemeal on one another. Lt. Jack Maas recalled it as a "hell of a scrap." Lieutenant Lynch's Grumman took a pounding from the agile Nakajimas but, paying back in kind, Lynch claimed a "Zero" destroyed. He then sparred with an Oscar pilot whose gunfire ripped off his canopy. Hunkering down against the armor-plated back of his seat, he dove out of the line of fire.

A single Ki-43 emerged from the sprawling dogfight and closed in on Lieutenant DeBlanc from high astern. The Oscar pilot—quite possibly Staff Sergeant Takahashi again—skillfully slid across the F4F's left rear quarter. Suddenly, machine-gun slugs punched through DeBlanc's Plexiglas, smashing into the instrument panel. The Wildcat's fuel primer and the unprotected auxiliary tank beneath the cockpit both ruptured, then flared up.

DeBlanc banked his fighter toward Kolombangara with flames licking back along the underside of its fuselage.

Embroiled in the ongoing dogfight, other F4F pilots could not come to their colleague's rescue. As the Oscar banked around for another pass, the wind wrenched the Grumman's damaged canopy loose when DeBlanc tried to slide it back, sending it tumbling into the slipstream. He was not long in following. Having espied the Oscar pilot repositioning himself to open fire, DeBlanc abandoned his stricken Wildcat at around two thousand feet. He descended into Vella Gulf, eventually washing on shore on Kolombangara after a grueling six-hour swim through shark-infested waters.

The air battle suddenly evaporated. While the remaining Cactus aircraft winged their way home in the gathering darkness, the third Japanese Pete lingered briefly over *Toa Maru 2* before heading back to Poporang to report the loss of two F1M2s. Six of the nine Oscar pilots eventually returned to Munda with or without their planes. Lieutenant Kimura survived DeBlanc's ambush but three of his pilots fell before the guns of the Wildcats—Sgt. Maj. Taisaku Miyamoto, Sgts. Kazuo Kondo and Saburo Yabuchi. The pilot who bailed out survived. VMF-112 pilots put in for two Petes and five "Zeros" shot down; DeBlanc also claimed Lieutenant Kimura as a probable.

The JAAF pilots submitted wild claims of *ten* F4Fs destroyed plus two probables. The 11 Sentai's 3rd Chutai was the most inexperienced of its units, and its pilots had never gone up against the tough Marine Corps fighters before. This not only helps account for their lackluster performance against VMF-112's Wildcats—it renders highly suspect their outlandish victory claims that may have been filed to save face after the shock of such a drubbing by Cactus pilots.

In fact, only Lieutenant DeBlanc and Staff Sergeant Feliton were shot down; Lieutenant Lynch's plane was the only other one seriously damaged. SSgt. Takao Takahashi remains the front-runner as the nemesis of both vanquished F4Fs since he subsequently put in a plausible claim for two Wildcats. A veteran ace of the China theater, Takahashi had been with the 3rd Chutai since February 1942, and was considered one of the 11th Sentai's best aviators. He would go on to rack up more than thirteen victories and be promoted to lieutenant before perishing on 13 November 1944 over Manila

Harbor. Like the great JNAF ace Hiroyoshi Nishizawa, Lieutenant Takahashi died trapped in a transport on a ferry run that was intercepted by U.S. fighters and ignominiously shot down.

Local natives guided both Feliton and DeBlanc to coastwatchers Josslyn and Keenan, who arranged to have them ferried back to Cactus via PBY on 12 February. For choosing to stay the course in a malfunctioning plane and successfully defending the SBDs and TBFs at great personal peril when he should have turned back, Lt. Jeff DeBlanc was later awarded the Medal of Honor.

In Vella Gulf crews on the escort vessels brought deck fires under control and prepared to rescue survivors from the disabled transport. The bombing of the *Toa Maru 2* had inflicted some forty casualties, half of them fatal. The *Hiyodori* and subchaser *Ch-30* picked up some 350 survivors as night closed in and took them to Vila-Stanmore, whence they were ferried to Bairoko Harbor on New Georgia by barge. Both escorts survived the Cactus attack, but not so the *Toa Maru 2*.

The preferred aiming point for torpedo drops was the bow of the target. Accordingly, Lieutenant Main's torpedo struck the port side of the *Toa Maru 2*'s bow, exploding as it entered the first cargo hold. One or two fish may have hit along her starboard side, but there were no other visible explosions. With water gushing into her forward half, she began to sink slowly by the head. The sea water worked its way into countless cement bags, turning their contents into solid concrete, whose escalating weight accelerated the flooding. Eventually abandoned, the stricken transport drifted toward the foot of Vella Gulf. Finally, with her bow now awash, she crunched into a sloping shelf "on the far side of Gizo-Kololokai Island." There she held fast about three hundred yards from shore. USN Avengers returning from a raid on Munda the next morning reported a "cargo ship beached and burning at S.E. End of Gizo Island." A passing PBY confirmed the TBF sighting at 0945 hours.

In the early hours of 4 January a PBY-5A from VP-12, on its way to harass Vila, was attracted to a distant glow off its left beam. Reaching the still-burning *Toa Maru 2*, the pilot decided to make a run on her. The shock wave of his 500-pound near-miss, exploding close to her port side, may have sufficed to capsize her, possibly causing her to pull free and drag backwards as she rotated about her bows. She slipped beneath the surface amidst a roar of hissing steam as seawater met flames and hot metal, coming to rest on her starboard side with her bow lying in fifteen fathoms of water, her stern in twenty fathoms.

Having managed to avoid Davy Jones' locker despite several close calls, the *Toa Maru 2* finally succumbed to at least one torpedo, a cargo of cement, and a Black Cat. Though jarred by several nearby earthquakes in recent years, her rusting hulk still rests on the shelf, more or less intact—and now is one of the most popular dive sites in the Solomons.

Fighter One (foreground) being resurfaced with coral, and Henderson Field (background). (U.S. National Archives, aka NARA)

Fighter Two in February 1943. (NARA)

Grumman F4F Wildcats at Fighter Two. The Wildcat was the only Cactus fighter that could meet the Zero on nearly equal terms. (NARA)

Mitsubishi A6M2 Zeros from the carrier *Zuikaku* on Lakunai Airfield, Rabaul, during Operation KE. (Thorpe Collection via Jim Lansdale)

Cactus airmen constantly mistook the JAAF's Nakajima Ki-43 Oscar for a variant of the JNAF's Mitsubishi A6M Zero. (USN National Museum of Naval Aviation, aka USNNMNA)

Ground crew services a Mitsubishi G4M Betty of the 705th Kokutai. (Jim Lansdale)

JAAF Kawasaki Ki-48 Lily lies derelict on Munda airstrip. (NARA)

JNAF Mitsubishi F1M2 Pete played a key role in Operation KE as a nocturnal fighter-bomber. (USNNMNA)

JNAF Kawanishi H8K Emily reconnaissance flying boat under air attack. (NARA)

Inferior in air combat, Bell's P-39/P-400 Airacobra found its niche at Cactus as a ground support aircraft. (USAF)

Torpedo attack by Grumman TBF Avengers. (NARA)

Douglas SBD Dauntless in a steep bombing dive. (NARA)

Japanese base at Gizo Island under air attack by Boeing B-17s. (NARA)

Swift Martin B-26 Marauder could carry the same bomb load as the larger B-17. (USAF)

Cactus-based RNZAF Lockheed Hudson on patrol over the Slot. (NARA)

VMF-112 at Guadalcanal after Operation KE: (1) Lt. John "J.B." Maas, (2) Capt. Mike Yunck, (3) Capt. Blaine Baesler, (4) Lt. Joe Lynch, (5) Lt. Jeff DeBlanc, (6) Lt. Jim Secrest, (7) Lt. R. Stack, (8) Lt. Stan Synar, (9) Lt. S. Richards, (10) Capt. Ken Kirk, (11) Capt. Bob Fraser, (12) Lt. Wayne Laird. (USMC)

Maj. (later Lt. Col.) Joe Bauer, CO of VMF-212. (NARA)

Brig. Gen. Francis Mulcahy, ComAirSols, commanded the Cactus Air Force. (NARA)

VMF-121 pilots in early 1943 (L to R): Lt. Roger Haberman, Lt. Bill "B" Freeman, Lt. Tom Furlow, Capt. Joe Foss, Capt. Greg Loesch, Lt. Frank "Skeezix" Presley, Lt. Bill Marontate, Lt. Oscar Bate. (NARA)

VMO-251 pilots at Espiritu Santo before deploying to Cactus on their first tour: (1) Lt. Phil Leeds. (2) Lt. Hank Sabatier, (3) Capt. Jim Anderson, (4) Lt. Jack Berteling, (5) Lt. Hank McCartney, (6) Lt. Bob Bryson, (7) Maj. Joe Renner. (Allan McCartney)

Capt. Pat Weiland of VMO-251. (C.P. Weiland)

Lt. Hank McCartney of VMO-251. (Allan McCartney)

VMSB-131 pilots at Espiritu Santo after Operation KE: (1) Lt. Frank Smith, (2) TSgt. George Nasif, (3) Lt. Barney McShane, (4) Lt. Marty Roush, (5) Lt. George "Bud" Main, (6) Capt. Jim McGuire, (7) Lt. Joe Warren, (8) Lt. Dean "Snuffy" Dalton. (Dave's Warbirds)

70th FS pilots before Operation KE: (1) Lt. Fred Purcell, (2) Lt. "Wally" Dinn, (3) Lt. Julius "Jake" Jacobson, (4) Lt. Dick Koenig, (5) Lt. (later Maj.) John Mitchell, (6) Lt. (later Capt.) Bill Shaw, (7) Lt. (later Maj.) Henry Viccellio. (347th FG Association via Jim Lansdale)

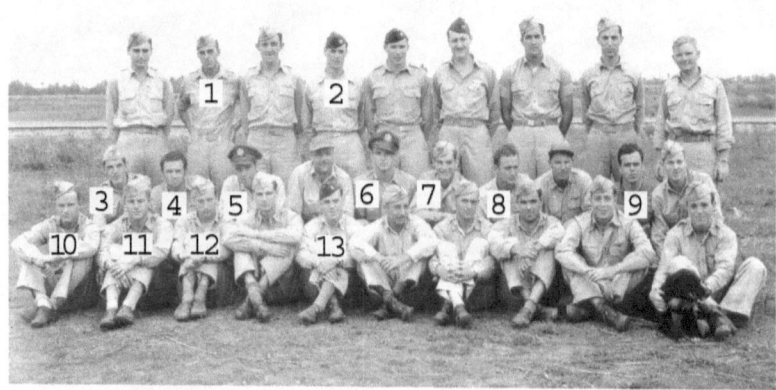

More 70th FS pilots before Operation KE: (1) Lt. Darrell Cosart, (2) Lt. (later Capt.) Jim Robinson, (3) Lt. (later Capt.) Albert Johnson, (4) Lt. Bob Petit, (5) Lt. (later Capt.) Tom Lanphier, (6) Lt. Larry McKulla, (7) Lt. Sam Barnes, (8) Lt. Dick Rivers, (9) Lt. Rex Barber, (10) Lt. Bill Daggett, (11) Lt. Bill Fiedler, (12) Lt. Harvey Dunbar, (13) Lt. George Topoll. (347th FG Association via Jim Lansdale)

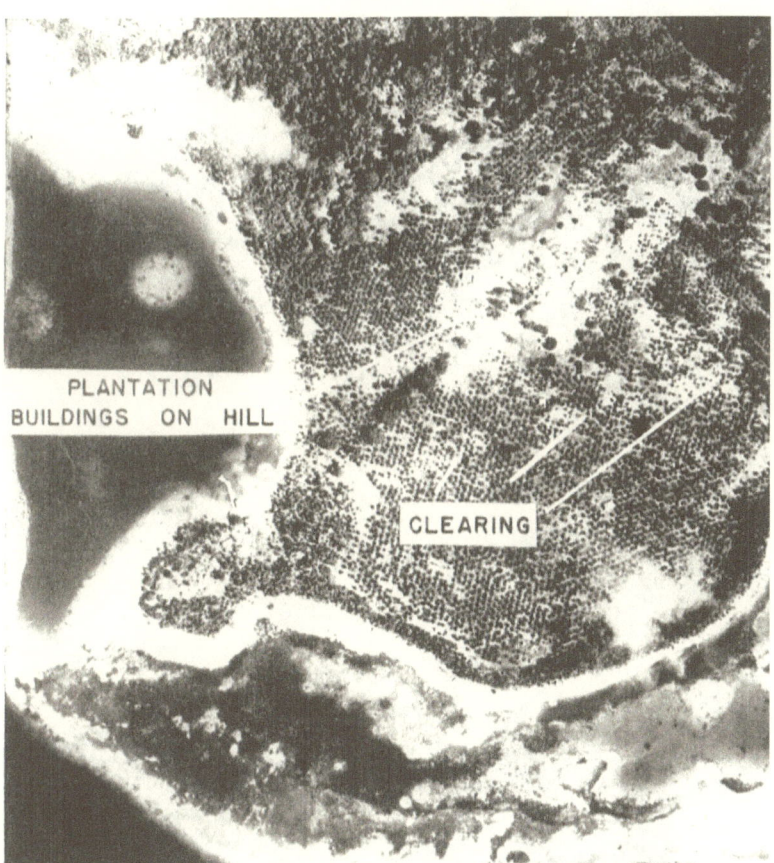

Reconnaissance photo of Munda Point in late 1942 reveals a Japanese airstrip under construction beneath an ingenious method of camouflage. (web site: Clipart.com)

HMNZS *Achilles* gets under way minutes after taking a bomb hit on her No. 3 turret. (NARA)

APD USS *Stringham*. (NARA)

Fletcher-class DD USS *DeHaven* off Savo Island, two days before her sinking. (NARA)

LCT 181 approaches rescue ship with *DeHaven* survivors. (NARA)

DDs of the Tokyo Express steam down the Slot. (NARA)

IJN single-funnel *Akizuki*-class DD under air attack. (NARA)

PT boats did their best to disrupt the Japanese evacuation operation off Cape Esperance. (NARA)

Fubuki-class DD. IJNS *Shirayuki* was the only DD of this class assigned to Operation KE. (NARA)

IJN seaplane tender at sea, loaded with Rufes and Petes. (NARA)

Japanese airstrip at Buka under air attack. (NARA)

IJN seaplane base at Rekata Bay under air attack. (NARA)

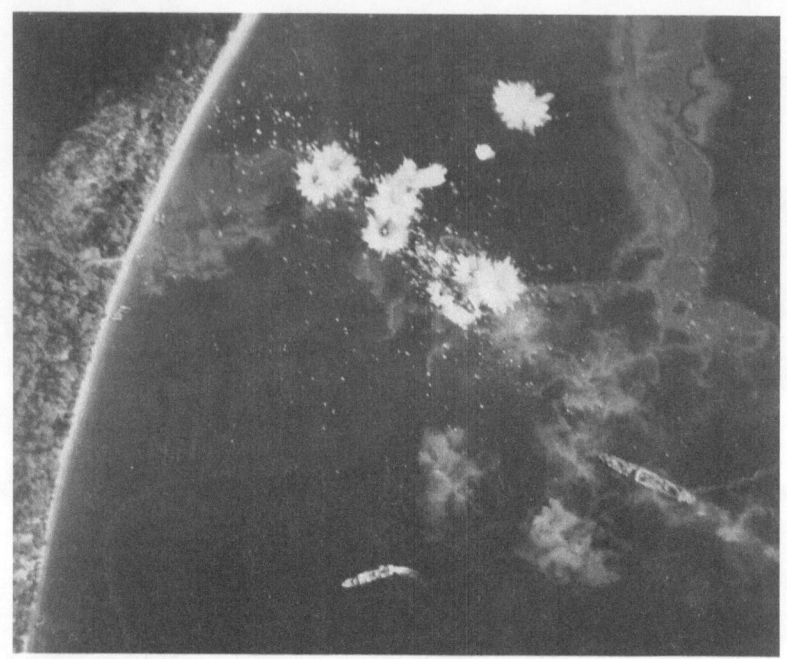

Japanese shipping in Tonolei Harbor under air attack by Boeing B-17s. (NARA)

Vila airstrip, bombed out and abandoned by late 1943. (NARA)

Zero awash on a reef in Coughlin Harbor, likely one of several ditched in severe weather by a *chutai* from the 252nd Kokutai on 25 Jan. 1943. (web site: Pacificwrecks)

Wreckage of a Zero in the Russells, probably flown by CPO Soji Chiba of the 252nd Kokutai who was shot down on 1 Feb. 1943. (NARA)

Abandoned Japanese barges and collapsible boats litter the beach around Cape Esperance after Operation KE. (NARA)

CHAPTER 11
GENERAL PATCH'S END RUN

Admirals Yamamoto, Kusaka, and Hashimoto were encouraged by the initial success of the Tokyo Express in transporting supplies and some nine hundred soldiers safely to Guadalcanal and another three hundred to the Russell Islands. At the same time, they were troubled by Cactus air attacks that netted serious damage to several of their destroyers. They were now forced to temporize while the naval–air engagement between TF GEORGE and torpedo-armed Betty and Nell bombers was played out off Rennell Island. The resulting minor but crucial Japanese victory precipitated the subsequent withdrawal of U.S. Navy task forces to safer waters and cleared the way for the first evacuation run. But an unexpected wrinkle cropped up to complicate matters anew.

Maj. Gen. Alexander Patch, commanding U.S. ground forces on Guadalcanal, sensed that he had his adversary, General Hyakutake, off balance. At least one intercepted Japanese message, originating from the Japanese 17th Army toward the end of November, indicated that Hyakutake was already contemplating the evacuation of his troops. Notwithstanding this hint of possible Japanese intent to pull out, Allied intelligence believed at this juncture that the Japanese were still leaning toward another all-out attempt to retake the Canal. General Patch and other American theater commanders began to suspect, mistakenly, that the Russell Islands might be the staging point for this renewed Japanese offensive. Determined to force the issue and win a decisive U.S. victory before a new threat materialized, General Patch made his move—cautiously and deliberately.

On 1 February, even before the destroyers of the Tokyo Express had cleared the Shortland Harbor on their first evacuation run, the destroyer-transport

USS *Stringham* sortied along with six lately arrived LCTs to land a battalion of infantry, supported by Marine artillery, on the far side of Cape Esperance—that is, on the flank of the retiring Japanese. Once established on the southwest coast, U.S. forces would be in a position to spoil any attempt to reinforce General Hyakutake's army; outflanked and isolated, the Japanese would be caught in a pincer closing in around Cape Esperance.

The value of the specially modified destroyer-transport for this type of operation was clearly understood by the USN. Designated as an assault purpose destroyer, the APD was the brainchild of Adm. Richmond Kelley-Turner. To bring his concept to fruition, the USN redesigned a number of World War I "flush-deck" destroyers—old "four pipers" like the *Stringham*—as full-fledged armed transports. Two each of their four boilers and funnels were removed, as well as all torpedo-related apparatus, to provide sufficient cargo space to carry a fully equipped infantry company—around 120 troops. Six of them could land an infantry battalion. With four 36-foot landing craft slung topside, these APDs could still make twenty-five knots. Their mottled green-and-grey camouflage earned them the sobriquet Green Dragons in U.S. Navy circles.

The compact Cactus landing force was to steam from Lunga Roads circa 0200 on 1 February in order to pass by the enemy-held coast west of the Bonegi River under cover of darkness. Thanks to major delays, the convoy did not leave until shortly after dawn, guarded by the four destroyers of the Cactus Striking Force and an umbrella of Wildcat fighters provided by VMF-112. Steaming leisurely at the ten knots dictated by the plodding LCTs, the convoy inched westward under the scrutiny of baleful eyes on shore—and in the air.

One of the 204th Kokutai's Dinah reconnaissance planes was over Iron Bottom Sound and Sealark Channel early that morning. As Lieutenant Miza swung his lithe, twin-engine craft from Tulagi over to Lunga Roads, he and his observer could not but have run into General Patch's amphibious force creeping along the coast. Flying high above the F4Fs of the fighter CAP, the Dinah crew radioed the ship types and numbers. From that altitude, they might have mistakenly reported the large *Fletcher*-class destroyers as light cruisers, for Rabaul was subsequently under the impression that Admiral Hashimoto's destroyers risked running into American cruisers if they tried an evacuation run that night. Regardless, the word was out that U.S. naval units were moving along the coast.

Twelve SBDs from VMSB-233 and VMSB-234 rose from Henderson Field at 0625 that morning; four TBFs from VMSB-131 followed at 0634 hours. After forming up over Lunga Point, the light bombers set a course of 300 degrees for the 185-mile trip up the Slot to Munda. A CAP of twelve F4Fs from VMO-251 joined up to provide air cover. Whether or not intended for that purpose, this raid may have served to distract the Japanese from General Patch's amphibious operation. It certainly put a temporary damper on the intended JAAF raid against Cactus scheduled for that morning.

While the Cactus strike force cruised toward New Georgia, coastwatcher John Keenan observed fourteen planes flying up the Slot past Vella Lavella "shortly after breakfast," only to see them return later. He puzzled over their identity, wondering if Munda's resident Oscars were speeding northwest to intercept an air raid in progress over Buin-Faisi? Or were they just running for safety? Regardless, some sixteen unprotected twin-engine Lilys still lingered at Munda when warning of the incoming raid was received, too late this time for any of them to scramble out of harm's way.

Rounding the northwestern cape of New Georgia, Captain Frazer led the Dauntlesses down for an attack out of the north on the primary target: the JAAF planes in their revetments at Munda airstrip. Frazer's division concentrated on revetment areas around the B loop at the east end of the field, where two twin-engine bombers—almost certainly Lilys—were parked.

Lt. H. Murphy followed Frazer in. Pushing over from ten thousand feet, he turned left into his dive. Almost at once he felt a heavy jolt in his right wing. Glancing over, he noticed a large hole that he attributed to flak. Unfazed by the incident, he continued his run, dropping his bomb.

Unseen by Murphy, Capt. Bill Moore was crossing with his second division to attack *his* assigned target: revetments at the *west* end of the strip. He passed too close beneath the first division, creating an overlap. Murphy's Dauntless "ran him down" from above, shearing off part of Moore's left wing. The captain's wingtip and pitot tube embedded themselves in the underside of Murphy's right wing. The impact threw Moore's damaged dive-bomber into a flat spin. His radio-gunner, Pfc. Dick Reed, went down with the twisting plane, but the pilot managed to get out. Wafting to earth, he landed on the airstrip and was captured by the irate Japanese. Captain Moore was never heard from again and is officially listed as MIA.

Captain Frazer's division scored three hits in the target area, causing smoke to well up around the bombers. Though shaken by the collision, the pilots of the second division rallied quickly to complete their runs. Focusing on the northwest corner of the south taxiway loop, Lieutenant Murphy loosed his 1,000-pounder on three parked bombers. When the missile exploded, flames broke out, emitting thick billows of smoke. Lieutenant Beebe hit a building with a galvanized roof at the head of the pier at Munda Point.

The tail-end Charlie of the second division was Lt. Abram Moss, who now approached his pushover point through intensifying AA fire. A burst of flak punched through his canopy, fatally wounding him in the head. As Moss slumped over, the Dauntless jerked and yawed. Radio-gunner Sgt. Gil Henze seized the auxiliary controls in the rear cockpit and called for help. Lieutenant Frazer instructed him to turn back down the Slot, flying parallel to the island chain. Maj. Ray Vroome of VMO-251 and his wingman volunteered to provide fighter cover for Henze.

Escorting the valiant sergeant as far as the Russells, the Wildcat pilots suddenly tensed when they saw the SBD's propeller windmill to a stop. Henze's plane had run dry, and there was no way he could switch fuel tanks from the rear cockpit. Major Vroome's radio had begun to malfunction, so he could only watch helplessly as the Dauntless dipped seaward. Sergeant Henze opened his safety harness, but, when the SBD plunged from under him, he failed to clear the aircraft's tailplane before it scythed into him, shearing off the lower part of one leg as the two fighter pilots gaped in shock. They watched Henze tumble through space before his chute finally opened. The luckless airman drifted down, trying to staunch the flow of blood. Landing in the water, he was still in his chute harness, his head awash, when the Wildcats buzzed him.

Miraculously, the resilient sergeant had merely passed out. He was soon pulled from the water by nearby islanders, who cauterized the leg wound. Two days later, a PBY picked Henze up. Having survived his horrific ordeal, he underwent surgery but died within two months, probably of a postoperative complication prehaps pneumonia, brought on by his weakened state.

VMSB-131's TBFs came out of the northwest hard on the heels of the SBDs. As per prescribed procedure, the pilots executed fast glides from 11,000 feet at angles between 40 and 50 degrees. Roaring diagonally across the airfield at upwards of 280 knots, they released their bombs at between 2,000 and 1,800 feet. Two heavy machine guns at either end of the runway spewed steady streams of 13-mm tracer at the oncoming planes as they zoomed by overhead.

First to descend was Capt. Art Molvik. Struggling with a temperamental intervalometer, he failed to release his four 500-pounders. Capt. Jim Maguire planed through light flak to unload his bombs on four twin-engine bombers dispersed at the northwest end of the field. Following him down, MTSgt. George Nasif toggled his bomb release, but only a single 500-pounder detonated in the same area. On their pullouts, both aircrews saw fires break out among the parked Lilys. Lt. Barney McShane got his ordnance away over the same target, but did not see the results.

Of the original sixteen Lily bombers, U.S. airmen spotted some ten to twelve dispersed around the airfield, preparing for an early-morning raid on Guadalcanal that had been rescheduled for this very day. These bombers had not been noticed by the Cactus fighter sweep of 31 January because they had been able to vamoose before the raiders struck. Observing from a high altitude through overcast skies, the U.S. fighter pilots had reported seeing no planes on the field below, incredulously oblivious to a bevy of revetments full of Oscars.

Its ordnance expended, the strike force rendezvoused at five thousand feet to disappear back down the Slot at 160 knots. Behind them, only six Lilys in revetments south of the runway at the west end of the field remained unscathed. Several other intact aircraft—likely some Oscar fighters parked in the open—were scattered around the field.

The returning strike force was passing over the Russell Islands when a pair of TBF crews caught a glimpse of something below. Receiving Captain Molvik's permission to break off, the two pilots glided down to investigate. They circled for fifteen minutes, observing "tents on East side of Bycee [Baisen?] Island and barges at South end." These signs confirmed the presence of the Japanese occupation force landed by the Tokyo Express on the night of 28 January.

Later that morning, while General Patch's amphibious force crept toward the far side of Cape Esperance, the Lilys and Oscars of the 6th Shidan finally sortied to raid Henderson Field, attempting once more to disrupt the operations of the Cactus Air Force in support of Operation KE. The mission had originally been planned for 30 January, but was scrubbed due to the foul weather plaguing the region. Postponed to the next day, it again failed to materialize. With the issue off Rennell Island still in doubt, the first evacuation run of the Tokyo Express had been put back from 31 January to 1 February. Accordingly, the JAAF raid was rescheduled a second time for the morning of 1 February. After TF GEORGE was clearly seen to withdraw, Admiral Hashimoto's destroyers got the green light, and the JAAF's Guadalcanal raid was on at last.

Now six bomb-laden Lilys—the only ones out of the original sixteen that had survived the morning's Cactus raid—took off from Munda to form up over Ranonga Island. They were joined by twenty-three Oscars of the 11st Sentai's 1st and 2nd Chutai out of Ballale. Those operable fighters of the 11th's 3rd Chutai that remained at Munda after the air battle over the *Toa Maru 2* were not available, having coincidentally scrambled to intercept a B-17 raid on Buin-Faisi before the Cactus raiders struck their airstrip. Neither did the JNAF Zeros scheduled to fly with the JAAF strike force on the scrubbed Guadalcanal raids sortie on 1 February; once again, this mission was exclusively an IJA show.

Vella Lavella coastwatcher Keenan recorded in his diary, "Twenty-two and possibly more [aircraft] sighted out to the S.W. bound S.E. Apparently another Nip raid on Guadalcanal." However, atmospheric conditions prevented him from alerting the Canal by radio until nearly 1000 hours. The JAAF raiders came in at 1030, unopposed by patrolling VMF-112 Wildcats; when the Japanese showed up, Captain Fraser's division found itself out of position to intercept.

The bombers and a low-flying CAP of six "Zero type fighters" were spotted by the escorting destroyers of General Patch's amphibious force as they flew into Iron Bottom Sound around the north shore of Savo Island to mask their approach from Cactus' radar and lookouts. Heading toward the Lunga perimeter, they banked right over Sealark Channel toward Henderson Field. A belated Condition Red sounded as the raiders went into their bombing runs.

A pair of F4F divisions on strip alert at Fighter Two scrambled to get airborne. First off were two sections of VMO-251. Capt. Walter Baran and Capt. Jim Anderson led wingmen Lt. Klas "Jack" Berteling and Lt. Hank McCartney into the sky in a northwesterly direction. Lieutenant McCartney was still scoreless after twenty-two missions. He had just cranked up his wheels and closed his hood when the retiring raiders passed beneath him, headed in roughly the same direction at one thousand feet. Anxious to break his jinx, the impetuous Marine flicked on his gunsight and arming switches; yanking the charging levers, he hastily pushed over. But buck fever kicked in. The adrenaline-charged youth held down the trigger, raking the rear of a twin-engine Kawasaki with .50-caliber fire. Flames spurted out as hunter and quarry roared over the American positions west of Fighter Two. Rapidly losing altitude, the Lily plowed into the hilly terrain beyond the Matanikau River.

Sliding to his right, Lieutenant McCartney lined up a second Lily. After a short burst his six fifties suddenly went silent. Out of ammo? Surprised, then perplexed, he broke off his attack to rejoin Lieutenant Berteling—in the nick of time as it turned out, for the low-flying Oscars of the Japanese escort had at last joined in the thick of things. McCartney climbed up behind a Ki-43 that was lining up his section leader and bluffed the enemy fighter off Berteling's tail. Even as the Oscar pilot broke away, one of his wingmen was already setting McCartney up for a high-side firing pass. Slugs thudded across the F4F's airfoil from wingtip to wingtip, tearing up the aluminum surface at three-foot intervals. The Wildcat shuddered under the fusillade as the startled youngster took evasive action. The Japanese fighter zoomed past, intent on pursuing another Wildcat stalking the Lilys.

Realizing that his controls and plane still functioned, McCartney hastened to link up with Berteling again. The two briefly scissored for mutual protection while they searched the quadrant for signs of attacking "Zeros," but no Oscars moved in to bait them into suicidal dogfights. As often happens in aerial combat, the sky was suddenly empty of enemy planes—to McCartney's great relief. The Oscar escort had broken contact to rejoin and protect the remaining bombers that were now flying just off the coast toward Cape Esperance.

Determined to have another crack at the raiders, McCartney screamed back down for a hasty downwind landing at Fighter Two. The battle-scarred Wildcat had hardly rolled to a stop before he climbed out, called excitedly for another plane, and tore off down the runway. Climbing at full throttle, he rejoined Berteling. The pair chased after the retiring Japanese, but failed to reestablish contact with the elusive enemy. Besides Lieutenant McCartney, two other VMO-251 pilots enjoyed some measure of success: Captain Baran claimed a bomber and a probable "Zero" destroyed; Captain Anderson was also credited with a "Zero."

Scoreless till now despite having participated in the two great brawls of 25 January and 27 January, Lieutenant McCartney had finally chalked up his first aerial victory as American infantrymen looked on approvingly. He was transferred out on 7 February, going on to fly with VMF-121 and achieve ace status with VMF-214—the fabled Black Sheep. But the odds nearly eclipsed such an eventuality. After landing, McCartney paused to examine the battle scars inflicted on his first F4F. Surveying its wing surfaces with some misgiving, he was able to put his fingers through a pair of ragged 12.7-mm holes that straddled his cockpit!

Capt. Mike Yunck's VMF-112 division took off too late to intercept the Japanese bombers. Scattered by the F4F attack, the surviving Lilys were now roaring westward, throttles wide open. Several happened to pass over the plodding U.S. convoy at five thousand feet. The destroyers *Radford* and *Nicholas* opened fire on the first "Mitsubishi 01," but the *Nicholas* checked her fire after a few rounds, unsure of the identity of the "two-motor" plane. A torrent of 5-inch and secondary AA fire from the *Radford* struck the Lily; nosing over, it plummeted toward the water.

This was enough for the *Nicholas* to rejoin the *Radford* in putting up another barrage when a second low-flying bomber unexpectedly broke out of the cloud cover. Damaged by AA fire, it stole away, trailing smoke. Shortly thereafter crewmen on the *Nicholas* observed "a whole flock of Zeros passing astern" at high altitude—probably the escorting Oscars hastening to rejoin the bombers. Unsure of what was happening, the two destroyers did not secure from general quarters until 1230. At some point they passed by the crash site of the first Lily. A smattering of debris and the lifeless bodies of several crewmen in life jackets bobbed aimlessly on the surface swell.

The raiders claimed four multiengine planes and four fighters destroyed *on the ground*, whereas Cactus acknowledged a single hit on Henderson's runway. Reality for the JAAF got even grimmer: VMO-251's Wildcats had gunned down two Lilys plus an Oscar and had claimed a probable Oscar; the destroyers had added another Lily and damaged a second. The Japanese inexplicably admitted the loss of an Oscar but no Lilys. Equally strange, the majority of the Ki-43s, which were flying high cover, had failed to engage the defending Wildcats. Perhaps the short but savage exchange ran its course before they could maneuver into a favorable position to intervene.

Arriving at Nugu Point in the forenoon, the USS *Stringham* began to disembark troops and equipment—undisturbed but not unnoticed by the Japanese. Alerted by Japanese ground observers that the Americans were landing troops to outflank the 17th Army, Rabaul dispatched a pair of reconnaissance planes, guarded by an escort of Zeros, to observe and report on U.S. activities at Guadalcanal. Likely flying separately, the two bombers and their CAPs triggered shifting blips on Cactus' radar screen. Cactus issued a red alert for the airfield complex twenty miles distant at 1130, causing general quarters to be sounded throughout the ships of the landing force. The alert precipitated a scramble of four Lightnings from the 339th FS at 1120 and another of eight Airacobras at 1155 hours. The P-38s stayed aloft until 1235, the P-39s until 1345, but neither flight made contact with the elusive enemy planes that had by now reconnoitered the hilly Esperance area and left.

The destroyers *Nicholas* and *Radford* turned back to sea to screen those LCTs still waiting to come in as the landing operation got under way. The destroyers *DeHaven* and *Fletcher* remained off the landing area with the fighter CAP as the *Stringham* finished unloading its company of troops. The three LCTs had begun to unload when the force commander decided to land the remainder of his troops some one and one-half miles to the north along a beach-fringed bay at Verahue. Capt. Robert Briscoe accordingly split his four escorting destroyers into two pairs: the *Nicholas* and *DeHaven* were detailed to remain behind while the *Fletcher* and *Radford* were sent to cover the Verahue landing group. Meanwhile, the empty *Stringham* weighed anchor and steamed away on her own.

Japanese ground observers had kept Rabaul appraised of the progress of the American amphibious landings around Cape Esperance. Admiral Kusaka and General Imamura had immediately interpreted the troops spilling ashore as a direct threat to Operation KE, for the Tokyo Express intended to embark at least a portion of the 17th Army in the same general vicinity that night. Furthermore, if even one of the reconnaissance Bettys radioed back its findings, its report would have confirmed that the Americans were coming ashore behind the Japanese defensive perimeter. Earlier misidentification by the reconnoitering Dinah of the escorting destroyers as American cruisers had already alarmed the Japanese because even light cruisers could easily outgun the destroyers of the Tokyo Express should the two forces clash off Cape Esperance. After receiving this stream of reports, there was no mistaking the fact that the Americans, supported by warships, were attempting a major flanking movement in the worst possible place.

Reacting to this unexpected and unwelcome news, Rabaul hastily ordered the Japanese airbase at Kahili to scramble a strike force to neutralize the American naval presence around Esperance before Admiral Hashimoto's evacuation convoy arrived in the area. Eighteen Aichi D3A dive-bombers, commanded by the 582nd Kokutai's Lt. Tensai Kitamura, rose to seek out the U.S. "cruisers." After takeoff, however, three malfunctioning Vals had to turn back. With the remainder flew Lt. Saburo Shindo's twenty-one Zeros from the 582nd, accompanied by another nineteen A6Ms from the *Zuikaku* detachment, led by Lt. Kenjiro Notomi.

While the *DeHaven* cruised slowly to and fro off the landing beach at Nugu Point, Cdr. Charles Tolman authorized two of his vessel's four boilers to be shut down for routine maintenance at 1200 hours. This decision left her with a maximum speed of twenty knots in an emergency. Evidently, no such emergency was expected. The amphibious operation was proceeding smoothly. "Tojo time"—the daily air raid over Henderson Field and Lunga Roads that had occurred with almost clockwork regularity since the beginning of the Guadalcanal campaign—had come and gone. No other raids were expected. Though Japanese submarines were known to be operating in the Slot, no sightings or other indicators had thus far betrayed the presence of a sub lurking in the immediate vicinity. Two boilers were considered more than adequate to carry out the current screening routine.

The *DeHaven* and most of her crew were relative newcomers to the combat zone, having arrived in the Solomons only the previous December. She had been initially assigned to important but tedious convoy escort duty on the New Caledonia–Espiritu Santo–Guadalcanal run; there her crew had experienced an adrenaline surge on but one occasion—when they sighted and depth charged a suspected enemy submarine with unknown results. Subsequently attached to the Cactus Striking Force, she helped shell Japanese positions on Guadalcanal and participated in the night bombardment of the new Japanese base and airstrip at Vila-Stanmore. All in all, the *DeHaven* had performed these routine tasks satisfactorily—an ideal baptism of fire for a new ship and a novice crew. But these operations hardly furnished sufficient combat experience to qualify the *DeHaven* and her crew as veteran old salts. So it was that a willing but relatively untried ship left Nugu Point at 1300 with sister *Nicholas* to escort three empty LCTs back to their base.

Meanwhile, twenty Japanese destroyers had begun to steam down the Slot toward Guadalcanal. Vigilant coastwatchers monitored their progress, passing the information to the Cactus Air Force by radio. When this first evacuation convoy of Operation KE came within range, Cactus Strike Command ordered out the air strike it had been preparing. Suddenly, word of an inbound air raid came in. Cactus issued a red alert at 1430, but then canceled it at 1435 hours. A standby flight of five P-39s from the 67th FS, led by Capt. Jerry Sawyer, had scrambled in the interim. The Cobras were still climbing when Henderson Field and its satellite airstrips again went to Condition Red at 1443 hours. Only a portion of the antishipping strike had gotten into the air when the incoming raid was finally confirmed. Strike Command quickly directed those light bombers already aloft to leave the vicinity, instructing them to rendezvous to the east before the enemy arrived to attack the usual target: Henderson Field and its satellites.

Over the USAAF channel, Cactus Recon ordered airborne fighters to circle over the Lunga perimeter to intercept the oncoming Japanese. Captain Sawyer's flight struggled to gain altitude in their slow-climbing Airacobras, corkscrewing their way up around the airfield complex. Sawyer and lieutenants Barnes, Bauer, Patterson, and Robinson at length leveled off to search all around the compass for the raid that never came.

Upon issuing its red alert, Cactus apparently ordered the VMF-112 fighter CAP to continue covering the landing beach at Verahue, where three very vulnerable LCTs were still unloading in the custody of the two remaining destroyers.

Arriving over Tulagi with their fighter escort, the Val dive-bombers turned and headed west over Iron Bottom Sound. They were passing by Lunga Point when they spotted five U.S. warships ahead. Three miles southeast of Savo Island, the *Nicholas* and *DeHaven* were still returning from the landing area without fighter cover, escorting the three empty LCTs. As the JNAF strike force approached Cape Esperance, the Vals rapidly deployed to attack their oncoming quarry.

The *DeHaven* went to general quarters when the first bogey alert flashed out from Cactus. Her third and fourth boilers were relit, but were not put on line before the red alert was rescinded. Now a formation of planes was clearly seen approaching from astern, flying at five thousand feet. Having also received the warnings from Cactus control, the *Nicholas* reacted instinctively to the possible threat of air attack once the unidentified flight was sighted. She went to battle stations, worked up to flank speed, and lunged into an evasive maneuver. The *DeHaven*'s claxon sounded "general quarters" a second time. She sped up, but, not unlike the *Nicholas* earlier, she hesitated to take further action until her lookouts could positively identify the planes. She slowed while gun crews apprehensively tracked the incoming raid, awaiting the order to open fire.

Perhaps lulled into a false sense of complacency by the familiar air activity building up over nearby Lunga Roads as the outgoing Cactus strike force began to gather, the officers manning the *DeHaven*'s bridge momentarily mistook the newcomers for Americans. Indeed, a flight of Airacobras had just overflown the convoy at low altitude around 1330—probably the eight P-39s scrambled by Cactus Recon at 1155, now on their way back to Fighter Two. Moreover, as seen from the *DeHaven*'s bridge, the planes still orbiting above Lunga Point appeared to be part of the same group as the approaching aircraft, signifying that the latter could be friendly. The *DeHaven* apparently did not receive radio warnings from the *Nicholas*. Another fateful minute elapsed before the lookouts and other crewmen recognized the oncoming bogeys as Japanese. By the time all doubt had vanished, it was too late: six Vals were pushing over to plunge down on the *DeHaven*.

Commander Tolman belatedly called for air support—a task he should have delegated to his communications officer—while gunners waited for his order to open fire. Some had barely opened up on their own with light automatic weapons when the *DeHaven* shuddered under the impact of the first bomb. It hit her amidships, detonating deep in the engineering area to break her back. Her main battery had fired its first salvos when a second missile struck directly aft of the forward funnel, knocking it over and lifting the 5-inch gun-director off its base. The explosion apparently did not penetrate below the stack as no men in the areas beneath it were hit. A near miss mushroomed off her port side, followed by another direct hit forward on her Number 2 turret. The resulting explosion detonated the magazines beneath both forward turrets, pulverizing the bridge and pilothouse, a mere dozen feet back. A sole bridge officer survived the fatal blast.

Almost torn apart, obscured by two columns of thick brownish-black smoke erupting from the first and third hits, the *DeHaven* plunged to the bottom in less than five minutes, taking nearly half her crew with her. Another 146 officers and men—38 of them wounded—survived long enough to be rescued by the LCTs.

Upon seeing the first six Vals dive on the *DeHaven*, the *Nicholas* opened fire at 1454 hours. The remaining Vals stalked the *Nicholas*, maneuvering to get the sun at their backs before closing in through scattered cloud cover to take her under attack. She was by now fleeing from her assailants flat out at thirty-two knots. Lt. Cdr. Andrew Hill conned her through a series of cornering maneuvers, desperately trying to evade his assailants. Above and below decks, men hung on as the *Nicholas* heeled over hard-a-starboard then canted hard to port. Her wild gyrations and hot AA fire, supported by the 20-mm mounts of the nearby LCTs, limited the enemy pilots to near misses until 1457, when a paint scraper caused the loss of steering control on the bridge. The rudder shifted from full-right to midships before steering was quickly shifted to the steering-motor room and full-right rudder regained. Bomb fragments cut down men on her decks, killing two, seriously wounding six, and inflicting flesh wounds on several others. All told, the Vals dropped sixteen 551-pound bombs on the two destroyers. When the attackers broke off, the *DeHaven* was gone, but the *Nicholas* was still afloat. She claimed three Vals shot down; the LCTs added a fourth.

A quartet each of 339th FS P-38s and 44th FS P-40s were already airborne, preparing to rendezvous with the TBFs and SBDs, when they, too, received the order from Cactus Recon to circle the airfields in anticipation of an air attack. Amidst clear skies, the Lightnings began to orbit at 22,000 feet, the Warhawks at 18,000 feet. From their vantage point, lieutenants Fred Purnell, Besby Holmes, Stan Cramer, and Murray Shubin of the 339th readily spotted eight to ten unidentified planes flying between Cape Esperance and Savo Island. Then they saw splashes from near misses and flashes from hits on the fore part of a destroyer that disappeared within five minutes. Once the attack on the *DeHaven* had begun, Cactus Recon radioed bearing and distance of the action to all USAAF fighters, no doubt in response to Commander Tolman's plea for help. But the Fighter Two controller came on the air, instructing the "escort fighters to carry on original mission." This totally confused the P-38 pilots.

Leading the P-40s, Maj. Kermit Tyler likely heard Cactus Recon's directive to head for Savo Island; if he picked up the Fighter Two controller's message to rendezvous with the strike force some ten miles to the east, he chose to ignore it. Major Tyler led Capt. Ken Taylor and lieutenants "Doc" Wheadon and Bob Westbrook over to Savo, but could find no enemy planes. All at once the Warhawk pilots saw a flash over a destroyer "off Cactus"— below to their right. Swinging to pass over the area, they observed little more than an oil slick. The Vals and escorting Zeros had reformed to the northwest of Savo by this time, and were now heading back up the Slot. Apparently Capt. Jerry Sawyer's P-39 flight did not receive Cactus Recon's order to head for Savo Island; once scrambled, Sawyer continued to circle the airfields until eventually called down at 1615 hours.

Captain Fraser's two divisions of VMF-112 Wildcats were preparing to join up with the antishipping strike when the attack on the two destroyers and three LCTs began. Apparently not receiving any instructions to the contrary over the USN–USMC channel, Fraser led his and Lt. Gil Percy's divisions, including section leaders Captain Mike Yunck and Lt. Sam Richards, toward the scene of the battle. They came close enough to witness the three fatal bomb hits. Fraser later recalled, "There was a black billow of smoke that hid the destroyer. Then I saw the bow, just the bow, coming slowly out from under. It sank. Like somebody had whacked the ship with a big fist."

VMF 112's Wildcats caught up to the Japanese about three miles west of Savo. There the F4F pilots fought it out with an estimated thirty Zeros from the 582nd Kokutai and the *Zuikaku* Hikokitai. Lt. Percy's Wildcat seemed to be everywhere at once. Twisting and turning among the enemy fighters, he claimed four Zeros destroyed. Two more Zeros apparently fell before Lt. Addison Raber's guns. Lt. Wayne Laird and Lt. Stan Synar each put in for one. Lt. John Stack's Wildcat was hit with 7.7-mm and 20-mm fire, but he claimed a Zero in return.

Lt. Otto Seifert also claimed a Zeke before another shot away his oil cooler. Seifert's faltering F4F fell away, but he grimly coaxed it back to Guadalcanal before ditching in shallow water, returning to base unharmed. One Zero bounced Lieutenant Richards before he could score, firing several cannon shells into his fuselage. A 20-mm round burst in his cockpit, pelting his legs with hot shrapnel. Richards, too, made it back to Cactus where his wounds were diagnosed as not serious. Captain Fraser, with lieutenants Laird and Synar, managed to break through to the vulnerable dive-bombers. Fraser claimed three Vals and, somewhere along the way, picked up a pair of 7.7-mm bullet holes in the tail of his F4F. Laird and Synar claimed one apiece.

One Val aircrew found itself under attack by Lt. John Moran, who had followed Fraser's flight. But the luck of the Irish seemed to desert him. By the time Moran lined up the dive-bomber, Fraser, Laird, and Synar had turned away to engage attacking Zekes. Suddenly all alone, Moran was jumped by CPO Saburo Saito and three other Zeros of the *Zuikaku*'s fighter *hikotai*. Hit in the motor, Moran's F4F emerged from the contest trailing thick smoke, and was last seen in a glide toward Savo Island, his attackers still in pursuit. One Zero pilot put down his flaps, methodically pouring machine-gun and cannon rounds into the lame Wildcat's tail. The desperate Marine hunkered down against his armor-plated seat as slugs tore away his canteen and safety belt.

Having coolly riddled the F4F, the Irishman's assailants broke off to claim a joint victory—Saito's first. Moran now began to ponder the intricacies of a water landing as the ocean rose swiftly up to meet him. The Wildcat slapped into the water and furrowed to a sudden stop. Moran pitched forward into his gunsight, fracturing his nose. Squirming out of the foundering plane's cockpit, he inflated his Mae West and swam to shore, where natives took him to the camp of an American Army detachment. There a corpsman treated his injuries. The downed aviator arrived back at Cactus on 2 February. He was further treated for his broken nose, cuts to his chin and mouth, a swollen right eye, and shrapnel wounds in his right leg. In truth he was fortunate to be alive: perhaps a shamrock had cast its lucky spell over Lieutenant Moran after all.

The Marine Corps pilots put in for ten Zeros and five Vals destroyed in addition to the four Vals claimed by U.S. warships. Admitted Japanese losses from both the air combat and air–sea action included one Val shot down plus four missing; another four were damaged. Five Zeros were destroyed, and another three were damaged. Among the Zero pilots lost were CPO Soji Chiba and PO2c Sakuji Tanaka from the *Zuikaku* detachment, plus PO2c Saburo Horida and PO2c Tatsuo Morioka from the 582nd Kokutai. The 582nd's LA Yoshio Ozawa was hit and forced to ditch, but was rescued. Most of the surviving Zeros made it back to Buin; five A6Ms landed at Ballale, and another five pushed on to Buka. One of the three damaged *Zuikaku* Zeros was forced to put in at Munda. At 1700 the remaining Vals pancaked at Munda to refuel before continuing on to Buin, where they finally landed at 1800 hours.

Japanese airmen submitted claims for thirteen out of twenty F4Fs destroyed, whereas the Cactus Air Force actually suffered two F4Fs shot down and two damaged.

The 347th Fighter Group's report pointedly summed up the obfuscating role played by Cactus fighter controllers in the demise of the *DeHaven*: "Confusion and chaos prevailed regarding instructions. Without doubt the destroyer would have been saved if logical instructions had been directed. TARFU."

The 347th may have overstated its case, but contradictory orders had undoubtedly stymied any timely interception by the USAAF pilots. Moreover, neglecting to detail even a section of F4Fs from the VMF-112 CAP to escort the returning ships was undoubtedly a pivotal factor in the loss of the *DeHaven*. Her violent demise earned her the dubious distinction of being the last major U.S. warship sunk in the Guadalcanal campaign. Just as unenviable was her record as having the most short-lived career of any U.S. destroyer in World War II—a mere 121 days.

This round went to the Americans, but it was a Pyrrhic victory. All the GIs and Marines made it on shore on the far side of Cape Esperance without any disruption by land or air from the Japanese. However, the sacrifice of the *DeHaven* and the damaged sustained by the *Nicholas* seriously undermined the ability of the Cactus Striking Force to oppose the Tokyo Express later that evening. Moreover, besides sinking one destroyer and damaging another, the two Japanese air raids inadvertently delayed the Cactus Air Force's strike on the incoming destroyers by several hours, making it all but impossible to launch any follow-up strikes as these would have arrived over the Japanese convoy after sunset.

CHAPTER 12
THE GREAT ESCAPE BEGINS

Maj. Earl Hall, CO of the 42nd BS(H), had brought the squadron's five operational B-17s from Button to Cactus between 29 and 31 January to undertake reconnaissance missions and to bolster any upcoming bombing forays against the fat shipping targets building up in Shortland and Tonolei Harbors. The fifth plane returned to Button on 30 January, allegedly for an unexpected major overhaul. During the evening of 31 January the ground crews of the 31st BS prepared three of the four remaining Forts for an early-morning mission up the Slot in the company of a flight of B-17s from the 72nd BS. Eight 500-pound bombs were hoisted into the racks next to the auxiliary fuel tank of each bomber.

Six 72nd BS Forts took off at 0535 on 1 February; with them went the three B-17s of the 42nd BS. Why the fourth 42nd BS ship missed the lineup is not known. Maj. Narce Whitaker's nine bombers rendezvoused at 0615 between Cape Esperance and Savo Island with Capt. Albert Johnson's five P-40s from the 44th FS and with four P-38s from the 339th FS, led by Capt. John Mitchell. Arriving over southern Bougainville at 0840, the strike force scanned the area from 15,000 feet for targets of choice: freighters, transports, and tankers. Between them, the harbors at Shortland and Tonolei had grown target-rich overnight; the strike force counted some thirty-two ships—the increase likely due to the arrival of the remaining destroyers assigned to the Tokyo Express evacuation run.

Capt. Jay Thomas of the 72nd, piloting the last bomber in the formation, called the attention of the two flight leaders to the especially large assemblage of shipping off Faisi. The Warhawks maintained low cover at 16,000 feet, with the Lightnings flying top cover at 18,000 feet while the big

Boeings made their bombing runs in two flights of five and four planes, respectively. Heavy flak from harbor and shore batteries burst dangerously close all around them. Unloading forty 500-pounders on the 6,853-ton seaplane tender *Kamikawa Maru*, riding at anchor in Shortland Harbor, the first flight banked to the left, followed by the fighter escort. Geysers of water leaped skyward, and an explosion flashed on the bow of the seaplane tender. A nearby freighter, the *Kanagawa Maru*, was hit twice. Both ships were last seen on fire. Heavy flak bracketed the five Forts, but all managed to remain in formation. When the lead flight emerged from the flak belt, five Zeros from the 204th Kokutai moved in to attack it.

Major Hall, who was leading the second B-17 flight, was accustomed to flying unescorted over Japanese territory. Trying to avoid the attacking Zeros and AA fire, he aborted his bomb run to lead his flight in a right turn for a run over Tonolei Harbor. In the South Pacific, this tactic, though not prudent, was not as risky as it would have been in Europe, where the key to the self-defense of B-17s against the lethal punch of Messerschmitts and Focke-Wulfs proved to be group integrity—best achieved by flying in large, tight formations. Aptly named, each Flying Fortress carried at least ten .50-caliber machine guns; these contributed to the cumulative firepower of close-flying bombers. To abandon this defensive umbrella was to court disaster.

But B-17 tactics in the South Pacific placed less stress on group integrity. Lightly armed Japanese fighters found the sturdy Forts difficult nuts to crack; many fell to the bombers' heavy machine guns in the attempt. Sporting only a 7.7-mm machine gun and a 12.7-mm machine cannon, JAAF Oscars tended to veer off when B-17 gunners opened up. Armed with a pair each of cannon and light machine guns, JNAF Zero pilots were more aggressive, attacking B-17s in individual, uncoordinated, high-side and low-quarter passes, making of their Zeros solitary targets for the concentrated fire of bomber gunners. Alternately, some tried snap rolls with triggers depressed, spraying the bombers with random fire as they curved through the formation. This shotgun tactic also achieved little. Japanese fighter pilots soon learned through experience that the surest way to down a B-17 was to hit the cockpit or other vital spots, such as the engines. Daring frontal runs to near-point-blank range were executed to neutralize the flight deck. Most enemy fighters were routinely delivering head-on attacks by the spring of 1942.

The B-17s opened their bomb bays as Major Hall's flight began its run over Tonolei Harbor. "Thirty-two 500-pound bombs were dropped in salvo from 13,000 feet at a concentration of ships in the harbor," noted Maj. W. H. McCarroll, the 347th Fighter Group's flight surgeon riding as an observer in the last Fort of the second flight. Three bombs were thought to have hit a transport. No sooner had the first two-plane element broken away to rejoin the main group than flak burst directly beneath the still-yawning bomb bay of Major Hall's wingman, Capt. Frank Houx of the 42nd BS. "Eager Beavers" disintegrated in a blinding flash when sizzling shrapnel punched into the auxiliary fuel tank, igniting volatile fumes.

Shaken by the violent explosion, the three surviving bombers in the second flight rallied to tighten up their formation. Possibly trying to escape intense and accurate AA fire, these B-17s made a 90-degree turn over Bougainville toward Choiseul—*away* from the rest of the formation. This time the flight leader's decision proved to be tactically unsound. The lone trio of unescorted Forts was halfway across the Slot when disaster struck in Spades: some thirty Mitsubishis swarmed all over them. "The Zeros were all 'square wing tip,'" reported Major McCarroll of the ones that went after his Fort. "The 'rising sun' was painted on the underside of each wing, but there was no insignia on the fuselage. They were painted a light khaki color with a slight sheen."

Major McCarroll identified the Hamps of the 204th Kokutai among the attacking fighters. The pilots from the 204th were led by ace Lt. (jg) Takeshi Morisaki. Leading Morisaki's second and third *shotai*, respectively, were aces CPO Yukiharu Ozeki and CPO Yoshimi Hidaka. Wingmen leading airmen Seiichi Kurosawa, Ryoji Ohara, Takeo Sakano, Shoichi Sugita, and Hideo Watanabe were all destined to become ace pilots. The observant flight surgeon also noticed that a third of the Zeros carried belly tanks. These particular A6Ms belonged to the 252nd Kokutai that was preparing to depart on the long journey to its new posting at Truk when it was scrambled out of Ballale—hence the drop tanks. Forty-seven Zeros intercepted the B-17s that day: eleven from the 204th, seventeen from the 252nd, five from the 253rd, and fourteen from the 582nd. Interestingly, all four squadrons subsequently put in separate claims for four Forts destroyed.

Major Hall managed to keep his three planes in formation until they approached Choiseul. During that time the flight's gunners apparently shot down four enemy fighters. The situation had grown desperate but not yet hopeless. Then, unexpectedly, Maj. Harold Hensley of the 42nd broke formation, turning southeast in an ill-advised solo attempt to cut back across the Slot to rejoin the main formation. A flock of clipped-wing Hamps immediately cut him off from the rest of his flight, then proceeded to shoot up "Yokahama Express." Hensley apparently managed to make a water landing, but he and his crew were never heard from again.

Major Hall and his remaining wingman now turned eastward, heading for Cactus. As he and Captain Thomas passed over the northern tip of Choiseul, another flak barrage enveloped the two B-17s. The CO's plane started to drop behind with a smoking engine, but managed to catch up again after five minutes. The tailing Hamps renewed their attacks, emboldened by the separation—first of the two bomber flights, then of the planes within the second flight. Pressing home their firing passes with daring and determination, these superb Zero pilots made coordinated runs from around the clock to split up the defensive fire of the B-17 gunners.

Not surprisingly, the favorite tactic of these seasoned veterans was to bore in head-on, guns blazing. Captain Thomas' copilot caught a spray of exploding 20-mm shrapnel from one Hamp. Other rounds punched through the Plexiglas nose of the B-17, grievously wounding Lieutenant Inman, the bombardier. Next, 7.7-mm and 20-mm fire walked along the bomber's fuselage, hitting the radio operator as he manned his gun. Farther back, Corporal Murphy recoiled from his waist gun and slumped down among empty shell casings. Major Hall's Fortress faltered once more under an equally devastating attack, dropping back as it lost speed. Finally, on fire with two Zeros circling above, the ravaged B-17 fell off toward the ocean near Ringana Point.

The lone survivor continued along the northern coast of Choiseul, pursued by some fifteen Hamps. A desperate Captain Thomas firewalled his engines. The four Wright R1820 radials howled in protest as Thomas thrust the bomber into a power dive from 13,000 feet. At 10,000 feet, the airspeed indicator was already passing through 250 knots with the engines drawing fifty inches of mercury. Leveling off at 1,200 feet, the Boeing managed to gain some respite from its tormentors whose dwindling numbers could now only attack in level passes or from above in shallow dives. The antagonists were passing over the eastern tip of Santa Ysabel when the last Hamps broke off.

By then twenty minutes had elapsed since the bomber's fifties last returned fire. The tail-gun position, the top turret, and the ball turret were all in a shambles; the other gunners had run out of ammunition; crewmen suffered from various wounds. The running fight had lasted fifty-five terrifying minutes. Try as they might, the shrinking group of Mitsubishis could not muster enough firepower to knock the Fort down—proof of the Zero's inadequacy as an interceptor when attacking large bombers in small numbers. Conversely, the bomber crew claimed they sent three more Zeros "crashing into the water." No A6Ms were lost, but five were hit by B-17 gunners.

Somehow the rugged Fort held together, but just barely. Engines one and two were running rough at about one-third their normal thrust. All trim-tab cables had been severed. Without the ability to trim the plane, the torque from the engines made it almost impossible to keep the damaged behemoth on an even keel. Captain Thomas began to look for a place to set his ship down in a water landing. But everyone on board except for him and Major McCarroll was wounded, the bombardier and the waist gunner grievously. These two crewmen would likely not have survived a water landing. Refusing to give up, the resourceful plane commander and his copilot managed to wedge their knees against their control columns, keeping the yokes forward while they wrestled to maintain sufficient left-rudder to offset the torque and keep the plane level. And this is how the flying sieve reached Guadalcanal. In the words of the good doctor, "After manually cranking down the landing gear and flaps, a near-perfect landing was made on Henderson Field even though both tires were flat." Only in the movies, you say?

With the way temporarily cleared of U.S. Navy task forces after the Battle of Rennell Island, the destroyers earmarked for the first evacuation run prepared to sortie for Guadalcanal as dawn broke over Shortland Harbor on 1 February 1943. Admiral Hashimoto's destroyer flotilla had been gathering while he and his superiors awaited the outcome of the clash off Rennell Island. Over the course of the evacuation phase of Operation KE, twenty-two destroyers in total were placed under Hashimoto's command: nine *Kagero* class, four *Yugumo* class, three each of the *Mutsuki* and *Asashio* classes, two *Shiratsu* class, and one *Fubuki* class. Of these, he assigned twenty to this first evacuation run.

A B-17 reconnaissance plane reported thirty-five ships in the Shortland-Tonolei harbor complex at 0820, just twenty minutes before the antishipping strike arrived, but took no particular notice of the concentration of destroyers preparing for their imminent departure. At 0950 the Fort was jumped by a *shotai* of 253rd Kokutai Zeros called down from Buka to stand in on local patrol duty for Kahili's and Ballale's exhausted fighters after their scrap with the B-17s. Thrown off course by attempts to evade their attackers, the B-17's crew claimed one Zero out of the six they estimated had jumped them. While no Zeros were lost, the intercept dissuaded the snooper from further examining the Shortlands-Tonolei harbor complex.

Having been fortunate not to attract the B-17 raiders or the reconnaissance Fort, Admiral Hashimoto set out from the Shortlands around midday with his twenty destroyers grouped in two divisions: the transports *Akigumo, Hamakaze, Isokaze, Kazagumo, Makigumo, Tanikaze, Yugumo,* and *Urakaze*—screened by the *Fumizuki, Kawakaze, Kuroshio, Maikaze, Makinami,* and *Shirayuki*—formed the Cape Esperance unit; the transports *Arashio, Oshio, Tokitsukaze,* and *Yukikaze*—screened by the *Nagatsuki* and *Satsuki*—formed the Kamimbo unit.

No luckier than General Patch's amphibious force, however, the Tokyo Express had little chance of passing the Central Solomons undetected. The first of two messages from Lt. Nick Waddell and Lt. Carden Seton on Choiseul alerted Cactus at 1222 that fifteen light cruisers and destroyers were leaving Faisi. Then they radioed that two heavy cruisers and two light cruisers were steaming past Choiseul in the company of sixteen destroyers. Alarm spread throughout the theater's high command. When Lt. Henry Josslyn reported that twenty destroyers were steaming east-southeast due north of Vella Lavella, his revised estimate set minds at ease. A Kiwi Hudson on patrol picked up the convoy abeam of Vella Lavella at 1320. It reported again at 1515, positioning the ships 210 miles from Cactus, further galvanizing Cactus into action.

Eighteen SBDs from VMSB-234, together with seven TBFs from VMSB-131, began taking off from Henderson Field at 1425. Less than five minutes into the takeoff routine, Cactus set Condition Red, but canceled it five minutes later. Then "Condition is red!" sounded again at 1443. At 1505 Henderson ordered all airborne bombers orbiting over Lunga Point to rendezvous ten miles to the east for protection from an untimely enemy air raid winging its way in beyond Savo Island. There the SBDs and TBFs circled impatiently, oblivious to the distant death knell of the *DeHaven* about to be sounded off Savo Island.

Initially ordered to protect the airfield complex by circling overhead, one flight of Airacobras and another of Warhawks were belatedly directed to the scene of the action, but only the P-40s responded. Wildcats also winged their way toward Savo Island. A flight of Lightnings, trying to unravel conflicting orders, watched from the sidelines as bomb explosions flashed in the distance, rending the *DeHaven* asunder.

It was 1530 when Condition Green was restored; Strike Command ordered the fledgling air strike, still orbiting out of harm's way east of Henderson Field, to pancake. The planes began touching down at 1545 with ground crews standing by to refuel them. Lt. Jack Malcolm and Lt. Arvid Blackmun of VMSB-234 had already landed shortly after takeoff, plagued by mechanical problems. Capt. Dick Blain and Lt. Dayton Swickard had also returned after their planes accidentally brushed each other as the SBDs were trying to rendezvous after lifting off. After their scrap with the attacking Vals and Zeros, the F4F escort also had to land, rearm, and refuel.

The shattered wreck of the *DeHaven* had hardly begun to settle into the seabed of Iron Bottom Sound when Strike Command ordered its preempted strike force back into the air. Between 1655 and 1725, seventeen VMSB-234 Dauntlesses and seven VMSB-131 Avengers roared back into the sky to join up with seventeen Wildcats from VMF-112 and VMO-251. With them went four Airacobras, four Warhawks, and four Lightnings from the 67th, 44th, and 339th FSs, respectively.

Wasting no time, the formation set off up the Slot in search of the twenty Japanese destroyers. Flying as an observer in MTSgt. Leon Julien's TBF was VMSB-131's intelligence officer, Lt. Bob Montgomery. A "frantic" message transmitted at 1700 on Rendova by Lt. Dick Horton, who was probably relaying information from Maj. Donald Kennedy based in eastern New Georgia, reported the Japanese to be 180 miles from Guadalcanal. Flying on a course of 303 degrees through a cumulus-sprinkled afternoon sky, the strike force easily located the Tokyo Express at 1820, steaming northeast of Vangunu Island—only 135 miles out (see map 5).

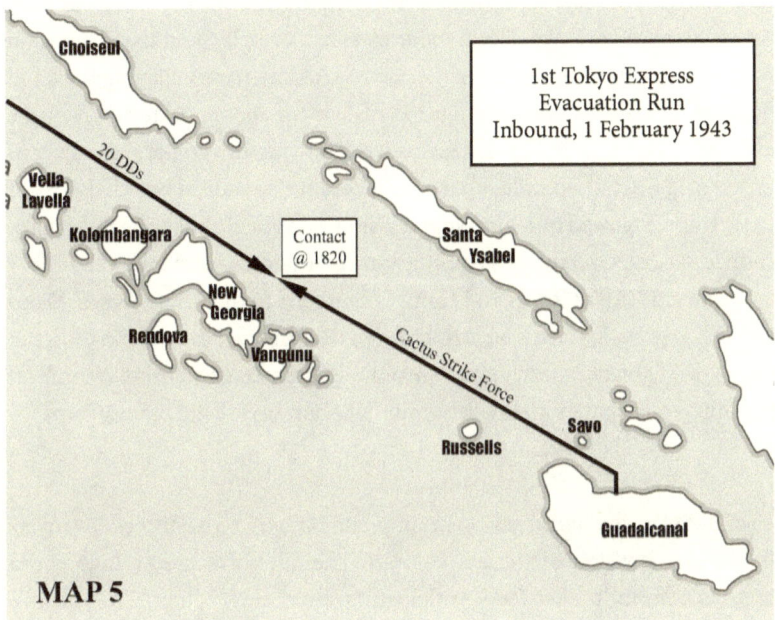

MAP 5

Some American pilots intimated they readily recognized "*Terutsuki*"-class destroyers knifing through the water below at close to thirty knots. The *Teruzuki* belonged to the *Akizuki* class—the largest Japanese destroyers afloat. Primarily designed as AA ships, these formidable, single-stack vessels boasted four pairs of 3.9-inch dual-purpose guns and upwards of fifteen 25-mm AA guns. The unfortunate *Teruzuki* herself had succumbed in early December 1942—not to air attack, but to a bold assault by Cactus PT boats while she helped guard the Tokyo Express as it unloaded supplies off Cape Esperance.

One would have expected to find *Akizuki*-class destroyers assigned to Operation KE, given the high risk of aerial attack, but this was not the case. Yet this fixation with "*Terutsuki*"-class destroyers on the part of Cactus fliers persisted, mission after mission, throughout Operation KE. "There appeared to be a destroyer leader of *Terutsuki* class . . . at the head of each column," remarked one combat report. "Other DD's [sic] were smaller and probably two stackers." Another noted, "There is some indication that the new single stack DD was represented."

Admiral Hashimoto would have undoubtedly been grateful for a specimen or two of the *Akizuki* class; as it was, he had to content himself with the nine *Kagero*-class and four *Yugumo*-class destroyers, both of which sported respectable AA batteries. The *Yugumo* class had actually been the inspiration behind the design blueprint for the *Akizuki* AA destroyers. Playing the hand dealt to him, the admiral configured his convoy for rapid dispersal in the event of an air attack. His destroyers were moving in two parallel columns of ten ships, each two miles apart. Each column contained two divisions of three ships, followed by a four-ship division, all spaced about one mile apart. Individual destroyers were steaming at three-hundred-yard intervals.

A mixed CAP of Zekes and Hamps belonging to the Ballale-based 252nd Kokutai kept vigil. Cactus airmen grossly overestimated the covering force at thirty-two fighters; in fact, there were only eighteen Zeros on hand to confront the thirty-one fighters and twenty-four light bombers flying against them.

VMSB-234's dive-bombers went in first, targeting the three destroyers in the first division of the left column. The SBDs executed a high-speed approach from 11,500 feet. Anticipating an enemy fighter CAP nearby, Capt. Dick Blain, the flight leader, leveled off momentarily at 8,000 feet for a quick glance around before pushing over into an off-beam attack. Plunging through the first angry bursts of flak, Captain Blain released his 1,000-pound bomb as his altimeter needle passed through 1,500 feet. The lead destroyer was careening to starboard when the 1,000-pounder struck her amidships. A ball of flame erupted skyward.

The other Dauntlesses then dropped toward the rapidly scattering ships in individual head-on dives. Lieutenants Don Russell, Carl Brorein, "Howie" Murphy, and John Beebe, and Capt. Otis Calhoun also dove on what appears to be Admiral Hashimoto's flagship—the *Makinami*. Lieutenant Russell scored a second hit amidships. Lieutenants Brorein and Murphy dropped their bombs into the cloud of smoke boiling upwards for what each believed to be a probable hit. Captain Calhoun's 1,000-pounder sent up a geyser of spume about fifteen feet astern, but Lieutenant Beebe's missile detonated squarely on the *Makinami*'s stern.

Steaming behind the *Makinami*, her guns spitting venom, the second destroyer reeled out of line to port, hoping to throw off an impending onslaught by three SBDs. Capt. Hoyle Barr's bomb smacked into the water some twenty-five feet short of the target's bow. Lt. Arvid "Art" Blackmun and Lt. Bob Ayers dropped their 1,000-pound bombs close off the starboard bow as the destroyer emerged from its 90-degree arc unscathed.

The third destroyer in line enjoyed an equally charmed life as she struggled to fend off attacks by six dive-bombers. Lieutenants Jack Malcolm and Andy Csaky loosed 1,000-pound bombs that exploded close on board the target's starboard beam as she canted into a sharp turn. Lt. Israel Boniske's salvo of one 500-pounder and two 100-pounders splashed into the same area. Boniske's rear gunner managed to strafe the destroyer during the SBD's pullout. Lieutenant Ayers zoomed past after diving on the second destroyer, enabling his gunner to spray the third destroyer with three hundred rounds of .30-caliber fire. Another 1,000-pounder, released by TSgt. Bob Fore, registered a near miss off her port quarter. Then the destroyer's stern lurched upward under the impact of Capt. George Wilcox' near miss off her fantail. Her luck somewhat tarnished, the beleaguered vessel churned away, having negotiated a complete 180-degree turn to starboard.

Neither captains Art Moran nor Sumner Whitten was able to drop his bombs due to faulty release mechanisms. Japanese AA fire intensified as the SBDs pressed home their attack. Lt. "I. J." Williams' Dauntless took a fatal hit. It immediately burst into flames and crashed into the sea, killing Williams and his gunner, Sgt. Amos Hawkes.

Within moments the torpedo bombers of VMSB-131 pushed over to begin their runs, but the tactical situation had already been altered. What had been an orderly convoy of two parallel columns now devolved into three unequal, ragged rows of squirming ships. The left column had swelled to eleven destroyers, including the damaged *Makinami*. The right column was down to a single four-ship division, its other members having swung to port to form a middle column of three destroyers, followed at a distance by two others. This column closed with the besieged left column to add its firepower to the latter's flak barrage.

Above, a *chutai* of Zeros flying low cover had streaked down to break up the SBD attack, but stopped short of penetrating the intimidating phalanx of Wildcats protecting the SBDs. The F4F divisions of Maj. John Renner and

Capt. Mike Yunck managed to keep the hesitant enemy interceptors at bay while the dive-bombers went in.

Flying high cover at 22,000 feet, Lt. Fred Purnell, leading the four P-38s, sighted two six-plane *chutai* of enemy fighters, flying slightly ahead—probably the Zeros of the 252nd. The Japanese turned sharply to get in behind the Lightnings, whereupon the P-38 pilots gunned their engines and climbed to lure their stalkers away from the light bombers at work below. The enemy pilots took the bait but only momentarily, following the Lockheeds up to 25,000 feet before breaking off the pursuit to dive back down.

Maj. Kermit Tyler's four P-40s were flying medium cover when they caught sight of, and were in turn spotted by, the dozen returning Zeros now cruising some 3,500 feet above them. Exploiting their altitude advantage, the Japanese pilots at first tried to harass the Warhawk flight in an attempt to break it up. Seeing that these tactics were not working, both *chutai* peeled off and dove for the P-40s. Individual dogfights broke out as the outnumbered Hawk pilots strove to drive Zeros off one another's tails. Inevitably, Lt. "Doc" Wheadon's P-40 caught a burst of 7.7-mm and 20-mm fire that ate through his stabilizer and wounded him in the calf, but he got away. Trying in vain to buy time for the TBFs, the P-40s were soon dispersed by their determined assailants.

Thanks to the sizable F4F contingent that stayed with the SBDs, the latter were not molested by other A6Ms waiting in the wings. Not so the torpedo bombers. With the four P-40s hopelessly engaged, some of the Zekes and Hamps seized the chance to bore through and intercept the TBFs and their four escorting P-39s.

The Cobras gamely followed the Avengers down to three thousand feet in a desperate attempt to shield them from the onrushing enemy. But it was no contest: quickly overwhelmed, the P-39 pilots simply could not handle that many Japanese fighters any more than the P-40s could—even at an optimal performance altitude for their Bell fighters.

One four-plane string of Zekes attacked together; the rest came in singly after the four P-39s. At one point Capt. Jerry Sawyer, the flight leader, found himself surrounded by no fewer than eight Mitsubishis. One Zero attempted a high-side pass on Sawyer. When the enemy pilot zoomed into his pullout, he poured on the coal and caught up. As the P-39's guns raked its fuselage, the A6M2 caught fire and fell into the sea. Lt. Bob Bauer of the

67th was less fortunate: fatally hit by enemy machine-gun and cannon fire, his faltering fighter disappeared below, taking him with it.

Eluding every effort of the valiant P-39 pilots to stop them, a dozen or so Zeros left the Cobras high and dry. Undeterred, the enemy fighters waded into the torpedo bombers, giving the seven Avengers scant opportunity to drop their ordnance accurately. Practically every TBF was attacked as it began its bombing glide or torpedo run.

Capt. Frank Smyth and Lt. Dean "Snuffy" Dalton were so busy dodging enemy fighters that neither could maneuver into a satisfactory release position. One Zero pumped a half-dozen rounds into the rear cockpit area of Smyth's Avenger, wounding both turret gunner Pfc. Larry Winkle and radio-gunner TSgt. Abe Leon. Gliding through eight thousand feet on his bombing run, Smyth was beset by heavy flak that registered hits on the Avenger's tail. Lieutenant Dalton "was attacked in gusto by Zeros." Shrapnel from an exploding 20-mm shell wounded him in the shoulder. Gunner Pfc. Oren Childress put finis to a Hamp firing from low astern, but not before explosive rounds chewed up the TBF's underside, creating gaping holes through which Childress could see the water below. The A6M3 absorbed a prolonged burst from Childress' .30-caliber "stinger," caught fire, and was last seen plummeting seaward, belching flames and smoke.

Lt. Barney McShane released his four 500-pounders on a destroyer near the rear of the left column, rocking it with near misses. Targeting the second destroyer in the left column, Capt. Jim Maguire claimed a probable hit and several near misses with his bomb salvo. In a parting gesture, the destroyer's gunners deposited a 25-mm round in the tail of his Avenger as he pulled out.

Flying a torpedo-armed Avenger, Capt. Bill Dean suddenly found himself in the unwelcome company of a Zero. The Japanese pilot raked the TBF with 7.7-mm and 20-mm fire as Dean began his torpedo run. A flurry of explosive rounds slammed into Dean's plane, wounding him and radio-gunner SSgt. John Bruder, who took a 7.7-mm slug through the buttock. The turret gunner finally exacted revenge on their tormentor; SSgt. Emmanuel DiTiberio's return fire flamed the Zero. The A6M fell off and splashed into the water, leaving DiTiberio slightly wounded with only three rounds left in his gun. Dean finally managed to drop his fish, but it went wide.

Lieutenant Dean's chagrin turned to shock when he saw MTSgt. Leon Julien's Avenger cartwheel into the water and disintegrate. Killed were the pilot, turret gunner Pfc. George Brown, radio-gunner Pfc. Gerry Shroeder, and the squadron intelligence officer. Capt. Art Molvik's TBF went in unobserved. Molvik, his turret gunner, SSgt. Bob Gough, and radio-gunner, Sgt. Gerry Chaplin, were last seen flying off the coast of Vangunu.

Now it became every man for himself. The remaining five Avenger pilots broke off, scrambling out of the area with throttles wide open. Of course Captain Dean brought along company: a Zero tailed him for what seemed like an eternity until, likely low on fuel, the enemy pilot turned away before he could administer the coup de grâce. With its hydraulic system inoperative and its flaps useless, Dean's battered TBF raced into Henderson Field in twilight at one hundred knots or more. Under the skillful coaxing of its injured pilot, it finally rolled to a stop. Seriously wounded as well, Lieutenant Dalton also managed to land his plane without cracking up. Scarred by some sixty-seven punctures, Captain Dean's Avenger resembled more a sieve than an aircraft. Not surprisingly, both it and Lieutenant Dalton's badly holed TBF were declared hors de combat and towed off to the bone yard.

Reporting on the mission, the pilots of VMSB-131 vented their frustration at the mauling inflicted upon them. The squadron war diary for February mentions poignantly, "The activity of our fighters was not observed." The combat action report for 1 February waxed more venomous: "None of our fighters made any effort to beat off Zeros which attacked before runs could be made." Reflecting further on the event, the vexed aircrews at length gleaned some reassurance from a report that "fighters were tangling Jap vs. U.S. at higher altitudes." But the squadron war diary hastened to add, "No planes were seen to be shot down in this fighter scrap."

In fact, the day had not gone well for the USAAF escort. Unable to score more than a single victory over the Japanese, the four P-40s and the quartet of P-39s were overwhelmed by superior numbers before the P-38 high cover could get back down to intervene, which it never did. Lieutenant Wheadon limped back to Cactus; he survived a crash-landing but wrote off his P-40 in the process. The Marines lost a pair of TBFs, converting two others into hangar queens. Japanese overclaiming totaled one P-38, two P-40s, four P-39s, and an SBD shot down, plus one P-40, four P-39s, and one SBD as probables.

VMSB-131 claimed a Zero and Hamp; the P-39s put in for a Zero. Japanese sources record the loss of Zero pilot CPO Korenobu Nishide. A second Japanese pilot was lost trying to set his seriously damaged Zero down on the water.

Capitalizing on effective tactics, the 252nd Kokutai's fighter pilots avoided the heavily protected SBDs and instead succeeded in disrupting VMSB-131's attack after shamming the P-38 top cover. Their aggressiveness and tenacity were undeniable, leaving the TBF aircrews with little to say save to gratefully affirm that their sturdy Grummans really could absorb a merciless pounding and still hang together long enough to make it back to base.

As for VMSB-234, after recovering from their bow-on bombing runs, the SBD pilots reversed course in a wide arc. Overtaking the Japanese destroyers, they rendezvoused far ahead for the return flight to Guadalcanal under their F4F umbrella. Upon landing, the dive-bomber pilots claimed two Japanese destroyers sunk and a third set on fire. SBD crews also reported erroneously that VMSB-131 may have scored a hit on the second destroyer in the right column, having likely observed Captain Maguire's probable on the second destroyer in the left column.

Regarding the bombing, thirteen 1,000-pound bombs, nine 500-pound bombs, two 100-pound bombs, and at least one torpedo had been dropped on the Tokyo Express. Only three bombs were claimed as definite hits, with the sole visible result being the *Makinami* in serious difficulty—afire and dead in the water, her engine room flooding. Somewhat less exhilarating was the sight of the Tokyo Express regrouping on a course of 120 degrees. Admiral Hashimoto transferred his flag to the *Shirayuki*—his only *Fubuki*-class destroyer. Detaching the *Fumizuki* to accompany the damaged *Makinami* back to the Shortlands, he steered resolutely for Guadalcanal with his eighteen remaining warships.

Even as the air–sea battle off Vangunu Island was reaching fever pitch, the first fifteen of fifty-one USN fighters detached from carriers for temporary shore duty were landing at Cactus—in the nick of time. Reorganized into a composite squadron under future ace Lt. Cdr. Charles "Whitey" Ostrom, the veteran carrier fliers immediately took over escort duties from the weary USMC squadrons. VMF-112 was reassigned to standby scramble duties. The advent of more U.S. fighters meant that the contest for control of the air could only get tougher for the Japanese.

A final series of Maytag Mike raids against the Canal's airfields took place from 1 to 4 February. Nells from the 701st Kokutai had to stand in for the Bettys of the decimated 751st. To coincide with the first two evacuation runs of the Tokyo Express, base harassment escalated to base suppression.

Eight Nells worked Cactus over for seven hours on the night of 1–2 February. The first Nell dropped ten bombs at random at 2009; the second followed about forty minutes later, dispensing another ten missiles. Things quieted down until 0210, when the third spread ten more bombs around the Lunga perimeter. A half-hour later the fourth unloaded some of its ordnance. Within five minutes, a fifth Nell made its run. The fourth G3M was back at 0300, followed by a fifth ten minutes later. A *shotai* of Nells attacked in unison at 0320. When these three bombers finally departed, it was all over. Altogether, 480 133-pound bombs had rained down on Henderson and its satellites.

This was nothing new to the inhabitants of the Lunga perimeter. These nightly tormenters were simply emulating the original Maytag Mike, Washing Machine Charlie, and Louie the Louse—those infamous sleep-molesters whose sometimes-unsynchronized engines sounded not unlike the old wringer washers of the era. Japanese bombers had been annoying the Americans from the time the latter first came ashore the previous August. This latest series of incursions caused minor damage to facilities and inflicted a few casualties amongst the men and planes, but mostly it deprived American servicemen of much-needed sleep.

CHAPTER 13
NIGHT ACTION AND DAYTIME PURSUIT

The sun set early behind a heavy bank of clouds. The dank scent of rain was in the air as flashes of heat lightning gamboled playfully on the horizon. Admiral Hashimoto's advance screen arrived off Guadalcanal at 2000 and proceeded to cruise ahead into Iron Bottom Sound south of Savo Island. The screen's job was to lure away or intercept any Cactus air or naval units that attempted to interdict the evacuation operation. An F1M2 floatplane patrolled ahead of the transports, which had slowed in anticipation of a signal to approach the embarkation beaches. The Pete's crew searched for signs of enemy activity on the surface of or above Iron Bottom Sound. The architects of Operation KE had not been remiss in their planning, and their diligence was about to pay dividends.

Having failed to stop the Tokyo Express on its way down the Slot, the Americans were resolved not to let the Japanese go unchallenged off Cape Esperance. USN ship dispositions after the battle of Rennell Island left Guadalcanal protected by the four destroyers of the Cactus Striking Force, one of which had been sunk that very afternoon! The remainder, plus three destroyer-minelayers and three small PT-boat squadrons, were all that could be mustered to oppose the approaching Japanese flotilla.

After a three-day trek at flank speed, the minelayers *Montgomery*, *Preble*, and *Tracey* arrived from Noumea in the nick of time to sow a field of mines parallel to the shoreline westward from Doma Cove. Some 255 of these deadly spheres had been lowered into the indigo-tinted depths when the vague outlines of the enemy destroyer screen loomed up about 12,000 yards distant, softly silhouetted against the rosy pyrotechnics illuminating the western skyline. The minelayers beat a hasty retreat.

Capt. Robert Briscoe had agreed to sweep the western approach to the Canal from north of Savo to the southwest with his destroyers while Lt. Cdr. Alan Calvert's PT boats covered the approach between Cape Esperance and Savo. Having already sortied from nearby Purvis Bay, just east of Tulagi, the *Nicholas*, *Radford*, and *Fletcher* rounded the northern side of Savo Island and headed toward the Russells to ambush the Tokyo Express, cognizant that they were outnumbered six to one. On board the *Nicholas*, the PA system blurted out a bravado message that nevertheless exuded discomforting overtones: "This is the Commodore speaking. It is our duty to inflict as much damage as we can with our small force. We will attack the enemy with torpedoes and gunfire and we will attempt to escape under a smoke screen." Note: *attempt* to escape!

The Japanese screening destroyers had almost passed Savo Island when the Cactus Striking Force spotted them, steaming some two thousand yards to the north. Captain Briscoe's tiny force had barely come about to head for the enemy when several Petes homed in on the destroyer trio. Having discovered them by their phosphorescent wakes, the tenacious floatplanes latched on to their quarry. In no time they were dropping flares and float lights to mark Briscoe's position and course for the benefit of Japanese gunnery and torpedo officers. These tactics forced the U.S. column to interrupt its attack and take evasive action. In return, the harried destroyers took the meddlesome snoopers under intermittent fire with their radar-guided, 5-inch main batteries. Five salvos from the *Nicholas* alone flashed into the night to ward off the Petes. Officers on her bridge claimed that her gunners "splashed one." Still, having now lost the element of surprise, the Cactus Striking Force was forced to stand well off while seeking an opportunity to move in.

Seeing that the screening force and air cover were successfully stymieing what little opposition Cactus had been able to muster, the transport destroyers approached from the Russells at 2245 to stand off Cape Esperance's two embarkation beaches. With no time to waste, landing barges and collapsibles began to ply between the ships and the shore while the destroyer vanguard continued to probe eastward into Iron Bottom Sound.

Undaunted, Lieutenant Commander Calvert's eleven PT boats lay patiently waiting in ambush off Savo Island, Cape Esperance, Doma Cove, and Lunga Roads. Coming into contact piecemeal with several of the Japanese pickets, they began to stalk their targets. Once discovered and taken under air attack by the Petes, they roared in to launch their torpedoes. As the PTs closed, most were instantly shelled by the screening destroyers, whose crews were masters at night fighting.

First to make contact at 2245 were Lt. (jg) John Clagett and Lt. (jg) Les Gamble. Commanding the *PT-111*, Lieutenant Clagett went after the dark silhouette of the *Kawakaze*, steaming about three miles east of Cape Esperance. The *Kawakaze* immediately spotted the oncoming PT boat and opened fire. With geysers spouting all around, the *PT-111* approached to within five hundred yards before firing all four torpedoes. Lieutenant Clagett whipped his boat around and was making good his escape when his luck ran out. Ten minutes after beginning its attack, the *PT-111* exploded in flames after a direct hit by the *Kawakaze* that killed the exec and one crewman. The rest of the crew went into the water where, against the light of a flaming gasoline slick, they began a nightlong vigil, warding off roving sharks till rescuers arrived. Clagett himself was eventually picked up by the *PT-124*.

Lieutenant Gamble took the *PT-48* in pursuit of a pair of destroyers west of Savo, one of which may have been the *Nagatsuki*. Under even heavier fire from *two* Japanese warships, Gamble only managed to close the range to nine hundred yards before decanting a pair of fish at each of his targets. Miraculously, the *PT-48* emerged unscathed from the cauldron of fire, retiring to Savo where Gamble gently beached her. The crew then made their way ashore to await the dawn.

A trio of PT boats, comprising the *PT-37*, *PT-59*, and *PT-115*, ran into the transport destroyers north of Cape Esperance. Closing to five hundred yards, Ens. Bart Connolly of the *PT-115* divided his four torpedoes evenly between a pair of targets before knifing his boat into a sharp turn. Enemy return fire grew hotter as Japanese gunners ranged in to track the receding *PT-115*. With geysers erupting all around him, Connolly coolly slowed down to conceal his telltale wake. The *PT-59*, commanded by Ens. Williams Kreiner III, also completed its run and, together with the *PT-115*, eluded the enemy's probing gunfire by ducking into the safety of a rainsquall that happened to be blowing across Iron Bottom Sound. Subsequently, Connolly also beached his boat off Savo Island.

The *PT-37* never made it. Having launched its fish, Ens. Jim Kelly's boat was speeding away when a shell tore into its fuel tanks, igniting several thousand gallons of high-octane gasoline. A spectacular explosion instantly blew the boat apart. MoMM1c Eldon Jenter was below deck at the time. The violent force of the detonation propelled him through the shredding hull, thereby saving his life. The sole survivor, he suffered severe burns and shrapnel wounds. Suddenly surprised by a brilliant flash astern, the crews of the other two boats erroneously surmised that someone had scored a hit on an enemy destroyer. However, none of the fish launched by the PTs thus far had found their target.

With Ens. Ralph Richards astern of him in the *PT-123*, Lt. Clark Faulkner stealthily conned the *PT-124* toward an enemy destroyer cruising south of Savo Island. The *Makigumo* had apparently pursued one of the other PT boats almost to Tulagi before turning back. Coming about, she was returning past Savo when Faulkner's two PTs started to stalk her. But, before the *PT-123* could launch its ordnance, it was struck by a Pete, whose pilot came out of nowhere and glide-bombed the creeping PT boat with either consummate skill or incredibly good fortune. The 133-pound missile chewed the *PT-123*'s stern to matchwood, killing four crewmen. Now also discovered, the *PT-124* boosted its engines and charged in. Manning the helm, Lt. (jg) Leighton Wood brought her to within eight hundred yards, whereupon Faulkner loosed all four torpedoes. The exec then veered away sharply. Treading water nearby, a *PT-123* survivor witnessed a single explosion that rocked the *Makigumo* as she maneuvered to evade the PT boat's attack.

Trying to avoid torpedoes, the disoriented *Makigumo* had strayed into the recently sown minefield where her stern brushed up against one of the deadly orbs. Badly holed, she began to flood rapidly in her crew quarters and her "auxiliary engine [steering?] room." Her crew suffered one dead, two missing, one seriously wounded, and six slightly injured. Unable to proceed, she was taken in tow by the *Yugumo*. The flooding could not be brought under control, however, and she had to be scuttled by a torpedo from her rescuer some nine miles south-southwest of Savo Island. She went under at 0327 as the crew of the *PT-109* looked on from a distance.

With Maytag Mike's Nells already making periodic bombing runs on Henderson, the *PT-109* and *PT-36* had initially taken up positions in Lunga

Roads at 2215 in case the enemy warships attempted to shell the airfield complex, but it soon became clear that the action was around Savo Island. Conning their boats westward into Iron Bottom Sound, Lt. Rollin Westholm and Lt. (jg) Charles Tilden approached the combat area to behold the three surface fires that attested to the violent fates of the *PT-111*, *PT-37*, and *PT-123*. They could also discern other PTs apparently being strafed by a Pete off Savo. Though neither boat arrived in time to intercept the enemy, they were soon occupied searching the area for survivors and missing colleagues. At daybreak the *PT-109* came upon Bob Searles' *PT-38* and Connolly's *PT-115*, both aground in the shallows off Savo. Before long, the *PT-109* had managed to drag them off their precarious perches. Continuing his search, Lieutenant Westholm recovered the body of one seaman before returning to base in the forenoon.

Flickering pyres of fuel and PT-boat debris were still pulsating at random intervals across the surface of Iron Bottom Sound when six dive-bombers from VMSB-234 arrived on the scene during the naval action. The Nells were still harassing Henderson Field to keep Cactus aircraft on the ground; however, these six SBD pilots managed to sneak off around midnight between raids, together with a U.S. Navy Black Cat assigned to detect the Japanese ships on its primitive radar and illuminate the target area with flares. Intermittent radio squealing disrupted communication between the PBY-5A and the SBDs. The Catalina could not coordinate its flare drops with the latter's bombing runs, so the SBDs had to attack vaguely defined targets, either sporadically illuminated by their own flares and by those of the Catalina or veiled in darkness.

One pilot dove from seven thousand feet to release his bomb "over one of three flaming targets." Pulling out at two thousand feet, he observed "that target was blown up." Another Dauntless dropped its bomb wide of its burning objective. Flying about one mile off Cape Esperance, a third pilot noticed something below him. When his flares revealed what appeared to be an enemy destroyer, he turned into his bombing run, releasing a 1,000-pounder that failed to explode. Somewhat chagrined but still of one mind, the pilot brought his plane around for a strafing run. He lined up his target and zoomed in with twin fifties blazing. Light, ineffective AA fire greeted his approach. After completing his run, he discerned what looked like a "PT boat firing on DD."

Altogether, the VMSB-234 aircrews noted six locations where fires seemed to be burning, though duplicate sightings were likely the case. But, due to recurring radio malfunctions, little could be done in the absence of coordinated flare drops by the Black Cat. In retrospect, that few bombs were dropped on these prospective targets was all for the best since three of the fires probably marked the graves of the unlucky PT boats, whose surviving crewmen were still in the surrounding water. Other fires probably burst sporadically from the funnels of speeding destroyers. After spending a half hour over the target area, the SBD aircrews reluctantly returned to Henderson without having achieved any concrete results. They, nevertheless, waxed optimistic about having attacked two "burning destroyers." At 0320 the Cat tried its own luck by dropping four 500-pound bombs on the *Arashio* as she was getting under way from Cape Esperance, claiming a near miss or a possible hit.

Witnessing the battle from afar, the crewmen on the shadowing U.S. destroyers observed that "the clouds above Savo were lighted for half an hour with the flash of guns and bombs and the flares dropped by the planes." The run-ins with the PTs no doubt threw Admiral Hashimoto's embarkation schedule out of whack. Having taken on board around 4,900 grateful Japanese troops, the admiral recalled his remaining picket destroyers, and quickly got under way in the early hours of 2 February. Some 1,270 crestfallen men were left behind on the beach at Kamimbo and another three hundred at Cape Esperance. Seeing that the Tokyo Express was leaving, the Cactus Striking Force attempted to close again, but the vigilant Pete swooped in with another flare drop to alert the Japanese destroyers. Wary of the fabled Japanese Long Lance torpedo, a frustrated Captain Briscoe backed off once more but refused to break contact. With dogged persistence, he followed Hashimoto for a time in the hope of picking off a careless straggler, but no such opportunity presented itself.

Even as the Tokyo Express weighed anchor for Bougainville, Cactus ground crews toiled feverishly to put together pursuing air strikes, their work periodically interrupted by recurring Nell raids. Notwithstanding these disruptions, six Hudson patrol bombers were sent into the Central Solomons before first light to track the retiring Japanese.

Next off the mark at 0540 was a 347th Fighter Group sweep. Hoping the fighters would give chase at high speed to catch Admiral Hashimoto's convoy before it withdrew out of range, the 70th FS put up eight P-39s armed with 500-pound bombs. Flying escort were four P-38s from the 339th. In their haste to get them away, ground crews had no time to fit them with the few drop tanks that were available. It was a gamble that failed to pay off. One hundred and thirty miles out, Captain Jim Robinson, leading the bomb-laden Airacobras, scanned his fuel gauge and made a difficult decision: he called off the pursuit. The fighter-bombers turned back—fewer than fifty miles short of their objective.

The Lightnings pushed on, overtaking a searching Hudson. Between the northern tip of New Georgia and Manning Strait, they located an estimated fifteen "enemy warships." But a strafing attack by two elements against that many destroyers would have been futile—especially if enemy fighters lurked above. Reluctantly, Capt. John Mitchell turned his flight away. Before heading back, the P-38s checked out Rekata Bay for any Japanese floatplane activity. Ongoing pandemonium must have greeted their arrival, for one of the patrolling Hudsons had already paid a brief visit to Rekata at 0630, leaving three 500-pound calling cards. Observing no sign of Petes, Rufes, or Jakes at the seaplane base, Mitchell led his flight back to Guadalcanal.

Meanwhile, one of the Hudson crews came upon a flotilla of eight destroyers at 0625, working their way up the Slot about 150 miles from the Canal. The New Zealanders shadowed the enemy ships up the coast of Santa Ysabel for nearly two hours, not realizing that their radio had begun to malfunction. Though messages were no longer being received by Cactus, their first signals had confirmed that at least one flotilla of the Tokyo Express was still within range of an air strike.

At 0630 Henderson Field prepared to put up ten Dauntlesses from VMSB-233, plus the three Avengers of VMSB-131 that could still fly. The USN torpedo-bomber squadron, posted on shore temporarily from the auxiliary carriers to operate with technical and administrative support provided by VMSB-131, flew off an additional seven Avengers led by Lieutenant Keighley. Detached with the TBFs, the composite USN fighter squadron contributed an escort of twenty-one Wildcats under Lt. Cdr. Whitey Ostrom.

The Cactus strike force caught up with the fleeing Japanese at 0810 near "Torpedo Junction," ten miles off Vella Lavella (see map 6). Steaming at an estimated thirty knots, the convoy had managed to put some 210 miles between itself and Guadalcanal and was now well within range of friendly fighter protection. Indeed, a Cactus search plane had observed "seven Zeros" circling just north of Santa Ysabel at 0703, likely searching for the earlier Hudson raider.

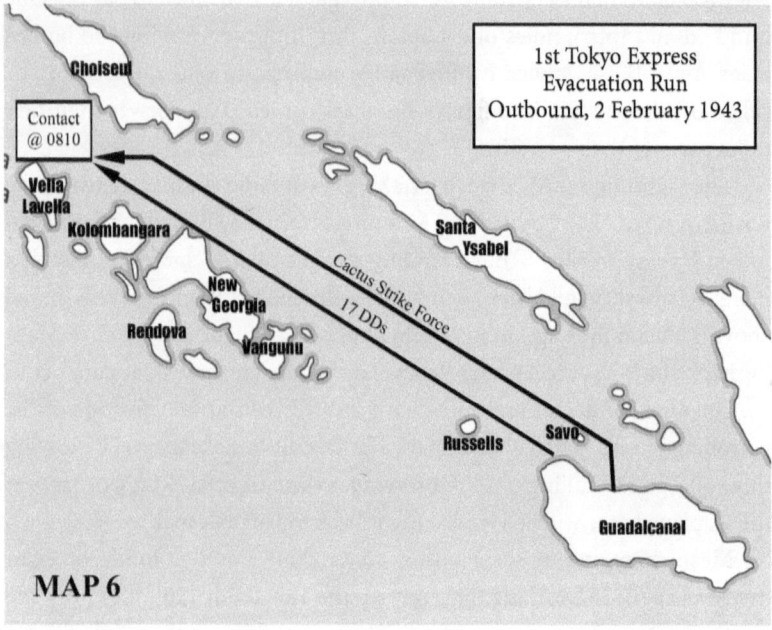

MAP 6

As expected, the swiftly moving destroyers were in two widely spread, though somewhat ragged, columns: a right column made up of six ships, and a left column with another five. A lone destroyer was stationed off the port bow of the flotilla; two more straggled behind the left column. Lagging far behind, the *Yugumo* and the two other destroyers with her had probably been passed over, masked beneath cloud cover as they returned back up the Slot after trying to rescue, then scuttling, the hapless *Makigumo*.

Cautious light-bomber pilots searched the empty skies for signs of Japanese fighters. Inexplicably, no enemy planes could be spotted. Unknown to them, a dozen 204th Kokutai Zeros had taken off from Kahili barely ten minutes before and were at this minute winging their way down the Slot. But they failed to arrive in time to interdict the air strike.

Not pausing to ponder their good fortune, the Cactus raiders hastened to move into the attack. VMSB-233's SBDs and VMSB-131's TBFs went after the rear of the convoy. The U.S. Navy TBFs fell upon the lead destroyers. Catching sight of the approaching aircraft, the Japanese abruptly "opened the column formation to either side . . . with slight zigzags on their turns."

Captain Frazer led VMSB-233 in a high-speed descent from 12,000 to 7,000 feet through light, inaccurate flak. Flying past the starboard quarter of the enemy flotilla, the SBDs banked into a shallow left turn toward the two destroyers abaft the left column to commence their attack. Frazer and Lieutenant Hays each registered close misses, though VMSB-131 pilots said they saw "two sure hits . . . on one of the trailing DDs." Captain Bercik's target was swinging around in a circle; Bercik could not line it up before passing through his bomb release point. Lieutenant Reed failed to make a drop because his bomb would not release. The remaining Dauntless pilots "missed their targets by varying distances" before withdrawing through intensifying flak.

Leading VMSB-131, Capt. Bill Hayter singled out the next-to-last destroyer in the right column and pushed over, the rest of his TBFs right behind him. Gliding through uncomfortably accurate flak, Hayter let loose four 500-pound bombs at two thousand feet. Flames flashed on the destroyer's stern. A hit! Next to dive, Lt. Marty Roush barely missed the bow of the last destroyer with his 500-pound-bomb salvo.

Carrying the only torpedo among the three Marine TBFs, Lt. "Bud" Main set up on what he perceived to be "a cripple" in the left column—probably one of the two destroyers shaken up by the SBDs' near misses—and dropped to three hundred feet for the run in. Closing at 195 knots, Main launched his fish at about one thousand yards. When he opened his throttle to pull out, the big torpedo bomber accelerated through a lethal storm of AA fire. Shrapnel from a bursting main-battery shell or a 25-mm explosive round tore through the Avenger's fuselage, mortally wounding the turret gunner, Sergeant Ganther. Lieutenant Main searched in vain for evidence of a torpedo hit.

What could be observed by VMSB-131 and VMSB-233 of the Navy TBF action around the front end of the convoy did not look too promising;

bombs were seen falling way wide of their targets. The flak may have proved too disruptive at that end to conduct accurate bombing. Overall, the USMC bomber crews noted that Japanese AA fire had been relatively light at first, but had become increasingly heavy and accurate as the attack developed.

Having expended their ordnance with lackluster results, the raiders withdrew. The strike force cruised back to Cactus at 170 knots, touching down at around 0930 hours. After landing, the unfortunate TBF turret gunner died of his wounds. The results of the mission were doubly disconcerting given the absence of enemy fighter interference. Between them, the two Marine Corps squadrons dumped ten 1,000-pound bombs, eight 500-pound bombs, and one torpedo on the Tokyo Express, netting a possible pair of bomb hits. The seven USN TBFs reportedly all missed, expending up to four 500-pound bombs each. Only a single destroyer was lightly hit, according to the Japanese.

The Tokyo Express had reformed into three columns by 0900 and was making twenty-five knots up the center of the Slot opposite the midpoint of Choiseul. A Cactus patrol bomber sighted "nineteen" destroyers, one of which appeared to be "in tow," indicating that the three stragglers had caught up to the main body, thanks to the delay caused by the air strike.

That afternoon Captain Sawyer led six P-39s of the 67th FS to strafe landing barges seen beached between Aruligo and the Tenamba River. Two Cobras covered while the other four made six passes at sixteen barges, setting two on fire and filling the others full of holes. Despite these latest attempts to interrupt the evacuation operation, the round belonged to the Japanese at the cost of the *Makigumo* and damage to the *Makinami*.

Again leaving the *Makinami* and *Fumizuki* behind in the wake of the morning's Cactus air attack, Admiral Hashimoto's seaworthy destroyers pushed on to the Shortlands. Coastwatcher Nick Waddell on Choiseul reported seeing them enter Shortland Harbor at 1100. Not long after, the *Fumizuki* towed the battered *Makinami* in to safety. The transport destroyers had to pause long enough to unload 4,940 sick, ragged, and emaciated soldiers before weighing anchor. Thirteen 582nd Kokutai Zeros flew CAP over the unloading operation from 1020 to 1220 hours.

Those evacuees needing medical attention were transshipped to other vessels to be transported directly to Rabaul for treatment. The rest were landed on tiny Erventa Island, where they were kept in isolation pending reassignment. Just as they did after Midway, the Japanese probably tried to hide the magnitude of the Guadalcanal disaster from the public for a time. The escort destroyers were the first to leave Buin for a safer haven, followed by the transport destroyers.

Earlier that morning a Cactus patrol bomber had already counted some twenty-four warships and merchantmen in the Shortland-Tonolei harbor complex—enough tonnage to warrant an air strike. Four Warhawks under the command of Lt. Dale Tarbet took off at approximately 1515 to escort Major Whittaker's six B-17s from the 72nd and 26th BSs to the Buin-Faisi area. Capt. John Mitchell brought along seven Lightnings as high cover. But all too soon, engine trouble whittled the escort down to three P-40s and four P-38s.

The Cactus raiders first came across the 6,441-ton seaplane transport *Keiyo Maru* at 1710, steaming with the subchaser *Ch-30* off Ballale. The pair of three-bomber elements proceeded to line up for a run at 14,000 feet, unloading forty-eight 500-pound bombs over the transport. Waterspouts all but enveloped her as bomb clusters saturated the surrounding area. *Keiyo Maru* was hit several times and began to burn fiercely. One hit on her stern damaged her steering gear, so the minelayer *Tsugaru* was sent out to tow her into the Shortlands after helping her get the fire under control. A destroyer, the *Yugiri*, assigned to Rabaul-Shortlands patrol and escort duties, was caught at anchor in Shortland Harbor and also bombed, suffering "minor damage."

The 44th FS's low cover cruised at 14,500 feet in anticipation of enemy interceptors while the 339th FS's high cover hovered at 25,000 feet. Although the morning search had revealed three Zeros at Ballale and twenty-four at Kahili, none rose to interfere with the bombing. Within five minutes, however, several groups of enemy fighters, totaling an estimated twenty to twenty-five planes in two groups, successively attacked the formation as it left the Shortlands.

First, a flight of ten Rufe floatplanes from the 802nd Kokutai jumped the trio of P-40s at six thousand feet. As the Hawks scrambled to evade their attackers, NAP1c Shinji Ishida claimed a "P-39" shot down. The P-38s plunged into the fray, careful not to get drawn too low to fight effectively. Captain Mitchell and Lt. Murray Shubin each claimed a float Zero destroyed before the remainder were quickly driven off. One of the victims, NAP3c

Kiyoshi Akizuki, parachuted to safety. Lieutenant Shubin would soon become one of the top P-38 aces in the Pacific with eleven victories, five of which he would shoot down in one day on 16 June 1943.

Next, a gaggle of eleven 252nd Kokutai Zeros scrambled out of Ballale, catching up to the B-17s twenty-five miles southeast of the Shortlands. Outnumbered, the P-40s and P-38s tried to head them off, but some of the A6Ms got through to the bombers. They came in head-on and fired, streaking past beneath the B-17s before climbing above the formation. Then, executing complete Immelmans, they swooped back down behind the less-maneuverable P-40s. The Warhawk pilots said they shot down three Zeros during the dogfight, with Lieutenants Tarbet, R. Morrisey, and John Wood claiming one apiece. Lt. Besby Holmes also hit the trigger button; the nose of his P-38 flickered, and he claimed yet another Zeke.

Lieutenant Wood turned around to find a Zero on his tail. The enemy pilot proceeded to pour 7.7-mm and 20-mm fire into the P-40 before himself being hit by a B-17 tail gunner. Shrapnel struck Wood in the left arm, side, and leg, but the wounded pilot persevered to bring his badly shot-up ship into Fighter Two. The optimistic 252nd pilot claimed Wood's "P-39" as a victory.

The B-17 crews observed eight enemy planes go down, claiming five Zekes destroyed by their own gunners. Duplicate claims by fighter pilots and bomber gunners abounded. In actuality, one Zero went missing and three more suffered damage. No Cactus planes were lost. The 26th BS's war diary remarked that the escort "did a beautiful job keeping enemy pursuit attacks off the formation."

Not knowing how the Americans would react to the success of the first evacuation run but expecting the worse, Admiral Yamamoto and Admiral Kusaka considered the Shortland-Tonolei anchorage to be far too risky a place for the destroyers of the Tokyo Express to sojourn between sorties. Therefore, after offloading their troops, Admiral Hashimoto directed his destroyers to head north along Bougainville's coast to the more remote, safer recesses of Buka Passage.

On 1 February Captain Carey of the 98th BS was over Buka Passage on a photoreconnaissance run when his B-17 was jumped by six "land type

Zeros." While the three fighters from the 253rd Kokutai attacked without much success, Carey's gunners claimed two Mitsubishis destroyed plus two probables—a neat trick considering none of the three was even hit. Despite the warm reception accorded them the previous day, Captain Carey's gutsy crew was back on 2 February, patrolling over northern Bougainville. The Fort came across nineteen destroyers riding at anchor in Buka Passage under the protection of fighters based at Buka and Bonis airstrips. Carey's plane was promptly subjected to a light barrage of inaccurate AA fire from the flotilla before retreating out of range.

Not surprisingly, no follow-up air strike was ever planned since the targets were beyond the range of anything Cactus could put in the air, save a B-17. Unescorted 13th Air Force Forts would have had to fight their way through Munda's and Bougainville's entire fighter contingent to get at Admiral Hashimoto's ships. As for the destroyers, they could rapidly disperse through open portals at either end of their anchorage if given sufficient warning. To protect their destroyer flotilla between runs, Japanese planners had wisely chosen a haven virtually immune from Allied air attack.

CHAPTER 14
COMAIRSOL'S VENDETTA

B rig. Gen. Francis Mulcahy was not one to be turned away empty-handed. Having failed to prevent Admiral Hashimoto from completing his first rescue mission, General Mulcahy ordered the Cactus Air Force to claim its consolation prize with a vengeance. ComAirSols and his staff had some time ago concluded from experience that no destroyer convoy scheduled for a nocturnal arrival off Cape Esperance would come within striking range before late afternoon. Strike Command decided to send a welcoming committee up the Slot, gambling that another Japanese destroyer convoy might have been dispatched to arrive at Guadalcanal on the night of 2 February. Accordingly, the three operable VMSB-131 Avengers sortied from Cactus at 1625 in the company of nine USN Avengers and a dozen Dauntlesses from VMSB-233.

Seven Airacobras of the 67th FS shared escort duties with fourteen USN Wildcats, but the Army air corps fighters were tardy getting airborne, so the strike force left without them. After flying up the Slot for 150 miles in an attempt to overtake the formation, the Cobra leader, Capt. Jerry Sawyer, called over the radio on a supposedly common channel. Typically receiving no answer from the Navy and Marine fliers who likely never heard his call, Sawyer led his pilots over to Viru Harbor, on the south coast of New Georgia, to carry out his secondary assignment—a strafing mission. Seeing no barges or landing craft, the P-39s skimmed over the water to make three runs on harbor facilities.

Minus the P-39s, the abbreviated strike force arrived in the Central Solomons circa 1833 hours. They diligently combed the waters of Kula Gulf over to Kolombangara, then back down through Vella Gulf and Blackett Strait to New Georgia—all to no avail. Coming up empty-handed, the pilots and aircrews consoled themselves by beating up on Munda airstrip before heading back.

Records for this mission are sketchy, but it is known that VMSB-233 was dealt more than its fair share of setbacks on the way up the Slot. No fewer than six of its pilots had to abort the mission due to faulty planes, leaving only half of the SBDs in the strike force. However, they acquitted themselves well during the actual attack on Munda. Captain Williamson, leading the flight, was the only one unable to release his bomb. Lieutenants Mitchell and Woodley both hit a supply dump adjacent to the copra storage shed and wharf. Lieutenant McCulloch's 1,000-pounder cratered the junction of the taxiways at the east end of the field. Lieutenant Cosley planted his 1,000-pound bomb in the "middle of—loop," starting a large, smoky fire. Lieutenant Otteson's bomb "hit 30 yards in from shelter #4P."

Lieutenant Commander Brunton then led the Avengers in. Five USN TBFs and one Avenger from VMSB-131 carried torpedoes, but the other Avengers were armed with four 500-pound bombs apiece. The torpedo-armed planes circled overhead while their bomb-laden colleagues glided down. All twenty-four missiles apparently struck in the target area. The runway, taxiways, and revetments were all hit, causing more large fires. Japanese flak was described as "light and ineffective."

No Japanese planes were on the ground amidst the evening shadows or in the air. Everyone returned safely to Cactus, but the USN F4Fs flew into a surprise as they circled the field at Fighter Two. Apparently the first six landed without incident, but, unknown to everyone on the ground or in the air, a 701st Kokutai Nell—operating as the first of that night's Maytag Mikes—had sneaked up on the formation. Tagging along in the fading twilight, the G3M escaped both visual and radar detection. At 1930 the enterprising enemy pilot turned on his landing lights and joined in the landing circle to make a run over Fighter Two. A few missiles from his five-bomb salvo fell along the northern edge of the field in the Army air corps area. The explosions knocked out field lights, set one of the 68th's P-39s ablaze, and peppered five more with shrapnel. His remaining bombs cratered the runway and taxiways.

Trying to land in the fading twilight without an illuminated flight path, four F4F pilots failed to see the bomb craters pockmarking the darkened field and wrecked their planes after touching down. Another four orbiting Wildcats were diverted to Henderson at 1955, but the Nell sneaked back before they could land. Within the next twenty minutes, the G3M made four runs over the bomber strip, dropping two single 133-pound bombs followed by two pairs of 133-pound missiles. Amidst the commotion, confused Americans swore they were under attack by one to four Bettys reportedly covered by at least two Zeros. A new taxiway was cratered, uprooting sections of Marston matting. Waiting above, low on fuel, the quartet of F4Fs finally received permission to land as Condition Green sounded.

Shortly after 2300 a second Nell began its night's work. It had barely unloaded three 133-pound bombs when Cactus gunners got the range, inflicting serious flak damage. The pilot broke off his attack. Coaxing his plane back toward Buka, he had to make a forced landing at 0255 at Kieta's desolate emergency strip on the coast of Bougainville. The next afternoon an 851st Kokutai flying boat put down in Kieta's modest harbor to rescue the Nell's seven crewmen.

The Cactus Air Force retaliated by raiding Munda airstrip on 3 February. Flying just ahead of a 70th BS strike force, the two P-40 pilots of Baker search arrived over Munda to report that the Japanese were still hard at work keeping the airstrip operational. Capt. Albert Johnson and Lt. Jack Bade observed three craters that recently had been filled in near the center of the runway.

The fast-flying Marauders showed up at 0850 in the slim company of three P-39s from the 67th FS and a pair of P-38s from the 339th FS, surprising seven twin-engine bombers on the field. These may have been JAAF Lilys, lingering under repair at Munda after having been damaged in the Cactus raid of 1 February or shot up while themselves attacking Cactus later that same morning.

The Two Warhawks from the 44th remained on station as added protection while the medium bombers made their runs from south to north at between 10,000 and 12,000 feet. The B-26s unloaded twelve 500-pounders about a quarter mile southeast of the runway beyond several planes parked near that end, starting a sizable fire on the fringe of Lambeti plantation. Flying low cover at 15,000 feet, Captain Sawyer's Airacobras observed moderate flak bursting 1,000 feet below them. Lieutenants Julius "Jake" Jacobson and Bill Griffith cruised undisturbed at 21,000 feet in their frigid Lightning gondolas while the attack went in, corroborating the results observed by the P-39s. Again, no enemy air opposition appeared.

A reconnaissance B-17 had just completed a photo run over the seaplane base at Rekata Bay when three gutsy "Nagoya Zeros" from the 253rd Kokutai out of faraway Buka intercepted it in midmorning. The Zeke *shotai* managed to work over the Fort pretty thoroughly in a sharp engagement, wounding three of the crew. Although B-17 gunners claimed they shot down a "black Zero with a belly tank" in return, all three Zeros were back in Buka by 1100 hours. Convinced they had seriously damaged the Fort, the Japanese pilots claimed a probable.

Twelve SBDs from VMSB-234 plastered the airfield at Vila-Stanmore under the protective umbrella of a dozen USN F4Fs at 1150 that same day. Before Japanese AA gunners realized what was happening, the two divisions of six dive-bombers winged over at 240 knots from the north. When they were opposite the field, they banked to the left behind Capt. Dick Blain. Swinging down from 12,000 feet into right echelon, the SBDs glided in over the reef, roughly at right angles to the runway, releasing their ordnance at only 5,500 feet. Eighteen bombs, ranging from 100 to 1,000 pounds, plunged earthward. Ear-splitting reports rent the air as a succession of explosions tore up construction equipment, building materials, and freshly packed coral across the length of the field.

Japanese gun crews rallied quickly. Several 75-mm and 40-mm guns barked angrily in reply, the bursting flak tracking the speeding Dauntlesses as the latter flew away to form up some fifteen miles to the northwest over Kula Gulf. Munda's fighters failed to intervene. All Cactus planes returned safely via the north coast of New Georgia and the Slot.

Having tried with dubious success to make life more difficult for enemy planes attempting to use Munda or Vila airstrips that day, the Cactus Air Force duly dispatched another antishipping strike up the Slot between 1515 and 1545 hours. Nine USN and two VMSB-131 TBFs cruised alongside twelve SBDs from VMSB-234 as far as the New Georgia Group at 125 knots to conserve fuel and stretch flying time. The bombers were heavily escorted by twelve USN F4Fs flying low cover, three P-40s from the 44th FS flying medium cover, and eight P-38s from the 339th FS flying high cover. The antishipping strike prowled the area amidst heavy rain clouds and towering thunderheads, retracing the route used the previous afternoon with equally negative results. The SBDs and TBFs then proceeded to work over the luckless airfield at Munda once more.

VMSB-234 made its approach from west-northwest at 13,000 feet, coming in out of the sun through low cloud cover. Gliding through a perfect break in the cumulus, the SBD pilots emerged over Munda airstrip at five thousand feet and toggled their bomb releases. Some four tons of bombs fell diagonally across the western two-thirds of Munda's runway. Several missiles failed to release; one 1,000-pounder got stuck temporarily before falling into the water. Observing from afar, the TBF crews believed they saw up to five bombs overshoot the target area, landing on the fringing reef. In general, the drop produced explosions, large fires, and billowing smoke.

Gliding in from 14,500 feet at around 45°, Lieutenant Commander Brunton led the Navy and Marine TBFs over the field from west to east. Four pilots each dropped four 500-pounders on the runway and taxiways at each end of the field. Another bombed the small peninsula off the west end of the runway, knocking out the AA battery located there. No actual fires were observed, though there was plenty of smoke. Lieutenant Keighley made his run but ended up bringing his four bombs back.

The Wildcats and Capt. A Johnson's Hawks, now flying close cover two thousand feet above the light bombers, went down with them to three thousand feet, observing bombs hitting the water and the airfield. From their vantage point high above, the Lightning pilots confirmed the bombing results on a field that appeared devoid of enemy planes.

Probably caught unawares by the sudden appearance of the raiders, enemy gunners opened up late. Light, inaccurate flak blossomed briefly at 20,000 feet, then in layers between 4,000 and 10,000 feet, managing to put a 25-mm shrapnel hole in the elevator of Lieutenant Shearon's TBF.

One Avenger crew reported seeing muzzle flashes from a new gun emplacement in the jungle located about a mile north of the airstrip and a half-mile in from the coast. The Japanese chose this location on a plateau above the airstrip for a battery of 75-mm guns because Cactus bombers had lately begun to make their runs over Munda from the north or the south. It was hoped U.S. pilots would be discouraged from attacking along this axis now that they had to pass directly over the new gun position. Although subsequently strafed and damaged, these two dual-purpose guns survived the war; they still stand in a forest clearing like a pair of sentinels, forever watchful, their rusting muzzles pointing toward an empty sky.

The afternoon of 3 February witnessed the arrival of veteran Navy fighter squadron 72 that came ashore with a further seventeen pilots commanded by Lt. Alberto "Al" Emerson. VF-72's Wildcats were immediately attached to the composite USN F4F squadron to share the brunt of the escort missions and fighter sweeps. VMF-123 also arrived at Cactus for its first combat tour. To help ease the untried men into their baptism of fire, Lieutenant Colonel Pugh, the new fighter commander, assigned the untested unit to patrol duty, Dumbo escort, convoy cover, and search missions.

A pair of Nells out of Vunakanau drew the Maytag Mike assignment that evening. One arrived over Cactus at 2102, the other at 2110 hours. The first, flown by Lt. (jg) Keizo Kondo, proceeded to torment Fighter Two, dumping a stick of ten 133-pound bombs just west of the field. The second Nell, piloted by CPO Kyo Fujimatsu, visited the Lunga perimeter, dropping its stick between the bomber field and Fighter Two. Returning independently, the pair flew into bad weather and was forced to pancake at Buka. Kondo landed safely at 2325, but in the course of touching down at midnight, Fujimatsu collided with another plane, seriously damaging his Nell. He and his crew had to book passage with Kondo when the latter took off for Rabaul at 0750 next morning.

A pair of Black Cats made their way up the Slot to the New Georgia group at around 0100 next morning. Splitting up, one headed toward Munda to drop four 500-pound bombs on the airstrip. The other was on its way to Kolombangara when it was sidetracked by a Japanese transport, aground and burning fiercely off the islet of Kololokai near Gizo Island. Dispensing a single 500-pounder on the blazing *Toa Maru 2*, the crew went on to bomb the enemy base at Vila-Stanmore. Light-caliber tracer wafted up into the night, but neither PBY was hit.

The Cactus Air Force paid another visit to Munda later that morning. Under CAVU skies, a dozen Dauntlesses from VMSB-234 and six USN Avengers climbed to 15,000 feet at 125 knots on a bearing of 288 degrees. Twenty-one USN F4Fs provided fighter cover. Reaching New Georgia at 0800, the SBDs banked to port, flew around the bottom of the island, and turned up Blanche Channel for an east-to-west attack. Flying over Rendova so as to approach Munda from the southeast, Captain Blain reformed his three divisions into left echelon before dropping to 13,000 feet. As the target hove into view, the Dauntless pilots banked into their final approach. Gliding by sections to 6,000 feet at 280 knots, each section released its bombs on its leader's signal.

Munda's air defenses opened up late, most of the flak coming from the Lambeti area east of the airstrip. The first rounds burst at 12,000 feet—an approach altitude frequently used on previous missions. Enemy gunners quickly began to layer the flak between 4,000 and 8,000 feet.

As the dive-bombers reached the release point, some five tons of bombs arced earthward, two 100-pound bombs failing to release. Columns of water and coral chunks erupted into the air when two bombs fell short; the remainder walked across the east end of the field. The dock at "Lilihina" (read Laiana) was damaged, and two large fires broke out just south of the runway. An AA gun fell silent after a 1,000-pounder showered its crew with shrapnel. Other missiles detonated among revetments and supply dumps in the woods north of the field.

Lieutenant Keighley's TBFs also came in from the east. Gliding down from 15,000 feet to 6,000 feet at an average 40-degree angle, the Avenger pilots dropped twelve 500-pound bombs on the western portion of the airfield. Lieutenant Routhbottom loosed his four 500-pounders on revetments north of the field. Lieutenant McKinney placed his missiles on the northwest corner of the north taxiway. Released at the northwest end of the field, two of Lieutenant Larkin's bombs fell on an AA position near the shore, and the other two landed in the water beyond. Lieutenant Saunders' drop went snafu: thanks to a faulty release mechanism, his bombs remained in their shackles.

Through a pall of smoke that obscured part of the airstrip, one pilot noticed two or three fighters in revetments south of the runway, suggesting that the Japanese Munda detachment was still using the airstrip. Possibly damaged in previous air raids, these planes either could not be flown to safety in advance of the incoming raid, or they were derelicts left to serve as distractions upon which Cactus raiders could waste their ordnance.

The Avengers duly rendezvoused with the Dauntlesses, circling to the northwest over Kula Gulf. The reassembled strike force rounded the northern tip of New Georgia for the trip back down the Slot. On their way, the American raiders probably passed, sight unseen, PO1c Takeshi Takahashi and his observer, who were returning to Kahili from a 204th Kokutai reconnaissance flight over Tulagi and Lunga Roads. Trying to cope with a troublesome engine, Takahashi decided to risk incurring the wrath of aroused and very twitchy AA gunners by pancaking at Munda in the wake of the Cactus air strike. Evidently, the attackers failed to inflict serious damage to the runway, nor did drifting smoke from the fires obscure the field enough to deter the twin-engine Dinah from touching down safely. A moot comment, perhaps, on the effectiveness of the day's bombing.

Finally, 4 February also saw the combat-weary crews of the USAAF's 70th BS take off from Henderson Field in their equally tired B-26s for a well-deserved rest in Fiji. Although necessary, the timing for this unit's rotation was most inopportune, coming as it did at the peak of the action involving Operation KE. The Marauder squadron had played no small part in the suppression campaign against Japanese bases and airstrips in the Central Solomons and the Bougainville-Shortlands area. The unit would be sorely missed, not being replaced until 7 February, when the 69th BS reported in for duty at Cactus. In the interim the hard-pressed Marine and Navy light-bombers proceeded to fill the void left by the Army mediums, flying a number of base-suppression missions in addition to their attacks on the Tokyo Express and other Japanese shipping.

CHAPTER 15

THE HALF-TIME SHOW

American ground forces cautiously closed in on the embattled rear guard of General Hyakutake's 17th Army. Although they did not fathom the nature of the Tokyo Express that had just run the gauntlet, U.S. theater commanders instinctively felt that something was afoot. Long-range JNAF reconnaissance missions flown during the first few days of February observed three of five potent USN task forces at sea east of Guadalcanal, including carriers. Admiral Halsey was evidently taking advantage of a heavy weather front to position these warships closer to the Canal—at least in the short term. Advancing the flattops clearly represented a calculated risk, but the stormy weather confounded any attempt by torpedo-laden Bettys to neutralize this threat. Rough weather slowed Japanese submarine movements as well. The Cactus Air Force's unrelenting base-suppression campaign against Munda and Vila further reinforced Admiral Kusaka's sense of urgency. Reacting to these ominous signs, he set in motion the next run of the Tokyo Express.

Gathering eleven transport destroyers and nine escorts, Admiral Hashimoto sailed from the Shortlands shortly before 1300 on 4 February. This time the Cape Esperance unit consisted of the transports *Akigumo*, *Hamakaze*, *Isokaze*, *Kazagumo*, *Tanikaze*, *Urakaze*, and *Yugumo*, screened by *Asagumo*, *Kawakaze*, *Kuroshio*, *Maikaze*, *Samidare*, and *Shirayuki*. In the Kamimbo unit sailed the transports *Arashio*, *Oshio*, *Tokitsukaze*, and *Yukikaze*, protected by *Fumizuki*, *Nagatsuki*, and *Satsuki*.

Sixteen Oscars of the 11th Sentai's 1st Chutai, likely staging through Ballale, were spotted over Buka at 1145 on their way to assume CAP duties over the convoy at 1500 hours. As an extra precaution, the 582nd Kokutai was apparently ordered to conduct a fighter sweep down the Slot to probe the route for nasty surprises. Early that morning sixteen Zeros took off from Buin, heading southeast. At 0820 Cactus received a report that an estimated fourteen aircraft were sighted flying over the Slot a mere hundred miles from Guadalcanal. The 582nd's search having turned up nothing ominous on the part of the U.S. Navy, Admiral Hashimoto's twenty destroyers proceeded undisturbed down the Slot. Fifteen Zeros from the *Zuikaku* detachment flew out of Buin to join the CAP at 1535, just as the Tokyo Express crept into striking range of the Cactus Air Force.

Alerted to the convoy's presence by coastwatchers on Choiseul and Vella Lavella, General Mulcahy and his men could only wonder at their adversary's dogged tenacity as they prepared to meet and defeat him. Eleven VMSB-233 and VMSB-234 Dauntlesses cleared the rendezvous area over Lunga Point at 1440 in the company of fourteen Navy Avengers. Flying with them were sixteen Wildcats, eight Airacobras, and four Lightnings. The F4Fs from VGS 11, 12, and 16 covered the SBDs; the P-39s from the 67th and 70th FSs had the TBFs in tow; the P-38s from the 339th flew high cover over the formation.

Back at Henderson, Lieutenant White of VMSB-233 fretted impatiently while a line crew fussed over a troublesome engine. Finally, White gunned his SBD down the runway in a gallant but futile effort to catch up. The gremlins that had held him back did catch up, however, and spread through the strike force like an epidemic. Savo Island had just passed below when Lieutenant Weber's engine began to run rough. Fellow VMSB-233 pilot Lieutenant Etheridge was unable to lean out his rich-flowing fuel mixture to prevent his motor from cutting out. Captain Bercik of VMSB-233 not only was cursed by engine trouble, but also discovered that his nose-mounted machine guns would not fire. Unreliable guns also plagued VMSB-234's Lieutenant Boniske, courtesy of a faulty firing mechanism. Reluctantly, one by one another four Dauntlesses dropped out of formation, and turned back for Henderson. The USN Avengers duly contracted their share of woes. Recalcitrant motors had already prevented two of the TBFs from taking off; now Ensign Speake touched down at 1520 with a troublesome rear turret.

Unfazed by this thinning of their ranks, the remaining seven SBDs and thirteen TBFs droned on beneath a bright tropical sun, their compass needles hovering about 303 degrees. An RNZAF Hudson pinpointed the Tokyo Express 220 miles away from Cactus at 1530 hours. The strike force was just to the northwest of Kolombangara when at the entrance to Vella Gulf, some twenty miles distant, pilots picked up traces of smoke and the long slivers of wakes trailing the inbound destroyers. The convoy was steering 122 degrees at an estimated thirty knots. The time was almost 1600 hours (see map 7).

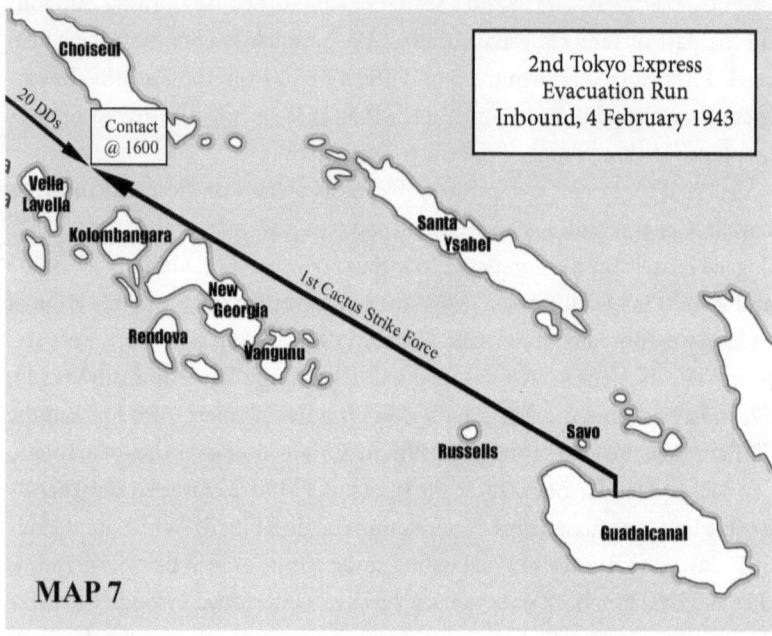

MAP 7

Drawing nearer, the Cactus airmen could discern the familiar parallel columns loosely spread about one mile apart. The Japanese destroyers were stationed line-astern in two rows of ten ships, each allegedly headed by a "*Terutsuki*"-class vessel. Individual destroyers did not even bother to zigzag in their haste to disperse via 90-degree turns. The TBFs accurately reported that the destroyers made outward turns, "North column to port and South column to starboard." U.S. Army escort pilots observed, "The first four or five in each column appeared to execute 90-degree turns to the inside, while those in the last half of each column turned outside."

Overhead, the SBDs and TBFs began to deploy for their attacks while the enemy fighter CAP—estimated by the Marine and Navy fliers at twenty-five to twenty-nine Zekes and Hamps—maneuvered to intercept them. Among the virtuoso pilots of the Zero *daitai* led by Lt. Kenjiro Notomi were WO Katsuma Shigemi, WO Yoshio Oishi, CPO Maseo Sasakibara, and CPO Saburo Saito.

Cruising at 24,000 feet, the USAAF high cover spotted another formation below at 12,000 feet—likely the 11th Sentai Oscars out of Rabaul. Before the Lightnings could drop down to intervene, around twenty Japanese fighters—by this time including the 11th Sentai's Munda-based detachment—slipped through to close with the dive-bombers as the covering Wildcats strove to intercept them. Several F4F pilots claimed victories in the ensuing air battle. Lieutenant Henry put in for two enemy planes; the smoking fifties of Lieutenant (junior grade) Timmes laid claim to two more. Lieutenants McKee and Dodds added one claim each. Ensign Woodcock fell victim to enemy fire, but not before he purportedly sent a "Zero" down ahead of him.

Capt. Otis Calhoun kept his formation of three-plane sections tight as the Dauntlesses descended at high speed from ten thousand feet to set up for stern-on runs on the three lead destroyers of the left column. Emerging from a shallow turn, Captain Calhoun wagged his wings, signaling for the attack to begin. First to push over, Calhoun selected the first destroyer as his target. He pulled his dive-bomber up over his inside wingman and dove in, dive brakes extended. Calhoun's inside and outside wingmen followed him down with the remaining SBDs.

The destroyer was still swinging sharply to port, forcing Calhoun to corkscrew his plane to stay on target. Try as he might, he only managed a near miss off the starboard bow with a 1,000-pound bomb. Maj. Bill Roberson's 1,000-pounder appeared to score a direct hit amidships, as did MTSgt. Bob Fore's 500-pounder and two 100-pounders. Lt. John Beebe was also on the mark: his 1,000-pound missile smacked into the stern of the elusive destroyer. Capt. Sumner Whitten's 100-pounders straddled the third destroyer's stern, but his 500-pounder held fast in its shackle.

Former carrier-based "dirty grey" Zeros, together with "orange" Zeros and mottled-green Oscars, were streaking past the covering USN Wildcats by this time. Wary of the heavy flak bursts floating up from their own ships, the enemy pilots took care to harass the SBDs only during the early moments of the latter's runs. Then, steering clear of the flak, they broke off to reposition themselves for a second bounce when the bombers pulled out. To defend against the swooping Japanese fighters, the Dauntless pilots executed fast pullouts, turning into their attackers to meet them head-on with their forward-firing twin fifties.

Lieutenant Bachtel managed a near miss off the bow of the second destroyer before three Zeros jumped him. Cannon fire shot away most of the SBD's tail surface, but rear gunner Sergeant Smith knocked down one of the Zeros.

Lt. Jim Murphy was midway into his dive on the same target when 20-mm slugs from several Mitsubishis hit his nacelle and fuselage, wounding gunner Cpl. Warren Williamson in the leg. Releasing his bomb, which he believed scored a probable hit, Murphy pulled out with smoke pouring from his engine and oil spattering his windscreen. His Dauntless began a shallow, controlled glide toward Ringi Island, lying off Choiseul. Army P-39 fliers confirmed his descent "near the SE tip of Choiseul." When Murphy ditched at 1607, he pitched forward, shattering his goggles against the bombsight; a shard of glass lodged in his eye. Deploying their life raft, the two men waited for a lingering pair of destroyers to leave before climbing in. Paddling steadily, they reached Choiseul early next morning. Natives thought that a pair of Japanese fliers had come ashore. A canoe of warriors arrived, bristling with machetes and clubs, to dispatch Murphy and Williamson to Nippon's warrior's shrine at Yasukuni. Fortunately, they recognized the fliers as Americans and took them safely to the local coastwatcher.

If the SBDs had received no small amount of attention from the defending Japanese fighters, Lt. Cdr. John Hulme's TBFs were about to go through sheer hell! Their torpedo runs began at 14,000 feet with a dive to 5,000 feet. The Avengers then went into their glides, leveling off at 200 feet to drop their missiles 1,000 yards from the target. To their credit, Capt. Jim Robinson's defending Airacobras stuck with their charges, diving with them from 5,000 feet down to between 50 and 100 feet above the water to intercept any Japanese fighters.

Almost immediately they were themselves bounced by Zekes, Hamps, and Oscars. Captain Robinson exploded one Zeke before a call for assistance from Lt. Nilo Inciardi, who was being swarmed, brought Robinson on the double. He scored hits on a Hamp that fell away smoking; a Grumman pilot later confirmed that it crashed in the water. The unfortunate enemy pilot could have been CPO Maseo Sasakibara. After successively tangling with two "carrier bombers" and a pair of fighters, claiming all four as certain kills,

Sasakibara faced off with another Cactus plane. As the two pilots approached head-on, their guns flashing, Sasakibara's Zero took fatal hits in its cowl. Struggling to maintain control as he descended rapidly toward the water, the young warrior managed to level off in time to ditch his steed. Upon impact with the steel-hard sea, he was thrown forward, gashing his head. Despite the concussion, he rallied in time to abandon his sinking plane. In due course Sasakibara was rescued by a ship and hospitalized.

Robinson managed to disperse Inciardi's assailants, but not before they had peppered the latter's Cobra. No fewer than thirty slugs tore ragged holes in Inciardi's fighter during the fracas. Another "Zero" went down at the hands of Lt. Bill Fiedler. Then lieutenants Inciardi and Bob Tullis each fired into enemy fighters. They set them to smoking, "but didn't observe final results."

Very few of the Navy Avenger pilots were able to carry out their torpedo attacks unmolested. One pilot had to break off his torpedo run altogether to shake off pursuing Japanese fighters. ARM3c Jesse Scott Jr., Ensign Peck's radio-gunner, tracked a Zero that rose up behind his TBF and, with cannons and machine guns blazing, closed to within fifty yards. As Scott and turret gunner S. Tefft returned the fire, a 20-mm shell whizzed past Scott to explode in the radioman's empty seat, folded against the bulkhead behind the torpedo. Firing tracer, AP, and incendiaries, the persistent TBF gunners started the Zero smoking. It dropped back, but not before raking the Avenger's underside. The TBF crewmen duly claimed a probable.

Still in control, Ensign Peck took the big Grumman down for his torpedo run. On the way in, another Zero pulled abreast slightly below, evidently lining up the TBF ahead of Peck. Neither Tefft nor Scott could bring their weapons to bear. Instinctively, the frustrated radio-gunner started to draw his side arm, but the Mitsubishi quickly pulled ahead. Leveling out, Peck tugged at his release handle, but the fish held fast. The first Zero's fusillade had done its work. Pulling up, Peck banked the TBF away amidst a hail of flak. All other torpedo drops missed.

Bursting flak sprayed Ens. Keith Hollandsworth's nacelle; his motor began to sputter, then it quit. Jettisoning his torpedo, Hollandsworth glided toward Choiseul, chased by four Hamps that took turns making overhead passes at his starboard side from out of the sun. The first pass knocked out the ball turret, and wounded radio-gunner Adcock in the leg. One Hamp tried to come up from below, but Adcock's stinger caught it in the engine nacelle, whereupon it veered away smoking.

Twisting and turning to shake off his pursuers, Hollandsworth realized that his heavy TBF was dropping too fast to reach land. Army P-39 pilots saw him ditching off the coast. After a wheels-up water landing, the crew went over the side amidst strafing attacks by a pair of Hamps. The pilot and his enlisted radio-gunner took refuge under a wing, but waterspouts engulfed the turret gunner as he tried to swim away from the foundering plane. He went under as the plane sank. After the A6Ms left, the two survivors inflated their dinghy and paddled some three miles to shore. Once on Choiseul, they were rescued by friendly natives and turned over to coastwatchers Seton and Waddell. They were soon joined by Lieutenant Murphy and his radio-gunner. Ironically, it had been Hollandsworth who had instructed the locals to kill Murphy and Williamson after being told they were a Japanese aircrew.

Things progressed no better among the bomb-carrying TBFs. With the P-39s now tied up below by the Oscars, they went in unprotected, gliding down to release their bombs at three thousand feet. Most were beset by Zekes and "dune-colored" Hamps that elected to stick with their quarry when the Avengers plunged through relatively inaccurate AA fire.

The Zeros attacked in *shotai* of three, making passes as each bomber started its dive to sea level. The enemy pilots gunned their nimble fighters from Grumman to Grumman, triggering bursts of 7.7-mm and 20-mm fire into each. Almost every TBF took hits. A mere five out of nine Avengers were able to drop their bombs. Only Ensign Beidelman and Ensign Riddle appear to have scored. Beidelman claimed one or more hits on the lead destroyer of the left column with his 500-pound and 100-pound bomb salvo. The observant Army escort reported direct bomb hits on only two destroyers.

Six Zekes attacked Ensign Riddle on his pullout. He dove for the deck with the enemy fighters on his tail, taking turns raking his aft fuselage. The turret gunner, AMM3c Herb Hopp, hosed the cowling, engine, and cockpit of one A6M as it pulled by. Heavily damaged, the Zero fell away. In turn the following Zero partially disabled the turret, and Hopp was wounded by splinters and shards of Plexiglas. Now making high-side passes, the enemy pilots concentrated on the forward half of the TBF. Before he was hit and killed, Riddle jinked his big bomber recklessly as he headed for the northwest tip of New Georgia, while Hopp tried to traverse his guns, spraying the

Zekes with sporadic barrages of lead. About three miles offshore, he hit one and it fell off, belching smoke.

With a dead pilot now at the controls, the faltering Avenger crossed the coast at speed, plowing into the rainforest on the side of a hill near the Masi River. Hopp crawled out of the wreckage as it burst into flames. Reaching the cockpit, he was unable to free Riddle's lifeless body before the spreading fire drove him back. Helpless, he found a nearby trail and stole away. AMM3c Bill Owen was thrown through the open bomb bay when the plane hit. Regaining consciousness a few feet away from the blazing wreck, he bandaged his wounds with strips of parachute silk and, still dazed, wandered away down the same trail. With the help of local villagers who rounded them up, Riddle's two surviving crewmen were safely delivered into the hands of coastwatcher Donald Kennedy. They were subsequently ferried back to Cactus via PBY.

The Navy aircrews continued to fight back as best they could. AEM2c H. Hadsell, Commander Hulme's turret gunner, let fly one hundred rounds at an attacking Zero, which caught fire and was last seen tracing a smoky arc toward the water. But the Zekes and Hamps exacted their pound of flesh from the ranks of the lumbering torpedo bombers. In addition to ensigns Riddle and Hollandsworth, ensigns Chessman and Teague were shot down. Chessman, Teague, and their two crews went in unobserved and were posted missing.

Their bombs and torpedoes expended, the American light bombers broke contact and headed for Guadalcanal, with the covering fighters following suit. The exhausted strike force made landfall at 1740 hours. Most of the Navy TBFs were found to be sporting anywhere from three to ten bullet holes each after they touched down.

Ensign Peck's Avenger was in grimmer shape. Nursing his badly shot-up plane back to Henderson, Peck and his crewmen, Scott and Tefft, were contemplating the merits of a landing attempt with bomb bay doors stuck open and with a torpedo that was on the verge of dropping out! The only other choice was to bail out. Peck decided to risk all and bring his heavily damaged ship in—without flaps and with his tail hook dangling down. Hearts were racing as the TBF's landing gear hit the Marston matting of Henderson's runway. Luckily, the torpedo was not jarred free, nor did it explode in its shackles upon impact. Praising their pilot, Scott and Tefft walked away from this, their first mission, shaking their heads and wondering if future sorties would all be like this one. Their Avenger was a shambles and barely salvable.

The 11th Sentai put in for two SBDs, two F4Fs, and one "P-40" destroyed in exchange for an Oscar, flown by Sgt. Koji Aoyama, shot down. Actual Cactus losses totaled one SBD, four TBFs, and one F4F. The Cactus fighter screen officially claimed seven victories for the loss of the F4F. The Navy TBF pilots, who bore the brunt of the onslaught, saw things slightly differently: "In all the fracas the fighter support was not too good," bluntly stated their combat report. However, it concluded, referring to their own lack of hits, "Not too good an average today although fighters did report the destruction of five Zeros."

In this first attack, American light-bomber pilots dropped four 1,000-pound bombs, twenty-one 500-pound bombs, four 100-pound bombs, and two torpedoes, claiming four certain hits on what was probably the *Maikaze*. She lay dead in the water while her crew assessed damage and fought a stubborn deck fire. One near miss flooded her engine room; another damaged her rudder, crippling her. The *Nagatsuki* circled nearby to lend assistance, while five Zeros orbited overhead. Towlines were soon secured, and the *Nagatsuki* began towing the *Maikaze* back to the Shortlands. The *Yugiri* was dispatched to meet the pair en route and escort them to safety.

The first strike force had been gone about an hour when Cactus ground crews scraped together enough planes for a second mission. However, this one was to be strictly a dive-bomber show. A pool of fifteen SBDs from VMSB-233 and VMSB-234 joined up with Lieutenant Emerson's dozen VF-72 F4Fs and four P-40s from the 44th FS for the trip up the Slot.

Four P-38s from the 339th FS were on their way to join up when Captain Dewey's flight glimpsed a pair of bandits between Henderson Field and Cape Esperance. Cactus Recon diverted the Lightnings to pursue the bandits. Having ordered external fuel tanks dropped, Dewey failed to intercept the bogeys. He and lieutenants Shubin, Cramer, and Richardson now had insufficient fuel to make the mission, so they reluctantly returned to Fighter Two. A second flight of P-38s, consisting of lieutenants Bob Rist, Fred Purnell, Jake Jacobson, and Ray Bezner, caught up to the strike force, taking up their customary station above the formation.

The raiders had not gone far when Lt. Andy Csaky of VMSB-234 dropped out with engine trouble, as did Lieutenant Reed and Master Technical Sergeant Olsen from VMSB-233. Twelve dive-bombers were now left to carry on. Knowing that Japanese fighters had intercepted the first strike force, the SBDs almost certainly flew to the attack in the prescribed tactical formation for defense—that is, in divisions where the second section of three planes positioned itself behind and slightly below the leading section to bring all twelve of their rear-firing machine guns to bear on assaulting Zeros.

Approaching 165 miles out from the Canal, Cactus airmen picked up eighteen enemy destroyers "north of the tip of New Georgia" at 1705 hours (see map 8). They also noticed a column of smoke drifting skyward from a burning ship on the horizon. Flying closer, Capt. Albert Johnson's P-40 pilots reported, "Another DD was observed on fire, heading back." Now on a course of 120 degrees, the Tokyo Express had reformed into two extended columns of nine ships each that were already breaking to port and starboard as the strike force closed to contact. This time the AA barrage rose hot and heavy.

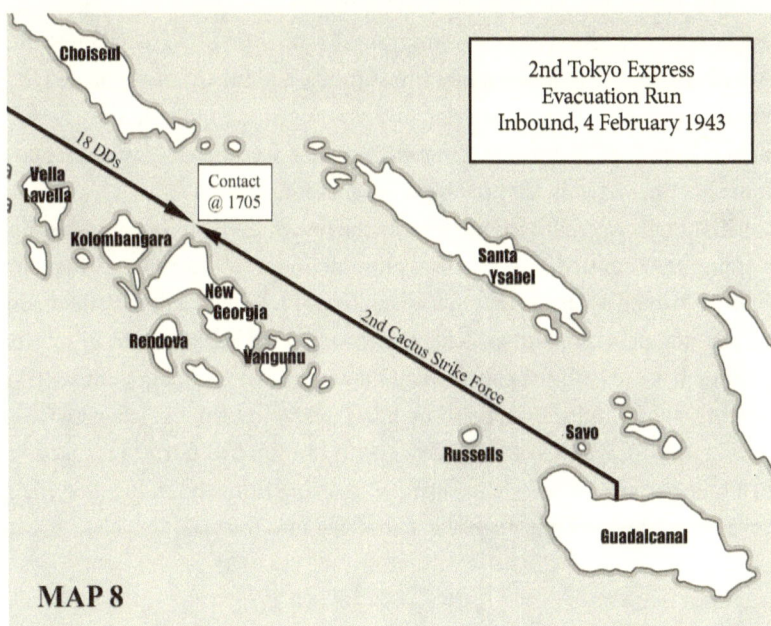

MAP 8

The Japanese fighter CAP lost fewer planes in the first engagement than the number claimed by Cactus pilots. Moreover, some of the defending

Oscars pancaked into Munda to refuel and rearm between the two strikes. In the wake of three consecutive days' bombings, Munda's ground echelon must have toiled like beavers to patch up the runway in time to launch its own Oscars, then service at least a portion of the combatants after the first fight. Thus, all told, an estimated twenty to thirty Japanese fighters were able to fly to this second intercept.

Uncharacteristically, the P-38 high cover descended from 24,000 feet, leveling out at 10,000 feet as the attack on the destroyers developed. The Lightning pilots spotted fifteen Zeros flying below them, but Lieutenant Rist refrained from attacking at lower altitudes, where his pilots would be fighting at a disadvantage. The Navy F4F fliers, however, tangled with the Zekes, Hamps, and Oscars without hesitation, claiming five "Zeros" destroyed. Ensigns Kinsella and Bob Jennings each put in for one and shared credit for another. Lt. "Red" Hessel also scored.

VF-72's Lt. Bob Sorensen jumped a Zero off Visu Visu Point, sending rounds into its cockpit. The A6M fell off into a vertical dive, and Sorensen claimed a probable. He then attracted the interest of a quartet of Zeros. Turning into one, he sent it away smoking, but the other three overwhelmed him. After his crippled Wildcat caught fire and splashed into Marovo Lagoon, he came ashore near Batuna Mission and was soon safe in the hands of Maj. Kennedy at Segi. Lieutenant Emerson was less fortunate: a Japanese pilot must have nailed him, for he was posted missing.

The P-40s were also in the thick of the brawl. Captain Johnson shot up a Hamp that emitted smoke before plummeting into the water. Lieutenant Matson flamed what he believed was a Zeke. Lt. Jack "Spyder" Bade made a high-side pass on another Zeke; tracers arced into the Mitsubishi's nose, flashing back toward the cockpit as it flew into his converging gunfire. The stricken fighter rolled over, crashing into the sea. In turn, the Japanese CAP sent Lt. Mike Carter's Warhawk down with cannon fire. Carter managed to bail out, but he was never seen again. Observing from above, the P-38 high cover estimated no fewer than six "Zeros" fell into the sea.

All the SBDs carried 1,000-pound bombs except for Lt. Eystein Nelson, who was armed with a 500-pounder plus two 100-pounders. Not waiting for the enemy fighters to pounce, Capt. Dick Blain led his group into a high-speed, turning dive from nine thousand feet. Reaching the release point, Captain Blain dropped his bomb on the *Kuroshio*, the second destroyer in the left column. A geyser of water shot up amidships off the port side. Most of the other pilots concentrated on the *Kuroshio* as well, inflicting several hits. Cornering desperately, she took a 1,000-pound bomb amidships from Capt. Hoyle Barr, followed by Lieutenant Nelson's three-bomb salvo in the same area. Her stern absorbed a 1,000-pounder from Lt. Dayton Swickard and a near miss from Lt. Art Blackmun. Lieutenant Woodley's missile sent up another geyser off her starboard bow. The *Kuroshio* was observed to be smoking and listing to port. Claims of three bomb hits jibe with the admission that she sustained three hits, causing a fire that led to the flooding of her magazines.

Lt. Carl Brorein planted his 1,000-pounder square on the fantail of the lead destroyer in the left column as it canted into a turn to port. Capt. Art Moran's bomb splashed near the starboard bow of the speeding vessel. The revelation that the *Kawakaze* "disclosed scratches" is an understatement; a number of her seams had split, flooding five of her compartments. Initially ordered to turn back, the order was rescinded when her captain reassured Admiral Hashimoto that she could continue on the mission.

Lt. Dale Thrasher, Lieutenant Otteson, and MTSgt. Ed Spencer went after the third destroyer—possibly the *Shirayuki*. Lieutenant Thrasher was unable to observe the result of his drop. A faulty release mechanism doomed Sergeant Spencer's bomb to remain in its harness. When Lieutenant Otteson went in, the *Shirayuki* was just pulling through a violent circle to port at thirty-four knots, her six 5-inch guns and a dozen 13-mm machine guns pouring out a heavy barrage. Otteson released his 1,000-pounder, but only managed a miss off the destroyer's port bow. The only *Fubuki*-class destroyer under command, she had been de rigueur in destroyer design in her heyday. But the detonation must have sent a severe tremor through her aged vitals; at 1725 Admiral Hashimoto's flagship glided temporarily to a stop with a faltering power train. The admiral transferred his flag to the *Kawakaze*. By 1830, however, temporary repairs had been made, and the *Shirayuki* was under way again.

A total of nine 1,000-pound bombs, one 500-pound bomb, and two 100-pound bombs were expended in the second air strike. The P-40 escort reported, "Direct hits were observed on the bow of one DD and amidships of another DD, both of which were left burning." The VMSB-234 combat report noted, "#2 DD was reported as smoking badly and seemed to have a list to port side." Flying high above the show, the Lightning pilots confirmed at least one direct hit on a destroyer.

Despite some mauling by the Cactus escort, enemy fighters broke through to the dive-bombers. The "silver" Zekes of the *Zuikaku*'s fighter *hikotai* were now joined by the "dirty brown" Hamps of the newly arrived 204th Kokutai. Lieutenant (junior grade) Morisaki's dozen Zeros did not leave Buin until 1630, arriving on the scene only after the air combat broke out. Following their leader, aces LA Ryoji Ohara and Warrant Officer Hidaka, together with other Zeros and Oscars, screamed down after the SBDs until the flak got too close for comfort. Zooming up, the Japanese pilots maneuvered to jump the Dauntlesses as the latter recovered from their dives.

"[Zeros] were thick," observed the SBD crews. "Attacked SBDs in sections of 3 and seemed to be all over the sky." One enemy fighter pulled up behind Lieutenant Blackmun as he came out of his bomb run. Blackmun took evasive action while the Zero pilot traded fire with his rear gunner. Rapidly expending a one-hundred-round magazine, his gunner ran out of ammo, leaving the A6M free to pour cannon and machine-gun fire into the temporarily defenseless dive-bomber. Luckily, Blackmun managed to join up with other reforming SBDs, thus avoiding the coup de grâce. Combined return fire from the Dauntlesses drove off the nettlesome Zero. Landing back at Henderson after an uneventful return trip, Blackmun's crew counted some two hundred holes in their plane.

Lt. D. Russell dove with a trio of Zeros on his tail. He got his bomb away before 7.7-mm and 20-mm fire from this *shotai* crippled his Dauntless on the pullout. He and his rear gunner, SSgt. Ray Stanley, perished when their plane nosed over and plowed into the ocean about a mile from the scene of battle.

Lieutenant Thrasher was more fortunate. Though Zeros thoroughly shot up his SBD, Thrasher somehow limped back to Henderson Field to face his next challenge: a landing on one wheel. Anxious eyes looked on as he touched down on the left landing gear, fighting gravity to keep the right wing level. As the Dauntless lost speed, the right wing dipped onto the runway, and the aircraft ground-looped to a stop amidst a swirl of dirt and debris. Thrasher's gunner, Cpl. John Blair, who was suffering from a deep wound that furrowed his forehead to the brain, was quickly extricated from the wreck and given immediate medical attention. Miraculously, he survived his grievous head wound.

The 204th Kokutai claimed four unspecified Cactus planes destroyed in the second engagement. The 11th Sentai listed three SBDs and one F4F destroyed. Actually, no fewer than six SBDs were seriously damaged by flak and enemy air action in this second exchange; another was shot down. The Cactus fighter screen lost one P-40 and two F4Fs.

In the two wild melees that had broken out over the Tokyo Express, the *Zuikaku* pilots alone claimed a phenomenal twenty-five Cactus planes destroyed, as well as numerous probables and damaged aircraft. CPO Masao Sasakibara claimed two fighters and a pair of bombers shot down, and CPO Saburo Saito claimed another two unidentified planes. Acknowledged *Zuikaku* losses for the entire day's aerial combat totaled two Zeros shot down—one flown by WO Katsuma Shigemi. Sasakibara had to ditch his Zero. Two more *Zuikaku* Zeros were damaged. On the other side of the ledger, Cactus pursuit pilots claimed seven enemy fighters shot down—three by the P-40s and four by the F4Fs. The 11th Sentai lost Sgt. Hiroshi Yuu of the 1st Chutai in this engagement. The 204th Kokutai reported no losses.

Coastwatcher Horton reported four fighters touching down at Munda from out of the east at 1718, followed by three more at 1830. At 1915 another dozen flew in from the east and landed—probably the last daytime CAP covering the Tokyo Express.

In this latest round, the Cactus Air Force had gotten in a few good punches, but had failed to deliver the elusive knockout blow. Admiral Hashimoto pushed on toward Guadalcanal.

At 2245 that night a Black Cat picked up ten of Admiral Hashimoto's destroyers on its airborne search radar about forty miles west of Guadalcanal. The PBY-5A tracked the first four until they arrived in the vicinity of Coughlin Harbor, then reestablished contact with the other six destroyers at a point between Visale and the mouth of the Aruligo River, alerting Cactus while it continued to shadow them.

The night of 4–5 February turned out to be especially disruptive for the Canal's airstrips: Nells from the 701st Kokutai furnished seven hours' airbase suppression while the Tokyo Express loaded troops. The ordeal began when the first Nell made its bombing run at 1930 hours. Another bomber showed up at 2135, then returned ten minutes later, followed by a third G3M at 2230 hours. The action wrapped up at 0240 when the last four Nells passed overhead, each one dumping ten bombs on Cactus' sleep-deprived inhabitants. The night's grief totaled seventy-five 133-pound bombs.

A division of five Marine SBDs once again loaded up with 1,000-pounders and managed to get safely off the ground between air raids. Vectored by the Black Cat, they headed for Aruligo. Upon their approach, the Cat's pilot obligingly illuminated one of the destroyers with a flare. Taking their cue, the Dauntlesses made their runs. A series of bright flashes followed by towering waterspouts bracketed the enemy ship, but no cigar. The Catalina dropped a flare over a target of its own at 0030. Proceeding to unload its four 500-pound bombs, it failed to score a hit.

The Tokyo Express continued to load up while an Aichi E13A floatplane from the 958th Kokutai cruised overhead. Without any forward-firing machine-guns, its crew understandably chose not to go after either the SBDs or the PBY. The Jake carried up to four 133-pound bombs, but neither American destroyers nor PT boats materialized.

The Japanese had inflicted terrible punishment upon Lieutenant Commander Calvert's PT-boat command two nights prior; few of his boats remained seaworthy. As for the Cactus Striking Force, on the afternoon of 1 February—even before his courageous but questionable sortie to confront the Tokyo Express on its first run—Captain Briscoe had petitioned Admiral Halsey to withdraw his remaining destroyers, arguing that the *Nicholas* needed to have her bomb damage repaired; alone, his other two ships could not take on a whole flotilla of Japanese destroyers. Halsey concurred. Briscoe's tiny force was back in Espiritu Santo by 5 February.

The 17th Army had been ordered to load its *daihatsu* and collapsibles beforehand so as to have them waiting offshore to speed up the embarkation process. Unmolested, apart from the brief U.S. air attacks, Admiral Hashimoto's destroyers proceeded to embark another grateful contingent of 3,902 Japanese troops, slipping away before Cactus could marshal enough resources to react. The Black Cat reported their withdrawal at 0100, shadowing its favorite six back up the Slot until it lost contact with them around 0325 hours. At around 0700 a CAP of fourteen 252nd Kokutai Zeros arrived overhead; they were relieved at about 0930 by fifteen Zeros from the 253rd.

Not all of that night's prospective evacuees appear to have boarded the ships. Perhaps rattled by the Cactus air strike, the Japanese cut short the embarkation, but evidently decided to ferry the leftover soldiers to the Russell Islands under cover of darkness. From there they would be staged back to New Georgia in accordance with the agreed-upon contingency plan. Perhaps beginning to believe that Operation KE was living on borrowed time, Rabaul wanted to remove all its men from Guadalcanal as soon as possible. It would be safer all around to load troops onto transports in the Russells rather than at Cape Esperance—providing that the evacuees actually made it to Baisen Island. But something stirring on the surface of the Slot prompted the crew of the departing Jake to drop a pair of 133-pound bombs at around 0240 hours. That the Jake's crew was perhaps unfamiliar with nocturnal evacuation protocol, which included the possibility of *daihatsu* plying the waters between Cape Esperance and the Russells, prompts no little speculation on the nature of the perceived target.

Indeed, Lt. Ray Williams and Lieutenant Inciardi, heading west in their P-39s at 0515 to carry out Baker search, came upon what they thought was an American "destroyer or cruiser" firing on two landing barges full of men about three miles off Cape Esperance. Since no destroyers were around, it must have been one of the similarly profiled minesweepers. Not long after, another pair of P-39s, piloted by Capt. Jim Robinson and Lieutenant Cunningham heading past Cape Esperance on Easy search, came upon thirty to fifty assorted landing craft—empty, adrift, and under fire from several PT boats that were in the process of scuttling them.

Paradoxically, the two evacuation runs of the Tokyo Express seemed to confirm suspicions that the Japanese were gearing up for a renewed offensive on Guadalcanal. The primary aim of U.S. strategy remained the same: to choke off the enemy's supply line, thereby depriving him of the wherewithal to continue the fight. By 5 February ComAirSol's staff had dragooned every available B-17, PBY, and RNZAF Hudson to expand Cactus' daily, long-range reconnaissance schedule from two sorties to twelve. An hour before dawn, ten B-17s now fanned out eight hundred miles to the north, west, and south of Guadalcanal, while a pair of Hudsons carried out the two remaining searches.

In its determination to pursue the Tokyo Express back up the Slot, Cactus Strike Command dispatched a force of dive-bombers and torpedo bombers at 0645, together with twelve USN Wildcats. Cruising at 125 knots to maximize range, the strike force covered 220 miles of empty ocean without catching up to Admiral Hashimoto's destroyers as expected. "The visibility was excellent," observed the TBF squadron's combat report, "and any DDs could have been located at least twenty or thirty miles away if they had been there." But they were not there. Thus thwarted, the Cactus strike force followed the well-worn search route around the New Georgia Group, pausing to visit its wrath on that convenient scapegoat, Munda airstrip.

Emerging from over Blackett Strait, VMSB-234's dive-bombers sped across the foot of Kula Gulf. Approaching Munda from the north at 12,000 feet, the eleven SBDs proceeded to glide-bomb without flaps at 6,000 feet. Heavy flak greeted the Dauntlesses, but failed to hit any. Pilots released by sections before quickly withdrawing to the rendezvous point. No fewer than six 1,000-pound bombs chewed up the runway and taxiways near the east end of the field, setting fire to a dump near the "C loop." Orbiting in the vicinity, TBF crews observed as many as five bombs falling beyond the shoreline to resculpture the fringing reef.

With Lt. Cdr. Charles Brunton in the lead, the nine USN Avenger pilots approached from the south at 14,500 feet. Gliding to their 6,000-foot release point, they rained down twenty-nine 500-pound bombs on the runway, taxiways, and revetments. Clouds of smoke rose up at random, though no fires could be seen. Lieutenant Speake struggled with a faulty release mechanism, but his bombs remained in their shackles. Bad luck also plagued Ensign McKinney, who managed to drop only a single bomb.

The heavier flak had dissipated by this time, but Japanese heavy-machine-gun nests energetically continued to spray the skies. One round punched a large hole in Lieutenant Shearon's wing. TBF crews reported three twin-engine bombers parked in revetments at the northeast end of the runway. Upon closer inspection, these planes looked to be little more than wrecked Lilys left there to draw fire. Having thus inflicted what damage they could, the raiders turned for home.

Under the protection of a dozen Navy F4Fs, nine SBDs from VMSB-234 joined up with six more from VMSB-144 to raid Vila at 0915 the following morning. An identical strike force of light bombers, escorted by twenty-two

Navy Wildcats, returned at 1515 that afternoon to deliver another blow to Munda. The bombings caused fires to break out on both airstrips. Seven 339th FS Lightnings, assigned to provide high cover on the afternoon strike, missed the rendezvous, but no airborne enemy fighters were encountered by either strike force.

The nagging question remained: Where *were* the Japanese destroyers?

The 72nd BS sent four separate B-17s aloft to probe the upper reaches of the Solomons as part of ComAirSols' enhanced search program. These long-range Forts, together with the RNZAF Hudsons, represented Cactus' last kick at the cans, but all they overflew were monotonous stretches of ocean.

One Fort from the newly arrived 23rd BS was among the reconnaissance planes ranging far into the Slot in search of the elusive Tokyo Express; the remainder of the squadron prepared to follow, if and when one of the snoopers ferreted out the enemy ships. This B-17 was probing the coast of Bougainville, some 420 miles out from Henderson and deep in enemy territory, when its number 2 engine windmilled to a stop. The pilot reluctantly turned about and set a course for faraway Guadalcanal, instructing his crew to empty the waist and tail guns and drag the ammo belts and extra cases forward from the aftersection to retrim the heavy bomber.

At 0910 a crewman spied another aircraft about five miles off the starboard beam, flying on a parallel course at the same altitude as if it were shadowing the temporarily defenseless B-17. Judging by its silhouette, the crew identified it as "a Mitsubishi 97, a light Japanese two engine bomber." What they really saw was a G4M medium bomber—probably one of four 705th Kokutai Bettys on solo morning patrol out of Rabaul. After thirty-five anxious minutes, during which the nervous gunners contemplated rearming their empty weapons, the enemy plane began to close as if to attack. The pilot of the Fort decided to bluff: unexpectedly, he banked toward the Betty. The B-17 had hardly completed its 90-degree turn when the Mitsubishi abruptly wheeled to the right and, in the words of radio operator Basil Debnekoff, "scooted away."

By then the evacuation convoy was actually far to the south of the Solomon Archipelago, steaming unmolested toward Bougainville. Its wily commander had headed south from Cape Esperance in the hope of melting into the vast expanse of open sea. Experience dictated that the Americans would not allow him to withdraw uncontested; he was, therefore, gambling that any air strike mounted against him would be directed to search the Slot first. The fox had skillfully thrown the hounds off the scent, escaping with another 3,900 troops.

Admiral Hashimoto's destroyers were eventually spotted by coastwatchers on Vella Lavella. At 0940 they reported picking up seventeen warships steaming north-northwest under fighter cover about five miles off the northern tip of Ranonga Island. The CAP comprised fifteen Zeros from the Kahili-based 253rd Kokutai.

At 0945 a PB4Y-1 crew on a photoreconnaissance mission to Buin-Faisi reported seeing only two destroyers amidst the shipping found there. However, they hit the jackpot twenty minutes later, spotting the seventeen destroyers as the Tokyo Express approached the south entrance to Shortland Harbor. Just then fifteen Zeros were seen to rise from Kahili, probably the CAP interrupting its descent toward the field to ward off the intruder. The patrol bomber and its five Lightning escorts from the 339th FS prudently elected to curtail their visit.

Just as well. Below, six Zeros from the 204th Kokutai took off on patrol at 1005 hours. While the 253rd Zeros landed, their CAP mission over, the 204th's *chutai* elected to lie in wait, cruising over the harbor complex, just in case. Coincidentally, after covering seven hundred miles of their search pattern, Captain Hawes' B-17 crew flushed a *chutai* of Zeros. The Mitsubishis gave chase, dogging the B-17 for forty-five tense minutes as the plane commander plowed through one rainsquall after another in a successful effort to shake off his pursuers. Since they were the only known Zeros aloft, and were up for fifty-five minutes, Hawes might have run into the orbiting 204th fighters over Buin-Faisi, though they reported neither sighting nor giving chase to a Fort.

In any event, Captain Hawes finished his reconnaissance and headed home. Passing over a lowly "minesweeper" about 237 miles out from Cactus, the Fort's crew paused to collect some payback, strafing the hapless vessel that they had first seen on their way up. Some three thousand rounds of .50-caliber fire, sprayed over several runs, at last caused a substantial explosion that nearly destroyed the stern of the ship, enveloping it in flames and smoke. Low on both ammo and fuel, the B-17 broke off the attack shortly after 1600 to resume its journey back to Henderson.

CHAPTER 16

THE FINAL TOUCHDOWN

Despite the successful completion of the second evacuation run, things remained critical for the Japanese: a sizable remnant of the 17th Army was still stranded on Guadalcanal in imminent danger of being overrun. Although Admiral Kusaka adamantly refused to abandon the troops clinging to hope at Cape Esperance, a jubilant but cautious Admiral Yamamoto suspected that after two evacuation runs, the Americans must be twigging on to the fact that something was afoot. Would they dispatch their capital ships to intervene on a grand scale should Admiral Hashimoto sortie again?

On 2 February a 705th Kokutai Betty on long-range patrol discovered one of several American task forces, including a carrier, lurking to the south and east of Guadalcanal. The A4M radioed Rabaul before being jumped by a fighter CAP. Fourteen Bettys were sent to attack these warships, but the mission was thwarted by inclement weather that ranged eastward beyond the Central Solomons.

When Operation KE's evacuation phase was about to begin, Yamamoto ordered Vice Adm. Nobutake Kondo to take his Advance Force to within 550 miles of Guadalcanal. Kondo was to distract the Americans and prepare to support the sorties of the Tokyo Express, should the U.S. Navy choose to contest the evacuation runs.

Admiral Yamamoto left nothing to chance. Early on 29 January the fleet carrier *Zuikaku*, accompanied by the smaller *Zuiho*, evidently steamed from Truk toward Rabaul to close the flying distance before the two flattops launched sixty-four aircraft assigned to land-based operations. The sortie was required to accommodate the shorter-ranging Vals that risked not reaching Rabaul from Truk if faced with strong head winds or bad weather.

At 1000 the carrier *Zuikaku* sent off thirty-six Zeros, and the *Zuiho* sent off eleven Zeros and seventeen Vals. The two carriers then returned to Truk in time for the *Zuiho* to sail with Admiral Kondo's Advance Force. The aircraft arrived in Rabaul at 1500 hours.

Yamamoto also beefed up Kondo's original task force with the cruisers *Agano, Atago, Haguro, Myoko, Nagara,* and *Takeo.* Thus reinforced, Kondo weighed anchor on 31 January, his sortie screened by an outer ring of submarines on picket duty in and around the Eastern Solomons. His mission was to cruise eastward to the north of Guadalcanal, eventually venturing as far south as Ontong Java Island. Two days later the fleet oiler *Kenyo Maru* refueled the cruiser *Agano* somewhere well north of the Solomons. That same day a radio intercept alerted admirals Nimitz and Halsey that Kondo was on the move.

A Liberator finally sighted sixteen warships southeast of the Carolines at 1037 on 5 February, steaming on a course of 240 degrees. Fifteen minutes later an update from the PB4Y-1 reported that the task force comprised two carriers, four battleships, six heavy and two light cruisers, plus a dozen destroyers. At 1207 a further revision from the shadowing plane enumerated one fleet carrier (the *Junyo*), one smaller carrier (the *Zuiho*), a battleship, four cruisers, and an escort of twelve destroyers. Kondo's task force had now advanced to a point two hundred miles north of Choiseul.

A 26th BS B-17 on patrol southeast of the Marshall Islands was reaching the limit of its eight-hundred-mile search at 1400 when it, too, came across the Japanese warships. The Fort reported one large and one small carrier, six heavy and six light cruisers, plus fourteen destroyers, steaming at eighteen knots. When sighted, the Advance Force had been roughly heading toward Japan but, upon recognizing the reconnaissance plane swooping over it at 3,500 feet, it executed an about-face and began to close on a provocative course of 110 degrees—southeastward.

Admiral Kondo must have continued in this general direction for a time; his task force was DF'd some 350 miles east of Ontong Java at 0600 on 6 February. Having made his presence known long enough to provoke a countermove on the part of the U.S. Navy, he now turned northwest, headed for Truk. He arrived there without incident on 9 February.

Other IJN warships were also on the move. A B-17 photoreconnaissance aircraft had sighted an "*Atago*-class" cruiser in Ysabel Passage and a

"*Mogami*-class" cruiser between Kobotteron and Monis Islands on 4 February; it further reported a single small "destroyer" at Kavieng. On the morning of 5 February a Cactus search plane reported two heavy cruisers or battleships anchored to the northeast of Erventa Island, off Buin. A photoreconnaissance PBY subsequently confirmed this sighting, but also failed to distinguish between battleships and heavy cruisers. As inconclusive as they are, these reports suggest that the heavy cruisers *Chokai* and *Kumano* had been ordered from Kavieng to Bougainville to back up the final run of the Tokyo Express in case Admiral Kondo's sortie stirred up a hornets' nest among the U.S. task forces operating east of Guadalcanal. As for the light cruiser *Sendai*, it had by now been recalled to Rabaul.

Should Admiral Kondo head for the Solomons, Admiral Nimitz was initially prepared to let Admiral Halsey advance his warships to the edge of the Coral Sea to ambush Kondo with his limited but significant carrier-based air power and then with his surface fleet. TF GEORGE was to advance up the Slot at the same time to interdict anticipated Japanese reinforcement convoys while acting as a distant screen for an American convoy headed for Lunga Roads.

But the unexpected reversal meted out to TF GEORGE off Rennell Island, including the uncalled-for loss of the *Chicago* and the equally needless loss of the *DeHaven* two days later at the hands of Japanese air power, must have dictated caution. Admiral Nimitz' resolve may have been further eroded by no fewer than a dozen sightings or electronic detections of Japanese subs in the South Pacific during January. The freighter *Samuel Gompers* was torpedoed just 115 miles south of New Caledonia on 30 January—a concrete indicator that Japanese subs were deployed to intercept any U.S. task force that made an overt move.

These developments, coupled to the loss of the fleet carriers *Hornet* and *Wasp* in the Solomons, may have sufficed to pressure Nimitz into cancelling the Coral Sea ambush. He chose, instead, to adopt a wait-and-see stance, thereby removing any immediate threat to Operation KE. While each side awaited a decisive, provocative move by the other side's fleet, Cactus continued to do battle alone with the Tokyo Express out of necessity. But unknown to U.S. theater commanders, the hiatus was only a day or two away from resolving itself once and for all.

Full of apprehension, Admiral Kusaka ordered the Tokyo Express out for the third and final time. The *Fumizuki, Satsuki, Tokitsukaze,* and *Yukikaze* were assigned to Kamimbo transport duties. Escorting them were the *Arashio* and *Oshio,* while the *Asagumo, Kuroshio, Samidare,* and the flagship *Shirayuki* acted as a roving cover force. The *Akigumo* and *Yugumo* made up the Russells transport group, with the *Hamakaze, Isokaze, Tanikaze,* and *Urakaze* serving as close escorts and the *Kazagumo* and *Nagatsuki* providing overall cover.

Setting out from Buka Passage early on 7 February with these eighteen destroyers, Admiral Hashimoto decided not to come down the Slot. Instead, he elected to retrace his detour route of 5 February, cruising eastward and then southward into the Solomon Sea. This time, however, the ruse did not succeed. Although a patrolling B-17 was discouraged from investigating the Buka area by three 253rd Kokutai Zeros scrambled at 0830, an F5A photoreconnaissance flight from the USAAF's Canal-based 17th Photographic Squadron (Light) reported at 1220 its sighting of "15 ships, probable DD" four miles southeast of the Shortlands. At 1342 the ever-vigilant coastwatchers on Vella Lavella reported "nineteen" destroyers bearing 293 degrees, headed south-southeast at thirty knots under low-hanging rain clouds, approximately 250 miles from Guadalcanal. The F5A counted "twenty" enemy ships bearing 286 degrees and still closing a half-hour later. The Cactus Air Force had wisely extended its "eyes" to monitor the more southerly approaches to Guadalcanal in anticipation of Admiral Hashimoto's deception. The extra surveillance had paid off.

The Army F5A pilot, who was flying only the second or third combat mission of the newly arrived unit, never returned to base. He was flying an unarmed, high-performance version of the P-38 Lightning. With a top speed of 360 knots at 25,000 feet and a service ceiling of 44,000 feet, the Lockheed was in its element, flying high-altitude reconnaissance missions of up to 2,260 miles return. Such sorties required brief periods of lower-level flying for photo work, but a climb rate of nearly 2,900 feet per minute could readily take the F5A up out of harm's way. Since no Japanese fighter *kokutai* mentions intercepting a lone P-38 this day, one must assume that the F5A pilot experienced a mechanical failure and either bailed out or ditched somewhere in the Solomon Sea.

Henderson Field buzzed with activity as a pool of eighteen SBDs from VMSB-234 and newly arrived VMSB-144 was readied for an interception mission. Takeoff began at 1546 but was marred by a mishap: one Dauntless strayed into a bomb cart inexplicably left on the taxiway, the wreck blocking the following plane until it could be cleared. The second SBD eventually took off, but never caught up to the strike force. Another SBD pilot found he could not retract his landing gear after getting airborne; chagrined, he had no choice but to circle around and land.

The remaining fifteen Dauntlesses—ten from VMSB-234 and five from VMSB-144—were away by 1630 hours. Joining up with twenty Navy Wildcats, the SBDs set out from Lunga Point beneath a low ceiling of heavy cumulus. They flew southwest of the Solomons under a moderate overcast in the direction of the last sighting reported by the F5A pilot. Near Rendova the weather began to clear, revealing a convoy about five miles off the southern tip of the island at 1735 hours. Banking westward toward the ships, the strike force could make out seventeen destroyers in two parallel columns between eight and ten miles away. A heavy storm front obscured the rear of the convoy, shielding the last destroyer (see map 9).

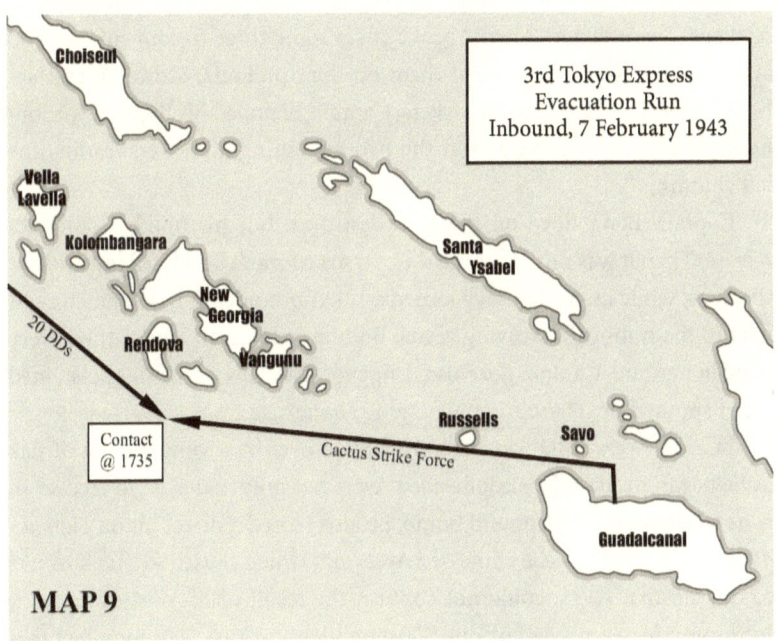

MAP 9

As the attacking planes approached to within four miles, the enemy vessels immediately lunged to port and starboard—all but the lead destroyer of the left column, that is. It executed a sharp about-face to starboard and steamed away between the columns. Capt. Dick Blain had directed his flight to split into three six-plane divisions for an attack on the three leading destroyers of the left column. With the first destroyer retreating posthaste, Blain redirected his first division to concentrate on the second destroyer. The first few ranging shells of 4.7-inch and 5-inch flak blossomed below at five thousand feet, but the dive-bombers ran into hot AA fire as they moved in.

At 1020 that morning, coastwatcher Jack Read had observed a large formation of fighters take off from Buka and head southeast, indicating that a *chutai* of 11th Sentai Oscars was on its way to Buin or Ballale, probably to take up CAP duties. That afternoon another fifteen Oscars out of Munda met the Tokyo Express en route to provide additional air cover.

Until now the JAAF fighter CAP had elected to remain hidden at the edge of the low ceiling to avoid the Cactus fighters while stalking the SBDs. The Dauntless pilots were about to push over into the flak when fifteen or so planes identified as "Zeros" broke cover some three or four miles ahead and zoomed down to intercept them on their pullouts. Sizing up the tactics of these would-be bushwhackers, Captain Blain led his flight in without hesitation for a head-on pass at the two remaining destroyers leading the left column.

Captain Blain dove on the lead destroyer, but his bomb would not release. Then it was miss after miss! Capt. Art Moran's bomb fell just wide of the mark while Lt. Andy Csaky loosed a 1,000-pounder that detonated right next to the frantically weaving vessel. Both missiles must have rattled every plate in her hull. Captain Barr also dropped wide. Geysers of smoke-stained water spouted up all around the lunging *Hamakaze*.

Lt. Bob Ayers' SBD was abruptly flipped over by a violent burst of flak as he began his dive. The coolheaded Ayers not only managed to recover in time to drop his 1,000-pound bomb, he also scored a direct hit on *Hamakaze*'s bow. Lt. John Beebe witnessed Ayers' hit, which caused so much smoke to boil up that Beebe could not confirm the result of his own drop. Lt. T. Johnson released a salvo of one 500-pounder and two 100-pounders that exploded next to *Hamakaze*'s starboard side amidships. Diving to his release point, Lt. Dayton Swickard toggled his bomb, but it held fast.

TSgt. A. Daniels, one of VMSB-144's novices, must have been very excited: he dove his SBD toward the deck, only releasing his ordnance as he pulled out a mere hundred feet or so above the water. He pulled his stick back into his groin, skimming the waves and barely clearing the onrushing *Hamakaze* as he zoomed up. Daniel's bomb salvo dropped into the target's lap! An incredulous Captain Moran watched Daniel's bombs arc into the forward gun turret and bridge areas, starting another fire that enveloped the ship from turret to bow.

Lt. Eystein Nelson of VMSB-234 also got into trouble: diving too steeply, he lost his original target but adjusted in time to register a near hit right next to the *Hamakaze*. Lt. W. Regan of VMSB-144 managed a miss off her stern. The *Hamakaze* emerged from her ordeal with much of her topsides redesigned by Cactus bombs. Confirming claims made by the SBD pilots, her captain radioed that his ship had received direct hits on her number one turret "and other parts of the ship," as well as a near miss on her starboard side. Her boiler room was flooding, but her engines were okay.

The destroyer next in line behind the *Hamakaze* came under attack at about the same time. Lt. Arvid Blackmun released his 500-pound and 100-pound salvo at 1,500 feet, claiming a probable hit. Another VMSB-144 neophyte, Lt. P. Carmichael, got a direct hit on the same destroyer with a 1,000-pound bomb. Last to dive, Lt. W. Miller confirmed Carmichael's hit, which struck the stern of the *Isokaze*, reportedly killing ten men. Then Miller dropped his own salvo just as the damaged destroyer slowed to a stop. Frustrated, he watched as spouts shot up just ahead of the *Isokaze*'s bow.

Both the *Hamakaze* and *Isokaze* were reported burning; one of them—likely the *Isokaze*—"was dead in the water when left." Admiral Hashimoto radioed at 1905 that the *Hamakaze* was still able to navigate under her own power. She left for the Shortlands shepherded by the *Kawakaze*, steaming at fourteen knots with an estimated arrival off Faisi at 0700 on the morrow. Floatplanes from the 11th Seaplane Tender Division joined the pair at 2000 to provide air cover.

Nor did the escaping first destroyer—likely the *Urakaze*—get away unchallenged. Lt. Carl Brorein went after her, but estimated his bomb salvo overshot by seventy-five feet or more. However, Lieutenant Brorein must have planted his bombs closer to *Urakaze* than he thought, for the detonations shook her enough to cause some damage. In the event, both the *Isokaze* and the *Urakaze* went on to complete the mission.

The flak grew thicker when destroyers in the right column, realizing that they were not being targeted, maneuvered closer to lend the left column the weight of their AA batteries. Every SBD was tracked by flak on its pullout, but only two Dauntlesses suffered minor shrapnel hits. Several pilots remarked that the dense barrage put up by these smaller destroyers was heavier than that normally expected from the larger "*Terutsuki*-class" AA destroyers. When the two columns converged, the combined main-battery fire of the *Kagero*-class and *Yugumo*-class destroyers might have conveyed this impression.

As the SBD attack went in, the fifteen Japanese fighters that were waiting in ambush several miles to the southwest emerged from cloud cover. Peeling off, they descended in a long column to intercept the Dauntlesses. As the SBDs recovered from their runs, the enemy delivered high-side passes against five of their number. One 7.7-mm slug punched through a cockpit, missing the pilot by fewer than two inches. One Japanese pilot attempted a head-on pass. Pulling out over the Dauntless, he was instantly bounced by four or more Wildcats. VMSB-144's aircrews reported that some seven out of the fourteen or fifteen attacking "Zeros" were shot down by U.S. fighters, but in fact duplicate sightings may have occurred.

When the Munda bushwhackers fell upon the SBDs at 1750, another thirty-odd fighters, including not only the 11th Sentai Oscars, but also fifteen Zekes and Hamps from the 582nd Kokutai that had just arrived from Kahili, engaged the outnumbered Wildcats to prevent them from breaking up the ambush. Furious aerial combat raged all over the sky. Notwithstanding the optimistic estimate of SBD aircrews, the Wildcat pilots claimed only three aircraft shot down plus three probables. Lieutenant Torkelson, Lieutenant (junior grade) Sperry, and Ensign Stalker received credit for the three Zeros.

For its part, the JNAF acknowledged the loss of veteran Zero pilot CPO Masami Takemoto of the 582nd Kokutai. JAAF losses are not known. Rendova coastwatcher Lt. Dick Horton reported that of the fifteen Japanese fighters he had observed taking off from Munda earlier that afternoon, only seven returned after the attack. A few of these planes may not have been Munda Oscars, but Bougainville-based fighters that were unable to go back for lack of fuel or due to battle damage.

CPO Saburo Saito of the *Zuikaku*, who flew with the 582nd that day, claimed a pair of victories, but the Americans incurred no losses, eliciting a compliment from the light-bomber crews that the Navy escort had furnished "excellent fighter protection."

Inexplicably, although fifteen Zeros from the 204th Kokutai had been flying CAP, they made no contact with the Cactus strike force, nor did the fifteen Zeros from the 252nd that also appear to have been present. Quite possibly these units may have been sent farther down the Slot in advance of the Tokyo Express to wait in ambush, emulating the tactic used on 11 January. If so, ironically, the Cactus strike force bypassed them in both directions without making contact.

Together, the VMSB-144 and VMSB-234 SBDs had rained down six 1,000-pound bombs, seven 500-pound bombs, and fourteen 100-pound bombs on the Tokyo Express, netting claims for five certain hits: four on the *Hamakaze* and one on the *Isokaze*. Unknown to them, near misses also damaged the *Urakaze*. The attack having petered out, the strike force rendezvoused seven miles off the port bow of the rapidly reassembling convoy. Japanese fighters were content to break off, having protected the destroyers from further harm.

Fourteen destroyers hove to off Cape Esperance that night, two others having been detached to retrieve the Japanese troops temporarily garrisoning the Russell Islands, in addition to those refugees that had managed to escape from Guadalcanal by barge or small craft. Cactus forces failed to intervene in the well-orchestrated embarkation process. Four groups totaling 1,730 soldiers were assembled on the beach at Kamimbo for loading into the twenty-six remaining *daihatsu* and collapsibles. Each group was funneled on board a cluster of five to seven boats, where they patiently rode the offshore swell until each cluster was summoned to either side of its assigned transport. Back on shore, several hundred men too ill or badly wounded to be moved peered over the sights of small arms and automatic weapons, waiting with patient resignation to embrace death at the hands of the advancing Americans. Weighing anchor shortly after midnight, the Tokyo Express evaporated into the night one final time with the last evacuees of the 17th Army.

Ever belligerent, the Cactus Air Force gave chase. Capt. R. Nelson led VMSB-144 up the Slot to the New Georgia group on a fruitless search. His squadron was flying its first mission as a full unit and, consequently, experienced the expected operational problems. Four pilots wound up turning back due to mechanical problems or because they became separated after misinterpreting their flight leader's signals. Arriving off northern New Georgia circa 0907, the fourteen remaining SBDs cruised the surrounding sea-lanes in the company of fifteen USN F4Fs and three 339th FS P-38s, but the Japanese destroyers were well beyond Vella Lavella, withdrawing under a CAP of 6th Shidan Oscars and then of 204th Kokutai Zeros. Coming up empty-handed, the strike force pummeled the Cactus Air Force's favorite whipping boy. You guessed it—Munda airstrip!

Instructed to release their bombs at six thousand feet, these gung ho Marines swooped down to three thousand feet before dropping their ordnance. Eleven SBDs unloaded 1,000-pounders, while the other three dropped standard three-bomb salvos, consisting of one 500-pounder plus two 100-pounders. Circling at 25,000 feet in their P-38s, lieutenants Bezner, Shubin, and Richardson observed four bombs splash harmlessly into the water. Two missiles hit the runway, and another plunged into a supply dump north of the west end of the runway, starting several large fires. The rest randomly cratered the field. The attackers encountered medium to heavy flak, but emerged unscathed.

One pilot spotted a single bomber in a revetment through thick smoke that shrouded the airstrip, but no one else saw any aircraft on the field. The Munda Oscar detachment had pulled out.

Lt. Wellman Huey of the 339th FS took off at 0610 behind Lt. Bob Kersteder, his element leader, to carry out Nan search—a new, daily reconnaissance patrol recently added, along with Fox, Baker, Dog, and Easy searches. Flying at 24,000 feet, the two P-38 pilots spotted thirteen of Hashimoto's destroyers under way some 250 miles up the Slot, steaming toward Bougainville. Neither seeing nor being spotted by the Zero *chutai* of Lt. Cdr. Mitsugu Kofukuda and WO Hatsuo Hidaka, Kersteder and Huey climbed away to the north. None the wiser, the fifteen pilots from the 204th Kokutai carried on with their CAP routine.

Nearing the Shortlands, Nan search came across four more destroyers. The leading pair was returning with the Russell garrison, having overtaken the much slower *Hamakaze* and *Kawakaze*. Operation KE officially came to an end at midmorning on 8 February 1943, when the Tokyo Express dropped anchor off Erventa Island to unload the last cadaverous remnants of General Hyakutake's decimated 17th Army.

Far to the east, lieutenants Kuehnle and Gill of the 70th FS were carrying out Baker search when they came across the abandoned legacy of Operation KE—"twenty or thirty new landing barges near Cape Esperance." But not all the barges and landing craft had been beached and left after loading up the Tokyo Express: some Japanese coxswains had conned their lumbering vessels—most probably loaded with the very last of the evacuees—through the darkness to Baisen Island, an outlying islet of the Russell group. During the morning of 9 February, two P-39s of the 70th FS, piloted by Capt. Jim Robinson and Lt. Richard Koenig, found them beached along Baisen's north shore. They proceeded to strafe them, sinking several before flying off. With their departure, the final curtain rang down on one of the more fascinating dramas of the Pacific War.

CHAPTER 17

OF MEN AND MACHINES

By mid-January 1943 Adm. Bull Halsey had already begun to fret over the effectiveness of his air arm and PT-boat flotillas against repeated sorties by the Tokyo Express. As for airborne interdiction, neither the light bombers of the Cactus Air Force nor the 13th Air Force's medium and heavy bombers had scored many hits on Japanese destroyers. That this deficiency continued to plague ComSoPac right through Operation KE helps explain why the IJN succeeded in rescuing the Japanese 17th Army from Guadalcanal. A review of the prevailing circumstances that affected the performance of the combatants during the evacuation operation is in order.

First, pilots and aircrew on both sides remained in short supply throughout Operation KE. In mid-January the estimated number of available pilots at Cactus barely topped 130; with the attachment of eleven VMF-112 pilots, plus the temporary addition of some sixty fresh naval pilots, it rose to around 200. Out of 180 fighter pilots at Cactus after Operation KE ended, only 100 on average were available for duty with Fighter Command. Of those U.S. airmen on active duty during KE, many were too ill or worn out—both physically and mentally—to remain on call indefinitely.

Lt. Paul Hansen alluded to combat fatigue as a partial cause of the shortage: "It is noticeable that pilots that have been here for a year or more are getting pilot fatigue." Fellow 68th pilot Lt. Allen Webb elaborated: "It is also my opinion that our pilots in this area are becoming tired. They are most willing at all times but most all units have been doing operational flying for a year or more and are stale, in some cases before being called upon for actual combat flying."

Lt. Henry Hackett, VMF-123's flight surgeon, perceptively cautioned his colleagues: "Pilots have a tendency to fly, or express a desire to do so, irrespective of whether they personally feel in condition to do so." Inevitably, if men flew the physically demanding combat planes of the day when they were exhausted or sick, fighting efficiency suffered. Maj. Joe Renner of VMO-251 had his finger on the pulse of the problem:

> In the Guadalcanal area, at least, pilots have been required to fly too many hours a day. For a period of six days, one group of fighter pilots [was] flying an average of six and one half hours a day. The time we weren't flying, we were on scramble standby. If we had to stand by, we were on that until noon, and then in the afternoon we flew a combat patrol over the area. Probably at 1645 we went out on a mission and came home after dark. It doesn't take long to burn the boys out at that clip.

Of course, the hectic activity shouldered during Operation KE made it more difficult to rotate men out on furlough. "If the going is tough, fighter squadrons should be relieved in three weeks' time," ventured Major Renner. "Otherwise they lose their desire to close with the enemy and their power to recuperate." Intimidating tales about superior enemy pilots and aircraft, blurted out by demoralized fliers coming off their tours, further impacted morale. Even seasoned pilots got a bellyful of combat. When forming Navy squadron VF-17 around the time of Operation KE, Lt. Cdr. Tom Blackburn took on two veterans who had fought in the Central Pacific and the Solomons. Despite furloughs home to recover from their ordeals on Guadalcanal during the dark days of October and November 1942, these men agreed to another tour only after being assured they would then be relieved from combat. Clearly, they had already served enough "time in Hell."

Combat fatigue plagued multiengine crews more than it did fighter pilots and light-bomber crews. Flying heavy bombers like the B-17 or temperamental medium bombers like the B-26 was more demanding of pilots, more so when these planes were numerically few, overworked, and prone to mechanical failure. The strain of having to fly long-range bombing missions in ticklish tight formations—especially when under air attack—added to the stress, as did the need to maintain a steady course during bombing runs through buffeting flak barrages.

Small wonder B-17 crews were rotated out of the combat zone every seven to ten days at first and then were rotated out every two weeks after the 5th BG joined the 11th in the forward area. But the pressing need to keep B-17 crews in the lineup during Operation KE disrupted this routine, with negative results. After it was over, barely enough men remained fit for duty to make up nineteen of the 11th BG's thirty-five aircrews; when this exhausted remnant departed the South Pacific on 7 February, the unit was simply disbanded. The 69th BS, flying B-26s, had its leave abruptly cancelled at the end of KE. "It was then that the squadron's morale was at a low ebb," recorded the unit's historian. The disappointment "was sufficient to discourage the most optimistic member of the squadron."

It was the psychological component of combat fatigue that played the pivotal role, affecting not only the mental health, but also the physical stamina of airmen. After Operation KE Lieutenant Hackett of VMF-123 argued that psychological exhaustion brought on physical debilitation by weakening the body's immune system, thereby increasing its susceptibility to disease. Lieutenant Hackett perceptively pointed out that the stress caused by operational flying had a "cumulative" effect. Though the overall outlook of pilots and aircrew improved after a furlough, the emotional residue of combat did not dissipate—it was merely pushed into the back of the mind. This suppressed litany of anxiety and fear rapidly resurfaced as the mind began to dwell on the next tour of duty, forming a fractured foundation upon which yet another round of harrowing experiences could chisel its psychological scars, further lowering combat efficiency.

Paradoxically, rehabilitation via rotation out of the combat zone focused on the symptoms to the neglect of the cause. Since each squadron was responsible for preparing its new arrivals for combat, Marine air echelons returning from furlough during Operation KE were confined to the rear area for two weeks or more to train replacements attached to their units. By the time these airmen got back to Cactus after this busman's holiday, the élan infused by their sojourn in Australia had been sapped by the boredom and frustration of being tied down to training duties.

Although USAAF squadrons serving in the South Pacific were rarely furloughed out as units, their pilots and aircrews were rotated out sporadically in small groups for two weeks' rest in rear areas—usually New Caledonia or Fiji. Few made it past Tontouta, New Caledonia, to reach Australia for quality R and R.

All things considered, this was still better than the mind-numbing Japanese practice of no pilot or aircrew rotation out of the combat zone unless replacements were available. One could escape only by being transferred to other duties or by being evacuated because of wounds or illness. Thus, in the Spartan tradition, one might return to Japan eventually *with* one's shield, or sooner, *on* it.

Second, along with the shortage of manpower in the air and ground echelons, aircraft availability proved to be an Achilles' heel of the Cactus Air Force and 13th Air Force. VMSB-131's war diary for 2 February aptly illustrates the dilemma: "After the fracas of yesterday we have three planes available to catch the Tokyo Express on her way back to the Shortlands." VMSB-131's pilots ended up flying occasionally available Navy torpedo bombers. On 28 January 1943 VMSB-234 listed ten SBD-4s in its inventory; by 5 February it was down to two aircraft and had to commandeer a portion of the newly arrived VMSB-144's twenty-two SBD-4s. It was no different for Cactus-based fighter squadrons. Major Renner of VMO-251 aptly summed up the need for more fighters: "We were always short of fighters; there never was a time when we had enough fighters to do our job." Army air corps fighter pilots concurred. Citing a 20 January mission to the Shortlands in which a formation of B-17s guarded by seven P-40s and a single flight of P-38s was overwhelmed by three large groups of Zeros, Rufes, and Petes, Lt. Lloyd Huff observed, "We do not have enough P-38's [sic] or P-40-F's [sic] at Cactus to run a mission successfully."

Despite the Solomon's newly assigned supply priority, the flow of replacement aircraft to the Canal was tantamount to a trickle until early 1943. Consequently, while squadrons rotated out periodically, their planes were kept in combat if they could fly, or they were flown back in by replacement squadrons or ferry pilots without adequate overhauls.

For example, twelve P-40F fighters were transferred to the 68th FS at Roses on 22 December; the 68th's pilots flew them to Button that same day.

Only ten Warhawks lifted off from Espiritu Santo for Guadalcanal the next morning. Of the two planes that had to stay behind, one had engine problems and the other, flown by Lt. Hansen, was down "for two days with battery and coolant trouble." One of the ten aviators that did leave for Cactus on 23 January was forced to make a water landing. A dinghy was dropped, and Lt. Wallace "Wally" Dinn paddled to a small island near San Cristobal and was picked up by a PBY two days later.

As for the rest of the flight, Capt. Stan Palmer observed, "Upon the arrival of the P-40s . . . it was necessary to ground them for three days while the prestone systems were cleaned out and the electrical systems checked." Added Lieutenant Hansen, "Because of poor maintenance at first, the P-40-F's [sic] didn't hold up like they should have and it was hard to keep half of them in commission."

A disturbing message dated 29 January from the noticeably distraught senior army aviator at Cactus, ostensibly sent to General Twining of the 13th Air Force, implied that all was not well with the B-17 operation either. Col. "Blondie" Saunders "reported that due to lack of adequate maintenance facilities the material condition of all B-17's [sic] at Cactus (striking force) had deteriorated to such an extent that effective strike was impossible and recommended planes be returned at once to Buttons [sic]."

The plight of the 67th FS poignantly illustrates the gravity of the USAAF's supply situation in the South Pacific. In March 1942 at New Caledonia the squadron took possession of forty-seven Airacobras—two P-39s and forty-five P-400s. Such was the shortage of spare parts that every fifth P-400 was earmarked for spares before it was even uncrated. Aircraft wrecked in training and operational accidents were immediately cannibalized for usable parts. Even then, many of the 67th's Cobras still had to fly with instruments missing, so critical was the shortage of gauges.

Operational accidents and combat casualties meant that fewer and fewer planes had to fly more and more missions, accelerating the wear and tear on those aircraft still left on the flight line. It was estimated that some 90 percent of needed spares could be salvaged locally from grounded planes, including wings, rudders, stabilizers, landing gear, radio equipment, and the precious instruments. But when it came to "striking" Marine Corps aircraft at Cactus, F4Fs were not considered beyond repair unless they were reduced to shattered hulks; damaged Wildcats were held indefinitely for repair pending the arrival of spare parts. Something simple like a shot-up fuselage could take up to a week to fix under these circumstances.

The new Marine engineering officer for Fighter One reported for duty on 5 October 1942. "When I arrived in Cactus," recalled Lieutenant DeFries of VMF-121, "no planes had been stricken and if a spare part was needed they just took it from the nearest plane that was not actually in commission and then, when they came to fix this plane up, they had to take the same part off another plane and this would go on and on." Lieutenant DeFries and his engineering chief, MTSgt. Harry Sobel, evaluated the damaged fighters, selecting those that could most easily be restored. They decommissioned the others, earmarking them for spares with instructions to cannibalize only these aircraft. In the case of the plane with the shot-up fuselage, DeFries was able to salvage the two wings for another pair of F4Fs; the motor was transferred "quick change fashion" to a third Wildcat, and other parts were donated to yet another. Thus, four fighters were rendered operational at the cost of writing off a single aircraft.

His successor tried to follow in his footsteps with questionable success. No fewer than ten F4Fs at Fighter Two were awaiting spare parts during Operation KE; several were ultimately out of commission for three months. Less than two weeks after KE ended, the enterprising Lieutenant DeFries—now the engineering officer for VMF-121—complained, "The number of planes out of commission for lack of parts was way out of proportion and I know of an instance where the striking of one plane would have given enough parts to put four planes in commission. Yet, I was not allowed to do so."

Not surprisingly, Japanese field repair units were even more strapped for parts and aircraft to maintain and replace their overworked air fleets than were their American counterparts, given the higher attrition rate of their planes and the comparatively limited production capacity of the Japanese aircraft and parts industry.

Third, if one considers the ongoing need for an understaffed ground echelon to service and maintain worn-out aircraft flying beyond prescribed overhaul limits, one quickly appreciates the personnel side of the maintenance problem that prevailed during Operation KE.

Squadron maintenance personnel remained administratively independent, but were loosely pooled to offset manpower shortages. Aircraft belonging to new units frequently had to be serviced by ground crews from other squadrons until their own maintenance personnel arrived. One entry for VMF-122's ground-echelon diary reads, "February 2 1943. No routine this day as 34 Navy fighters came in and we got the job so have plenty to do what with trying to help out with VMO-251 ... [and] our planes."

Squadron maintenance cadres routinely exchanged tips on how to solve common problems. For instance, according to Master Technical Sergeant Hanley, VMF-122's engineering chief, there came from VMO-251 a solution to reduce wing-tank feeding problems in the Wildcat. And the engineering officer of VGS-11, who had served in the Aleutians, passed on a way to ensure that F4F engines would start in damp Canal weather.

Such neighborliness was not always forthcoming, however. Surprisingly, bickering among units and one-upmanship found their greatest expression within Cactus' ground echelon. Often one squadron's ground crew would not work on a sister outfit's planes after their own work was done, even though the other squadron lagged behind because more of its fighters had been shot up.

The ad hoc integration of manpower inevitably strained the command structure as well. With their backs up, VMF-122's line crews, who were temporarily officerless at one point, bristled because VMO-251's officers tended to take over, making the sister unit's NCOs report to *their* privates first class. To their credit, the VMF-122 techs kept the planes flying under protest until VMF-251's CO, Major Renner, changed this unpopular policy in response to complaints from VMF-122 after he heard about it.

Surly attitudes and short tempers were fueled by the cumulative effects of months spent on the flight line, abject working and living conditions, and monumental boredom during off-duty hours. The rotation policy for ground crews was far worse than the one established for pilots and aircrew; ground crews served *six-month tours* in the forward area, whereas aircrews served considerably shorter stints. Not surprisingly, combat fatigue took a heavier toll among the ground echelon than within the air echelon. Master Technical Sergeant Hanley had this to say about Operation KE: "Under combat conditions ... existing during January and February, a tour of three months for a ground crew should be the limit because of the strain engendered by the lack of sleep, nerves, sickness and the like."

The quality of workmanship simply *had* to suffer from time to time as a result of such lengthy and exhaustive tours. Shoddy workmanship meant defective planes on the flight line, which was another impediment to providing sufficient aircraft for air operations during Operation KE. The following nightmare from VMSB-142 is a case in point: "TSgt. Milby had engine trouble and took off . . . with a substitute plane. MTSgt. Thornbury could not take off because his brakes locked; and Lt. Finch found that the first plane given him had no bomb mounted. The first substitute had gas in the oil tank, the second contained no parachute and had generator and transmitter trouble, and the rudder of the third was locked by the tail strut."

Out of approximately 150 light-bomber sorties ordered out over the ten missions that actually made contact with the six KE-related Tokyo Express runs, at least twenty planes never delivered their ordnance or conveyed only partial payloads to the target due to various mechanical failures. Problems ranged from engine trouble to faulty guns and turrets to malfunctioning bomb-release mechanisms. Other antishipping strikes, as well as base-suppression missions against Munda, Vila, and Bougainville, exhibited similar failure rates in placing ordnance on the target.

As for the Japanese, the technical training of their maintenance personnel was decidedly substandard; apart from Rabaul there were no bases equipped to perform major aircraft overhauls in the theater. In fact, Rabaul's ability to undertake major aircraft rebuilds remains questionable to this day. Thus, though they had more planes to begin with, it was still more difficult for the Japanese to muster enough operable aircraft to meet the exigencies of Operation KE than it was for the Cactus Air Force to marshal sufficient planes to defend against it.

Fourth, further aggravating the ground echelon's problems, newly trained, know-it-all pilot "tyros" tended to disregard the practical savvy of ground crewmen, which often led to needless accidents. For instance, plane captains riding on the wings of taxiing aircraft could better see mud holes and obstructions, yet hotshot pilots often ignored their signals.

Pilots were not expected to double as mechanics, but a basic familiarity with their aircraft's technical aspects would have taken pressure off overstretched ground crews. Japanese aircrew, on the other hand, were given sufficient rudimentary mechanical training to enable them to fix the most common basic problems with their aircraft, without the help of a technician if necessary. Precisely how much of this knowledge pilots actually learned is another matter.

Many Cactus pilots could not start their planes properly; they frequently overprimed and flooded their motors. Lieutenant DeFries rightly observed, "All this resulted in an unnecessary strain being put on the starting mechanism and therefore much more starter failure[s] than should have been."

Other cockpit problems included prop trouble, drops in fuel or oil pressure, and brake problems. Most of these glitches could be attributed to pilot oversight or ignorance of proper procedures, according to Capt. J. Scott, VMF-123's engineering officer. "Minor oil leaks and brake trouble are the two principal causes of planes being out of commission," remarked Maj. Bill Millington, VMF123's exec, who went on to explain that largely unknown to pilots, oil pressure in the blower automatically fluctuated when the blower was engaged at varying altitudes. "As for brake trouble," Major Millington ruefully concluded, "this is up to the pilot more than the brake."

Gun and radio malfunctions usually boiled down to switches that had not been set in the proper position by excited pilots in the midst of combat. Regarding generators, Lieutenant DeFries observed that F4F pilots "often missed hops because of so-called generator trouble." Had they bothered to learn, these fliers would have known to "reach in the junction box and flash the field of the relay and the generator would work."

Pilot ignorance simply made the ground echelon's job that much harder, but the consequences of not knowing were far more serious for the pilot—even fatal. A pilot might not be able to get into the air quickly, if at all, during a scramble, or he might abandon or crash a plane that he might have been able otherwise to bring back from a mission. Ultimately, the lack of practical knowledge might cost him his life in combat.

Squadron ground echelons insisted on separate dispersal areas for their respective aircraft because Operations assigned aircraft to a flight without knowing where on the field the planes were located. Pilots had to chase around trying to find the one assigned to them, then they converged from all over the field to vie for taxiing and takeoff position, thereby wasting precious time in a scramble. This practice also complicated the servicing of aircraft: fuel bowsers, ordnance trucks, and trouble-shooter vehicles had to spend time hunting down randomly dispersed fighters to ready them for a given mission.

Fighter planes were not assigned to specific pilots at this time, either. In terms of operational efficiency, if a pilot were assigned his own plane, mechanical problems would be halved since a pilot who was held accountable would be less prone to abuse his aircraft. Also, from the servicing perspective, with one pilot regularly flying a given aircraft, the line crew would become familiar with his traits and habits in the cockpit, which would help the techs anticipate and deal with the plane's particular maintenance needs in a timely manner. When Operation KE debuted, these arguments were still falling on deaf ears.

Fifth, throughout Operation KE, both the Japanese and the Americans were plagued by technical design problems that hampered the efficient prosecution of air operations.

At the highest tactical level, Rabaul and other Japanese air bases found themselves unable to communicate with airborne formations. Unreliable atmospheric conditions, coupled to an insular topography, rendered HF and LF radio bands especially vulnerable; the MF band as a substitute, was hard to use with existing TM-type airborne HF sets, though the airbases could use small self-contained MF sets. The growing need to fly between dusk and dawn in enemy-dominated skies made radio communication susceptible to additional, nighttime "atmospherics."

The problem was exacerbated by certain policy decisions. For example, radio telegraphy extended the range of airborne sets over that of voice communication, but in lieu of formal radio telegraphy training, aircrew had to learn code procedures on their own. Only an estimated 50 percent of JNAF fighter pilots ever became proficient in communication by key. Moreover, the TM-type transceiver set fitted to the Zeros of JNAF fighter *kokutai* was well built with quality components, but it was so compact that it defied easy servicing. Subjected to shoddy maintenance, these radios became so unreliable that frustrated pilots stripped them from their planes to save weight. Unless individual *daitai*, *chutai*, and *shotai* leaders chose to keep their sets, any direct radio link with their bases was effectively severed.

Since bomber *kokutai* retained their radios and, thereby, their land–air link, in mixed formations fighters could theoretically communicate indirectly with their bases. However, without radios, most Zero *daitai*, *chutai*, and *shotai* leaders relied on hand signals to communicate—a haphazard, woefully deficient method at best. In bad weather or during air combat, this manual signaling proved highly impractical. Indeed, the lack of airborne radios may have contributed to the tactical snafu experienced by the 252nd Kokutai during the JNAF raid of 25 January on Cactus.

As attrition from illness and other causes decimated the ranks of the ground echelon's experienced radio officers, operators, and techs, the single communications training school could not supply enough replacements. Cutting corners on training programs produced partially trained newcomers who could not operate or maintain airborne and land-based radio sets properly, further stymieing ground–air communication and, by corollary, an airbase's tactical control over its *kokutai*.

The Telefunken DF set used for direction finding via the LF band was an especially vexing piece of equipment; its intricacies were seldom mastered by its inadequately prepared users, leaving a critical deficiency in a base's ability to recover wayward aircraft.

On the U.S. side, IFF sets used in USMC aircraft were heat-sensitive. VMF-123, for one, removed its airborne sets; eventually, a general order was issued sanctioning the practice of not replacing defective sets once these were taken out.

According to VMO-251's Capt. Pat Weiland, "Communications [were] always problematic between ground and air due to reception and maintenance.... In the clearest of enunciated tones, the emissions were either guttural or warbling." Airborne radio sets were problem-plagued. When they worked, they could transmit up to a hundred miles over the open water under ideal "atmospherics," but over the insular topography of the Solomon Archipelago, whose larger islands could rise to five thousand feet or more, transmission range could and did fall off sharply. Solar activity and turbulent weather further aggravated radio communications.

Then there was the problem of compatibility. Unbelievably, Navy and Marine Corps fighters could not talk to Army air corps fighters because the USA and USN had been assigned different radio frequency bands during peacetime. After the war began, their radios were fitted with an overlapping band of common channels for joint communication. This was crucial to maintain tactical control over Cactus' multiservice air arm, but the commonly assigned frequencies worked poorly in the Solomons.

Newly trained USN fighter directors began operating at Cactus on 8 October 1942. Their job was to control and coordinate the operation of Fighter Command's planes by assigning missions, CAPs, searches, and patrols. Initially, limited-range, ground-to-air contact was tenuously maintained via a radio set salvaged from a Wildcat. At one point the Navy fighter director at Cactus Recon tried working with a *pair* of base radio sets. He communicated with his USN and USMC pilots over the F4F set and used a low-power cockpit set that had been scrounged from an Army fighter to talk with his USAAF aviators. By speaking into the two microphones, he was able to address both groups of pilots.

On joint missions where pilots had to communicate via the Cactus base sets, the Navy and Marine pilots could not talk even indirectly to their Army counterparts once a mixed formation had flown out of range of Cactus' radio. Messages had to be relayed by hand signals—an impractical, frustrating exercise with squadrons flying at different altitudes. The probability of a tactical snafu on such missions was high.

To sum up, the upshot of having a small inventory of aircraft in constant use was mechanical failure of near-epidemic proportions. Inadequate spares due to the "no striking" policy further compounded the paucity of operable aircraft. This worsening crisis was temporarily relieved by several USN carrier squadrons that were posted on shore with fresh planes to boost the shrinking assets of the Cactus Air Force.

Interunit bickering among ground echelons that led to on-again, off-again maintenance efficiency further reduced aircraft availability. Flight operations were hindered by dispersal policies that prevented the rapid servicing and deployment of fighter aircraft—especially in the event of a scramble. Cooperation between the air and ground echelons was not always as smooth as it could have been, adding to the hardship of ground crews by unnecessarily swelling their workload.

On the personnel side, during Operation KE both the air and ground echelons served extended tours of duty in an inhospitable and disease-ridden environment that sapped their strength. Long hours in the air or fixing planes, interspersed with fitful snatches of sleep or rest interrupted by nuisance raids, weakened their will to carry on. Pilots and aircrew were in short supply and hard to come by. Having to deal leniently with the weak stomachs among them created a serious morale problem among the sturdier hands and threatened to erode both unit integrity and combat efficiency.

Deficiencies in the technology then in use, such as substandard radio designs and incompatible radios, further challenged the smooth operation of General Mulcahy's command, as did a shortage of technicians properly trained to perform specific jobs.

One can only speculate on the precise extent to which these serious deficiencies affected the ability of the Cactus Air Force to oppose Operation KE, but affect it they did. Had the Japanese not been beset by similar problems, the playing field would have undoubtedly been tilted even more in their favor.

CHAPTER 18

GOOD LUCK OR GOOD MANAGEMENT?

The Japanese plan for KE effectively exploited the strengths of the JNAF, JAAF, and IJN, as well as the limitations of the Cactus Air Force, 13th Air Force, and USN. This chapter reviews these respective strengths and limitations and their contributions to the success of Operation KE. A number of intertwined elements stand out here: (1) the optimal concentration and deployment of assets by the Japanese to confuse the enemy, (2) the establishment of local air superiority in areas controlled by enemy air power, (3) the employment of an experienced cadre of veteran pilots in a leadership role, (4) the exclusive use of destroyers to carry out the evacuation, (5) the recourse to tactical changes in routing and timing, and (6) the lack of sophistication in weapons and weapon-delivery systems.

First, consider the optimal concentration and deployment of assets by the Japanese. Advancing the fleet carrier *Zuikaku* and the super-dreadnoughts *Yamato* and *Musashi* to Truk, in addition to assembling and readying Admiral Kondo's powerful task force for sea, drew admirals Nimitz and Halsey first into marshaling every available warship in the South Pacific to counter another Japanese attempt to reinforce the 17th Army as the prelude to a new Guadalcanal offensive.

Though the air-minded Admiral Yamamoto still yearned for the elusive battle that would break the back of the U.S. Navy in the Pacific, he realized that it would now have to be primarily a surface action in which his marginal superiority in naval fire power would be clearly offset by a deficiency in carrier-based air power, for the Americans would not be limited to a surface action alone.

Yamamoto might have been prepared to gamble that his modest carrier fleet—*Zuikaku, Junyo*, and *Zuiho*—if used in a defensive role with the help of a submarine screen, could keep U.S. carrier planes off center stage long enough for his mega-battleships to deal successfully with their U.S. Navy counterparts. Realistically, he probably deemed it more prudent to feign belligerency with a bold sortie by Admiral Kondo's task force, and the overt deployment of a submarine screen, in order to force Admiral Nimitz to hesitate long enough for the Tokyo Express to execute Operation KE.

Whether intentional or not, the bluff worked. Though the U.S. Navy had placed seven battleships, two fleet carriers, three auxiliary carriers, nine cruisers, and numerous destroyers at Admiral Halsey's disposal in the South Pacific, Admiral Nimitz procrastinated, awaiting a clear commitment to fight on the part of major Japanese naval units or a more vulnerable positioning of Kondo's sizable task force—neither of which Admiral Yamamoto offered him. Instead, the Rennell Island fiasco jeopardized Admiral Halsey's one real attempt to move his task forces into the Solomons. Thus, no American capital ship ever intervened to stop the evacuation runs of the Tokyo Express save for a single, desultory sally by the three surviving destroyers of the Cactus Striking Force.

Second, the marshaling of fighter planes to establish local numerical superiority enabled Japanese air power to achieve its first KE objective: protection of the Tokyo Express convoys.

Coral Sea and Midway had taught both combatants the inestimable value of adequate fighter cover to protect vulnerable surface vessels and bomber formations from air attack. Throughout most of Operation KE, the JNAF's 11th Koku Kantai, supported by the JAAF's 6th Shidan, provided the Tokyo Express with very adequate protection in the Slot. When enough Zeros and Oscars were mustered, fighter CAPs managed to achieve control of the airspace over the destroyer convoys entrusted to their protection.

In five out of nine major clashes with Cactus strike forces between 10 January and 7 February, experienced Japanese pilots exploited their superior numbers and the maneuverability of their Zero and Oscar fighters to break through Cactus fighter screens and disrupt the SBDs and TBFs, causing them either to miss their targets or, in at least thirteen cases, to miscarry their runs altogether. In the first engagement of 15 January, although the SBDs did get through to damage a pair of destroyers, determined Japanese CAP pilots clashed with a substantial Cactus fighter escort in a violent and sanguinary donnybrook. The U.S. pilots had their hands full trying to keep the Zeros off the backs of the dive-bombers.

But command of the air over the Tokyo Express proved difficult to maintain whenever insufficient fighters were mustered or inferior aircraft were enlisted to fly CAP.

During the B-17 antishipping strike of 15 January a large group of Pete floatplanes, assigned to support frontline fighters, proved no match for the Cactus fighter escort. Moreover, the modest force of Zeros seemed unwilling to test the heavy combined firepower of the Forts and escorting P-38s. On 28 January nine Zeros flying CAP over the six destroyers transporting the Russell Island garrison were caught between a rock and a hard place when they tried to protect two separate convoys at once; the deterrent value of two Pete floatplanes covering the smaller but more vulnerable freighter and tanker convoy proved insignificant. Similarly, weak CAPs of Petes were encountered and defeated over a freighter and one escort on 27 January and over the small *Toa Maru 2* convoy on 31 January. A Zero CAP was requested on 31 January but was never sent.

On its return leg, the first Tokyo Express evacuation convoy ran into a Cactus strike force that vastly outnumbered the Zero CAP. Rather than tackle both the SBDs and TBFs, the Zeros ignored the heavily protected SBDs. Easily breaching the weak screen of USAAF fighters guarding the TBFs, they thoroughly broke up the bombing and torpedo runs of the attacking Avengers. In this case, the CAP prudently settled for partial success rather than risk total failure. Reaching the Central Solomons on 2 February, the destroyers found no friendly fighters overhead to intercept the oncoming Cactus raiders. Although a Zero fighter CAP had been dispatched to escort the destroyers back to Bougainville, it was inexplicably delayed. Fortunately for the Japanese, the destroyers pulled through the Cactus air attack relatively unscathed, thanks to their agility in evading bombs and torpedoes delivered by modest strike forces using hit-or-miss technology. When the Tokyo Express had been attacked on 28 January after its CAP had flown to the rescue of a nearby merchant convoy, Japanese destroyers had also managed to outmaneuver the Cactus raiders.

Inexplicably, the lesson regarding adequate CAP protection initially went unheeded on the part of the Americans, who lost both the cruiser *Chicago* and the destroyer *DeHaven* for lack of adequate fighter cover. Cactus air strikes against the Tokyo Express also suffered more than once from a paucity of escorting fighters needed to protect the attacking SBDs and TBFs. Maj. Joe Renner of VMO-251 affirmed both the numerical superiority of Japanese CAPs and the critical deficiency in Cactus escort fighters:

> I have seen sixteen SBD's [sic] and six TBF's [sic] go off with eight Grummans for escort. You could protect part of them and get embroiled with probably sixteen or twenty Zeros, but there would be enough Zeros left to pick up the planes that were without fighter protection. . . . It's criminal to send dive-bomber pilots and torpedo pilots unescorted against a Jap surface force when we know there is a probability the Japs will have fighter protection above them. We should have at least six to one fighter planes for every dive-bomber and torpedo plane we have in the area.

Indeed, the lessons learned in the great carrier battles of 1942 dictated the following ratio for a balanced naval air group: 40 percent fighters, 40 percent dive-bombers, 20 percent torpedo bombers. But even when the Cactus Air Force managed to muster something approaching this ratio, opposing fighters frequently outnumbered U.S. fighters escorting air strikes against the Tokyo Express.

Third, the Japanese air arms brought together twenty-nine JNAF and JAAF fighter pilots who were already aces or who would achieve ace status to participate in Operation KE. These men helped redress the technological and doctrinal deficiencies plaguing the Japanese in the air during the evacuation of the 17th Army. CAP duty over the Tokyo Express primarily meant capitalizing on numerical superiority and pilot expertise to outmaneuver and bypass Cactus' escorting fighters in order to get at the light bombers—a task for which the Zero and Oscar were especially well suited when flown by more-talented pilots. It was here that ability came to the fore.

The performance of the 11th Koku Kantai's Zero pilots in particular must have come as a mild surprise. Veteran IJN airmen had been decimated repeatedly by early 1943 and were succeeded by replacements rushed into combat with substandard training. Nevertheless, thanks to a sprinkling of veteran aces among its pilots, this unit's *kokutai* flew with an unanticipated degree of skill and aggressiveness. By way of illustration, recall 1 February, when several *chutai* of Hamps from the 204th Kokutai intercepted some B-17s on an antishipping raid over the Tonolei-Shortland harbor complex. Riding in one of the Forts as an observer, Maj. W. H. McCarroll had this to add to his earlier comments about these JNAF pilots: "Bold tactics were used. Some of the enemy planes approached to within ten yards of the wing tips of the B-17. They came in from every direction, more often toward the front of the bomber. . . . This appeared to be a new team with a new coach. Their tactics were different and bolder . . . than those observed previously in this area. The Zero pilots showed no fear of the B-17's guns; when they started a pass, they completed it."

This particular group of 204th Kokutai Hamps contained an unusually high proportion of veteran pilots. Three of the twelve men in these *chutai* were already aces; five more were destined to become aces. That such highly experienced pilots were able to lead the defense of the Tokyo Express against U.S. air attacks explains much of Operation KE's success.

However, the successful defense of the destroyer convoys can probably be viewed as the swan song of the JNAF's fighter arm; never again was it able to marshal sufficient planes and talented pilots to achieve such a degree of good fortune. After Guadalcanal the arrival of better-trained Allied squadrons, flying superior and better-maintained aircraft and employing more-effective combat tactics, precipitated a downhill spiral of enfeebled Japanese naval air power that culminated in the desperate kamikaze campaign of April 1945.

Indications of this degenerative trend were already in evidence during Operation KE. On 7 February, although Japanese fighters outnumbered Cactus fighters, less-experienced pilots may have made up a high proportion of this particular CAP, giving rise to the failure of several units to engage and an overall lackluster performance on the part of those that did.

Only six JAAF ace-quality fighter pilots flew in Operation KE; other IJA fliers proved less competent because they were still unlearning the lessons taught in air combat over China and the Far East—lessons that did not apply when dueling with unfamiliar USN and USMC Wildcats in the Solomons. Part of the 11th Sentai's 3rd Chutai that intercepted a Cactus strike force over Vella Gulf on 31 January likely contained a mere smattering of veteran pilots amongst a host of relative greenhorns. These airmen had never encountered Grumman Wildcats before. For these reasons, six aggressive leatherneck pilots gave their nine JAAF counterparts a severe mauling. Ambushing the three enemy *shotai* first from below and then from above, the F4Fs first disabled the leader's fighter before proceeding to shoot down four more and damage several others. After Guadalcanal, the JAAF's ability to resist the onslaught of Allied air power also declined rapidly.

Fourth, the Japanese learned through trial and error the futility of trying to maintain the 17th Army using slow, poorly armed transports. Unable to wrest command of the air from the Cactus Air Force, they had to resort to smaller destroyer-transports supplemented by submarines and air drops. Thus, by default, destroyers played the key role when it came to evacuating the remaining 12,000 Japanese troops from the island.

The three key characteristics of the destroyer—slim, swift, sinuous—greatly increased its chances of survival. By design able to travel at upwards of thirty knots, the vessel was fast; its light tonnage and narrow girth also made it exceptionally maneuverable. A destroyer could turn completely about in the minute that it took for a dive-bomber to reach its bomb-release point from level flight. When the Tokyo Express destroyers were zigzagging at high speed, they presented an onerous challenge to light bombers attacking in small groups.

Ship for ship, the destroyer also delivered a much heavier AA punch than any Japanese *maru*. This was especially true of the *Kagero*, *Yugumo*, and *Akizuki* classes, as these had been designed to play an enhanced AA role. When under threat of Cactus air attack, there was nothing new or unique about a convoy steaming in parallel rows of loosely spread, fast-moving ships; such a formation furnished the latitude needed for the fast destroyers to disperse, zigzag, and execute sharp turns to evade bombs and aerial torpedoes. Conversely, it also facilitated the practice of closing with other destroyers under attack to beef up the AA barrage.

On the down side, destroyers on both sides were comparatively thin-skinned. Three well-placed bomb hits were more than enough to send the *DeHaven* to the bottom in record time; a single mine or torpedo put finis to the *Makigumo*. The operative term of course is "hit." And hits against destroyers proved hard to get during Operation KE. Attacking aircraft were forced to concentrate on a few specific destroyers to ensure hits.

SBD, TBF, B-17, and PBY crews claimed some nineteen direct bomb and torpedo hits, seven or more probable hits, and at least thirty-three near misses against elusive Tokyo Express destroyers on KE-related runs. At the same time, they dropped at least 182 and perhaps as many as 200 misses. Even then it is doubtful that all the hits claimed actually scored, judging by the comparative lack of destroyers sunk or disabled.

In other words, between 10 January and 7 February ten Cactus air strikes and three single-plane sorties intercepted six return runs of the Tokyo Express. During the run of 10–11 January Cactus light bombers never even got the chance to drop their ordnance. Of the aggregate 133 potential destroyer targets available during the attacks on the other five runs, SBDs, TBFs, B-17s, and PBYs inflicted damage to seventeen destroyers—or roughly 10 percent. None was sunk by air attack. After Operation KE, VMSB-131 flatly concluded, "The Commanding Officer and pilots of this squadron are of the firm opinion that it is useless to send TBF planes equipped with torpedoes to attack fast and highly maneuverable ships such as DDs and fast, light cruisers."

The four antishipping attacks of 23, 27, and 31 January on regular transports and freighters also exhibited low hit-to-ordnance-dropped ratios; all but one garnered better results than attacks on the Tokyo Express, however. Why?

On 23 January twelve SBDs and four TBFs dropped at least twelve bombs and four torpedoes on a merchantman and its escort without scoring a hit. Not impressive. But, when ten SBDs and six TBFs attacked a freighter and its escorting subchaser on 27 January, the dive-bombers netted three hits on the freighter and a near miss on the *Ch-17*, leaving them both damaged though not in a sinking condition. Twelve SBDs rained down fourteen bombs of various sizes on a tanker and a freighter the next day, claiming to have left both ships "smoking and dead in the water" with the freighter "probably sunk." Actually, although four TBFs failed to score with their torpedoes, both ships *were* hit by bombs. Twelve SBDs managed to score one bomb hit on the *Toa Maru 2* on 31 January. TBFs added another hit and scored two bomb hits on the escorting torpedo boat. The TBFs also achieved at least one fatal torpedo hit on the *Toa 2*.

In all four cases, the Cactus Air Force put up typical strike forces that proved sizable in proportion to the number of ships attacked. Here, the results generally justified the more-concentrated effort. In sharp contrast, when a similar number of light bombers sortied against the much larger destroyer convoys of the Tokyo Express, the result was a paucity of vessels sunk or damaged. One cannot escape the conclusion that much larger and more-frequent air strikes than those strikes mounted by the Cactus Air Force were required to neutralize six to twenty destroyers in a convoy. Air-Sols never mounted a strike force potent enough even to deter, let alone scuttle, the Tokyo Express during Operation KE.

Fifth, in deploying the Tokyo Express convoys, as well as their merchant shipping, the Japanese attempted to deceive the Americans with tactical changes in routing, and timed their sorties to stymie any attempts to disrupt the evacuation routine.

Regarding routing, as early as 2 January the destroyers of the Guadalcanal Reinforcement Unit steamed toward the Canal through the Solomon Sea rather than down the Slot. On 29 January the destroyer convoy delivering the Japanese garrison to the Russell Islands also elected to return to the Shortlands via the open sea south of the Solomon Islands. Two days later the transport *Toa Maru 2* sailed down the west side of Bougainville rather than along the sub-infested east side.

By avoiding the familiar routes through the Solomons, the Japanese hoped to throw off both U.S. subs and Cactus strike forces, as these would naturally search up the Slot. Similarly, Admiral Hashimoto avoided at least one round of Cactus air attacks by heading south and then west around the Solomons on his way back to Bougainville on the morning of 5 February. A second attempt to utilize this route two days later did not succeed: coastwatchers and an American photoreconnaissance aircraft spotted the Tokyo Express, which led to the Cactus Air Force intercepting it.

As for scheduling the Tokyo Express, the IJN timed its destroyer convoys to arrive at Guadalcanal after sunset. This tactic posed severe limitations on the Cactus Air Force's ability to deliver multiple air strikes. It also hampered the initiatives of Cactus' surface forces—its destroyers and PT boats—to obstruct evacuation operations.

The floatplanes of the R Homen Koku Butai rendered sterling service by night against American PT boats during Operation KE. Cactus fighter pilots would have had to know how to stalk and beat off the covering Petes and Jakes in nocturnal combat to give not only the PTs, but also the SBDs and TBFs, a reasonable chance of disrupting the embarkation process. Not only floatplane pilots, but in fact *all* JNAF fighter pilots received some training in night flying and nocturnal combat.

Overnight nuisance-bombing forays—several of them by Bettys or Nells in force—constituted yet another useful, though less-pivotal, contribution to the unmolested loading of Japanese troops off Cape Esperance.

In fact, the Japanese military machine per se was largely nocturnal in the Solomons. Even without the benefit of radar the IJN enjoyed its greatest successes against Allied warships at night during the Guadalcanal campaign. The IJA and IJN *rikusentai* excelled in both nocturnal infiltration and banzai attack tactics; indeed, the major ground offensives on Guadalcanal were nearly all mounted after dark.

Of great significance to Operation KE was the repulsion of TF GEORGE by three determined JNAF Betty and Nell bomber squadrons that pressed home their attacks around the clock. The sinking of the cruiser *Chicago*, with the resulting withdrawal of all major U.S. warships from around Guadalcanal, was a pivotal factor in clearing the way for the Tokyo Express runs. The bomber crews of the 11th Koku Kantai's 701st and 705th Kokutai were experienced in delivering low-level torpedo attacks at night. Three U.S. warships were struck on 29 January, but only one torpedo exploded—against the *Chicago*'s hull. Three bombers were lost in two attacks. In contrast the 751st's Betty crews sortied by day against TF GEORGE. As a result, this *kokutai* suffered staggering losses at Rennell Island, though it managed to administer the coup de grâce to the crippled *Chicago*.

On the other hand, American nocturnal capabilities left much to be desired. "The field at Cactus was not easy to operate from—Fighter Strip #2," noted Maj. Dick Baker of VMF-123. "Some [fighter] pilots had no night flying and some had but one hour, whereas many night take-offs and landings were required." Regarding the light bombers, Major Joe Renner says,

"We found through experiment at Guadalcanal that night dive bombing was not only unsuccessful but very costly. We tried at first to send our dive-bombers out at night to drop flares, or to get an enemy surface force in the path of the moon, and dive bomb it, . . . and we lost several airplanes and several pilots. I don't recall any hits."

VMSB-234's two attempts to bomb the Tokyo Express off Cape Esperance at night came to nothing. On the night of 27 January three TBFs from VMSB-131 tried to catch five ships reported coming into Munda. Arriving over Munda Point at 0100, Captain Aggerbeck called off the attack "due to insufficient visibility for dropping torpedoes on the targets."

If Cactus fighter pilots and bomber crews had been skilled enough to deliver waves of nocturnal strafing and bombing attacks against the Tokyo Express while its destroyers were trying to embark General Hyakutake's troops, the resulting carnage might have caused the Japanese to abandon the initiative altogether. Unfortunately, it would take another three months before U.S. light-bomber crews could comfortably carry out overnight raids up the Slot as far as Bougainville.

Sixth, as for weapons and delivery systems, though the obsolescent Douglas SBD Dauntless and the more-versatile Grumman TBF Avenger proved successful as light bombers, when reduced to their lowest common denominators, dive-bombing, glide-bombing, and torpedoing a moving target remained hit-or-miss propositions. Trying to aim a bomb-laden plane diving at a twisting sliver of metal moving at breakneck speed far below while surrounded by bursting flak or attacking Zeros amounted to no mean feat, nor did skimming over the water through a gauntlet of flak to line up a fast-moving target in a torpedo attack. Both scenarios were hands-on exercises and thus susceptible to human error in both judgment and execution.

Many light-bomber crews had not been fully trained before going into combat. VMSB-131 had barely converted from the Dauntless to the Avenger before leaving Hawaii for the South Pacific. The first time Lt. Marty Roush took off in a combat-ready TBF fully loaded with ordnance was on an actual combat mission; he had never launched a single torpedo in practice.

In early 1943 the combat capabilities of pursuit planes further favored the Japanese when their agile fighters were flown by good pilots. USAAF,

USMC, and USN aviators fought courageously and skillfully, utilizing the bold combat doctrine of Maj. Joe Bauer and others, but they flew fighters that were outclassed by nimbler Zekes, Hamps, and Oscars. When flying CAP, their Wildcats, Warhawks, and Airacobras could all be bypassed momentarily by a skilled Japanese pilot who would have executed at least one free pass at the bombers before U.S. fighters caught up.

The newest USAAF fighter—the Lightning—frequently failed to protect Cactus strike forces if intercepting Japanese fighters fell among the lower-flying bombers before the P-38 top cover could engage them at higher altitudes. Fully aware of their fighter's limitations, P-38 pilots were reluctant to descend in defense of the light bombers below. Moreover, flying way above a strike force, the top cover sometimes lost contact while passing through heavy cloud banks, leaving the bombers partially unprotected. Such problems undoubtedly spurred the derogatory reference to the P-38 pilots as "the high-cover foxhole boys" by Marine Corps airmen.

As for the P-39 and P-400 Airacobra variants—an inferior combat performer above 12,000 feet—the mere fact that it was recruited out of sheer necessity to fly escort missions testifies to the desperate measures resorted to by the Cactus Air Force to furnish adequate fighter protection for its bombers during Operation KE.

Regarding the Japanese air arm's second aim, the JNAF and JAAF failed to wrest supremacy of the air over the Slot from the Cactus Air Force. There are three noteworthy reasons for this failure.

First, even if all four *kokutai* of available Japanese twin-engine bombers had been massed in one or more strike forces, their vulnerability to U.S. fighters would have resulted in unacceptable losses. Knowing this, the Japanese simply used their bombers as bait to draw Guadalcanal's fighters up. While this ruse clearly succeeded, Japanese fighter pilots failed to gain the upper hand in three ensuing air battles because the tactical implications of this scenario better favored Cactus fighter pilots. The Japanese flew fighters that were more maneuverable though lightly armed; these fighters excelled in mass dogfighting, but American pilots refused to dogfight with them. Relying instead on the tactical lexicon devised by Bauer and others, the Americans fought on their own terms, which explains in part why they shot down approximately seventy planes to the Japanese' fifty between 23 December and 8 February—the period covered in this narrative. In other words, during the three massed air attacks against Cactus (a fourth raid was scrubbed by the JNAF), the Cactus fighters stalemated the Japanese over Henderson Field despite the numerical odds.

Second, and not unrelated, the Cactus Air Force fielded around thirty-six ace-quality fighter pilots of its own during Operation KE. In their absence the JNAF and JAAF might very well have achieved greater success than they did, but the presence of aerial virtuosos like Joe Foss, Bob Westbrook, John Mitchell, Murray Shubin, Jack Conger, Herb Long, Joe Lynch, Jeff DeBlanc, and Charles Ostrom, among others, provided a leavening effect that partially offset the advantage gained by numerical superiority and the presence of Japanese ace-quality fighter pilots.

Incidentally, regarding the phenomenon of overclaiming, Cactus fighter pilots claimed two planes shot down for every one actually destroyed while their JNAF and JAAF counterparts claimed a whopping *four* victories for every plane actually shot down. A number of aircraft believed destroyed on both sides survived with varying degrees of damage. Even at that, a significant number of Japanese claims have no basis in fact; that is, even the inclusion of damaged U.S. planes cannot substantiate all their claims. On the other hand, total U.S. claims of aircraft destroyed equals the total number of admitted Japanese planes shot down *and* damaged.

Third, neutralizing Cactus' airfield complex required a period of sustained area-saturation bombing, as well as ongoing naval bombardment and shelling by heav, land-based artillery. Not only were JAAF and JNAF twin-engine bombers too few and too vulnerable, but they also carried insufficient payloads—even collectively—to put Henderson and its ancillary fields out of business. Neither was the IJN able to deliver concentrated naval bombardments with sufficient regularity to have a long-term effect. The 17th Army had too few heavy artillery pieces like "Pistol Pete" to bring anything beyond harassing fire down on Henderson and its satellites. And, in all three massed air attacks against Cactus, the Cactus Air Force could almost always provide sufficien, via air, sea, or land to neutralize its airbase complex.

Turning now to American initiatives, a strategic misallocation of resources ordered by ComAirSoPac served to limit the scope of the Cactus Air Force's attacks against Operation KE convoys, contributing to the Japanese success in evacuating the 17th Army. Rear Adm. Aubrey Fitch and his staff, among others, believed that Operation KE constituted the enemy's new Guadalcanal offensive. Consequently, he ordered ComAirSols to attack all Japanese shipping plying the Slot as well as neutralize all Japanese airbases throughout the Solomons in an effort to disrupt Japanese naval supply lines. It was a tall order for Brig. Gen. Francis Mulcahy.

The issue that arises out of this strategy revolves around the use of long-range heavy and medium bombers to bomb shipping while, conversely, employing light bombers to bomb enemy bases. During Operation KE, Cactus' priority target was or should have been the Tokyo Express; the 13th Air Force's main target was or should have been the system of bases supporting the destroyer convoys. The disproportionate attention paid to Munda and Vila airstrips by the Cactus Air Force merits special scrutiny in this context.

No sooner were these two bases discovered than Munda and Vila-Stanmore came under regular bombardment and shelling by Allied air and naval forces. So systematically were they worked over that by the time Operation KE entered the planning stage the Japanese had downgraded both airstrips to standby status. Thanks to the ongoing disruption of Munda's operation, the airstrip never became a permanent bomber base; the JNAF was forced to keep its bombers out of harm's way at Rabaul and Buka. Dispatching Bettys, Nells, and Lilys from Rabaul and Buka, and staging them through Kahili and Ballale, meant longer flying times, a greater need for fuel, and smaller bomb loads. These handicaps blunted the impact Japanese bombers had on suppressing Allied air, land, and sea operations in the Eastern Solomons, but by no means negated it altogether.

As an advance base, Munda, supported by Vila, could have helped intensify and sustain the Japanese air offensive down the Slot and beyond, but its permanent use would not have greatly altered the overall course of the war in the South Pacific. However, raiding these Central Solomon bases became second nature to the Cactus Air Force, which ultimately gave them more attention than they probably deserved. Even then, though some strategic value was obtained, American air power never succeeded in totally shutting down Munda during Operation KE despite the considerable energies devoted to this goal. It was this rabid persistence on the part of U.S. commanders that led to two serious errors in their judgment.

First, the most appropriate assets for suppressing the Munda and Vila airstrips were the 13th Air Force's B-26s and B-17s. USAAF medium bombers detached for duty with the Cactus Air Force managed to hit the airstrips, supply dumps, and other installations at Munda and Vila a dozen times between 16 January and 30 January. Such a strategic bombing role was both logical and appropriate for medium bombers. Regrettably, the mediums did not keep up these base-suppression raids during the crucial evacuation phase of Operation KE. The B-26s attacked Munda only once in February— on 3 February—and Vila not at all. The following day the 70th BS's Marauders were rotated out of Henderson Field to Fiji. This unit had been in the line at Cactus since 9 January and might no longer have been able to continue its offensive due to the attrition inflicted on its small aircraft inventory by the brutal pace of the previous weeks.

The misuse of the 5th and 11th BG(H)s' B-17s in an antishipping role reflected an erroneous belief in the nearly unlimited versatility of the heavy bomber. Only when the Forts came down to between six thousand and eight thousand feet—in range of Japanese flak—did they have even minimal success bombing stationary or moving ships. The B-17's forte proved to be area-saturation bombing in large formations, operating at medium and high altitudes; Forts were far more effective for bombing sprawling land targets, such as airfields, supply bases, and harbor facilities. While Japanese fighters attacked B-17s on several occasions, Japanese fighter *kokutai* did not relish intercepting flights of the heavily gunned Forts; they and often gave them a wide berth—especially if the heavies were escorted. B-17s attacked Kahili, Ballale, and Buka airfields several times throughout January 1943, but more often tried to bomb shipping at anchor in Shortland and Tonolei Harbors with middling success.

The B-17 also proved to be especially well-suited to long-range reconnaissance missions over Bougainville and the Bismarck Archipelago, where the risk of Japanese fighter interception was high. B-17s on solo reconnaissance missions were often assaulted by a *chutai* or *shotai*, but were seldom shot down. As a result, the Cactus Air Force grossly underutilized its slower but adequately defended Catalinas in the reconnaissance role, as did the 7th AF, which commanded B-17 and PBY squadrons in the Central Pacific. Thus, the overworked Forts were stretched even more thinly across the Pacific, performing reconnaissance work when they should have been released to intensify strategic bombing in the South Pacific.

Underemployment of the 13th Air Force's bombers against Munda-Lambeti and Vila-Stanmore had far-reaching consequences for the Cactus Air Force. While struggling to juggle enough aircrews and planes to mount an effective antishipping campaign against the Tokyo Express, Cactus SBD and TBF squadrons flew nine missions targeting either Munda or Vila between 10 January and 8 February, not counting antishipping strike forces that bombed Munda on the way back as their assigned secondary target. Indeed, light bombers flew no fewer than one hundred individual base-suppression sorties against Munda and Vila during Operation KE; at least 125 escorting fighters as well as fighters carrying out sweeps were also dispatched. The Japanese themselves realized the anomaly. "We were not often attacked by heavy bombers at MUNDA," recalled Lt. Cdr. S. Yunoki, "but the dive-bombers and torpedo bombers made very serious attacks."

The 13th Air Force should have husbanded its limited bomber force, focusing its destructive power exclusively on appropriate strategic targets like the bases at Munda and Vila, which were hit only five times by B-17s during all of Operation KE. This would have liberated the Cactus Air Force's light bombers to mount heavier and more-frequent antishipping strikes against its priority target: the Tokyo Express. Perhaps Admiral Fitch and General Mulcahy should not be faulted for trying to keep Munda, Vila, and their airstrips off balance. Rather, it is their choice of assets to do this that merits criticism.

Second, regarding the Cactus Air Force's actual execution of its campaign against the Tokyo Express, one of the tactics employed proved additionally wasteful.

Search-and-destroy missions dispatched on speculation used up valuable men, aircraft, and fuel that ought to have been allocated to meaningful missions against clearly located and well-tracked Tokyo Express convoys. For example, on 19 January a vague radio intercept and a single sighting by an unspecified source of "7 DD, 1 CA (air escort)" steaming down the Slot at fifteen knots about halfway between the Shortlands and Vella Lavella set in motion a pair of air strikes out of Cactus. First off at 1427 was a flight of B-17s, escorted by six P-40s and six P-38s. Eighteen SBDs and ten TBFs, escorted by eleven F4Fs and eight P-39s, followed at 1645 hours. Neither group made contact with the phantom destroyers in the heavy weather, returning to Cactus empty-handed. More than sixty aircraft ultimately participated in the missions—a colossal waste of personnel, assets, and resources. Perusal of Japanese destroyer movements on 19 January reveals no such convoy steaming down the Slot that day.

Though strictly speaking not necessarily an asset misallocation, the use of the P-39 in an escort role remains questionable. The 67th FS is a case in point. Although circumstances dictated the need for the 67th FS to fly CAP on air strikes, this decision may have been ill-advised. Flying its inferior Bell P-400 Airacobras, the 67th had operated almost exclusively as a ground support unit during most of its stay on Guadalcanal. The fighter-bomber role proved to be a highly dangerous and thankless job in which the 67th's pilots and planes undeniably excelled.

By mid-January, however, the pilots of the 67th found themselves increasingly reassigned to air-combat duties. Realistically, even their newer Airacobra variants limited them to flying low cover, but they were called upon occasionally to fly CAP missions at altitudes that did not favor the pedestrian performance of even the later P-39 models. There is no question that these Cobra pilots, though lacking in combat experience, did their best against superior Japanese fighters. Their courage and audacity were never in doubt. A review of their performance during Operation KE suggests, however, that they fought their duels at a disadvantage and, but for the lack of any feasible alternative, should not have been thrown into the savage air battles that raged over the Solomons. From its combat debut in the fall of 1942 to June 1944, the 67th racked up only fifteen aerial victories—almost all of them after the squadron reequipped with Lightnings for air combat.

An examination of the significance of Munda airstrip as a contributing factor to the success of Operation KE deserves some discussion. At least one treatise on the Guadalcanal campaign contends that because the airstrips at Munda and Vila were downgraded to standby status, they were not consciously integrated into the KE operation. However, the Japanese categorically stated as one of their KE operational goals, "To make efforts for the expansion and the strengthening of air defense bases at MUNDA, KOLOMBANGARA, BUIN, BUKA and RABAUL in the SOLOMON area, and to expedite the use of air strength."

The airstrip at Munda Point was relatively compact and basic in design, yet it fairly bristled with AA guns: eighteen 75-mm dual-purpose guns; twenty 40-mm flak guns, comparable to the Allies' Bofors; fifty 25-mm rapid-fire guns, equivalent to the Allies' 20-mm Oerlikon; and copious nests of 13-mm heavy machine guns, like the Allies' .50-caliber weapon, in both single and twin mounts. No facility meant to stay in standby service would have been kept this well protected. In fact, Munda airstrip, in particular, was destined to play several noteworthy roles in support of Operation KE.

First, once Munda became operational, it failed to host any permanently based air units, but it repeatedly operated small *chutai* or even single *shotai* of Zeros prior to KE in spite of obsessive U.S. efforts to put both it and uncompleted Vila out of business. JNAF fighters made use of Munda's facilities throughout the month. Taking up short-term residence, pilots dispersed their planes away from the derelicts spread at random around the airstrip and periodically rearranged them to confound aerial surveillance and attract strafing planes. On 12 January a B-17, on its way back from a photoreconnaissance mission over New Georgia's Wana Lagoon, observed four Zeros taking off from Munda, leaving eight other Zeros plus a medium bomber on the field. B-26 raiders counted at least twelve planes at Munda the next day.

JNAF fighter units regarded Munda as a convenient oasis that not only enabled them to fly CAP over the Tokyo Express with greater confidence, but also presented them with tactical opportunities that could not otherwise have been exploited without considerable risk to men and machines. For example, the proud samurai who taunted MG Ed Zielinski would never have dared to vindicate his honor had Munda airstrip not been there. Having flown down from Bougainville, patrolled over the destroyers, fought against VMF-121, and followed Zielinski partway home, he would likely have run out of fuel before making Kahili.

Second, Munda was singled out to play a role in the actual provision of fighter CAPs for KE evacuation convoys. Thirty JAAF Oscar fighters from the 1st Sentai flew into Munda on 18 January and were relieved toward the end of the month by the 3rd Chutai of the 11th Sentai. Lieutenant Keenan on Vella Lavella observed a noticeable increase in air activity at Munda after 18 January, as did Cactus reconnaissance flights.

For instance, the camera of a photoreconnaissance plane recorded ten planes on the airstrip on the 22nd, seven of them possibly damaged. Coastwatcher Horton reported from Rendova on 25 January that four fighters from the west landed at 1700; within a few minutes, one took off toward Vila. Two days later, he saw ten "Zeros" arrive, nine of which landed. They were part of a fifteen-Oscar contingent that paused at Munda on their way back from Guadalcanal. That evening five Oscars prepared to escort a Lily to harass Cactus, but the raid was cancelled, according to Munda's narrative, and its twenty-seven resident Oscars retired temporarily to Rabaul due to a fuel shortage. The next day, 28 January, a flight of Lilys and Oscars took off at 0745 and returned later; these may have been the seven Oscars and seven Lilys that touched down around 1800 hours. Lieutenant Horton saw the fighters land, followed at 1830 by another seven fighters coming off patrol. Munda recorded on 29 January that seven Lilys landed with six Oscars. Later, Horton noted that another eight "Zeros" flew in from the west to land at 1845 while three others orbited in the vicinity; these were likely the first of the 11th Sentai's Munda detachment to arrive. Eight "small planes" escorted eleven "transports or bombers" to Munda from the northwest on the evening of 30 January, according to coastwatchers Keenan and Horton.

Since Zero *kokutai* war diaries make scant mention of operations into, out of, or through Munda after mid-January, Munda's beehive of mixed fighter and bomber activity—especially the early evening touchdowns and overnight sojourns—suggests that Oscars, initially from the 1st Sentai and then from the 11th Sentai, were using Munda as a temporary home base.

Third, in a secondary role, these resident JAAF Ki-43s and visiting Zeros preyed upon Cactus patrol bombers. A Zero that scrambled after the Black Cat on 4 January, as well as three that tried to catch up to a straggling Marauder after the Munda raid of 5 January, likely flew out of Munda. An RNZAF Hudson pilot, patrolling the Slot on 13 January, reported that he unexpectedly ran into "six" Zeros at 1530 hours. Before the three-plane *shotai* from the 204th Kokutai even saw the snooper, the Kiwi plane commander eluded them by wheeling into the nearest cloud cover. The crew came away convinced these enemy pilots had been lying in wait over the southern tip of Choiseul to ambush them—a stone's throw away from Munda airstrip. Another RNZAF Hudson, searching the Central Solomons on 24 January, was jumped by an estimated five "Hamps," but escaped by ducking into clouds. These misidentified clipped-wing fighters were almost certainly Munda-based Oscars, since no Zeros were operating in the area that day.

Fourth, Munda served as a potential staging base for Tokyo Express CAPs and bomber strike forces and reconnaissance runs. At 1250 on 9 January a *chutai* of Zeros from the 204th Kokutai paused at Munda for servicing and refreshments after a mission to Rendova. They were on their way back to Kahili again by 1545 hours. The 204th returned next evening; between 1930 and 1937 a dozen Zeros put down for the night after coming off convoy escort duty. They were off early next morning to fly CAP over the Tokyo Express. At 0935 seven Zeros set back down after tangling with a Cactus strike force; they stayed until 1110, when they took off for Buin. CAP duty over the Tokyo Express again brought a *chutai* of 204th Kokutai Zeros for an overnight sojourn between 14 January and 15 January. Another 204th *chutai* pancaked at 0815 on 15 January, having again fought off a Cactus air attack on the destroyers. Within twenty minutes they had resumed their flight back to Kahili. The 21st saw a *shotai* of Vals from the 582nd Kokutai on a reconnaissance mission from Buin stop off for thirty-five minutes before returning.

JAAF Lily bombers were continually coming and going between 22 January and 1 February in preparation for bombing Guadalcanal's airfields. Laying over in the New Georgia group, however, did entail a strong risk of being caught on the ground by frequent American air attacks, or even another naval bombardment. The JAAF strike force of 1 February was pruned down to six Lilys by just such a raid. As an emergency landing strip, Munda hosted both strike-force members and Maytag Mike bombers. If they consumed too much fuel and ammo or sustained battle damage, these planes, pilots, and crews could pancake for temporary repairs or emergency medical treatment.

During January, Munda-Lambeti suffered a naval bombardment, twenty-five air strikes, and thirteen nighttime harassment raids. Given the modest quantity of ordnance dumped on both Munda and Vila in any light-bomber raid, their ground echelons—operating late into the night to fill bomb craters and repair runway, taxiways, and revetments—rendered them usable within a day after a raid. The airstrips could be fully operational in a day or two after a raid by medium or heavy bombers or after a naval bombardment. Though no planes were based at Munda on a full-time basis apart from the JAAF's Oscars, the airstrip was never shut down. It took a full-scale amphibious assault and six weeks' bitter fighting to wrest Munda from the Japanese in the summer of 1943. When U.S. troops finally overran the airstrip, they found fourteen wrecked Zeros, four Oscars, several Bettys, seven Lilys, and four Vals—a poignant testimonial to the unrelenting tenacity of the Japanese to keep Munda open at all costs.

With the fall of Guadalcanal, the New Georgia group became Japan's first line of defense in the Solomons. Within this context it appears that Japanese intentions for Vila airstrip were at least as grandiose as those for Munda. Vila was to be developed into a major fighter and bomber airbase for the JAAF and would presumably function alongside a rejuvenated JNAF fighter and bomber facility at Munda in support of a determined defense of the New Georgia group aimed at thwarting any Allied advance into the Central Solomons. Instead, intensified air raids by the Cactus Air Force and the 13th Air Force throughout the spring and early summer of 1943—in conjunction with the rapid Allied advance upon Munda in the summer and the unanticipated bypassing of Kolombangara with a landing on Vella Lavella in the fall—effectively stymied the consummation of these plans.

Admiral Ainsworth aptly summed up the problem posed by the existence of Munda and Vila airstrips and pointed to the only real solution: "The fact is inescapable that the Japs have gone right ahead and built two airfields in spite of constant bombing by aircraft and two bombardments by surface vessels. We may destroy large quantities of gasoline and stores, and we may render these fields unusable at critical times, but the only real answer is to take the fields away from them."

At the risk of giving imperial GHQ's planners more credit than they deserve, it is tantalizing to speculate if the Japanese entertained an ulterior motive for reactivating Munda airstrip after December. Was sending two successive *daitai* of JAAF Oscar pilots to take up residence at Munda a deliberate ploy to lure the Cactus Air Force's attention away from the evacuation convoys? Did Japanese planners purposefully distract Admiral Fitch and General

Mulcahy into weakening their already limited antishipping strike capability? Whether or not such a strategy was intended, this is more or less what happened. Begun the previous December, the Cactus Air Force's campaign against Munda continued without letup throughout Operation KE.

Something similar occurred on a larger scale between late 1943 and early 1944, when the Allied juggernaut began to pound Rabaul itself. Flushed with Operation KE's unexpected success, Rengo Kantai decided in the spring of 1943 to commit most of its remaining carrier *hikokitai* to land-based operations out of Rabaul. Admiral Yamamoto planned to launch a surprise April offensive against the burgeoning Allied air and naval armadas that were massing for an invasion of the Central Solomons. But Operation I-GO—the initial phase of the plan—was judged a failure by Rengo Kantai HQ. Despite glowing reports from JNAF airmen that they had sunk many Allied ships and downed scores of planes, the actual results were far more modest. Thus, after only a few weeks, the survivors of those carrier *hikokitai* that participated in I-GO were withdrawn to Truk to await the American invasion of New Georgia.

As the air battles over the Solomons, the Bismark Archipelago, and New Guinea continued to take their toll, Allied fighter sweeps were no longer contested; intercepts against bombers were carried out with great caution. Rabaul's fighters were ordered not to stray from New Britain's coast in pursuit of the enemy. Clearly, the Japanese were husbanding their meager fighter assets to maintain a presence at Rabaul that would tie down Allied air power, even after all bombers and transport aircraft had been evacuated.

In the spring of 1944 Rabaul's remaining fighters were withdrawn to defend Truk, but several damaged Zeros were made airworthy, phoenix-like, by cannibalizing wrecks lying about. Once back in service, they simply tried to survive by escaping aloft whenever Allied air raids arrived. Even after Rabaul ceased to host any resident air contingent, a skeleton ground echelon kept its major fields operable, forcing the Allies to continue diverting considerable air resources and copious quantities of ordnance to keep this bypassed bastion neutralized until the war's end.

Similarly, air activity out of Munda and construction activity at Vila, though interrupted sporadically during Operation KE, never really ceased. Munda hosted Zeros on a day-to-day basis throughout January 1943. Once they took up temporary residence, Munda-based Oscars carried out their assigned role to defend Admiral Hashimoto's destroyers. Thus, whether intentional or not, this small echelon of resident planes, coupled to bombers and fighters staging through Munda, was able to maintain an ongoing presence that partially distracted Cactus' attention away from its more important targets—the convoys of the Tokyo Express.

Things had changed dramatically for the Japanese by the fall of 1943. Superior U.S. fighters, like the Chance Vought F4U Corsair and the Grumman F6F Hellcat, now flew out of no fewer than ten Allied airbases stretching from Guadalcanal to Vella Lavella. In the interim, Japanese air power in the Solomons had been systematically and inexorably smothered. Without air cover, even swift Japanese destroyers fell prey to hordes of American and New Zealand land-based aircraft that roamed at will throughout the South Pacific. The Japanese were forced to rely increasingly on motorized barges that could slip furtively by night from island to island in an attempt to furnish some measure of short-range transportation.

Despite the shifting balance of military power in the Solomons by early 1943, Operation KE proved to be the opportunity for the Japanese to triumph over their enemies under adverse circumstances one final time. The evacuation of Guadalcanal cost the IJN one destroyer sunk and seventeen more damaged to varying degrees, including several that were hit on more than one occasion. Nearly seventy aircraft were recorded lost in KE-related air combat. Operation KE cost the USN one cruiser, one destroyer, and three PT boats; two other destroyers and several PT boats were damaged. In addition, some fifty U.S. planes were lost or written off. Thus, both sides just about broke even in a material sense.

However, the Americans were obliged to concede a qualified strategic victory that for the Japanese turned out to be more a humanitarian gesture than a military coup. The Tokyo Express, according to Japanese statistics found in Gen. Douglas MacArthur's reports, rescued 10,572 troops, who the Imperial Japanese Army hoped would recuperate from their debilitating ordeal on "Starvation Island" and rally to fight another day. In reality, however, not all of them fought for Hirohito again.

The healthier evacuees were quickly transferred from the Solomons to Rabaul. There the 38th Division was reorganized for the defense of New

Britain. The 2nd Division and the 35th Brigade were transferred to other theaters. Only the reconstituted Japanese 229th and 230th Infantry Regiments returned to the Solomons, where within six months they found themselves pressed into the defense of the New Georgia group.

Elements of the 229th had already been in New Georgia for several months when the 230th staged in via Kolombangara in July 1943, fielding far less than its full complement. Its 2nd Battalion could scrape together a mere four hundred soldiers to defend Munda airstrip. Nevertheless, colonels Genjiro Hirata's and Wakichi Hisashige's veteran jungle fighters, reinforced by many new replacements, offered bitter resistance to U.S. troops advancing on Munda Point.

Though initially more robust than the 230th, the tough-minded 229th had already been whittled down by the savage fighting before it was assigned to retake Kelley Hill, virtually on the doorstep of the contested airstrip. Even so, the remnants of this regiment unleashed a surprisingly determined assault to retake the high ground and, overall, helped retard the Allied campaign against Fortress Rabaul by delaying the capture of Munda for a month or more.

Operation KE was a watershed moment of the Pacific War: the end of the beginning and the beginning of the end. On the one hand, it marked the end of the Guadalcanal campaign—a blood-drenched saga that had begun six months before with the landing of the 1st Marines on Beach Red. On the other hand, Operation KE heralded the beginning of an agonizing retreat back across the Pacific—an odyssey of death and destruction that finally ended for the Dai Nippon Teikoku Kaigun two and a half years later in Tokyo Bay on the deck of the USS *Missouri*.

NOTES

General

For ease of usage, notes to chapters are presented in an informal style instead of the rigid format traditionally found in scholarly publications, dissertations, and theses. The titles of some works have been abbreviated, but the full titles of these sources can be found in the bibliography. Quotations have not been directly annotated in the text, but their sources are recognizable in the appropriate topical chapter notes.

Regarding websites, précised titles of sites are given; full titles and site addresses can be found in the bibliography. When no title is given, the address is cited.

Some Japanese sources were initially researched by Allan Alsleben and Henry Sakaida, who shared their data with us. These sources were identified as per the reference information provided by these contributors.

Japanese documents are generally dated in the following sequence: year (of the emperor's reign)/month/day. For example, the Japanese date of 17/12/23 is equivalent to the Allied date of 42/12/23 or 23 Dec. 1943.

Introduction

Pages 1–2

The discussion of Operation KE and the propensity of the Japanese to evacuate their troops during the Solomons campaign

Altobello, *Into the Shadows Furious*, 2, 4–9. Bergerud, *Fire in the Sky*, 85–86. Hammel, *Munda Trail*, 7–10.

Pages 2–3

The uniqueness of Operation KE

Bergerud, *Fire in the Sky*, 41, 75, 86–87, 89–90, 423–425. Lundstrom, *The First Team*, 525–526.

Pages 3-4
Postcombat reporting and aircraft misidentification anomalies
Foss, *Flying Marine*, 31, 34. Frank, *Guadalcanal: The Definitive Account*, 314–315. Hammel, *Guadalcanal: Starvation Island*, 314–315. HQ, 347th Ftr Gp, Pilot's Combat Report: Capt. Stanley A. Palmer, 2. Izawa, "IJN Float Fighter Units," 12. Lundstrom, *The First Team*, 300. Miller, *The Cactus Air Force*, 34. Sakaida, *JAAF Aces*, 87–88; Sakaida, *IJN Aces*, 87–88. Salecker, *Fortress Against the Sun*, 319–320. VMF-121, *War Diary*, 13 Oct. 1942.

Chapter 1. The Genesis of Operation KE-GO
Pages 5-10
The general discussion in this chapter
Altobello, *Into the Shadows Furious*, 1–9. Bergerud, *Fire in the Sky*, 12–15, 17–18, 28, 34, 36–44, 73–75, 77–78, 81–82, 421–423, 425, 532, 558, 570–571. Cleveland, *Grey Geese Calling*, 15–16. Crenshaw, *South Pacific Destroyer*, 21–22, 23–24, 60. Ferguson, *Guadalcanal: The Island of Fire*, 2–5, 41–51. Frank, *Guadalcanal: The Definitive Account*, 206, 498–499, 526–527, 534–539, 540–541, 544–547, 559–562, 582, 598–601. Hammel, *Munda Trail*, xv–xvi. Hara, *Japanese Destroyer Captain*, 160–166, 171–173. Historical Section, G-2, "General Situation o/a Nov. 1942," in Japanese Monograph #32. Hoyt, *Guadalcanal*, 251–256. Kennedy, *Pacific Onslaught*, 118–135. Lord, *Lonely Vigil*, 36–38, 40. Lundstrom, *The First Team*, 525–526. Paschall, "A Fateful Six Minutes," in *Battle of Midway*, 76–77. Sakaida, *IJN Aces*, 20–21, 23–24. 2nd Demob Bureau, Japanese Monograph #98 (IJN), 56–58, 59, 60, 63; 2nd Demob Bureau, Japanese Monograph #122 (IJN), 1–2, 16. Tuleja, "The Miracle of Midway," in *Battle of Midway*, 10–12. Vader, "Japan Goes to War" and "Coral Sea and New Guinea," in *New Guinea*.

Page 10
The movement of the three IJN cruisers to Kavieng for Operation KE
Hackett et al., TROM for *Chokai, Kumano, Sendai* in web site Junyokan.
The American belief that a new Japanese offensive was in the offing on Guadalcanal 2nd Demob Bureau, Japanese Monograph #122 (IJN), 14. Wolf, *13th Fighter Command*, 108–109.
John Prados' article ("U.S. Intelligence and the Japanese Evacuation of Guadalcanal, 1943") in *Intelligence and National Security*, Apr. 1995, aptly summarizes the U.S. intelligence dilemma in early 1943.

Chapter 2. Japanese Aircraft and Air-Combat Doctrine

Page 11
The goals of the JNAF/JAAF air armada in support of Operation KE
Bergerud, *Fire in the Sky*, 601. MacArthur, Reports: Japanese Operations in the SW Pacific Area, 196. Frank, *Guadalcanal: The Definitive Account*, 540–541, 543, 547. Historical Section, G-2, Japanese Monograph #32, 4. 2nd Demob Bureau, Japanese Monograph #122 (IJN), 38.

Pages 11–12
Specifications and characteristics of the Zeke and Hamp variants
Barker, *Pearl Harbor*, 18–19. Bergerud, *Fire in the Sky*, 199–212. Caidin, *Zero Fighter*, 68, 72–75. Crawford, "Zero: Flimsy Killer," in *WWII Air War: The Men, the Machines, the Missions*, 68–73.

Pages 12–13
Specifications and characteristics of the Oscar
"Alexander, Nakajima Ki-43 Hayabusa (Oscar)," in web site WWII Tech: WWII History. "Joe Baugher's Hayabusa Files," in web site danford.net/hayabusa. ht. Bergerud, *Fire in the Sky*, 219–221. Dunn, Nakajima Ki-43 Armament—A Reassessment (Abstract), 1–9, in web site j-aircraft.com/research/rdunn/Nakajima_ki43arm.htm. Francillon, *Japanese Aircraft of the Pacific War*, 206–214. G-2: Historical Section, Japanese Monograph #32, 2. Heiferman, *Flying Tigers*, 44–45.

Pages 13–14
Japanese fighter doctrine, the *shotai*, and Lieutenant Miyano's preference for the *rotte*
HQ USAFISPA, POW Report #121, 6. Hata et al., *Japanese Naval Aces*, 272. "Japan," in web site East Asian/Pacific Area Minor Air Forces. ONI, POW Report: WO Mitsunori Nakajima, 96–97. 204th Kokutai, Combat Report, 18/1/11, 18/1/15, 18/1/19, 18/1/20, 18/1/25 in web site Japan Center.
See also Terms, Acronyms, and Abbreviations entries for *chutai, daitai, hikodan, hiko shidan, kokutai, koku sentai, koku kantai, shotai.*

Page 13
Maj. Joe Renner's comment
Bureau of Aeronautics, Interview of Maj. J. N. Renner, USMC, 11.
See also Ferguson, *Guadalcanal: The Island of Fire*, 78–79, 80.

Pages 14–15
Japanese pilot habits and tactics
Bergerud, *Fire in the Sky*, 194–195, 198–199, 412–413, 448–449, 459–462, 475, 479, 505–507. Blackburn, *The Jolly Rogers*, 130, 131, 148–149, 220. Brand, *Fighter Squadron at Guadalcanal*, 48. Ferguson, *Guadalcanal: The Island of Fire*, 178. Foss, *Flying Marine*, 79, 82. Frank, *Guadalcanal: The Definitive Account*, 524–525. Gamble, *The Black Sheep*, 203. Heiferman, *Flying Tigers*, 13–14, 29. HQ USAFISPA, POW Report #121, 6. Izawa, Japanese Navy Float Fighter Units, 5–6. Sakaida, *JAAF Aces*, 6–11; Sakaida, *IJN Aces*, 21, 25, 54. Vader, *New Guinea*, 14–15.

Page 15
Specifications of the Rufe
Brand, *Fighter Squadron at Guadalcanal*, 89–90. Caidin, *Zero Fighter*, 68, 70–71. Horton, *New Georgia: Pattern for Victory*, 104–105.
The role of the Rufe in the Solomons and tactics used by Rufe pilots
Aircraft SoPac Force, War Diary, 30 Dec. 1942: Air Strikes. Izawa, "Fighting Floatplanes," in *Air Enthusiast*; Izawa, Japanese Navy Float Fighter Units, 1, 7, 12.

Pages 15–16
Rekata Bay seaplane base
"Rekata Bay," in web site PacificWrecks.com. Ferguson, *Guadalcanal: The Island of Fire*, 181. Izawa, Japanese Navy Float Fighter Units, 7–8. Lord, *Lonely Vigil*, 51, 82. *Senshi Shoho*, Vol. 83, 557.
Specifications and characteristics of the Pete and its role in Operation KE
Alexander, "F1M (Pete)," in web site WWII Tech: WWII History. Frank, *Guadalcanal: The Definitive Account*, 547. Izawa, "Fighting Floatplanes," in *Air Enthusiast*, 11. Radio intercept from IRO 7, 3 Jan. 1943 at unspecified time.

Page 16
The description of the Aichi Jake
"Aichi E13A," in web site combinedfleet.com/ijna/e13a.htm.
Specifications of the Val
Barker, *Pearl Harbor*, 66–67. Kennedy, *Pacific Onslaught*, 102–103.

Pages 16–17
Specifications of the Betty
Barker, *Suicide Weapon*, 86–87. Horton, *New Georgia: Pattern for Victory*, 62–63. Macintyre, *Leyte Gulf*, 34–35.

Characteristics of the Betty and its assigned role during Operation KE
  Bergerud, *Fire in the Sky*, 558–559. MacArthur, Reports: Japanese Operations in the SW Pacific Area, 196. Brand, *Fighter Squadron at Guadalcanal*, 75–76. Crenshaw, *South Pacific Destroyer*, 61. Lundstrom, *The First Team*, 201. USAAF HQ: G-2, "Pacific Counterblow," in web site Guadalcanal Air War at USD History Server.

Page 17
Specifications of the Nell
  "G3M 'Nell'," in web site Realism Counts. Swinson, *Defeat in Malaya*, 106–107.

Pages 17–18
Specifications of the Lily
  "Kawasaki Ki-48 'Lily'," in web site resourcegroup.org/IJARG/kawasakiki-48.html.

Page 18
Specifications and role of the Dinah
  "Ki-46 Army Type 100 (Dinah)," in web site PacificWrecks "Mitsubishi 'Dinah' (Army Type 100 Command Recon aircraft)," in web site csd.uwo.ca/~pettypi/elevon/gustin_military/db/ap/KI46MITS.html. 2nd Demob Bureau, Japanese Monograph #122 (IJN), 38.
Specifications for the Mavis and Emily flying boats
  "Kawinishi H6K Mavis," in web site warbirdsresourcegroup.org/IJAR/Kawinishih6k.html. "Kawinishi H6K," in web site combinedfleet.com/ijna/h6k.html. "Kawinishi H8K Emily," in web site warbirdsresourcegroup.org/IJAR/Kawinishi h8k.html. "Kawinishi H8K," in web site combinedfleet.com/ijna/h8k.html.

Pages 19–20
Deployment of the several JNAF *kokutai* and their aces to Rabaul and bases in the Western Solomons
  Hata et al., *Japanese Naval Aces*, 49–50, 114–115, 148, 150, 151, 157, 158–159, 160–161, 242, 249–250, 256, 261, 269, 272–273, 274, 279, 284, 290, 306, 308, 310, 314, 319, 320, 322, 324, 349, 351, 372, 373. HQ USAFISPA, POW Report #121, 3, 4, 7. Lundstrom, *The First Team*, 471–472, 473. Radio intercept from NU SA 06, 15 Jan. 1943 @2035L; from CinC 3rd Fleet, 23 Jan. 1943 @2223L; from NU TI 0, 24 Jan. 1943 @2103L; from NI SO 12, 27 Jan. 1943 @2203L. Sakaida, *IJN Aces*, 11, 45, 48–49, 51, 52, 54, 60, 64, 89. *Senshi Sosho*, Vol. 83, 557.

Pages 20–23
Estimated dispositions of JNAF and JAAF aircraft on the eve of Operation KE
Aircraft SoPac Force, War Diary, 27, 29, 31 Jan. 1943: Enemy Contacts; 4, 7 Feb. 1943: Enemy Contacts. Alsleben, emails to D. Letourneau: 23 Oct. 2002, 23 Jan. 2004. Bergerud, *Fire in the Sky*, 23–24, 425. Dunn, Nakajima Ki-43-1 Armament—A Reassessment, 3 in web site j-aircraft.com/research/rdunn/ Nakajima_ki43arm.htm. Frank, *Guadalcanal: The Definitive Account*, 198, 410, 543, 545–546, 758 (footnote for pages 582–588). Hackett et al., TROM for *Kamikawa Maru, Kiyokawa Maru, Kunikawa Maru, Sanyo Maru*, in web site Tokusetsu Suijoki-Bakan! G-2: Historical Section, Japanese Monograph #32, 2–4; Japanese Monograph #35, 36. Izawa, "Fighting Floatplanes," in *Air Enthusiast*, 18; Izawa, Japanese Navy Float Fighter Units, 7, 9, 10, 11. Lundstrom, *The First Team*, 471–472, 473. Nevitt, TROM for *Fumizuki, Nagatsuki, Satsuki*, in web site Long Lancers. MacArthur, Reports: Japanese Operations in the SW Pacific Area, 196. Radio intercept from YO YU 4, 20 Jan. 1943 @1410L. Sakaida, *IJN Aces*, 54, 55. *Senshi Sosho*, Vol. 28: 562–563; Vol. 83: 537–538. 2nd Demob Bureau, Japanese Monograph #122 (IJN), 38. 204th Kokutai, Combat Diary excerpt.

Page 23
JAAF aces who participated in Operation KE
"Japanese Aces," in web site World War II Vehicles. Magnus, in web site Air Aces. Web site WWII Aces of the IJA.

Page 24
The Yamamoto and Kondo task forces
Frank, *Guadalcanal: The Definitive Account*, 542, 545–546.

Chapter 3. American Aircraft and Air-Combat Doctrine
Page 25
The estimate of U.S. aircraft in the South Pacific and at Cactus
Frank, *Guadalcanal: The Definitive Account*, 542–543.

Pages 25–26
U.S. Marine/USN fighter strength at Cactus
Aircraft SoPac Force, War Diary, 17 Jan. 1943: (4) Ship Movements; 30 Jan. 1943: (3) Other Operations; 31 Jan. 1943: (3) Plane Movements, (5) Other Operations; 1, 2, 3 Feb. 1943: (3) Plane Movements. Frank, *Guadalcanal: The Definitive Account*, 542. Kiethly, Memo: Info. on . . . VMO-251, unnumbered

page. Lundstrom, *The First Team*, 329–330. MAG 12, Record of Events of MAG 12, unnumbered page. VGSs-11, 12, 16, War Diary, 31 Jan. 1943; 1, 3 Feb. 1943. VMF-112, Daily Ops Reports, 25 Jan.–12 Feb. 1943. VMF-121, Daily Ops Report, 29 Jan. 1943. VMF-122, War Diary of Ground Echelon, 25 Jan.–12 Feb. 1943. VMF-123, Chronology, 3 Feb. 1943; Summary of War Duty, 2. VMF-124, Squadron History, 2. VMO-251, War Diary, 4, 6, 7 Feb. 1943.

Page 26
Specifications and characteristics of the Wildcat and its comparison to the Zero
Brand, *Fighter Squadron at Guadalcanal*, 45, 47, 94, 105, 117, 153, 156, 167. Macintyre, *Aircraft Carrier*, 105.
Claire Chennault's air combat doctrine and its dissemination throughout U.S. air arms
Bergerud, *Fire in the Sky*, 450–451. Foss, *Flying Marine*, 80. Heiferman, *Flying Tigers*, 6–33.

Pages 26–27
Japanese bombing and fighter-sweep tactics against slow-climbing Cactus fighters
Bergerud, *Fire in the Sky*, 502–504. Brand, *Fighter Squadron at Guadalcanal*, 94–95. Cleveland, *Grey Geese Calling*, 22. Feliton, phone interview with the writers, 22 Feb. 2002. Ferguson, *Guadalcanal: The Island of Fire*, 82. Foss, *Flying Marine*, 54–55, 69, 70, 72. Lundstrom, *The First Team*, 186. Mann, "So Far ... A Pilot's Dream," in *Aces Against Japan*, 82. Wesolowski, "Snap Shot," in *Aces Against Japan*, 70.

Page 27
The Thach weave and its scissor derivatives
Astor, "The Master Weaver," in *Battle of Midway*, 34–35. Bechtel, "The Christmas Present," in *Aces Against Japan*, 88. Bergerud, *Fire in the Sky*, 451, 455–456, 457. Blackburn, *The Jolly Rogers*, 111, 220–221. Sulzberger, Summary of VMF-121 War Diary, 6.

Pages 27–28
Joe Bauer's air combat philosophy and pilot-training regimen
Bergerud, *Fire in the Sky*, 490–492. Brand, *Fighter Squadron at Guadalcanal*, 42–48. Feliton, phone interview with the writers, 22 Feb. 2002. Foss, *Flying Marine*, 80–81. Lundstrom, *The First Team*, 331.
For a classic example of a Wildcat-versus-Zero scissoring duel see Conger's account in Brand, *Fighter Squadron at Guadalcanal*, 95.

Pages 29–30

Specifications and characteristics of the P-39/P-400 Airacobra, its inadequacy as a fighter, the use of the P-400 as a ground-support aircraft, and deployment of the P-39/P-400 at Cactus

> Bergerud, *Fire in the Sky*, 602. Cleveland, *Grey Geese Calling*, 17, 24. Ferguson, *Guadalcanal: The Island of Fire*, 5–6, 78–79, 80–81, 92–93, 130–131, 159, 175. King, Bombing and Strafing by P-39's on Guadalcanal, 1, 3–6. Musell, "The Bell P-39 Airacobra," in web site chuckhawks.com/p39.htm (P-39D). USAAF HQ, G-2, "Pacific Counterblow," in web site Guadalcanal Air War at USD History Server.

Pages 30–31

Specifications and characteristics of the P-40 Warhawk and its deployment at Cactus

> Aircraft SoPac Force, War Diary, 30 Jan. 1943: (3) Other Operations. "AETC Office Webmaster," in web site aetc.randolph.af.mil/ho/upt_hanges/@_p39.htm. Bergerud, *Fire in the Sky*, 492–493. Cleveland, *Grey Geese Calling*, 78. Ferguson, *Guadalcanal: The Island of Fire*, 186, 190. Heiferman, *Flying Tigers*, 56–57. Musell, "P-40 Warhawk," in web site chuckhawks.com/p40.htm. Vader, *New Guinea*, 101.

Pilot assessment of the P-40 HQ, 347th Ftr Gp. Pilot's Combat Report: Lt. A.S. Webb, 1; Capt. S.A. Palmer, 3.

Pages 31–32

Specifications and characteristics of the P-38 Lightning and its deployment at Cactus

> Aircraft SoPac Force, War Diary, 27 Jan. 1943: (3) Other Operations. Bergerud, *Fire in the Sky*, 262–268. Davis, *Get Yamamoto*, 88–90. Cleveland, *Grey Geese Calling*, 78. Ferguson, *Guadalcanal: The Island of Fire*, 167–168. Tillman, "P-38," in *Pacific Fighters*, 25. USAAF HQ, G-2, "Pacific Counterblow," unnumbered pages, in web site Guadalcanal Air War at USD History Server. WRG-USAAF Resource Center, "Lockheed P-38," in web site warbirdsresourcegroup.org/urg/p38.htm.

Page 33

John Mitchell's development of combat tactics for the P-38 Lightning

> Bergerud, *Fire in the Sky*, 479–480, 481–482. Davis, *Get Yamamoto*, 90. Ferguson, *Guadalcanal: The Island of Fire*, 176–178, 197. "John W. Mitchell," in web site American Air Aces of WWII.

Pages 33–34
Total fighter strength at Cactus
ComSoPac, Message to CinCPac, 27 Jan. 1943. Davis, *Get Yamamoto*, 88. Ferguson, *Guadalcanal: The Island of Fire*, 48. HQ, 347th Ftr Gp, Pilot's Combat Report: Capt. S.A. Palmer, 1; Lt. A.S. Webb, 1. Lundstrom,*The First Team*, 329–330. McKillop, USAAF Combat Chronology, Fri. 29 Jan. 1943: South Pacific Theater, 13th AF.

Page 34
The perception of their aircraft held by Cactus fighter pilots and its utility in the Guadalcanal campaign.
Bergend, Fire in the Sky, 198-199, 489.

Pages 34–35
Specifications, characteristic and deployment of the SBD Dauntless
Aircraft SoPac Force, War Diary, 2 Jan. 1943: Plane Movements; 28 Jan. 1943: (4) Other Operations. Bechtel, "The Christmas Present," in *Aces Against Japan*, 88. Macintyre, *Aircraft Carrier*, 91. McEniry, *A Marine Dive-Bomber Pilot at Guadalcanal*, 17, 19, 21–24. VMSB-132, War Diary, 2, 3, 13 Feb. 1943. VMSB-142, War Diary, Aircraft. VMSB-144, Squadron History, 2. VMSB-234, War Diary, Jan. 1943: Composition: (a) Aircraft; Log of Events 1, 2, 16, 27, 28, 30 Jan. 1943.

Page 35
Specifications of the TBF-1 Avenger
Macintyre, *Leyte Gulf*, 60–61.
An informative article on the Avenger is Jerry Scutts,"Avenger!" in *WWII Air War*, 82–92.

Pages 35–36
The arrival at Cactus and subsequent deployment of VMSB-131
Aircraft SoPac Force, War Diary, 3 Jan. 1943: Plane Movements; 18 Jan. 1943: (5) Plane Movements. Frank, *Guadalcanal: The Definitive Account*, 410. Hammel, *Guadalcanal: Decision at Sea*, 334, 368–369. VMSB-131, War Diary, 18, 19 Jan. 1943; 2 Feb. 1943.

Page 36
The authorization, dispatch, and arrival of the USN TBFs at Cactus
Aircraft SoPac Force, War Diary, 30 Jan. 1943: (3) Other Operations; 31 Jan. 1943 and 1, 2, 3 Feb. 1943: (3) Plane Movements. VGSs-11, 12, 16, War Diary, 1, 3 Feb. 1943.

Pages 36–38
Specifications and characteristics of the B-17 and its evolving role and deployment in the Guadalcanal campaign

Aircraft SoPac Force, War Diary, 31 Dec. 1942; 2 Jan. 1943; 3, 4, 5, 14 Jan. 1943: Plane Movements; 26, 29 Jan. 1943: (2) Air Strikes. Bergerud, *Fire in the Sky*, 272–276. Cleveland, *Grey Geese Calling*, 11, 17, 23, 24, 25, 26, 37–38, 39, 64, 65, 78. ComSoPac, Message to CinCPac, 27 Jan. 1943. Ferguson, *Guadalcanal: The Island of Fire*, 48, 95, 102, 175, 188. 5th BG(H), Narrative: 19 May, 1918–31 Dec. 1943, 7–11. Horton, *New Georgia: Pattern for Victory*, 90–91. Lundstrum, *The First Team*, 301. McKillop, USAAF Combat Chronology, Sun. 3, Sun. 17, Tues. 19 Jan., Sat. 6 Feb. 1943: SoPac Theater, 13th AF. Salecker, *Fortress Against the Sun*, 300, 318–319, 320, 321, 323. USAAF HQ, G-2, "Pacific Counterblow," in web site Guadalcanal Air War at USD History Server.

Pages 38–39
Specifications and characteristics of the B-26 and its role and deployment in the Guadalcanal campaign

Aircraft SoPac Force, War Diary, 27 Dec. 1942; 29 Dec. 1942: Plane Movements; 31 Dec. 1942: Plane Movements; 4 Jan. 1943: Air Strikes; 6 Jan. 1943: Miscellaneous. "American Combat A/C of WWII," in web site Historycentral.com. ComSoPac, Message to CinCPac, 27 Jan. 1943. Bergerud, *Fire in the Sky*, 281–284. Cleveland, *Grey Geese Calling*, 17. Ferguson, *Guadalcanal: The Island of Fire*, 48, 186. "Martin B-26 Marauder," in web site Yahoo. McKillop, USAAF Combat Chronology, Sat. 9 Jan., Thurs. 4 Feb., Tues. 9 Feb. 1943: SoPac Theater, 13th AF.

Pages 39–40
The specifications and characteristics of the Consolidated PBY

Bergerud, *Fire in the Sky*, 207. "Cats Are Night Creatures," in web site Black Cat PBYs. Horton's *New Georgia: Pattern for Victory*, 36–37. "Early Operations," in web site Black Cat PBYs. Mills, *Blue Catalinas of WWII*, 5–7. Vader, *New Guinea*, 26.

Pages 40–41
The specifications and characteristics of the Lockheed Hudson

"Lockheed Hudson MkIII," in web site Air-Navy. Bergerud, *Fire in the Sky*, 302. Rooney, *Stillwell*, 40–41.

Page 41

The specifications, characteristics and role of the Consolidated B-24/PB4Y-1 Liberator

>Bergerud, *Fire in the Sky*, 277–280. Salecker, *Fortress Against the Sun*, 324, 325. Swinson, *Mountbatten*, 122–123.

Pages 41–42

Total available Cactus aircraft estimates were compiled from weighing and combining the various sums for each type of plane found throughout the chapter. See also Bergerud, *Fire in the Sky*, 21–22, 341.

Chapter 4. Of Pilots and Preparedness

Pages 43–44

U.S. isolationism, disarmament and rearmament, and training of airmen and the effect on morale

>Astor, "The Master Weaver," in *Battle of Midway*, 36. Bergerud, *Fire in the Sky*, 327, 330–331, 333–340, 366–367. Blackburn, *The Jolly Rogers*, 5. Hammel, *Carrier Clash*, 20–22; *Aces Against Japan*, 1–3, 45. McEniry, *A Marine Dive-Bomber Pilot at Guadalcanal*, 37–38. Paschall, "A Fateful Six Minutes," in *Battle of Midway*, 76.

Pages 44–45

The saga of VMO-251's reorganization and ersatz pilot training prior to its tour of duty at Cactus

>Kiethly, Memo: Info. on ... VMO-251, 3, 8. Bureau of Aeronautics, Interview of Maj. J. N. Renner, USMC, 1–3.

For complementary information, see Bergerud, *Fire in the Sky*, 476–477.

Pages 45–46

The competence of USAAF pilots at Cactus and Navy/Marine training

>Davis, *Get Yamamoto*, 76–77. Ferguson, *Guadalcanal: The Island of Fire*, 16, 21 23, 36–37. "John W. Mitchell," in web site American Air Aces of WWII.

Page 46

Rear-area training of pilots for the 339th FS

>Aircraft SoPac Force, War Diary, 21 Dec. 1942: Other Ops. "Memo from Maj. Gen. Millard F Harmon to LtGen. H. H. Arnold, 20 Oct. 1942," in Ferguson, *Guadalcanal: The Island of Fire*, 224–225.

Lieutenant Hansen's comment
HQ, 347th Ftr Gp, Pilot's Combat Report: Lt. P.M. Hansen, 1.

Pages 46–48
JNAF pilot training and proficiency
Bergerud, *Fire in the Sky*, 142, 322–330, 344–347, 412–413, 462, 489, 505–507, 523, 666–667, 668. Frank, *Guadalcanal: The Definitive Account*, 524–525, 747 (note for pages 524–25). Hara, *Japanese Destroyer Captain*, 260. Hata et al., *Japanese Naval Aces*, 152, 273, 371, 383. HQ USAFISPA, POW Report #121, 1–3, 5, 8. Lundstrom, *The First Team*, 529. ONI, POW Report: WO Mitsunori Nakajima, 96, 97. Sakaida, *IJN Aces*, 45, 54, 104, 105. 347th Ftr Gp, Adv Echelon, Account of Experience of Maj. W. H. McCarroll, 3. "U.S. Pacific Fleet and Pacific Ocean Areas Wkly Intelligence Report, 1, 14, 13 Oct. 1944," in Doll, *Marine Fighting Squadron 121*, 18–19.

Pages 48–49
JAAF pilot training and proficiency
Bergerud, *Fire in the Sky*, 325, 326, 327. Foss, *Flying Marine*, 82. Frank, *Guadalcanal: The Definitive Account*, 524–525. Sakaida, *IJN Aces*, 25.
The assignment of pilots to the *daitai* of the 11th Sentai
Alsleben, email to D. Letourneau, 6 Nov. 2002.

Pages 49–50
The discussion of U.S. pilot combat aptitude, "giggle girls," and morale
Bergerud, *Fire in the Sky*, 334, 355–357, 360–363, 366–368. Bureau of Aeronautics, Interview of Maj. J. N. Renner, USMC, 5–6, 9, 11. Foss, *Flying Marine*, 89. Tom Mann, "So Far ... A Pilot's Dream," in *Aces Against Japan*, 82.

Pages 50–51
The impact of malaria and other tropical illnesses
Bergerud, *Fire in the Sky*, 128, 130–131, 133–135, 135–137. Ferguson, *Guadalcanal: The Island of Fire*, 136–137. Hata et al., *Japanese Naval Aces*, 322. Historical Section, G-2, Japanese Monograph #35, 45. Sakaida, *IJN Aces*, 25, 52.

Pages 51–53
The discussion of problems within the Cactus Air Force's chain of command
Bergerud, *Fire in the Sky*, 29–33. Bureau of Aeronautics, Interview of Maj. J. N. Renner, USMC, 7–8. Cleveland, *Grey Geese Calling*, 38. Ferguson,

Guadalcanal: The Island of Fire, 185–186. MAG 12, Record of Events of MAG 12, unnumbered page. Wolf, 13th Fighter Command, 100–101.

Page 53
The issue of competence versus rank or seniority
VMF-123, Summary of War Diary, 5, 17.
The ways by which pilots kept up their will to fly
Bergerud, Fire in the Sky, 346–347, 360–362.

Chapter 5. Pregame Warm-ups: Munda and Vila
Pages 55–56
Japanese airfield development at Buka and Bonis, Kahili and Kara, and Ballale
Aircraft SoPac Force, War Diary, 5 Jan. 1943: Photo Missions. Bergerud, *Fire in the Sky*, 25–26, 468, 621, 636. Blackburn, *The Jolly Rogers*, 138–139. Frank, *Guadalcanal: The Definitive Account*, 275–276, 609–611. Hammel, *Aces Against Japan*, 86. "Kahili" and "Kara," in web site PacificWrecks. Lord, *Lonely Vigil*, 81, 82. Lundstrom, *The First Team*, 261.

Pages 56–59
The rationale behind and the building of Munda and Vila airstrips
Altobello, *Into the Shadows Furious*, 6–7. Bergerud, *Fire in the Sky*, 85. Blackburn, *The Jolly Rogers*, 113–114. Frank, *Guadalcanal: The Definitive Account*, 525–526. Hammel, *Munda Trail*, 4–7. Hata et al., *Japanese Naval Aces*, 151. Horton, *Fire Over the Islands*, 183–184. Izawa "Fighting Floatplanes," in *Air Enthusiast*, 11. Lord, *Lonely Vigil*, 115–116. Lundstrom, *The First Team*, 261. Sakaida, *IJN Aces*, 24. 2nd Demob Bureau, Monograph #98 (IJN), 56; 2nd Demob Bureau Monograph #122 (IJN), 15.

Page 58
Lieutenant Horton's attempts to set up a coastwatcher outpost to monitor Munda airstrip
Horton, *Fire Over the Islands*, 185, 187–190; Report on Coastwatcher Station PWD.

Page 60
Japanese observation outposts and Joe Foss' attack on the radio-equipped schooner
Aircraft SoPac Force, War Diary, 7 Jan. 1943: Air Strikes. Foss, *Flying Marine*, 141. Horton, *Fire Over the Islands*, 127, 148–151, 184, 196. Lord, *Lonely Vigil*, 92, 93, 111, 116, 216. Military History Section, Japanese Monograph #118, 298–299. Radio intercept: U.S. intel comment, 20 Jan. 1943.

Pages 60–62

The JNAF's attempt to base fighters at Munda on 23 Dec. and the first Cactus air raids
Aircraft SoPac Force, War Diary, 23 Dec. 1942: Air Strikes, Contacts Reported by Other Commands; 24 Dec. 1942: Air Strikes. Bechtel, "The Christmas Present," in *Aces Against Japan*, 88. Bergerud, *Fire in the Sky*, 104. Frank, *Guadalcanal: The Definitive Account*, 526. HQ, 347th Ftr Gp Det, Daily Ops Report, 23 Dec. 1942: 12th Mission. Hata et al., *Japanese Naval Aces*, 115, 284. Horton, *Fire Over the Islands*, 189–190. MAG 14, Guadalcanal: Escorted Bomber Missions, 7, 9. Munda War Diary, Ops Report, 17/12/23 in web site Japan Center. 252nd Kokutai, Combat Report, 17/12/23 in web site Japan Center. Weiland, email to D. Letourneau, 26 Jul. 2003.

Pages 63–64

The Cactus raids of 24 Dec. at Munda, and the nocturnal Rabaul raid of 24-25 Dec.
Air Force History Support Office, web site USAAF in WWII: Combat Chronology, 01/24/43, SoPac. Aircraft SoPac Force, War Diary, 24 Dec. 1942: Air Strikes, Enemy Contacts. Bechtel, "The Christmas Present," in *Aces Against Japan*, 87–91. Bowman, *B-17 Flying Fortress Units*, 82–83. "Camouflage and Markings: Bell P-39," in web site: IPMSStockholm.org. Cressman, "Chronology of USN in WWII," Chap. 5: Thurs. 24, Fri. 25 Dec. 1943, Pacific, in web site Hyperwar. Debnekoff, email to D. Letourneau, 18 Aug. 2003. Frank, *Guadalcanal: The Definitive Account*, 526. HQ, 347th Ftr Gp, Ops Report, 24 Dec. 1942: 1st, 4th, 5th Missions. Hata et al., *Japanese Naval Aces*, 381. Salecker, *Fortress Against the Sun*, 304. 252nd Kokutai, Combat Report, 17/12/24 in web site Japan Center. Wolf, *13th Fighter Command*, 96.

Page 64

Three replacement Zeros arrive at Munda
   252nd Kokutai, Combat Reports, 18/1/24, 25 in web site Japan Center.
Examples of Baker, Dog, and Easy searches
   347th Ftr Gp Det, Daily Ops Reports throughout the period under study, 1 Jan.–8 Feb. 1943.

Pages 65–66

The events of 26 Dec. at Munda and Wickham anchorage
   Alsleben, email to D. Letourneau, 19 Oct. 2002, 1. Aircraft SoPac Force, War Diary, 26 Dec. 1942: Air Strikes, Contacts Reported by Other Commands; 28 Dec. 1942: Air Strikes. Cressman, "Chronology of USN in WWII," Chap. 4: Sat.

26 Dec. 1942, Pacific in web site Hyperwar. Doll, *Marine Fighting Squadron 121*, 46–47. Frank, *Guadalcanal: The Definitive Account*, 526. HQ, 347th Ftr Gp, Ops Report, 26 Dec. 1942: 3rd, 4th, 6th, 7th Missions. Military History Section, Japanese Monograph #116, 183. Munda War Diary, Ops Report, 17/12/26 in web site Japan Center. Salecker, *Fortress Against the Sun*, 304. 2nd Demob Bureau, Japanese Monograph #122 (IJN), 11. 252nd, 582nd, 802nd Kokutai, Combat Reports, 17/12/26 in web site Japan Center. VMF-12, War Diary, 26 Dec. 1942.

Pages 67–68
The events of 27 Dec. at Munda
Aircraft SoPac Force, War Diary, 27 Dec. 1942: Air Strikes. HQ, 347th Ftr Gp, Ops Report, 27 Dec. 1942: 6th, 7th, 8th Missions. Hata et al., *Japanese Naval Aces*, 344, 381. Munda War Diary, Ops Report, 17/12/27 in web site Japan Center. 252nd Kokutai, Combat Report, 17/12/27 in web site Japan Center. Weiland, *Above and Beyond*, 52–54; Log Book, 27 Dec. 1943.

Pages 68–69
Lt. Rex Barber's exploit of 28 Dec. at Munda
Aircraft SoPac Force, War Diary, 28 Dec. 1942: Air Strikes, Contacts Reported by Other Commands. Frank, *Guadalcanal: The Definitive Account*, 526. HQ, 347th Ftr Gp, Ops Report, 28 Dec 1942: 5th Mission. "Mitsubishi G3M Nell," in web site Realism Counts. 701st Kokutai, Combat Report, 17/12/28 in web site Japan Center. "USAAF Aces Scoring with Airacobras," in web site tmg.obc/watel.pl/articles/. Wolf, *13th Fighter Command*, 97.

Page 69
The second Cactus raid of 28 Dec. on Munda
Aircraft SoPac Force, War Diary, 28 Dec. 1942: Air Strikes. HQ, 347th Ftr Gp, Ops Report, 28 Dec. 1942: 7th, 9th Missions. *Senji Senpakushi*, 57. VMF-121, War Diary, 28 Dec. 1942.

Page 70
The antishipping strikes of 29 Dec. against Wickham anchorage
Aircraft SoPac Force, War Diary, 29 Dec. 1942: (2) Air Strikes. HQ, 347th Ftr Gp, Ops Report, 29 Dec. 1942: 1st, 2nd, 4th, 5th, 7th Missions. McKillop, USAAF Combat Chronology, Tues. 28 Dec. 1942. SoPac Theater, 13th AF. Military History Section, Japanese Monograph #116, 83. 347th Ftr Gp, Info from Flight Leader Reports, 29 Dec. 1942. VMF-121, War Diary, 29 Dec. 1942.

Interception of the PB4Y-1 by Hamps on 29 Dec.
    Aircraft SoPac Force, War Diary, 29 Dec. 1942: (2) Air Strikes. 204th Kokutai, Combat Report, 17/12/29 in web site Japan Center.

Page 71
The Cactus raid of 30 Dec. against Wickham anchorage
    Aircraft SoPac Force, War Diary, 30 Dec. 1942: (2) Air Strikes. HQ, 347th Ftr Gp, Ops Report, 30 Dec. 1942: 6th Mission. VMF-121, War Diary, 30 Dec. 1942. Weiland, *Above and Beyond*, 56; Log Book, 30 Dec. 1943.
Note that Weiland describes this event as a fighter sweep against Munda on New Year's Day. In fact, he raided Rekata Bay on 1 Jan. 1943. See below in the narrative.

Pages 71–72
The Cactus raids on Munda on New Year's Eve, New Year's Day, 2 Jan. and 3 Jan. 1943
    Aircraft SoPac Force, War Diary, 31 Dec. and 1, 2, 3 Jan. 1943: Air Strikes. Bergerud, *Fire in the Sky*, 104. Hackett et al., TROM for *Sanyu Maru*, in web site Tokusetsu Suijoki-Bakan!
The operational drawbacks plaguing the Tokyo Express
    Hara, *Japanese Destroyer Captain*, 160–161, 162.

Pages 72–75
The air strikes of 2 Jan. 1943 on the Tokyo Express
    Aircraft SoPac Force, War Diary, 1 Jan. 1943: Contacts Reported by Other Commands; 2 Jan. 1943: Air Strikes, Contacts Reported by Other Commands. Crenshaw, *South Pacific Destroyer*, 52. Cressman, "Chronology of USN in WWII," Chap. 5: Sat. 2 Jan. 1943, Pacific, in web site Hyperwar. Frank, *Guadalcanal: The Definitive Account*, 547. HQ, 347th Ftr Gp, Ops Report, 2 Jan. 1943: 9th, 12th Missions. MAG 14, Guadalcanal: Escorted Bomber Missions, 7. McKillop, USAAF Combat Chronology, Sat. 2 Jan. 1943: SoPac Theater, 13th AF. *Sanyo Maru*, "War Diary" 18/01/02 in web site Japan Center. 204th Kokutai, Combat Report, 18/1/2 in web site Japan Center. VMF-121, War Diary, 2 Jan. 1943. VMSB-233, War Diary, 2 Jan. 1943: Attack Mission. Weiland, *Above and Beyond*, 56.

Page 74
Damage to the *Suzukaze* caused by the SBDs
    Military History Section, Japanese Monograph #116, 184. Nevitt, TROM for *Suzukaze*, in web site Long Lancers.

Page 75
The PT-boat attack of 2–3 Jan. 1943 against the Tokyo Express
  Aircraft SoPac Force, War Diary, 2 Jan. 1943: Air Strikes. Crenshaw, *South Pacific Destroyer*, 52. Frank, *Guadalcanal: The Definitive Account*, 547–548. Hara, *Japanese Destroyer Captain*, 166. Salecker, *Fortress Against the Sun*, 317. Sanyo Maru, War Diary, 18/1/2 in web site Japan Center.

Pages 75–76
The activities of the Black Cats on the nights of 2–3 and 3–4 Jan. 1943
  Aircraft SoPac Force, War Diary, 3, 4 Jan. 1943: Air Strikes.

Page 76
The Cactus air strikes of 3 and 4 Jan. 1943 on Munda
  Aircraft SoPac Force, War Diary, 3, 4 Jan. 1943: Air Strikes. HQ, 347th Ftr Gp, Ops Report, 3 Jan. 1943: 4th Mission; 4 Jan. 1943: 6th, 7th Missions.
Admiral Halsey's decision to resort to a naval bombardment to reduce Munda
  Frank, *Guadalcanal: The Definitive Account*, 548.

Chapter 6. Bombarding the Phoenix
Pages 77–80
TG AFIRM's bombardment sortie of 4–5 Jan. 1943 against Munda
  Aircraft SoPac Force, War Diary, 5 Jan. 1943: Air Strikes, Other Operations. Crenshaw, *South Pacific Destroyer*, 52–54. Vice Adm. Aubrey Fitch, "Operation Order 1–43," 1–2, Annex "A" in Aircraft SoPac Force War Diary. Foss, *Flying Marine*, 137, 138–139. Frank, *Guadalcanal: The Definitive Account*, 548–549. Publication Branch, ONI, Bombardments of Munda and Vila-Stanmore, 5–8, 9, 11–17. Radio intercept from EO YU 9, 5 Jan. 1943 @0330L. 204th, 582nd Kokutai, Combat Reports, 18/1/4, 5 in web site Japan Center. VMF-121, War Diary, 5 Jan. 1943. Weiland, *Above and Beyond*, 56.

Page 81
The progress of construction at Munda, the intermittent presence of Zeros, and the Cactus air strikes of 5–23 Jan. 1943
  Aircraft SoPac Force, War Diary, 5, 7, 9, 11, 12, 13, 14, 16 Jan. 1943: Air Strikes; 23, 24 Jan. 1943: (2) Air Strikes; 7, 16, 19, 22, 24 Jan. 1943: Photo Missions. 582nd Kokutai, Combat Reports, 18/01/15, 21 in web site Japan Center. Munda War Diary, Narrative, 1301; Ops Reports, 18/1/09, 10, 11; 18/1/27: sketch of Munda 27 Jan. 1943 in web site Japan Center. 347th Ftr

Gp Det, Daily Ops Reports, 5, 7, 9, 11, 12, 13, 14, 16, 19, 23, 24 Jan. 1943: Relevant Missions.

The SBD and B-26 raids of 25 Jan. 1943 on Munda

Aircraft SoPac Force, War Diary, 25 Jan 1943: (2) Air Strikes. Air Force History Support Office, USAAF in WWII: Combat Chronology, 25 Jan. 1943, 13th AF. 347th Ftr Gp Det, Daily Ops Report, 25 Jan. 1943: 6th, 9th Missions. VMSB-233, War Diary, 25 Jan. 1943: Attack Mission, 51–52.

Pages 81–82

The VMSB-142/233 raid of 26 Jan. 1943 on Munda

Aircraft SoPac Force, War Diary, 26 Jan. 1943: (2) Air Strikes. 347th Ftr Gp Det, Daily Ops Report, 26 Jan. 1943: 7th Mission. VMSB-142, War Diary, 26 Jan. 1943. VMSB-233, War Diary, 26 Jan. 1943: Attack Mission.

Page 82

The B-26 raid of 27 Jan. 1943 on Munda

Aircraft SoPac Force, War Diary, 27 Jan. 1943: (2) Air Strikes. Air Force History Support Office, web site USAAF in WWII: Combat Chronology, 27 Jan. 1943, 13th AF. McKillop, USAAF Combat Chronology, Wed. 27 Jan. 1943: SoPac Theater, 13th AF. 347th Ftr Gp Det, Daily Ops Report, 27 Jan. 1943: 6th Mission.

The B-26 raids of 28 and 29 Jan. 1943 on Munda

Air Force History Support Office, USAAF in WWII: Combat Chronology, 28, 29 Jan. 1943, 13th AF. Aircraft SoPac Force, War Diary, 28, 29 Jan. 1943: (2) Air Strikes. McKillop, USAAF Combat Chronology, Thurs. 28, Fri. 29 Jan. 1943: SoPac Theater, 13th AF. 347th Ftr Gp Det, Daily Ops Reports, 28, 29 Jan. 1943: 4th Mission.

Page 83

Munda's ability to recover quickly from Cactus air raids

Munda War Diary, Narrative, 1301.

The Val air attack, the Zero fighter sweep, and the troop landing to knock out the coastwatchers on Rendova

Munda War Diary, Narrative, 1287, 1289; Ops Report, 18/1/04; Selected Radio Messages: from Munda 18/1/04 @1830L, 18/1/05 @1220L and 1050L, 18/1/06 @0300L, @1306L, @1400L, @1800L, @2250L, 18/1/07 @0200L, @1200L, 18/1/08 @0530L, @0800L, @0840L, @1430L, 18/1/09 @0900L, 18/1/11 @1240L, 18/1/13 @1010L; from unspecified originator 18/1/05 @1535L,

18/1/07 @1305L; from FBG 18/1/@1614L in web site Japan Center. Horton, *Fire Over the Islands*, 192, 196, 198; Report on Coastwatcher Station PWD. 958th Kokutai, Combat Report, 18/1/15 in web site Japan Center. 204th Kokutai, Combat Reports, 18/1/08, 09 in web site Japan Center.

Pages 83–85
The Cactus USAAF raids of 1, 2, 7, 9, and 13 Jan. 1943 on Rekata Bay
Aircraft SoPac Force, War Diary, 2, 7, 9, 13 Jan. 1943: Air Strikes. History of the 69th BS(M). HQ, 347th Ftr Gp, Ops Reports, 2 Jan. 1943: 5th, 9th Missions; 7 Jan. 1943: 5th Mission; 9 Jan. 1943: 6th, 7th Missions; 13 Jan. 1943: 7th, 8th, 12th Missions. VMF-121, War Diary, 1 Jan. 1943. Weiland, *Above and Beyond*, 56.

Page 85
The combat of 14 Jan. 1943 over Rekata Bay
Aircraft SoPac Force, War Diary, 14 Jan. 1943: Other Operations. Hackett et al., TROM for *Tsugaru*, in web site Fusetsukan. HQ, 347th Ftr Gp, Pilot's Combat Report: Lt. G. G. Topoll and Lt. H. L. Dunbar, 1. Nevitt, TROM for *Mochizuki*, in web site Long Lancers. 958th Kokutai, Combat Report, 18/1/14 in web site Japan Center.

Page 86
The 339th's fighter sweep of 26 Jan. 1943
347th Ftr Gp Det, Daily Ops Report, 26 Jan. 1943: 6th Mission.

Pages 86–88
The encounter of 5 Jan. 1943 between the P-38s and the R Homen Koku Butai, plus the brush with the 204th Kokutai Zeros
Aircraft SoPac Force, War Diary, 5 Jan. 1943: Air Strikes. Hammel, *Aces Against Japan*, 11. HQ, 347th Ftr Gp, Ops Report, 5 Jan. 1943: 6th Mission. HQ, 347th Ftr Gp, Pilot's Combat Report: Capt. S. A. Palmer, 2. Izawa, "Fighting Floatplanes," in *Air Enthusiast*, 15. Izawa, "Japanese Navy Float Fighter Units," 12. MAG 14, Guadalcanal: Escorted Bomber Missions, 7. McKillop, USAAF Combat Chronology, Tues. 5 Jan. 1943: SoPac Theater, 13th AF. 347th Ftr Gp Det, Combat Report, Cactus, 5 Jan. 1943. 204th Kokutai, Combat Report, 18/1/5 in web site Japan Center. USAAF Victories Over Seaplanes. Wolf, *13th Air Command*, 99.

Pages 89–91
The B-17 antishipping strikes of 17–20 Jan. 1943
Aircraft SoPac Force, War Diary, 17–20 Jan. 1943: Air Strikes. 802nd Kokutai, Combat Report, 18/1/18 in web site Japan Center. 582nd Kokutai, Combat Report, 18/1/19 in web site Japan Center. HQ, 347th Ftr Gp, Pilot's Combat Report: 1st Lt. Lloyd Huff, 2; 1st Lt. Robert B. Kennedy, 1, 2; Capt. Stanley A. Palmer, 2. *Kamikawa Maru, Sanyo Maru,* War Diaries, 18/1/20 in web site Japan Center. Salecker, *Fortress Against the Sun,* 319–320. 347th Ftr Gp, Cactus, Action Report, 18 Jan. 1943. 347th Ftr Gp Det, Report of Escort Missions, 19, 19 [should be 20], 20 Jan. 1943. 204th Kokutai, Combat Reports, 18/1/18, 19, 20 in web site Japan Center.

Page 91
The B-17 raids of 26 Jan. 1943 on Ballale and 29 Jan. 1943 on Kahili
Aircraft SoPac Force, War Diary, 26 Jan. 1943: (2) Air Strikes. Air Force History Support Office, USAAF in WWII: Combat Chronology, 26, 29 Jan. 1943; 13th AF. McKillop, USAAF Combat Chronology, Tues. 26 Jan. 1943: SoPac Theater 13th AF. 26th BS(H), War Diary, Tues. 26 Jan. 1943.

Pages 91–92
The development of Vila's airstrip
Aircraft SoPac Force, War Diary, 22 Jan. 1943: (3) Photo Missions. Nevitt, TROM for *Otori,* in web site Long Lancers. 958th Kokutai, Combat Report, 18/1/19 in web site Japan Center. Radio intercept from NO KO SO 2, 18 Jan. 1943 @00214L.

Pages 90–93, 94–98
The four Cactus air strikes against Munda, detachment of the *Saratoga*'s air group, the bombardment of Vila-Stanmore by TG AFIRM on 23–24 Jan. 1943, Japanese retaliation, and the Maytag Mike raids of 23–24 Jan. 1943
Aircraft SoPac Force, War Diary, 19 Jan. 1943: Contacts Reported by Other Commands; 22 Jan. 1943: (3) Photo Missions; 23 Jan. 1943: (2) Air Strikes, (3) Other Operations; 24 Jan. 1943: (2) Air Strikes, (3) Photo Missions, (5) Other Operations. Horton, Coastwatcher NLO, Vila, Report, 28 Jan. 1943. Crenshaw, *South Pacific Destroyer,* 57–58. Frank, *Guadalcanal: The Definitive Account,* 572–573. *Kamikawa Maru,* War Diary, 18/1/23 in web site Japan Center. Munda War Diary, Narrative, 1302; Ops Report, 18/1/25 in web site Japan center. Nevitt, TROM for *Otori,* in web site Long Lancers. Publications Branch, ONI, Bombardments of Munda and Vila-Stanmore, 21, 22, 23–26, 28–31. Radio

intercept from MO FU YA, 23 Jan. 1943 @2201L; from Chief of Staff, 6th Air Fleet, 23 Jan. 1943 @2206L; from M I A, 23 Jan. 1943 @2230L; from I FU 08, 23 Jan. 1943 @2250L; from TA TE 1, 23 Jan. 1943 @2000L; from TE WA 61, 24 Jan. 1943 @0230L; from SO US IK, 26 Jan. 1943 @0825L. 2nd Demob Bureau, Monograph #98 (IJN), 65–66. 705th, 751st, 851st Kokutai, Combat Reports, 18/1/23 in web site Japan Center. 347th Ftr Gp, Ops Report, 24 Jan. 1943: 10th Mission. VMF-121, War Diary, 24 Jan. 1943. "VAdm. Aubrey Fitch's Operation Order No. 2–43," 1–2, Annex "A" in Aircraft SoPac Force War Diary. VMO-251, Report of Destruction of Enemy Ships and Planes and Loss of Our Own Aircraft, Month of Jan. 1943.

Pages 93–94
The air strike of 23 Jan. 1943 on *Toa Maru 2*
Aircraft SoPac Force, War Diary, 23 Jan. 1943: (2) Air Strikes. Hata et al., *Japanese Naval Aces*, 381. Keenan, Diary of a Coastwatcher, Thurs. 28, Fri. 29 Jan. 1943. 958th Kokutai, Combat Report, 18/1/23–24 in web site Japan Center. 204th Kokutai, Combat Report, 18/1/23 in web site Japan Center. Radio intercept from NO E 6, 22 Jan. 1943 @0921L. VMSB-233, War Diary, 23 Jan. 1943: Attack Mission.

Page 98
The ongoing reinforcement of Vila-Stanmore
Aircraft SoPac Force, War Diary, 24 Jan. 1943: (2) Air Strikes. Horton, Coastwatcher NLO, Vila, Report, 28 Jan. 1943. Nevitt, TROM for *Arashio, Hiyodori, Isokaze,* in web site Long Lancers. Radio intercept from HE SO 98, 24 Jan. 1943 @1417L.
The B-26 raid of 28 Jan. 1943 on Vila
Aircraft SoPac Force, War Diary, 28 Jan. 1943: (2) Air Strikes. Air Force History Support Office, USAAF in WWII: Combat Chronology, 28 Jan. 1943, 13th AF. McKillop, USAAF Combat Chronology, Thurs. 28 Jan. 1943: SoPac Theater, 13th AF. 347th Ftr Gp Det, Daily Ops Report, 28 Jan. 1943: 6th mission.

Pages 98–99
Baker search mission and the SBD raid of 29 Jan. 1943 on Vila
Aircraft SoPac Force, War Diary, 29 Jan. 1943: (2) Air Strikes. Air Force History Support Office, web site USAAF in WWII: Combat Chronology, 29 Jan. 1943, 13th AF. McKillop, USAAF Combat Chronology, Fri. 29 Jan. 1943: SoPac Theater, 13th AF. 347th Ftr Gp Det, Daily Ops Report, 29 Jan. 1943: 3rd, 5th Missions.

Page 99
The future role of Vila as a JAAF airbase abandoned
   Munda War Diary, Narrative, 1302. "Vila Airfield," in web site PacificWrecks.
Watermelons at Vila-Stanmore
   Sabel, email to D. Letourneau, 19 Oct. 2002. "Vila Airfield," in web site PacificWrecks.

Chapter 7. Kickoff!
Pages 101–106
The Tokyo Express run of 10–11 Jan. 1943, the PT-boat attack, and the Cactus air strike
   Aircraft SoPac Force, War Diary, 10 Jan. 1943: Contacts Reported by Other Commands; 11 Jan. 1943: Air Strikes, Other Operations, Enemy Contacts. "Black Cats and PT boats," in web site Black Cat PBYs. Crenshaw, *South Pacific Destroyer*, 54–55. Doll, *Marine Fighting Squadron 121*, 47–49. Cressman, "Chronology of USN in WWII," Chap. 5: Mon. 11 Jan., Tues. 12 Jan. 1943 in web site Hyperwar. Foss, *Flying Marine*, 142. Frank, *Guadalcanal: The Definitive Account*, 549–550.MAG 14, Guadalcanal: Escorted Bomber Strikes, 7. Military History Section, Japanese Monograph #116, 184. Nevitt, KE Operation, 1; TROM for the *Hatsukaze, Kawakaze, Kuroshio, Naganami, Tokitsukaze*, in web site Long Lancers. Sakaida, *IJN Aces*, 48–49. 2nd Demob Bureau, Japanese Monograph #98 (IJN), 61. SoPac Force Intel Div, "Operational Difficulties at Guadalcanal," in Air Battle Notes #11, 10. 204th Kokutai, Combat Reports, 18/1/10, 11 in web site Japan Center. VMSB-233, War Diary, 11 Jan. 1943: Attack Mission. VP-12, *The Old Black Cats*, 8–9.

Pages 106–107
The two unsuccessful antishipping strikes of 11 January and 14 January, 1943.
   Foss, *Flying Marine*, 143.
General Hyakutake's dilemma and the dispatch of Major Yano's rearguard
   Frank, *Guadalcanal: The Definitive Account*, 559–560. Historical Section, G-2, Japanese Monograph #35, 29. Jersey, *Hell's Islands*, 386–387. Mil Intel Div, Japanese Field Artillery, 3, 4, 42–43. 2nd Demob Bureau, Japanese Monograph #98 (IJN), 60, 61.

Pages 107–110
The Tokyo Express run of 14–15 Jan. 1943 and the PT boat and PBY actions
   Aircraft SoPac Force, War Diary, 15 Jan. 1943: Air Strikes. "Early Operations," in web site Black Cat PBYs. Crenshaw, *South Pacific Destroyer*, 55. Cressman,

"Chronology of USN in WWII," Chap. 5: Thurs. 14 Jan. 1943 in web site Hyperwar. Foss, *Flying Marine*, 144–147. Frank, *Guadalcanal: The Definitive Account*, 559–560. Munda War Diary, Ops Report, 18/1/14 in web site Japan Center. Nevitt, email to D. Letourneau, 27 Sept. 2010; TROM for *Akizuki, Hamakaze, Isokaze, Maikaze, Urakaze*, in web site Long Lancers. *Kamikawa Maru, Sanyo Maru*, War Diaries, 18/1/14, 15 in web site Japan Center. Radio intercept from O WO 76, 14 Jan. 1943 @1205L; from Cdr. Reinforcement Forces, 16 Jan. 1943 @1200L, @2135L. 204th Kokutai, Combat Report, 18/1/14–15 in web site Japan Center. VP-12, *The Old Black Cats*, 7–8.

Pages 110–114

The Maytag Mike raid of 14–15 Jan. 1943 and the first Cactus air strike of 15 Jan. 1943
Aircraft SoPac Force, War Diary, 15 Jan. 1943: Air Strikes, Enemy Operations. Doll, *Marine Fighting Squadron 121*, 49–50. Foss, *Flying Marine*, 143–144. Frank, *Guadalcanal: The Definitive Account*, footnote to 559–560, on 754. HQ, 347th Ftr Gp, Ops Report, 15 Jan. 1943: 9th, 10th, 11th Missions. MAG 14 Guadalcanal: Escorted Bomber Missions, 7. McKillop, USAAF Combat Chronology, Fri. 15 Jan. 1943: SoPac Theater, 13th AF. Military History Section, Japanese Monograph #116, 184. Nevitt, email to D. Letourneau, 27 Sept. 2010; TROM for *Arashi, Hamakaze, Isokaze, Tanikaze, Urakaze*, in web site Long Lancers. Radio intercept from RK TO 16, 15 Jan. 1943 @0740L, plus U.S. Intel Comments; from RE TO 1, 15 Jan. 1943 @0800L; from ME NU 5, 15 Jan. 1943 @1300L. Salecker, *Fortress Against the Sun*, 319. *Senshi Sosho*, Vol. 28, 472. 204th Kokutai, Combat Report, 18/1/15 in web site Japan Center. VMSB-142, War Diary, 15 Jan. 1943. VMSB-233, War Diary, 15 Jan. 1943: Attack Mission. Wolf, *13th Fighter Command*, 101–102.

Pages 114–117

The morning B-17 recon run and the Cactus B-17 strike of 15 Jan. 1943 on five destroyers

Aircraft SoPac Force, War Diary, 15 Jan. 1943: Air Strikes, Contacts Reported by Other Commands. Cressman, "Chronology of USN in WWII," Chap. 5: Fri. 15 Jan. 1943 in web site Hyperwar. Foss, *Flying Marine*, 144. Frank, *Guadalcanal: The Definitive Account*, 560. HQ, 347th Ftr Gp, Monthly Mission Report, 15 Jan. 1943. HQ, 347th Ftr Gp, Pilot's Combat Report: Lt. Allen S. Webb, 1. MAG 14, Guadalcanal: Escorted Bomber Missions, 7. McKillop, USAAF Combat Chronology, Fri. 15 Jan. 1943: SoPac Theater, 13th AF. Military History Section, Japanese Monograph #116, 184. Salecker, *Fortress Against the Sun*,

319. *Kamikawa Maru, Sanyo Maru*, War Diaries, 18/1/15 in web site Japan Center. Radio intercept from the *Hiyodori*, 15 Jan. 1943 @1538L; from RE TO 1, 15 Jan. 1943 @1542L. 252nd Kokutai, 958th Kokutai, Combat Reports, 18/1/15 in web site Japan Center. Wolf, *13th Fighter Command*, 102.

Pages 117–121
The *Giyu Maru*'s sortie and the Cactus antishipping strike of 15 Jan. 1943 against the *Yamashimo Maru* and the *Hiyodori*
Aircraft SoPac Force, War Diary, 15 Jan. 1943: Air Strikes, Enemy Operations, Other Operations, Contacts Reported by Other Commands. Alsleben, email to D. Letourneau, 1 Sept. 2010. Bergerud, *Fire in the Sky*, 488. Cressman, "Chronology of USN in WWII," Chap. 5: Fri. 15 Jan. 1943 in web site Hyperwar. Doll, *Marine Fighting Squadron 121*, 50–51. Foss, *Flying Marine*, 144–147. Frank, *Guadalcanal: The Definitive Account*, 560. Hata et al., *Japanese Naval Aces*, 38. HQ, 347th Ftr Gp, Pilot's Combat Report: 1st Lt. Lloyd D Huff, 1; 1st Lt. Robert D. Kennedy, 1; 1st Lt. Martin L. Smith, 1. Hackett et al., TROM for the *Yamashimo Maru*, in web site Kosakukan!, *Kamikawa Maru*, War Diary, 18/1/14–16 in web site Japan Center. MAG 14, Guadalcanal: Escorted Bomber Missions, 7. McKillop, USAAF Combat Chronology, Fri. 15 Jan. 1943: SoPac Theater, 13th AF. Military History Section, Japanese Monograph #116, 184. Nevitt, TROM for *Hamakaze, Hiyodori, Urakaze*, in web site Long Lancers. 958th Kokutai, Combat Report, 18/01/15–16 in web site Japan Center. Radio intercepts from the *Hiyodori*, 15 Jan. 1943 @1538L, @1822L, @1825L, @1915L; 16 Jan. 1943 @1130L. *Sanyo Maru*, War Diary, 18/01/15 in web site Japan Center. 204th Kokutai, 252nd Kokutai, Combat Reports, 18/1/15 in web site Japan Center. VMSB-142, War Diary, 15 Jan. 1943. VMSB-233, War Diary, 15 Jan. 1943: Attack Mission.

Chapter 8. Blitzing the Quarterbacks
Pages 122–128
The JNAF air raid of 25 Jan. 1943 and the resulting combat action
Aircraft SoPac Force, War Diary, 25 Jan. 1943: (3) Enemy Activity; 26 Jan. 1943: (3) Other Operations. Cressman, "Chronology of USN in WWII," Chap. 5: Mon. 25 Jan. 1943 in web site Hyperwar. Foss, *Flying Marine*, 150–153. Frank, *Guadalcanal: The Definitive Account*, 574. HQ, 347th Ftr Gp, Monthly Ops Report, 25 Jan. 1943. HQ USAFISPA, POW Report #121, 1, 3. Lord, *Lonely Vigil*, 48, 56–57, 96. Lundstrom, *The First Team*, 261. Munda War Diary, Ops Report, 18/1/25; Radio Messages: from Munda @0735 and 0740, 18/1/26 in web

site Japan Center. 2nd Demob Bureau, Japanese Monograph #98 (IJN), 65. 2nd MAW: Fighter Command Cactus, Combat Report, 25 Jan. 1943. SoPac Force Intel Div, "Scramble at Guadalcanal," in Air Battle Notes #11, 1–4. 347th Ftr Gp Det, Daily Ops Report, 25 Jan. 1943: 10th, 11th, 12th Missions. 347th Ftr Gp, Adv Echelon, Combat Report, 25 Jan. 1943. 204th, 252nd, 253rd, 582nd, 705th Kokutai, Combat Reports, 18/1/25 in web site Japan Center. VMF-121, Sqn Ops, 25 Jan. 1943. VMF-122, War Diary of Ground Echelon, 25 Jan. 1943. VMO-251, Report of Destruction of Enemy Ships and Planes and Loss of Our Own Aircraft, Month of Jan. 1943. Wolf, *13th Fighter Command*, 103.

Pages 128–130
The events of Fiedler and McKulla's search mission and the 204th Kokutai sortie Aircraft SoPac Force, War Diary, 26 Jan. 1943: (3) Other Operations. Hirayama, account in "Dramatic Rescue off Choiseul," in web site PacificWrecks.com. Bergerud, *Fire in the Sky*, 623. 347th Ftr Gp Det, Daily Ops Report, 25 Jan. 1943: 1st Mission; 26 Jan. 1943, 4th Mission. 347th Ftr Gp, Adv Echelon, Combat Report, 26 Jan. 1943. 204th Kokutai, Combat Report, 18/1/26 in web site Japan Center. 204th Kokutai, S18 (1943): Combat Diary, 23. 252nd Kokutai Combat Report 18/1/26 in web site Japan Center. "USAAF Aces Scoring with Airacobras," in web site tmg.obywatel.pl/articles/a. Wolf, *13th Fighter Command*, 104.

Pages 130–139
The JAAF air raid of 27 Jan. 1943 against Cactus and the resulting combat action Aircraft SoPac Force, War Diary, 27 Jan. 1943: (4) Enemy Activity. "Joe Baugher's Hayabusa Files," in web site danford.net/hayabusa.htm. 11th Sentai, Chronology, 26–27 Jan. 1943. Bergerud, *Fire in the Sky*, 596. Horton, Coastwatcher NLO, Vila, Report, 27/1/43. Doll, *Marine Fighting Squadron 121*, 51. Dunn, "Nakajima Ki-43-1 Armament—A Reassessment (Abstract)." Ferguson, *Guadalcanal: The Island of Fire*, 193–194. Frank, *Guadalcanal: The Definitive Account*, 574. Hata et al., *JAAF Fighter Units and Their Aces*, 38. "Ki-43-1 Oscar, Manufacturer's #572" and "Munda Airfield," in web site PacificWrecks. Historical Section, G-2, Japanese Monograph #35, 34. Munda War Diary, Ops Reports, 18/1/26, 27. Sakaida, *IJN Aces*, 25. 347th Ftr Gp, Adv Echelon, Combat Report, 27 Jan. 1943. 347th Ftr Gp Det, Daily Ops Report, 27 Jan. 1943: 4th, 5th Missions. 347th Ftr Gp Monthly Ops Report, 27 Jan. 1943. 12th Shidan, 12th Air Sector Operations Order #94, 28 Jan. 1943. VMF-112, Daily Ops Report, 27 Jan. 1943: Items 2, 3. VMF-121, Sqn Ops, 27 Jan. 1943. VMF-122, War Diary of Ground Echelon, 27 Jan. 1943. Wolf, *13th Fighter Command*, 104–105.

Pages 136–137
The sluggish performance of the P-38 Lightning at lower altitudes
  Bergerud, *Fire in the Sky*, 263, 493. Ferguson, *Guadalcanal: The Island of Fire*, 176–178. McEniry, *A Marine Dive-Bomber Pilot at Guadalcanal*, 84. Sakaida, *IJN Aces*, 25, 81.

Pages 137–138
The amoral code of conduct of Japanese and American airmen and their behavior toward each other
  Bergerud, *Fire in the Sky*, 521–528. HQ USAFISPA, POW Report #121, 6. Izawa, "IJN Float Fighter Units," 12. Weiland, email to R. Letourneau: 4 Oct. 2003.

Pages 139–140
JAAF bomber activity at Munda 28–30 Jan. 1943
  Horton, Coastwatcher NLO, Vila, Report, 30 Jan. 1943. Munda War Diary, Ops Reports, 18/01/28, 29, 30 in web site Japan Center.

Chapter 9. Turnovers
Pages 141–142
The antishipping strike of 27 Jan. 1943 at Torpedo Junction
  Aircraft SoPac Force, War Diary, 27 Jan. 1943: (2) Air Strikes. 8th Fleet, War Diary, 18/1/27 in web site Japan Center. *Kunikawa Maru*, War Diary, 18/1/27 in web site Japan Center. 6th Kure Sp Naval Ldg Force, War Diary, 18/1/25, 27 in web site Japan Center. 347th Ftr Gp Det, Daily Ops Report, 27 Jan. 1943: 7th Mission. VMSB-131, War Diary, 27 Jan. 1943; Intelligence Report, 27 Jan. 1943. VMSB-233, War Diary, 27 Jan. 1943: Attack Mission.

Pages 142–147
The Cactus air strike of 28 Jan. 1943 against the mercantile convoy and the Russells garrison convoy, plus the latter's return route
  Aircraft SoPac Force, War Diary, 28 Jan. 1943: (2) Air Strikes, Contacts Reported by Other Commands; 29 Jan. 1943: Contacts Reported by Other Commands; 30 Jan. 1943: (4) Enemy Activity. Air Force History Support Office, web site USAAF in WWII: Combat Chronology, 28 Jan. 1943, 13th AF. Eschenberg, letter to E. Stevenson, 27 May 1995. McKillop, USAAF Combat Chronology, Thurs. 28 Jan. 1943: SoPac Theater 13th AF. Frank, *Guadalcanal: The Definitive*

Account, 582. *Kamikawa Maru*, War Diary, 18/1/28 in web site Japan Center. Nasif, letter to E. Stevenson, 9 June 1996. Nevitt, KE Operation, 2. 26th BS(H), War Diary, Thurs. 28 Jan. 1943. 204th Kokutai, Combat Diary, 23. 204th, 582nd Kokutai, Combat Reports, 18/1/28 in web site Japan Center. VMSB-131, War Diary, 28 Jan. 1943; Intelligence Report, 28 Jan. 1943. VMSB-142, War Diary, 28 Jan. 1943. VMSB-234 War Diary, 28 Jan. 1943. (Good description, although this squadron did not participate.) Wolf, *13th Fighter Command*, 106.

Page 147
Coastwatcher activities in the Russell group
Aircraft SoPac Force, War Diary, 30 Jan. 1943: (3) Other Operations. Horton, *Fire Over the Islands*, 157–164, 207–208.

Pages 147–150
Account of the first phase of the Battle of Rennell Island
Crenshaw, *South Pacific Destroyer*, 61–64. Cressman, "Chronology of U.S. Navy in WWII," Chap. 5: Fri. 29 Jan. 1943 in web site Hyperwar. Frank, *Guadalcanal: The Definitive Account*, 577–579. Office of Naval Intel, Japanese Evacuation of Guadalcanal, 26–36, map opposite 28. Jacobsen, web site The Battle of Rennell Island. "Rennell Island," in web site USS *Enterprise:* CV-6. 701st, 705th, 751st Kokutai, Combat Reports, 18/1/29, 30 in web site Japan Center. Wukovits, "Battle of Rennell Island: Setback in the Solomons," in web site Historynet.com.

Page 149
The monitoring of Japanese radio traffic by Cactus Crystal Ball
Jacobson, web site The Battle of Rennell Island.

Pages 150–151
The aborted predawn Cactus SBD raid of 30 Jan. 1943 on Munda
Aircraft SoPac Force, War Diary, 30 Jan. 1943: (2) Air Strikes. VMSB 233, War Diary, 30 Jan. 1943: Special Attack Mission.

Page 151
The 13th USAF B-26 raid of 30 Jan. 1943 on Munda
Aircraft SoPac Force, War Diary, 30 Jan. 1943: (2) Air Strikes. McKillop, USAAF Combat Chronology, Sat. 30 Jan. 1943: SoPac Theater 13th AF. 347th Ftr Gp Det, Daily Ops Report, 30 Jan. 1943: 4th Mission.

The details of the air traffic passing over Vella Lavella on 29 and 30 Jan. 1943
    Keenan, Diary of a Coastwatcher, 31–32. Radio intercept from MD RE 3, 29 Jan. 1943 @2146L.

Pages 151–152
The Baker search mission, Pat Weiland's "Recon" anecdote, and the incident with the Japanese flying boat
    Crenshaw, *South Pacific Destroyer*, 63–64. Frank, *Guadalcanal: The Definitive Account*, 579–580. 347th Ftr Gp det, Daily Ops Report, 30 Jan. 1943: 5th Mission. Weiland, email to D. Letourneau, 28 Aug. 2002.

Pages 152–156
The B-26/B-17 raid of 30 Jan. 1943 on Munda and the midair collision over Cactus, the separation of the four P-39s and the sighting of the Betty bombers, the sinking of the *Chicago*, and the Cactus search mission
    Aircraft SoPac Force, War Diary, 30 Jan. 1943. (2) Air Strikes, Contacts Reported by Other Commands. Cressman, "Chronology of USN in WWII," Chap. 5: Sat. 30 Jan. 1943 in web site Hyperwar. Crenshaw, *South Pacific Destroyer*, 64–65. Frank, *Guadalcanal: The Definitive Account*, 579–581. McCartney, email to R. Letourneau, 24 Nov. 2003. McKillop, USAAF Combat Chronology, Sat. 30 Jan. 1943: SoPac Theater 13th AF. 751st Kokutai, Combat Report, 18/1/30 in web site Japan Center. Office of Naval Intel, Japanese Evacuation of Guadalcanal, 36–44. 347th Ftr Gp Det, Daily Ops Report, 30 Jan. 1943: 7th, 8th Missions. Wood, email to D. Letourneau, 15 Sept. 2003.

Pages 156–158
The campaign of Maytag Mike raids against Henderson and Espiritu Santo
    Aircraft SoPac Force, War Diary, 20 Jan. 1943: (5) Enemy Operations; 22 Jan. 1943: (5) Enemy Activity; 23 Jan. 1943: (4) Enemy Activity; 27 Jan. 1943: (4) Enemy Activity. 851st Kokutai, Combat Reports, 18/1/20, 22, 27 in web site Japan Center. Bergerud, *Fire in the Sky*, 79–80. Frank, *Guadalcanal: The Definitive Account*, 573–574, 588, 591. Lundstrom, *The First Team*, 237. Radio intercepts from MI A, 23 Jan. 1943 @2250L, 24 Jan. 1943 @0050L; from I FU 00, 24 Jan. 1943 @2230L, 25 Jan. 1943 @ 0030L. 751st Kokutai, Combat Reports, 18/1/20, 23, 25–26, 26–27 in web site Japan Center. 705th Kokutai, Combat Report, 18/1/21 in web site Japan Center. 701st Kokutai, Combat Reports, 18/1/22, 22–23 in web site Japan Center. 253rd Kokutai, Combat Report, 18/1/27 in web site Japan Center. 204th Kokutai, Combat Report,

18/1/26 in web site Japan Center. VMF-122, War Diary of Ground Echelon, 20, 21, 22, 23, 24, 26, 27 Jan. 1943.

Pages 158–159
Capt. Mitchell stalks Washing Machine Charlie 28–29 Jan. 1943
 Davis, *Get Yamamoto*, 91, 94. Ferguson, *Guadalcanal: The Island of Fire*, 194. Historical Section, G-2, Japanese Monograph #35, 36. Munda War Diary, Ops Report, 18/01/29 in web site Japan Center. 751st Kokutai, Combat Report, 18/1/26–27 in web site Japan Center. 347th Ftr Gp Det, Daily Ops Report, hand-written entry at bottom of page. VMF-112, Daily Ops Report, 29 Jan. 1943, Item 1. VMF-122, War Diary of Ground Echelon, 29 Jan. 1943.

Pages 159–160
The Black Cat raids on Vila and Munda, and the JNAF raids on Button
 Aircraft SoPac Force, War Diary, 28, 29 Jan. 1943: Air Strikes.

Page 160
The departure of Admiral Kondo's task force from Truk
 Hara, *Japanese Destroyer Captain*, 172.

Chapter 10. Pass Interception
Page 161
The arrival of JNAF bombers and fighters at Munda on 30 Jan. 1943
 Radio intercept: 30 Jan. 1943: message @1427L. Keenan, Diary of a Coastwatcher, Sat. 30 Jan. 1943. Munda War Diary, Ops Report, 18/01/30 in web site Japan Center.

Pages 161–162
The B-17 solo raids on Munda and Vila and the B-17 recon missions of 31 Jan. 1943
 Aircraft SoPac Force, War Diary, 31 Jan. 1943: (1) Searches, (2) Air Strikes, Enemy Contacts. Debnekoff, email to D. Letourneau, 18 Aug. 2003. McKillop, USAAF Combat Chronology, Sun. 31 Jan. 1943: SoPac Theater, 13th AF.
Baker search
 347th Ftr Gp Det, Daily Ops Report, 31 Jan. 1943: 4th Mission.

Pages 162–165
The Cactus fighter sweep of 31 Jan. 1943
 Aircraft SoPac Force, War Diary, 31 Jan. 1943: (5) Other Operations. ATIS, MOTO #19: 8th Area Army. HQ, 347th Ftr Gp, Det, Daily Ops Report, 31 Jan.

1943: 5th, 6th, 7th Missions. McKillop, USAAF Combat Chronology, Sun. 31 Jan. 1943: SoPac Theater, 13th AF. Hata et al., *JAAF Fighter Units and Their Aces*, 255. Radio intercept: U.S. intel report, 31 Jan. 1943. VMF-112, Daily Ops Report, 31 Jan. 1943: Item 2.

Page 165

The earlier departure from Bougainville of the unescorted freighter and the subsequent attack by the PBY

Aircraft SoPac, War Diary, 31 Jan. 1943: (5) Other Operations, Contacts Reported by Other Commands. JICPOA #1072: intercept from Hawaii.

Information on the *Toa Maru* 2, her escorts, and fighter CAP

Alsleben, email to D. Letourneau, 7 Nov., 2002. Cressman, "Chronology of USN in WWII," Chap. 4: Thurs. 10 Dec. 1942, Pacific in web site Hyperwar. JOMS #116: Ship Assignments, Harbor Master Logs Rabaul (8th Fleet), Jan. 25, 28, 29, 1943. Hackett et al., TROM for subchaser *Ch-30*, in web site Kusentai! Lord, *Lonely Vigil*, 95. McFadyen, "*Toa Maru No. 2*," in Michael McFadyen's Scuba Diving web site, 1, 2–4. McKillop, USAAF Combat Chronology, Sun. 31 Jan. 1943: SoPac Theater 13th AF. Military History Section, Japanese Monograph #116, 15. WDC 01742: 1st Base Force (Buin), 8th Fleet, 2 Feb. 1943.

Pages 165–166

Coastwatcher reports and recon aircraft sightings of the *Toa Maru* 2 convoy near Bougainville and the New Georgia group

Aircraft SoPac Force, War Diary, 29 Jan. 1943: Contacts Reported by Other Commands; 31 Jan. 1943: Enemy Contacts. Horton, Coastwatcher NLO. Vila, Report, 31/1/43. Keenan, Diary of a Coastwatcher, Sun. 31 Jan. 1943.

Page 166

The composition of the Cactus strike force and its departure

Alsleben, email to D. Letourneau: 9 Jan. 2003, 1. DeBlanc, *Genealogical Excerpts*, 20–21. HQ, 347th Ftr Gp, Ops Report, 31 Jan. 1943: 8th Mission. Irwin, interview with D. Letourneau, 18 Jan. 2003. McEniry, *A Marine Dive-Bomber Pilot at Guadalcanal*, 22. Miller, *The Cactus Air Force*, 41. VMF-112, Daily Ops Report, 31 Jan. 1943: Item 3. VMSB-131, War Diary, 31 Jan. 1943. VMSB-233, War Diary, 31 Jan. 1943: Attack Mission. VMSB-234, War Diary, 31 Jan. 1943.

Aircraft problems and aborts

DeBlanc, *Genealogical Excerpts*, 21–22. VMSB-131, War Diary, 31 Jan. 1943.

The interception of the *Toa Maru 2* and the SBD attack

Aircraft SoPac Force, War Diary, 31 Jan. 1943: (2) Air Attacks. Bergerud, *Fire in the Sky*, 581. McEniry, *A Marine Dive-Bomber Pilot at Guadalcanal*, 19–23. ATIS, MOTO #19: 8th Area Army. 347th Ftr Gp Det, Daily Ops Report, 31 Jan. 1943: 8th mission. VMSB-131, War Diary, 31 Jan. 1943. VMSB-233, War Diary, 31 Jan. 1943: Attack Mission. VMSB-234, War Diary, 31 Jan. 1943.

Pages 166–167

The action between DeBlanc and the Petes

DeBlanc, phone interview with D. Letourneau, 30 Jan. 2003; DeBlanc, *Genealogical Excerpts*, 22–23. Feliton, email to R. Letourneau, 4 Feb. 2002; phone interview with the writers, 22 Feb. 2002.

Page 167

Secrest's and DeBlanc's strafing attacks

DeBlanc, email to D. Letourneau, 26 May 2002; DeBlanc, *Genealogical Excerpts*, 22; phone interview with D. Letourneau, 30 Jan. 2003. Feliton, phone interview with the writers, 22 Feb. 2002. Secrest, letter to C. Darby, 12 Mar. 1990.

Pages 167–168

The TBF attack

Aircraft SoPac Force, War Diary, 31 Jan. 1943: (2) Air Strikes. Eschenberg, letter to E. Stevenson, 27 May 1995. Nasif, letter to E. Stevenson, 9 June 1996. VMSB-131, War Diary, 31 Jan. 1943.

Pages 168–173

The combat between the VMF-112 Wildcats and the 11th Sentai Oscars

Alsleben, emails to D. Letourneau: 23 Oct. 2002, 1–2; 26 Oct. 2002, 1; 1 Nov. 2002, 1–2; 2 Nov. 2002, 1. Bergerud, *Fire in the Sky*, 455–456, 508. DeBlanc, emails to D. Letourneau, 1 Feb. 2001, 26 May 2002; DeBlanc, *Genealogical Excerpts*, 23–27; *Once They Lived by the Sword*, 10, 15–16; phone interview with D. Letourneau, 30 Jan. 2003; phone interview with the writers, 31 Mar. 2003. Feliton, email to R. Letourneau, 4 Feb. 2002; phone interviews with the writers, 1 Feb. 2001, 22 Feb. 2002. Hata et al., *JAAF Fighter Units and Their Aces*, 154, 262, 284, 294. Horton, *Fire Over the Islands*, 184; Horton, *New Georgia: Pattern for Victory*, 24. Honan and

Harcombe, *Solomon Islands*, 148–149. Hubler and Doubleday, *Flying Leathernecks*, unnumbered page. Lord, *Lonely Vigil*, 116, 216. ATIS, MOTO #19: 8th Area Army. Secrest, letters to C. Darby, 12 Mar. 1990, 26 Mar. 1990. VMF-112, Daily Ops Reports, 31 Jan. 1943. VMF-112, Official Squadron History, 40–41.

Pages 173–174

The fates of the *Hiyodori, the* subchaser *Ch-30,* and the *Toa Maru 2*
    Aircraft SoPac Force, War Diary, 3 Feb. 1943: Contacts Reported by Other Commands; 4 Feb. 1943: (2) Air Attacks. CIC SoPac Force, PW Interrogation Report #134: PO2c Nobutaro Yada, 2. Horton, *Fire Over the Islands*, 154. Cressman, "Chronology of USN in WWII," Chap. 5: Sun. 31 Jan. 1943 in web site Hyperwar. Keenan's Diary of a Coastwatcher, Mon. 1 Feb., Tues. 2 Feb., Sat. 6 Feb. 1943. ATIS, MOTO #19: 8th Area Army. Military History Section, Japanese Monograph #116, 184. Nevitt, TROM for the *Hiyodori,* in web site Long Lancers. *Senji Senpakushi,* 174.

Chapter 11. General Patch's End Run

Pages 175–176

General Patch's flanking strategy
    Crenshaw, *South Pacific Destroyer,* 65. Frank, *Guadalcanal: The Definitive Account,* 583. Hoyt, *Guadalcanal,* 266–267.

Page 175

The intercepted Japanese message concerning withdrawal from Guadalcanal
    Twining, *No Bended Knee,* 166.

Page 176

The U.S. Navy's APDs
    Crenshaw, *South Pacific Destroyer,* 28, 84.
The sortie of Patch's amphibious force and the Dinah recon patrol
    Crenshaw, *South Pacific Destroyer,* 65–66. Frank, *Guadalcanal: The Definitive Account,* 583. Hoyt, *Guadalcanal,* 266. 204th Kokutai, Combat Report, 18/2/1 in web site Japan Center. VMF-112, Daily Ops Report, 1 Feb. 1943: Item 1.

Pages 177–179

The Cactus raid of 1 Feb. 1943 on Munda
    Aircraft SoPac Force, War Diary, 1 Feb. 1943: (2) Air Attacks. SoPac Force Intel Div, "Pilot Killed, SBD Gunner Attempts Return," in Air Battle Notes #11, 8–9.

Keenan, Diary of a Coastwatcher, Mon. 1 Feb. 1943. Munda War Diary, Ops Report, 18/02/01 in web site Japan Center. VMO-251, War Diary, 1 Feb. 1943. VMSB-131, War Diary, 1 Feb. 1943; Intelligence Report, 1 Feb. 1943. VMSB-233, War Diary, 1 Feb. 1943: Attack Mission. VMSB-234, Action With Enemy, 1 Feb. 1943; SBD Intelligence, 1 Feb. 1943; War Diary, 1 Feb. 1943.

Pages 179–183
The JAAF raid of 1 Feb. 1943 on Cactus
Aircraft SoPac Force, War Diary, 1 Feb. 1943: (5) Enemy Activity. Crenshaw, *South Pacific Destroyer*, 65–66. 11th Sentai, Chronology, 1 Jan. 1943. Frank, *Guadalcanal: The Definitive Account*, 583. Historical Section, G-2, Japanese Monograph #35, 44. McCartney, email to D. Letourneau, 21 Jul. 2002; email to R. Letourneau, 18 Aug. 2002. "H. Allan McCartney," in web site American Air Aces of WWII. "Munda Airfield: Captured Japanese Aircraft," in web site PacificWrecks.com. Radio intercept from MU WI 31, 29 Jan. 1943 @1200L; from RE SO 6, 30 Jan. 1943 @1427L.

Page 183
The amphibious force's sojourn at Nugu Point, the red alert, and the Lilys
Dailey, "Pacific Battle Line," excerpt in web site USS *DeHaven* Sailors Assn. Frank, *Guadalcanal: The Definitive Account*, 583. Herr, web site The Last Days of the *DeHaven*. Virgil Wing, account in web site USS *DeHaven* Sailors Assn.

Pages 183–184
The amphibious force's sojourn at Verahue and the dispatch of the JNAF air strike
Frank, *Guadalcanal: The Definitive Account*, 583. Herr, web site The Last Days of the *DeHaven*.

Pages 184–185
Background information on the *DeHaven*
Crenshaw, *South Pacific Destroyer*, 56, 57.

Pages 185–187
The events involving the *DeHaven* and the *Nicholas* on 1 Feb. 1943
Breining, "Bye Bye DD," in web site USS *DeHaven* (*DD-469*). Crenshaw, *South Pacific Destroyer*, 66. Cressman, "Chronology of USN in WWII," Chap. 5: Mon. 1 Feb. 1943 in web site Hyperwar. Daly, "*Pacific Battle Line*," excerpt in web site USS *DeHaven* Sailors Assn. Elam, account in web site USS *DeHaven* (*DD*-

469). Frank, *Guadalcanal: The Definitive Account*, 583, 585. 582nd Kokutai, *Zuikaku* Hikokitai, Combat Reports, 18/2/1 in web site Japan Center. Herr, web site The Last Days of the USS *DeHaven*. Hoyt, *Guadalcanal*, 266. Hubler and Doubleday, *Flying Leathernecks*, unnumbered page. "*Nicholas II*: DD449," in web site Navy History. Wing, account in web site USS *DeHaven* Sailors Assn.

Pages 187–190
The actions of the various fighter squadrons during the attack on the *DeHaven*
Hubler and Doubleday, *Flying Leathernecks*, unnumbered page. 347th Ftr Gp Det, Daily Ops Report, 1 Feb. 1943: 7th, 8th, 9th, 10th, 11th Missions. VMF-112, Daily Ops Report, 1 Feb. 1943: Items 1, 2, 3; Official Sqn History, 41.

Chapter 12. The Great Escape Begins
Pages 192–196
The B-17 raid of 1 Feb. 1943 on Shortland and Tonolei Harbors and Japanese interception tactics
"Summary of Report of B-17 Raid on Shortland-Tonolei" in *History of the 5th BG(H)*. Bergerud, *Fire in the Sky*, 551–552, 553–554. Cleveland, *Grey Geese Calling*, 60, 77, 78, footnote 16 on 120. 42nd BS(H), Log, 29 Jan.–1 Feb. 1943. Frank, *Guadalcanal: The Definitive Account*, 583; endnote for 582–83 on 758. Hackett et al., TROM for *Kamikawa Maru*, in web site Tokusetsu Suijoki-Bakan! MAG 14, Guadalcanal: Escorted Bomber Missions, 8. McKillop, USAAF Combat Chronology, Mon. 1 Feb. 1943: SoPac Theater, 13th AF. Military History Section, Japanese Monograph #116, 185. Salecker, *Fortress Against the Sun*, 193, 201, 210. 2nd Demob Bureau, Japanese Monograph #98 (IJN), 23. SoPac Force Intel Div, "Four Forts and Thirty Zeros," in Air Battle Notes #11, 5–7. 347th Ftr Gp, Adv Echelon, Account of Experience of Maj. W. H. McCarroll, 1–3. 347th Ftr Gp, Adv Echelon, Daily Ops Report, 1 Feb. 1943: 3rd, 5th Missions. 204th, 252nd, 582nd Kokutai, Combat Reports, 18/2/1 in web site Japan Center.

Page 194
The loss of Capt. Houx's B-17
5th BG(H), Narrative, excerpt. Cleveland, *Grey Geese Calling*, 78, 120. Salecker, *Fortress Against the Sun*, 321. 347th Ftr Gp, Adv Echelon, Account of Experience of Maj. W. H. McCarroll, 2.

Pages 196–205
The first evacuation run of the Tokyo Express and the Cactus air strike
Aircraft SoPac Force, War Diary, 1 Feb. 1943: (2) Air Attacks, (5) Enemy Activity, Enemy Contacts. Crenshaw, *South Pacific Destroyer*, 66. Frank, *Guadalcanal: The Definitive Account*, 585–586. Hoyt, *Guadalcanal*, 267. McKillop, USAAF Combat Chronology, Mon. 1 Feb. 1943: SoPac Theater, 13th AF 347th Ftr Gp, Monthly Ops Report, 1 Feb. 1943: 9th, 10th, 12th, 13th, 14th Missions. 347th Ftr Gp, Adv Echelon, Combat Action Report, 1 Feb. 1943. 252nd, 253rd Kokutai, Combat Reports, 18/2/1 in web site Japan Center. VMF-112, Daily Ops Report, 1 Feb. 1943: Items 3, 4. VMSB-131, Intelligence Report, 1 Feb. 1943; War Diary, 1 Feb. 1943. VMSB-131, entries for 1 Feb. 1943 in VMSB-131. VMSB-234, Action With Enemy, 1 Feb. 1943; SBD Intelligence, 1 Feb. 1943; War Diary, 1 Feb. 1943. Wolf, *13th Fighter Command*, 107.

Page 205
Battle damage to Japanese destroyers
Frank, *Guadalcanal: The Definitive Account*, 586. Military History Section, Japanese Monograph #116, 184. Hoyt, *Guadalcanal*, 267. Nevitt, TROM for *Makinami*, in web site Long Lancers.
The arrival of the USN squadrons at Cactus and the reassignment of VMF-112
VGSs-11, 12, 16, War Diary, 1 Feb. 1943. VMF-112, Daily Ops Reports, 2, 3, 6 Feb. 1943: Items 3, 2, 1, respectively. VMF-122, War Diary of Ground Echelon, 2 Feb. 1943.

Page 206
The Maytag Mike raids of 1–2 Feb. 1943 in support of Operation KE
Aircraft SoPac Force, War Diary, 2, 3 Feb. 1943: (5) Enemy Activity; 4 Feb. 1943: (6) Enemy Activity. 701st Kokutai, Combat Report, 18/2/1–2, in web site Japan Center. VMF-122, War Diary of Ground Echelon, 1 Feb. 1943.

Chapter 13. Night Action and Daytime Pursuit
Pages 207–208
Info on U.S. preparations, the sortie of the Cactus Striking Force, and the arrival of the Tokyo Express
Crenshaw, *South Pacific Destroyer*, 66. Dailey, *Pacific Battle Line*, excerpt in web site USS *DeHaven* Sailors Assn. Frank, *Guadalcanal: The Definitive Account*, 587, 588. Hoyt, *Guadalcanal*, 267. Wing, account in web site USS *DeHaven* Sailors Assn.

Pages 209–211
The PT-boat action of 1–2 Feb. 1943
Crenshaw, *South Pacific Destroyer*, 66–67. Frank, *Guadalcanal: The Definitive Account*, 587. Hoyt, *Guadalcanal*, 267. Radio intercept from unspecified originator, 2 Feb. 1943 @0935L. Stevenson, World War II Vessels Sunk in the Solomon Islands, 3. Wood, letter to editor, *Naval History*, 10 May 1999, 1; letter to Bob(R. Baldwin?), 3 June 1999, 1; letter to R. Baldwin, 6 Nov. 1999, 1; phone interview with the writers, May 2003.

Page 210
Battle damage to the Japanese destroyer *Makigumo* at Guadalcanal
Frank, *Guadalcanal: The Definitive Account*, 588. Hoyt, *Guadalcanal*, 267–268. Military History Section, Japanese Monograph #116, 185. Nevitt, TROM for *Makigumo*, in web site Long Lancers. Radio intercept from unreadable originator, 2 Feb. 1943 @0251L; from TE FU 9, 2 Feb. 1943 @0900L.

Pages 211–212
The night attack by VMSB-234 and the Black Cat
Aircraft SoPac Force, War Diary, 2 Feb. 1943: (2) Air Attacks. Frank, *Guadalcanal: The Definitive Account*, 587–588. Radio intercept from unspecified originator, 2 Feb. 1943 @0935L. VMSB-234, War Diary, 2 Feb. 1943.

Pages 212–213
The RNZAF Hudson search for the Tokyo Express
Aircraft SoPac Force, War Diary, 2 Feb. 1943: Enemy contacts. Ross, RNZAF, 156.

Page 213
The unsuccessful fighter sweep of 2 Feb. 1943 by the P-39s and P-38s of the 347th FG
347th Ftr Gp Det, Daily Ops Report, 2 Feb. 1943: 1st, 2nd Missions.

Pages 213–216
The Marine/USN SBD/TBF air strike of 2 Feb. 1943 on the Tokyo Express
Aircraft SoPac Force, War Diary, 2 Feb. 1943: (2) Air Attacks. MAG 14, Guadalcanal: Escorted Bomber Missions, 5. 347th Ftr Gp Det, Daily Ops Report, 2 Feb. 1943: 10th Mission. 204th Kokutai, Combat Diary, 2 Feb. 1943. 204th Kokutai, Combat Report, 18/2/2 in web site Japan Center. VGSs-11, 12, 16, War Diary, 2 Feb. 1943. VMSB-131, War Diary, 2 Feb. 1943; Intelligence Report, 2 Feb. 1943. VMSB-233, SBD Intelligence, 2 Feb. 1943:

Daylight Attack Mission #1, VMSB-233, War Diary, 2 Feb. 1943: Daylight Attack Mission #1.

Page 216
The 67th FS's barge-strafing attack
   347th Ftr Gp Det, Daily Ops Report, 2 Feb. 1943: 7th Mission.

Pages 216–217
Erventa Island was apparently chosen as the destination of the evacuation convoys. Numa Numa, located farther northeast along the coast of Bougainville, was also considered
   Lord, *Lonely Vigil*, 188, 192. Twining, *No Bended Knee*, 166. MacArthur, Reports: Japanese Operations in the SW Pacific Area, 196. Jersey, *Hell's Islands*, 400.

Pages 217–218
The B-17 raid of 2 Feb. 1943 on Buin-Faisi
   Aircraft SoPac Force, War Diary, 2 Feb. 1943: (2) Air Attacks, Enemy Contacts. Cressman, "Chronology of U.S. Navy in WWII," Chap. 5: 2 Feb. 1943 in web site Hyperwar. Ferguson, *Guadalcanal: The Island of Fire*, 197. Hackett et al., TROM for *Keiyo Maru* in web site Kokui Umpansen. Izawa, Japanese Navy Float Fighter Units, 12. McKillop, USAAF Combat Chronology, Tues. 2 Feb. 1943: SoPac Theater, 13th AF. Military History Section, Japanese Monograph #116, 185. Nevitt, TROM for *Yugiri*, in web site Long Lancers. Salecker, *Fortress Against the Sun*, 321–322. "Murray Shubin," in web site American Air Aces of WWII. Stevenson, WWII Vessels Sunk in the Solomon Islands, 3. 347th Ftr Gp, APO 709: Feb. 1943. 347th Ftr Gp, Adv Echelon, Report of Ftr Escort, 2 Feb. 1943. 347th Ftr Gp Det, Daily Ops Report, 2 Feb. 1943: 8th, 9th Missions. 26th BS(H), Log, Tues. 2 Feb. 1943. 252nd Kokutai, Combat Report, 18/2/2 in web site Japan Center. Wolf, *13th Fighter Command*, 107.

Pages 218–219
The movements of the Tokyo Express upon arrival off Bougainville and the B-17 recon missions over Buka
   Aircraft SoPac Force, War Diary, 2 Feb. 1943: Enemy Activity, Enemy Contacts, Contacts Reported by Other Commands. 98th BS, Operational Diary, 1–2 Feb. 1943. MacArthur, Reports: Japanese Operations in the SW Pacific Area, 196. "Shortland Island," in web site PacificWrecks. 253rd Kokutai, Combat Report, 18/2/1 in web site Japan Center.

Chapter 14. ComAirSol's Vendetta

Pages 220–222
The unsuccessful Cactus search mission of 2 Feb. 1943, the air strike against Munda, and the retaliatory Nell raids on Fighter Two and Henderson Field
Aircraft SoPac Force, War Diary, 2 Feb. 1943: (2) Air Attacks, (5) Enemy Activities. Ferguson, *Guadalcanal: The Island Of Fire*, 197. 701st Kokutai, Combat Reports, 18/2/2–3, 3–4 in web site Japan Center. 347th Ftr Gp Det, APO 709: Feb. 1943. VGSs-11, 12, 16 War Diary, 2 Feb. 1943. VMF-122 Ground Echelon, War Diary, 2 Feb. 1943. VMSB-131, Intelligence Report, 2 Feb. 1943; War Diary, 2 Feb. 1943. VMSB-233, War Diary, 2 Feb. 1943: Attack Mission.

Pages 221–223
Baker search and the B-26 strike of 3 Feb. 1943 on Munda
Aircraft SoPac, War Diary, 3 Feb. 1943: (2) Air Attacks. 347th Ftr Gp Det, Daily Ops Report, 3 Feb. 1943: 2nd, 3rd, 4th Missions.

Page 223
Interception of the B-17 recon plane by Zeros near Rekata Bay on 3 Feb. 1943
Aircraft SoPac Force, War Diary, 3 Feb. 1943: (5) Enemy Activity. 253rd Kokutai, Combat Report, 18/2/3 in web site Japan Center.
The VMSB-234 raid of 3 Feb. 1943 on Vila-Stanmore
Aircraft SoPac Force, War Diary, 3 Feb. 1943: (2) Air Attacks. VGSs-11, 12, 16, War Diary, 3 Feb. 1943. VMSB-234, Action With Enemy, 3 Feb. 1943; War Diary, 3 Feb. 1943.

Pages 223–225
The SBD/TBF evening strike of 3 Feb. 1943 on Munda
Aircraft SoPac Force, War Diary, 3 Feb. 1943: (2) Air Attacks. 347th Ftr Gp Det, Daily Ops Report, 3 Feb. 1943: 5th, 6th Missions. VGSs-11, 12, 16, War Diary, 3 Feb. 1943; Intelligence Report, 3 Feb. 1943. VMSB-234, Action With Enemy, 3 Feb. 1943; War Diary, 3 Feb. 1943.

Page 225
The dispatch and arrival of the USN F4F/TBF squadrons and VMF-123
Aircraft SoPac Force, War Diary, 30 Jan. 1943: (3) Other Operations; 31 Jan. 1943, 1, 2, 3 Feb. 1943: (3) Plane Movements. VGSs-11, 12, 16, War Diary, 31 Jan. 1943, 1, 2, 3 Feb. 1943. VMF-122 Ground Echelon, War Diary, 2 Feb. 1943. VMF-123, Chronology, 3 Feb. 1943.

The Maytag Mike raids of 3 Feb. 1943 on Cactus and the Black Cat raids of 4 Feb. 1943 on Munda and Vila
    Aircraft SoPac Force, War Diary, 3 Feb. 1943: (5) Enemy Activity; 4 Feb. 1943: (2) Air Attacks. 701st Kokutai, Combat Report, 18/2/3 in web site Japan Center. VMF-122 Ground Echelon, War Diary, 3 Feb. 1943.

Pages 225–227
The Cactus morning raid of 4 Feb. 1943 on Munda
    Aircraft SoPac Force, War Diary, 4 Feb. 1943: (2) Air Attacks. 204th Kokutai, Combat Diary, 4 Feb. 1943. 204th Kokutai, Combat Report, 18/02/04 in web site Japan Center. VGSs-11, 12, 16, Action With Enemy, 4 Feb. 1943; Intelligence Report, 4 Feb. 1943; War Diary 4 Feb. 1943. VMSB-234, Action With Enemy, 4 Feb. 1943.

Page 227
The relief of the 70th BS(M)
    McKillop, USAAF Combat Chronology, Thurs. 4 Feb., Tues. 9 Feb. 1943: SoPac Theater, 13th AF.

Chapter 15. The Half-Time Show
Pages 228–229
Background information for the second evacuation run
    Frank, *Guadalcanal: The Definitive Account*, 589–590. 2nd Demob Bureau, Japanese Monograph #98 (IJN), 67.

Page 229
The progress of the Tokyo Express
    Aircraft SoPac Force, War Diary, 4 Feb. 1943: (6) Enemy Activity, Enemy Contacts, Contacts Reported by Other Commands.

Pages 229–236
The first air strike of 4 Feb. 1943 against the second evacuation run
    Aircraft SoPac Force, War Diary, 4 Feb. 1943: (2) Air Attacks. Dunn, emails to D. Letourneau, 26 Jul.–16 Sept. 2010. Frank, *Guadalcanal: The Definitive Account*, 591. Hata et al., *Japanese Naval Aces*, 314. Horton, *Fire Over the Islands*, 234. Lord, *Lonely Vigil*, 167–169. McEniry, *A Marine Dive-Bomber Pilot at Guadalcanal*, 19–20. Interview with Lieutenant Murphy, USMCR, in web site: Rescued Pilots Intelligence, 1. Military History Section, Japanese

Monograph #116, 185. Nevitt, TROM for *Maikaze, Nagatsuki,* in web site Long Lancers. Radio intercept from: NI NO 1, 4 Feb. 1943 @1625L; from SO KO 6, 4 Feb. 1943 @1715L; from YU TA 4, 4 Feb. 1943 @1854L. 347th Ftr Gp, Adv Echelon, Combat Report, 4 Feb. 1943: Takeoff @1440. 347th Ftr Gp Det, Daily Ops Report, 4 Feb. 1943: 5th, 6th Missions. 20th Kokutai, Combat Diary, 4 Feb. 1943. U.S. Pacific Fleet, Air Battle Notes, #12, 5-8. VGSs-11, 12, 16, Action With Enemy, 4 Feb. 1943; Intelligence Report, 4 Feb. 1943. VMSB-233, War Diary, 4 Feb. 1943: Attack Mission #2 [should be #1]. VMSB-234, Action With Enemy, 4 Feb. 1943: @1600; SBD Intelligence, 4 Feb. 1943: Attack Mission #2; War Diary, 4 Feb. 1943. Wolf, *13th Fighter Command,* 109.

Pages 236–241
The second strike of 4 Feb. 1943 against the second evacuation run

Aircraft SoPac Force, War Diary, 4 Feb. 1943: (2) Air Attacks. Horton, Coastwatcher NLO, Vila, Report, 4 Feb. 1943. Dunn, emails to D. Letournean, 26 Jul.–16 Sept. 2010. Frank, *Guadalcanal: The Definitive Account,* 591. Hata et al., *Japanese Naval Aces,* 261. Lord, *Lonely Vigil,* 167. McEniry, *A Marine Dive-Bomber Pilot at Guadalcanal,* 19. Military History Section, Japanese Monograph #116, 185. Nevitt, TROM for *Kawakaze, Kuroshio, Shirayuki,* in web site Long Lancers. Radio intercepts from RO NO 4, 4 Feb. 1943 @1830L, @1710L, @1830L. 347th Ftr Gp, Adv Echelon, Combat Report, 4 Feb. 1943: Takeoff @1555. 347th Ftr Gp Det, Daily Ops Report, 4 Feb. 1943: 7th, 8th Missions. 20th Kokutai, Combat Diary, 4 Feb. 1943. 204th Kokutai, *Zuikaku* Hikokitai, Combat Reports, 18/2/4 in web site Japan Center. U.S. Pacific Fleet, Air Battle Notes, #12, 9. VGSs-11, 12, 16, War Diary, 4 Feb. 1943. VMSB-233, War Diary, 4 Feb. 1943: Attack Mission #2 [should be #1]. VMSB-234, Action With Enemy, 4 Feb. 1943 @1705; SBD Intelligence, 4 Feb. 1943: Attack Mission #3; War Diary, 4 Feb. 1943. Wolf, *13th Fighter Command,* 109.

Pages 241–242
The Maytag Mike raids of 4–5 Feb. 1943

Aircraft SoPac Force, War Diary, 4 Feb. 1943: (6) Enemy Activity. 701st Kokutai, Combat Report, 18/2/4–5 in web site Japan Center. VMF-122 Ground Echelon, War Diary, 4 Feb. 1943.

Page 242
The Black Cat and SBD nocturnal encounters of 4–5 Feb. 1943 with Tokyo Express destroyers

Aircraft SoPac Force, War Diary, 4 Feb. 1943: (2) Air Attacks, (6) Enemy Activity. Cressman, "Chronology of USN in WWII," Chap. 5: Thurs. 4 Feb. 1943 in web site Hyperwar.

Pages 242–243
Cactus' failure to contest the Tokyo Express' arrival off Cape Esperance on the night of 4–5 Feb. 1943, plus the return trip
Crenshaw, *South Pacific Destroyer*, 68. Dailey, *"Pacific Battle Line,"* excerpt in web site USS *DeHaven* Sailors Assn. Frank, *Guadalcanal: The Definitive Account*, 589, 591. 252nd, 253rd, 958th Kokutai, Combat Reports, 18/2/5 in web site Japan Center.

Page 242
The number of Japanese troops evacuated by the second destroyer run
MacArthur, Reports: Japanese Operations in the SW Pacific Area, 196.

Page 243
The barge and landing craft incidents of 5 Feb. 1943 off Cape Esperance
Crenshaw, *South Pacific Destroyer*, 68. 347th Ftr Gp Det, Daily Ops Report, 5 Feb. 1943: 1st, 4th Missions.

Pages 243–244
The Cactus strike force's fruitless search of 5 Feb. 1943 for the Tokyo Express, and the bombing of Munda
Aircraft SoPac Force, War Diary, 5 Feb. 1943: (2) Air Attacks. VGS-11, 12, 16, Action With Enemy, 5 Feb. 1943; Intelligence Report, 5 Feb. 1943; War Diary, 5 Feb. 1943. VMSB-234, Action With Enemy, 5 Feb. 1943.

Pages 244–245
The raids of 6 Feb. 1943 on Vila and Munda
Aircraft SoPac Force, War Diary, 6 Feb. 1943: (2) Air Attacks. 347th Ftr Gp Det, Daily Ops Report, 6 Feb. 1943: 5th Mission. VGSs-11, 12, 16, War Diary, 6 Feb. 1943. VMSB-144, Sqn History, 3; War Diary, 6 Feb. 1943.

Pages 245–246
The B-17/B-24 recon missions, and the progress of the Tokyo Express
Aircraft SoPac Force, War Diary, 5 Feb. 1943: (1) (D) Searches from Cactus,

(2) Air Attacks, (4) Other Operations, Enemy Contacts, Contacts Reported by Other Commands. Debnekoff, email to D. Letourneau, 18 Aug. 2003. 204th, 253rd Kokutai, Combat Reports, 18/1/5 in web site Japan Center.

Chapter 16. The Final Touchdown
Page 247
The Japanese search for U.S. task forces
2nd Demob Bureau, Japanese Monograph #122 (IJN), 19. 705th Kokutai, Combat Report, 18/2/2–4 in web site Japan Center.

Pages 247–248
The final composition of Admiral Kondo's task force included at least seventeen warships, including CV: *Junyo, Zuiho*; BB: *Haruna, Kongo*; CA/CL: *Agano, Atago, Haguro, Jintsu, Myoko, Nagara, Takeo*; DD: *Asagumo, Hatsuyuki, Samidare, Shigure, Shikinami, Suzukaze*.

Page 248
The sortie of Admiral Kondo's Advance Force from Truk
Aircraft SoPac Force, War Diary, 4 Feb. 1943: (4) Other Operations; 5 Feb. 1943: (4) Other Operations, Enemy Contacts; 7 Feb. 1943: Contacts Reported by Other Commands. Crenshaw, *South Pacific Destroyer*, 68. Frank, *Guadalcanal: The Definitive Account*, 582, 594. Hara, *Japanese Destroyer Captain*, 172. Tulle, TROM for *Junyo, Zuiho, Zuikaku*, in web site Kido Butai. 26th BS(H), Log, Fri. 5 Feb. 1943. *Zuikaku, Zuiho*, War Diaries 18/2/5, in web site Japan Center.

Pages 248–249
The standoff between Admirals Yamamoto and Nimitz
Aircraft SoPac, War Diary, 1, 2, 5, 10, 13, 21, 24, 26, 27, 28, 29, 30 Jan. 1943: Contacts Reported by Other Commands; 2 Feb. 1943: Contacts Reported by Other Commands; 4 Feb. 1943: (6) Enemy Activity, Enemy Contacts; 5, 6 Feb. 1943: Enemy Contacts; 8 Feb. 1943: Contacts Reported by Other Commands. Crenshaw, *South Pacific Destroyer*, 68. Cressman, "U.S. Navy Chronology in WWII," Chap. 5: Sat. 30 Jan. 1943 Pacific in web site Hyperwar. Frank, *Guadalcanal: The Definitive Account*, 546, 582, 594, 596. Miller, *The Cactus Air Force*, 36. 2nd Demob Bureau, Japanese Monograph #98 (IJN), 60, 66, 67; Japanese Monograph #122 (IJN), 19.

Pages 249–250

The sortie of the final evacuation convoy on 7 Feb. 1943

> Aircraft SoPac Force, War Diary, 7 Feb. 1943: (A) Contacts Reported by Other Commands. Crenshaw, *South Pacific Destroyer*, 68. Frank, *Guadalcanal: The Definitive Account*, 594. Nevitt, KE Operation, 4–5. 253rd Kokutai, Combat Report, 18/2/7 in web site Japan Center.

Pages 250–251

The F5A recon flight

> Frank, *Guadalcanal: The Definitive Account*, 594, 595. 204th, 252nd, 253rd, 582nd Kokutai, *Zuikaku* Hikokitai, Combat Reports, 18/2/7 in web site Japan Center. VMSB-144, Combat Action Report, 7 Feb. 1943.

Details were sparse; the account is, therefore, to a degree conjectural.

Specifications of the F5A were very similar to those of the P-38L, a recon variant of the Lightning used in the European theater

> Whiting, *Patton*, 33. Tillman, "P-38," in *Pacific Fighters*, 26.

A short treatise of the Lightning as a recon plane can be found in Bergerud, *Fire in the Sky*, 545–547.

Pages 251–255

The Cactus air strike of 7 Feb. 1943 against the last evacuation convoy

> Aircraft SoPac Force, War Diary, 7 Feb. 1943: (2) Air Attacks. Dunn, emails to D. Letourneau, 26 Jul.–16 Sept. 2010. Frank, *Guadalcanal: The Definitive Account*, 594–595. Hata et al., *Japanese Naval Aces*, 261. Military History Section, Japanese Monograph #116, 185. Nevitt, TROM for *Hamakaze, Isokaze, Urakaze* in web site Long Lancers. Radio intercepts from WA RE 9, 7 Feb. 1943 @1802L, @1808L; from MO I/KO I 5, 7 Feb. 1943 @1840L; from YU TO 0, 7 Feb. 1943 @1900L; from TO YA 6, 7 Feb. 1943 @1905L. VGSs-11, 12, 16, War Diary, 7 Feb. 1943. VMSB-144, Action With Enemy, 7 Feb. 1943; Sqn History, 3–4; War Diary, 7 Feb. 1943. VMSB-234, Action With Enemy, 7 Feb. 1943.

Pages 255–256

Details of the loading operation off Cape Esperance and the leaving of a sacrificial rearguard

> Frank, *Guadalcanal: The Definitive Account*, 589, 594. Hara, *Japanese Destroyer Captain*, 172. MacArthur, Reports: Japanese Operations in the SW Pacific Area, 196. *Senshi Sosho*, Vol. 28: diagram opposite 558.

Page 256
The withdrawal of the Tokyo Express from Guadalcanal on 8 Feb. 1943, its pursuit by the Cactus strike force, and the latter's raid on Munda
   Aircraft SoPac Force, War Diary, 8 Feb. 1943: (2) Air Attacks, Enemy Contacts, Contacts Reported by Other Commands. Historical Section, G-2, Japanese Monograph #35, 48. 347th Ftr Gp Det, Daily Ops Report, 8 Feb. 1943: 5th Mission. VGSs-11, 12, 16, War Diary, 8 Feb. 1943. VMSB-144, Action With Enemy, 8 Feb. 1943.

Pages 256–257
The details of Nan and Baker searches of 8 Feb. 1943
   Aircraft SoPac Force, War Diary, 8 Feb. 1943: Enemy Contacts. 347th Ftr Gp Det, Daily Ops Report, 8 Feb. 1943: 2nd, 3rd Missions.

Chapter 17. Of Men and Machines
Page 258
Admiral Halsey's concerns
   Crenshaw, *South Pacific Destroyer*, 55–56.
Estimates of the pilots and aircrew remaining at Cactus at the end of Operation KE
   MAG 12, Record of Events of MAG 12, unnumbered page. Salecker, *Fortress Against the Sun*, 323.

Pages 258–261
The discussion about combat fatigue, physical and mental health, and the rotation system
   Bergerud, *Fire in the Sky*, 186, 201–203, 243, 244–245, 325, 344–345, 352–353, 354–355, 357, 360–363, 533, 539, 542, 666. Blackburn, *The Jolly Rogers*, 41–42, 45–46. Brand, *Fighter Squadron at Guadalcanal*, 198–199, 207. Bureau of Aeronautics, Interview of Maj. J. N. Renner, USMC, 3–4, 8–9. Cleveland, *Grey Geese Calling*, 38, 60. Davis, *Get Yamamoto*, 80. Ferguson, *Guadalcanal: The Island of Fire*, 113, 121, 136–137, 190. HQ, 347th Ftr Gp, Pilot's Combat Report: Lt. P. M. Hansen, 1; Lt. Allan Webb, 1. McEniry, *A Marine Dive-Bomber Pilot at Guadalcanal*, 86–87. Hackett's remarks in Sulzberger, Summary of VMF-123 War Diary, 13–14. Salecker, *Fortress Against the Sun*, 205. VMF-112, Daily Ops Report, 30 Jan. 1943: Item 3; 9 Feb. 1943: Item 3. Web site: History of the 69th BS (M).

Page 261
Aircraft availability at Cactus
    Bureau of Aeronautics, Interview of Maj. J. N. Renner, USMC, 6. HQ, 347th Ftr Gp, Pilot's Combat Report: Lt. L G Huff, 2. VMSB-131, War Diary, 2 Feb. 1943. VMSB-234, War Diary, 3, 5–8, 10–12, 13, 15, 18–21, 23, 25–28 Feb. 1943; Jan. 1943: Composition, (a) Airplanes; Feb. 1943; Composition, (a) Airplanes. 1–31 Jan. 1943.

Pages 261–262
The experiences of the USAAF's 44th FS, heavy bomber, and 67th FS
    Aircraft SoPac Force, War Diary, 24 Dec. 1942: Air Strikes; 29 Jan. 1943: (3) Other Operations. Ferguson, *Guadalcanal: The Island of Fire*, 22, 26; HQ, 347th Ftr Gp, Pilot's Combat Report: Capt. S. A. Palmer, 2; Lt. P. M. Hansen, 1.

Pages 262–263
Operational accidents, aircraft striking policy, and defective aircraft
    Brand, *Fighter Squadron at Guadalcanal*, 121, 122. DeFries, Report on Fighter Maintenance, Section B: 4, 6. Diepenbrock, undated note to R. Letourneau re: ground echelon. Hanley, observation in Sulzberger, Summary of VMF-123 War Diary, 9; see also 5–6, 12.

Pages 264–265
The discussion of cooperation, rivalry, and friction among ground echelons
    Bergerud, *Fire in the Sky*, 349–352. DeFries, Report on Fighter Maintenance, Section A: 1, 2–3. Sulzberger, Summary of VMF-121 War Diary, 8. VMF-122, History of VMF-122: Narrative, 2. VMF-122, War Diary of Ground Echelon, 18, 19 Jan. 1943.

Page 265
VMSB-142's experience with defective aircraft
    VMSB-142, War Diary, 20 Jan. 1943.
Japanese problems with aircraft maintenance
    Bergerud, Fire in the Sky, 22–23, 341. 582nd Kokutai Combat Report, 18/02/01, in web site Japan Center.

Pages 265–266
Bad habits among pilots, cockpit troubles due to pilots' ignorance of technical characteristics and operational traits of their aircraft, and mechanical training for Japanese aircrew
    DeFries, Report on Fighter Maintenance, Section A: 1–2; Section B: 1. HQ USAFISPA, POW Report #121, 7. Millington and Scott in Sulzberger, Summary of VMF-123 War Diary, 5, 8, 11, 12. SoPac Force Intelligence Division, "Operational Difficulties at Guadalcanal," in Air Battle Notes, #11, 10.

Pages 266–267
Aircraft dispersal, and pilot and plane assignments
    DeFries, Report on Fighter Maintenance, Section B: 1. SoPac Force Intelligence Division "Operational Difficulties at Guadalcanal," in Air Battle Notes #11, 10. Sulzberger, Summary of VMF-123 War Diary, 8.

Pages 267–268
Japanese radio-communications problems
    HQ USAFISPA, POW Report #121, 6, 7. Military History Section, Japanese Monograph #118, 294-298.

Pages 268–269
U.S. radio-communications problems
    Bergerud, *Fire in the Sky*, 456–459. Bureau of Aeronautics, Interview of Maj. J. N. Renner, USMC, 4, 7. DeFries, Report on Fighter Maintenance, Section B: 5. Horton, *Fire Over the Islands*, 109. Lundstrom, *The First Team*, 192. McEniry, *A Marine Dive-Bomber Pilot at Guadalcanal*, 103. Sulzberger, Summary of VMF-123 War Diary, 10–11. Weiland, email to R. Letourneau, 4 Oct. 2003.

Chapter 18. Good Luck or Good Management?
Pages 271–272
The discussion of Admiral Yamamoto's asset concentration and deployment strategy for Operation KE
    King, "First Report to the Secretary of the Navy," 23 Apr. 1943 in web site Hyperwar.

Page 274
The lack of sufficient fighter cover for Cactus air strikes
    Blackburn, *The Jolly Rogers*, 71. Bureau of Aeronautics, Interview of Maj. J. N. Renner, USMC, 6.

Pages 274–276

The relative competence of JNAF and JAAF airmen and their decline in combat aptitude
  Bergerud, *Fire in the Sky*, 666–667, 669–676. Sakaida, *IJN Aces*, 8. 347th Ftr Gp, Adv Echelon, Account of Experience of Maj. W. H. McCarroll, 2.

Page 276

The use of destroyers as transports by the IJN
  Bergerud, *Fire in the Sky*, 568–569. Cleveland, *Grey Geese Calling*, 23. McEniry, *A Marine Dive-Bomber Pilot at Guadalcanal*, 17–18, 108. USAAF HQ, "Destroyers Hard to Hit," in web site Guadalcanal Air War, at USD History Server. VMSB-131, Action of VMSB-131 at Cactus, 4.

Page 277

Hits and misses were estimated using primarily the war diaries and combat action reports of the bomber squadrons involved in addition to selected secondary sources. The aggregate potential targets of 133 DDs and 14 DDs damaged was arrived at as follows:

- 15 Jan. 1943: Black Cat (night attack). Potential target: 1 DD/damaged: 1 DD
- 1st air strike. Potential targets: 9 DDs/damaged: 5 DDs
- 2nd air strike. Potential targets: 5 DDs/damaged: 0 DDs
- 28 Jan. 1943: 1st air strike. Potential targets: 6 DDs/damaged: 1 DD
- 1 Feb. 1943: 1st air strike. Potential targets: 20 DDs/damaged: 1 DD
- 2 Feb. 1943: SBDs (night attack). Potential targets: 3 DDs/damaged: 0 DDs
- 2 Feb. 1943: Black Cat (night attack). Potential targets: 15 DDs/damaged: 0 DDs
- 2 Feb.1943: 1st air strike. Potential targets: 17 DDs/damaged: 0 DDs
- 4 Feb.1943: 1st air strike. Potential targets: 20 DDs/damaged: 2 DDs
- 2nd air strike. Potential targets: 18 DDs/damaged: 2 DDs
- 5 Feb.1943: Black Cat (night attack). Potential target: 1 DD/damaged: 0 DDs
- 7 Feb.1943: 1st air strike. Potential targets: 18 DDs/damaged: 2 DDs

Pages 278–280

The discussion about Japanese prowess in nocturnal combat and the Cactus Air Force's comparative weakness
  Bureau of Aeronautics, Interview of Maj. J. N. Renner, 6–7. Crenshaw, *South Pacific Destroyer*, 56. HQ USAFISPA, POW Report #121, 6. VMSB-131, Action of VMSB-131 at Cactus, 5. Lord, *Lonely Vigil*, 61, 82.

Pages 280–281
Dive-bombing, glide bombing, and torpedo-bombing
   Bergerud, *Fire in the Sky*, 533–534, 571–573, 573–574, 576–578. McEniry, *A Marine Dive-Bomber Pilot at Guadalcanal*, 19–23.

Page 281
The anecdote of the USAAF P-38 flight leader's refusal to defend Marine SBDs at low altitude
   McEniry, *A Marine Dive-Bomber Pilot at Guadalcanal*, 84.

Page 282
U.S. ace-quality pilots at Cactus during Operation KE
   "American Aces of WWII and Korea" in web site Aerofiles. Olynyck, *USMC Credits for the Destruction of Enemy Aircraft in Air-to-Air Combat, World War 2*, List #1, 15-17, 76-79. Web site American Air Aces of WWII. Wolf, 13th Fighter Command, 279.
A complete listing can be gleaned from web site American Air Aces of World War II, and "American Aces of WWII and Korea," in web site Acrofiles.

Pages 283–284
The Cactus Air Force's misallocation of resources regarding its airbase suppression campaign against Munda and Vila
   Bergerud, *Fire in the Sky*, 412, 531–532, 537–538, 543–544, 573, 621–622, 624–625. Cleveland, *Grey Geese Calling*, 11. Salecker, *Fortress Against the Sun*, 300–301. 2nd Demob Bureau, Japanese Monograph #98 (IJN), 56.

Pages 284–285
The misuse of B-17s
   Bergerud, *Fire in the Sky*, 273–274, 544–545, 586–588. Cleveland, *Grey Geese Calling*, 23–24, 78. Keenan, Diary of a Coastwatcher. Salecker, *Fortress Against the Sun*, 195, 197–198, 21. Wolf, *13th Fighter Command*, 107.

Pages 285–286
Misallocation of resources in search-and-destroy missions
   Aircraft SoPac Force, War Diary, 19 Jan. 1943: (2) Airstrikes, Contacts Reported by Other Commands. Radio intercept from NA HA 6, 19 Jan. 1943 @ unspecified time, plus U.S. Intel Comments. 347th Ftr Gp, Ops Report, 19 Jan.

1943, 8th, 10th Missions. VMSB-131, Mission Charts, 19 Jan. 1943. VMSB-233, War Diary, 19 Jan. 1943: Attack Mission.

Page 286

The 67th FS's readiness to assume a combat role during Operation KE and its lack of combat experience

Bergerud, *Fire in the Sky*, 508. Caidin, *Zero Fighter*, 157. Ferguson, *Guadalcanal: The Island of Fire*, 80–81.

Pages 286–290

Discussion of Richard Frank's comment on Munda airstrip, including some aircraft comings and goings

Aircraft SoPac Force, War Diary, 15 Jan. 1943: Other Operations; 22, 23, 24 Jan. 1943: (3) Photo Missions; 25 Jan. 1943: (3) Enemy Activity. Horton, Coastwatcher NLO, Vila, Report, 25, 26, 27, 28, 29, 30, 31 Jan. 1943. Frank, *Guadalcanal: The Definitive Account*, 573. Munda War Diary, Narrative, 1289, 1302; Ops Reports, 18/01/22, 27, 28, 29, 30, 31; Radio Message: from Munda 18/1/19 @1720L in web site Japan Center. Radio intercepts: U.S. Intel Report, 13 Jan. 1943; from I FU 00, 23 Jan. 1943 @1920L; U.S. Intel Report, 28 Jan. 1943. 2nd Demob Bureau, Japanese Monograph #98 (IJN), 56; Japanese Monograph #122 (IJN), 8, 11, 18. 12th Hikodan, "Results of Important Operations of the 6th Air Division, from Dec. 1942 to Mar. 1943," in Japanese Monograph #32. 204th Kokutai, Combat Report, 18/01/09, 10, 11, 14, 15 in web site Japan Center. USSBS(P). USSBS #195: Interrogation of Lt. Cdr. S Yunoki; USSBS(P), USSBS #224: Interrogation of Cdr. Yasumi Doi. VGSs-11, 12, 16, War Diary, 4 Feb. 1943. VMSB-131, Intelligence Report, 2 Feb. 1943.

Page 290

Wrecked Japanese planes at Munda airstrip

"Munda Airfield: Captured Japanese Aircraft," in web site PacificWrecks.

Admiral Ainsworth's last word

Publications Branch, ONI, Bombardments of Munda and Vila-Stanmore, 31.

Pages 291–292

The Munda conspiracy theory and the similarity between the Munda and Rabaul experiences

Bergerud, *Fire in the Sky*, 48: 425–427, 640–655. Blackburn, *Jolly Rogers*, 178–179, 215–221, 227–228, 229, 236–237, 243, 247, 254–255, 260, 263, 272–274, 278, 280, 287, 290–294.

Page 292
Allied airfields in the Solomons in the fall of 1943 included four on Guadalcanal (Henderson, Fighter Strips One and Two, Carney), two in the Russell Islands (North Field, South Field—called Banika), two on New Georgia (Segi, Munda), one on Arundel (Ondongo), and one on Vella Lavella (Barakoma).

The writers have consistently maintained that approximately 10,600 Japanese were rescued from Guadalcanal, based on actual Japanese statistics found in General MacArthur's reports. A total of 10,652 evacuees is recorded in the U.S. Navy's chronology of WW II: 4,935 rescued by the first evacuation run; 3,921 by the second; 1,796 by the third. Other sources give various figures, most differing on the high side. For example, Capt. Tamiechi Hara lists precisely 12,198 IJA and 832 IJN evacuees. Regardless of the numbers actually saved, the Japanese regarded the feat as a phenomenal success.

Pages 292–293
The deployment of the Guadalcanal evacuees
  Hara, *Japanese Destroyer Captain*, 172. Cressman, "Chronology of USN in WWII," Chap. 5: 2, 5, 8 Feb. 1943 in web site Hyperwar. Hammel, *Munda Trail*, 41, 42, 46, 55, 72, 96–97, 114, 119, 140, 147, 158–159, 163–165, 172–175, 184, 190, 191, 237, 258, 268, 286–287. MacArthur, Reports: Japanese Operations in the SW Pacific Area, 196–197.

BIBLIOGRAPHY

**Documents and Unpublished Manuscripts,
National Archives and Records Administration, College Park, MD**
NOTE: *RG = Record Group*
2nd MAW: Fighter Command, Cactus. Combat Report, 25 Jan. 1943. (RG 18, Box 3355.)
26th Bomb Squadron (Heavy). Log. U.S. Pacific Fleet: South Pacific Force Intelligence Division. Air Battle Notes from the South Pacific No. 11, 17 Feb. 1943. (RG 38.) (Courtesy of Ewan Stevenson.)
347th Fighter Group, Advanced Echelon. Account of Experience of Maj. W. H. McCarroll, Flight Surgeon, USAAF, in B-17 #41–2524. (RG 18.)
347th Fighter Group, Advanced Echelon. Daily Operations Reports, 25 Jan.–1 Feb. 1943. (RG 18.)
347th Fighter Group Headquarters: Office of the Group Intelligence Officer. Action Reports/Combat Reports/Reports of Escort Missions, Jan.–Feb. 1943. (RG 18, Box 3355.)
347th Fighter Group Headquarters: Office of the Group Operations Officer. Monthly Operations Reports, 25 Jan.–8 Feb. 1943. (RG 18, Box 3354.)
347th Fighter Group Headquarters: Office of the Group Intelligence Officer. Operations Reports, 23 Dec. 1942–24 Feb. 1943. (RG 18, Box 3354.)
347th Fighter Group Headquarters: Office of the Group Intelligence Officer. Pilots' Combat Reports, 16 Jan.–27 Sept. 1943. (RG 18, Box 2365.)
Aircraft South Pacific Force (U.S. Pacific Fleet). War Diary, 23 Dec.–8 Feb. 1943. (RG 38.) (Courtesy of Ewan Stevenson.)
Bureau of Aeronautics. Interview of Maj. J. N. Renner, USMC, 17 Jul. 1943. (RG 127, Box 47.)
Combat Intelligence Center, South Pacific Force. Prisoner of War Interrogation Report #134: PO2c Nobutaro Yada. (RG 38.) (Courtesy of Ewan Stevenson.)

DeFries, H. O., Capt. USMC. A Report on Fighter Maintenance and Operations in Combat Area 19 Feb. 1943. (RG 127, Box 7.)

Fitch, Aubrey, W., Vice Adm., Commander Task Force Sixty-three. Operation Order No. 1–43: 1 Jan. 1943, and Operation Order No. 2–43: 20 Jan. 1943. (RG 38.) (Courtesy of Ewan Stevenson.)

Intercepted Enemy Radio Traffic and Related Documents. (RG 38, Box 525.)

Kiethly, Glen F., Capt., USMC. Memo: Information on History of VMO-251. (RG 127, Box 47.)

King, J. P., Lt., Intelligence, 347th Fighter Group Detachment. Cactus: Bombing and Strafing by P-39's on Guadalcanal. Report dated 26 Jan. 1943. (RG 18.)

MAG 12—1st MAW—Fighter Command. Record of Events of MAG 12 for 1 Feb.–25 Jul. 1943. (RG 38, Box 1614.)

MAG 14. "Missions, Dates, Numbers of Our VB and VF, Enemy Opposition, Enemy Losses and Our Losses." In Guadalcanal: Escorted Bomber Missions during Months of Dec. 1942 and Jan. 1943 through 24 Feb. 1943. (RG 127, Box 6–7.)

Office of Naval Intelligence. POW Field Interrogation Report (Guadalcanal): WO Mitsunori Nakajima, JNAF, 12 Feb. 1943 (RG 38). (Courtesy of Rick Dunn.)

Office of Naval Intelligence. Solomon Islands Campaign, VIII: Japanese Evacuation of Guadalcanal. Washington, DC: Publications Branch, Office of Naval Intelligence, 1944. (RG 38.)

Office of Naval Intelligence. Solomon Islands Campaign, IX: Bombardments of Munda and Vila-Stanmore. Washington, DC: Publications Branch, Office of Naval Intelligence, 1944. (RG 38.)

Sulzberger, Myron Jr., Capt., Intelligence Officer, VMF-123. Summary of War Diary to 15 Jun. 1943 with Comments and Observations. (RG 127, Box 8.)

26th Bomb Squadron (Heavy). Log.

U.S. Pacific Fleet: South Pacific Force, Intelligence Division. Air Battle Notes from the south Pacific, # 11:17 Feb. 1943, #12: 2 Mar. 1943 (RG 38.)

VGS-11, VGS-12, and VGS-16. War Diary, 31 Jan.–19 Feb. 1943. (RG 38, Box 1668.)

VMF-112. Daily Operations Reports, 1 Jan.–12 Feb. 1943. (RG 127, Box 2.)

VMF-121. Official Squadron History, 1 Mar. 1942–15 Dec. 1944. (RG 127, Box 3.)

VMF-121. Pilots' Box Score while in Combat in the Solomon Islands Area: First Tour (25 Sept.–15 Dec. 1942) and Second Tour (19 Dec. 1942–29 Jan. 1943). (RG 127.)

VMF-121. Squadron Operations while at Guadalcanal, S.I., 15 Dec. 1942 ... 29 Jan. 1943. (RG 127, Box 7.)

VMF-121. War Diary, Oct. 1942–Jan. 1943. (RG 127.)

VMF-122. War Diary of Ground Echelon, Jan.–Feb. 1943. (RG 127, Box 8.)

VMF-123. History of Marine Fighting Squadron One Twenty-Three: Chronology. (RG 127, Box 8.)
VMF-123. Schedule II—Flying Activities of the Squadron at Cactus from 4 Feb. to 17 Mar. 1943. In Combat Flying Information from Marine Fighting Squadron One Twenty Three. (RG 127, Box 8.)
VMF-123. Summary of War Duty to 15 Jun. 1943. (RG 127, Box 8.)
VMF-124. Squadron History: For Period 7 Sept. 1942–1 Dec. 1944. (RG 127, Box 9.)
VMO-251. Report of Destruction of Enemy Ships and Planes and Loss of Own Aircraft: Month of Jan. 1943. (RG 127, Box 47.)
VMO-251. War Diary, 1 Jan. 1943–31 Jan. 1943 and 1 Feb. 1943–28 Feb. 1943. (RG 127, Box 47.)
VMSB-131. Intelligence Reports, 27 Jan.–2 Feb.1943. (RG 38, Box 1666.)
VMSB-131. Intelligence Summary: Action of Marine Scout Bombing Squadron 131 at Cactus, from 11 Nov. 1942 to 2 Feb. 1943. (RG 38, Box 1666.)
VMSB-131. Manuscript containing summary of historical highlights. (RG 38, Box 1666.)
VMSB-131. Miscellaneous Correspondence and Reports, 1941–47. (RG 127, Box 6.)
VMSB-131. War Diary, 28 Jan.–9 Mar. 1943. (RG 127, Box 9.)
VMSB-141. Unit History. (RG 127, Box 10.)
VMSB-142. War Diary, 1 Mar. 1942–1 Jul. 1944. (RG 127, Box 10.)
VMSB-143. War Diary, 7 Sept. 1942–1 May 1944. (RG 17, Box 15.)
VMSB-143. Log, Feb. 3–28 1943. (RG 38, Box 1651.)
VMSB-143/VGSs-11, 12, 16. Combat Action Reports, Feb. 1943. (RG 38, Box 1668.)
VMSB-144. Combat Action Reports, Feb. 1943. (RG 38, Box 1668.)
VMSB-144. War Diary, 7 Sept. 1942–31 May 1943. (RG 38, Box 1651.)
VMSB-144. Squadron History, 7 Sept. 1942–7 Dec. 1944. (RG 17, Box 16.)
VMSB-233. Combat Action Report, 2 Feb. 1943. (RG 38, Box 1673.)
VMSB-233. Squadron Monthly Report of Friendly and Enemy Losses. (RG 127, Box 35.)
VMSB-233. War Diary, 1 Jan. through 28 Feb. 1943. (RG 127, Box 35; RG 38, Box 1651.)
VMSB-234. U.S. Aircraft—Action with Enemy, 1–7 Feb. 1943. (RG 38, Box 1673.)
VMSB-234. War Diary, 28 Jan.–28 Feb. 1943. (RG 127, Box 37.)

Documents and Unpublished Manuscripts, Other

NOTE: Several documents are listed in the section Internet Sources.
5th Bombardment Group (Heavy), USAAF. Narrative: 19 May 1918–31 Dec.

1943. Maxwell Air Force Base, Alabama: Air Force Historical Research Agency. (Excerpts courtesy of Joanne Emerick.)

12th Hiko Shidan. 12th Air Sector Operations Order #94, 29 Jan. 1943. (Excerpt courtesy of Richard Dunn.)

42nd Bomb Squadron (Heavy). Log. (Courtesy of Ewan Stevenson.)

98th BS(H). Operational Diary: 98th Bombardment Squadron. (Courtesy of Ewan Stevenson.)

204th Kokutai, JNAF. S18: Combat Diary. (Handwritten/typewritten copies of 25 Jan.–19 Feb. 1943.) (Courtesy of Ryoji Ohara and Henry Sakaida.)

ATIS Enemy Publications Series: JOMS #116. Maxwell AFB, Alabama: Air Force Historical Research Agency. (Excerpts courtesy of Allan Alsleben.)

ATIS Enemy Publications Series: JICPOA #1072. Maxwell AFB, Alabama: Air Force Historical Research Agency. (Excerpts courtesy of Allan Alsleben.)

ATIS Enemy Publications Series, MOTO #19: 8th Area Army. Maxwell AFB, Alabama: Air Force Historical Research Agency. (Excerpts courtesy of Allan Alsleben.)

ATIS Enemy Publications Series: WDC #1742. Maxwell AFB, Alabama: Air Force Historical Research Agency. (Excerpts courtesy of Allan Alsleben.)

ComSoPac. Message to ComCPac, 27 Jan. 1943. Annapolis, MD: Nimitz Library, U.S. Naval Academy. (Courtesy of Rick Dunn.)

Eschenberg, Russ. Letter to Mr. E. M. Stevenson, 27 May 1995. (Courtesy of Ewan Stevenson.)

Flahavin, Peter. Henderson Field—"The Pagoda" Flight Operations Centre and Communications Tunnel. Melbourne, Australia: Pamphlet. (Courtesy of Peter Flahavin.)

Historical Section, G-2, GHQ. Japanese Monograph No. 32: Southeast Area Air Operations Record, Nov. 1942–Apr. 1944. Washington, DC: Department of the Army, n.d.

Historical Section, G-2, GHQ. Japanese Monograph No. 35: 17th Army Operations, Vol. II. Washington, DC: Department of the Army, n.d.

Horton, D. C. "Coastwatcher NLO, Vila, Reports." In Reports from Coastwatchers in the Solomon Islands Area. Melbourne: Archives of Australia. (Series B3476 and B3477A.)

HQ, U. S. Army Forces in South Pacific Area. POW Interrogation Report #121: WO Mitsunori Nakajima, JNAF. 14 May 1943. (Courtesy of Rick Dunn.)

Irwin, John. Line Chief's Notebook. (Select excerpts courtesy of John Irwin.)

Izawa, Yasuho. Japanese Navy Float Fighter Units. (Manuscript courtesy of Henry Sakaida.)

Keenan, J. H., Lt., RANVR. Diary of a Coastwatcher (Vella Lavella Island), 30 Jan.–16 Feb. 1943. (Excerpts courtesy of Jeff DeBlanc.)

Kirkland, Gene. PT 109: The Early Days, Jul. 1942–Apr. 1943. (Manuscript, copyrighted in 2003 by the author.) (Courtesy of Leighton Wood.)

MacArthur, Douglas, Lt. Gen. Reports of General MacArthur: Japanese Operations in the Southwest Pacific Area. Vol. II, Part I. Tokyo, 1950. (Facsimile reprint by U.S. Army Center of Military History, 1994.)

McKillop, Jack. Combat Chronology of the U.S. Army Air Forces, 1 Jan.–28 Feb. 1943. n.p.: USAF (Airways and Air Communications Service), 1955–1959.

Military History Section, GHQ, Far East Command. Japanese Monograph No. 116: The Imperial Japanese Navy in World War II. Washington, DC: Department of the Army, Feb. 1952.

Military History Section, GHQ, Far East Command. Japanese Monograph No. 118: Operational History of Naval Communications, Dec. 1941–Aug. 1945. Washington, DC: Department of the Army, n.d.

Military Intelligence Division. Special Series No. 25: Japanese Field Artillery. Washington, DC: War Department, Oct. 1944.

Nasif, George, Lt. Col. Letter to Ewan Stevenson, 9 Jun. 1996. (Courtesy of Ewan Stevenson.)

Nevitt, Allyn. KE Operation: The Evacuation of Guadalcanal. (Courtesy of Allyn Nevitt.)

Secrest, Jim. Letters to C. Darby, 12, 26 Mar. 1990.

Senji Senpakushi. Maxwell AFB, Alabama: Air Force Historical Research Agency. (Translated excerpts courtesy of Ewan Stevenson.)

Senshi Sosho (BKS), Vols. 28 and 83. Maxwell AFB, Alabama: Air Force Historical Research Agency. (Excerpts courtesy of Allan Alsleben.)

Senshi Sosho (BKS), Vol. 28, opposite page 558. Diagram of Japanese loading operation at Cape Esperance. Maxwell AFB, Alabama: Air Force Historical Research Agency. (Courtesy of Ewan Stevenson.)

Second Demobilization Bureau. Japanese Monograph No. 98 (IJN): Southeast Area Naval Operations, Part I, May 1942–Feb. 1943. 2nd ed. Washington, DC: G-2 Historical Section, June 1949.

Second Demobilization Bureau. Monograph No. 122 (IJN): Outline of Southeast Area Naval Air Operations, Part III, Nov. 1942–June 1943. Washington, DC: G-2 Historical Section, June 1950.

Stevenson, Ewan M. Manuscript of Dumbo Rescues. (Courtesy of Ewan Stevenson.)

Stevenson, Ewan M. World War II Vessels Sunk in the Solomon Islands. (Courtesy of Ewan Stevenson.)
Summary of Report of B-17 Raid on Shortland-Tonolei. In History of the 5th Bombardment Group (Heavy). Maxwell AFB, Alabama: Air Force History Research Agency. (Excerpts courtesy of MSgt. Craig Mackay.)
USAAF Victories Over Seaplanes. Maxwell AFB, Alabama: Air Force Historical Research Agency. (Courtesy of Allan Alsleben.)
U.S. Navy. List of Aircraft Lost: Pacific Theater, Dec. 1942–Mar. 1943. Washington, DC: Naval Historical Center.
U.S. Navy. Location of U.S. Naval Aircraft, 17 Feb. 1943. Washington, DC: Naval Historical Center.
VMF-112. Official Squadron History, 1 Mar. 1942–15 Dec. 1944. (Courtesy of Jack Maas.)
VMSB-234. Working Roster, 4 Feb. 1943. NAS Ft. Worth, TX: VMGR-234 Archives. (Courtesy of Lt. Col. D. Stumpf, USMC.)
VP-12. The Old Black Cats, 29 Jun. 1943. (Courtesy of Ewan Stevenson.)
Walton, Capt. Frank (Executive Officer: VMF-214). War Diary—VMF-214: First Tour, Russell Islands–Munda. (Courtesy of Allan McCartney.)
Weiland, Pat. Pilot's Log Book. (Copy in email to R. Letourneau, 9 Oct. 2003.)
Wood, Leighton. Letter to Editor, *Naval History*, 10 May 1999; Letter to Bob [Baldwin?], 3 June 1999; Letter to R. Baldwin, 6 Nov. 1999. (Courtesy of Leighton Wood.)

Correspondence and Interviews with Veterans
Joe Conrad, pilot VMSB-131
John Cook, ground crewman, 44thFS
Jeff DeBlanc, pilot, VMF-112
Basil Debnekoff, B-17 radio operator, 23rd BS(H)
Robert Diepenbrock, ground crewman (unspecified unit)
George Dooley, pilot, VMSB-131
Jim Feliton, pilot, VMF-112
John Irwin, line chief, VMO-251
Jack Maas, pilot, VMF-112
Allan McCartney, pilot, VMO-251, VMF-214
Barney McShane, pilot, VMSB 131
Ryoji Ohara, pilot, 204th Kokutai, JNAF (via Henry Sakaida)
Marty Roush, pilot, VMSB-131

William Sabel, Lt., engineering officer, U.S. Army Corps of Engineers
Richard Watson, ground crewman, VPB-44
Pat Weiland, pilot, VMO-251
Leighton Wood, commander, *PT-124*

Correspondence with Military Historians and Students of Military History

Allan Alsleben
Charles Darby
Rick Dunn
Peter Flahaven
Bruce Gamble
John Innes
Danny and Kerrie Kennedy
Jim Lansdale
Allyn Nevitt
Ragnar Ragnarsson
Luca Ruffato
Henry Sakaida
Ewan Stevenson
Justin Taylan
Ryan Toews

Books

Altobello, Brian. *Into the Shadows Furious: The Brutal Battle for New Georgia*. Novato, CA: Presidio Press, 2000.
Bailey, Dan E. *WWII Wrecks of Palau*. Redding, CA: North Valley Diver Publications, 1991.
Barker, A. J. *Pearl Harbor*. New York: Ballantine Books, 1969.
Barker, A. J. *Suicide Weapon*. New York: Ballantine Books, 1971.
Bergerud, Eric M. *Fire in the Sky: The Air War in the South Pacific*. Boulder, CO: Westview Press, 2000.
Blackburn, Tom. *The Jolly Rogers*. New York: Pocket Books, 1990.
Bowman, Martin. *B-17 Flying Fortress Units of the Pacific War*. Oxford: Osprey Publishing, 2003.
Brand, Max. *Fighter Squadron at Guadalcanal*. Toronto: Pocket Books, 1996.
Caidin, Martin. *Zero Fighter*. New York: Ballantine Books, 1970.

Clemens, Martin. *Alone on Guadalcanal: A Coastwatcher's Story*. Annapolis, MD: Naval Institute Press, 1998.

Cleveland, W. M., ed. *Grey Geese Calling: Pacific Air War History of the 11th Bombardment Group (H) 1940–1945*. Ascov, MN: American Publishing, 1981.

Crenshaw, Russell S. Jr. *South Pacific Destroyer: The Battle for the Solomons from Savo Island to Vella Gulf*. Annapolis, MD: Naval Institute Press, 1998.

Dann, Richard. *Walk Around: F4F Wildcat*. Carrollton, TX: Squadron/Signal Publications, 1995.

Davis, Burke. *Get Yamamoto*. London: Arthur Barker, 1969.

DeBlanc, Col. Jefferson, USMC (Ret.). *Once They Lived by the Sword*. St. Martinsville, LA: Jeff DeBlanc, 1988.

Doll, Thomas. *Marine Fighting Squadron One-Twenty-One (VMF-121)*. Carrollton, TX: Squadron/Signal Publications, 1996.

Ethell, Jeffrey, and Warren M. Bodie. *WWII Pacific War Eagles: China/Pacific Aerial Combats in Original Color*. Fort Royal, VA: Widewing Publications, 1997.

Ferguson, Robert Lawrence. *Guadalcanal: The Island of Fire: Reflections of the 347th Fighter Group*. Blue Ridge Summit, PA: Aero, 1987.

Foss, Joe. *Joe Foss, Flying Marine: The Story of His Flying Circus in World War II (as Told to Walter Simmons)*. Washington, DC: Zenger Publishing, 1979. (Originally published E. P. Dutton & Co., 1943.)

Francillon, Rene. *Japanese Aircraft of the Pacific War*. London: G. R. Putnam, 1970.

Frank, Richard B. *Guadalcanal: The Definitive Account of the Landmark Battle*. Toronto: Penguin Books, 1992.

Hammel, Eric. *Carrier Clash*. Pacifica, CA: Pacifica Military History, 2004.

Hammel, Eric. *Guadalcanal: Decision at Sea*. Pacifica, CA: Pacifica Military History, 1998.

Hammel, Eric. *Guadalcanal: Starvation Island*. Pacifica, CA: Pacifica Military History, 1987.

Hammel, Eric. *Munda Trail*. New York: Avon Books, 1989.

Hara, Tameichi, Capt. *Japanese Destroyer Captain*. New York: Ballantine Books, 1961.

Hata, Ikuhiko, Yasuho Izawa, and Don Cyril Gorham. *Japanese Naval Aces and Fighter Units in World War II*. Annapolis, MD: Naval Institute Press, 1989.

Hata, Ikuhiko, Yasuho Izawa, and Christopher Shores. *Japanese Army Air Force Fighter Units and Their Aces: 1931–1945*. London: Grub Street, 2002.

Heiferman, Ron. *Flying Tigers: Chennault in China.* New York: Ballantine Books, 1971.
Hibbert, Christopher. *Anzio: The Bid for Rome.* New York: Ballantine Books, 1970.
Honan, Mark, and David Harcombe. *Solomon Islands.* Victoria, Australia: Lonely Planet Publications, 1988.
Horton, D. C. *Fire Over the Islands: Coast Watchers of the Solomons.* Sydney, Australia: A. H. & A. W. Reed, 1970.
Horton, D. C. *New Georgia: Pattern for Victory.* New York: Ballantine Books, 1971.
Hoyt, Edwin P. *Guadalcanal.* New York: Stein and Day, Publishers, 1981.
Hubler, Richard, and John De Chant Doubleday. *Flying Leathernecks.* Garden City, NY: Doran and Company, 1944.
Humble, Richard. *Japanese High Seas Fleet.* New York: Ballantine Books, 1973.
Hunt, E. Howard. *Limit of Darkness.* New York: Stein and Day, Publishers, 1985. (Originally published 1944.)
Jersey, Stanley C. *Hell's Islands: The Untold Story of Guadalcanal.* College Station, TX: Tamu Press, 2007.
Kennedy, Paul. *Pacific Onslaught, 7th Dec. 1941/7th Feb. 1942.* New York: Ballantine Books, 1972.
Lord, Walter. *Lonely Vigil: Coastwatchers of the Solomons.* New York: The Viking Press, 1977.
Lundstrom, John B. *The First Team and the Guadalcanal Campaign: Naval Fighter Combat from August to November 1942.* Annapolis, MD: Naval Institute Press, 1996.
Macintyre, Donald. *Aircraft Carrier: The Majestic Weapon.* New York: Ballantine Books, 1968.
Macintyre, Donald. *Leyte Gulf: Armada in the Pacific.* New York: Ballantine Books, 1969.
McEniry, Col. John Howard Jr. USMC (Ret.). *A Marine Dive-bomber Pilot at Guadalcanal.* Tuscaloosa, AL: The University of Alabama Press, 1987.
Miller, Thomas G. *The Cactus Air Force.* Fredericksburg, TX: Admiral Nimitz Foundation, 1969.
Mills, James C. *Blue Catalinas of World War II.* Manhattan, KS: Sunflower University Press, 1995.
Olynyk, Frank J. USMC Credits for the Destruction of Enemy Aircraft in Air-to-Air Combat World War 2. Ohio: Frank J. Olynyk, Apr. 1982.
O'Neill, Richard. *Suicide Squads: Axis and Allied Special Attack Weapons of World War II.* New York: Ballantine Books, 1984. (Originally published by Salamander Books, 1981.)

Rentz, Maj. John N., USMCR. *Marines in the Central Solomons*. Nashville, TN: The Battery Press, 1989. (Originally published 1952.)

Rooney, D. D. *Stillwell*. New York: Ballantine Books, 1971.

Ross, J. M. S., Squadron Leader. *Royal New Zealand Air Force*. Wellington. War Historical Publications Branch, 1955.

Sakaida, Henry. *Imperial Japanese Navy Aces 1937–45*. Oxford: Osprey Publishing, 1998.

Sakaida, Henry. *Japanese Army Air Force Aces 1937–45*. Oxford: Osprey Publishing, 1997.

Salecker, Gene Eric. *Fortress Against the Sun: The B-17 Flying Fortress in the Pacific*. Boston: Da Capo Press, 2001.

Swinson, Arthur. *Defeat in Malaya: The Fall of Singapore*. New York: Ballantine Books, 1969.

Twining, Merrill B., Gen., USMC, and Neil Carey, ed. *No Bended Knee: The Battle for Guadalcanal*. Novato, CA: Presidio Press, 1997.

Vader, John. *New Guinea: The Tide Is Stemmed*. New York: Ballantine Books, 1971.

Walton, Frank. *Once They Were Eagles: The Men of the Black Sheep Squadron*. Lexington, KY: University Press of Kentucky, 1986.

Weiland, Pat. *Above and Beyond*. Pat Weiland. Pacifica, CA: Pacifica Press, 1997.

Wolf, William. *13th Fighter Command in World War II: Air Combat over Guadalcanal and the Solomons*. Atglen, PA: Schiffer Military History, 2004.

Articles and Parts of Books

Allmore, William B. "Midway Atoll's Undaunted Defenders." In *Battle of Midway: Special Collector's Edition*, edited by C. J. Anderson, 20–26, 92. Leesburg, VA: Primedia, 2002.

Astor, Gerald. "The Master Weaver." In *Battle of Midway: Special Collector's Edition*, edited by C. J. Anderson, 34–40. Leesburg, VA: Primedia, 2002.

Bechtel, Paul, Maj., USAAF. "The Christmas Present." In *Aces Against Japan: The American Aces Speak*, edited by Eric Hammel, 87–91. New York: Pocket Books, 1995. (Originally published 1992.)

Crawford, Bruce. "Zero: Flimsy Killer." In *WWII Air War: The Men, the Machines, the Missions*, edited by Roger L. Vance. Leesburg, VA: Cowles Enthusiast Media/Creative Publishing, 1996, 68–73.

Cupp, Jim, Capt., USMC. "Tail Chase." In *Aces Against Japan: The American Aces Speak*, edited by Eric Hammel, 112–120. New York: Pocket Books, 1995. (Originally published 1992.)

DeBlanc, Jeff, 1st Lt., USMC. "Point of No Return." In *Aces Against Japan: The American Aces Speak*, edited by Eric Hammel, 92–103. New York: Pocket Books, 1995. (Originally published 1992.)

Gresham, John D. "Ordnance: Douglas SBD." In *WWII History*, edited by Brooke C. Stoddard, 12–17. Reston, VA.: Sovereign Media, 2002.

Holloway, Don. "Cactus Air Force: A Thorn in Japan's Side." In *WWII Air War: The Men, the Machines, the Missions*, edited by Roger L. Vance, 126–135. Leesburg, VA: Cowles Enthusiast Media/Creative Publishing, 1996.

Izawa, Yasuho. "The Fighting Floatplanes of the Imperial Japanese Navy." *Air Enthusiast Magazine* 31 (1986): 7–18.

Mann, Tom, 2nd Lt., USMC. "So Far ... A Pilot's Dream." In *Aces Against Japan: The American Aces Speak*, edited by Eric Hammel, 81–85. New York: Pocket Books, 1995. (Originally published 1992.)

Margry, Karel. "Guadalcanal." *After the Battle*, no.108 (2006): 2–28.

Paschall, Rod. "A Fateful Six Minutes." In *Battle of Midway: Special Collector's Edition*, edited by C. J. Anderson, 74–80. Leesburg, VA: Primedia, 2002.

Prados, John. "U.S. Intelligence and the Japanese Evacuation of Guadalcanal, 1943." *Intelligence and National Security* 10, no. 2 (1995): 294–305.

Pricer, Douglas. "Dante's Final Flight." *World War II*, 16, no. 5. (2002): 50–56.

Scutts, Jerry. "Avenger!" In *WWII Air War: The Men, The Machines, The Missions*, edited by Roger L. Vance, 82–92. Leesburg, VA: Cowles Enthusiast Media/Creative Publishing, 1996.

Swett, Jim, 1st Lt., USMC. "Seven and Down." In *Aces Against Japan: The American Aces Speak*, edited by Eric Hammel. New York: Pocket Books, 1995, 104–110. (Originally published 1992.)

Tillman, Barrett. "P-38." *Pacific Fighters*, Winter 2003, 22–29.

Tuleja, Thaddeus V. "The Miracle of Midway." In *Battle of Midway: Special Collector's Edition*, edited by C. L. Anderson, 10–16, 82–89. Leesburg, VA: Primedia, 2002.

Wesolowski, John, Ens., USN. "Snap Shot." In *Aces Against Japan: The American Aces Speak*, edited by Eric Hammel, 70–75. New York: Pocket Books, 1995. (Originally published 1992.)

Internet Sources

NOTE: The following websites were all accessible as of 30 Jun. 2011.

6th Kure Special Naval Landing Force. "War Diary." In website Japan Center for Asian Historical Records. http://www.jacar.go.jp

Advanced Japanese Destroyers of WWII. http://www.friesian.com/destroy.htm

"Aichi E13A." In website WWII Imperial Japanese Navy Page. http://www.combinedfleet.com/ijna/e13a.htm

Air Force History Support Office. U.S. Army Air Forces in World War II: Combat Chronology. In website Air Force History. http://www.airforcehistory.hq.af.mil/PopTopics/chron/42dec.htm and www.airforcehistory.hq.af.mil/PopTopics/chron/ 43jan.htm

Alexander, Paul D. "Mitsubishi F1M (Pete)." In website WW II Tech: World War II History. http://www.net/main/japan/F1M/index.html

Alexander, Paul D. "Nakajima Ki-43 Hayabusa (Oscar)." In website WW II Tech: World War II History. http://www.net/main/japan/ki-43/index.html

"American Aces of World War II and Korea." In website Aerofiles. http://www.aerofiles.com/acesww2.html

American Aces of WW II. http://www.acepilots.com

"American Combat Aircraft of World War II." In website Historycentral.com.

"B-26B 'Krejan' Serial Number 41–17550." In website PacificWrecks. http://pacificwrecks.com/aircraft/b-26/41–17550.html

"The Battle of Rennell Island: Setback in the Solomons." In website Historynet. http://www.historynet.com/magazines/world_war_2/3026046.html

Baugher, Joe. Joe Baugher's Hayabusa Files, Part I: Ki-43-1. http://www.warbirdforum.com/hayabusa.htm

"Bell Airacobra." In website RAAF Museum. http://www.raafmuseum.com

"Black Cats and PT Boats." In website The Black Cat PBYs. http://www.daveswarbirds.com/blackcat/historyp.htm

"Camouflage and Markings: Bell P-39 Airacobra in USAAF Service." In website IPMSStockholm.org. http://www.ipmsstockholm.org/magazine/2003/05/stuff_eng_profile_p39.htm

"Cats Are Night Creatures." In website The Black Cat PBYs. http://www.daveswarbirds.com/blackcat/history7.htm

Combat Reports (Kodochosho) for 204th, 252nd, 253rd, 582nd, 701st, 705th, 751st, 802nd, 851st, 958th Kokutai. In website Japan Center for Asian Historical Records. http://www.jacar.go.jp

Cressman, Robert J. "A Chronological History of the U.S. Navy in World War II, Vol V: January and Feb. 1943." In website Hyperwar: A History of the U.S. Navy in World War II. http://www.ibiblio.org/hyperwar/USN/index.html

Dailey, Foster, USS *DeHaven* Sailors Association. *Pacific Battle Line.* New York: MacMillan Co. 1944. Excerpt in website USS *DeHaven* Sailors Association http://www.ussdehaven.org

"Dramatic Rescue off Choiseul." In website PacificWrecks. http://www.pacificwrecks.com/history/mavis_rescue

Dunn, Richard L. Nakajima Ki-43-1 Armament—A Reassessment (Abstract). http://www.j-aircraft.com/research/rdunn/Nakajima_ki43arm.htm

"Early Operations." In website The Black Cat PBYs. http://www.daveswarbirds.com/blackcat/history.htm

Eighth Fleet, IJN. "War Diary." In website Japan Center for Asian Historical Records. http://www.jacar.go.jp

Elam, Leonard. "469 Survivor." In website USS *DeHaven* Sailors Association. http://www.ussdehaven.org/elam.htm

Grinnell, Roy. "American Fighter Aces: Series 1." In website Zero Fighter Sweep. http://www.airartnw.com/zerofighter.htm

"G3M Nell." In website Realism Counts. http://geocities.ws/realismcounts/G3m.html

Hackett, Bob, Sander Kingsepp and Peter Cundall, with Erich Muehlthaler. "Fusetsukan." http://combinedfleet.com/Fusetsukan.html

Hackett, Bob, and Sander Kingsepp. "Junyokan." http://www.combinedfleet.com//Junyokan.htm

Hackett, Bob, Sander Kingsepp, and Peter Cundall. "Kokui Umpansen!" http://www.combinedfleet.com//Keiyo_t.htm

Hackett, Bob, Sandar Kingsepp, and Peter Cundall. "Kusentai!" http://www.combinedfleet.com/CH-23_t.htm

Hackett, Bob, Sander Kingsepp, Allan Alsleben, and Peter Cundall. "Tokusetsu Suijoki-Bakan!" http://www.combined fleet.com/Suijoki-Bokan!.htm

Herr, Ernest A. "The Last Day of the USS *DeHaven*." In website Combat Stories of World War II. http://bellsouthpwp2.net/e/a/ea_herr/dehaven_.htm

History of the 69th Bombardment Squadron (M). http://www.b26.com/page/historyofthe69thbombardmentsquadron.htm

Jacobsen, Phillipp H. The Battle of Rennell Island. http://microworks.net/pacific/battles/rennell_island.htm

"Japan." In website East Asian/Pacific Area Minor Air Forces. http://world.std.com/~Ted7/minorafp.htm

"Japanese Aces." In website World War II Vehicles. http://www.wwiivehicles.com/japan/aircraft/aces.asp

"Kawanishi H6K." In website WWII Imperial Japanese Naval Aviation Page. http://www.combinedfleet.com/ijna/h6k.htm

"Kawanishi H8K." In website WWII Imperial Japanese Naval Aviation Page. http://www.combinedfleet.com/ijna/h8k.htm

"Ki-43-1, Manufacturer's Number 572." In website PacificWrecks. http://www.pacificwrecks.com/aircraft/ki-43/572/index.html

"Ki-46 Army type 100 (Dinah)." In website PacificWrecks. http://www.pacific-wrecks.com/resources/tech/aircraft/dinah.html

"Kawasaki Ki-48 Lily." In website Imperial Japanese Aviation Resource Center. http://www.warbirdsresourcegroup.org

King, Fleet Adm. Ernest J., USN. "U.S. Navy at War 1941–1945: Official Reports by Fleet Admiral Ernest J. King, USN." In website Hyperwar: A History of the U.S. Navy in World War II. http://www.ibiblio.org/hyperwar/USN/USNat-War/index.html

"Lockheed Hudson Mark III." In website Air-Navy: Naval Aircraft. http://www.home.att.net/-jbaugher4/a28_6.html

Magnus, A. Air Aces. http://users.accesscomm.ca/magnusfamily/airaces1.htm

McFadyen, Michael. "*Toa Maru No. 2*." In Michael McFadyen's Scuba Diving website. http://www.michaelmcfadyenscuba.info/viewpage.php?page_id=390

Mitsubishi G3M Nell. http://www.aviastar.org/air/japan/Mitsubishi_g3m.php

"Mitsubishi Ki-46 Dinah." In website Military History Encyclopedia on the Web. http://www.historyofwar.org/articles/weapons_Mitsubishi_ki-46.html

"Munda Airfield: Captured Japanese Aircraft." In website PacificWrecks. http://www.pacificwrecks.com/60th/1943/1-43.html#26

Munda Base. "Detailed Engagement Report and Wartime Log Book, From Dec. 1942 to Feb. 1943." In website Japan Center for Asian Historical Records. http://www.jacar.go.jp

Nevitt, Allyn D. Long Lancers. http://www.combinedfleet.com/lancers.htm

"Nicholas II: DD449." In website Navy History. http://www.multied.com/Navy/destroyer/NicholasIIdd449.html

Office of Asst. Chief of Staff, Intelligence, USAAF HQ. "Pacific Counterblow: The 11th Bombardment Group and the 67th Fighter Squadron in the Battle for Guadalcanal." In website USAAF in WWII. (Original pamphlet published during WWII.) http://www.usaaf.net/ww/vol3/index.htm

Office of Naval Intelligence, U.S. Navy HQ. "Untitled Narrative of B-17 #41–2524 (Capt. Jay Thomas), Feb. 1 1943." In website Hyperwar: A History of the U.S. Navy in WWII. http://www.ibiblio.org/hyperwar/USN/USN-CN-Solomons/USN-CN-Solomons-17.html

Payne, Lt. H. G. Jr., USMC. "Rescued Pilots Intelligence: Interview with Lt. H. J. Murphy, USMC." In website Australian War Memorial. http://www.awm.gov.au

"Rennell Island: January 29–30 1943." In website USS *Enterprise*: CV-6. http://www.cv6.org/1943/rennell/default.htm

Rickard, J. 23 May 2008. *Lockheed Hudson Mk.III*. http://www.historyofwar.org/articles/weapons_lockheed_hudson_III.htm

Royal Australian Navy. "Report on Coast Watching Station PWD." In website Australian War Memorial. http://www.awm.gov.au

"Shortland Island." In website PacificWrecks. http://www.pacificwrecks.com
Tulle, Anthony P. *Kido Butai*. http://www.combinedfleet.com/cvlist.htm
USAAF HQ, G-2. In "Pacific Counterblow." In website Guadalcanal Air War at USD History Server. http://www.history.acusd.edu/gen/ww2text/wwtoo4o
U.S. Strategic Bombing Survey (Pacific). "Interrogation of Lt. Cdr. S. Yunoki, IJN." In website Hyperwar: A Hypertext History of the Second World War. http://www.ibiblio.org/hyperwar/AAF/USSBS/IJO/IJO-46.html
U.S. Strategic Bombing Survey (Pacific). "Interrogation of Cdr. Yasumi Doi, IJN." In website Hyperwar: A Hypertext History of the Second World War. http://www.ibiblio.org/hyperwar/AAF/USSBS/IJO/IJO-52.html
USS *DeHaven* (DD469). http://www.destroyerhistory.org/fletcherclass/ussdehaven
VMF-112. http://marines.centreconnect.org/vmf112/index.html
War Diaries for *Kamikawa Maru, Kunikawa Maru, Sanyo Maru*. In website Japan Center for Asian Historical Records. http://www.jacar.go.jp
War Diary for Munda. In website Japan Center for Asian Historical Records. http://www.jacar.go.jp
War Diary for *Zuikaku Hikokitai*. In website Japan Center for Asian Historical Records. http://www.jacar.go.jp
WWII Aces of the Imperial Japanese Army Air Force. http://www.billybishop.net/jaaf.html
Wukovits, John. "Battle of Rennell Island: Setback in the Solomons." In website Historynet.com. http://www.historynet.com/battle-of-rennell-island-setback-in-the-solomons.htm

INDEX

Achilles (New Zealand), 79
Ackerman, Ralph, 93–94
aerial gunnery, 14, 45–46
Agano (Japan), 248
Ainsworth, Waldon, 76, 77, 93, 95, 96, 290
air-combat doctrine and tactics: American, 14, 27–28; Chung-king method, 13; corkscrew dive maneuver, 28; deflection shooting, 45–46; Japanese, 13–15; Lufbury circle, 105; night attacks, 279–80; overhead pass maneuver, 27, 131; *rotte* system, 14; scissoring maneuver, 27–28; shadow gunnery, 46; Thach weave maneuver, 27, 35, 134
air supremacy, 281–82, 292
Airacobra fighter aircraft (P-39), 28–30, 281
aircraft availability: American, 261–63; Japanese, 272–74
aircraft carriers: American, 25–26, 228–29, 249; Japanese, 247–48, 272
aircraft communications, 267–69
aircraft maintenance personnel, 263–65
aircraft misidentification, 3–4
aircraft weapons and delivery systems, 280–81
airfields: intermediate, Japanese, 56–57; in support of Tokyo Express runs, 55–56. *See also* base-suppression campaign; *specific airfields*
Akigumo (Japan), 197, 228, 250
Akizuki-class destroyer, 199–200

Akizuki (Japan), 107, 108, 109, 113, 114, 117, 143
Altamaha, 35
Ames, Roger, 113
Anderson, Jim, 132, 134, 180
antishipping campaign, 2, 81, 86, 165, 283; effectiveness of, 277–78; misuse of bombers in, 284–85
Arashi (Japan), 101, 107, 108, 113, 114, 115, 117
Arashio (Japan), 98, 101, 197, 212, 228, 250
Asagumo (Japan), 228, 250
assault purpose destroyer (APD), 176
Atago (Japan), 24, 248
Avenger bomber (TBF-1), 35–36
aviators: characteristics of aces, 125; chute strafing by, 137–38; combat fatigue and, 258–61; combat shirkers, 49–50; mechanical knowledge of, 265–67; overclaiming by, 282; proficiency of Japanese, 274–76; shortage of, 47, 258–59; tropical illnesses and, 50–51. *See also* training and readiness
Ayers, Bob, 201, 252
Azusa Maru (Japan), 70

Bade, Jack, 151, 222, 238
Baesler, Blaine, 61
Baisen Island, 143
Baker, Dick, 43, 53, 279
Ballale Island airfield, 55, 88, 91
Baran, Walter, 112, 180, 182

361

Barber, Rex, 68–69
Barr, Hoyle, 201, 239
base-suppression campaign, 2, 81, 228, 265; impact on Operation KE, 228, 283–85; Japanese, of Henderson, 206, 211, 241–42. *See also specific airfields*
Bate, Oscar, 119, 121
Battle of Midway, 5, 27
Battle of Rennell Island, 156, 196, 272, 279
Battle of the Coral Sea, 6, 27
Bauer, Bob, 202–3
Bauer, Harold "Indian Joe," 27–28, 105, 281
Bechtel, Paul, 62, 63, 70, 72
Beebe, John, 178, 200, 231, 252
Berteling, Klas "Jack," 180, 181
Betty torpedo bomber (G4M), 17
Bezner, Ray, 126, 136, 236, 256
Black Cat patrol aircraft (PBY-5A), 40
Blackburn, Tom, 259
Blackmun, Arvid, 198, 201, 239, 240, 253
Blain, Dick, 198, 200, 223, 226, 238, 239
Blair, John, 240–41
Blotnick, Joe, 142
bomber aircraft: heavy, 36–39; Japanese, 16–18; light, 34–36; misuse in anti-shipping role, 284–85
Bonis airfield, 122
Boniske, Israel, 201
Brannon, Dale, 31, 33, 45, 46
Briscoe, Robert, 183, 208, 242
Brorein, Carl, 200, 239, 254
Brown, George, 204
Bruder, John, 203
Brunton, Charles, 36, 221, 224, 244
Bryson, Bill, 154
Buin-Faisi airfields, 55, 86
Buka airfield, 55, 122, 126

Cactus Air Force: aircraft availability, 261–63; command structure, 51–53; composition of, 25–26; daily reconnaissance flights, 64–65, 256; fighter strength of, 33–34, 41–42; maintenance personnel shortage, 263–65; misallocation of assets by, 285–86; USN squadron, 205, 213, 215–16, 223. *See also* Henderson Field
Cactus Crystal Ball, 149
Cactus flight controllers, 151–52
Cactus Striking Force, 207–8, 212, 242
Calhoun, Otis, 200, 231
Calvert, Alan, 101, 108, 208, 209, 242
Campbell, Bill "Soupy," 44, 104, 105
Cannon, Joe, 106
Carl, Marion, 28
Carter, Irwin, 61, 67, 74, 80
Carter, Mike, 145, 238
Catalina PBY flying boat, 39–40
Ch-17 (Japan), 141, 143, 145, 277
Ch-26 (Japan), 98
Ch-30 (Japan), 165, 167, 173, 217
Chaplin, Gerry, 204
Chenango, 148
Chennault, Claire, 26
Chicago, 150, 152, 153, 249, 274, 279; sinking of, 154–55, 156
Childress, Oren, 203
China, 13
Chokai (Japan), 10, 24, 249
Christian, Wayne, 154
chute strafing, 137–38
Claggett, John, 109, 209
Clemens, Martin, 6
coastwatchers, 57, 61, 83, 122, 143, 147, 150, 151, 165, 180
Cobra. *See* Airacobra fighter aircraft (P-39)
Coleman, Harry, 69
ComAirSoPac, 141, 165, 283
combat air patrol protection, 273–74
combat fatigue, 258–61, 264
Conger, Jack, 282
Copahee, 35
Cramer, Stan, 188, 236
Crum, Youell "Joe," 74
Csaky, Andy, 201, 237, 252

Index ★ 363

Daggitt, Bill, 68–69
Dalton, Dean "Snuffy," 203, 204
Dauntless dive-bomber (SBD-4), 34–35
Dean, Bill, 203, 204
DeBlanc, Jeff, 166–67, 169, 170–73, 282
Debnekoff, Basil, 162, 245
DeFries (VMF-121), 263, 266
DeHaven, 93, 96, 183, 184–87, 190, 191, 198, 249, 274, 277
destroyers, Japanese, 162, 176, 196–97, 199–200, 245, 276–77
Dinah reconnaissance aircraft (Ki-46), 18, 22
Dinn, Wally, 68, 86, 262
disease and illnesses, 50–51
DiTiberio, Emmanuel, 203
dive-bombers: American, 34–36; Japanese, 16
Dunbar, Harvey, 85

Emerson, Alberto "Al," 225
Emily flying boat (H8K), 18
Enterprise, 42, 148, 152, 154

Faulkner, Clark, 102, 210
Feliton (staff sergeant), 167, 169, 170, 171, 172, 173
Fiedler, Bill, 128–29, 233
Fitch, Aubrey, 92, 93, 141, 283, 285
Fletcher, 77, 183, 208
floatplanes, 15–16, 21, 279
flying boats, 18
Flying Fortress bomber (B-17), 36–38; misuse in antishipping role, 284–85; shortage of, 37–38; tactics in South Pacific, 193
Foeller, Jack, 74
Fore, Bob, 201, 231
Foss, Joe, 28, 60, 106, 107, 110, 118, 120, 121, 124–25, 127, 282
Fraser, Bob, 145, 158–59, 180, 188
Freeman, Bill "B," 79, 80
Fumizuki (Japan), 197, 205, 216, 228, 250

Gamble, Les, 109, 209
Gardner, Harvey "Fateye," 67
Giffin, Richard, 148, 149
Gifford, Jack, 79, 80
Giyu Maru (Japan), 92, 114, 118
Gough, Bob, 204
Greyback, 78
Griffith, Bill, 223
Grouper, 129
Guadalcanal campaign: aircraft misidentification in, 3–4; Japanese airbase construction in, 6–7; Japanese decision to evacuate and, 9; U.S. "sitzkrieg" posture in, 2; U.S. strategy for, 243
Guadalcanal Reinforcement Unit, 9–10, 72, 75, 108, 142

Haberman, Roger, 121
Hackett, Henry, 259, 260
Haguro (Japan), 248
Hakaze (Japan), 57
Hall, Earl, 192, 193, 194, 195
Halsey, William, 42, 76, 92, 147–48, 228, 242, 248, 249, 258, 271, 272
Hamakaze (Japan), 107, 113, 114, 197, 228, 250, 253, 255, 257
Hamp fighter aircraft (A6M3), 11, 12, 56
Hansen, Paul, 46, 133, 139, 258, 262
Haruna (Japan), 24
Hashimoto, Shintaro, 10, 24, 142, 143, 162, 175, 180, 196, 200, 205, 212, 228, 229, 239, 250, 253, 278
Hatsukaze (Japan), 101, 102, 103
Hawkes, Amos, 201
Hayter, Bill, 142, 167, 215
Hearn, Alex "Sandy," 67, 68
Helena, 77, 79, 80, 93, 95, 97
Henderson Field, 7, 38, 110, 121, 147, 198; air attacks on, 16–17, 110, 130, 156–57, 179–80; Japanese observation of, 60; massed daylight raid against, 122–27; naval bombardment of, 37;

"Tojo time" at, 184. *See also* Cactus
    Air Force
Hendrix, Phil, 117
Hensley, Harold, 195
Hidaka, Hatsuo, 19, 91, 123, 147, 257
Hiyodori (Japan), 91, 99, 116, 117, 120,
    165, 167, 173
Hollandsworth, Keith, 233–34
Holmes, Besby, 86, 87, 90, 126, 128, 136,
    162, 188, 218
Honolulu, 79, 93
Hopp, Herb, 234–35
Hornet, 249
Horton, Dick, 58, 83, 94, 130, 161, 198,
    241, 255, 288
Houx, Frank, 194
Hubbell, Bob, 87, 88, 89, 90, 128, 133
Hudson medium patrol bomber
    (MkIII), 39, 40–41
Huey, Wellman, 256
Huff, Lloyd, 89, 91, 116, 117, 261
Hughes, Tom, 168, 169, 171
Hulme, John, 232
Hyakutake, Harukichi, 8, 175, 228

I-9 (Japan), 96
IJA Directive 184, 107
Imamura, Bunzaburo, 150, 183
Imamura, Hitoshi, 1–2, 8, 9
Inciardi, Nilo, 232, 233, 243
Isokaze (Japan), 98, 107, 113, 114, 197,
    228, 250, 253, 254, 255
Iwami Maru (Japan), 66
Izumi Maru (Japan), 66

Jacobson, Julius "Jake," 65, 143–44, 163,
    222, 236
Jake patrol floatplane (E13A), 16, 21, 56
Japanese Advance Force, 247–48
Japanese Army Air Force, 8; aircraft in
    Operation KE, 22–24; pilot training,
    48–49
Japanese cipher codes, 10, 141

Japanese Navy: destroyers' role in Tokyo
    Express, 72–73; pilot shortage, 47; pi-
    lot training, 46–47
Japanese observation post network, 60
Japanese 17th Army, 7, 8, 9, 107, 143,
    156, 183, 228, 242, 247, 256, 257, 276,
    292–93
Japanese 8th Combined Special Naval
    Landing Force, 165
Japanese Destroyer Squadron 2, 72
Japanese 4th Engineer Detachment, 93
Japanese 76th Independent Chutai, 22, 130
Japanese 11th Koku Kantai, 8, 11, 46–47,
    115, 156, 161, 272, 275, 279
Japanese 204th Kokutai, 11, 19, 47, 51,
    70, 72, 73, 74, 79, 80, 83, 86, 87, 89, 93,
    94, 101, 103, 104, 106, 111, 113, 114,
    118, 121, 126, 127–28, 147, 151, 176,
    193, 194, 214, 227, 240, 241, 246, 255,
    256, 257, 275, 289
Japanese 252nd Kokutai, 11, 19, 20, 60,
    65, 111, 114, 115, 117, 118, 121, 123,
    127, 129, 194, 200, 205, 218, 242
Japanese 253rd Kokutai, 11, 19, 123, 124,
    126, 127, 128, 194, 197, 219, 223, 242,
    246, 250
Japanese 582nd Kokutai, 11, 19–20, 65,
    79, 80, 83, 89, 123, 144, 145, 184, 189,
    190, 194, 216, 228, 229, 254, 255, 289
Japanese 701st Kokutai, 22, 150, 156,
    206, 221, 241, 279
Japanese 705th Kokutai, 22, 94, 96, 97,
    122, 149, 156, 245, 247, 279
Japanese 751st Kokutai, 22, 97, 121, 130,
    148, 154, 155, 156, 157, 206
Japanese 802nd Kokutai, 18, 21, 86, 88,
    217
Japanese 851st Kokutai, 18, 96, 222
Japanese 956th Kokutai, 21, 79
Japanese 958th Kokutai, 21, 85, 92, 93,
    114, 118, 165, 242
Japanese 6th Kure Special Naval Landing
    Force, 141

Japanese 8th Mountain-gun Company, 38th Howitzer Regiment, 107
Japanese 6th Sasebo Rikusentai, 57
Japanese 11th Seaplane Tender Division, 86, 115, 253
Japanese 1st Sentai, 22, 23, 111, 130, 134, 139
Japanese 11th Sentai, 22–23, 48–49, 111, 130, 131, 132, 135, 138, 172, 180, 228, 231, 236, 241, 252, 254, 276
Japanese 45th Sentai, 96, 130, 134, 158
Japanese 6th Shidan, 12, 113, 130, 141, 179–80, 256, 272
Jintsu (Japan), 24
Johnson, Albert, 146, 151, 192, 222, 224, 237
Josslyn, Henry, 57, 150, 151, 197
Julien, Leon, 198, 203–4
Junyo (Japan), 24, 248, 272

Kahili airfield, 55, 88, 184
Kaku Maru (Japan), 91
Kamikawa Maru (Japan), 16, 21, 96, 108, 117, 118, 141, 142, 165, 193
Kanagawa Maru (Japan), 193
Kawakaze (Japan), 101, 102, 143, 197, 209, 228, 239, 253, 257
Kazagumo (Japan), 197, 228, 250
Keenan, John, 57, 94, 150, 151, 153–54, 161, 162, 164, 177, 180, 288
Keiyo Maru (Japan), 217
Kelley-Turner, Richmond, 176
Kennedy, Bob, 90, 91, 117
Kennedy, Donald, 57, 66, 101, 130, 198, 235
Kersteder, Bob, 256
Ki-43 Hayabusa fighter. *See* Oscar fighter aircraft
Kimura, Susumu, 108, 109–10, 114, 142, 143
Kimura, Toshio, 168, 169, 170, 172
King, Ernest, 6, 7
Kirk, Ken, 62, 63

Kiwi (New Zealand), 102
Koenig, Richard, 257
Kofukuda, Mitsuga, 19, 257
Kondo, Keizo, 69, 225
Kondo, Nobutake, 24, 148, 247, 248, 249, 272
Kongo (Japan), 24
Kosaka, Magoichi, 65–66
Koyanagi, Tomiji, 9, 72, 73, 75, 101, 103, 108, 142
Kumano (Japan), 10, 24, 249
Kunikawa Maru (Japan), 16, 21, 95, 114, 117, 165
Kuroshio (Japan), 101, 107, 114, 117, 143, 197, 228, 250
Kusaka, Jinichi, 8, 9, 10, 175, 183, 218, 228, 247, 250

Laird, Wayne, 189
Lanphier, Tom, 63, 67, 71
LaVellette, 154–55
League of Nations, 43
Leeds, Phil, 94
Leon, Abe, 203
Liberator bomber (B-24), 39, 41
Lightning fighter aircraft (P-38): combat tactics, 33; F5A version of, 250; poor performance of, 86–88, 136, 281; specifications, 31–32
Lily bomber aircraft (Ki-48), 17–18
Loban, Glen, 94, 112, 154
Loesch, Greg, 79, 117, 124, 125, 127
Long, Herb, 104, 105, 111, 112, 282
Louisville, 80
Lundin, Bill, 112–13
Lynch, Joe, 89, 132, 139, 167, 169, 171, 172, 282

Maas, Jack, 25, 168, 171
Maguire, Jim, 142, 179, 203, 205
Maikaze (Japan), 107, 113, 114, 115, 197, 228, 236
Main, Charlton "Bud," 146, 167, 173, 215

Makigumo (Japan), 197, 210, 214, 216, 277
Makinami (Japan), 101, 197, 200, 201, 205
Malcolm, Jack, 198, 201
Marauder attack bomber (B-26), 38–39, 81
Marontate, Bill, 79, 119, 121
Marshall, George, 6, 7
Mason, Paul, 123
Matson, H. "Mat," 145
Mavis flying boat (H6K), 18
Maytag Mike raids, 62, 97, 110, 121, 206, 225
McCarroll, W.H., 47, 194, 196, 275
McCartney, Allan "Hank," 44, 124, 134, 154, 180–81
McCormick, Harlan, 52
McGlothlin, Joe, 61
McKulla, Larry, 128, 129
McMahon, John, 105
McNeese, George, 64, 67, 68
McShane, Barney, 146, 179, 203
Mikage Maru (Japan), 141, 142
Millington, Bill, 266
mine warfare, 207–8
Mitchell, John "Mitch," 33, 68, 87, 89, 132, 133, 137, 158, 159, 162, 192, 213, 217, 282
Miyamoto, Taisaku, 170, 171, 172
Miyano, Zenjiro, 14, 19, 74, 118, 119, 120, 121, 123, 147
Mochizuki (Japan), 85
Molvik, Arthur "Art," 144, 179
Montgomery, Bob, 198
Moore, Bill, 177
Moore, Jack, 112, 113
Moran, Art, 201, 239, 252
Moran, John, 145, 189–90
Moravec, Joe, 80
Morisaki, Takeshi, 90, 123, 147, 194, 240
Morrisey, R., 152, 218
Moss, Abram, 178
motor torpedo boats, 75
Mueller, Elton, 105, 112, 131
Mulcahy, Francis, 34, 51, 52, 53, 220, 229, 283, 285

Munda airfield, 61–64, 66, 76, 77–79, 81–83, 92–93, 161, 177, 222, 224–25, 256; construction of, 57–59; as principal focus of attack, 283–85; in success of Operation KE, 286–90; unescorted hit-and-run strike on, 150–51
Murphy, "Howie," 177, 178, 200
Murphy, Jim, 232, 234
Musashi (Japan), 24, 271
Myoko (Japan), 248

Naganami (Japan), 101
Nagara (Japan), 24, 248
Nagatsuki (Japan), 197, 209, 228, 236, 250
Nakajima, Bunkichi, 19, 65–66
Nakajima, Mitsunori, 126–27
Nashville, 77, 78, 79, 93, 95
Nasif, George, 146, 167, 179
Nassau, 35
Nautilus, 143
Navajo, 152, 155
Nell attack bomber (G3M), 17
Nelson, Eystein, 238, 239, 253
New Zealand No. 3 Squadron, 40–41, 64, 103, 110, 128, 197, 213, 229, 243, 245, 288, 289
Nicholas, 93, 95, 182, 183, 185, 186, 187, 191, 208, 242
Nichols, Cyril, 98, 99, 113, 163
Nimitz, Chester, 7, 42, 147, 248, 249, 271, 272
Norris, Emmett, 86, 87, 90
Noshiro Maru (Japan), 98
Notomi, Kenjiro, 184, 230

O'Bannon, 77, 93, 95
Ohara, Ryoji, 19, 147, 194, 240
oil supply lines, 5–6
Operation I-GO, 291
Operation KE-GO, 265; air units assigned to, 18–20, 22–24; aircraft availability, 272–74; alternative plan

for, 143; approval of plan for, 9; asset deployment in, 271–72; aviator proficiency as factor in, 274–76; Cactus impact on initial sorties, 142–43; combatant loses in, 1, 292; destroyers in, 162, 176, 196–97, 199–200, 245, 276–77; diversionary initiatives, 10; official ending of, 257; options for, 107; planning for USN response to, 247–48; rearguard reinforcements for, 107–10, 111f; routing and scheduling in, 278–80; U.S. amphibious landing to counter, 175, 180, 183; vessels assigned to, 9–10, 24. *See also* Tokyo Express runs
Operation MI-GO, 5
Operation Watchtower, 7
Oscar fighter aircraft (Ki-43), 12–13, 22, 23, 56, 83
Oshio (Japan), 93, 101, 197, 228, 250
Ostrom, Charles "Whitey," 205, 213, 282
Otori (Japan), 91
Ozeki, Yukiharu, 19, 194

Palmer, Stan, 31, 88, 89, 262
parachute strafing, 137–38
Patch, Alexander, 8, 175, 180
patrol aircraft, allied, 39–41
Pearl Harbor attack, 5
Percy, Gil, 162, 163, 188, 189
Pete floatplane (FiM2), 16, 21, 56
Peters, Herb, 123–24
Peterson, Bob "Pete," 74
Petit, Robert, 71
Pierce, Frank, 105, 119
Pierce, Tom, 112
Ploetz, Fred, 90
Presley, Frank "Skeezix," 79, 121
PT boat, 75
PT-36, 210–11
PT-37, 109, 209, 210, 211
PT-38, 211
PT-40, 102

PT-43, 101–2
PT-45, 109
PT-48, 209
PT-59, 209
PT-109, 210–11, 211
PT-111, 209, 211
PT-112, 101, 102
PT-115, 209, 211
PT-123, 210, 211
PT-124, 209, 210
Pugh, Edward, 51–52, 225
Purnell, Fred, 90–91, 137, 138, 188, 202, 236

R Homen Koku Butai, 15–16, 21
Rabaul base, 1, 5, 10, 59, 265, 291
Raber, Addison, 162, 163, 189
Radford, 93, 96, 97, 182, 183, 208
radio communications, 267–69
Read, John "Jack," 122, 252
Reed, Dick, 177
Reinburg, Hunter, 65, 71, 80, 83, 104, 105, 111, 112, 131–32, 139
Rekata Bay seaplane base, 83–85, 213
Renner, Joe, 13, 44, 49, 50, 52, 53, 94, 111, 112, 201, 259, 264, 274, 279–80
Richards, Ralph, 210
Richards, Sam, 188, 189
Ridings, Don, 37
Rist, Bob, 236, 238
Robertson, Bill, 231
Robinson, Jim, 82, 155, 156, 213, 232, 233, 243, 257
Robinson, Robbie, 147
Roush, Marty, 167, 215, 280
Rufe floatplane (A6M2-N), 15, 21
Russell, Don, 200
Russell Islands garrison, 143, 147

Sabatier, Henry "Hank," 124, 142
Sabel, Bill, 99
Saito, Saburo, 136, 189, 230, 241, 255
Samidare (Japan), 228, 250

Samuel Gompers, 249
Sanders, Warren, 74
Sanyo Maru (Japan), 16, 21, 75, 108, 118, 166
Saratoga, 42, 45, 92, 94, 97, 148
Sasakibara, Maseo, 20, 230, 232–33, 241
Satsuki (Japan), 197, 228, 250
Saunders, "Blondie," 262
Sawyer, Jerry, 185, 188, 202, 216, 220, 222
Scott, Jesse Jr., 233, 235
Searles, Bob, 211
Secrest, Jim, 166–67, 169, 170
Seifert, Otto, 189
Sendai (Japan), 24
Seton, Carden, 197, 234
Shaw, Bill, 136, 137
Shaw, Dave, 65, 67, 73, 90–91
Shigemi, Katsuma, 20, 230, 241
Shimakawa, Masaaki, 19, 104, 106, 147
Shirayuki (Japan), 143, 197, 205, 228, 239, 250
Shiromoto, Naoharu, 23, 163, 164
Shortland-Tonolei harbor complex, 55, 114, 162, 192, 197, 217, 218; antishipping strikes on, 66, 86–88, 89–91, 193–95, 275
shotai air-combat doctrine, 13–14
Shroeder, Gerry, 204
Shubin, Murray, 90, 143–44, 188, 217, 218, 236, 256, 282
Smith, John, 28, 90
Smith, Marty, 117, 128
Smyth, Frank, 203
Sobel, Harry, 263
Solomon Islands fortification, 6
Sorenson, Bob, 238
Southeast Asia Co-prosperity Sphere, 5
Spencer, Ed, 239
Spurlock, Roy, 67, 68
St. Louis, 77, 79, 80, 93
Stack, John, 189
Stamp, Clyde, 74

Stringham, 176, 183
Strother, Dean, 52
submarines, 149, 184, 249
Sugita, Shoichi, 19, 74, 194
Suho, Motonari, 19, 60, 124, 127
Suwanee, 148
Suzukaze (Japan), 74
Swickard, Dayton, 198, 239, 253
Synar, Stan, 189

Takahashi, Takao, 23, 170, 171, 172–73
Takashima Maru (Japan), 66
Takeo (Japan), 248
Tanaka, Raizo, 9, 75
Tanikaze (Japan), 107, 113, 114, 143, 197, 228, 250
Tarbet, Dale, 137, 138, 217, 218
Task Force AFIRM, 76, 77–79, 83, 92, 94–96, 148
Task Force GEORGE, 180, 249; Japanese reconnaissance of, 148–49, 151; mission of, 148; sinking of Chicago, 154–55, 156, 279
Task Force LOVE ONE, 148
Task Force ROGER, 148
Task Force SUGAR, 148
Task Group TARE, 77
Taylor, Ken, 98, 99, 135, 188
Tefft, S., 233, 235
Teruzuki (Japan), 9, 199
Thach, John "Jimmy," 27
Thomas, Jay, 192, 195, 196
Thompson, John, 45
Thrasher, Dale, 239, 240
Tilden, Charles, 101, 102, 211
Toa Maru 2 (Japan), 93, 94, 95–96, 165, 166, 167, 168, 172, 225; sinking of, 173–74
Tokitsukaze (Japan), 101, 102, 107, 114, 117, 143, 197, 228, 250
Tokyo Express runs: advance screen for, 207; assessment of, 3–4; combat air patrols escorting, 56; destroyers' role

in, 72–73; final evacuation convoy, 250, 251f, 273; first evacuation convoy, 197, 199f, 212; first sortie, 101–7, 104f; rearguard reinforcements for, 107–10, 111f; second evacuation convoy, 228, 230f, 237f. *See also* Operation KE-GO

Tolman, Charles, 184, 186, 188

Topoll, George, 85

Toyota, Sandai, 94–95

training and readiness: acceleration prior to war, 43–44; Army Air Force aviators, 45–46; of combat shirkers, 49–50; Japanese aviators, 46–49, 274–76; Marine aviators, 44–45. *See also* aviators

Tsugaru (Japan), 85, 217

Tsukamoto, Yuzo, 67, 68, 114, 129

Tulagi Harbor seaplane base, 6

Tullis, Bob, 233

Twining, Nathan, 52

Tyler, Kermit, 126, 133, 134, 148, 163, 188, 202

Urakaze (Japan), 107, 108, 109, 110, 113, 114, 143, 197, 228, 250, 254, 255

U.S. Army Air Force training, 45–46

U.S. Marine fighter squadrons, 25–26; accelerated training for, 44–45

U.S. Navy: auxiliary aircraft carriers, 25–26; in bombardment of Munda airfield, 76, 77–79; squadrons at Cactus, 205, 213, 215–16, 223

U.S. 13th Air Force, 36, 39, 41–42, 52, 261, 285

U.S. 5th BG(H), 36, 37, 260, 284

U.S. 11th BG(H), 36, 37, 260, 284

U.S. 26th BS, 38, 91, 147, 217, 218, 248

U.S. 31st BS, 38, 192

U.S. 69th BS, 227, 260

U.S. 72nd BS, 115, 192, 217, 245

U.S. 431st BS, 73, 91

U.S. 23rd BS(H), 162, 245

U.S. 42nd BS(H), 38, 162, 192, 195

U.S. 98th BS(H), 66, 218

U.S. 69th BS(M), 39, 81, 83, 84

U.S. 70th BS(M), 39, 81, 82, 222, 227, 284

U.S. 347th FG, 33–34, 47, 85, 190, 213

U.S. 12th FS, 29, 30, 62, 113, 117

U.S. 44th FS, 81, 133, 134, 135, 142, 145, 151, 152, 162, 187–88, 198, 222, 223, 236

U.S. 67th FS, 29–30, 33, 45, 99, 152, 162, 185, 198, 216, 220, 222, 229, 262, 286

U.S. 68th FS, 29, 30, 31, 89, 97, 116, 128, 133, 142, 261

U.S. 69th FS, 151

U.S. 70th FS, 29, 30, 45, 68, 82, 98, 99, 151, 152, 213, 229, 257

U.S. 339th FS, 31, 33, 46, 65, 66, 69, 86, 97, 125, 132, 135, 139, 158, 162, 183, 187–88, 198, 213, 222, 236, 246, 256

U.S. 1st Marine Division, 7, 8

U.S. 17th Photographic Squadron (Light), 250

U.S. VF-72, 26, 225, 236, 238

U.S. VGS-11, 229

U.S. VGS-12, 229

U.S. VGS-16, 229

U.S. VMF-112, 25, 132, 143, 145, 158, 162, 163, 172, 182, 185, 188–89, 190, 198, 258

U.S. VMF-121, 25, 60, 65, 66, 69, 70, 71, 74, 77, 79, 80, 83, 104, 105, 106, 111, 113, 117, 124, 126, 131, 182

U.S. VMF-122, 25, 156, 264

U.S. VMF-123, 25, 53, 225, 260, 268

U.S. VMF-212, 45

U.S. VMF-214, 182

U.S. VMO-151, 44

U.S. VMO-251, 25, 44, 61, 69, 71, 81, 83, 94, 111, 112, 113, 123, 132, 153, 154, 162, 180, 182, 198, 261, 264

U.S. VMSB-131, 35, 36, 93, 94, 141, 143, 146, 167, 177, 178, 197, 198, 201, 204, 205, 213, 215, 220, 221, 223, 261, 277, 280
U.S. VMSB-132, 34
U.S. VMSB-141, 43–44
U.S. VMSB-142, 81–82, 111, 120, 143, 145, 265
U.S. VMSB-144, 244, 251, 253, 254, 255, 256, 261
U.S. VMSB-233, 34, 73–74, 81, 82, 93, 94, 104, 106, 143, 145, 167, 177, 213, 215, 220, 221, 229, 236, 237
U.S. VMSB 234, 229
U.S. VMSB-234, 34, 99, 177, 197, 198, 200, 205, 211, 212, 223, 224, 225, 229, 236, 239, 244, 251, 253, 255, 261, 280
U.S. VP-12, 77, 103, 108

Val dive-bomber aircraft (D3A), 16, 21
Vandergrift, Archer, 7
Vila-Stanmore airfield, 59, 59f, 81, 92, 96–98, 159, 163, 223; condition following TF AFIRM attack, 98–99; construction of, 91–92; postwar use of, 100; as principal focus of attack, 283–85; purpose of, 99, 290; TF AFIRM attack on, 94–96
Vroome, Ray, 124, 178

Waddell, Nick, 165, 197, 216, 234
Warhawk fighter aircraft (P-40), 26–28, 30–31
Warren, Joe, 167
Wasp, 249
Webb, Allen, 30–31, 88, 117, 258–59
Weiland, Pat, 67, 68, 71, 83, 138, 151–52, 268
Westbrook, Bob, 98, 99, 102, 135, 139, 188, 282

Westholm, Rollin, 101, 211
Wheadon, Elmer "Doc," 134, 139, 148, 188, 202, 204
Whitaker, Narce, 192, 217
White, Phil, 65, 70
Whitten, Sumner, 201, 231
Wickham, Harry, 58, 61, 62, 69, 83
Wickham anchorage barge base, 66, 70–71
Wilcox, George, 201
Wildcat fighter aircraft (F4F-4), 25, 26–28
Williams, I.J., 221
Williams, Ray, 243
Williamson, Warren, 232, 234
Winkle, Larry, 203
Wisner, Ben, 61
Wood, John, 218
Wood, Leighton, 210

Yamamoto, Isoroku, 5, 9, 24, 69, 148, 175, 218, 247, 271–72, 272, 291
Yamashimo Maru (Japan), 91–92, 117, 120
Yamato (Japan), 24, 271
Yost, Don, 60–61, 62, 63, 66, 70, 77, 126
Yugiri (Japan), 217
Yugumo (Japan), 197, 210, 214, 228, 250
Yukikaze (Japan), 197, 228, 250
Yunck, Mike, 132, 182, 188, 202

Zeke fighter aircraft (A6M2 and A6M3), 11, 12, 56
Zeroes: color variations in, 4; model variants, 11–12. *See also specific models*
Zielinski, Ed, 63, 105, 106, 287
Zuiho (Japan), 20, 24, 247, 248, 272
Zuikaku (Japan), 20, 24, 247, 248, 271, 272

ABOUT THE AUTHORS

Roger Letourneau is a retired businessman and former member of the Canadian armed forces. He earned an MA in history and an MBA.

Dennis Letourneau is a professional engineer who obtained his engineering degree from McGill University in Montreal, Quebec.

The Naval Institute Press is the book-publishing arm of the U.S. Naval Institute, a private, nonprofit, membership society for sea service professionals and others who share an interest in naval and maritime affairs. Established in 1873 at the U.S. Naval Academy in Annapolis, Maryland, where its offices remain today, the Naval Institute has members worldwide.

Members of the Naval Institute support the education programs of the society and receive the influential monthly magazine *Proceedings* or the colorful bimonthly magazine *Naval History* and discounts on fine nautical prints and on ship and aircraft photos. They also have access to the transcripts of the Institute's Oral History Program and get discounted admission to any of the Institute-sponsored seminars offered around the country.

The Naval Institute's book-publishing program, begun in 1898 with basic guides to naval practices, has broadened its scope to include books of more general interest. Now the Naval Institute Press publishes about seventy titles each year, ranging from how-to books on boating and navigation to battle histories, biographies, ship and aircraft guides, and novels. Institute members receive significant discounts on the Press' more than eight hundred books in print.

Full-time students are eligible for special half-price membership rates. Life memberships are also available.

For more information about Naval Institute Press books that are currently available, visit www.usni.org/press/books. To learn about joining the U.S. Naval Institute, please write to:

Member Services
U.S. Naval Institute
291 Wood Road
Annapolis, MD 21402-5034
Telephone: (800) 233-8764
Fax: (410) 571-1703
Web address: www.usni.org

One New Humanity takes a thorough and important look at a major blind spot in Western theology—namely, how a corporate perspective in the core salvation text of Ephesians 2:11–22 helps us appreciate the grace of God and our calling to be one. In doing so, it reveals that salvation and the call to be God's people have a broader scope than many realize. In most cases, the book avoids generalizations that plague how we see salvation. The book shows there is more to our faith than personal salvation. It helps us see that the work of God is more marvelous than many imagine.

Darrell L. Bock, PhD
Executive Director for Cultural Engagement and Senior Research Professor of New Testament Studies, Dallas Theological Seminary

Kristin's story about finding the weight of glory during her mom's accident hit me hard. That sense of glory being raw, heavy, and redemptive—not shiny or manageable—felt so honest. It reminded me of those moments in my own life when God's presence wasn't flashy but deeply comforting in the most challenging times. The reflections on Werner's German roots and the trauma passed down through generations also really struck me. Asking tough questions about complicity and violence isn't easy, but it is necessary. The vulnerability in those stories made the call to peace in Ephesians 2 feel even more urgent and real.

What I love most is how the book doesn't shy away from the messiness of life or faith. It's not about quick fixes or feel-good answers—it's about walking the hard road with Jesus toward a unity that can transform us and the world. This feels like such an important message for our time. It's clear this book isn't just words on a page—it's hope for what the church can be. I'm grateful to have had the chance to read it.

David H. Beyda, MD
Ethics Committee Member, Christian Medical and Dental Association
Author, *Border Crossings*

One New Humanity is a powerful and timely call for the church to rediscover its role as a reconciling presence in a divided world. Werner and Kristin offer profound insights into reconciliation, identity, and peace in the midst of both global and personal conflict. They effectively show how Christ's redemptive work forms a "new humanity" that confronts and dismantles systems of division, hostility, and shame. The result is a well-written, intellectually stimulating, and profoundly inspiring vision of restored glory, healed shame, and embodied peace. Love it!

Alan Hirsch
Founder, Movement Leaders Collective and Forge Missional Training Network
Award-winning author on missional spirituality, leadership, and organization

Oh, how readily we conform to the pattern of this world! As tribalism takes hold of global Christianity and separatist theologies threaten to create new apartheids, we are in desperate need of a transformative biblical theology of unity in diversity. Nothing stunts Christian maturity like individualism wrapped in homogeneity. *One New Humanity* reveals biblical roots able to nourish a healthier future for Jesus's bride—the global church—her local expressions, and her participation in God's purposes both locally and globally. In Christ, we are called to mutual submission, allowing the Holy Spirit to bring about relational harmony in the tensions of difference. This is our greatest witness to the world, and in *One New Humanity*, Caynor and Mischke reveal why.

JAY MATENGA, DIS
Executive Director, World Evangelical Alliance Mission Commission

One New Humanity is a profound exploration of human identity, glory, and peace through the lens of Ephesians 2. The authors, representing two different generations, bring unique depth to this oft-neglected theme. The diverse cultural backgrounds of the wide range of sources they draw from also lend significant credibility to their work. This book reminds us that the gospel is not just about saving sinners from sin but, more importantly, about God's greater plan to restore shalom to the world and humanity as he intended. This work is a timely resource as we seek to understand the transformative power of the gospel of peace in our fractured world.

I'CHING THOMAS
Associate International Director, Operation Mobilization

The authors have sought to bring principles of sociology, such as polarization, depolarization, and theology into dialogue. They assert that we are in a moment of crisis, not primarily one of ideology, thought, theology, or political power, but a crisis of glory—and therefore, a crisis of community and belonging. This work is Christ-centered, deals with brutal honestly about sin, and expresses the hope of God's shalom in light of the new humanity we have become, are becoming, and will fully be one day. In this book, you will find practical examples of both the failures of humankind and the breaking in of the glory of God in the new humanity.

DR. TIMOTHY A. VAN AARDE
Senior Pastor, Australind Baptist Church
WA and Associate, Faculty of Religion, University of Pretoria

This is much more than just another missions book. These pages comprise a seminal, in-depth, and thorough consideration of Ephesians 2:11–22 from important missiological and exegetical perspectives. Yet, its core message is practical in application as the two authors expertly weave current events and issues into what should entail the praxis of missions today, centered on "making peace" to forge "One New Humanity." Caynor and Mischke masterfully bring a comprehensive—and at times uncomfortable—exposure to the true application of this missional passage today.

MARVIN J. NEWELL, DMiss
Ambassador at Large, Missio Nexus
Author, *A Third of Us*

This remarkable book brings together deep biblical study with the fruits of both sociological analysis and contextualized fieldwork to offer a compelling case that reconciliation and peacemaking are at the very heart of the gospel. The pursuit of peace is not an optional vocation for some Christians but a baptismal calling for us all. It is a book I will be returning to again and again.

HELEN PAYNTER
Director, Center for the Study of Bible and Violence
Author, *Blessed Are the Peacemakers*

As a Palestinian Christian who has suffered from Christian racism and racial inequality due to misinterpretations of the Bible, reading this book gives me hope for a better future. I envision a time when my Jewish brothers and sisters in Christ and I will be treated as equals, united in the love of Jesus, who broke down the barriers of hatred that divided us. Thank you, Werner and Kristin, for writing *One New Humanity* at this crucial time—our world is in desperate need of the gospel of peace.

MAHER HADDAD
Palestinian American Author, Christian Media Producer,
and International Missionary

Kristin Caynor and Werner Mischke have written a beautiful book for all who long for peace in a broken world. Richly theological, practically missiological, and deeply personal, *One New Humanity* connects the dots between divine and human glory, and sin and violence, and it makes a compelling case for how peace is central to the good news of Jesus to which we bear witness in a broken world. Highly recommended!

AL TIZON, PhD
Affiliate Associate Professor of Missional and Global Leadership,
North Park Theological Seminary

One New Humanity is an essential book for us to read as we try to reaffirm God's glory in a world that has lost perspective of the divine and of the truth. If we are to understand and embody Christ's ministry of reconciliation, peace, and restoration in the context of all humanity, we must return to Scripture. Kristin and Werner have invested more than four years researching the subject and exploring it through exegesis, history, consultations, and engaging the global church. I highly recommend a thorough study of *One New Humanity* as our world enters a new era with all its changes—politically, culturally, technologically, and spiritually.

PAUL R. GUPTA, PhD
Chairman, Hindustan Bible Institute & College, Chennai, India

Werner and Kristin offer a prophetic voice for the church in our times of conflict and rage. With fresh eyes examining the teachings in Ephesians concerning the new humanity formed in Christ Jesus, they call us to pursue unity across all human barriers. Readers may agree or disagree with applications to current events or missiological practice, but that is the point, isn't it? We will never have uniformity in beliefs and opinions in the church, yet Christ calls us to unity that transcends individual and corporate humanity. *One New Humanity* builds a biblical foundation to stimulate spiritual motivation toward oneness in Christ.

YVONNE W. HUNEYCUTT, DMin
Global Teacher, Trainer, and Author with the
Perspectives on the World Christian Movement Course
Author, *Propelled by Hope*

One New Humanity delivers a theological gut-punch that moves readers to worship through tears and excitement. Exposing humanity's divinely given yet distorted drive for glory, Caynor and Mischke show how life in Christ radically reverses human shame, trauma, and violence. The vision of God's people being human as we are intended to be is compelling, convicting, and catalyzing.

CAMERON D. ARMSTRONG, PhD
Program Director, ThM/PhD Orality Studies,
Asia Graduate School of Theology, Philippines

This book focuses on Jesus himself as fulfilling Isaiah's prophecy, interpreted by Paul in Ephesians, that God's people would speak and become God's peace to peoples far from him. While I found a few points of disagreement, there is much to learn from the experience and exegesis of the authors.

STEVE HAWTHORNE
Editor, *Perspectives on the World Christian Movement*

In a world characterized by divisions, moral decline, and pervasive consumerism—where achieving unity and peace appears increasingly unattainable—Caynor and Mischke's *One New Humanity* emerges as a timely and essential contribution. It provides profound insights into God's plan of salvation, highlighting its universal inclusivity for people of all ethnicities and cultural backgrounds. Through a rigorous examination of Scripture and the application of compelling illustrations, the book elucidates how God establishes a "new humanity" in Christ, integrating them as members of his household. This new humanity exists in harmonious coexistence within the divine family, reflecting shared glory, rejecting violence, and addressing the wounds of shame through the transformative power of the gospel of peace.

JOHNSON RAJENDRAN, PhD
Principal, Hindustan Bible Institute and College, Chennai, India

Ephesians is where Paul sets out his most simple and central vision: belief and practice, theology and relationships, can never be severed—they must be held together for dear life (and the life of the world). With urgency, Paul moves through all of human experience, showing again and again how our ordinary lives can be drawn into the large, all-encompassing work of Christ. In tribute to Paul, Mischke and Caynor personalize Ephesians in every nook and cranny of their own history and experience—just as a true biblical commentary should. And should it surprise us that the message is nothing short of revolutionary?

JULIE CANLIS, PhD
Seasonal Lecturer, Regent College
Author, *A Theology of the Ordinary* and *Calvin's Ladder*

One New Humanity is a groundbreaking and deeply compelling work that speaks directly to the heart of the church's calling in a divided and polarized world. This book doesn't just inform—it transforms. As a Christian from the Middle East, I found its message both convicting and hopeful. In a region where honor, shame, and reconciliation shape our daily lives, Caynor and Mischke's insights resonate profoundly. They do not offer abstract theology, but a deeply biblical vision of peace rooted in Christ. This book forces us to wrestle with history, power, and exclusion while presenting the gospel's radical alternative—unity in Christ that transcends all barriers. It is an urgent call for the global church to embody the reconciling love of Jesus, healing wounds, confronting injustice, and reimagining community in his name. Many churches have lost credibility in their communities due to internal divisions and political conflicts. If you long for a vision of the church that embodies Christ's reconciling love, this book will stir your heart and strengthen your faith.

BASSEM MELKI, PhD
Assistant Professor of Peace Studies
Arab Baptist Theological Seminary

In *One New Humanity*, Werner Mischke and Kristin Caynor raise a deeply spiritual question: *What does it mean to be human?* They reveal sin as more than just personal failure; it is a force interwoven through generations, cultures, and systems. They highlight how these distort our sense of harmony and well-being by confronting shame, violence, and individualism. Drawing from early Christian thought and social science, they illustrate how Jesus's Gospel of Peace transforms cycles of conflict and violence, offering a new way to embrace humanity. Their reference to the *True Human Being* for Jesus resonates with the Indigenous worldview underlying the First Nations Version, portraying him as the model of restored humanity, one who embodies the Creator's vision of peace, dignity, and reconciliation. In this timely book, the authors invite readers to walk this path, seeking the Creator-given way of being truly human.

TERRY M. WILDMAN
Lead Translator and Project Manager, First Nations Version New Testament

ONE NEW HUMANITY

Glory, Violence, and the Gospel of Peace

Kristin Caynor & Werner Mischke

with Brad Vaughn

Afterword by D. Zac Niringiye

visit us at missionbooks.org

One New Humanity: Glory, Violence, and the Gospel of Peace
© 2025 by Mission ONE, Werner Mischke, Kristin Caynor.
All Rights Reserved.

No part of this book may be reproduced, stored in a retrieval system, or transmitted in any form or by any means—electronic, mechanical, photocopy, recording, or otherwise—without prior written permission from the publisher, except brief quotations used in connection with reviews. This manuscript may not be entered into AI, even for AI training. For permission, email permissions@wclbooks.com. For corrections, email editor@wclbooks.com.

William Carey Publishing (WCP) publishes resources to shape and advance the missiological conversation in the world. We publish a broad range of thought-provoking books and do not necessarily endorse all opinions set forth here or in works referenced within this book.

The URLs included in this workbook are provided for personal use only and are current as of the date of publication, but the publisher disclaims any obligation to update them after publication.

Scripture quotations are from the ESV® Bible (The Holy Bible, English Standard Version®), Copyright © 2001 by Crossway, a publishing ministry of Good News Publishers. Used by permission. All rights reserved.

Scripture quotations marked NRSV are taken from New Revised Standard Version Bible, copyright © 1989 National Council of the Churches of Christ in the United States of America. Used by permission. All rights reserved worldwide.

Published by William Carey Publishing
10 W. Dry Creek Cir
Littleton, CO 80120 | www.missionbooks.org

William Carey Publishing is a ministry of Frontier Ventures
Pasadena, CA | www.frontierventures.org

Cover and Interior Design: Werner Mischke

ISBNs: 978-1-64508-610-9 (paperback)
        978-1-64508-612-3 (epub)

Printed Worldwide

30 29 28 27 26   2 3 4 5 6   IN

Library of Congress Control Number: 2025930809

About the cover image

The image is called "Anastasis" (*Gk*: resurrection). It shows that as Jesus rises in victory over death, he pulls Adam and Eve out of their coffins, delivering them from sin and the grave while stomping on hell and the devil. Jesus is also pulling Adam and Eve *together*—he is reconciling and reuniting them. This rhymes theologically with Ephesians 2:15—"that he might create in himself one new man in place of the two, thus making peace." Adam and Eve together represent humanity; this image speaks of horizontal reconciliation and the "one new humanity" of Ephesians 2:15 (*ktisē en autō eis hena kainon anthrōpon* / create in himself a unified, brand-new kind of humanity). "Anastasis" pictures Jesus as Creator, Victor, Reconciler, and Peacemaker for "One New Humanity."

According to Wikimedia Commons, the image is titled, "Anastasis, Harrowing of Hell and Resurrection." Photographed by GunnarBach, February 2004, the image is of a fresco painting from the Chora Church (now Kariye Mosque) in Istanbul, Turkey. According to Wikipedia, the original Chora Church dates to the fourth century. This work has been released into the public domain by its author, GunnarBach; this applies worldwide.

 https://commons.wikimedia.org/wiki/File:Chora_Anastasis1.jpg

 https://en.wikipedia.org/wiki/Chora_Church

To Udo Heintz (b. 1934)
of Hanover, Germany,
of grace and peace
in ever following Jesus.
Lieber Onkel, Danke.
—*wm*

¹³ But now in Christ Jesus
you who once were far off have been brought near
by the blood of Christ.
¹⁴ For he himself is our peace, who has made us both one
and has broken down in his flesh
the dividing wall of hostility,
¹⁵ by abolishing the law of commandments expressed in ordinances,
that he might create in himself one new man
in place of the two, thus making peace,
¹⁶ and might reconcile us both to God in one body
through the cross, thereby killing the hostility.
¹⁷ And he came and preached peace to you who were far off
and peace to those who were near.
¹⁸ For through him we both have access in one Spirit to the Father.
¹⁹ So then, you are no longer strangers and aliens,
but you are fellow citizens with the saints
and members of the household of God.

Ephesians 2:13–19

CONTENTS

Preface & Acknowledgments		xvii
Introduction		xxi
Section I	**GLORY and Shame**	
1	Longing for Glory	3
2	Jesus, Our Glory	11
3	Defining (and Defending) Shame	19
Section II	**VIOLENCE and Sin**	
4	Sin Is Not Simple	31
5	Shame, Violence, and Individualism	47
6	Powers and Principalities	65
7	Status Games	85
8	Group Versus Group Hostility	105
Section III	**The GOSPEL OF PEACE and Its King**	
9	Resurrection in Rwanda	125
10	*Pax Romana* Versus *Pax Christi*: Contrasts in Peace	137
11	Perfection in Weakness: Contrasts in Power	169
12	Homogenous Unit Principle: What Peace?	183
13	Being Human, and the Gospel	221
14	Gospeling Peace with King Jesus	239
Afterword	By D. Zac Niringiye	265
APPENDICES		
Appendix 1	Reconciling Atonement in Ephesians 2: An Exegetical Study, by Brad Vaughn	269
Appendix 2	Word Study: Son of Man, First Adam, and Last Adam, Humanity	295
Appendix 3	Comparison Exercise: *Pax Romana, Pax Christiana, Pax Christi*	297
Bibliography		299
Scripture Index		319
Topic Index		325

FIGURES

Fig. 3.1	The cycle of shame, stigma, violence, trauma	25
Fig. 4.1	Reductionism has two factors—importance and complexity	36
Fig. 4.2	"Sin"/ "sins"/ "sinned"/ "sinning" in the New Testament (ESV)	38
Fig. 4.3	Range of human groupings in the Bible critiqued or judged by God	40
Fig. 4.4	Depicting levels of power while centering the individual	41
Fig. 4.5	Depicting levels of power while relativizing the individual	41
Fig. 5.1	Five categories of comparison between individualism and collectivism	50
Fig. 5.2	John Braithwaite's Reintegrative Shaming Theory (RST) says shame can be used to disintegrate or to reintegrate	58
Fig. 5.3	Characteristics of community in Acts 2 and 4	60
Fig. 6.1	Levels of power in a biblical worldview	66
Fig. 6.2	All are born under sin, enslaved to various Powers	67
Fig. 6.3	Christ above all Powers	68
Fig. 6.4	A cosmology of the early church: Christ has descended and ascended (Eph 4:8–10); Christ is enthroned far above all rule and authority (Eph 1:20–23)	69
Fig. 6.5	"In" the old humanity vs. "in" Christ's new humanity	76
Fig. 7.1	Types of honor-status reversal	96
Fig. 7.2	Humiliation and exaltation of Christ as honor-status reversal	97
Fig. 7.3	Salvation is at the crux of two dimensions of honor-status reversal in Ephesians 2	99
Fig. 7.4	Honorific gospel beliefs and subverted beliefs	102
Fig. 8.1	Left to right political spectrum	107
Fig. 8.2	Group of persons moderately right in political stance	107
Fig. 8.3	Deliberation moves the group toward the extreme	108
Fig. 8.4	Group polarization—both left and right move to their own extremes	109
Fig. 8.5	Contrasting views of diversity— the bottom based on Ephesians 2:13–16	113
Fig. 8.6	The Ethical Paradox of Group Loyalty	116
Fig. 10.1	Isaiah's vision of peace echoed in Ephesians 2	150
Fig. 10.2	Kingdom of the world versus Christ's kingdom of the cross	159

Fig. 12.1	The Homogenous Unit Principle—large factor in global Christianity's growth since the 1970s	186
Fig. 12.2	General statistics about Unreached People Groups, 2025	188
Fig. 12.3	Two uses of "gentiles" / *ethnos* in the New Testament	192
Fig. 12.4	The HUP contributes to polarization	201
Fig. 12.5	Heterogeneous groups offer varied perspectives from a "wide argument pool" thus tending toward depolarization	201
Fig. 12.6	The Ethical Paradox of Group Loyalty	202
Fig. 12.7	Loyalty to an in-group relative to an out-group vs. loyalty to Christ relative to an out-group	205
Fig. 12.8	Depolarization through allegiance to Christ the King	207
Fig. 12.9	Comparing impacts—Doctrine of Discovery, Dispensationalism, HUP	216
Fig. 12.10	A three-part people group missiology—initial ideas	218
Fig. A.2	Word study: Son of Man, first Adam, last Adam, humanity	295

For introductory videos relating to each chapter,
plus other relevant resources, go to
onenewhumanitybook.com.

PREFACE & ACKNOWLEDGMENTS

Ephesians 2 Gospel Project—
Origin of this Book

In 2019, I (Werner) was invited to present at a regional meeting of the Evangelical Missiological Society. The conference theme was "Mission Amid Global Crisis." My presentation was centered on Ephesians 2:11–22, and was called "An Honor-Bearing Gospel for Shame-Fueled Crises."[1] It was the first time I presented a view of contemporary issues of conflict, division, and violence seen through the lens of this Ephesians 2 text. If there's one phrase in Ephesians 2 that has captured me, it's this: "through the cross, thereby killing the hostility" (v. 16).

Ephesians 2:11–22 addresses the reconciliation of Jews and gentiles. Despite their long history of division and violence, together they comprise the multicolored people of God unified in Christ. Does this text address the challenges of the global refugee crisis, or the problems of racism, tribalism, or nationalism? Could this text play a role in the church's vocation of discipling all the nations and blessing all the peoples of the earth? How does this text speak to our world?

I had begun a journey exploring the meaning and relevance of Ephesians 2. I longed to know how this text was understood by scholars throughout church history. In December 2019, I wrote a two-page document that formed the basis for the Ephesians 2 Gospel Project, which included this key idea: *There is a social and horizontal dimension to the gospel of Christ because there is a social and horizontal dimension to the atonement of Christ (Eph 2:13–16).* We envisioned participating in a conversation in the global church to address collective identity conflict—theologically and missiologically.

A Collaboration Begins

Kristin Caynor and I met in the fall of 2020. As I shared about the project with Kristin, I discovered she had a story, an educational background and a skill set unlike mine. Kristin grew up in Southeast Asia. Kristin has a graduate degree in theology and is proficient in Hebrew and Greek. I soon learned Kristin has another important ability: She knows the online tools to explore the writings of the Church Fathers relative to specific Scriptures. So, I invited Kristin to begin a research project on Ephesians 2 with funding from the ministry I served with, Mission ONE.

---

1 Mischke, "An Honor-Bearing Gospel."

Thus, a research-and-book-project collaboration was born. The numerous conversations which Kristin and I have had over the past four years have been inspirational, creative, learning experiences. I was the one learning more from her than she from me.

In the summer of 2021, Kristin and I spent two days with Mako Nagasawa, founder of The Anastasis Center. Our conversations were rich and resonant. He has done extensive explorations of the theology of the "one new man" ("new humanity") of Ephesians 2. Mako's insights about early Christianity were most helpful. He and his team also embody their theology in beautiful ways in their interethnic urban setting. Mako was for us an early conversation partner saying *press on*. Thank you, Mako.

Also encouraging were early conversations with longtime Mission ONE friend and ministry partner Dr. Paul R. (Bobby) Gupta. As president of Hindustan Bible Institute & College (HBI), Chennai, India, Bobby offered for Kristin and me to present papers of our earliest research on Ephesians 2 in HBI's monthly academic webinar series. That webinar came to fruition October 8, 2021.

Two years later (December 7–8, 2023), HBI hosted a consultation of Indian scholars, "Ephesians 2: Reconciliation and Unity," from which came a five-article monograph. Dr. Gupta and HBI offered their support and academic involvement in this exploration of Ephesians 2; this has been an honor for us and a great kindness. *What a treasure to collaborate in the global church.* I am deeply grateful.

In October of 2022, we gained another conversation partner—Dr. D. Zac Niringiye, former assistant bishop of the Anglican Church of Uganda. He was at one time the pastor in Kampala of a church where current Mission ONE president Olivia Mulerwa was a faithful member. Olivia has remained friends with "Bishop Zac" (as he is known to many). A God-ordained opportunity arose in the US whereby Zac could serve as a scholar-in-residence at Fuller Seminary for one year. Olivia made the introductions, and we have been the beneficiaries.

It was a special honor for the three of us (Kristin, Zac, and me) to meet quarterly for one year in Phoenix on behalf of this book project. Kristin and I are profoundly grateful for Zac's mind-stretching insights, practical suggestions, Jesus-centered influence, and joyful friendship. *Brother Zac, you are to us a gift from God. We are honored to have your afterword in this volume.*

Like most book projects, this one has been a journey of conversations, readings, excursions, and writings. A six-day research trip to Rwanda in April 2022 was especially significant. In addition to diverse people in America, our conversations have included people from Ethiopia, Venezuela, Germany, India, Kenya, Mexico, Rwanda, Spain, Uganda, and the United Kingdom. Our conversation partners come from a variety of tribes, ethnicities, social classes, and backgrounds. You will meet some of them in this book.

The authors who have informed our work include both ancients and moderns. You will encounter writings from the Fathers, who wrote in the earliest centuries of the church, as well as numerous authors of our modern world.

William Carey Publishing deserves our thanks for agreeing to publish this work. Vivian Doub and Melissa Hicks have been encouraging, professional, and kind in all our interactions. *Thank you.*

My deep gratitude also goes to Mission ONE, the organization founded by my dear friend Bob Schindler, of which I was a part from 1992 until the end of 2024. Mission ONE's purpose is *to partner with the global church in making communities more like the kingdom of God*. I sincerely hope that this exploration in Ephesians 2 will ultimately help many communities be *more like the kingdom* through Christ's reconciling gospel of peace. To the Mission ONE board of directors, staff, and the many friends and donors who financially sustain the ministry, I acknowledge this work is part of the larger work of Mission ONE.

Although my thirty-two year journey with Mission ONE ended at the end of 2024, I remain profoundly grateful for the innumerable ways I have been nourished in that journey. What an honor to play even a small role in the global church in Christ's ministry of blessing the nations! We stand on the shoulders of giants in an interweaving of relationships and interdependence that only God clearly sees. Accordingly, this book was only possible because others pray, others labor, others give sacrificially, others serve, others study and research and write, others have given their lives. I offer my heartfelt thanks to God.

Werner Mischke
Phoenix, Arizona
January 2025

INTRODUCTION

Christ is our peace; Christ makes peace; Christ preaches peace.
  —*Ephesians 2:14–15, 17*

One New Humanity argues that Ephesians 2 offers a radical vision of human glory and peace that challenges cycles of shame and violence—from the Roman Empire to the contemporary world. In conversation with early Christians, the global church, social sciences, and the biblical narrative, we show that through Christ's life, death, and resurrection we gain a peaceful way of being human *for the world*—impacting identity, relationships, church, and vocation.

In the process of examining glory, violence, and the gospel of peace, we explore the question, "What does it mean to be human?" Our journey culminates in the Son of Man, True Human Being—Jesus. We join the early Christians in proclaiming that Christ alive, crucified, risen, and exalted is truly the ultimate antidote, rebuke, and alternative to violence. With Jesus we embody his gospel of peace near and far—*for the world*.

One New Humanity is divided into three sections following the subtitle: *Glory, Violence, and the Gospel of Peace*. The theme of section I is Glory; section II is Violence; section III is the Gospel of Peace. Each section responds to the query—What does it mean to be human?—with a set of explorations that make up the chapters of that section.

We believe the material in this book is relevant to readers in various cultural contexts and regions of the world. Nevertheless, we recognize our audience will be primarily American.

Werner's Dreadful Question

Circa 1970 ...

"Mom, how could Germany do what they did in the war, murdering millions of innocent Jews?"

My mother hears a dreadful question from her teenage son.

Hannelore Just had lived as a teenager through the war in Germany in the city of Hannover. As I grew into my teen years, I remember her talking matter-of-factly about war terrors. *Regular bombing raids for three years. Fleeing to bomb shelters. Playing a game with friends: Who can find the biggest piece of shrapnel?*

When I ask the question, I am fourteen or fifteen years old, probably in ninth grade. Children first learn about America and its allies winning World War II in middle school. In high school, they learn more about the War and the horrors of Germany and the Holocaust.

The photos. The grim black-and-white photos in my high school history textbook. The Allied forces liberated the concentration camps in Germany and Poland. They documented these events with photographs of human beings, eyes wide open, barely alive, like skeletons, peering out from stacked wooden shelves in a warehouse for the not-quite-dead. Other photographs I see later in my life are of mass burials and wide mounds of the dead. Etched into my memory are the images in a textbook—piles of whitish human bones and other messy remains of men, women, and children murdered *en masse.*

As I write these words, it is fifty-plus years since I asked my mother the dreadful question: "How could Germany do what they did in the war, murdering millions of innocent Jews?"

I remember my mother's answers, accrued from conversations across my teen and adult years.

Before Hitler, we couldn't put bread on the table. We had the black market. Hitler did a lot of good. Hitler put Germany back to work. He gave Germany the Autobahn and the Volkswagen ... Killing all the Jews? We didn't know. Yes, it is terrible, but we didn't know. What about America? Look how America treats black people. Is America much better?

My mother loved God. She was much loved by her family, church, and community. She suffered much and endured many hardships over her seventy-three years. She died in 2004. With affection and respect, I honor her memory.

But I am unsatisfied. Her answers to my dreadful question now seem like evasions. But how do you answer the unanswerable, the mystery of evil, the unspeakable memories? Perhaps my question triggered her memories of trauma, preventing conscious reasoning. Could she have responded any other way?

In 2015, the evil and horror of World War II Germany became more real to me. My wife, Daphne, and I visit Germany. She wants to visit Bergen Belsen, the concentration camp memorial. *I don't want to go there.* But we go. We are with my relatives, Onkel Udo, and cousins Peter and Claudia. We walk outside on concrete sidewalks, alongside mound after mound of mass graves with concrete signage. I have the photos. *Hier Ruhen 5000 Tote* (Here Rest 5000 Dead), *April 1945*; *Hier Ruhen 1000 Tote, April 1945;*

Hier Ruhen 800 Tote, April 1945. Mound after mound. The silence is penetrating. Mass death after mass death. How is this possible?

Kristin's View

Werner and I believe in a God who makes an end of violence. We believe that this is the God who Jesus reveals. So, for us, the apparent embrace of Jesus as God by a nation that perpetrated the horrors of the Holocaust is a deeply troubling contradiction.

The world is troubled by violence in God's name from many religious traditions, including Christianity. For many, our track record has not left a good resumé for the Bible, Christianity, or religion in general.

We want to ask how Christians become complicit in mass violence. But in doing so, we need to understand why violence happens in the first place. This understanding also helps to answer other pressing questions: Why are addiction and deaths of despair on the rise? What can we do about the violence in our streets? Why do so many countries feel more politically polarized than ever? Is there any good news?

Jesus Invites Us to the Great Feast

Initially, this project set out to see what the gospel of peace (Eph 2:17; 6:15) says to these things, and especially to the contradiction of mass violence perpetrated in Jesus's name. The initial idea was that maybe Christian societies have perpetrated mass evil in part because they've sidelined important gospel texts like Ephesians 2:11–22. And maybe, if we could convince people to preach Ephesians 2:14 as often as we preach John 3:16, that would make a difference.

Ephesians 2:11–22 has indeed been sidelined in much evangelical teaching on "the gospel." But what we have found is something more serious and beautiful. It is not a matter of simply adding Ephesians 2 back into the "gospel equation" so we can get the right answer. Rather, the Scriptures call to us with an ongoing invitation from Jesus to follow him "further up and further in," to continually more expansive views of the Peace he is.

This invitation arrives to us in the form of the cross, intervening right in the middle of the worst of human evil. It arrives as a magnificent message of good news, written with the blood of state, religious, and mob violence.

The good news is that we have been invited to a party—to the Great Feast of the King, to a seat at his table (Luke 14:16–24). To each of us, Jesus says, "Come, and follow me." If we are blind, he promises to lead us there (Isa 42:16). If we are crippled, he will carry us (2 Sam 9:13; Isa 40:11; 46:4). If we have no name—or maybe one that isn't very good—he will introduce us as his own when we arrive (Isa 62:2; Rev 3:12). And if we are not whole, he will heal us (Isa 57:19; Jer 30:17).

Of course, we can refuse the invitation. Maybe we are *too* whole—we can walk ourselves to a party any time we want. Or maybe we are too busy with more important matters. Maybe we have our own feast, with our own table, and our own name to worry about (Matt 24:4–5). Or maybe we're upset because of who else has been invited to share the place of honor. We're not sure everyone has earned the right (Luke 15:28–30), or that they've put in their fair share of work (Matt 20:11–12). In fact, being seen among such a motley group might be bad for us, and *our* name. Yes, we're aware that the King has given them all new names—but we know who these people are out there in the world (Luke 7:39). And what if the King should insist on giving *us* a new name, when the one we have now is working quite well for us?

We must realize, deep down, that we are being invited to no ordinary, respectable dinner party. In fact, it is a new world, where we can *no longer regard anyone according to the flesh* (2 Cor 5:16). To enter this Feast, we must check everything at the door. We must forsake all we have built, with no promise of getting it back. We must be reborn into a new family, where the most unexpected people become brothers and sisters. We must become one, even as Jesus and the Father are one (John 17:22). And we must become a new humanity—a new way of being human entirely (Eph 2:15). In the end, if we're not willing to relate to one another on entirely new terms, we cannot come to this party.

So, our prayer is not that you find a formula for preventing violence or creating church unity. Rather, we invite you to walk along the road with us for a little while. We pray that you would hear the invitation of peace in your own life. And we pray that you would not only hear, but that your feet would be ready to follow the way of Jesus.

Who We Are

Kristin:

I've lived in three countries, eighteen cities, and forty-five houses at the last count. My ethnic background is a mix of Anglo and Hispanic American, and my cultural background also includes Thailand. Among the people I have lived with are Mexican, American, Kenyan, Liberian, Thai, Lao, Haitian, South African, Native American, and Russian.

Answering the questions "Who am I?" and "Where do I belong?" has been a lifelong journey. Loyalty is complicated. Home is even more complicated.

Everywhere I've lived, my belonging has been in doubt for one reason or another. In Thailand, I'm a white foreigner (until they hear me speak Thai with a Bangkok accent). In Spain, I'm a Spaniard (until they hear my broadly "pan-American" accent). In the US, I'm an "American," but I don't feel like one, and my deepest friendships tend to be with people from immigrant families or other global nomads like me.

On the other hand, I have had true friendships with people who don't share any language in common with me. I have more friends outside the church than within it. Even though I'm committed to following Jesus, I never find it difficult to discuss spiritual things with those who do not identify as "Christian."

I love a broad cross section of people, and I feel a sense of loyalty to all of them. At times, I've been aware that people I love think the world would be better off if others I love were dead. This makes the question of loyalty complicated and painful. Recently, this pain has been felt most keenly in having both Palestinian and Israeli friends.

And then, there is the question of "home." Jesus said,

> There is no one who has left house or brothers or sisters or mother or father or children or lands, for my sake and for the gospel, who will not receive a hundredfold now in this time, houses and brothers and sisters and mothers and children and lands, with persecutions, and in the age to come eternal life. (Mark 10:29–30)

While I didn't always have a choice in the matter, I have found this to be true. Giving up the usual sense of home, family, and belonging has led to many homes and many families. But the "giving up" is still real, and costly.

Werner:

I speak English, but my first language was German. As mentioned above, I grew up in a German American immigrant family. My ethnic background is German. I am pro-immigration.

There is much intergenerational trauma connected to Germany's history in World War II. I'm referring to the trauma and death Germany inflicted on others and endured itself—as well as the shadow of guilt and shame that was cast over succeeding generations of Germans.[2] This trauma has touched me and my family.

We were a Christian family attending a Baptist church. My family blended into white suburbia in Rochester, New York. My father began suffering from severe mental illness (bipolar disorder) when I was a teenager. This brought about embarrassment and stigma, creating in me a shadow of shame.[3]

My wife, Daphne, and I are currently part of an evangelical church in Scottsdale, Arizona, reflecting the demographics of a mostly white upper-middle-class community. We have many friends there. We're part of a small group that meets regularly. We participate in various ministries. The church supports my ministry.

My family has been affected by addiction with its trials and sorrows. We have survived and grown. I'm in my late 60s. By American standards our household is wealthier than the majority. I have enjoyed many advantages not available to others.

Being evangelical means emphasizing the Bible, the cross, conversion, and activism.[4] I believe this book is rooted in these emphases, although in ways that are unconventional. I am amazed by Jesus and his ways—what he teaches, what he does (and has done!), where he goes.

Two primary influences in my adult life are the *global church* and *books*. I've learned and benefited enormously from relationships in the international community of people involved in global Christian mission. These influences are much the result of a vocational-and-learning journey in serving the global church that began in 1992. I am profoundly grateful for what God has so graciously given through the many generous people who have made it possible.

---

2 Lindahl, *The Pendulum*.

3 Mischke, "Shadow of Shame."

4 Godfrey, "Bebbington's Four Points."

SUMMARY OF SECTIONS AND CHAPTERS
Section I: "Glory and Shame"

What does it mean to be human? Because of God our Creator, being human means that we are made in the image of God—*imago Dei*—"crowned with glory and honor" (Ps 8:6); this is humanity's Original Glory, or "relational beauty." Humanity's longing for glory is according to God's design, and Original Glory precedes Original Sin. This mosaic of glory-related truth—*our Original Glory, our longing for glory by God's design, Jesus our glory, and the loss of glory felt in shame*—comprises the foundation for understanding the cycle of toxic shame and violence. It also helps us to see that while shame often leads to violence, it is fundamentally a healthy response to brokenness in the world, which can lead to transformation.

- **Chapter 1, "The Longing for Glory,"** reexamines the biblical depth of the concept of glory as "relational beauty." This glory described by Scripture is a deep human need and is far-reaching in its implications. God desires to share his own glory with us in Jesus.
- **Chapter 2, "Jesus Our Glory,"** explains that Jesus, the ideal human being, is simultaneously God's glory and humanity's glory—as revealed in the Gospels and in Pauline texts such as Ephesians 1 and 2.
- **Chapter 3, "Defining (and Defending) Shame,"** explores how humanity's sin-and-shame is properly understood and grieved against the backdrop of our Original Glory.

Section II: "Violence and Sin"

What does it mean to be human? Because of sin, *being human* means that we often respond to problems with conflict. We live in a broken world plagued by the traumas of division, hostility, and violence. The Bible and the gospel speak to all the dynamics at the root of violence.

- **Chapter 4, "Sin Is Not Simple,"** considers an overall biblical witness concerning sin as a personal, social, multi-generational, and systemic tangle of individual, corporate, and cosmic forces.
- **Chapter 5, "Shame, Violence, Individualism,"** compares individualistic with collectivistic cultures, and examines the limits individualism places on how we respond to violence. We explore how these limits can be overcome.

- **Chapter 6 is "Powers and Principalities."** This chapter presents surprising findings on how Powers and Principalities were understood in the ancient world. This sheds new light on Ephesians' four references to cosmic beings (1:21; 2:2; 3:10; 6:12), and on the implications for God's people.
- **Chapter 7 is "Status Games."** Humanity's competition for status and recognition are major drivers of social hostility and international conflict, but in Ephesians 1–2, by the glory of being "in Christ" we embody a gospel that subverts traditional conflict-fueling beliefs about identity and status.
- **Chapter 8, "Group vs. Group Hostility,"** examines social science insights about group-based conflict, for example, the Law of Group Polarization and the Ethical Paradox of Group Loyalty; these contrast starkly with Christ's gospel of peace and the depolarizing of Jews and gentiles embodied in Ephesians 2.

Section III: "The Gospel of Peace and Its King"

What does it mean to be human? Because of Christ the True Human, being human means that God restores our humanity through saving us from sin, violence, and dehumanizing idolatries. Christ is our peace; Christ makes peace; Christ preaches peace (Eph 2:14–15, 17). Being human means participating with Christ in proclaiming the gospel of peace *for the world* and to all peoples—near and far.

- **Chapter 9, "Resurrection in Rwanda,"** recounts our experiences in Rwanda and the way that our deepest longings for glory can be met through the cross, even in the most difficult places to forgive and find reconciliation.
- **Chapter 10, "Pax Romana vs. Pax Christi: Contrasts in Peace,"** compares Rome's imperial propaganda about global peace through conquest and dominance, with Christ's peace through the humility of the cross, which subverts imperial notions of violence-based "peace."
- **Chapter 11 is "Perfection in Weakness: Contrasts in Power."** We explore the complexities of Christianity in partnership with empire—"Pax Christiana." Power is unavoidable, but humanity's lust for power is often pathological; indeed, Pax Christiana is often complicit with violence, greed, and idolatry, contra Pax Christi and Ephesians 2.

- Chapter 12 is "Homogenous Unit Principle: What Peace?" Since the 1970s, the Homogenous Unit Principle has been at the crux of two movements (Church Growth and Unreached Peoples). The HUP can be seen *in continuity* and *in discontinuity* with the Doctrine of Discovery and Dispensationalism, theologizing or reinforcing social division and racial inequality, contra Ephesians 2 and the gospel of peace.
- Chapter 13, "Being Human, and The Gospel," examines Jesus Christ as the True Human Being. What if our aim in being human is Jesus himself? What if the Sermon on the Mount was our guide for discipleship—including enemy-love and peacemaking? What if Christ Jesus preaches the gospel of peace? What if the gospel is primarily not about going to heaven, but about being truly human with King Jesus—for his kingdom on earth as it is in heaven?
- Chapter 14, "Gospeling Peace with King Jesus," opens space to imagine practical ways of living out the Good News of Peace. It reflects on whether obeying the simple teachings of our Lord is the path to right belief and offers "four principles" plus "four provocations" on how churches can live more fully into one new humanity.

Appendix 1: "Reconciling Atonement in Ephesians 2" by Brad Vaughn

Vaughn's article was commissioned for this book. Here's why: The text of Ephesians 2:11–22 contains an extensive amount of material about Christ's reconciling work on the cross; nevertheless, many of our theological traditions largely ignore it relative to cross-and-atonement doctrine. Especially widely ignored is reconciliation "through the cross" (2:16) between Jews and gentiles. As stated above, an early key idea for this project was: *There is a social and horizontal dimension to the gospel of Christ because there is a social and horizontal dimension to the atonement of Christ (Ephesians 2:13–16).* We therefore wanted an experienced theologian to write an article focused on atonement in Ephesians 2. Brad Vaughn expertly filled this need. His article offers robust theological support to an important message of this book, namely:

> The cross of Christ reconciles vertically and horizontally; therefore,
> Christ's gospel offers to us reconciliation with God,
> and simultaneously, reconciliation with hostile others—
> thereby creating one new humanity in Christ.

The glory that you have given to me,
I have given to them that they may be one,
even as you and I are one—
I in you and you in me—
that they may become perfectly one,
and that the world may know that you sent me,
and loved them, even as you loved me.
–John 17:22–23

And we have seen his glory,
glory as of the only Son from the Father,
full of grace and truth.
–John 1:14

And we all, with unveiled face,
beholding the glory of the Lord,
are being transformed into the same image
from one degree of glory to another.
For this comes from the Lord
who is the Spirit.
–2 Corinthians 3:18

SECTION I

GLORY
and Shame

Chapter 1: Longing for Glory

Chapter 2: Jesus, Our Glory

Chapter 3: Defining (and Defending) Shame

Chapter 1

LONGING FOR GLORY

"Glory is the relational beauty that every person's heart yearns to behold and even to enter."
—Steve Hawthorne

IN THIS CHAPTER

- Humans have a built-in longing for glory, for the deep experience of relational beauty, in a story larger than ourselves.
- The story finds its climax in the glorious God-Man, Jesus.

Kristin:

Jesus says there is a connection between God's glory and the peace and unity of his disciples. And the social sciences affirm the other side of the same coin: connections between shame, division, and violence. We define shame as our human response when glory has been lost, degraded, or despised by sin. We will say more about this in chapter 3. But first, we need to understand the foundational, created glory for which we are made.

Both the Scriptures and the social sciences draw a connection between shame and violence—and glory and peace. And even in "secular" violence studies, there are those who advocate for including spirituality in the discussion. But we haven't found many places where the two have been read together on the crucial topics of violence and division. And we have found fewer places bringing non-Western perspectives.

If Jesus says that the glory of the Father will cause us to be one—even as he and the Father are one—what is this glory?

Growing up in church, I thought of "glory" as bright and shiny. I might have imagined rays of light shining from the face of Jesus, or maybe an American football player who makes a touchdown and points to the sky to say, "Glory to God!" I knew that we should give God glory and not seek our own. Overall, I thought glory was about attention, flashiness, or getting credit.

And then when I was sixteen, my mom, my brother, and I were in a car accident near our home in Thailand. We were all hospitalized, and my mom suffered a traumatic brain injury which left her in a coma. Our whole world was upended.

I was wheelchair-bound for nearly three months while we waited for what would happen to my mom. At any moment we might hear that she had woken up and was waiting to see us, that she had died, or almost any possibility in between. What if she woke up and couldn't remember who we were? What if she woke up severely impaired or with a different personality?

Every afternoon, I wheeled myself up to the hospital's seventh floor where a rooftop garden overlooked the city of Bangkok. As the sun set in the monsoon sky's incredible arrays of cloud and color, I would read. One afternoon, I opened my Bible to Romans 8, and the words leapt from the page: "For I consider that the sufferings of this present time are not worth comparing with the glory that is to be revealed to us" (8:18). Suddenly, I knew that glory wasn't quite what I had thought. The glory of Romans 8 was not pristine, sparkly, or pretty. Here, glory was battered, wounded, limping, and grieving. It was less about "success" and more about suffering.

I turned to my Bible's concordance and searched for "glory":

For this light momentary affliction is preparing for us an eternal weight of glory beyond all comparison. (2 Cor 4:17)

But we see him who for a little while was made lower than the angels, namely Jesus, crowned with glory and honor because of the suffering of death. (Heb 2:9)

My idea of glory now carried a weight it never had before. Sitting in a wheelchair on the hospital rooftop, with my mom lying in the ICU two floors below me, and the magnificent sun setting behind the monsoon clouds—I had begun to taste glory. The glory for which creation longs (Rom 8:19–21) is not about scoring a touchdown at the Super Bowl. Glory is heavy—almost unbearably so.

And furthermore—contrary to what I grew up believing—glory is something that we were made to long for and to seek. "To those who by patience in well-doing seek for glory and honor and immortality, he will give eternal life" (Rom 2:7).

How we define glory, and *where* we seek it, will become the stuff and substance of our lives. Whose table do we want to be invited to? Who do we want to celebrate us, and what do we want to be celebrated for? What are we willing to suffer for? This will become who and what we are. It will determine how we respond when the worst trials come, and when the fate of our souls depends on it.

Defining Glory in the Hebrew Scriptures

For the earth will be filled
with the knowledge of the glory of the Lord
as the waters cover the sea.
—Habakkuk 2:14

In the Hebrew Scriptures, the word for "glory" is *chabod*, often translated as "weight" or "heaviness." The apostle Paul might have had this in mind when he contrasted our light and momentary affliction with an eternal *weight* of glory (2 Cor 4:17).

God will not give his glory to another, nor his praise to an idol (Isa 42:8). Glory is given to God for what he has done in the world (Isa 42:12-13). It is sung and shouted with joy as a spontaneous reaction to his revelation (Isa 24:14-16; 42:11). It is an expression of gratitude (Ps 86:12), reverence, humility, and fear (Isa 25:3; Ps 22:23; Jer 13:16). Glory has to do with authority, significance, status (Ps 8:5; Jer 48:17-18), majesty, and splendor (Job 40:10; Ps 21:5).

Glory is connected to fruitfulness, wealth, and abundance (Gen 31:1). When the glory of Jacob is brought low, it results in leanness, scarcity, and lack (Isa 17:4-6). By contrast, when the dry land blossoms, glory is given to it (Isa 4:2; 35:1-3).

But glory also has to do with moral uprightness and beauty (Isa 62:2; Ps 97:6). When Moses makes the bold request to be shown the glory of the Lord, the Lord replies, "I will cause all of my goodness to pass before you" (Exod 33:19)—not "my power," or "my impressive acts," but *my goodness*.

Steve Hawthorne says that "Glory is the relational beauty that every person's heart yearns to behold and even to enter." This relational beauty is the fullest expression of the inherent worth of the Creator himself, of every human being, and of every created thing.[1] Glory can be individual, but it is also shared (Ps 21:5). God's glory makes people glorious. And the reverse is also true—God stakes some of his own glory and reputation on his people (Isa 43:7; 48:9-11; Ps 79:9).

Finally, glory is often synonymous with the *honor, being, essence,* and *presence* of a person (Gen 49:6; Ps 7:5; 30:12). God's glory first appears in the form of a cloud in the wilderness (Exod 16:10) and remains on Sinai while the covenant and the Torah is given (Exod 24:16). Deuteronomy describes darkness, gloom, and fire on the mountain (Deut 4:11). The people are terrified at what they see and hear (5:24). When Moses

---

[1] Hawthorne, "The Story of His Glory," in Winter and Hawthorne, *Perspectives*, 49.

makes the bold request to be shown God's glory, God confirms that "man shall not see me and live." Nevertheless, he says, "While my glory passes by I will put you in a cleft of the rock, and I will cover you with my hand until I have passed by. Then I will take away my hand, and you shall see my back, but my face shall not be seen" (Exod 33:20–23).

When Moses returns from this encounter, his face shines with an overwhelming radiance. Even the face which has seen *the back* of God's glory becomes almost unendurable to behold (Exod 34:29–30). For the rest of his life, he must wear a veil whenever he is among the people (34:34).[2]

Eventually, the cloud of glory will rest in the tabernacle (Exod 40:34). When the Temple of Solomon is consecrated, the cloud appears again, filling the place so that no one inside can stay on their feet (1 Kgs 8:10–11).

After the people are exiled, God's glory gets wheels. The temple has been destroyed, but this does not limit the presence of the Lord. Now the glory makes an unexpected move, appearing to the prophet Ezekiel in faraway Babylon (Ezek 1:3). Unlike the gods of the nations, the Lord does not dwell in a house made by hands (Isa 66:1), nor does he have a single territory where he reigns. He is the God of heaven and earth (Gen 24:3); indeed, all of heaven and earth are filled with his glory (Isa 6:3). Ezekiel sees a vision of four living creatures with wheels covered in eyes, whose sound is like the sound of armies. Over the frightening heavenly chariot is a throne, and seated on it is a likeness in human appearance with fire and brightness all around (Ezek 1:15–26). "Such was the appearance of the image of the glory of the Lord," says Ezekiel, "And when I saw it, I fell on my face … " (v. 28).

Glory in the New Testament

Then we come to the New Testament. John's Gospel begins with the astonishing claim that God's glory *took on flesh* and that *we have seen it*— "glory as of the only Son from the Father, full of grace and truth" (1:14). The glory which no human being can behold and live has been seen in a human being: Jesus, Mary's son from Galilee.[3] He is the image of the

---

[2] This links with the concept of "face," connected with glory and honor in many cultures. See Flanders, *About Face*. Relatedly, "Those who look to him are radiant, and their faces shall never be ashamed" (Ps 34:5).

[3] In the New Testament, glory—or *doxa* in Greek—has many of the same meanings as in the Old Testament; however, it also adds some special emphases. The first emphasis is eschatological. In the New Testament, glory is frequently associated with the fuller revelation of Jesus Christ at the end of the age. So, for instance, in the Synoptic Gospels, the second coming of Jesus is referred to as "when the Son of Man comes in his glory" (Matt 25:31; Luke 9:26; Mark 10:30). This represents a time when he will be seen fully for who he is and will establish his rule and reign on earth.

invisible God (Col 1:15), the radiance of the glory of God, and the exact imprint of his nature (Heb 1:3).

It's easy to see how these claims could have amazed and scandalized a faithful Jew. But John's Gospel takes things further. On the eve of his passion, Jesus makes his final prayer to the Father. He says:

> The glory that you have given to me, I have given to them, that they may be one, even as you and I are one, I in you and you in me, that they may become perfectly one, so that the world may know that you sent me and loved them even as you loved me. (John 17:22–23)

The glory that Jesus received from the Father has been given to us so that *we would be one* even as Jesus and the Father are one, and so that Jesus's true nature may be seen by the world. While there is a sense in which we "give glory to God" or "glorify" him, it is perhaps better to say that we need God to share his glory *with us* so that we can fulfill our purpose in becoming like him.

Remembering Moses, Paul says that now, "we all, with unveiled face, beholding the glory of the Lord, are being transformed *into the same image* from one degree of glory to another" (2 Cor 3:17–18). Peter adds that we ourselves have become partakers of the divine nature (2 Pet 1:4).

As we behold the glory of the Lord, we are transformed into the same image—the image of our Creator, which he gave us from the beginning. While the image was marred through sin, Jesus comes to restore it to us.

At this time, "what we will be has not yet appeared; but we know that when he appears we shall be like him, because we shall see him as he is" (1 John 3:2). To truly behold the glory of God in Christ is to be radically transformed into the same.

The fourth-century theologian Gregory of Nyssa connected John 17:22 and Ephesians 2 in his commentary on the Song of Songs. He writes:

> He who invested himself with humanity received this glory before the cosmos existed, and when that humanity had been glorified by the Spirit, the further gift of the Spirit's glory was passed on to the entire heredity [of that humanity], beginning with the disciples. That is why he said, "The glory that you have given me, I have given to them, so that they may be one, even as we are one: I in them and you in me, that they may become perfectly one." Therefore, the person who has left immaturity behind, and by growing attained to mature manhood, and achieved the measure of the intelligible stature, who from being a slave and a concubine has come to share the status of kingship.[4]

---

4 Norris, *Gregory of Nyssa: Homilies on the Song of Songs*, 495–97.

The "status of kingship" we share comes from Christ, with whom we have been seated "in heavenly realms" (Eph 2:6). Furthermore, this glory is never an individual matter based on our individual achievements or uprightness. Rather, it is *our* glory, found when we are in unity within the body of Christ. This is the great and awesome "relational beauty" we were made to yearn for.

BEING HUMAN: Seeking Glory

Growing up, I was taught that we shouldn't seek glory for ourselves but instead should "give glory to God." While Scripture supports this idea in some contexts, Paul points us in a different direction: "to those who by patience in well-doing seek for glory and honor and immortality, he will give eternal life" (Rom 2:7). In fact, he will go on to say that the longing we have for this glory is shared by the whole universe (Rom 8:19–23).

We are *made to seek for glory and honor and immortality*—if we do so through patience and well-doing. Considering the connection between glory and righteousness,[5] it makes sense that Romans 2:7 casts the quest for this glory in a positive light.[6]

---

5 In addition to special eschatological emphasis, the New Testament also enhances the Old Testament association of glory with moral uprightness. In his letter to the Philippians, Paul says that being "filled with the fruit of righteousness" is to the glory of God, picking up both the themes of ethics and of abundance (1:11). In multiple places, we are urged to "walk in a manner worthy of God." 1 Thessalonians further adds, "who has called us into his own kingdom and glory" (2:12). As Romans 3:23 famously says, "All have sinned and fallen short of the glory of God," and in Romans 1:23 we are told that through their ungodliness and unrighteousness (v. 18), people "exchanged the glory of the immortal God for images resembling mortal man and birds and animals and creeping things." This passage suggests a connection between the glory of God, true worship, and how we live with one another.

6 Scripture connects *being made in God's image* with *sharing in God's glory*. In Paul's sermon in Acts 17, he affirms the Greek poets who say that "we are indeed [God's] offspring." Paul sees these pagan poets as in agreement with the Scriptures. In Genesis, God makes humankind in his own image and likeness. Just as Adam and Eve are made in God's image, so they also bear children who in turn, share the same image and likeness (Gen 5:3). Paul goes on to say: "Being then God's offspring, we ought not to think that the divine being is like gold or silver or stone, an image formed by the art and imagination of man" (Acts 17:29). Since we ourselves carry God's image as offspring, to think that God is like gold or silver is to fall below our own true status, and to "fall short of the glory of God" (Rom 3:23). We could thus understand the "exchange of the glory of God for images" as both an affront to God's divine nature as it has been displayed in creation as a whole (1:20), *and* as a confusion and degradation of our own glory as God's offspring.

Werner:

In Ephesians the word Christ (*christos*) occurs forty-six times. The word Lord (*kyrios*) occurs nineteen times. That's astounding: sixty-five times the titles for Jesus—Christ or Lord—appear in this compact letter. Christ means Messiah-King, "anointed One." Lord means master or ruler. The regal, glorious Christ towers over the letter and its six chapters. A phrase that occurs ten times is "in Christ." Those who give allegiance to Christ are mystically joined into Christ in a regal identity of glory.

When Jesus is our glory[7]—our very source of honor—a journey of transformation begins. This transformation can set us free from competing loyalties to family, tribe, nation, social status, or another source of identity that may restrict obedience to Jesus.

Our study of Ephesians 2:11–22 has led us to challenging questions and truths. In this book, we will go on to explore how they rhyme with our world. We will consider the social dynamics of honor competition, Jew versus gentile, identity and diversity, race and ethnicity, tribalism and nationalism, the church's complicity with violence, and how these matters speak to God's ancient purpose to bless all the peoples of the earth (Gen 12:1–3).

Exploring these thorny issues may make some readers wary and defensive. Perhaps in some cases we have not struck the right balance or achieved the proper charitable tone. We believe that some of these thorny issues lose much of their thorniness in knowing Jesus—in focusing on his reconciling work on the cross, his social and relational ways, his incredibly challenging ethical teachings.

As ever in the church, the Lord Jesus Christ is our "true north," our rock, our example, our security, our glory and honor, the one "who fills all in all" (Eph 1:23).

Indeed, King Jesus is God's glory unveiled in a human being; we'll explore this further in the next chapter: "Jesus, Our Glory."

---

7 John 17:22; Col 1:27; Eph 2:6; etc.

CHAPTER 1 SUMMARY

- Glory is relational. We were made for glory—in relationship to God and with one another.
- The Bible offers a thick, comprehensive narrative about the unavoidable bond between God's glory and humanity's longing for glory.
- Paul's letter to the Ephesians[8] has much to say about God's glory, the glory of salvation in Christ, human glory in Christ, the problem of human division and hostility, and the glory of human beings reconciled in the love of Christ.
- Glory is foundational to human identity—while shame is at the crux of violence. Studying humanity's God-given glory is thus foundational to addressing the problem of violence.

FOR FURTHER REFLECTION

- God creates humanity "in his own image" *(imago Dei)*—giving them regal responsibility over the earth (Gen 1:26–28). How might this help us understand humanity's longing for glory?
- In our world, where do you see humanity's "longing for glory" either as an expression of goodness or brokenness?
- David has a longing for glory when he prays, "Awake, my glory" (Ps 57:8). According to Psalm 57:7–11, what does *David's glory awakened* look like?

---

[8] We recognize that the Pauline authorship of Ephesians is disputed by scholars. In referring to Paul as the writer, we are not taking sides on this complicated debate, which is outside our purview. Our view is that—regardless of authorship—the book has been read for most of history within the Pauline tradition, and so we are doing likewise. The reader can thus consider "Paul" to be shorthand for the author Paul and/or the Pauline tradition in which we are reading this book.

Chapter 2

JESUS, OUR GLORY

IN THIS CHAPTER

- Jesus is the unveiling of God's glory as a human being. He embodies divine glory and is humanity's hope of glory.
- Our longing for glory is fulfilled in the Son of Man, Jesus the Christ, True Human Being.

Kristin:

Jesus is God's glory and our hope of glory.

As we explore this, it can be tempting to think of Jesus as a theological functionary more than as a Person. We can focus on Jesus as part of God's salvation formula and miss the man from Nazareth who walked among us. We can get caught in the weeds of popular theology debates. And we can forget that no theology would be possible if Jesus did not live a real human life.

God came in flesh as our Child, Brother, and Friend to reach us with this good news. He even let himself be treated like a criminal (Rom 5:6–8). This was how he proved God's love to us—perhaps knowing that some could find it hard to believe how much God loves us (Rom 5:8).

Jesus demonstrates his glory through power over the forces of nature and over Satan and demonic entities. But it is also revealed in the way he exercises power. Compassion sends him to the sick, the sinner, the outcast, and the marginalized. In Luke 4, he announces himself as the one who brings good news to the poor, the captives, the blind, the oppressed (Luke 4:16–21; Isa 61:1–2). John the Baptist also recognizes Jesus not only by miracles, but by his concern for the marginalized (Luke 7:22).

The fullest revelation of beauty and glory comes through the act of Jesus humbling himself, becoming obedient to the point of death, even death on the cross. For this reason, God has highly exalted him and given him a name above every other name (Phil 2:6–11). His display of divine glory runs contrary to all the human ways of seeking it; humans are ever exchanging God's glory for what ultimately prove to be lesser things (Rom 1:23).

God's glory came down and filled all things with himself (Eph 4:9–10). He chose the sinner, the fool, the enemy, the low and despised, even "things that are not" (1 Cor 1:28–30). In this unlikely gathering, he is displaying the rich variety of his great wisdom (Eph 3:10). Because he came for the least, we all have hope of glory. Matthew Bates says it this way: "God intends everlasting honor for us through the gospel.... . The purpose of the gospel is that we might *share in the glory*."[1]

Jesus Goes with the Marginalized

Jesus is willing to be a scandal (Rom 9:33). He proclaims that the meek, persecuted, peacemaking, and poor in spirit are truly blessed (Matt 5:2-12). In so doing, he proclaims that many things which cause shame in the world are not at all shameful by God's standards, but actually a source of glory.

The religious leaders despise Jesus for accepting sinners (Luke 7:39). He touches people who are unclean through illness (Luke 5:13) and afflicted by demons (Mark 5:1-13). He associates with the politically and socially ostracized. He's willing to bear the shame of those who fell on hard times through no fault of their own—but he's also not afraid to be seen among prostitutes, drunkards, and tax collectors, and to bear the same reproach (Matt 11:19).

Jesus's ministry stood in continuity with the Hebrew Scriptures. God's people already knew that he desired mercy rather than sacrifice (Matt 9:11-13), and reams of parchment were dedicated to God's concern for the poor, oppressed, and vulnerable. We are to show our love and gratitude for God through caring for such as these.[2]

God's people were also commanded to remember their former shame—they were slaves in Egypt, so they should be careful to uphold the cause of the poor, the immigrant, and the enslaved.[3] Proverbs adds that "whoever mocks the poor insults his Maker" (17:5), and Jesus teaches that whatever we do to the least of these we have done to him, our King (Matt 25:40). In Ephesians 2, we are told, "Therefore, remember ... " (Eph 2:12).

Jesus loved the socially marginalized and was unconcerned with how this impacted his own social standing. "If you want to know what God is like, look at Jesus."[4] Could it be that how Jesus conducts himself *relationally and socially* displays the divine nature—just as much as his miracles?

---

[1] Bates, *Why the Gospel?*, 40-41; emphasis in original.

[2] Deut 15:11-15; 16:11-12; 24:17-22; Job 29:11-16; Ps 72:4; Prov 14:21, 32; 19:17; 21:13; 22:9, 16; 28:27; 29:7; 31:20; Isa 3:14-15; 58:6-7; Ezek 16:49; Amos 5:11.

[3] Deut 15:11-15; 16:11-12; 24:17-22.

[4] Folsom, *Karl Barth's Church Dogmatics*, 79.

Jesus Is Help from Outside

In the Synoptic Gospels, Jesus "leaves the crowds" for the other side of the Sea of Galilee (Matt 8:28–34; Mark 5:1–20; Luke 8:26–39). While sailing, Jesus falls asleep and a great storm arises. When the disciples cry out, he rebukes the wind and the waves.

As soon as they land, they are met by a demon-possessed man. He may be the most marginalized and "undeserving" person Jesus encounters in the Gospels. First, the man was probably a gentile.[5] Second, he was possessed by an "unclean spirit" (Mark 5:2). Third, he was naked ("he had worn no clothes," Luke 8:27; Lev 18). Fourth, he lived not in a house but among the tombs, among the dead (Luke 8:27; Num 19:11–16). Fifth, he was "cutting himself with stones" (Mark 5:5; Lev 19:28; 21:4–5). Altogether, this made him an extreme outcast at the lowest level of uncleanness, defilement, and oppression. His condition was debilitating shame.

Not only was this man an outcast, but attempts to restore him had proven impossible (Mark 5:3–4). He was too violent for others to even come near (Matt 8:28). But Jesus came "to destroy the works of the devil" (1 John 3:8). He commands the unclean spirits to come out of the man. They confess Jesus as the Son of God and beg to be sent into a large herd of pigs instead. In cinematic fashion, the herd rushes over a cliff and into the sea.

Where others had tried and failed to bind this man, Jesus finally and fully freed him. This man had no way to fix his problems on his own. His only hope was for someone to rescue him from outside. Christian psychiatrist Curt Thompson says that "when I'm in the middle of [shame], I'm not very able to pause [and] be aware, 'Oh this is my problem, and here are the things that I'm going to do to reconcile and resolve this. In fact, when [shame] becomes too intense, what we really need is for someone else to come and find us."[6]

Going to rescue this one lost sheep would be Jesus's only errand on the other side of the lake. When the local people hear what's happened,

---

[5] Matthew's account says, "When he came to the other side" (Matt 8:28). "'Other side' often marks the movement from a Jewish to a gentile territory and vice versa." *ESV Study Bible*, 1836. The fact that there were pigs nearby also strongly suggests this was a gentile area that Jews avoided. Moreover, when they returned to the other side, they encountered "a man named Jairus, who was a ruler of the synagogue" (Luke 8:41), obviously a Jew; this reinforces the contrast that one side of Lake Galilee was dominated by Jews, the other side by gentiles.

[6] Thompson, interview.

they beg him to leave the region. The man who is freed from the demons, on the other hand, begs to go with Jesus. Instead, Jesus restores him to his community and appoints him to tell others what God has done.

While we see an earnest desire to follow Jesus on the part of the restored man, there is hesitation on the part of others. In Matthew, two people approach Jesus as he is preparing to cross the sea. The first is a scribe who says, "Teacher, I will follow you wherever you go." Jesus tells him that foxes have dens and birds have nests, but the Son of Man has nowhere to lay his head. The other is a disciple who asks to first bury his father. Jesus replies, "Let the dead bury their own dead" (Matt 8:19–22).

This is not only a story about Jesus seeking the lost. It's also about the struggle of a theologian and an everyday Jesus-follower—to get on the boat, confront the waves, and go to the dead and lost places of society. It's about how Jesus comes for us when no one else can or will. And it's about following him—even toward danger, shame, homelessness, or death.

Whenever people tell me that they long to see the power of God at work today, I only have one answer: If you want to see God working, start obeying him. And if you want to know how to obey him, look at Jesus in the Gospels. Jesus shows us exactly where to go if we want to see God and his blessing (Matt 5:8). This is not a list of rules for God or religious leaders to hold over our heads. It's a map showing us the Way to green pastures, where the Shepherd is already waiting.

Jesus Is Above Human Glory

Just as Jesus gives hope of glory to those who have none in the world, so he also rearranges status and glory for those who think they do have it. He chose the foolish things to shame the wise, and the weak to shame the strong. And he brought the "glory" which seemed great to nothing (1 Cor 1:25–31).

The mother of Jesus was the first person to see the good news that was coming. And when she did, she sang,

> He has shown strength with his arm;
>> he has scattered the proud in the thoughts of their hearts;
> he has brought down the mighty from their thrones
>> and exalted those of humble estate;
> he has filled the hungry with good things,
>> and the rich he has sent away empty. (Luke 1:51–53)

To say that Jesus is unconcerned with "networking" or "image" is an understatement. Instead of seeking the favor of the influential, he often reserves his harshest condemnations for them (Matt 3:7; Luke 20:16-19). The blessings pronounced on the meek, the peacemakers, the persecuted, and the poor in spirit are contrasted by *woes against* religious leaders (Matt 23:13-29). They are infuriated (Luke 20:19). As time goes on, they work to undermine him (Mark 12:13) and finally plot to kill him (Matt 26:3-4).

Jesus often tells those who have experienced a miracle not to say anything (Matt 17:9; Mark 7:36; 8:30; Luke 5:14; 8:56). When the crowds try to make him king, he flees (John 6:15) and begins to say "hard things" which even many of his disciples cannot accept (6:60). Finally, when only the twelve are left, he asks if they too want to leave (v. 66)! "I do not receive glory from people," Jesus says (John 5:41). "I do not seek my own glory; there is One who seeks it, and he is the judge" (John 8:50).

Consider the "status game"[7]—how humans play in the quest for glory. Little has changed since the time of Jesus. We still look to the strong, attractive, cunning, and successful. People go into debt to have cars, clothes, technology devices, and luxuries they don't need—all in pursuit of status and human glory. Those who rise highest achieve wealth and fame—but the standards flux and shift from one moment to the next. Sometimes those who rise highest fall lowest, and fame turns to infamy. (We will further explore status games in chapter 7.)

The glory of Jesus is that he does not play the status game. Throughout the Gospels, Jesus refuses to be motivated by human standards of status. And yet, he is clearly motivated by glory—the true glory which comes from the Father.

Right after Jesus is affirmed as the "beloved" Son of God, he is led into the wilderness. There he is tempted by Satan, who offers him "all the kingdoms of the world and their glory" (Matt 4:8). He knows the Scriptures and refuses to receive the glory of the world's kingdoms. And yet, immediately after this, we see tantalizing hints of the kingdom he will receive with all the nations, as Jesus withdraws to "the way of

---

[7] Concerning the status game, Will Storr writes: "We need it. Status is an essential nutrient found not in meat or fruit or sunlight but in the successful playing of our lives. When we feel chronically deprived of it, or disconnected from the game, our minds and bodies can turn against us. To our brains, status is a resource as real as oxygen or water. When we lose it, we break." Storr, *Status Game*, 19.

the sea, beyond the Jordan, Galilee of the nations.[8] The people walking in darkness have seen a great light ..." (Matt 4:15–16). Jesus is the King, and he will one day receive a kingdom of magnificent diversity (Rev 5:9) and marvelous light (1 Pet 2:9).

Jesus's Purpose for All Peoples

John's Gospel also begins with a sign of this purpose for all peoples. Jesus "manifested his glory" first through the sign of turning water into wine at the wedding of Cana, "and his disciples believed in him" (John 2:11). In doing this, he also filled the role of the bridegroom (2:1–10). In Revelation, the Feast of the Lamb envisions people from every tribe, tongue, and nation united as God's people and wedded to him (Rev 5:9; 19:7). Isaiah 25:6 also describes how the Lord will make a feast with the best wine which will be for all peoples. From here, Jesus goes to cleanse the temple. While it is not recorded in John's Gospel, Mark tells us that he quotes Isaiah saying, "my house shall be a house of prayer for all peoples" (Mark 11:17).

The arc of glory in John's Gospel begins with the wedding at Cana, a foreshadowing of the wedding of the Lamb and the Feast for all peoples. And it concludes as Jesus prays to the Father, declaring that the same glory is given to his disciples "that they may be one, even as we are one" (John 17:22).[9]

Through the carpenter Jesus of Nazareth, God reveals a new way of being human, where love is no longer constrained by social boundaries. In Christ, God brings to crescendo "the story of his glory"[10] to bless every people for the sake of his name. The King of the Jews has come to fulfill Abraham's promise to bless all the peoples of the earth (Gen 12:1–3).

---

8   The word often translated as "gentiles" can also be translated as "nations," since it simply refers to any non-Jewish people groups.

9   The other Gospels and the Hebrew Scriptures also testify to this plan for all peoples. Mark tells the story of Jesus's discussion with the Syrophoenician woman (7:26). Luke has the parable of the good Samaritan, and Simeon prophetically declares that Jesus is God's salvation for all peoples, and a light of revelation to the gentiles (Luke 2:32). Matthew references the prophecy that the Messiah will proclaim justice to the gentiles, and that they will hope in his name (12:18–21).

10 Hawthorne, "The Story of His Glory."

Jesus Creates the Glorious New Humanity

All the nations are found, dignified, and transformed in this Palestinian Jew, and reconciled in him. He creates in himself *one new humanity* (Eph 2:15) to share his glory. We were created for glory beyond our imagining. We were created to share in the "status of kingship"[11] of the Son of God himself, and to steward the world (Gen 1:26-28) after the example of the Creator. We were set in the garden, given the image of God and the crown of dominion. This was our Original Glory.

But all of this was lost.

And now we wander in exile, through a land overshadowed by death, darkness, and fear. Now, we are degraded, and we degrade others. Now, we are slaves to our pathologies, bound in the body of death. And we all live with the sense that something is missing, that all is not as it once was, or could be. This is the experience of shame. We can have no understanding of glory without understanding this—not as long as we walk through the veil of tears.

> You have made us for yourself, and our hearts are restless until they can find peace in you.[12]

BEING HUMAN: Original Glory

The Scriptures make a radical testament to the glory of being human, showing us that glory is far more than simply getting credit or praise; it is the end that we were made for, and it's only found when we are in relationships of harmony with God and others. It isn't something we can have or experience alone. It's *the way of being* that holds all things together, and which Jesus came to restore us to.

Indeed, glory is foundational. We explored our *longing for glory* in chapter 1, and *Jesus, our glory* in chapter 2. Just ahead in chapter 3, "Defining (and Defending) Shame," we'll explore humanity's degradation of glory.

---

11 Norris, *Gregory of Nyssa: Homilies on the Song of Songs*, 496.
12 St. Augustine, *Confessions*, 17.

CHAPTER 2 SUMMARY

- Jesus is God's glory and our hope of glory. Jesus is what God looks like.
- Jesus loved the socially marginalized and was unconcerned with how this impacted his own social standing.
- Jesus did not play the status game; he was unconcerned about his social status. At the same time, Jesus rearranges status and glory for those who think they have it.
- God reveals a new way of being human in Jesus, who is compelled by love to cross many social boundaries.
- In Christ, God brings to crescendo "the story of his glory" to bless every people for the sake of his name.

FOR FURTHER REFLECTION

- Repeatedly, Jesus refuses power, influence, and accolades. Why might Jesus's example be particularly challenging to us today?
- "If you want to know what God is like, look at Jesus."[13] Does this challenge your view of God? If so, how?
- In Mark 5:1–20, Jesus crosses social boundaries. He crosses the Sea of Galilee to visit a demon-possessed gentile living among the tombs. *Jesus sets him free.* In your journey with Jesus, to what extent are you crossing social boundaries with your faith community?

---

13 He is the radiance of the glory of God and the exact imprint of his nature" (Heb 1:3). Cf. John 1:1–3, 8.

Chapter 3

DEFINING (AND DEFENDING) SHAME

IN THIS CHAPTER

- There is a deep human need for glory and wholeness in community.
- Violence is an affront to human glory—against both soul and body. The result is shame, which in turn often leads to violence.

Kristin:

We were made in Original Glory. In any sense that the commonly held doctrine of "Original Sin" is true, Original Glory is still where the story began *and* where the story is headed. The degradation of glory in humanity is not our true nature, but rather a failure to live up to our true nature. Jesus is here to save us from the cycles of degradation we are caught in, and from which we cannot escape on our own. As we are transformed into his image from one degree to another, glory must redefine everything—in ways we cannot now imagine.

Shame can be defined in many ways.[1] For the purposes of this chapter we define it as the sense that Original Glory has been degraded, lost, or despised (Hab 2:16). We can experience shame because of what we have done, but also because of things that have been done to us, or even because of things being done and suffered by others in our community. We can even feel shame on behalf of total strangers. It is a natural and even healthy emotional response to the brokenness and disconnection in the world because of sin—in ourselves and in our community. It is related to terms like rejection, disgrace, embarrassment, unworthiness, loneliness, misunderstanding, dishonor, insignificance, failure, and guilt.

Deep in our souls, we yearn for a relational beauty which we rarely experience. The grief we feel in this yearning is part of what we mean by *shame*. All of this exists to let us know that we are made for more. C. S. Lewis speaks of the mingled joy and pain in the great desire we all have for "our proper place" at the Feast of the Nations:

> I am trying to rip open the inconsolable secret in each one of you—
> the secret which hurts so much that you take your revenge on it

---

1 For nuanced definitions on shame and honor from a missiological perspective, see Flanders and Mischke, "'Top Ten Statements' Concerning Honor, Shame, and the Gospel," in *Honor, Shame, and the Gospel*, xxi–xxiv.

by calling it names like Nostalgia ...; the secret also which pierces with such sweetness that when, in very intimate conversation, the mention of it becomes imminent, we grow awkward ... the secret we cannot hide and cannot tell, though we desire to do both. We cannot tell it because it is a desire for something that has never actually appeared in our experience. We cannot hide it because our experience is constantly suggesting it, and we betray ourselves like lovers at the mention of a name.[2]

In fact, glory and shame are close together. Our yearning for Original Glory is an "inconsolable secret." It's an awesome thing we cannot escape—and yet, it's also an embarrassment because it points to something we don't fully know, and maybe are not sure we can really believe in. It's the site of our greatest and sweetest joys, and of our greatest pain.

But like all stories, the story of shame does not begin with brokenness.

Where Does Shame Come From?

Life is fundamentally relational and created for the relational beauty of Original Glory. We come to be through the relationship of man and woman. The emerging embryo grows only when it becomes embedded in the mother's uterine wall, and the life of the mother is sustained only through a relational web of other human beings, plants, and animals. The needs of the human child are not only physical but social and emotional.[3]

After we are born, we are even more dependent. We are not born on our feet, or with any capacity to survive on our own, and in the first years of our lives we need eye contact, caresses, and play to develop properly. We are not born with the ability to regulate emotions. Others help us, through their love, to form a sense of who we are and our connection to the world.

In a perfect situation, children would be raised by emotionally healthy adults, and parents would have a "village" to support them. As vulnerable people, children would be held as more precious, not less.

Over time, they would differentiate themselves from their parents with their own unique gifts and perspectives. In the beginning, God made distinctions to create space for life to flourish—between light and dark, sky and sea, dry land and water, and ultimately between man and woman. As they grew, children would replicate this process of glorification to become distinct members of the community. But the distance would not

---

2 Lewis, "Weight of Glory," 29–30.

3 National Institutes of Health, "Will Stress During Pregnancy Affect My Baby?"

mean disconnection. Instead, it would create space to be filled by love and rejoicing. As Adam said, "This at last is bone of my bone and flesh of my flesh!" (Gen 2:23). Adolescents would be affirmed and guided in finding their own irreplaceable roles in a larger, shared story. This Grand Narrative would show the glory of the community's connections to other communities (Eph 3:14–15), to the nonhuman creation, and to God. All these distances would be filled with love.[4]

As children continued to grow, a great sense of glory, meaning, and interconnectedness would grow with them (Eph 3:16). They would feel proud to be themselves, to belong to their family, and to their community. They would also feel proud of their connection to other communities with different languages and customs. All the splendor of God's diverse wisdom would be made manifest to them (Eph 3:10) and would fill them with an increasing openness to give and receive love (Eph 3:16–19). The basic needs of being seen, safe, soothed, and secure would be met.[5]

This ideal state of fearless love and intimate connection is symbolized by the phrase *naked and without shame* (Gen 2:25). But in our lives, we never really know what this is like. Our earliest experiences in community might give us a taste of the glory we need—but they also bring us pain, dysfunction, shame, and fear.

"Who told you that you were naked? Have you eaten from the tree I commanded you not to eat from?" This is God's question when he finds our first parents hiding in the garden (Gen 3:11). Their shame is a sign that sin has broken their glory. It is a sign that instead of the distance being filled with love, it has been filled with shame, fear, violence, and finally death.

Defining Violence

The World Health Organization defines violence as the "intentional use of physical force or power, threatened or actual, that either results in or has a high likelihood of resulting in injury, death, psychological harm, maldevelopment or deprivation."[6] Violence causes harm in various ways. It's multidimensional. Violence is not merely physical. We believe that at its root, violence begins in the garden—violating God's purpose for humanity's glory.

---

4 Ephesians 3:14–19 envisions a thriving community in which people grow. This family of families is sustained by the riches of the Father's glory (v. 16).

5 Thompson, *Soul of Desire*, 31.

6 Lee, *Violence*, 4, citing Krug et al. *World Report on Violence and Health*, 5.

At first glance, it may seem like taking the forbidden fruit was not really an act of violence. After all, who was really hurt? But if we define violence as harm done to the whole human person—harm done to *humanity-made-for-glory*—things become clearer. The taking of the fruit was violence against the human soul, against Original Glory. Although it may not show itself immediately in the body, it is no less violence.

In 2019, I (Kristin) was living in Spain when war broke out in Venezuela. One night, a new lady came to Bible study. She looked like a Spaniard, but somehow I knew she had come from Venezuela. She had the look of a wounded soul. Her body was intact, but profound violence had been done to her soul because of what she had seen, and because she was powerless to help those she had left behind.

> Then the eyes of both were opened, and they knew that they were naked. (Gen 3:7)

Vulnerable, exposed, and helpless.

Our first parents ruptured their intimacy with God, creation, and each other. They did violence *to their own souls* by denying their glory and worshiping a created thing rather than the Creator (Rom 1:22). They held the power and beauty of the fruit in higher regard than the relational beauty they already shared with the Creator. But in the end, the fruit only exposed their own weakness. For the first time, they saw something ugly, degraded, and truly frightening. This dysfunction now lay between them and lived inside of them. All they could do was cover themselves and hide from the glory of which they had fallen short (Rom 3:23).

The ripple effects spread quickly. In further attempts to distance themselves from the shame, they blamed each other and God. Finally, the loss of relationship also led to displacement and disconnection from the land. And very soon, it led to death when their firstborn son felt shame with his brother. God seemed to reject Cain's offering, and "his face fell." To put it another way, he lost face (Gen 4:5). But rather than seeking to do good and regain a sense of dignity,[7] Cain chose the ultimate denial of the glory of his human soul. He killed his brother—one made in the image of God, and so close to his own. [8]

A cycle of shame and violence was unleashed in Eden, and it continues to this day.

---

7 The phrase often translated "If you do well, will you not be accepted?" (v. 7) could be translated, "Will you not be dignified through doing good?"

8 Gen 9:6.

Anthony's Story

At twenty-seven years old, Anthony has a lot of years ahead of him. He's attractive, physically fit, and reasonably intelligent. But Anthony is a lost child. A week ago, he was released from prison after an eight-year sentence, where he spent the last eighteen months alone in a windowless cell in solitary confinement. He now leans against a wall, exhausted from another sleepless night on the streets.

Anthony was born substance-exposed and grew up in foster care. His speech was delayed because of drugs his mother used while pregnant, and his early inability to regulate emotions and express himself led to regular outbursts. Foster parents responded either with more violence, or by returning him to the state. He never had a reliable caretaker and often faced physical, emotional, and sexual abuse from foster siblings.

His violent tendencies did not lessen as he grew. With little else to hang his identity on, he clung to cultural ideals of masculinity to cover the sense of worthlessness he felt. Violence proved the surest means of gaining at least a form of respect as a man. He never felt so respected as when he stood behind a gun.

Deep within him, Anthony longed to be cared for and to meaningfully connect with others. But when held up against the ideals of masculinity, this longing only made him feel more ashamed. Even little things could set him off. And the very fact that he reacted so emotionally caused him to feel ashamed of his shame. At thirteen, he began turning to drugs for relief. As a teenager, he found comfort from occasional stints in juvenile detention. There, at least three meals, a bed, and some attention could be relied on. For him, this was the closest he came to feeling "care" as a child.

At sixteen, he became a father to a child he's rarely seen. He longs to know his daughter but has no idea how he can. Most of the time, he thinks it's better this way. After being in prison, he owes years of child support which he would have to begin paying once he gets a job—if he gets a job.

Prison was the first place he found a strong sense of fitting in. Being white was enough for other white inmates to have his back. Every day, he learned to see other races as the enemy and developed deep-seated prejudices. And then, he went into solitary confinement. As with many who endure isolation,[9] this further devastated his mental health. With everything he'd been through before, he had never engaged in self-harm. But in solitary, his mental torment became unbearable, and he began to

---

[9] Solitary confinement stands in violation of the United Nation's "Mandela Rules" for humane treatment of prisoners, to which the United States is not beholden.

cut himself. At first, it was just to feel alive. But soon, he *wanted* to be transferred to the psych ward—again, to experience even that miserable form of "care."

He was released straight from solitary onto the street, with nothing but the clothes he had when he went in, and a dead cell phone. He cannot describe, let alone identify, the maelstrom of disorders he could now be diagnosed with.

In Anthony's case, the violence he suffered and committed in prison was far worse than before he went in. Shame and secrecy about these experiences make them "unshareable." The gap between himself and his society yawns deeper and further than ever. He feels sure it's only a matter of time before he falls back into the abyss. And anyway, he has no family, no support, and no one who would care much if he lived, died, thrived, or got locked up for life.

"Every child is born into the world looking for someone looking for them," says Curt Thompson.[10] But no one has ever come looking for Anthony, except the police. And they are the only ones he can make sure will come looking again.

> And he came, and preached good news of peace to you who were far off, and to you who were near (Eph 2:17) ... Now, in the world of Jesus the Coming King, you who were once far off have been brought near, in the blood of the Coming King (Eph 2:13) ... He himself is our peace, who has created in his body an entirely new way of being human—a new way to see our worth, our identity, and our purpose (Eph 2:15) ... With him, we all have a Father whose door is always open. So you are no longer just a face in the crowd or an outcast—you have citizenship in the world ruled by Jesus, along with everyone else that he has called. You belong completely to the family of God (Eph 2:19). *(Author's translation)*

"Anthony" is not a real person. But his story is based on real, firsthand accounts from among the 10 percent of Americans who've been locked up at some point in their lives. Many of these accounts are from family and friends of mine who have healed enough to tell them. Each sentence has a face behind it for me. I know many more for whom these topics remain completely off limits.

I am convinced that the good news Jesus preached is good news for the world, good news for people like Anthony, and good news for our communities. It's good news because it cuts straight to the heart of violence at all levels. Jesus enters the cycle of death and overcomes it.

---

10 Quoted in Kiyomi, "The Stranger in My House."

Shame > Stigma > Violence > Trauma

Violence denies the glory of the soul. The denial of this fundamental truth about us creates trauma. As we struggle to make sense of trauma, we often narrate it through the lens of shame, a "frequent, often poorly recognized sequel to trauma."[11]

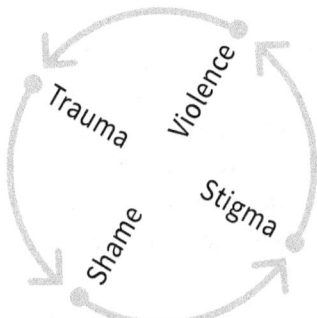

Figure 3.1: The cycle of shame, stigma, violence, trauma

The various forms of shame which can follow a traumatic experience are natural responses. Trauma forces us to question our view of ourselves and the world around us. At this point, shame can go in one of two directions—either toward healing and resilience, or stigma and disintegration. We will say more about this in chapter 5.

For now, we simply need to acknowledge that when shame leaves the soul wounded, people begin to live out their shame narratives as a stigma. They may begin to withdraw from their community, and their community may also push them out, causing disintegration. If stigma deepens, and people begin running out of ways to cover their shame or regain a sense of any kind of glory, they become more likely to also commit acts of violence to cover up or eliminate the apparent source of their shame.[12] This violence could be against others, or themselves in the form of addiction and self-harm. Most often, it is both.

The cycle of violence takes place within the individual, but always interacts with cycles taking place in the whole community as well. Violence traumatizes others, and so perpetuates the cycle. A family, a culture, or a community can hold collective shame, and be caught in a collective cycle of violence.[13] We will say more about this in the coming chapters.

---

11 Taylor, "The Influence of Shame on Post-Trauma Disorders," in the Abstract.
12 Gilligan, *Violence*, 110–11.
13 Scheff, Daniel, and Sterphone, "Shame and a Theory of War and Violence," 109–15. See also Gerodimos, "Humiliation, Shame, and Violence," 1–12.

BEING HUMAN: Sin and Shame

This chapter shows us the deep longing for glory which shame exposes. C. S. Lewis understood this fundamental human longing as evidence that there had to be more than what we experience now. We can see that we do not exist on our own, nor do we experience glory or shame on our own. Our self-understanding is built by the communities around us and our experiences in relationships. That self-understanding determines the narratives we live out in our actions with others.

When we are degraded, we degrade others in a vicious cycle of longing for glory, and despair about ever having what we can't stop longing for. If we see our own humanity as worthless, we compulsively treat all humanity as worthless, both in ourselves and others. All of this is connected.

Scripture gives us many examples of how the pattern of sin and shame works at all levels. These stories invite us to wrestle with the complex nature of sin and its tragic effects. Scripture shows how sin and shame move individually, corporately, and generationally.

This brings us to the end of Section I. We have examined "Our Longing for Glory" (ch. 1), "Jesus, Our Glory" (ch. 2), and just-completed "Defining (and Defending) Shame" (ch. 3). Just ahead is Section II: "Violence and Sin" which opens with chapter 4: "Sin Is Not Simple."

CHAPTER 3 SUMMARY

- Life is fundamentally relational and created for relational beauty, reflecting God's glory.
- A cycle of shame and violence was unleashed in Eden, and it continues to this day.
- "Anthony's story" depicts the complexity of sin and brokenness—individually, socially, institutionally.
- Christ's gospel speaks to the heart of violence at all levels—individually and socially.
- Jesus enters humanity's cycle of shame/violence/death—and overcomes it.

FOR FURTHER REFLECTION

- If we were created for relational beauty, what does human brokenness look like?
- How might the story of Cain and Abel (Gen 4:1–10) serve as a prototype for humanity's shame and violence?
- Have you observed the cause-and-effect connection between shame and violence?

SECTION II

VIOLENCE
and Sin

Chapter 4: Sin Is Not Simple

Chapter 5: Shame, Violence, and Individualism

Chapter 6: Powers and Principalities

Chapter 7: Status Games

Chapter 8: Group Versus Group Hostility

Chapter 4

SIN IS NOT SIMPLE

"Nathan said to David, 'You are the man!'"
−2 Samuel 12:7

IN THIS CHAPTER

- The Bible reveals a complex view of sin. Sin is a tangled mess of personal, familial, social, institutional, systemic, and cosmic realities.
- Sin, in all its complexity, is the number one ally of violence.

Werner:

In 2 Samuel 11, the rich and mighty King David covets his neighbor's wife and takes the beautiful Bathsheba for himself (11:1–4). She becomes pregnant. David tries to cover up his sin by lying, manipulating, and trying to get Bathsheba's husband Uriah the Hittite to lie with his wife. When that doesn't work, he orders the murder of Uriah (11:6–14). David wraps the entire affair in self-protective lies. After Uriah's death, Bathsheba becomes David's wife and bears him a son (11:27). "But the thing that David did displeased the Lord" (11:27).

"And the Lord sent Nathan to David" (12:1). The prophet Nathan goes to David's house. It is the Bible's classic example of speaking truth to power. Nathan tells a story. "There were two men in a certain city, the one rich and the other poor." The rich man had "very many flocks and herds." Despite his great wealth, the rich man steals the poor man's one and only beloved ewe lamb and kills it to be eaten. David plainly sees the injustice. He is outraged: "As the Lord lives, the man who has done this deserves to die" (12:5).

Nathan replies, "You are the man."

David replies humbly, "I have sinned against the Lord." He acknowledges his sin and repents. Nathan immediately comforts David: "The Lord has put away your sin; you shall not die" (12:13).

But David's sin has consequences: "Thus says the Lord, 'Behold, I will raise up evil against you out of your own house.[1] And I will take your wives

---

[1] Robert Alter writes, "As Bar-Efrat notes, David's rather callous message to Joab, 'the sword sometimes consumes one way and sometimes another,' is now thrown back in his face. The story of David's sons, not to speak of his descendants in later generations, will in fact turn out to be a long tale of conspiracy, internecine struggle, and murder.

before your eyes and give them to your neighbor, and he shall lie with your wives in the sight of this sun" (12:11). Yes, David repents; nevertheless, "because by this deed you have utterly scorned the Lord, the child who is born to you shall die" (12:14). The ripple effects are immediate with the death of the infant, but David's sin has national and multi-generational impact.[2]

After this, David's son Amnon rapes his half-sister, Tamar. Years later, her full brother Absalom kills Amnon in revenge and goes into exile. Absalom will later be brought back, but will organize a coup against his father, during which he rapes his father's concubines in broad daylight. Absalom is finally killed in the civil war which ensues, and David loses yet another son.

Psalm 51 is considered a record of David's repentance. His sorrow is obvious. "Have mercy on me, O God ... blot out my transgressions ... cleanse me from my sin ... my sin is ever before me." David plainly accepts responsibility for his individual actions and feels the pangs of a deeply troubled conscience. His sins are many. His sins are *against many*:

1. **David sinned against Bathsheba.** By abusing his power as king he committed not just adultery, but sexual assault. Bathsheba had no opportunity to refuse, especially with her husband at war. Moreover, Nathan's prophetic narration depicts Bathsheba as utterly powerless, a victim-pawn in what occurs. She is not just a ewe sheep, but a "ewe lamb." The ewe lamb does not willingly follow the wicked rich man but is forcibly taken by him.

2. **David sinned against Bathsheba's husband Uriah the Hittite.** David abused his power. He debased Uriah by sexually assaulting his wife; he lied to him, manipulated him, and finally gave orders to murder him.

3. **David sinned against his general, Joab.** David lied to him, involving him in the plot to kill a very honorable soldier, Uriah.[3]

One of the most extraordinary features of the whole David narrative is that this story of the founding of the great dynasty of Judah is, paradoxically, already a tale of the fall of the house of David. Once again, no one has grasped this tragic paradox more profoundly than William Faulkner in his recasting of the story in *Absalom, Absalom!* The author of the David story continually exercises an unblinking vision of David and the institution of the monarchy that exposes their terrible flaws even as he accepts their divinely authorized legitimacy." Alter, *The Hebrew Bible: A Translation*, 2650–51.

2 "David himself will not be condemned to die, but death will hang over his house. As the Talmud (Yoma 22B) notes, the fourfold retribution for Uriah's death will be worked out in the death or violent fate of four of David's children: the unnamed infant son of Bathsheba, Tamar, Amnon, and Absalom." Alter, 2649.

3 1 Samuel 23:39 reads, "Uriah the Hittite: thirty-seven in all." Uriah is listed as the last of David's thirty-seven "mighty men" of valor. The author of Samuel could have excluded

4. **David sinned against his own family.** David became an unforgettable example of a family leader who allows sexual lust to drive his behavior. Others followed his example.

5. **David sinned against his people.** David failed to be a righteous leader and failed to uphold justice.

6. **David sinned against the Hittites.**[4] God intended for Abraham's family to bless all peoples, including the Hittites. David represents the people as king; with his series of blatant law-breaking actions (coveting your neighbor's wife, lying, adultery, murder) against Uriah the Hittite (a gentile more honorable than himself), David violates God's overarching purpose to make a name for himself among the nations.[5]

7. **David sinned against God.** In all of the above, David sinned against God's holiness, love, honor, law, and global purpose.

But in Psalm 51 David says: "Against you, you only, have I sinned, and done what is evil in your sight" (Ps 51:4). What about all those people listed above against whom he sinned? In what sense is it possible that David's sins are "only against God"? I can think of three possibilities:

First, since God's laws were broken in every aspect of David's behavior, in every aspect David sinned against the character, honor, and law of God.

Second, David lived in the ancient Near East; every nation had its own national, tribal god or deity. David's abuse of power and sexual lust was not atypical or deviant for the kings or the gods of the ancient Near East. But David manifestly deviated from the laws of Yahweh. One can say that against *no other god* did David commit sin. His sins were exclusively against the God of Jacob, the Almighty God, Yahweh.

Third, no human being saw every sinful imagination of David's heart or every action, but God did (I have "done what is evil in your sight"). Therefore, it was only God who knew the full extent of David's iniquity.

While affirming that our sins *as individuals* are against God, we also affirm that sin and evil are *social*. As in David's story, sin can be familial, corporate, tribal, and national. Sin is a tangled mess. It has ripple effects

---

Uriah from the list, thus permitting the reader to avoid recalling the stinging dishonor of David's sin. The author of Samuel has the reader remembering the gravity of David's sin as a thread in Israel's family story as the people of God.

4 In 2 Samuel 11, "Uriah" is mentioned fifteen times, of which five he is called "Uriah the Hittite." His identity as a Hittite was important to Uriah, to the author of the books of Samuel, and to God.

5 "You who boast in the law dishonor God by breaking the law. For, as it is written, "'The name of God is blasphemed among the Gentiles because of you'" (Rom 2:23-24). This text could certainly be applied to David's sin against Uriah the Hittite.

and repercussions everywhere. This story reveals the long, tragic fallout of an individual's sin (despite his repentance), and correspondingly, sin's inevitable cascade of familial, social, and systemic effects over time.

In his book *Missing the Mark: Sin and Its Consequences in Biblical Theology*, Mark Biddle writes, "David, as father and king, has created a system of interactions that will ultimately bring one of his daughters, and three of his sons to ruin at the hands of other members of the king's family. The nation will experience civil war and long-term political unrest. The royal court will be torn by intrigue (1 Sam 13; 1 Kgs 2)."[6]

Robert Alter says regarding this story (as noted above), "the fourfold retribution for Uriah's death will be worked out in the death or violent fate of four of David's children: the unnamed infant son of Bathsheba, Tamar, Amnon, and Absalom." Moreover, "the story of David's sons, not to speak of his descendants in later generations, will in fact turn out to be a long tale of conspiracy, internecine struggle, and murder."[7]

"Against you, you only have I sinned"?

Yes. But at the same time, it's not that simple.

Kristin: **Retelling the Story**

The story of David and Bathsheba could be retold in different ways.[8] One way is to start with David and show the ripple effects of his individual choices, as Werner has done above. But we could also begin with the larger historical structures which David inherited. We could see the story as a kind of performance of a bigger and older "script,"[9] a reenactment of the past where David simply "plays the role" of a king in his day.

---

6 Biddle, *Missing the Mark*, ix.

7 Alter, *Hebrew Bible*, 2649.

8 Whenever we interpret a story, we do our own retelling. The Gospels show us that the same story can be told in a variety of different ways, depending on the perspective of the storyteller. And as John the Evangelist points out, it is never possible to share everything (John 21:25). Every story is retold by choosing certain details that suit the purposes of the storyteller and the needs of their audience. John tells us that the world could not contain the books that would be written if everything about Jesus's life were written down (John 21:25). And yet, he wrote down the things he thought would help his readers to "believe that Jesus is the Christ, the Son of God, and that by believing you may have life in his name" (John 20:31). By contrast, Luke has the specific purpose of "writing an orderly account" for a reader named Theophilus (Luke 1:3). His perspective is often thought of as more of a historian who gathers other people's eyewitness accounts. Likewise, whenever we teach or preach Scripture, we naturally select what things to emphasize for our audience and our purposes. If we do this faithfully, we will be aligned with the purpose of the authors—helping us to believe, to have life, and to be transformed in Jesus's name.

9 Personal conversation with Bishop Zac Niringiye on Feb. 6, 2023.

Generations before, David's ancestor Judah also took a woman who was forbidden, though for different reasons. She was a Canaanite, the daughter of Shua, or "bath-shua" in Hebrew (Gen 38:2). Judah also loses two sons because of sin. The sin of the first son is unnamed, but the sin of the second son is (with twisted irony) his refusal to impregnate Judah's daughter-in-law, Tamar (Gen 38:9–10). In Samuel, Tamar (David's daughter) is deceived by her half-brother, who ends up sexually assaulting her. In Genesis, Tamar (Judah's daughter-in-law) deceives *him* in order to finally bear children.

The connections are not coincidence. The writers show how the pattern of sin repeats from generation to generation. David is not judged for Judah's actions—but his sin is not entirely his own either. It is also a choice not to depart from the sins of his fathers *and* to imitate the corrupt ways of kings from surrounding nations (1 Sam 8:5).[10]

In addition to his failure to repent of generational sin, David also follows the normal script for power's corruption. When the tale with Bathsheba begins, we do not find him on the battlefield delivering the people as he did before, nor studying God's teaching (Deut 17:18–20). Instead, he is relaxing at his palace while other men go out to fight. Now he is a man of power, a king with a citadel. And it is here where he begins turning into the type of leader the Lord warned the people about (1 Sam 8:11–18.) At this moment, he looks just like one among history's many liberators-turned-dictators.

Werner: ### The Danger of Making Things Too Simple

What is the point of delving into the tragedy concerning David's sin? Simply this: Sin is an individual reality, but it is not *merely* an individual reality. Sin is complex. Sin is a personal, social, and systemic tangle of individual, corporate, and cosmic forces. In my book *The Global Gospel*, I simplify the complex subject of honor-shame dynamics in the Bible.

But there is a danger in making too simple something that is both extremely important and complex: the danger of reductionism. *Importance* and *complexity* are two primary factors in grappling with the risks of reductionism. Figure 4.1 illustrates the idea that as the importance of an issue increases and the degree of complexity increases, there is increasing risk associated with reductionism:

---

10 In a similar fashion, we are told that the kings of Israel, from generation to generation, "clung to the sin of Jeroboam" (2 Kgs 3:3) or "walked in the ways of the sin of Jeroboam" (1 Kgs 16:26; 22:52) or simply "did not depart from all the sins of Jeroboam" (2 Kgs 13:11).

- The more important an issue, the greater the risk for a negative impact in our world if our understanding of it is too simplistic.
- The more complex an issue, the greater the temptation to reduce its complexity to understand it and communicate about it.
- The greater the reductionism, the more likely the risk for an imbalance or other negative effect—even if unintended.

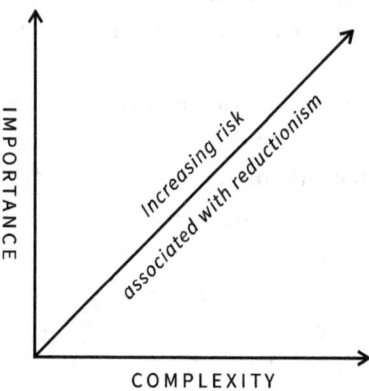

Figure 4.1: Reductionism has two factors—importance and complexity

For example, consider the vexing issue of violence in our world. It is both extremely important and complex. An example of a reductionist view says the answer is in criminal justice reform. Others might say the answer is in psychology … or biology … or another field of science. A Christian might say the answer is spiritual.

Violence expert Dr. Bandy X. Lee observes that no single approach, no one discipline is enough to solve the important and vexing problem of violence. The vast complexity of the human mind … the winding intricacies of family stories … the clashing of cultural forces … local, national, and international powers … spiritual dynamics, both dark and light … the myriad horrors … the bewildering beauty of our life together as human beings … *It is all far too complex.*

Lee proposes that the only truly workable approach is one that *integrates* various disciplines. Lee urges that we must avoid reductionisms and *embrace complexity.*[11] But we evangelicals like reductionisms. It is

---

11 "We now know that this reductionism by favoring lower levels no longer holds for physics, much less for the study of human beings: reductionistic biology fails to explain life, as reductionistic psychology fails to explain the human mind. Human beings are far more complex than this approach will allow, and a proper understanding lies in embracing complexity rather than in finding a way to explain it away." Lee, *Violence*, 45–46.

our habit to shun complexity.¹² In their outstanding book *Reframation*, Hirsch and Nelson seek to overcome reductionism in the church concerning "God and gospel":

> We want to throw a torchlight on the many *reductions* of how we understand and experience both God and gospel. On the one hand we believe many of our problems in engaging missionally … are rooted in *reduced* understandings of God that have severely limited the ways in which we think he is to be encountered and communicated in the world. On the other hand we are equally limited by a severely *diminished* anthropology (understanding of the human condition) and have therefore failed to fully understand the complex, existential, religiously motivated elements common to all human beings—desire, longing, and search.¹³

What is our hope as authors? That readers would *long for and desire, proclaim and embody* Christ's gospel of peace with more of its beauty and complexity. But the stunning beauty of the gospel cure is only revealed in considering the profound pathology of the human condition. This means we must further diagnose humanity's sin, along with our tendency to minimize its complexity.

Reductionism about Sin

A popular *Systematic Theology* offers this definition of sin:

> Sin is any failure to conform to the moral law of God in act, attitude, or nature. Sin is here defined in relation to God and his moral law. Sin includes not only individual acts, such as stealing, lying, and committing murder, but also attitudes that are contrary to the attitudes God requires of us.¹⁴

Sin is any failure to conform to the moral law of God in act, attitude, or nature. The definition assumes that sin is primarily located in the individual person. Individuals fail to conform to the moral law of God. Individuals steal. Individuals lie and commit murder. Individuals have selfish attitudes.

---

12 Historian Mark Noll critiqued the anti-intellectualism of American evangelicals in his 1994 book, *The Scandal of the Evangelical Mind*. Noll approvingly quotes N. K. Clifford who wrote in 1973: "The Evangelical Protestant mind has never relished complexity. Indeed, its crusading genius, whether in religion or politics, has always tended toward an over-simplification of issues and the substitution of inspiration and zeal for critical analysis and serious reflection." Who would doubt that Clifford's 1973 quote still rings true in 2025? See Noll, *Scandal*, 19–20, citing Clifford, "His Dominion," 323.

13 Hirsch and Nelson, *Reframation*, 50–51 (emphasis mine).

14 Grudem, *Systematic Theology*, 965.

The Bible emphasizes the sinfulness of sinners—*individual* sinners. A series of word studies shows how wide-ranging this emphasis is in the New Testament. Here are some results:

Number of verses in New Testament with "sin" / "sins" / "sinned" / "sinning"	198
Number of words, aggregate: "sin" / "sins" / "sinned" / "sinning"	219
Number of occurrences referring to individual sinner, directly or indirectly	186
Number of occurrences referring to sins of a specific group	33

Figure 4.2: "Sin" / "sins" / "sinned" / "sinning" in the New Testament (ESV)

Out of 219 occurrences of the words *sin, sins, sinned,* and *sinning,* 186 occurrences related directly or indirectly to individual persons.[15] That amounts to 85 percent; the vast majority focus on the individual.[16] Only 33 occurrences referred to a specific group. The New Testament plainly speaks about individual sin[17] and the saving work of Christ for sinners.

But to teach about the problem of sin as only an individual matter is a *reduction*. Consider the vast narrative material in the Bible about empires (for example, Babel, Egypt, Babylon,[18] Persia, Rome). These empires are consistently presented as opposed to the One Creator God and to God's people.[19] The biblical writers describe the sinfulness of these empires not so much by using the word *sin,* but in colorfully describing their arrogance, oppression, violence, and idolatry—often in story form. Fully the first fifteen chapters of Exodus—all 404 verses—attest to the empire's sinfulness in a complex, dramatic narrative. God delivers his people from Egypt's idolatry and violence so they can freely worship the true and living God as a witness to the nations (Exod 9:13–16; 15:14–15).

---

15 Mischke, "'Sin' ... an Analysis."

16 The "Jesus Prayer" has been used for centuries in various Christian traditions. Based in part on Luke 18:13, the Jesus Prayer emphasizes the individual sinner: "Lord Jesus Christ, Son of God, have mercy on me, a sinner."

17 This emphasis on the individual sinner in need of salvation is consistent with the passage about the white throne judgment (Rev 20:13–15) in which "each one of them"—of the dead—are judged, and "if anyone's name is not found written in the book of life, he was thrown into the lake of fire." However, verse 14 says, "Then Death and Hades were thrown into the lake of fire." This suggests that all enemies of humanity—all systems of evil—will be judged. "The fiery lake is the place where all evil—the dragon, the wild things, the false prophet, and their armies—is eradicated." McKnight and Hatchett, *Revelation,* 144.

18 "While most English translations distinguish between 'Babel' and 'Babylon,' Hebrew has one word for both: babel." Sprinkle, *Exiles,* 38.

19 Wink, *Engaging the Powers,* 11–109. See also Howard-Brook, *Come Out My People*; this extensive work argues that the entire biblical narrative offers an ongoing comparison between the good, peaceable "religion of creation" and the oppressive, idolatrous "religion of empire" (27).

Sin Is Not Just about Individuals

It's not just individuals who sin. "God did not spare angels when they sinned" (2 Pet 2:4); "the devil has been sinning from the beginning" (1 John 3:8); and the sins of Babylon "are heaped as high as heaven" (Rev 18:4–5). Sin is a human problem entangled with dark forces—fallen angels, the devil, the various empires.

Consider again the story of David in 2 Samuel 11–12. The word *sin* never appears in chapter 11, and only once in chapter 12. As the David-narrative progresses in Samuel, his individual sin overlaps with moral failures at the family and national levels in a complex tangled mess. Clearly, these dynamics rhyme with our own world—institutional tragedies born of sexual lust, family dysfunction and brokenness, sin as a multi-generational system—these are as modern as they are ancient.

The Bible reveals that sin and judgment happen at the individual level, but also at the supernatural cosmic realm, as well as the familial, civic, corporate, national, and imperial levels. Consider Figure 4.3 (on the following page), which offers examples from the Bible of various human group types who are critiqued or judged by God.

The diagram illustrates that in the Bible, sin occurs across the full range of person-to-group types—beginning at left with the individual, then moving to the family and tribe, next the local church, then the city, next the people group or nation, then the empire (the largest non-universal group), and lastly, all humanity.

The judgment of groups is not merely an Old Testament dynamic; in every category there are examples from the New Testament as well. The biblical evidence is plain: Evil and sin are personal, social, and systemic.

A Tale of Two Diagrams

On page 41 we compare two diagrams. The first diagram (Figure 4.4) centers the individual and "magnifies" the individual relative to social and cosmic forces. I made this diagram thinking of the individual sins of David in the story of David and Bathsheba. I attempted to represent the complex social and cosmic forces that operate on the individual.

Figure 4.4 suggests a world revolving around "me"—a single human being. Here the individual person is pictured at the center, alone. Some readers might think of the Enlightenment credo of individualism of the philosopher René Descartes, "I think, therefore I am."

When an African friend saw this diagram, he saw my Western bias. He saw a view of human life that overrepresented the individual in relation to social and cosmic powers. That was for me no small insight.

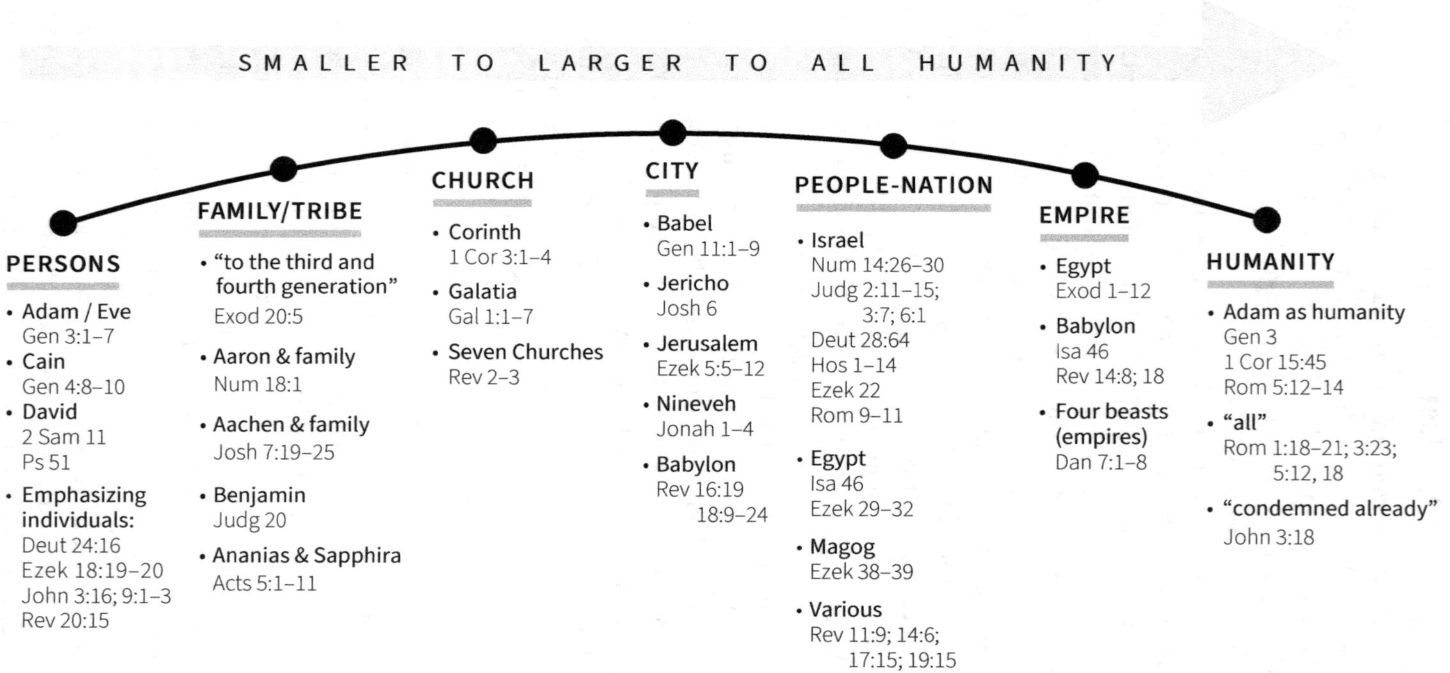

SMALLER TO LARGER TO ALL HUMANITY

PERSONS
- Adam / Eve
  Gen 3:1–7
- Cain
  Gen 4:8–10
- David
  2 Sam 11
  Ps 51
- Emphasizing individuals:
  Deut 24:16
  Ezek 18:19–20
  John 3:16; 9:1–3
  Rev 20:15

FAMILY/TRIBE
- "to the third and fourth generation"
  Exod 20:5
- Aaron & family
  Num 18:1
- Aachen & family
  Josh 7:19–25
- Benjamin
  Judg 20
- Ananias & Sapphira
  Acts 5:1–11

CHURCH
- Corinth
  1 Cor 3:1–4
- Galatia
  Gal 1:1–7
- Seven Churches
  Rev 2–3

CITY
- Babel
  Gen 11:1–9
- Jericho
  Josh 6
- Jerusalem
  Ezek 5:5–12
- Nineveh
  Jonah 1–4
- Babylon
  Rev 16:19
  18:9–24

PEOPLE-NATION
- Israel
  Num 14:26–30
  Judg 2:11–15;
  3:7; 6:1
  Deut 28:64
  Hos 1–14
  Ezek 22
  Rom 9–11
- Egypt
  Isa 46
  Ezek 29–32
- Magog
  Ezek 38–39
- Various
  Rev 11:9; 14:6;
  17:15; 19:15

EMPIRE
- Egypt
  Exod 1–12
- Babylon
  Isa 46
  Rev 14:8; 18
- Four beasts (empires)
  Dan 7:1–8

HUMANITY
- Adam as humanity
  Gen 3
  1 Cor 15:45
  Rom 5:12–14
- "all"
  Rom 1:18–21; 3:23;
  5:12, 18
- "condemned already"
  John 3:18

Figure 4.3: Range of human groupings in the Bible critiqued or judged by God

I appreciate the viewpoint of my African friend. While recognizing the social and cosmic forces surrounding the individual, this diagram exaggerates the power of the individual in two ways—first by the human head being *centered,* and second, by the human head being *too big,* relatively speaking. This reminds us: diagrams (like words) are useful but limited symbols for expressing reality.

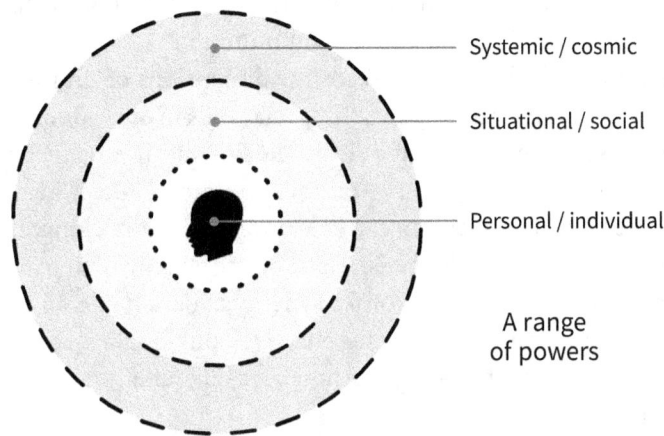

Figure 4.4: Depicting levels of power while centering the individual

Figure 4.5 attempts to illustrate the powers, peoples, nations, institutions, corporations, families, and communities that influence individuals. My world does not revolve around me, the individual. This truth is so simple, it is almost embarrassing.

Figure 4.5: Depicting levels of power while relativizing the individual

The second diagram (Figure 4.5) represents the social and cosmic forces in levels of magnitude and as having far greater influence than the individual human.

With this diagram we amplify the cosmic and social dynamics of sin. The weight of sin at higher levels presses down onto lower levels as we follow "the course of this world." Miroslav Volf rightly states, "sin is both the rot deep in our souls and a prowling beast of exclusion that holds captive entire societies, cultures, and communities."[20]

Grappling with the social and cosmic dimensions of sin is especially important for comprehending massive social evils in our world. Consider the Holocaust under Germany's Third Reich, the Rwandan Genocide (1994), or the history of slavery and racism in the United States. What about the perpetual problems of extreme poverty, sex trafficking, abortion, the refugee crisis, or homelessness? These all are evils involving individual human agents, but they also involve a synergy of dark forces and systems.

Isn't it therefore important to see ourselves, our families, communities and nations, our global neighborhood, inside and underneath this complexity?

Is It Both-And?

The first diagram recognizes social and cosmic powers while magnifying the individual. The second diagram recognizes the individual while magnifying cosmic and social powers. Is one more "biblical" than the other?

On the one hand, the Bible affirms individual personhood and agency. Bible stories often involve individuals whose predicaments have made them extremely vulnerable in life-and-death political rivalries. Sometimes they have faith in God and follow God; sometimes they become depressed; sometimes they fail and fall into sin; sometimes their circumstances are utterly bleak.

Jesus is revealed as the Son of Man, God-in-the-flesh, fulfilling ancient prophecies. In perfect faithfulness to the Father, he chooses to submit to unimaginable suffering and injustice because of self-giving love for humanity and God's glory. This is Jesus of Nazareth, the apparent victim of Roman crucifixion. He is the One whose great inversions change the course of history. He lovingly submits to God while loving his enemies. He redefines manhood and leadership as humble fearless servanthood. He relativizes traditional sources of honor and identity.

---

20 Volf, *Exclusion and Embrace*, 314.

Despite massive cosmic, political, and social forces that cause unimaginable suffering, Jesus the Christ rises again on the third day over death and over all sin and darkness. To humanity as a whole and to every person individually, he bequeaths a transcendent dignity, and the possibility of eternal life. Jesus idealizes individual agency.

On the other hand, the Bible gives robust and routine witness to the myriad cosmic, national, and communal forces that challenge individuals and peoples. What character in the Bible is not beset by social, imperial, or spiritual forces that employ rejection, shame, violence, or death in opposition to God and the *shalom* he intends for his world? As N. T. Wright says, "Sin in the human heart, darkness in the human mind, dehumanized behaviour in the human life: all went together with the rule of dark forces that operated through idols, including empires and their rulers, to thwart the purposes of the one creator God."[21]

Again, consider Jesus. Through birth, life, death, and resurrection Jesus interacts with: his own family and hometown; other families and individuals; friends and followers; enemies, rivals, traitors; cities and villages of first-century Palestine; national, tribal, religious allegiances; dreadful forces of empire; and demonic powers of darkness. And he does this all while submitting to and agreeing with the Father's will (John 5:17–19). He "in every respect has been tempted as we are, yet without sin" (Heb 4:15).

Jesus redefines the moral standard for humanity and the potential glory of the individual; at the same time Jesus exposes both the great power and the ultimate impotence of the world's massive structures of sin—rulers, authorities, and cosmic powers of evil (Eph 6:12). "The Son of Man came to seek and to save" lost sinners (Luke 19:10); Jesus also came "to destroy the works of the devil" (1 John 3:8).

In Luke 19:41–44, Jesus weeps over Jerusalem. He sees what the multitudes cannot—their collective blindness "to the things that make for peace." He knows their tragic destiny—"the days will come upon you" when the Roman Empire, Jerusalem's overlord, will destroy the city and its inhabitants. It will be a time when individual moral agency will be useless in preventing that destruction.[22]

We humans are immortal beings in a moral universe. We have agency in the story of God. Our choices are weighty. Like Jesus, we are imbued with glory. At the same time the Bible reveals hierarchies and structures

---

21 Wright, *Paul and the Faithfulness of God*, 771.
22 Jesus is referring to the destruction of Jerusalem in AD 70.

of power—familial, spiritual, social, political, tribal, national, imperial. These forces and influences, for good or ill and everything in between, are part of our world. We are shaped by them knowingly and unknowingly, even as we follow Jesus.

Kristin:

Werner has emphasized a definition of sin from a popular systematic theology—"the failure to conform to the moral law of God." I want to emphasize a definition in relation to glory, that "all have sinned and *fallen short of the glory of God* (Rom 3:23)."[23] David violated God's covenant, but he also fell short of the glory God intended for himself and for his people. Ironically, at the moment of his highest worldly honor, David found himself at the lowest point of shame before the One who had raised him up from the sheepfold (1 Chr 17:7). He rejected the one source of glory that really counts—the Lord's.

Thinking in terms of glory can help us see things holistically. Returning to the story of Anthony, we can see how the various forces of sin and shame work: Anthony is accountable for the violence he perpetrated, but the people who perpetrated violence against him are also accountable. The people who did violence to his soul and body are accountable. The people who sold him drugs—all the way from the pushers up to the cartels—are also accountable. So is the corruption of the American government, which greatly exacerbates Latin America's drug wars. The brokenness of the foster care system and our cultural lack of care for children are also accountable. And the truth is, none of us can say what we would have done when put into the same circumstances.

The patterns of dysfunction and fallen glory that we see at larger levels, we also see at smaller and smaller levels, all the way down to the individual. Rather than imitating God, the "Father from whom every family in heaven and on earth is named" (Eph 3:15), we humans follow the false "father," the devil (John 8:44). His pattern leads to a cycle of lies, violence, and shame that we cannot transcend—not without help from the outside.

---

23 In Romans 1–3, Paul describes sin and its universality. Rather than arguing his case using the language of guilt and innocence, Paul primarily uses the language of shame and honor (Rom 1:23; 2:23; 3:23). See Vaughn, *Reading Romans with Eastern Eyes*, 39–51.

BEING HUMAN: Under the Complexity of Sin

Our exploration of sin and its effects in the life of King David shows us that we cannot reduce the degradation of glory—or its restoration—to individual guilt and innocence. Scripture calls us to see sin as a multilayered oppression on every level of human existence.

In this chapter, we have seen how our typical theological approaches to sin can train us to overlook crucial insights on violence offered by biblical narratives. In the next chapter, "Shame and Individualism," we will take a closer look at the individual and communal dynamics of violence, shame, and glory. In so doing, we will see how the individualism which predominates in much of our theology also places cultural limits on how we understand and respond to the violence in our world.

CHAPTER 4 SUMMARY

- In the story of David and Bathsheba, sin is much more than an individual affair. David's personal sin rippled—*physically*, *emotionally*, *spiritually*, *politically*—across his family and nation, intergenerationally and systemically, resulting in death and division.
- Western theology tends to locate sin exclusively in the individual; this obscures the Bible's robust material about the social, corporate, cosmic, and systemic nature of sin.
- Scripture affirms the responsibility and agency of individuals while simultaneously recognizing the various levels of sinful powers under which we live.
- The Bible critiques families and tribes, cities, churches, peoples, nations, and empires—all examples of collective identity sin.
- The biblical narrative describes sin as a tangled complexity of personal, social, and cosmic forces. This begs the question: Does the Bible reveal a gospel which corresponds to this complexity, offering hope for humanity?

FOR FURTHER REFLECTION

- If you were to teach a Bible lesson on the complexity of sin, where would you begin?
- How does Western theology's emphasis on the individual (despite its many blessings) restrict us in addressing collective identity sins such as tribalism, racism, or nationalism?
- How might you use your individual agency to communicate in your arena of influence the biblical truths about *collective identity sin*?

Chapter 5

SHAME, VIOLENCE, AND INDIVIDUALISM

*I need to know there is justice / That it will roll in abundance
And that you're building a city / Where we arrive as immigrants
And you call us citizens / And you welcome us as children home.*
–"Citizens" by Jon Guerra

IN THIS CHAPTER

- The toxic cycle of *shame > stigma > violence > trauma* is common in many social systems. These social systems are marked by disintegrative shame.
- *Disintegrative* shame—in contrast to *reintegrative* shame—reinforces the toxic aspects of shame and the brokenness of a community.
- The early church and Paul can be seen as practicing reintegrative shame—for the health of the individual and community.

Kristin:

Anthony's story shares a lot in common with the man among the tombs (Mark 5:1–20). We know that he was both violent toward others and afflicted by forces outside his control. The man who Jesus visited on the other side of Lake Galilee had an entire legion of demons against him and could not be restrained by mere physical force. Both were caught in cycles of shame and violence similar to the one we introduced in chapter 3, and both needed help from the outside to escape.

But what about the shame-and-violence cycles of the entire human race? How do we transcend these cycles, especially when we see that they are also perpetuated by supernatural powers of darkness?

The world itself needs help from the outside. And in Christ, God came to us as help from outside—outside of our calculations of worthiness, or honor, or shame. He came to us from outside the universe altogether, and we have seen his glory, full of grace and truth (John 1:14).

> For while we were still weak, at the right time Christ died for the ungodly. For one will scarcely die for a righteous person—though perhaps for a good person one would dare even to die—but God shows his love for us in that while we were still sinners, Christ died for us. (Rom 5:6–8)

And now, Jesus comes to us and says, "As the Father has sent me, even so I am sending you" (John 20:21). Just as Jesus said to the man among the tombs, "Go home to your friends and tell them how much the Lord has done for you, and how he has had mercy on you" (Mark 5:19–20).

Now we are emissaries proclaiming peace to those who need deliverance. Paul writes, "All this is from God, who through Christ reconciled us to himself and gave us the ministry of reconciliation; that is, in Christ God was reconciling the world to himself, not counting their trespasses against them, and entrusting to us the message of reconciliation" (2 Cor 5:18–19). Because the cycle of shame and violence exists at every level, whatever is good news for one must become good news for a community. And whatever is good news for a community will become good news for individuals.

Sin, Shame, and Individualism

While Western culture has its gifts, it also has limitations. In individualistic cultures, people are less used to thinking in terms of community. Perhaps no culture in history has taken the experiment of individualism so far as the majority culture of the United States.

Understanding cultural biases in theology helps us grapple with this "I-versus-we" distinction in the biblical text. In their book *Misreading Scripture with Individualist Eyes,* Randolph Richards and Richard James write about the differences between individualistic and collectivistic societies:

> Individualist societies tend to think of community as being the sum of the individuals. We bring our individual identities, characteristics, values, and talents, and the sum of this becomes our community. Individuals gather to make a community. In collectivist societies, however, the individual is the sum of the community. The community identity, characteristics, values, and talents form the identity of those who all belong to that community. Collectives are defined by the things they share with others, things such as shared blood, shared interests, shared history, shared land, and shared loyalty. They define their core identity as being part of a group, in distinction to other groups.[1]

All cultures can be placed on a spectrum from individualistic to collectivistic.[2] To help us see what this means, we will make some generalizations about the extreme ends of the spectrum:

---

[1] Richards and James, *Misreading Scripture,* 22.

[2] What follows was originally shared in "Telling Our Western Stories" at Rio Vida Torchbearer's School, El Campello, Spain, March 6, 2023.

INDIVIDUALISM: Life is about the individual—
my achievements, failures, rights, freedoms, distinctions, and property.

COLLECTIVISM: Life is about the community—
our achievements, failures, rights, freedoms, distinctions, and property.

Individualists emphasize the importance of private property, whereas collectivists emphasize the importance of shared/community property. Individualism is associated with ideals like equal opportunity, equal treatment under the law, freedom of self-determination, self-reliance, and the economic system of capitalism.

In questions of ethics, individualists ask if the actions of an individual have infringed upon the rights of another individual. Collectivists believe that the whole community has rights, and ask how behavior affects the whole community's way of life and social harmony.

Consider different approaches to addiction. Individualists can argue that someone in addiction only harms themselves. But collectivists emphasize that harm against one person's body really does affect others in profound ways.[3] Scripture supports this idea: "For if one member suffers, all suffer together; if one member is honored, all rejoice together" (1 Cor 12:26). This is often missed with the Western bias toward individualism and the limitations of English Bible translations.[4]

While individualists emphasize equal treatment under the law, for collectivists a person's responsibility changes based upon their social position, age, or wealth.

In individualism, the desire to respect choice tends toward secularism: the creation of "religiously neutral" spheres where differing individuals can (in theory) agree on laws and on matters tied to "reason alone" apart from "faith." For some Christians, this means that many daily activities have no spiritual significance and little bearing on Christian identity. A job is just a job, unless it is a directly religious vocation.

---

3 Lau, *Defending Shame*, 199.

4 Another example of this is found in 1 Cor 6:16–20. Verse 16 (ESV) reads, "Or do you not know that he who is joined to a prostitute becomes one body with her?" In this verse, the "you" being addressed is plural, and the "he" whose body is spoken of is singular. But, when we get to v. 19, there is a transition from speaking of a single person's body, to speaking of the collective body, where the body being addressed is plural: "Do you not know that y'all's body is a temple of the Holy Spirit within all of you, whom you all have from God? ... So, glorify God with y'all's body" (my translation). The nuance here can easily be missed. My body can be joined with a prostitute; but my body is not a temple of the Holy Spirit—*ours is*. So, in sinning against my own body, I'm also sinning against *our* body. More will be said on this in the next chapter.

	INDIVIDUALISM	COLLECTIVISM
COMMUNITY	The primary claim that the community makes on me is to keep me as an individual from violating other individuals' rights.	Because I would not be alive or be who I am without my community, I owe my life to my community. I do not want to violate the rights of my community.
THE NONHUMAN CREATION	The material world belongs to humans as property. As property, it doesn't necessarily have any rights of its own.	Other created things are part of our community/kinship network. Because they are related to us and supply us what we need to live, we have a responsibility to them.
LAW	Because everything comes down to individual choice and difference, enforcement of the rule of law by power is vital for maintaining order. The law exists to keep individuals from infringing on other individuals' rights.	The "laws" of state government are mostly irrelevant—but social contracts and norms are strictly enforced by the community in an informal way. These norms exist to maintain the honor of self and others. Social harmony is more important than being "guilty" or "innocent" by law.
GOD	Because "law" and objectivity are so important, God is associated with law, objectivity, reason, etc. God is primarily a judge and an enforcer of law. Humanity owes God perfect law observance.	God is our greatest ancestor and the Giver of all things. God is therefore the highest standard for honor. Humanity owes honor to God—to live with him and his other family members in a manner worthy of him.
COSMOLOGY	Characterized by humanism: Westerners tend to view everything in terms of humans and law (in some cases including the "laws of nature"). If a person does believe in God, God still operates primarily by laws, usually without the intervention of other spiritual beings or forces.	Characterized by supernaturalism: The spirit world is full, and active in both nonhuman and human affairs. The kinship network may extend to include ancestors (spiritual or physical), as well as gods, demons, and other spiritual entities. For some, this leads to an animistic view where everything has a spirit or spiritual life.

Figure 5.1: Five categories of comparison between individualism and collectivism

A 2007 survey by the Barna Group showed that a large number of Americans took Bible stories "at face value." However, the same survey found that "a minority of the people who believe these stories to be true consistently apply the principles embedded in these stories within their own lives. It seems that millions of Americans believe the Bible content is true but are not willing to translate those stories into action."[5] Is it any surprise that fifteen years later, belief in the Bible's validity has dropped, in part due to this inconsistency?[6]

Seeing the limitations of Western culture is not to diminish its gifts. But gifts from people of other cultures can supply what we are lacking. To that end, we turn now to look at how individualism affects the way we deal with violence.

Violence in American Culture

The United States has a culture of violence. Walter Wink says provocatively: "Violence is the ethos of our times. It is the spirituality of the modern world. It has been accorded the status of a religion, demanding from its devotees an absolute obedience to death." Wherever the violence originates, whether from the right or the left, Wink argues that "violence … and not Christianity, is the real religion of America."[7]

Americans tend to think about violence and ethics in terms of individuals and their choices.[8] We often speak about "guilt" and "innocence." We are less accustomed to describing the human condition in relational, honor-shame terms like "glory" or "shame."[9] But the experience of shame hinges on the community. This is true spiritually, physically, psychologically, emotionally, socially, and even environmentally.

---

5 Barna Group, "Most Americans Take Well-Known Bible Stories at Face Value."
6 Newport, "Fewer in US Now See Bible as Literal Word of God."
7 Wink, *Engaging the Powers*, 13. Wink equates the religion of violence with the religion of Babylon.
8 As anthropologist Margaret King put it, "We are, it is argued, a nation of unique individuals … we believe this, of course, because our shared culture tells us to believe it. We are all different—exactly like everybody else." King, "Deep Culture," 687–94.
9 Cohen connects the silence around American shame to the American priority on "self-esteem," for which he says, "No one else is (theoretically) required" versus concepts of "face" and "honor" which depend on "being claimed from and given by other people." He cites studies where 70% of American high school students believe they are above average in leadership, and where a full 25% believe they are in the top 1% in their ability to get along with others. By contrast, studies conducted with students in Japan and other East Asian societies show that they do not display these "better than average" tendencies. In fact, the Japanese language did not even have a serviceable word for "self-esteem," forcing researchers to invent one in order to conduct their study. See Cohen, "The American National Conversation about (Everything but) Shame," 1085–86.

Failing to acknowledge this reality can have dire consequences. Although we are the wealthiest nation in the world, we are also the most violent among all industrialized nations—three times over.[10] In spite of the fact that our prison population is currently at a twenty-year low, the US still holds 2.3 million people behind bars, making up *over 25 percent of the world's prisoners* for only 4.25 percent of its population.[11]

Many people view these staggering numbers in terms only of individuals and their choices to commit crimes.[12] We talk as if it's a coincidence that we have more individuals who make bad choices. Or perhaps we imagine it's a failure of the law. But what happens when we think about this in terms of Original Glory?

James Gilligan conducted thousands of hours of interviews with violent offenders in the United States prison system. He concluded that unaddressed, toxic shame is a deciding factor leading to violence.[13] Heinous crimes are committed by people with profoundly wounded souls. Often, violence is seen as the only way to gain a form of respect or attention, or to protect against further shame. Gilligan writes:

> I have yet to see a serious act of violence that was not provoked by the experience of feeling shamed and humiliated, disrespected and ridiculed, and that did not represent the attempt to prevent or undo this "loss of face"—no matter how severe the punishment, even if it includes death. ... The secret [that violent men would die in order to not reveal] is that they feel ashamed—deeply ashamed, chronically ashamed, acutely ashamed, over matters that are so trivial that their very triviality makes it even more shameful to feel ashamed about them, so that they are ashamed even to reveal what shames them. And why are they so ashamed of feeling ashamed? Because nothing is more shameful than to feel ashamed.[14]

---

10 Cohen, "The American National Conversation about (Everything but) Shame," 1080. It is worth noting that although America's combined wealth is greater than any other nation, this does not mean that the average American gets to reap the benefits. Income disparities continue to grow, and the wealthiest among us enjoy a disproportionate amount of power in spite of our democratic ideals. Nevertheless, meaningful comparisons can be made between cities such as Seattle, WA, and Vancouver, BC. These cities are geographically close and demographically very similar, but Seattle sees far higher rates of violence and incarceration than Vancouver. Numbeo, "Crime Comparison Between Vancouver, Canada and Seattle, WA, United States. Safety Comparison."

11 World Population Review, "Prison Population by State 2022."

12 Gilligan, *Violence*, 89–91.

13 Gilligan, 110–11.

14 Gilligan, 110–11.

As Americans, most of us believe that we *should* be independent, confident, self-assured, and self-made. When feelings of shame reveal dependence, vulnerability, and the need for love, we can even feel ashamed of our shame (this is particularly true for men). This is what psychologists call a "recursion of shame."[15]

Western approaches to therapy can exacerbate the problem. Counselors often encourage a person to objectify emotions in terms of guilt, and not shame. This is meant to distance people from shame—but it can deepen shame about feeling shame.[16] Furthermore, while the standard Western approach is to remove shame, some now argue that increasing crime rates in Western cultures come partly from the uncoupling of shame from criminal punishment.[17]

Shame in and of itself is only a symptom of relational brokenness and degraded glory. But it can be difficult to acknowledge because it requires us to embrace dependence, creatureliness, and our desperate longing for the care and recognition of others.

It also requires us to grapple with the complex realities of sin and guilt, and to think about these things beyond an individualist legal framework.

Werner: **Humans—Always "Participating"**

Susan Eastman's *Paul and the Person* peers deeply into the limits of individualism. Eastman's interdisciplinary approach combines theology with the findings of neuroscience. She shows that human beings are both "embodied and embedded in their world"[18] and that "the self is intensely vulnerable to its relational matrix."[19] This corresponds to Paul's complicated ideas about human identity, says Eastman, especially in Paul's "participatory theology." That phrase, *participatory theology*, refers to those texts written by Paul indicating that as a human, he is influenced by, *he participates with*, "agents." These agents are *sin* and *Christ*, and they are simultaneously internal and external.[20]

---

15 Scheff, "The Ubiquity of Hidden Shame in Modernity," 129.
16 Lau, *Defending Shame*, 1.
17 Braithwaite, *Crime, Shame*, 1.
18 Eastman, *Paul and the Person*, 4
19 Eastman, 81.
20 Eastman, 6–7.

According to Eastman, in Romans 7, Paul's writings indicate that sin was an *internal-and-external agent* having profound influence on his life:

> Now if I do what I do not want, I agree with the law, that it is good. So now *it is no longer I who do it, but sin that dwells within me.* For I know that nothing good dwells in me, that is, in my flesh.... Now if I do what I do not want, *it is no longer I who do it, but sin that dwells within me.* (Rom 7:16–18, 20, emphasis added)

In Galatians 2, Paul writes of another agent, both internal and external—*Christ.*

> For through the law I died to the law, so that I might live to God. I have been crucified with Christ. *It is no longer I who live, but Christ who lives in me.* And the life I now live in the flesh I live by faith in [or by the faith of] the Son of God, who loved me and gave himself for me. (Gal 2:19–20, emphasis added)

As Paul writes of these "agents" influencing his life he reveals himself as a thoroughly embedded person. Eastman debunks the idea of the "freestanding self." She argues persuasively that a common belief—that *the individual comes first* and that autonomous individuals join together to form relationships and community—is unsupported by Scripture or science. Absent nurturing relationships and connection, humans struggle to become healthy "selves." In other words, "individuality presupposes relationality."[21] Relationality and *inter*dependence are always first.

Contrary to Enlightenment views of the human person as an autonomous, free moral agent, Eastman writes:

> For Paul, there is no place where an autonomous individual can stand aside and evaluate, let alone choose, between different possible identities. There is no freestanding "self" in Paul's cosmos, nor is there a neutral environment within which human beings may act out their personal lives. Rather, Paul's anthropology is participatory all the way down.[22]

Eastman shows that "Paul's participatory logic" has three parts. Humans participate in the "realm of sin and death"; Christ participated "in that realm of human bondage," and humans can participate in a new realm—the kingdom of God—"inaugurated and indwelt by Christ."[23]

---

21 Chappell, "Knowledge of Persons," 3–4. Quoted in Eastman, *Paul*, 16.

22 Eastman, 9.

23 Eastman, 10.

Limits of a Legal Framework

Mark Biddle writes, "In the West, the dominant model of sin and salvation—developed especially in the thoughts of Paul, Anselm, and Abelard—has long relied on a courtroom analogy. Human beings in willful rebellion against God's authority violate God's law. Their crime incurs the penalty of death."[24]

We sometimes refer to the courtroom analogy as a legal framework. It includes the violation of God's law, the "crime" of sin, individual guilt, spiritual death, and the resulting punishment of eternal separation from God. Biddle says this framework "addresses certain aspects of the problem of human existence. Yet, although dominant in the Western popular mind, it does not fully reflect the biblical witness."[25]

American evangelist Billy Graham often used the courtroom analogy. It was well received by his American audience. Americans have historically had a high view of judges and the ideal of equal justice under the law in which the two options are guilt and innocence. And indeed, God is described as a judge in Scripture (Dan 7:9–10; Rev 20:11–15).

But the eternal God is more than a judge. God is also the personal Creator. He is the Savior who gave his life for the person standing before the Judge, and indeed for the whole world. In both Daniel and Revelation, God as Judge is simultaneously King with a kingdom. This King reigns in love over his people, his dominion, his cosmos.

A biblically faithful gospel does not require a legal framework in which the overriding emphasis is on sin-and-guilt and the remedy is penal substitutionary atonement. For example, the gospel sermons in the book of Acts are more focused on *the regal* (Jesus is the risen, victorious King) than *the legal*.[26] Having an understanding of the honor-shame dynamics of first-century Palestine aids the student of Scripture in seeing a multifaceted *regal-framework gospel* in the New Testament.[27] Therefore, while affirming that the courtroom analogy is one way of communicating the seriousness of sin and the beauty of the gospel, we also acknowledge its limitations. Because our courtrooms deal with people as individuals, the courtroom

---

24 Biddle, *Missing the Mark*, viii.
25 Biddle, viii.
26 McKnight, "Gospeling the Gospel in Acts."
27 In *The Global Gospel*, Section III is "A Global Gospel for Our Multicultural World," containing ten chapters that offer honor-shame-based gospel contextualizations employing primarily a regal-framework; see Mischke, *The Global Gospel*, 206–78. Cf. McKnight, *The King Jesus Gospel*; Bates, *Salvation by Allegiance Alone* and *Why the Gospel?*; Vaughn, *One Gospel for All Nations*.

analogy does not allow us to address the sin dynamics comprising social, collective, cultural, or systemic realities. Why does this matter?

- If we limit our view of sin to a legal framework and courtroom analogy, it unnecessarily narrows our gospel focus to individual sinners, their individual salvation, and their vertical reconciliation unto God.
- This narrower view obscures our vision of the Bible's broad, thick witness concerning social, systemic, and cosmic evil and sin—and the degree to which the cross and gospel of Christ address these evils.
- This individual/legal framework provides theological sanction for Christian teachers to:
  » Ignore horizontal reconciliation in the church between previously hostile groups through the cross of Christ and the gospel of peace (Eph 2:13–17).
  » Sideline Christ's victory over the hostile principalities and powers (Col 2:14–15) as part of his work on the cross.
  » Dismiss as mere "social gospel" or "wokeness" attempts to portray horizontal reconciliation and the church's *one new humanity* as thoroughly grounded in Scripture.
- This narrower view limits our peripheral vision. It hinders the church in addressing some of the church's (and humanity's) most pressing concerns. Among these concerns are those evils, injustices, and sins related to group division and conflict, such as racism, political tribalism, and nationalism.

Brueggemann writes, "There is a relentless *communitarian* tilt to the gospel that refuses the mistaken American creed of 'individualism.' The good news is that we cannot and need not be self-sufficient."[28] Moving beyond individualism and embracing the Bible's other gospel frameworks requires that we grapple with shame, and with the relational nature of the good news which addresses shame.

Kristin: ## Defending Shame

Just as physical pain tells us that something in the body is wrong, so shame can indicate that something in our social body is wrong. Shame may point to a social pathology. It may be because of our sin, or sins against us. It may be from something that our community or someone close to us has done or has suffered. It may even come from fear of further shame.

---

28 Brueggemann, *Ancient Echoes*, 83.

In this sense, we cannot say that shame in and of itself is a bad thing.[29] In many cases, shame is a healthy and appropriate response to brokenness. People who feel no shame (the "shameless") are dangerously disconnected from the social body and lack a conscience for how the actions of one affect others.

But shame can move in different directions—toward transformation and reintegration in a community—or toward further disintegration and violence. According to criminologist John Braithwaite, this largely depends on the nature of the community in which it occurs. Braithwaite observed how different cultures deal with violence. He distinguished between *reintegrative* and *disintegrative* shame and developed an approach called "Reintegrative Shaming Theory" (RST).[30]

Reintegrative shame transforms offenders and strengthens communities. "The key to crime control," says Braithwaite, "is cultural commitments to shaming in ways that I call reintegrative. Societies with low crime rates are those that shame potently and judiciously; individuals who resort to crime are those insulated from shame over their wrongdoing."[31]

Disintegrative shaming, on the other hand, is "applied injudiciously and counterproductively." This kind of shaming promotes further crime and breaks social bonds through a process Braithwaite calls "stigmatization."[32]

Braithwaite observes that in Western culture, punishment is meted out by an anonymous system which treats defendants according to the crime they are accused of. The desire for "objectivity" and "equal treatment under the law" means that justice is usually dealt with outside of a person's community and relational network. Crime is seen more as a violation of impersonal law than as a violation of a person or a community's dignity.[33]

---

29 This is contrary to the view among some social scientists who hold an "asymmetry thesis" that guilt is good but shame is always bad for human flourishing. "The most direct measures of guilt- and shame-proneness fail to support the asymmetry thesis. They fail to adequately challenge the global historical consensus that shame—no less than guilt—contributes meaningfully to human flourishing when it finds healthy expression." Ten Elshof, *For Shame*, 58.

30 RST has since been applied in communities in the West and around the world, both by secular organizers and leaders, and by Christian organizations like Prison Fellowship.

31 Braithwaite, *Crime, Shame*, 1.

32 Lau, *Defending Shame*, 178.

33 Highly relevant is the conversation about retributive vs. restorative justice. For an in-depth exploration of the links between theology and forms of justice, see The Anastasis Center: "Christian Restorative Justice: A Study Guide." For a secular view about restorative justice, see Tamler Sommers's chapter "Honorable Justice" in *Why Honor Matters*, 153–83.

As a result, shame may not happen in a way that helps a person to grasp the *meaning* of their actions, feel remorse, and be transformed.[34]

When shame comes from persons the offender does not know or respect (like criminal justice officials), this increases the likelihood that they will not acknowledge the shame. When shame is unacknowledged, an offender does not accept responsibility and may direct blame and anger at others.

Figure 5.2: John Braithwaite's Reintegrative Shaming Theory (RST) says shame can be used to disintegrate or to reintegrate*

But it's also possible for shame to be acknowledged and never discharged. When shame has nowhere to go for restoration, it leads to "depression, confusion, alienation, and a loss of self-esteem."[35] Simply meting out "just deserts" is counterproductive, because it creates "a degradation ceremony with maximum prospects for stigmatization." Incarceration then breaks up meaningful relationships that could later help reintegrate an offender into the community.

Disintegrative Shame in Prison

Punitive measures, uncoupled from shame, also deny the moral capacity and dignity of the offender. Simply putting someone in prison without providing meaningful ways to be restored treats a person as fundamentally broken and unworthy of restoration. It is yet another denial of Original Glory. Gilligan observes the ritualistic shame of entering prison. Psychologically, this process deprives people of their identity and

---

34 Lau, *Defending Shame,* 177.

35 Gilligan, *Violence,* 153–59.

* Figure conceived and produced by Kristin Caynor and Werner Mischke.

status as a human being step-by-step, beginning by removing them from society and assigning them a number instead of a name.

Consider Anthony's story. Prison cut him off from the few social connections he had. These were quickly replaced with the social bonds available in prison and their standards for belonging. And then, after years of "punishment," he is simply left on the street with the same clothes he came in with—whether they fit him or not, whether they are in good condition or poor, whether they are appropriate for the season and the weather or not.

His identity and dignity were ceremonially stripped from him by society—*but no ceremony exists to restore it to him*. Nothing is in place to reaffirm his value and potential to be a blessing to his community.

Braithwaite claims that some communities work *against* reintegrative shaming. When social bonds are weak or fractured, shame has a maximum potential for stigmatization and a low potential for transformation. In individualistic cultures, the prospect of stigmatization makes it much harder to acknowledge shame.

Disintegrative Shame in "Cancel Culture"

Another example is "cancel culture." A person can be permanently stigmatized based on just one mistake. Social media further exacerbates the situation, creating maximum shame with minimal accountability and human connection. We say things online that we would never say face to face. In such a heightened shame environment, a person is either in or out. There is no room for both total truth about wrongdoing *and* full forgiveness for the wrongdoer.

On the other hand, such "labeling" is far less likely to occur among people who see each other's complexity as human beings. Reintegrative shaming can only happen in communities which are communitarian, interdependent, and socially cohesive. In these communities, shaming does not come from an impersonal system of law. Instead, it comes from people who share significant relationships.[36] Those shaming the offender are in the best position to see the extent of the harm they have caused, and this makes the shame stronger. But the community can also see that person for more than their crime, which makes the possibility for true restoration greater.

---

36 Lau, *Defending Shame*, 180.

ACTS 2 & 4	COMMUNITY CHARACTERISTICS
And how is it that we hear, each of us in his own native language . . . ? (Acts 2:8)	The first Christian community was very diverse, from day one.
And they devoted themselves to the apostles' teaching . . .	The word of God and the good news was preached and sought after.
and to [the shared life], to the breaking of bread and the prayers (v. 42).	They had *koinonia* in shared meals and praying together.
And awe came upon every soul, and many wonders and signs were being done through the apostles (v. 43).	They lived in awe and expectation for the works of God.
And all who believed were together and had all things in common. And they sold their possessions and belongings and distributed the proceeds to all, as any had need (v. 45).	Believing meant belonging to each other in heart, soul, and material possessions.
And day by day, attending the temple together and breaking bread in their homes . . .	They met together daily for worship in public places, and in their homes to share life and food.
they received their food with glad and generous hearts (v. 46) . . .	They were marked by celebration and generosity.
praising God and having favor with all the people.	They were marked by praise and by a unique reputation with others.
And the Lord added to their number day by day those who were being saved (Acts 2:42–47).	They were prepared to multiply and did.
Acts reiterates the *koinonia* again in ch. 4, and further adds that *"there was not a needy person among them"* (4:34).	No human needs were unmet in the first Christian community. This was their glory!

Figure 5.3: Characteristics of community in Acts 2 and 4

Shame in the Interdependent Community of Acts 2

New Testament scholar Te-Li Lau looks at shame language in the writings of Paul. He shows how Paul used shame in ways that were reintegrative. He also notes that the early church was a community conducive to reintegrative shaming. The household setting limited the size of congregations to around thirty or less, "thus promoting intimacy and accountability."[37]

---
37 Lau, 185.

Acts 2:42–47 and 4:32–37 bear this out (see Figure 5.3, left). These chapters show us how the new way of being human in Christ was first lived out. Early believers were far less hierarchical than surrounding cultures. Radical abandonment of property and status meant there was a high level of interdependency, equality, and an "all in" commitment to the shared vision of the kingdom over individual achievement and power. The fellowship they shared was not merely an abstract "spiritual" agreement based on affirming a creed. It was a *local, embodied* interdependence, which meant sharing time, space, and material goods.[38]

In Jesus, we have a new way to pursue glory *and* to experience shame. He has perfectly revealed God's plan for a new social body being transformed in his image and glory.

Lau demonstrates that Paul makes ample use of shaming language in his letters. But he does so in a particular way. One example is 2 Corinthians 2:5–11:

> Now if anyone has caused pain, he has caused it not to me, but in some measure—not to put it too severely—to all of you. For such a one, this punishment by the majority is enough, so you should rather turn to forgive and comfort him, or he may be overwhelmed by excessive sorrow. So I beg you to reaffirm your love for him. For this is why I wrote, that I might test you and know whether you are obedient in everything. Anyone whom you forgive, I also forgive. Indeed, what I have forgiven, if I have forgiven anything, has been for your sake in the presence of Christ, so that we would not be outwitted by Satan; for we are not ignorant of his designs.

Without naming the person, Paul publicly acknowledges the one who has "caused pain" ... "to all of you." Paul is indirectly calling out the offender. He is using shame *together with* the Christian call to forgiveness. Why? To restore *both* the offender *and* the social harmony of the Corinthian body of believers.

What does it mean to truly belong to each other? What would it look like for someone like Anthony, who is "far off," to hear good news and to be drawn near in the body of Christ? What would it mean for someone like him to truly belong to us, and for us to truly belong to him?

---

38 My translation of *koinonia*, which I believe more nearly approximates the use of this word in Koine Greek, and especially in Acts. For more on defining *koinonia*, see Jordan, "Christian Fellowship Isn't Just Being Nice."

BEING HUMAN: In Community

Taking a closer look at what the Bible has taught us about glory and shame helps us to see that the realities of sin are far more complex than simply assigning individual guilt or innocence to the various parties. Jesus comes to undo the power of sin and to restore us to glory. Because we were created as relational beings, the way that we relate matters. Because the glory Jesus gave us is inherently communal, sin cannot be faced only as an individual matter. Peacemaking requires that we grapple with more than just individuals.

As Westerners, we tend to favor categorization, individualism, and reductionism. While some of this has brought its benefits, it has created serious problems for us in many areas. It makes it difficult to grapple with realities that are interconnected, interdependent, and holistic.

It can also make it hard for us to face things that defy our categorizations and efforts at human control. It can make it hard for us to speak about the mysterious, larger-than-human spiritual realities of evil beyond our imagining, and of goodness beyond our imagining, too.

We have explored in this chapter the role of the community as an ally of violence—versus the community as a social environment that heals brokenness and shame. Just ahead is chapter 6, "Powers and Principalities," in which we'll examine the emphasis in Ephesians on rulers, authorities, and dark forces.

CHAPTER 5 SUMMARY

- The glory Jesus gave us is inherently communal and a catalyst for healing. But violence denies the glory of the human being, creating trauma and division.
- A family, culture, community, or nation can hold collective shame and be caught in a collective cycle of violence.
- Following Jesus or doing theology with an individualistic bias (as is common in the West) can inhibit a community-oriented demonstration of the beauty of the gospel.
- The New Testament reveals being human as both embodied and embedded.
- Shame can be a healthy response to brokenness. People who feel no shame (the "shameless") are dangerously disconnected from the social body.
- *Disintegrative* shame damages individuals and communities; *reintegrative* shame transforms offenders and strengthens communities.

FOR FURTHER REFLECTION

- Twice in 1 Corinthians, Paul writes, "I say this to your shame" (5:6; 15:34). Why is Paul using "shaming language" as he writes to the Corinthian believers?
- What's the difference between healthy, appropriate shame and toxic shame?
- What would you observe in a community that uses *reintegrative shame* to restore a person to the community?

Chapter 6

POWERS AND PRINCIPALITIES

*"For we do not wrestle against flesh and blood,
but against the rulers, against the authorities,
against the cosmic powers over this present darkness,
against the spiritual forces of evil in the heavenly places."*
–Ephesians 6:12

IN THIS CHAPTER

- Ephesians offers four relevant texts describing an interplay of rulers, authorities, and dark cosmic forces which are catalysts for division, hostility, and violence.

- No understanding of violence and of our identity in Christ is complete without this: Ephesians 2 presents two ways of being human—one *in flesh,* cooperating with the Prince of the Power of the Air—the other *in Christ, in his flesh,* that is, his body.

Kristin:

Certain kinds of evil defy categorization. I had studied the theory of violence before going to Rwanda. I had read books about the psychology of shame and violence, countless articles on sociology, and reams of history and theology. But none of this could prepare me for my visit to Nyamata Church in Rwanda.

In the 1994 genocide, approximately ten thousand people were slaughtered in the church building or on its property. That experience cannot be fully described in words, let alone explained, not with scientific research, nor with the dictums of theology.

Evil that is especially heinous poses deeper questions. We struggle to make sense of it. Scientific research can help, but it can only go so far. We are confronted with what seems larger than our categories and larger than individual human choices. It is massive and world-shattering—what we might call "the spiritual." Secular researchers also acknowledge that an integrated approach to violence will include other forms of knowledge which are of a spiritual and "mythological"[1] nature.

---

1 Mythological, in this sense, does not mean untrue. As C. S. Lewis helpfully explains, there are myths which are true. Myths in this sense are simply the grand metanarratives we use to explain the world and who we are within it.

Ephesians grapples with these "larger-than-nature" mysteries through the framework of Powers and Principalities, "spiritual forces of evil in the heavenly places" (Eph 6:12). Although this theme is often deemphasized in the modern West, it was important for the early church and continues to be a major concern for Christians from traditional cultures.

Ephesians makes four explicit references to Powers and Principalities (1:21; 2:2; 3:10; 6:12). We will look at each of these references to see what they tell us about the good news of peace. Cultural context will also help us to see how Ephesians presents us with two distinct ways of being human: one "in flesh" and "following the prince of the power of the air," and the other "in Christ" and in his flesh as members of his body.

We will explore how the Powers and Principalities were understood in the ancient world in relation to ethnic, national, and religious loyalties.[2] We will examine how the glory of God reconfigures our identities "in flesh." And we will discuss idolatry and violence within the context of the human quest for glory and the sacrifice of Jesus.

"Raised to Life and Seated Above" (Eph 1:21)

Ephesians 1 says that when Christ was raised from the dead, he was seated "far above all rule and authority and power and dominion, and above every name that is named, not only in this age but also in the one to come" (v. 21).

Figure 6.1: Levels of power in a biblical worldview

---

2 See Heiser, *The Unseen Realm,* for an accessible introduction to the ancient worldview of the biblical authors. Heiser calls this as the "divine council worldview."

In chapter 4, we introduced Figure 6.1, "Levels of power in a biblical worldview." The diagram represents various levels of power, influence, or agency: principalities and powers ... peoples and nations ... institutions, governments, corporations ... families and communities ... individuals.

Below is a modified version, emphasizing the effects of sin. Sin corrupts or bends every level of power. The umbrellas or coverings represent "the covering that is cast over all peoples" (Isa 25:7). All are born "under sin" (Rom 3:9; Gal 3:22), "under the Law" (Gal 2:23), and under enslavement to Powers. As Paul says, "Formerly, when you did not know God, you were enslaved to those that by nature are not gods" (Gal 4:8).[3]

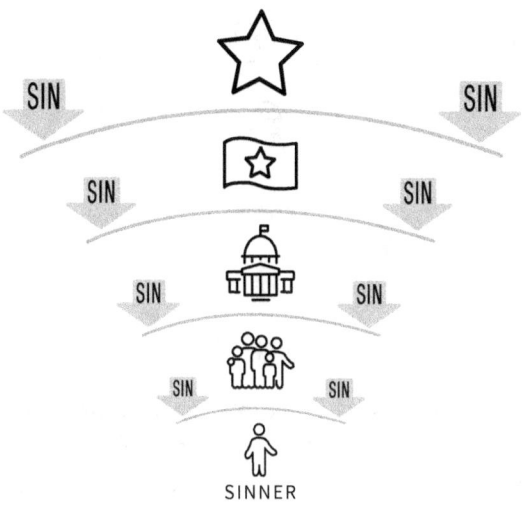

Figure 6.2: All are born under sin, enslaved to various Powers

All the different structures of glory, at all "levels," are bent by sin and death in similar ways. The smaller umbrellas model themselves after the larger "course of this world, following the prince of the power of the air, the spirit that is now at work in the sons of disobedience" (Eph 2:2). In the Roman Empire, family life was explicitly modeled after the imperial structure, which in turn was upheld by the cults of the gods.[4] Family, culture, and institutions are not bad in and of themselves. But when they derive their own power and glory in part from those above them, they

---

[3] Elsewhere, Paul says that there are many so-called gods in heaven and on earth as indeed there are many "gods" and "lords" though for us there is but one God (1 Cor 8:5-6). In these verses, Paul seems to be acknowledging the existence of these hostile Powers, and yet that they are "nothing" next to the One "through whom are all things."

[4] Gupta, *Strange Religion*, 9–23.

become similarly bent by the weight of sin. So, while we are oppressed by systems of power, we also take pride in our associations with nation, school, work, family, etc.

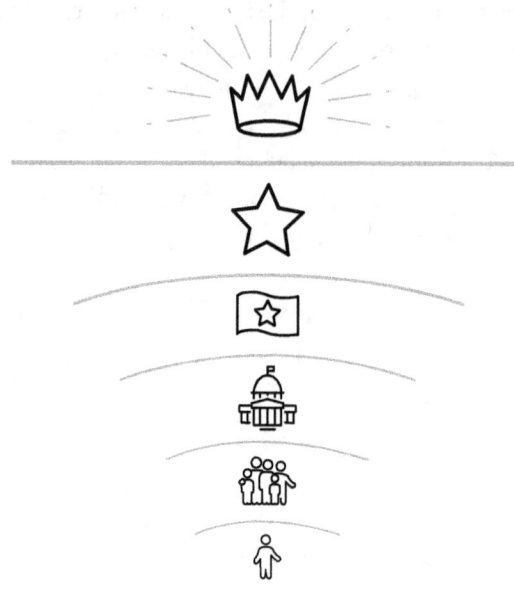

Figure 6.3: Christ above all powers

But the Godhead is far above all Powers. In Figure 6.3, this is represented by the crown of glory. The weight of sin and death does not bend God's power in any way. In fact, all power and glory is derived from him, although the many veils of sin distort our view of God's glory.

This is where the good news comes in. Jesus descended from the heavenly places (Eph 4:10; John 3:13; Phil 2:6–8), sent by the Father of glory (Eph 1:17–18). He was "born of woman, born under the law, to redeem those under the law that we might receive adoption as sons" (Gal 4:4–5).

Although Christ "was in the form of God, he did not count equality with God a thing to be grasped, but emptied himself, taking the form of a servant and being born in the likeness of men." And he went further still and humbled himself by becoming obedient to the point of death—even death on a cross (Phil 2:6–8)!

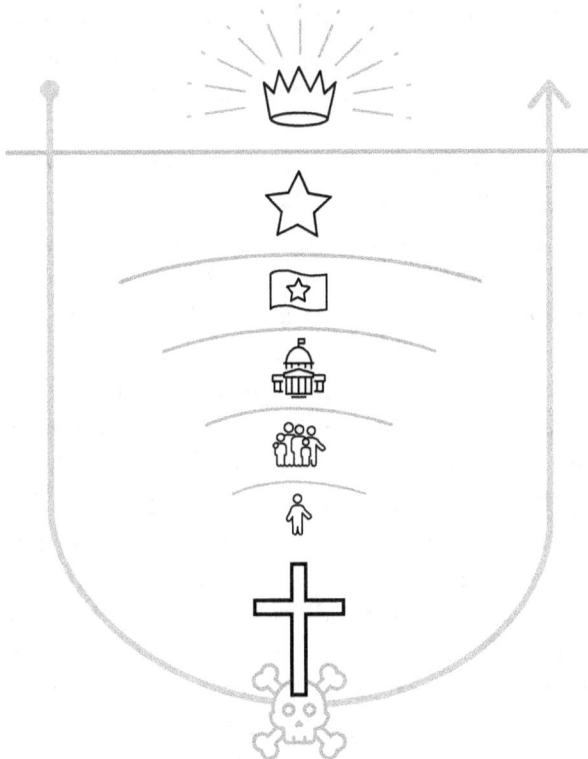

Figure 6.4: A cosmology of the early church: Christ has descended and ascended (Eph 4:8–10), Christ is enthroned far above all rule and authority (Eph 1:20–23)

> Therefore, God has highly exalted him and given him the name that is above every name, so that at the name of Jesus every knee should bow, in heaven and on earth, and even under the earth. (Phil 2:9–10)

As Ephesians also says,

> Therefore, when it says, "When he ascended on high he led a host of captives, and he gave gifts to men." (In saying, "He ascended," what does it mean but that he had also descended into the lower regions, the earth? He who descended is the one who also ascended far above all the heavens, that he might fill all things). (Eph 4:8–10)

Earthly Kingdoms with Cosmic Backing

Ephesians chapter 1 begins with Christ's ascension from the realm of death, "under the earth." And then he was lifted even further, to be seated "far above all rule and authority and power and dominion."

What might this have meant in the Greco-Roman context? In ancient Near Eastern thought, earthly kingdoms had cosmic backing. All the major cosmologies reflect this belief, including the biblical one.[5] While wars between kingdoms raged, heavenly ones were also taking place.[6] Each nation was named by its god, and so were the people of the LORD (Deut 32:8; Num 6:27; 1 Kgs 8:16). The LORD is described as a great King above all gods (Ps 95:3), and his judgment of the nations corresponds to the judgment of the gods in his council (Ps 82:1, 6; 86:8–9).

In the ancient Near East, a nation's gods gave it divine assistance with technology, law, agriculture, and war. The king was the god's earthly representative and could be seen as the god's direct descendant. The laws of a kingdom were displayed to show the wisdom of its king and its gods.[7] The biblical writings also reflect this understanding, though in a different way. The king of the Jewish people is not the LORD's descendant, but God says he will treat the king as his son (Ps 2:6–7; 1 Chr 22:10), and he commands the king to study his Torah and live by it (Deut 17:19).

Jesus is the Anointed King and true Son of God. He is both a human and a cosmic being, who has been set over every human dominion and every heavenly one. As the Son of God and the radiance of God's glory, he is greater than any angel (Heb 1:2–3). And, as the Head over all things, he is given to the church, "the fullness of him who fills all in all" (Eph 1:22–23).

"Following the Prince of the Power of the Air" (2:2)

Ephesians 2 then describes how this body is formed in the resurrected One. Though we were also once "dead," following "the prince of the power of the air," we are now his (2:2). Because Jesus was seated above every Power, we who are in him are also raised to sit with him in the heavenly places (2:6).

Returning to Figure 6.4, we see how Jesus descended to "the lower regions" and to death to gather those who are "in him." We are the "captives" freed from the reign of death, sin, and the powers, and brought to be seated above. The new, reconciled humanity in the verses that follow comes from the conquest of the Prince of the Power of the Air, and the deliverance of his captives.

---

5 Heiser, *Demons*, Kindle loc. 568.

6 Most explicitly in Dan 10:13, 20. See Heiser, loc. 542.

7 One key example of this is the famous "Code of Hammurabi." See King, "Code."

Ethnicity, the Powers, and the Peace Treaty

In light of the cultural connection between the nations and the Powers and Principalities, Ephesians 2:1–22 gains greater significance. In the Greco-Roman world, people groups were thought to share biological kinship with their gods, who mated with humans in the ancient past (think Hercules). This made the Jewish people unique. Their God never had sexual relations with human beings, or with anyone. He was not in any way related to the gods of the pantheon.

This could create more than one problem for Jews. One was that their religion didn't fit within the polytheistic religious policy of the empire. But the challenges were also political.

In the Greco-Roman world, "the making of peace" or ratification of a peace treaty could only be made by calling upon the gods of each side. Because the gods were related to one another, and to their respective kings and peoples, they would guarantee the treaty and punish anyone who broke it. Family ties were everything. To break the treaty would be to dishonor your god and incur their wrath. This was such an important belief that in one instance, a story had to be fabricated about Hercules having sex with a Jewish woman, so that the Greeks would accept a treaty with the Judaeans.[8]

Making a Peace Treaty in Ephesians 2

As other commentators have pointed out, when Ephesians 2 speaks of Jesus "making peace" (v. 15) this is treaty-making language. Now when we read Ephesians 2, we notice new things. First, Paul says we all once lived among the sons of disobedience (2:2–3). This seems to show that the condition of being *in flesh, in the world, in that time, and dead in trespasses and sins* applied to both Jews and non-Jewish peoples. But now, we are raised up with Christ above the Powers, so that we may walk in the good works God has prepared for us (Eph 2:10).

Second, King Jesus ratifies the peace between nations. He can do this because there is a new creation in him, and with it a new divine kinship and citizenship in the household of God (Eph 2:19). This reorders all forms of identity, not just the "religious."[9] It makes a claim about the gods,

---

8 Fredriksen, "Power, Politics, and God."

9 Contemporary ideas about "religion" and "ethnicity" are not reflective of how these realities were understood in the ancient world. For more information, see Buell, *Why This New Race*. Buell argues that in the era of early Christianity, ethnicity was understood to be on a spectrum between "fixed and fluid."

but also about politics, family, ethnicity—in short, everything (Eph 1:22). It's an entirely new way of being human.

The Great King proclaims the peace treaty far and wide (Eph 2:17). He is "gospeling peace."[10] In fulfillment of Isaiah 52:7,[11] Jesus proclaims the good news that Peace has been won. This meant that the violence of the gods, the nations, families, and individuals is ended.[12]

Now the nations are restored to their true status with the Father from whom every family—both in heaven, and on earth—is named (Eph 3:14). According to early apologist Irenaeus, Jesus "announces the gathering together in peace, through the name of Christ, of men of unlike races."[13] Likewise, Justin Martyr (circa AD 100–165) wrote:

> We who hated and slaughtered one another, we who would not welcome to our homes people of a different race because of their customs, now, since the coming Christ we live and eat with them, and we pray for our enemies, and we try to persuade those who hate us, unjustly, to live according to the good counsel of Christ.[14]

As the reign of apostate angels is undone, hostility comes to an end. According to Irenaeus, this is the meaning in the prophecy also cited in Ephesians: "He ascended on high and led captivity captive" (Ps 68:18; Eph 4:8).[15] To violate this treaty is to dishonor our King, God, and Father.[16] According to the Greek fathers, we do so to our peril. Disunity within the church spits on the sacrifice of the King who made Peace with his own

---

10 In Eph 2:17 ESV, "preached peace" is εὐηγγελίσατο εἰρήνην / *euēngelisato eirēnē*. The word *euēngelisato* is the verb form of gospel. The phrase *euēngelisato eirēnē* means "gospeled peace" or "preached the gospel of peace/harmony."

11 "How beautiful upon the mountains are the feet of him who brings good news, who publishes peace, who brings good news of happiness, who publishes salvation, who says to Zion, 'Your God reigns'" (Isa 52:7).

12 This was also the overwhelming majority view of the early church in its first three hundred years. We will say more about this in chapter 9 on the Pax Romana.

13 St. Irenaeus of Lyons, "The Demonstration of the Apostolic Preaching."

14 Kalantzis, *Caesar and the Lamb*, 82.

15 St. Irenaeus of Lyons, 63.

16 There are both active and passive ways of violating this treaty. An example of a passive form of peace treaty violation is to build a church based on the Homogenous Unit Principle: most people prefer to be with people like themselves (see ch. 12). But building a church around the preferences of human beings to be with "their" people in their social status and their race has huge risks: namely, it leads to sacralizing attitudes of social class division, racism, or other separations contrary to the ways of Jesus. The history of white evangelicalism in America has proven this to be true. See, for example, Emerson and Smith, *Divided by Faith*, and Tisby, *Color of Compromise*.

body, in his flesh, and in his blood. When we allow another identity with its standards for glory to rule us, we return to slavery. As Colossians says, we choose to serve the elemental spirits of the earth again (Col 2:20–3:1).

The Diverse Wisdom of God Made Known (3:10)

The biblical narrative advocates for harmonious diversity under the creative purposes of a glorious loving God. The diversity of human cultures has a cosmic purpose in God's work of restoring his glory. Paul says,

> To me, though I am the very least of all the saints, this grace was given, to preach to the Gentiles the unsearchable riches of Christ, and to bring to light for everyone what is the plan of the mystery hidden for ages in God, who created all things, so that through the church the manifold wisdom of God might now be made known to the rulers and authorities in the heavenly places. (Eph 3:8–10)

The word translated "manifold" has the sense of diverse, variegated, and multicolored. As the mysterious unity of all peoples under one King is brought to light, the church becomes a revelation of the wisdom of God in all its rich variety to the Powers. God's diverse people display God's diverse wisdom.

Jesus and His Body

According to Ephesians, the Good News of Peace means that we are bound together in Jesus, and that we now belong to one body and one Spirit in one holy temple. Being in the new humanity means that we belong to the Coming King, and that we also belong to one another, just as the hand belongs to the wrist. To put it another way, being a child of my Father automatically makes me a sister to my brother. The new humanity is nothing short of a new birth and a new creation,[17] in which we no longer regard anyone according to the flesh (2 Cor 5:16).

In the flesh, we regarded people according to old human standards for glory, acceptance, and belonging. On this basis, we excuse violence and treat people as less than human. But in *his* flesh, we no longer look at anyone the same way. In him, there is no longer Jew or Greek, slave or free, male or female.[18] We might also add that there are no longer criminals

---

17 We note here that the word for "create" in 2 Cor 5:16 is (in the Septuagint) the same word used in Genesis for God's original creative act. In two other places, Paul also refers to a new creation in the context of "regarding no one according to the flesh" any longer (2 Cor 5:16), and says that "neither circumcision nor uncircumcision counts for anything" (Gal 6:15).

18 The phrase "old humanity" is also used in the passage here referenced from Col 3:9–12.

or free citizens, no longer disabled or able-bodied, citizen or immigrant, worthy or unworthy.[19] Every label we hold "in the world" is nullified—but our true diversity and individuality is honored and upheld in Christ.

Chrysostom on Ephesians 2

The fourth-century theologian John Chrysostom quotes Ephesians 2 when writing about the body of Christ. He laments that those whom Christ brought near from so far away would dare to separate themselves from their brothers and sisters over what he calls "natural differences."[20] In fact, says Chrysostom, these natural distinctions are the very things which enable unity in the body. As Paul says, "If all were the same thing, where would the body be" (1 Cor 12:19)? A pile of hands could not be a body. And so, the very differences which make us think we are unequal in honor are actually the things which give us all equal belonging in the body. This glory that we share comes not from our individual traits, but from the way those traits fit together in Christ.

In other words, glory comes from a certain way of being truly human, the way of relating in Jesus. Those who are held as less-than by society, find glory in the body of Jesus.[21] This is a mystery of glory worth suffering for (Eph 3:1–3, 13). This is why Paul begs us to "walk in a manner worthy of the calling to which you have been called, eager to maintain the unity of the Spirit in the bond of peace" (4:2–3). With all of this in mind, we return to Ephesians 2:11–16.

In Flesh versus in *His* Flesh

Verse 11:

> Therefore remember that once you peoples in flesh—so-called the foreskinned by those so-called the circumcision in flesh, made by hands,

Verse 12:

> that you were in that time without the Coming King, alienated from the citizenship of Israel, and foreigners of the covenant of promise, not having hope and godless in the world.

---

19 Obviously, in the social realm, Jew and Greek, slave and free, male and female do still exist; likewise, criminals, disabled and able-bodied, citizen and immigrant, continue to exist. The point is that, in Christ, in his body the church, these identity markers are no longer to be determinative of value, worth, or honor. Paul is teaching a radical truth: identity formation begins with being in Christ as our primary source of belonging and honor.

20 Chrysostom, "Church Fathers: Homily 5 on Ephesians," 378.

21 Chrysostom, 375–76.

Verse 13–14a:

> But now, in the Coming King Jesus, you who once were far off have come to be near in the blood of the Coming King. Indeed, he is our peace, who makes the two one, and destroys the dividing wall of the breach, the hostility,

Verse 14b–15a:

> in his flesh, nullifying the torah of commandments in dogmas

Verse 15b–16:

> so that he might create in himself the two into one new humanity, making peace, and reconcile both in one body to God through the cross, killing the hostility in it. *(my translation)*

When I read Ephesians 2:11–22 in Greek I noticed that the word *en* ("in") occurs fifteen times in these eleven verses. Verses 11–12 call the reader to remember that once they were *in flesh, in that time,* and *in the world.* These verses describe a certain condition, a world one could live "in."

Being *in that time* and *in the world* means shame and hostility— separation from the King, alienation, estrangement, hopelessness, and being without God. "But now, *in* the Coming King Jesus you were once far off have come to be near." Now, we are in the Coming King, in the blood of the Anointed, and *in his flesh.*

Later, Paul will say to "put off the old humanity which belongs to your former way of life and to put on the new humanity, created after God" (Eph 4:22–24, my translation). Here he refers to the new humanity *(kainon anthrōpon)* which Jesus creates in 2:15. This makes it clear that Paul is referring to two different ways of being human, in both Ephesians 2 and 4.[22] We also note that *in his flesh* Jesus nullifies "the torah of commandments in dogmas" (vv. 14–15). This seems to be another description of being "in" the old humanity.

In all, these verses give us the following list of *en* uses associated with the new and old humanities:

---

22 We can see this theme of the two humanities throughout Ephesians and in other Pauline writings. In addition to "in flesh" and "in the world" we could also add "dead in trespasses and sins" (2:1), "in whom we all once lived" (2:3) vs. "in heavenly realms in the Anointed" (2:6). We also see the phrase "old humanity" used in Col 3:9, and the references to "a new creation" in 2 Cor 5:17 and Gal 6:15.

OLD HUMANITY	NEW HUMANITY
In flesh (2:11, 2x)	*In the Coming King Jesus* (2:13)
In that time (2:11)	*In the blood of the Anointed* (2:13)
In the world (2:12)	*In his flesh* (2:14)
In dogmas (2:15)	*In himself* (2:15)
	In one body (2:16)
	In one Spirit (2:18)
	In whom (2:21–22, 2x)
	In the Spirit (2:22)

Figure 6.5: "In" the old humanity versus "in" Christ's new humanity

Here we make two observations about the old humanity:

1. Both Jews and gentiles were *in flesh*. Those of us from the gentiles *in flesh* were godless, hopeless, and separated from the covenant. But the Jewish people are also referred to as the "circumcised *in flesh*." This means that the designation *in flesh*—together with *in that time*, *in the world*, and *in dogmas*—applies to both groups.

2. Being *in flesh* and *in the world* creates a certain way of relating to one another. The non-Jewish nations were called "the foreskinned" by those who called themselves "the circumcision." Here, the relationship boils down to the bare facts: *circumcision* or *foreskin*, *clean* or *unclean*, *included* or *excluded*. These are terms of mutual shaming: "We are who we are because we are not who you are." Being *in flesh* creates a false glory where status comes from deriding the other to build up ourselves. From the Jewish standpoint, the nations are "the foreskinned," without covenant, strangers, and godless (Eph 2:11–12). *In flesh*, and *in dogmas*, Jewish law observance becomes a false way of constituting identity and seeking glory.

Ultimately, the old way creates hostility (2:14), disobedience, subjugation to Principalities, wrath (2:1–3), estrangement, alienation, division, hostility (2:12–14), all kinds of evil (2:1), and death (4:17–19, 28–31).

Jesus is the New Humanity—the new way of being human. Without losing our individuality, we are enfolded in him, so that where he goes, we go (Eph 2:6). As he descends to death, we die in a death like his, that we may be raised in a resurrection like his (Rom 6:5). As he is in the world, so are we (1 John 4:17). We put on the new humanity by living together in diversity as members of Christ's body (Eph 4:25; 5:20), so that together we may be able to withstand the schemes of the devil (6:11).

"We Wrestle Not against Flesh and Blood" (6:12)

Put on the whole armor of God, that you may be able to stand against the schemes of the devil. For we do not wrestle against flesh and blood, but against the rulers, against the authorities, against the cosmic powers over this present darkness, against the spiritual forces of evil in the heavenly places. (Eph 6:11–12)

Growing up, I heard that I, *as an individual,* need to put on the whole armor of God. But the image in Ephesians is not of a solitary Christian suiting up as a lone warrior. Rather, *we* are encouraged to put on the armor of God *together,* as one body. *I* am not expected to be always ready with the breastplate of righteousness or the helmet of salvation—but *we* are. *I* cannot extinguish all the flaming darts of the evil one with the shield of faith—but *we* can. *I* may not be capable of walking my life out with the beautiful, good news of peace on my feet—but *we* are.

There is no such thing as a super Christian who can do it all on their own. Only one person has ever taken up the whole divine armor alone.[23] And the only way we can take up the same divine armor is inside of Christ, connected with his body, abiding in the Vine (John 15:4), rooted and grounded in love (Eph 3:17), and joined—through him—with all his holy people. Only then can we hope to comprehend what is the breadth and length and height and depth, and to know the love of Christ which surpasses knowledge, that we may be filled with all the fullness of God (Eph 3:18–19).

---

23 Ephesians 6:11–17 makes several key references to Isaiah, all of which point to a moment where the Lord himself decides to rise and act in the face of injustice and oppression. In Isaiah 59:14–17, the Lord sees justice turned back, righteousness far away, and truth lacking. "The Lord saw it, and it displeased him, that there was no justice. He saw that there was no man, and wondered that there was no one to intercede; then his own arm brought him salvation, and his righteousness upheld him. He put on righteousness as a breastplate, and a helmet of salvation on his head."

The "readiness given by the gospel of peace" (6:15) refers famously to Isaiah 52:7. Here too, we see a decisive moment in Isaiah. In 6:8 the Lord famously asks, "Whom shall I send, and who will go for us?" and Isaiah says, "Here am I! Send me."

In Isaiah 52:6, the same turn of phrase is flipped. The Lord describes the oppression of his people and then says, "Therefore, on that day, they shall know that it is I who speak: here am I. How beautiful upon the mountains are the feet of him who brings good news! Who proclaims peace, who announces good news of happiness, who proclaims salvation, who says to Zion 'Your God reigns'!" (my translation). Since we know that it is Jesus who announces the good news of peace in Eph 2:17, and that it is the Lord who speaks and acts in Isaiah 52 and 59, we can conclude that the armor of God represents things first taken up by God himself in Christ, and then by us as we become part of his body.

Glory and Idolatry

We were made to long for glory—the relational beauty in which we find love, acceptance, value, and the purpose for our existence. Inside of individuals, this longing can go dreadfully wrong. But it can also go wrong on large scales. Mass evil and injustice—larger than any individual choice—happen in part because people continue to serve and sacrifice to Powers and Principalities.

We seek glory and salvation from our shame in idols. We create images of the glory we desire, and will sacrifice to them if we think they will give us a sense of identity in return. And we will sacrifice anything or anyone who seems to threaten the glory of that idol.

The sexual abuse and cover-ups in prominent Christian ministries are a tragic example of how this sacrificial system works. It is scandalous enough when those we trust as spiritual leaders turn out to be abusers. But we also know it only continues because many others ignored, denied, and covered it up. We find *entire structures* involved. In most cases, people did not think of themselves as supporting abuse—instead, they thought that they were protecting a ministry, a church, or a reputation. In the end, they continued to support a structure or a leader because they offered a sense of purpose, status, security. Their institutions became idols. And the result of idolatry is always the same: *idols require human sacrifice*. They ask for violence against the souls or bodies of human beings to preserve their own lives. They assign a greater meaning to the violence, convincing their followers that it's necessary to preserve what's really important. And the more seemingly "worthy" the cause is, the easier it is to make the sacrifice.

To promote our own glory, we insult and degrade others—or simply forget about them if they don't add to our own agenda. In the end, violence against the soul often leads to violence against the body too. Jesus pointed to this when he taught,

> You have heard that it was said to those of old, "You shall not murder; and whoever murders will be liable to judgment." But I say to you that everyone who is angry with his brother will be liable to judgment; whoever insults his brother will be liable to the council; and whoever says, "You fool!" will be liable to the hell of fire. (Matt 5:21–22)

When we degrade others, we also degrade our own glory. As true glory is further lost, the desperation to cover ourselves only grows, along with our willingness to commit the most heinous of crimes. Often, that violence is against individuals. But sometimes, the violence is against a whole group of people perceived to be a threat to our group, identity, culture, or way of life.

René Girard says that Jesus unmasks the true reasons for human violence. Whatever the supposed "cause," it is a facade.[24] The true desire is to be *like* our idols, to be like our sources of glory.[25] As a matter of fact, we want to *become* our idols. The good desire to share God's glory with him gets bent toward images, toward lesser copies of the real thing: "Those who make them become like them, and so do all who trust in them" (Ps 115:8). We begin to follow standards written by human hands and their dogmas (Col 2:14).

We long for a way out of shame and loathe ourselves for it. We desire the glory of the idol, and we loathe the idol for it. The desire and the loathing become insatiable. Since we cannot believe that God truly offers his glory to us, we sit down to eat the sacrificial meals with our idols, consuming the glory of those made in his image.

But Jesus says, *this is my body, which is broken for you*. He comes and takes the place of all human sacrifice, once and for all. He comes as true God of true God and offers himself to us with all of his glory. He comes right in the middle of the idolatry and the sacrificial system and says,

> Come, everyone who thirsts, come to the waters; and he who has no money, come, buy and eat! Come, buy wine and milk without money and without price. Why do you spend your money for that which is not bread, and your labor for that which does not satisfy? Listen diligently to me, and eat what is good, and delight yourselves in rich food. Incline your ear, and come to me; hear, that your soul may live. (Isa 55:1–3)

Jesus comes under the Powers and Principalities and is sacrificed to their system—but in the end, his glory and his life prove to be limitless. He alone provides limitless satisfaction for a limitless desire.

> For my flesh is true food, and my blood is true drink. Whoever feeds on my flesh and drinks my blood abides in me, and I in him. As the living Father sent me, and I live because of the Father, so whoever feeds on me, he also will live because of me. (John 6:55–57)

When we eat the life of Christ and satisfy our longing for glory in him, the power of death itself is undone. When he invites us, seats us, and gives us himself to eat, the Feast never ends. He is the only one who can provide enough for everyone.

---

24 Girard, *The Girard Reader*, 183.

25 Marion, *God Without Being*, 94.

> But if you bite and devour one another, watch out that you are not consumed by one another. But I say, walk by the Spirit, and you will not gratify the desires of the flesh … Now the works of the flesh are evident … but the fruit of the Spirit is love, joy, peace, patience, kindness, goodness, faithfulness, gentleness, and self-control. Against [feeding on] such things there is no law. (Gal 5:15–23)

Indeed, what we ate in the garden was not just a piece of fruit—what we ate was our own glory. What we ate was each other—*our* human soul.

And yet, this does not mean that walking out the gospel of peace with integrity will not demand sacrifice. To find our glory *in Christ* is to go where he went in this world. Serving the true God and steadfastly refusing to engage in the sacrifice of any human soul or body is costly. We must often relinquish a role we love, status we feel secure in, a purpose we've been living for, or relationships we cherish. As Daniel Berrigan said,

> We cry peace and cry peace, and there is no peace. There is no peace because there are no peacemakers. There are no makers of peace because the making of peace is at least as costly as the making of war—at least as exigent, at least as disruptive, at least as liable to bring disgrace and prison and death in its wake.[26]

Jesus laid down the glory of heaven so that he could serve us—so that his glory could become our source, our food, and our hope. And so to take up his glory, we must also lay ours down. But he has already gone ahead to show us the way. And he has promised to be with us always.

Two Ways of Being Human

Ephesians presents two distinct ways of being human—two realms, two kingdoms in which we can live. One realm is ruled by hostility, division, and wrath. The other is ruled by Christ who is our Peace. And the transfer of allegiance from one to the other—*salvation*—changes everything.[27]

Even when mass violence happens, not everyone will be complicit. While we were in Rwanda, we met two pastors who *did* resist the genocide, and who chose to hide people, risking their lives and the lives of their families. One of them felt compelled to hide targeted people, but he could not make the decision alone. It might cost his entire extended family their lives. As the choice was placed before them, they sat in silence, until his young daughter spoke up: "I am ready to die," she said.

---

26 Berrigan, *No Bars to Manhood*, 49.
27 Bates, *Salvation by Allegiance Alone*.

"That was a proud moment for me," he told us. "I told my family that I too would rather die innocent than live guilty." So the family hid people in their homes. They prayed and waited on words from God to know where to move them from place to place as men came to search them out.

The other pastor and his family hid hundreds of people on the church property. They too relied on words from the Lord telling them when and where to hide people. Finally, the property was surrounded by fifty armed men. The pastor put everyone inside of the church and stood in front with his family.

"If you want to kill these people," he told them, "First you will have to kill me, my wife, and my small children. Then you can do what you want with these people."

Surprised, and perhaps amazed, the men argued amongst themselves about what they should do with these defiant people. And since they could not agree, they left.

Our time with these two pastors ended with a sobering assessment. They said, "We've talked about this, and we both agreed that if we had had only twenty other pastors who were willing to do the same thing, we could have stopped the genocide entirely."

Many in this world are willing to die fighting for their loyalties to nation, clan, and family. But very few are willing to let Jesus take away their swords. When this happens, it is evidence of the New Humanity. It is evidence of people who have been transferred from the dominion of darkness to worship in the light of the crucified God.

A Warning from the Rwandan Church

There is great encouragement to be had from the church in Rwanda. But there are also serious warnings about the Old Way of being human. As I have shared about Rwanda in the US and in other parts of the world, I've found that I don't have to draw the connections between what happened there and what is happening in many of our countries. Most people see it right away.

"I know that you were here to speak about Rwanda," said one lady, "but the whole time you were talking, all I could think was *this is about the United States! This is about us!*"

"What you shared was so moving," said one man. "But I'm also emotional because I'm worried about what's happening here, and how the church has been involved."

"Thank you so much for telling us about Rwanda! But do you think we could have dinner and talk about America? And could we talk about our community in particular?"

While we were in Rwanda, we also received many direct warnings about our country, especially from those who have spent a lot of time in the United States:

> Forgive me, but I must be very honest with you—over the past several years, I've become very concerned for the United States. Every time I am there, I become more worried. And the propaganda I see on CNN and Fox, and what I hear from pulpits—it reminds me of Rwanda before the genocide.
>
> There were Christians who wanted to do something about the division in Rwanda—but it was too little, too late. Don't let the church in the United States make the same mistake!
>
> Do not compartmentalize the gospel. Do not pretend that some things have to do with the cross, and other things have to do with politics. If you do, and if the church does not learn to raise its prophetic voice, I'm worried for where you will end up.
>
> Do you think that what happened here could not happen in your country? I watch your country very closely, and I know you very well. I know your history, your laws, and your politics. Do not think that you could not have another civil war!

Another civil war? The possibility might be more real than we think.

BEING HUMAN: Engaging the Powers

In this chapter, we explored the "Powers and Principalities" as allies of violence who were, nevertheless, shamed and defeated through Christ's crucifixion and resurrection.

Just ahead in chapter 7, we'll examine "Status Games." We'll discover that humanity's God-given longing for glory—which we first discussed in chapter 1—shows up in all human beings as a powerful desire for status and recognition. And because of humanity's sin and brokenness, something as seemingly benign as *status* can be a major "ally" of violence.

CHAPTER 6 SUMMARY

- The evil of gratuitous violence defies logic; to grapple with this evil we need ways of knowing beyond the natural. The forces of darkness are allies of violence.
- Ephesians presents two ways of being human.
  - » The first way is conventional: *"in flesh"* ... "following the prince of the power of the air" (Eph 2:2), creating division and hostility—through wrath, anger, slander (4:31).
  - » The second way is *"in Christ," in his flesh* (2:14) as members of his body, creating peace—it is *kainon anthrōpon* (Eph 2:15; 4:24)—a brand new way of being human, a new way of community.
- In Ephesians 2:13–17, King Jesus is proclaiming a peace treaty far and wide—he is "gospeling peace" in fulfillment of Isaiah 52:7. The violence of gods, of peoples and nations, of families and individuals—is ended.
- To violate this peace treaty is to dishonor our King, God, and Father.

FOR FURTHER REFLECTION

- If Christ is proclaiming a peace treaty far and wide within the church, what hostile groups today do you imagine could be reconciled?
- What might be the role of lament and confession in experiencing the reconciliation of formerly hostile groups? Why is this so rare?
- In Ephesians 3:8–10 Paul says that the church, the *Jew-and-gentile-new-humanity-in-Christ,* is "the manifold wisdom of God ... [being] made known to the rulers and authorities in the heavenly places." What is Paul getting at?

Chapter 7

STATUS GAMES

*So then you are no longer strangers and aliens,
but you are fellow citizens with the saints
and members of the household of God.*
–Ephesians 2:19

*He has brought down the mighty from their thrones,
and exalted those of humble estate.*
–Luke 2:52

IN THIS CHAPTER

- Humanity's fundamental need for status is a potential "ally" of violence.
- The desire for status (or recognition) drives humans to compete and fight to gain status and to prevent the loss of status, individually and collectively.
- The Bible offers many status-oriented stories, pithy truths, and the shame-to-honor status-reversal of knowing Christ, which meets humanity's need.

Kristin:

We begin this chapter by returning to the biblical Feast of the King, to explore how it subverts humanity's traditional norms concerning status.

Scripture uses many words to describe the Feast. Jesus often called it "the kingdom of God." It is a feast for all the nations, the table of the King, the wedding supper of the Lamb, the River of Life (Isa 25:6; 2 Sam 9:11; Rev 19:9; 22:1–2; John 10:10), the Feast where God swallows up death forever.

With no fear of death and no fear of lack, there is no longer fear of shame—or of violence.

> Nation shall not lift up sword against nation, neither shall they learn war anymore; but they shall sit every man under his vine and under his fig tree, and no one shall make them afraid, for the mouth of the Lord of hosts has spoken. (Mic 4:3–4)

He will swallow up death forever; and the Lord GOD will wipe away tears from all faces, and the reproach of his people he will take away from all the earth, for the Lord has spoken. (Isa 25:8)

In God's world, his generous nature is the First, and the Last. The story which begins with the glory of the Garden will end with the glory of the Great Feast.

But most of the world's founding stories do not begin this way. They more often begin with violence and butchery, sex and jealousy, competition and hostility. In the oldest myths, it is the gods who compete. In the newer ones, it is living organisms competing for "survival of the fittest." But in nearly all of them, there is no life or order as we know it without violence and chaos.[1] Catholic philosopher and theologian John Milbank sees violence as *the* link between antiquity and modernity—"from the perspective of Christian virtue, there emerges to view a hidden thread of continuity between antique reason and modern, secular reason. This thread of continuity is the theme of 'original violence.'"[2]

Ancient Origin Stories: Enuma Elish Compared to Genesis

The ancient Mesopotamian epic of the Enuma Elish is too long to elaborate here. But we will outline a few of the similarities to the story of Genesis 1–3, along with the striking differences. Those contrasts show a distinct story about where we came from, and a different message about where we're going.

Both stories begin with watery chaos. In the Enuma Elish, the chaos divides into Tiamat, the goddess of saltwater, and Apsu, the god of freshwater. As they intermingle, other gods are born. When the first generation mates, more gods are born, of sky and earth and dry land.

Soon, the younger gods become noisy. This irritates Apsu, who plots to kill them. Tiamat hears of this, and sends one of her sons to kill Apsu instead. The story takes many twists and turns, but in the end, Tiamat goes to war against the god Marduk. He defeats her and uses half of her body to create heaven and the other half to create earth. Marduk then orders the cosmos. He creates humans from the corpse of another deity and tasks them with assisting the gods in continuing to order and maintain the world.

---

[1] Stonestreet and Baer, "Is Genesis Just One of the Many Creation Myths?" See also Howard-Brook, *Come Out My People*, 37–38; Watkin, *Biblical Critical Theory*, 54–55; Wink, *Engaging the Powers*, 13–16.

[2] Milbank, *Theology and Social Theory*, 5.

Genesis gives several hints at the presence of divine beings other than the Lord. As we discussed in chapter 6, "Powers and Principalities," these are likely members of the divine council (Ps 82:1–2). But in Genesis they are "a silent chorus."[3] They are present with God, but not active in creating or ordering the cosmos. Certainly, they are not in conflict, and we see no cosmic battle between chaos and order.

Instead, we see a Creator God who "hovers" over the chaos. The Hebrew word connotes the gentle fluttering of a bird's wings over her young. Rather than turning into gods, the waters divide as the Creator's Spirit speaks over them. The entire ordering of creation unfolds without violence of any kind. Primarily, it happens through the response of the natural elements to the Creator's voice. God speaks, and the earth responds actively by bringing forth life (1:11–12). He sees the goodness of this work, names the things he has made, and blesses them.

As in the Enuma Elish, humanity is tasked to join the continued ordering of creation. But the human being does not come from the mutilated corpse of a god. Instead, they come from the earth and are shaped by the hands of God, who breathes breath into them. They are then placed in a garden, already fruitful and ready with food. As Watkin points out,

> In contrast to other ancient creation myths, Genesis 1 is remarkably calm and ordered. No one gets hurt, no one loses a corporeal appendage, and no one dies. The universe is not created in war and through fighting but in peace and through speaking.[4]

The creation of the world ends with the Woman, and the Man's joyful response to her. Proverbs 8 also tells of the joy and exultation in God's creative acts. Lady Wisdom says, "I was beside him, like a master workman, and I was daily his delight, rejoicing before him always, rejoicing in his inhabited world and delighting in the children of man" (vv. 30–31). Again, Watkin:

> The universe did not lurch into being through conflict or stumble into being by chance. God had a plan, and that plan faced no opposition. This further reinforces the pattern laid down by the Trinity: the bedrock reality of our universe is peace, harmony, and love; not war, discord, and violence.[5]

---

3 Zank, "Enuma Elish and Genesis."
4 Watkin, *Biblical Critical Theory*, 55.
5 Watkin, 55.

The story of Genesis also stands in contrast with the great creation myths of the modern West,[6] founded on competition and on the logic of "survival of the fittest."

All these myths start with the assumption that there is only so much to go around. This is sometimes referred to as the "image of limited good," fostering an intensely competitive win-lose environment.[7] If one eats, another might not. If one person gets a good seat at the table, someone else will get a lesser seat, or maybe no seat at all. This creates a situation where existence is only secured by competition. And the gatekeepers of power decide who is worthy of resources and places of honor.

In some cultures, your place is inherited through birth and preserved through strength. In the West, it is (in theory) earned through hard work and merit. We compete for good grades, good jobs, and a place in the mythical "Market"—a larger-than-human reality both as powerful and capricious as the gods of Olympus, Valhalla, or Ayodhya.[8]

Feast of the King—Abundance and Glory for All

But the Feast of the King is not like this. John says that Jesus is the Logos—the Word or the Logic of the universe. *He* is how the world was created (John 1:1–2), and the *true* laws of nature are revealed in him.

The Creator is not bound by scarcity, and his way of self-giving love contradicts the logic of competition. He can give everything, and still have more to give. He does not exercise power through force, but rather with the word of life: "A bruised reed he will not break, and a faintly burning wick he will not quench; he will faithfully bring forth justice" (Isa 42:3). Like the earth, we can respond and bring forth life as he begins the work of reconciling all things in himself (Matt 13:3–9).

At his Feast, the abundance is only increased as more people come to the Table. It is a Feast of multiplication as each one brings what they have to the hands of Jesus. As we return the gifts of the Creator back to him, he makes them new and frees them from scarcity and death. And each new guest only adds to the glory of all. Paul understood this from the many

---

6 By calling them "myths" I am not commenting on whether they are true or not. I am only indicating that they are the type of big stories, or metanarratives, that we use to understand the world.

7 See Neyrey, *Honor and Shame in the Gospel of Matthew*, 17–18; Mischke, *The Global Gospel*, "Honor/Shame Dynamic #3: Image of Limited Good," 98–103. In Christ there is no "limited good."

8 Cox, "The Market as God."

passages in Isaiah which saw the ingathering of the nations as a sign of the restoration of Israel's glory (Isa 25:7–8), so that "the latter glory will be greater than the first" (Hag 2:7–9).

For Paul, *the unity of the nations is a sign that God is making peace and bringing death to an end* (Hag 2:9; Isa 25:8; 60:1–5). As Cyril of Alexandria put it, when the "mutually exclusive attitudes" of the peoples are destroyed, "the enemy will then be completely ashamed, astounded at the magnitude of the fame accorded them, the permanence of the satisfaction, and the reliability of the hope."[9]

When the nations come in, we will see our enemy ashamed. We will have astounding *fame*, permanent satisfaction, and a reliable hope.

Werner:

Defining Status

As we discussed in chapter 1, glory is a multifaceted concept. It encompasses terms like belonging, acceptance, beauty, worthiness, value, prestige, excellence, honor, authority, and *status*. Status is one dimension of glory.

Status means "the relative social, professional, or other standing of someone or something."[10] For example, one might discuss "an improvement in the status of women" in a particular social context. The word *status* used this way can refer to a social standing that varies. It is high or low or in between.

The word *status* can also be used to signify class. One might say that a person *has* status, referring to their "high rank or social standing: those who enjoy wealth and status."[11] These definitions refer to "someone or something." Both people and things can have status. For example, Rolls Royce is a very costly brand of car (a thing) that signifies the highest status. A house in Beverly Hills, California, signifies a top-tier-status neighborhood (other neighborhoods are below).

Status can be thought of as a form of social capital. But it isn't only a thing we desire. It is a thing that—in a very real way—we need for our health and well-being.

---

9   Cyril of Alexandria helped bring this to our attention in his writings on the glory of the temple. The image is of a great house filled with treasures from all over the world showcasing the extent of the reign of God, and glorying in the peace he has accomplished. St. Cyril of Alexandria, *Commentary on the Twelve Prophets*, 341.

10 *New Oxford American Dictionary* (Version 2.3.0). Copyright © 2005–2022 Apple Inc. All rights reserved.

11 *New Oxford American Dictionary.*

Status and Health

We now examine some key insights from the social sciences concerning status and health. Will Storr's *The Status Game: Our Social Position and How We Use It* is most helpful. Storr's research shows that what he calls "the status game" is universal to the human family. Status competition is apparently woven into our DNA—from the most remote, prehistoric tribes to the most tech-savvy urbanite family. "Our need for status is ... fundamental."[12]

Storr references the work of Professor Sir Michael Marmot.[13] Across decades, Marmot collected health and demographic data about various populations. In 1976, he began researching the relationship between health and social status among people serving in the highly stratified British civil service. It led to a major discovery: "The rates of disease increased progressively down the social ladder."[14] As he researched the wider population of the UK he found the same status syndrome at work: the further down people were on the social ladder, the greater the rate of disease, and the earlier they died. The same also held true in other nations studied.

Dr. Marmot found that disease increases progressively down the social ladder. As Will Storr says in his book—*our need for status is fundamental.* This is yet another example of how social sciences come into meaningful conversation with the insights of Scripture on the human need for glory. We do not merely need a connection with the material world through food—we need meaningful connection with others. We not only need to eat, but we also need a *seat* at a glorious Feast.

In reading *The Status Game*, I became more aware of my own concern for status. Storr writes, "When asked why we do the things we do, we rarely say, 'It's because of status. I really love it.'"[15] This made me smile. It is

---

12 Storr writes, "If moral truth exists anywhere, it's in our DNA: that ancient game-playing coding that evolved to nudge us into behaving co-operatively in hunter-gatherer groups. But these instructions—strive to appear virtuous; privilege your group over others—are few and vague and open to riotous differences in interpretation. All the rest is an act of shared imagination. It's a dream we weave around a status game." Storr, *Status Game*, 137–39. Contra Storr, this author (as a Christian) believes that moral truth exists objectively in the Triune Creator God, and that we live in a moral universe. Storr's views are presented here because this author believes that humanity's fundamental, pathological drive for status is profoundly influential on human behavior, and Christianity's history reveals a struggle with the pull of status and power.

13 Marmot, *The Status Syndrome*.

14 Marmot, 2

15 Storr writes, "It can be distasteful to think of [status] as any kind of motivating force, let alone a vital one. It contradicts the heroic story we like to tell of ourselves. When we pursue the great goals of our lives, we tend to focus on our happy ending. We want the qualification, the promotion, the milestone, the crown. If our need for status is so

embarrassing to admit that status has a bearing on my choices: where I live, the car I drive, the clothes I wear, the mobile phone I use, the church I attend. Writing this book has status implications—the hope of favorable reviews, an increase in reputation. "To admit to being motivated by improving our rank is to risk making others think less of us, which loses us rank."[16]

> This inbuilt need to achieve and maintain status gives us a thirst for rank and a fear of its loss that deforms our thinking … Always on alert for slights and praise, we can be petty, hateful, aggressive, grandiose and delusional. We play for status, if only subtly, with every social interaction, every contribution we make to work, love or family life and every internet post. We play with how we dress, how we speak and what we believe [17]

Status, Caste, Segregation

The status game is played in many ways. It is one thing to play the status game, for example, as a sports fan. Who doesn't enjoy using their "bragging rights" when their favorite team wins? But the status game is also played in ways that have profoundly negative, even deadly, impacts on other persons, peoples, and races. In India, for example, the status game has been played through the caste system for millennia.

> The evil of India's caste practice is almost as old as the gods, and is the most noxious and evolved example today of how humans attempt to impose superiority and suffering on others by virtue of their birth. Hindu texts speak of four tiers, or varnas, making up a broader caste pyramid in society. On top are the Brahmins or priestly caste, the Kshatriyas or warrior class and the Vaisyas or merchant class. At the bottom come the Shudras or labouring castes. The rest do not even count: outcastes.[18]

Caste is "the arbitrary construction of human divisions,"[19] writes Isabel Wilkerson in her much-awarded book *Caste: The Origins of Our Discontents*. Wilkerson examines the similarity between caste systems in three nations: India, America, and Nazi Germany. Caste is "the policing of roles expected of people based on what they look like, and, second,

---

fundamental, this discomfort we feel towards it may seem surprising. But that's the game." Storr, *Status Game*, 11.
16 Storr, 11.
17 Storr, 2.
18 Ziegler (Banyan), "India's caste system remains entrenched."
19 Wilkerson, *Caste*, 37.

the monitoring of boundaries—the disregard for the boundaries of subordinate castes or the passionate construction of them by those in the dominant caste, to keep the hierarchy in place."[20]

Historically, the American version of caste was stated in this racial creed, "Let the lowest white man count for more than the highest Negro."[21] The statement is saturated with an all-too-human instinct—love of domination merged with fear of losing status and power. Wilkerson refers to this as "dominant group status threat."[22] It is the built-in and sometimes fierce impulse to protect the social position (or wealth or power or sense of superiority) of one's group.

Protecting the social status of one's group is a powerful dynamic all over the world. One way this happens in the United States is by constructing "walls." Consider, for example, redlining: "a discriminatory practice that puts services—usually financial services—out of reach for residents of certain areas based on race or ethnicity."[23] Redlining was particularly widespread after World War II and into the 1960s in cities and towns all over America. Credit-worthy black families were unable to get mortgages to "move up" and buy a house in middle-class neighborhoods.[24] Forced to remain in impoverished neighborhoods, redlining prevented innumerable black families from accruing intergenerational wealth.[25]

After the Fair Housing Act of 1968 made race-based redlining illegal, concerned citizens—shall we call them the dominant caste?—came up with a new way of erecting walls through zoning laws. Matthew Desmond powerfully argues in *Poverty, by America*, that communities all over the country passed zoning laws to restrict and prevent the construction of affordable housing.[26] And the net result? Exclude families and individuals from the community who are lower-status, lower-income earners. This kind of exclusion doesn't necessarily mean racial exclusion. But Desmond argues it's still a form of segregation driven by an undertow of racism. And I would add—*status-anxiety* or *fear of "the other."*

---

20 Wilkerson, 216.
21 Wilkerson, 25.
22 Wilkerson, 332, referencing Mutz, "Status Threat, Not Economic Hardship."
23 Hayes, "What Is Redlining?"
24 Rothstein, *The Color of Law*.
25 Rothstein, 185.
26 Desmond, *Poverty, By America*; see especially chapter 9, "Tear Down the Walls," 161–82.

My point here is simple. Love of status drives us as humans. (Aristotle would say it is *love of honor*.[27]) The desire to gain and preserve status shapes us as individuals, families, communities, and nations far more than we may admit. Christians are not immune from the contagious virus of dominant-group-status-anxiety. Herd immunity from the virus seems impossible. But King Jesus offers a cure: His sin-forgiving, shame-covering, glory-restoring, reconciling-with-God-while-reconciling-with-neighbor-and-enemy ... gospel of peace.

Status of Nations

Francis Fukuyama is an American political scientist, scholar, and writer. For decades he has been writing about this idea: "The desire for recognition is the motor of history."[28] Fukuyama describes three types of human drives related to status and identity-recognition. He uses three Greek words to describe these drives: *thymos, isothymia, megalothymia*.

Thymos is the part of the soul that craves recognition or dignity; *isothymia* is the demand to be respected on an equal basis with other people; while *megalothymia* is the desire to be recognized as superior.[29] Fukuyama argues that these dynamics are enormously significant in national and international affairs. "Demand for recognition of one's identity is a master concept that unifies much of what is going on in world politics today."[30]

> Modern liberal democracies promise and largely deliver a minimal degree of equal respect, embodied in individual rights, the rule of law, and the franchise [voting rights]. What this does not guarantee is that people in a democracy will be equally respected in practice, particularly members of groups with a history of marginalization. Entire countries can feel disrespected, which has powered aggressive nationalism, as can religious believers who feel their faith is denigrated. *Isothymia* will therefore continue to drive demands for equal recognition, which are unlikely to ever be completely fulfilled.[31]

---

27 As quoted in Neyrey, *Honor and Shame in the Gospel of Matthew*, 5.

28 Fukuyama, *The End of History and the Last Man*; also, *Identity: The Demand for Dignity and the Politics of Resentment*. He names the German philosopher Friedrich Hegel as the originator of the idea: "Hegel put recognition of that moral agency at the center of his account of the human condition. In *The Phenomenology of Spirit*, he argued that human history was driven by a struggle for recognition." *Identity*, Kindle loc. 626.

29 Fukuyama, *Identity*, Kindle loc. 73.

30 Fukuyama, Kindle loc. 109.

31 Fukuyama, Kindle loc. 73.

Fukuyama says, "Twentieth-century politics had been organized along a left-right spectrum defined by economic issues, the left wanting more equality and the right demanding greater freedom." He points out that while economic matters are important to voters, bread-and-butter issues are now secondary to a more fundamental driving force: collective dignity or status. He calls this the "politics of resentment":

> In a wide variety of cases, a political leader has mobilized followers around the perception that the group's dignity had been affronted, disparaged, or otherwise disregarded. This resentment engenders demands for *public recognition of the dignity of the group in question*. A humiliated group seeking restitution of its dignity carries far more emotional weight than people simply pursuing their economic advantage.[32]

Consider ISIS, which carried out a mass execution in 2015 of twenty-one Coptic Christians on the coast of Libya. A video was made of the beheading event. The ISIS propaganda magazine *Dabiq* recruited soldiers using the language of honor-shame and heroism:

> The time has come for those generations that were drowning in oceans of disgrace, being nursed on the milk of humiliation, and being ruled by the vilest of all people, after their long slumber in the darkness of neglect—the time has come for them to rise... . The time has come for (all Muslims) to wake up from its sleep, remove the garments of dishonor, and shake off the dust of humiliation and disgrace, for the era of lamenting and moaning has gone, and the dawn of honor has emerged anew.[33]

Commenting on Dabiq's propaganda, political theorist Yara Damaj writes, "The IS claims to offer the disenfranchised—who see no way to live in honor in the West—a chance to reinvent themselves as heroes in the IS's dystopic reality. It does so by concocting *fantasies of belonging* that are presented in the form of relief from what is experienced in the lived real."[34]

Consider Putin's Russia. As we write this book, Russia is engaged in a war with Ukraine. What motivated Russian President Vladimir Putin to invade Ukraine? An American defense analyst writes that honor is a major factor.

---

32 Fukuyama, Kindle loc. 87. (Emphasis mine)

33 Dabiq, 2014. "The Return of Khilafah," July 5, 2014, 3. (As referenced in Damaj, "Fatal Attraction.")

34 Damaj, "Fatal Attraction: The Islamic State's Politics of Sentimentality." (emphasis mine)

Leaders make some decisions that appear irrational when viewed from a strictly transactional perspective but less so when taking into account perceptions of honor and justice. In Putin's case, he seems convinced that his war is a mission to *restore Russia's national honor*, redeeming the country from the *humiliation* that followed the end of the Cold War and the disintegration of the Soviet Union. In his annual state of the nation address to parliament in 2005, he referred to the Soviet Union's collapse as *"the greatest geopolitical catastrophe of the century"* and viewed as unacceptable that "tens of millions of our fellow citizens and countrymen found themselves beyond the fringes of Russian territory." For Putin, *Russia's honor requires the recovery of these "lost" Russians and the land they occupy,* even if he must run high risks to achieve this.[35] (emphasis mine)

Recall Fukuyama's concept of *isothymia* is "the demand to be respected on an equal basis with other people." Can we not see this dynamic in the examples given above? The American government has also been accused of "the desire to be recognized as superior," with attitudes and behaviors that do not make for peace. The roots of the current Russia-Ukraine war comprise one example where there is heated debate.[36] While I find the debate confusing, the fact that *there is a debate* proves our point: The competition for status and recognition exists not merely between persons, families, and communities. The desire for recognition and status writ large exists between peoples and nations, sometimes resulting in bloodshed and all-out war.

The world's great power competitions revolve around much more than economic interests. Identity and recognition, honor and dignity, are major factors in international rivalry and war.

Ancient Dynamics: Honor-Status Reversal in the Bible

The word *status* does not appear in most English translations of the Bible. But we contend that honor-status reversal is a Bible motif. We will observe that Ephesians 2 offers two examples of honor-status reversal, while

---

35 Krepinevich, "Is Putin a Rational Actor?"
36 Economist, diplomat, and author Jeffrey Sachs considers Putin's war against Ukraine to be in response to America's reneging on a commitment to Russia not to expand NATO. See "Jeffrey Sachs: The Untold History of The Cold War." For an opposing view, see Jeff Neal, "There was no promise not to enlarge NATO." Anne Appelbaum argues that Putin is like other dictators who comprise a mutually supportive global network of autocrats; Putin wants to ignore the rule of law, human rights, and accountability through "kleptocracy and autocracy." See Appelbaum, *Autocracy, Inc.*, 27–42, 98–121.

simultaneously speaking to collective identity conflict, reconciliation, and peace. What is honor-status reversal? It is when a person, family, or people have whatever degree of esteem, respect, privilege, power, or authority before a community turned the other way around.[37]

The honor-status of a person or group can be high or low or in-between, ranging from the lowest honor-status of a leper or a slave community, to the immensely powerful high honor-status of a mighty king or empire. Generally, persons and groups are keenly aware of their level of honor-status in their community.

We classify honor-status reversal according to the result: (1) *Result is honor:* Honor-to-shame-to-honor, or simply, shame-to-honor; and (2) *Result is shame:* Shame-to-honor-to-shame, or simply, honor-to-shame. These variations are illustrated in Figure 7.1 below.

I have written extensively about the Bible motif of honor-status reversal. A twenty-three-page excerpt from my volume *The Global Gospel* is available to the reader as a free PDF.[38] Below is a sampling of that material.

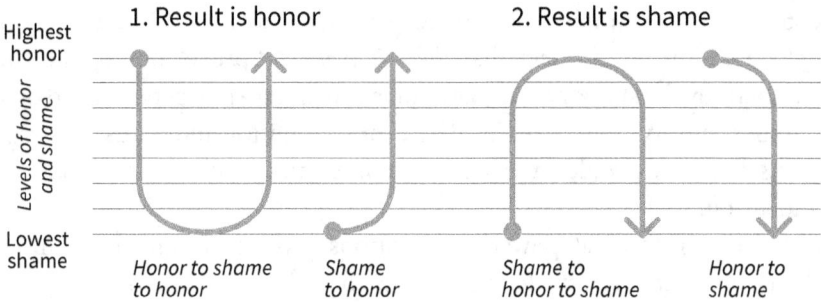

Figure 7.1: Types of honor-status reversal

---

37 Adapted from Mischke, *The Global Gospel*, 181.

38 See Mischke, "Honor-Status Reversal as a Motif of the Bible," in *The Global Gospel*, https://wp.me/a39vTO-235.

Examples of Honor-Status Reversal

The U-shaped honor-status trajectory of Jesus Christ in Philippians 2:5–11 depicts honor to shame to exalted glory as in figure 7.2, below.[39]

The U-shaped pattern repeats in Scripture at both the micro level (short pithy verses[40]) and macro level (long stories, grand narratives[41]). Moreover, the U-shaped pattern of status reversal exemplified by Christ is a pattern for Christian living (Matt 16:24; John 20:21; Rom 6:3–5; Gal 2:20). Honor-status reversal is a central dynamic in the Bible, and symbolic of the whole life of Jesus. Honor-status reversal is a pattern for following Christ.

Similar U-shaped trajectories of honor-to-shame-to-honor are found in the stories of Abraham, Job, Joseph, Nebuchadnezzar, and the prodigal son (Luke 15:11–32). Isaiah discloses numerous examples of honor-status reversal. Judah and Jerusalem lose their honor and are brought low. The arrogant peoples and nations are brought low. In Isaiah's suffering servant we see honor-to-shame-to-honor, as well as the future shame-to-glory of the Jewish people. Isaiah reveals, "Every valley shall be exalted, and every mountain and hill made low" (Isa 40:4).

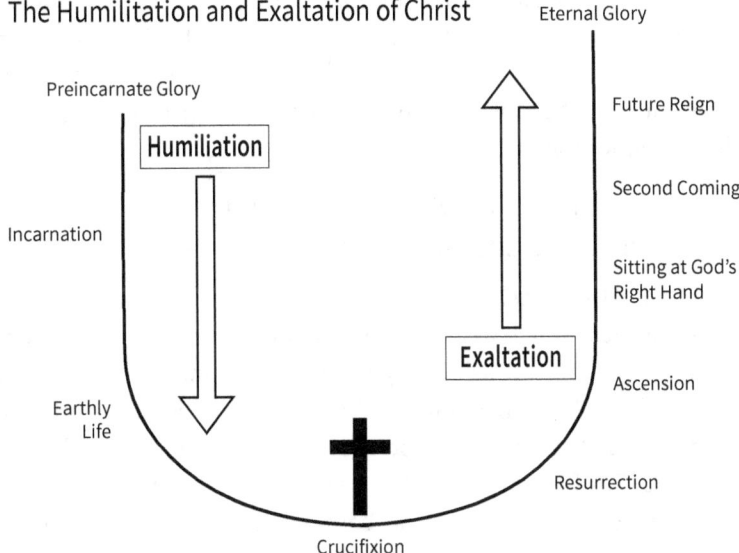

Figure 7.2. Humiliation and exaltation of Christ as honor-status reversal

---

39 Adapted from *ESV Study Bible*, 2525.

40 For example, in Luke 1:52; 7:28; 9:48; 13:30; 14:11; 17:33; 18:14; 20:17; 24:26.

41 For example: the book of Job; the story of Joseph (Gen 37–50); the Exodus (Exod 1–15). Daniel has a variety of honor-status reversal stories (Daniel and friends, chs. 1–3; Nebuchadnezzar (ch. 4); Belshazzar (ch. 5). Likewise, Esther is a single drama of interwoven honor-status-reversal stories.

When Christ descends, he conquers sin and death and restores glory to his creation at every level. The final victory is when Christ ascends even from death, taking with him people from every nation. He draws us into his own self, so that as he ascends, we ascend with him. He is the new humanity. And we only become part of it by being found "in him" (Phil 3:9).

This change in status and restoration to God's glory causes a change in our status with one another as well. No matter how far apart we may have seemed before, we are now "one in Christ Jesus" (Gal 3:28).

Honor-Status Reversal in Ephesians 2

In Ephesians 2 we observe two dimensions of honor-status reversal—vertical and horizontal—as indicated by figure 7.3.[42]

First, in the personal-vertical dimension, believers *in relation to God* experience an honor-status reversal (vv. 1–7); they were God's sin-captured enemies, but God rescues them by his saving grace; as a result, they are "seated above with Christ" (v. 6) in a position of regal honor. What a reversal!

Second, in the social-horizontal dimension, believers *in relation to God's people* experience an honor-status reversal (vv. 11–12, 19): "So then you are no longer strangers and aliens, but you are fellow citizens with the saints and members of the household of God (v. 19): From shameful outsiders to honorable insiders.

Redefining Honor and Shame, Insiders and Outsiders, in Ephesians 2

In verse 11, Paul the Jewish Christ-follower reminds the gentile Christians in Ephesus of their non-Jewish, non-people-of-God background. He tells the gentile males in his audience they are "called the uncircumcision by the circumcision" (v. 11). Lynn Cohick writes, "Circumcision took on special importance in the Hellenistic period as an indication of Jewish identity."[43] According to Tet-Lim Yee, "Circumcision was of prime importance" to the Jewish community; it was a "confessional sign in harmony with the maintaining of the status of the covenant people of God."[44] Paul is grappling with the identity and status of God's people.

---

42 Diagram adapted from Mischke, *The Global Gospel*, 198.
43 Cohick, *The Letter to the Ephesians*, 283.
44 Yee, *Jews, Gentiles and Ethnic Reconciliation*, 80.

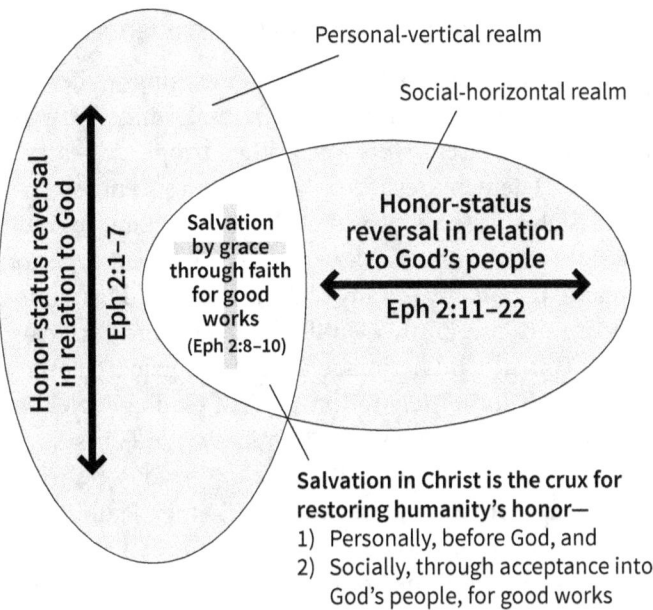

Figure 7.3: Salvation is at the crux of two dimensions of honor-status reversal in Ephesians 2

Recall David's bold, derogatory question regarding Goliath: "For who is this uncircumcised Philistine, that he should defy the armies of the living God?" (1 Sam 17:26). For David, the military battle was an honor-shame-and-status contest as much as a life and death struggle.

In Ephesians 2:11, Paul indirectly claims honor status for his Jewish ancestry; at the same time, he seems to put all gentiles into the category of "uncircumcised Philistine." This is who the gentile believers "were at one time" before Christ intervened in their lives. Although Paul's words might be read as an insult, it is likely that this is a more complex relational dynamic.

What is Paul doing? Paul is *relativizing status*. He is downgrading the importance of honor status based on the world's values. It turns out that because of Christ, "the relative social, professional, or other standing of someone or something" is far less weighty than our relationship to God and God's people. How can this be? *Here's how:* In Christ we have all the honor and glory we'll ever need.

Whatever social status they held as gentiles adds not one iota to their actual, eternal social capital. The only thing that matters is this: Who they are in relation to God in Christ and his people. These gentiles are reminded of their identity *now* by what *before* they were not: they were not in Christ. They shared no ancestry with God's people or their covenant promises. They were outside of God's family.

Critiquing Group-Based Arrogance

Concerning Ephesians 2:11–20, Willie James Jennings writes, "The power of this account of gentile status radically undermined any distinction gentiles held for themselves vis-à-vis other peoples. It is the ultimate deconstructive statement regarding gentile ethnocentrism."[45] Whether in the honor-status-obsessed world of the Roman Empire or of our own world today, this text critiques every stance of arrogant superiority based on race, wealth, nationality (or any other group-based haughtiness).

Why does Paul describe this gentile identity in outsider terms? God has intervened in Christ! God has made a way for outsider-gentiles to locate their own stories *honorifically* in the story of God's people. This honor-status reversal happens through the humiliation of Christ's incarnation, his perfect life, shameful cross, atonement, glorious resurrection, and exaltation as king—all in fulfillment of Israel's story. Paul writes, "So then you are no longer strangers and aliens, but you are fellow citizens with the saints and members of the household of God, built on the foundation of the apostles and prophets, Christ Jesus himself being the cornerstone" (Eph 2:19–20).

This is the kingdom-of-God program of identity formation. God is "democratizing" honor—it's equally available to *everyone*—to all persons and peoples. Regardless of one's family, wealth, status, or position in society, through King Jesus all have access to God's family (Eph 2:19), God's throne (Heb 4:16), God's honor (1 Pet 2:7), God's Great Feast (Luke 14:12–24).

God is relativizing every other form of social capital. Mark Roberts writes: "Notice that the recipients of the letter *were* ... gentiles 'by birth' (literally 'in flesh,' *en sarki*). They did not become Jewish when they received God's grace through Christ. Rather, Christ made them into something different from ordinary gentiles and Jews."[46] In other words, Christ gave them a new identity, a new source of eternal honor.[47] McNall writes, "This transformation [by the reconciling cross of Christ] is seen ... in the tearing down of ethnic and cultural boundaries ('the dividing

---

45 Jennings, *The Christian Imagination*, 271.
46 Roberts, *Ephesians*, 77; emphasis in original.
47 The early Christian writing known as the *Epistle to Diognetus* expresses this point when it calls Christians a new race, "neither Jewish nor Gentile." This informs how we think about the phrase "one new man" (Eph 2:15), *hena kainon anthrōpon* in the Greek. The phrase is also translated "one new humanity" (NIV), and "one new people" (NLT). Believers from Jewish backgrounds as well as gentile backgrounds, believers from every social class together, gain the ultimate insider status: "members of the household of God." Christ-followers have a new family-based core identity in King Jesus.

wall of hostility' [2:14]). This demolition results in a new community comprised of a new people who do not look like they belong together. Only Jesus and his spirit can account for this strange lot."[48]

To Whom Do We Belong?

This idea of "a new race, neither Jewish nor gentile," is helpful. In the Ephesian church, Jewish believers share both biological and historical continuity with their historic Jewish people; nevertheless, they are new-in-Christ, part of his body. They testify to this newness by worshiping God and doing so with people who, in former days, they strenuously avoided, even hated!

To the question, *to whom do we belong?* Jewish believers answer: We belong in King Jesus and we are part of a completely new community of intimacy with gentiles. Because Jewish loyalty to God had historically been expressed (in part) by their exclusion from gentiles, it represents a profound shift indeed.

To whom do we (gentiles) belong? For gentiles, could there be an even greater newness to their identity? Because of Christ, they are now bound together with believers of Jewish heritage. Together, they form a "new humanity," or simply a new divine way of being human. This colorful humanity is a new community whose Father is God, whose King is Jesus, and whose bond is the Holy Spirit—the Trinity of diversity in unity.

All who give their loyalty to King Jesus gain the honor margin and shame resilience to maintain loyalty to Christ and his people. This requires new beliefs and behaviors. Figure 7.4 (next page) compares "honorific gospel beliefs" with "subverted beliefs." As traditional forms of social status lose their sway over the believer's identity, our honor in Christ subverts traditional beliefs and notions of honor.

We find that we are freed from the vicious ups and downs of the status game to walk in the newness of life. Now our status is found not from achievement over and against others, but from our belonging to Christ and to one another. Now I do not rest in my own glory alone, but as relational beauty is restored, I enjoy the glory of God, united in all things.

Ignatius of Antioch, who was born in the apostolic era, is the earliest writer who references Ephesians. He says that "in his death Christ made a new standard for all ages, one that could apply to all his holy people, whether Jew or gentile."[49] In the Coming King—in his flesh and in his blood—we have a new standard for seeking glory. This standard binds

---

48 McNall, *The Mosaic of Atonement*, 243–44.
49 St. Ignatius of Antioch, "Church Fathers: Epistle to the Smyrnaeans (St. Ignatius)."

us together rather than driving us apart. It is this new reality—fresh and original, little used, often resisted—that makes possible the banquet of the Great King. Amid our world's darkness and division, *the party is on.* Do we see it breaking into our own communities?

HONORIFIC GOSPEL BELIEFS		SUBVERTED BELIEFS
We gain an enormous honor surplus as believers, along with strong shame resilience. Our honor and dignity as human beings abounds by: • the surpassing worth of knowing Jesus Christ our Lord (Phil 3:8); • being adopted into the family of God, whose king is Jesus the Christ (Rom 8:14–17; Eph 1:5); • experiencing the love of God "poured into our hearts through the Holy Spirit" (Rom 5:5); • humbly serving in God's kingdom (Mark 9:35; 10:43)—and being ambassadors of Christ (1 Cor 5:20); • being part of the royal priesthood, the church, the community of faith, the body of Christ (1 Pet 2:9).	Compared to the surpassing worth of knowing Jesus Christ our Lord and king: whatever level of wealth, honor, reputation, social capital, or majority status we may have inherited or earned, it is worthless and odorous (Phil 3:4–8; see also Eph 2:11–12, 19).	Our ascribed or achieved honor, social position, social capital, or majority status permit us to separate from, dominate, or oppress others.
	Because of the atonement of Christ (Eph 2:13–16), our new humanity (v. 15) gives us capacity and desire for communion and intimacy with "other" persons, families, peoples.	Our honor status, face, or social capital, whether high, low, or in between, is determinative of our true, essential honor and dignity.
	Because of the atonement of Christ (Eph 2:13–16), God has broken down the wall of hostility between believers differing in tribal identity, nationality, social class, or other classification. The cross has "killed the hostility" between Jew and gentile believers, and by extension, other Christian communities that may be in a state of division or conflict.	The default relational dynamic between Jew and gentile—or God's people and "others"—is separation, revenge, or violence.

Figure 7.4: Honorific gospel beliefs and subverted beliefs

BEING HUMAN: Status-Driven

In this chapter, we've explored some of the personal and international dimensions of "Status Games." We considered how *desire for recognition* often allies with hostility or violence. We also looked at some of the Bible's hope-filled truths about status, including our status reversal through Christ in Ephesians 2. Just ahead in chapter 8, "Group versus Group Hostility," we'll explore some special features about groups which can make them easy allies—and targets—of violence.

CHAPTER 7 SUMMARY

- The Bible's Feast of the Great King relativizes all traditional sources of status, honor, and glory.
- Humanity's need for status is fundamental; it's apparently woven into our DNA.
- Honor-status reversal is a motif or theme of the Bible from Genesis to Revelation.
- Status games are often an ally of violence. "The desire for recognition is the motor of history." *Desire for status writ large* drives nations to gain or regain honor, power, or glory via international competition, hostility, even war.
- Ephesians 2 and Christ's gospel of peace speak directly to humanity's need for status and recognition, offering to alleviate hostility in Christ.
- By grace through faith, believers gain a new source of honor or status: personally with God (Eph 2:1–6) and socially with God's people, the church (Eph 2:11–12, 19).

FOR FURTHER REFLECTION

- Where in the church might you observe the drive to gain or regain status—"the desire for recognition"? What about your own life?
- How would you communicate the gospel offering salvation that includes a new source of eternal honor based on allegiance to King Jesus (Eph 2)?
- Considering how powerfully humanity's drive for status affects individuals, families, communities, and nations—and the Bible's widespread relevance concerning honor status—why is there so little preaching on the subject?

Chapter 8

GROUP VERSUS GROUP HOSTILITY

Is there a way to love always? / Living in enemy hallways
Don't know my foes from my friends and
I don't know my friends anymore
Power has several prizes / Handcuffs can come in all sizes
Love has a million disguises / But winning is simply not one.
–"Citizens" by Jon Guerra

IN THIS CHAPTER

- Groups are often "allies" to violence. Families, tribes, nations, empires—social groups—have their own unique dynamics that fuel unethical and, often, violent behavior.
- The Law of Group Polarization and the Ethical Paradox of Group Loyalty demonstrate humanity's propensity for group hostility. Does the gospel address these social dynamics?

Kristin:

What happened in Rwanda could happen in your country. The same could be said in countries the world over. In America, we see increasing polarization over politics, ethnicity, religion,[1] or all the above.[2]

Americans are almost twice as unlikely to critique their own political party today than they were in the 1970s.[3] As Ezra Klein says in his book *Why We're Polarized,*

> We became more consistent in the party we vote for not because we came to like our party more—indeed, we've come to like the parties we vote for less—but because we came to dislike the opposing party more. Even as hope and change sputter, fear and loathing proceed.[4]

Klein calls this "negative partisanship."[5]

---

1 Pallavi Rao, "Which Countries Are the Most Polarized?"
2 Carothers and O'Donohue, "How to Understand the Global Spread of Political Polarization."
3 Brown University, "US Is Polarizing Faster Than Other Democracies, Study Finds."
4 Klein, *Why We're Polarized,* 10.
5 Klein, 9–10.

It's not just that Americans of opposing political parties differ in opinion. The language and attitude of politics have become war-like—*the opposing party is the enemy; I love my country; people of the other party are enemies of our country.* In a recent survey, 40 percent of people said they view their political opponents as "evil" and 20 percent admitted to having thought that the country would be better off if the majority of their political opponents were dead.

For many partisan political activists in America, the thing that matters is domination. What if someone acknowledges that an opposing argument has some points of merit? The extremist says, *No! That's giving comfort to the enemy.* Moderation, respectful listening, and compromise are condemned. "For angry activists, speech is a sword ... Activists wield the sword to slice and dice opponents, and wield the shield to protect themselves from the pain of disagreement, or—heaven forbid—the wrenching pain of being exposed as wrong or misguided."[6]

In addition to disturbing trends in violence against others,[7] we see an astonishing rise in violence against oneself. Mental health is particularly poor in English-speaking countries. In the United States, we see a large increase in teenage girls reporting sexual assault and worsening mental health.[8] Overall, deaths of despair have risen by 287 percent among youth in the last decade alone. Some have attributed this rapid rise to the COVID-19 pandemic.[9] But the previous decade shows that it began well before 2020.[10] This encourages us to look at deeper social causes.

The statistics for churches are also concerning. In 2023, 40 percent of evangelical pastors reported seriously considering leaving the ministry in the past year. That was up from 29 percent the year before, an 11 percent increase. The major reasons named were stress, loneliness, and political division in the church.[11]

Moreover, we see an increase in young people leaving the church—not because the church has failed to align with secular knowledge, but because the church fails to align with its own teaching.[12] Churches are

---

6   See French, *Divided We Fall*, 115.
7   United Nations, "A New Era of Conflict and Violence."
8   Naím, "The Other Deadly Pandemic."
9   Graham, "America's Crisis of Despair."
10 BMJ, "Disease of Despair Have Soared."
11 Chang, Moore, and French, "The After Party."
12 David Brooks, "The Dissenters Trying to Save Evangelicalism from Itself."

often not places for civil dialog like many young people would hope them to be.[13]

Why do we see ideological, political, religious, and ethnic polarization, even among those who claim that their identity in Jesus comes first? We've found a few principles in the social sciences which shed some light.

Werner: ### The Law of Group Polarization

Most democratic nations organize themselves on a political spectrum from left to right. Generally, the left emphasizes equality between groups and the positive role of government intervention; the right emphasizes freedom for individuals and limited government. This spectrum is represented below:

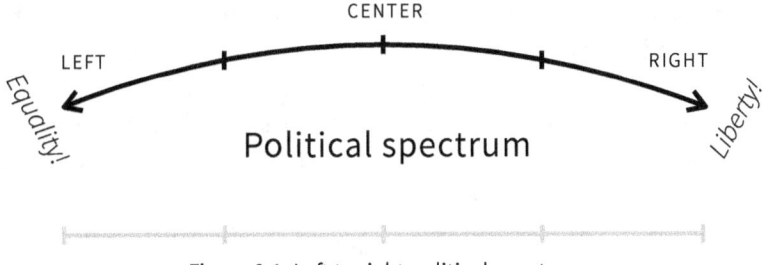

Figure 8.1: Left to right political spectrum

Now let's imagine a group of friends from the same church at a weekend get-together. Everyone in the group is white. Everyone is middle class, or upper middle class. Everyone is evangelical. Everyone is enjoying themselves. When it comes to political and social views, there is much agreement. Everyone mostly watches the same TV news channel. Everyone holds similar political views. Where they stand on the political spectrum of left-to-right is largely the same—moderate-right—as indicated below.

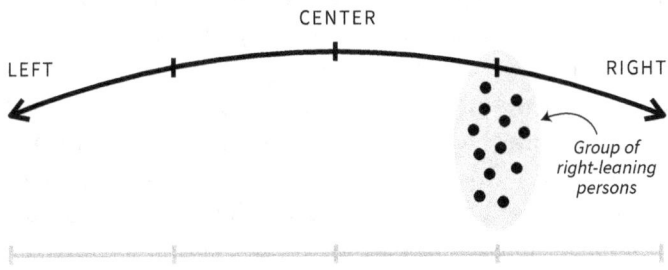

Figure 8.2: Group of persons moderately right in political stance

---

13 Caleb Nelson, "Millennials & Gen Z Are Leaving Church."

When the group conversation turns to politics—left versus right—two or three people are a little more to one side. But pretty much everyone has the same opinion. As the group ends its discussion, there is a strong sense of agreement and solidarity. This sense of solidarity and its effects on the group and its individuals—this is the subject of Cass Sunstein's 1999 article, "The Law of Group Polarization." Here's the opening statement:

> In a striking empirical regularity, deliberation tends to move groups, and the individuals who compose them, toward a more extreme point in the direction indicated by their own predeliberation judgments.[14]

When a group of like-minded persons discusses and deliberates about an issue (e.g., social issues and politics), something curious happens—they consistently move toward a more extreme position in the direction of where they began talking about it. This applies to the group as a whole and to the individuals in the group.

Below is a diagram depicting the behavior of a group "after deliberation," that is, after they have discussed the issues, stated their perspectives, and reached conclusions. They are surer of their stance. They move in the direction of a more extreme position.

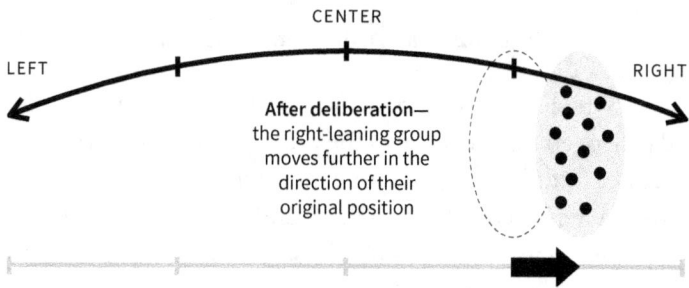

Figure 8.3: Deliberation moves the group toward the extreme

This phenomenon has been observed in all groups, left and right, liberal and conservative, and other types. Sunstein says, "Two principal mechanisms underlie group polarization. The first points to social influences on behavior; the second emphasizes limited 'argument pools,' and the directions in which those limited pools lead group members."[15]

In other words, two factors are particularly significant in group polarization. First, we often underestimate the role of the group on the behavior of individuals. Adults are often just as prone as teenagers to the pressures of peers in shaping their views and behaviors. Second, the more

---
14 Sunstein, "The Law of Group Polarization," 1.
15 Sunstein, 4.

homogenous and like-minded a group, the smaller the "argument pool." This means there is a limited range of perspectives from which to draw knowledge and insight. It therefore can lead to conclusions and behaviors which may be nearsighted at best, or foolishly destructive at worst.

As mentioned already, The Law of Group Polarization can apply to anyone. Figure 8.4 (below) shows the effects on both left and right. In both cases, the groups move further to the extreme, thereby increasing polarization and division.

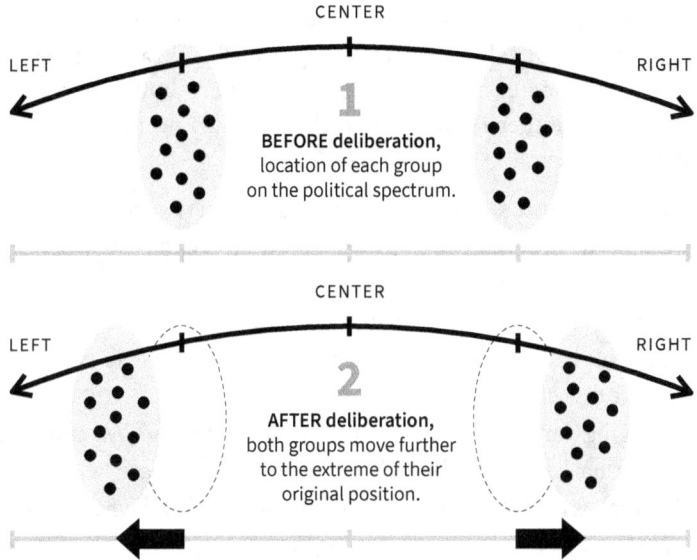

Figure 8.4: Group polarization—both left and right move to their own extremes

Without perspectives from people "on the other side," groups and individuals simply get more and more polarized. Sunstein writes, "When people are hearing echoes of their own voices, the consequence may be far more than support and reinforcement. Another lesson is that particular forms of homogeneity can be breeding grounds for unjustified extremism, even fanaticism."

Kristin: **Polarization and Politics**

The acceleration of division has been keenly felt in American politics. Data from Pew Research on the United States Congress shows that both parties have grown "more ideologically cohesive," and that there is less diversity of thought within the parties than fifty years ago. Between both parties, "there are now only about two dozen moderates left on Capitol Hill, versus more than 160 in 1971–72."

According to Pew, "Both parties have moved further away from the ideological center since the early 1970s. Democrats on average have become somewhat more liberal, while Republicans on average have become much more conservative." Since the '70s, the "middle"—where moderate Republicans could sometimes find common ground with moderate Democrats on contentious issues—has vanished.

> Five decades ago, 144 House Republicans were less conservative than the most conservative Democrat, and 52 House Democrats were less liberal than the most liberal Republican, according to the analysis. But that zone of ideological overlap began to shrink, as moderates in both parties—increasingly out of step with their caucuses and their constituents—either retired, lost reelection bids or, in a few cases, switched parties.[16]

Since 2002 "there's been no overlap at all between the least liberal Democrats and the least conservative Republicans in the House."[17] The Law of Group Polarization shows why this gap is widening. The less diverse our circles become, the more prone we are to moving toward ideological poles. And the further we move toward those poles, the less diverse our social circles are.

The longing for glory includes the need to belong. We reinforce our belonging by shared stories about "our glory"—who we are, where we came from, what makes us distinct, why we belong together, and why we are worthy of power, resources, and prestige. Ideology easily becomes part of that story.

Identity, Belonging, Glory

The Law of Group Polarization also shows that ideological battles are not won primarily on the plane of intellectual argument. They are won first on the plane of identity, belonging, and glory.

In 2016, I met someone in the far-right group known as "the Alt-Right." Before I knew this about them, they told me, "I don't really care who wins the election. I'm only voting for Trump to stand with my tribe." Very few people are so self-conscious in their decisions. We prefer to believe that we vote because we've educated ourselves on the issues. But the reality of how we form opinions is usually more complicated and often takes something more drastic to unmask.

---

16 Drew Desilver, "The Polarization in Today's Congress Has Roots That Go Back Decades."
17 Desilver.

The day after Trump won the 2016 election, a good friend approached me in the hallway at Duke. "Can we pray together?" she said. "I have something I need to confess." We sat down together. "This morning, I saw that Trump won," she said. "And I thought about all those people who voted for him. I never understood how a Christian could vote for Trump. But I realized that most of them were just voting for what they thought represented *their* people. At the core, they were voting to belong. And even though I thought I was voting for issues I cared about, I was really voting to belong too. I was voting for Hilary because that's what 'people like me' do. I'm not really any better, and all this time I've been thinking I was."

A little later, I would hear a similar confession from a friend who voted for Trump. "I don't actually want this man in office," he said. "People kept saying he would change when he became president, but I knew that wasn't true. Maybe it would have been better not to vote. But I felt like as a conservative Christian from the working class, I *had* to vote for him. I'm just as much a victim of identity politics as anyone."

Political polarization is not primarily a crisis of intellect, education, or decency. Our polarization represents *a crisis of belonging and a crisis of glory*. We can see signs of this crisis everywhere—of the shocking rise in opioid overdoses, worsening mental health among the young, increases in pornography addiction and sexual dysfunction, mass shootings and extremist violence by so-called "loners," the general epidemic of loneliness, and so much more.

And technology has thrown fuel on the fire. It is both easier to experience shame, and to shame others, without having to face them "in real life." Media also pushes ever-shifting standards for what it means to be worthy of attention and praise, or worthy of belonging in one ideological group or another.

Perhaps most frighteningly, social media and polarized news outlets reinforce increasingly smaller argument pools. The algorithms are designed to give us what we look for most—usually, whatever makes us ready to spend money or emotional energy. Few things do that as effectively as *reinforcing belonging.*

Werner: **The Illusion of the User**

Technology is not morally neutral. Our social media apps are not merely technologies that we use. Social media companies use us. Tech companies use us to generate profits without regard to the harm they cause to society. As Jason Thacker says, "technology is not simply a tool; technology is a force that can radically shape our lives, often by pushing us toward specific ends that clash with the goals of the Christian life." Thacker provokes: *Are Christians being "discipled by algorithms"?* [18]

Business school professor Scott Galloway was queried, "The Internet promised the democratization of business and culture. The reverse seems to have been the case. What's gone wrong?" In his answer, Galloway focuses on the business model of social media companies:

> If you were to try and reverse-engineer, the one thing that's done a ton of damage is that their underlying business models tap into a very tribal instinct and that we're very drawn to conflict and rage and the underlying business model of Google and Facebook is to sell as much advertising as possible, so as a result the algorithm has a vested interest in creating conflict and rage. They talk about engagement as a key metric, and what they really refer to is an enragement.... . We have a business model that quite frankly is just meant to agitate and tear at the fabric of society.[19]

The word *engagement* is a "nice" way to describe what social media companies do. The word *enragement* is more descriptive of their business model. Their business model is simple: Social media content is provided freely by its users; when it is characterized by anger and outrage it generates more clicks (more engagement) than if characterized by peace and harmony; more clicks mean more advertising revenue; more revenue means more profit; more profit means more power. Stated formally, "Social media platforms have played an increasing role in the spread of extremist content that translates into real world violence, due in part to business models that incentivize user engagement over safety."[20]

Social Media, Social Violence?

Social media allows people to easily connect around violent ideology. The Islamic group ISIS recruited some "40,000 foreign nationals from 110 countries to join the group" through their "strategic use of social media."[21] Groups like Al Qaeda and the Taliban also used social media platforms widely.[22]

---

18 Thacker, "Discipled by Algorithms: Where Is 'Big Tech' Leading You?"
19 Keen, "Scott Galloway: Tech Companies Should Be Broken Up."
20 Peters, "The Rising Threat of Domestic Terrorism."
21 Ward, "ISIS's Use of Social Media Still Poses a Threat to Stability in the Middle East and Africa."
22 Ward, "ISIS's Use of Social Media."

American citizens also use social media to spread the threat of violence within America's borders. "Virtually all domestic extremists use the internet and social media platforms to issue propaganda, coordinate training, raise funds, recruit members, and communicate with others."[23] Unfortunately, absent regulations and penalties, and given their enormous profits, there is little incentive for these mammoth companies to modify their business models. "Major social media companies … continued to prioritize growth and engagement and have not taken sufficient action to address this threat."[24] Politically motivated threats and violence in the US have grown dramatically.

I've never explored the so-called dark web: online communities where the values of tribalism, polarization, love of weapons, hatred of the "other," right-wing white supremacy, left-wing anarchy, or any other form of hostility are what holds a group together. But I have read Andrew Marantz's book *Antisocial: Online Extremists, Techno-Utopians, and the Hijacking of the American Conversation*. It made me anxious. I learned how the convenience and near-global accessibility of social media platforms make it easy for persons with violent motivations to find each other, exchange ideas, and organize.

Most troubling for me was this anecdote about the spread of taboo opinions on the internet: "One taboo opinion tended to beget another. Roissy, for example, was no longer just a pickup artist; he was now a full-blown anti-Semite and white nationalist whose slogan was 'Diversity + Proximity = War.'"[25] I was stunned. I wrote in the page margin: "Contra Ephesians 2:13–16! Diversity + Christ = Peace / new humanity / glory!"

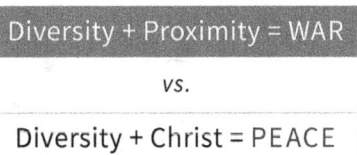

Figure 8.5: Contrasting views of diversity—the bottom concept is based on Ephesians 2:13-16

Of course, the formula cited by "Roissy" is extreme. Perhaps relatively few hold this view. But Marantz is making the point that taboo opinions and ideas grow easily on the internet. Moreover, the social media

---

23 Doxsee et al., "Pushed to Extremes," 80.
24 Doxsee et al., 5.
25 Marantz, *Antisocial*, 156.

algorithms of Twitter [now, "X"] are set up to lead people down a "rabbit hole" of ever more extreme content, to keep them "engaged."[26]

Social media addiction is common—addiction to the screen, the interactivity, the social reinforcement, the dopamine hit.[27] How did I just waste an hour scrolling, posting "Likes," accomplishing little to nothing? When alienated, angry, aggrieved persons follow their social media "engagement" toward darkness and join a like-minded online community, what happens? *En-rage-ment*. As Jason Thacker describes it, social media platforms "function like jet fuel poured on a society already aflame with self-seeking sin and pride."[28] A former Facebook vice president confesses, "The short-term, dopamine-driven feedback loops that we have created are destroying how society works."[29]

Compared to the millennia of the human story, the amazing technologies in our devices and social media platforms are barely twenty years old. Meanwhile, the "old way of being human" of which Paul wrote (Rom 3:13–17) stubbornly persists. Furthermore, the effects of the old way of division, hostility, corruption, and violence can be accelerated by these new technologies. And when large group dynamics are involved, it's especially dangerous.

Many have argued that as religion in America fails to provide a sense of belonging and transcendence on its own, politics has ascended as the next best thing. The American political story is particularly apt to provide a sense of transcendence which can be quasi-religious for the secular person and can easily blend itself with religion for the person of faith.[30]

---

26 "Twitter generates a list of accounts it recommends users follow based on the user's engagement with similar accounts and topics, creating a 'rabbit hole' effect that can promote conspiracy theories and extreme content." Peters, "Rising Threat of Domestic Terrorism," 5.

27 "Although not as intense as a hit of cocaine, positive social stimuli will similarly result in a release of dopamine, reinforcing whatever behavior preceded it. Cognitive neuroscientists have shown that rewarding social stimuli—laughing faces, positive recognition by our peers, messages from loved ones—activate the same dopaminergic reward pathways. Smartphones have provided us with a virtually unlimited supply of social stimuli, both positive and negative. Every notification, whether it's a text message, a 'like' on Instagram, or a Facebook notification, has the potential to be a positive social stimulus and dopamine influx." See Haynes, "Dopamine, Smartphones & You."

28 Thacker, "Discipled by Algorithms."

29 Haynes, "Dopamine." Referencing the November 2017 interview with Chamath Palihapitiya, a former Facebook VP; see Stanford Graduate School of Business, YouTube channel.

30 See Hamid, "America without God." His key point—"As religious faith has declined, ideological intensity has risen." See also Fatal, "Is Politics Filling the Void of Religion?"

The Ethical Paradox of Group Loyalty

Group honor competition and conflict usually begin with the family. Jerome Neyrey examines the importance of loyalty to one's family in the ancient context of the biblical world.

> Relatives who press for the advantage of family members are simply doing their duty to the kinship group, which is an honorable thing. Hence solidarity and loyalty among family members go without saying. Blood replicates the honor of the family.[31]

"Blood replicates the honor of the family." Yes, and anyone familiar with a blood feud will agree. The definition of a blood feud is: "a lengthy conflict between families involving a cycle of retaliatory killings or injury." The cycle of violence is fueled by honor competition.

An internet search of "blood and honor" or "blood feud" brings out the ugly prevalence of this global scourge. Whether it is the Hatfields and the McCoys … or Sunni versus Shiite … Aryan race against Jewish race … Chinese against Japanese … white race versus any others, it is, in essence, all honor-based violence fueled by blood.

What about giving your life out of loyalty to the cause of your people or nation?

As an American I have a critical view of the Japanese kamikaze pilots who, out of honor and loyalty to their people, flew suicide missions crashing into American battleships in World War II. What about 9/11? Islamic radicals hijacked commercial aircraft, killed the pilots, and crashed into the World Trade Center towers and the Pentagon. These "suicide pilots" caused the deaths of 2,753 persons in New York City alone, plus all those who died in Washington, DC, and Pennsylvania. Why did they do it? One explanation: it was out of honor and loyalty to their people's cause. From one perspective: *loyalty*. From another perspective: *evil*.

Contrast, Tension, Paradox

So, we observe a contrast in perspective, a tension, a paradox between the "good" of group loyalty and ethical evil. This is why we are exploring the Ethical Paradox of Group Loyalty.

I first learned about this "ethical paradox" in the book *Divided by Faith* by Emerson and Smith. The authors address the problem of racial division and injustice reflected by America's white evangelical church. Here's how the authors describe the "Ethical Paradox of Group Loyalty" applied to church congregations:

---

31 Neyrey, *Honor and Shame in the Gospel of Matthew*, 53.

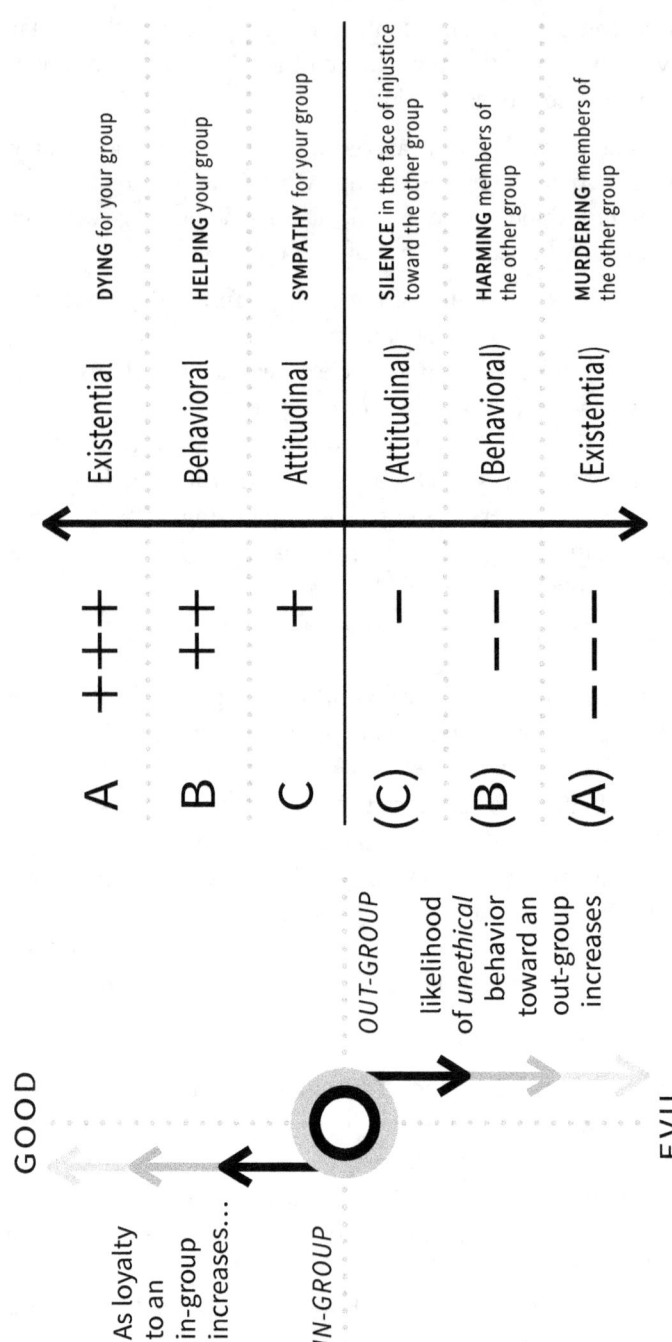

Figure 8.6: The Ethical Paradox of Group Loyalty

Given human limitations, racially exclusive identities and congregations necessitate bias. We might call this the ethical paradox of group loyalty. The paradox is that even if made up of loving, unselfish individuals, the group transmutes individual unselfishness into group selfishness.[32]

Stated more broadly: The greater the *unselfishness* or loyalty toward one's in-group (e.g., family, church, tribe, race or ethnic group, political party, people, nation), the greater the potential *selfishness* toward the out-group (e.g., *other* family, *other* church, *other* tribe, *other* race or ethnic group, *other* political party, *other* people, *other* nation).

It is conventional that humans show a preference for their own family and people. This is often benign, even healthy. In fact, failure to "take care of your own" is unethical (1 Tim 5:8). But this benign human tendency can turn. Social scientists observe that as loyalty to one's own group increases, the likelihood of unethical behavior toward an out-group increases. Figure 8.6 on the previous page illustrates how the dynamic works.

Observe the right side of the diagram, beginning with "C," just above the middle horizontal axis, then moving up:

- Level C represents the first stage (+) of goodness as defined by the in-group. At this level, one's loyalty and moral goodness is passive, merely an *attitude*—sympathy for one's group.

- Level B represents the second stage (++) of goodness as defined by the in-group. At this level, one's loyalty and moral goodness is more than an attitude—it is *behavioral*—helping one's group. This may include giving, supporting, volunteering, collaborating in all kinds of ways.

- Level A represents the third and highest stage (+++) of goodness as defined by the in-group. At this level, one's loyalty and moral goodness is more than an attitude, and more than helping. It is *existential;* that is, one's loyalty to the group is so great, that giving one's life, dying for the group, is a valid option.

---

32 Emerson and Smith, *Divided by Faith,* 158.

Now, observe the right side of the diagram, beginning with "(C)," just below the middle horizontal axis, then moving down:

- Level (C) represents the first stage (-) of unethical behavior resulting from minimal in-group loyalty. At this level, loyalty to your own group results in a passive, attitudinal form of unethical behavior—*silence* in the face of injustice to the other group. But this indifference is often foundational for greater injustice. Miroslav Volf writes, "Especially within a large-scale setting, where the other lives at a distance, indifference can be more deadly than hate."[33]

- Level (B) represents the second stage (- -) of unethical behavior resulting from in-group loyalty. At this level, one's unethical behavior moves past mere silence and becomes *active harm* to members of the other group. This may include violence in various forms—physical, psychological, financial, environmental.

- Level (A) represents the third and worst stage (- - -) of unethical behavior resulting from the greatest in-group loyalty. At this level, the unethical behavior is neither passive and attitudinal, nor is it merely active and behavioral in harming the other group. It is *existential*. Life is at stake. Loyalty to the group is so great that killing members of the other group is valid.

In 1932 American theologian Reinhold Niebuhr wrote a book on how a society can be pathological and immoral, despite the so-called morality of its individuals. He titled his book *Moral Man and Immoral Society*. He examined numerous examples of how fervent loyalty to one's own group or nation resulted in bad outcomes for other groups. He wrote, "The whole history of mankind bears testimony to the fact that the power which prevents anarchy in intra-group relations encourages anarchy in intergroup relations."[34]

Example: Nazi Germany

On the one hand, the forces of identity, power, and honor hold a group or nation together and keep it from falling apart. On the other hand, these same dynamics—identity, power, and honor—are often at the root of hostility, immorality, and anarchy between groups or nations.

Niebuhr's 1932 book was prophetic about the World War to come. On August 19, 1934, Germany voted to merge the posts of Chancellor

---

33 Volf, *Exclusion & Embrace*, 77.
34 Niebuhr, *Moral Man and Immoral Society*, 16.

and President, confirming Hitler as Germany's supreme authority. Adolf Hitler became the sole leader of The Third Reich. All political opposition was eliminated. Absolute loyalty was demanded.

Loyalty was conceptually framed as "blood and honor" *(Blüt und Ehre)*. To be loyal to Germany's Führer was to be loyal to the German *Volk* (people). Patriotism became nationalism with an intense religious fervor. Germany's government, military, and citizenry designed and carried out Hitler's barbaric vision: the systematic murder of six million Jewish men, women, and children. Millions of other persons were also murdered who were considered "undeserving of life" *(lebensunwertes leben*—"life unworthy of life").[35]

Through propaganda and other means, loyalty to the German-Aryan "in-group" gave sanction to demonizing, radical othering, and murder en masse of the "out-group." And the church was complicit. Theologians in the German Christian Movement created theology[36] to support the murderous Nazi pogroms. Siegfried Leffler, a leader in the German Christian Movement, said in a large meeting of theologians in 1936:

> As a Christian, I can, I must, and I ought always to have or to find a bridge to the Jew in my heart. But as a Christian, I also have to follow the laws of my nation [Volk], which are often presented in a very cruel way, so that again I am brought into the harshest of conflicts with the Jew. Even if I know "thou shalt not kill" is a commandment of God or "thou shalt love the Jew" because he too is a child of the eternal Father, I am able to know as well that I have to kill him, I have to shoot him, and I can only do that if I am permitted to say: Christ.[37]

These words are jaw-dropping. Nazi violence against the Jews was not merely rationalized, but rationalized in a most persuasive and self-exonerating way: *by theology*, by the sanction of Christ. It was an extreme version of the Ethical Paradox of Group Loyalty in which the "submersion of the individual into *das Volk*"[38] made it truly difficult to resist the Nazi regime. However, as we shall see in chapter 10, theologizing violence in the name of Christ did not begin in 1930s Germany. It has been part of church history since the fourth century. And it continues today.[39]

---

35 Sciolino, *The Holocaust*, Kindle loc. 2076.
36 Heschel, *The Aryan Jesus*.
37 Heschel, 21–22.
38 Bultmann, as quoted in Eastman, *Paul and the Person*, 102.
39 See Neumann, *Kingdom of Rage*, ch. 6: "A Corrupted Faith," 109–33.

BEING HUMAN: The Group's Magnetic Pull

Groups are far too often an ally of hostility and violence. That's why we've been exploring the Law of Group Polarization and the Ethical Paradox of Group Loyalty.

We are bringing *group dynamics* to the surface; we are identifying their power to shape a person, community, or nation. From the group side it can be described as a magnetic-like pull; from the side of the individual, it can be described as loyalty and belonging.

However we describe it, our embeddedness in the group—family, social class, community, political tribe, ethnic group, people, nation—powerfully shapes us all. This includes the thinking, desires, attitudes, and behaviors that move groups toward virtue—or toward hostility and violence.

With this chapter, we come to the end of Section II: "Violence and Sin." We've covered "Sin Is Not Simple" (ch. 4), "Shame and Individualism" (ch. 5), "Powers and Principalities" (ch. 6), "Status Games" (ch. 7), and the just-completed "Group vs. Group Hostility" (ch. 8). Our goal has been to peer through the lens of violence and ask what it means to be human. We have seen that sin is a systemic complexity. We observe that persons and groups all too often respond to problems by violence.

We have also encountered biblical hope in these chapters. We have seen the Bible grapples with violence; it refuses to whitewash the problem. Neither does the Bible minimize the utter severity and mystery of the solution: True God condescends, becoming True Human, enduring and subverting violence.

The Bible reveals a thick, complex narrative of good news—offering to fully heal the pathology and cleanse the sin at the heart of humanity's violence in creating One New Humanity (Eph 2:15-16).

Just ahead is Section III: "Gospel of Peace and Its King." We will explore more fully Christ's depolarizing gospel in Ephesians 2.

CHAPTER 8 SUMMARY

- Social media companies manipulate users through algorithms designed to engage *and enrage*—stoking division and extremism.
- The Law of Group Polarization helps us know that the danger of hearing only one side of an issue can lead to extremism. It's healthy to hear a variety of views.
- The Ethical Paradox of Group Loyalty: as loyalty to one's own group increases, the potential for unethical behavior toward an out-group also increases.
- Polarization represents a crisis of belonging and glory.
- Christian leaders are sometimes complicit in supporting state-sponsored violence.

FOR FURTHER REFLECTION

- Have you observed the Law of Group Polarization at work in your own life? How so?
- Why does the issue of group hostility and reconciliation (as found in Eph 2) represent a delicate matter for pastors to address in their preaching? What risks do pastors face?
- What are the different stances Christian leaders in your community take relative to hostility and violence—through theology and teaching, or silence?

SECTION III

THE GOSPEL OF PEACE
and Its King

Chapter 9: Resurrection in Rwanda

Chapter 10: Pax Romana Versus Pax Christi: Contrasts in Peace

Chapter 11: Perfection in Weakness: Contrasts in Power

Chapter 12: Homogenous Unit Principle: What Peace?

Chapter 13: Being Human, and the Gospel

Chapter 14: Gospeling Peace with King Jesus

Chapter 9

RESURRECTION IN RWANDA

IN THIS CHAPTER

- Readers will visit Rwanda, listen to Christian leaders who lived through the aftermath of the genocide, and enter the Nyamata church memorial where thousands of people were massacred.
- Kristin and Werner share their experiences. They encounter the memory of Rwanda's violent horrors—as well as Rwanda's beauty in a surprising community of reconciliation.

Kristin:

Antoine Rutayisire looked like a man forged from steel. And like most people we met in Rwanda, he didn't pull any punches in conversation. Thankfully, we had not gone there to hear easy sayings. We had gone to learn about the 1994 genocide, of which Pastor Antoine was a survivor.

As we sipped on cappuccinos, he leaned across the coffee table: "Do you think America is a great nation?" he asked. "Tell me, how does your country measure greatness? I will give you my definition of greatness: first, there is *love*. Is your nation full of love? Then there is joy and peace. Does your nation have joy? Does it have peace? Is your nation gentle, patient, or self-controlled? If not, then you do not have a great nation. You are powerful, yes. And you are rich. But you are not great."[1]

What is greatness? What if greatness were truly defined by coming to the table of the Great King and feasting on the fruit of the Spirit? What would it mean for a community in America or Rwanda or Cambodia to be truly great?

The events leading up to 1994 are complex and contested. What we do know is that in the postcolonial years (following 1962) historic ethnic and class divisions—compounded by colonial "divide-and-conquer" policies[2]—led to increasing hostility and fear between those classified

---

1 From an interview conducted on April 13, 2022, with Antoine Rutiyisire in Kigali, Rwanda.
2 It was official colonial policy throughout East Africa to pit existing tribal, ethnic, or class groups against each other in order to make it easier for colonial governments to maintain sole power. The exact nature of Hutu and Tutsi identities in pre-colonial times is historically unclear, but the colonial strategy of pitting the two groups against one another is well-documented; this continues to have effects in many previously colonized countries to this day.

as "Hutus" and "Tutsis." What we might call "ethnicity," "class," and "ideology" all came to bear in this divide.[3] In fact, the only area without significant divide was religion.[4] Smaller skirmishes and attacks had led to various waves of refugees leaving Rwanda in the '60s, '70s, and '80s, as tension continued to escalate.

And then, in April of 1994, a series of events led to a sudden eruption of violence on a mass scale. Hundreds of thousands perished within the space of one hundred days. Ever since then, violence has not stopped spilling over throughout the region—today, most notably in the Democratic Republic of Congo. Arguably, millions have perished since then, in a war that may have never really ended.

The 1994 violence was horrific both for the incredible swiftness and brutality of the violence and for its intimacy. During the Holocaust, many people knew what was happening to their neighbors as they were taken away. But most people did not have a hand in personally killing their neighbors.

In Rwanda, things were different. Neighbor rose up against neighbor, teacher against student, and student against teacher. Sometimes people even killed their relatives—often, with garden tools. Almost overnight, the country turned into a living hell. Bodies were left where they lay, shoved into mass graves, or dumped into rivers. For many in the outside world, the full magnitude of what was taking place was not even guessed until over ten thousand mutilated bodies washed downstream to neighboring Uganda and began piling up in Lake Victoria.[5]

Solemn and Grave—Our Visit to Nyamata

We came to Rwanda in April of 2022, twenty-eight years after the genocide began, during the National Week of Remembrance. We also happened to be there in a year when that week corresponded exactly with Holy Week—the time when Christians remember Jesus's passion and journey to the cross. For three days we visited mass graves, heard stories about what

---

3 Katongole, *Who Are My People?*, 69–74.

4 While the larger debates in society certainly cut through the church, the country was overwhelmingly Christian and Catholic. Just 35 years before the genocide began, Rwanda declared itself a Christian nation and was held up as the example of a successfully evangelized African nation, with over 90% in regular church attendance. At the time of the genocide, over 90% of the country identified as Christian. See Carney, *Rwanda Before the Genocide*, 52; Longman, *Christianity and Genocide in Rwanda*, 4.

5 Lorch, "Thousands of Rwanda Dead Wash Down to Lake Victoria."

happened in 1994, and talked with Christian leaders who had worked in reconciliation. And then, on Good Friday—the final day of the Week of Remembrance—we visited Nyamata Church.

As the genocide began, many fled to churches. In past conflicts, churches had been places of refuge. People hoped that church leaders would protect them as they had in the past. They hoped that no one would dare to kill them in a holy place.

Tragically, they were often wrong on both counts.[6] Stories abound of church leaders' complicity or outright support of mass murder. We spoke to an Anglican bishop who was commissioned to spend six months investigating church involvement in the genocide (both Catholic and Protestant). As he put it, "It was the most shameful time of my life." Instead of sanctuaries, churches became convenient killing grounds. In one instance, a priest even gave the orders to bulldoze his own church, with two thousand people inside. Although Rwanda was overwhelmingly Christian at the time of the genocide, hundreds of thousands of people found more glory in being a Hutu or a Tutsi in flesh. It is believed that up to ten thousand people died in one day at Nyamata Church. The original building has been preserved as a memorial, and rows of mass graves lie outside.

The clouds were dark overhead as we walked down the driveway to the church, the air heavy with the threat of rain. We visted the church in 2022, on a day which was both Good Friday and the final day of the week of remembrance of the genocide. A large event was taking place nearby, where survivors of the massacre told their stories over loudspeakers. Although we couldn't understand the words, we could hear their voices cracking with emotion sometimes unable to go on.

Inside the church, much has been left as it was. The front door still hangs off its hinges. Bullet holes and grenade shrapnel remain lodged in the walls. The bodies of the dead were buried outside, but the clothing of the victims were left inside, stacked in piles on top of the pews, and lining the walls. Pairs of jeans, baseball hats, and a blood-stained child's shirt featuring the Teenage Mutant Ninja Turtles remind me that this is not the distant past.

Words fall dreadfully short.

How? How is something like this possible?

As I walked around that sanctuary, there were moments when I felt like I couldn't breathe.

---

6 Katongole, *Who Are My People?*, 68–69.

And yet, I didn't want to leave. I felt like I could have stayed there for days, just to sit in the silence—in a place where only silence can really speak. As I sat stunned by the desolation, I realized that I had never been so close to the horrific mystery of evil—but that I had also never felt so terribly close to the cross, and the heavy, unbearable presence of my God. I have never felt so powerfully the nearness of Jesus in his affliction.

My Lord and my God! My Lord and my God!

These were the only words I could think—half as a cry, half as a plea. How could I possibly explain the dreadful weight of holiness in that place?

> I saw Mother Mary there, looking on just as she was on the day those people died—*and just as she was on the day when Jesus died, on Good Friday all those years ago ...*
>
> Church and state had conspired to kill these people—*and they conspired to kill him too.*
>
> They were cut down by their friends and neighbors—*he was betrayed by his friends and condemned by the crowds.*
>
> So many Rwandans were tortured and humiliated—*he died a long and humiliating public death.*
>
> *He became sin, who knew no sin, so that in him, we might become the righteousness of God.*

Outside, I read a story from one little girl who survived:

> "I hid under the dead bodies of my mother and my little sister. Later, the wives of the men came to pick clothes"—*They divided my garments among them and cast lots for my clothing.*
>
> "I asked Jesus to have mercy and let me hide inside His gown. I felt like I had really gotten in there. I felt Him holding me. The women pulled at my clothes, but they turned to others ..."

Directly beside it was another survivor's story, also a young girl:

> "It was the day I concluded that God no longer protected us, the day when I saw newborn babies smashed against a wall ... a grenade exploded, killing my younger sisters, injuring my shoulder and tearing off part of my mother's face ... after [they] left, she called for me, asking for some water. She took it in both hands, looked at me and said, 'I'm going to die, my child. And you, are you okay?' She drank the water and straightaway breathed her last breath." *And when he had drunk it, he said, "It is finished" and gave up his spirit.*

A Resurrection at Reconciliation Village

Later that day, we drove to a nearby village, known by many as "Reconciliation Village." In this village, survivors and perpetrators of the Nyamata massacres live side by side and have a farming co-op together.

As our car bumped along the dirt road, chickens ran and children played around us. "Muzungu! Muzungu!" they shouted as they jumped and waved. A cool breeze blew with the scent of rain.

We were invited into a small living room. As children and chickens continued to run here and there, we were greeted by a woman named Jacquline, a survivor of the genocide at Nyamata. We were also introduced to Frederic, who had been a perpetrator of genocide in the same community. Others came around to listen. A woman sat down in one corner and began to weave a basket. I watched as she pulled differently colored threads from different piles, bringing them together one at a time as we talked.

In 1994, Jacqueline was seventeen years old. Her family was among the first targeted in the Nyamata area. When she left to milk the cows that morning in April, it was an ordinary day. But when she came home, she found her entire family slaughtered.

She fled to the church and found an uncle there, the only other survivor in their entire extended family. Together, they fled from there into the forest, where they survived for over three months as their country descended into chaos.

"We thought we were just doing our job for our country," said Frederic. "But we were told so many lies that it's hard for us to understand what really happened."

After the genocide ended, the new government put thousands of perpetrators in prison. "At first, we were sure that they were only holding us to kill us later," said Frederick. "We lived in constant fear."

And then, God gave a special call to a group of survivors who were also preachers. Among them was Pastor Antoine. These men were burdened to go into the prisons and preach—sometimes, to the very men who had killed their own families. They told them that they could find forgiveness and healing at the foot of the cross of Jesus. Like Zacchaeus, Jesus was passing their way, wanting to go to their house. But they would need to come down from their sycamore trees if they wanted to eat with him.

"When the preachers came saying that we needed to confess what we had done, we thought they were only trying to find out who had killed their own families so they could take revenge."

Meanwhile, the same preachers were also ministering in the ruins of Rwanda, preaching to other survivors, and telling them that they too needed to find their healing at the cross of Jesus. But if they wanted to eat with the Lord, they would need his help to forgive.

"I was a devout girl," Jacquline told us. "I used to pray to God throughout the day. But after the genocide, I didn't want to hear anything about God or forgiveness. I decided that maybe he did not exist—and if he did exist, he had stopped caring about Rwanda."

Pastor Antoine told us how some people responded to him: "You are a survivor," said one woman, "But you are a man. You could never understand the humiliation we women endured." She had been raped in front of her children and her village.

"I may not understand you," he replied. "But Jesus understands you! Do you know that he was hung naked and humiliated on the cross, in front of everyone?"

I had to wonder: who else could *really* say these things, *except another survivor?* Who else could really extend forgiveness to wrongdoers—and ask for others to extend forgiveness—besides one who had also suffered?

> For Christ also suffered once for sins, the righteous for the unrighteous, that he might bring us to God. (1 Pet 3:18–19)

St. John Chrysostom put it this way: Christ stretched out his arms on the hard wood of the cross so that he could take the hand of each side of the hostility and bring them together in him.

> He became sin who knew no sin, so that in him, we might become the righteousness of God.... For he is our peace; in his flesh he has made both into one and has broken down the dividing wall, that is, the hostility between us ...

In a very real way, these preachers stretched themselves out—over their own crosses of pain, trauma, and agony—to take the hand of each, just like Jesus did.

We continued to talk, and it began to rain. As heavy drops of water splashed in the mud outside the door, I looked and saw the woman's basket beginning to take shape.

The preachers labored for ten years. Then, in 2004, the president of Rwanda made a declaration: If any prisoner would fully confess all that he had done, face the survivors, and show them where their relatives' bodies were left, he could get out of prison and serve the rest of his time rebuilding the country in community service.

The prisoners were still afraid of revenge. But a few decided it was worth the risk. And then, a few became a flood. The regular courts could not handle the number of confessions, and so the meetings were held in traditional-style *gacaca* courts.[7] In these gatherings, the whole community would come together with survivors and perpetrators to hear the confessions, to talk, and to decide together on a path forward.[8]

In Jacquline's case, the meeting was also attended by the preachers who had been ministering to both sides for so many years.

"The first day, we couldn't even look at each other," she said. "We had to go home and try again. But very slowly, we began to talk. And as we talked, we began to understand each other."

Over time, the perpetrators were able to fully confess what they had done, and the survivors were able to ask their questions. Some were able to gather the bones of their relatives and rebury them. And many were also able to publicly extend forgiveness.

As these conversations continued, both sides realized that they had a common problem: the men leaving prison had nowhere to live and no way to make a living. And ten years later, many of the survivors were still homeless. So someone put forth the suggestion—what if we built a village together?

When Prison Fellowship heard about the idea, they said, "If you really want to do this, we will raise money for building materials."

At first, only three homes were built. Survivors moved into one, former perpetrators into another, and returning refugees into the third. They lived in them for one year just to see—could this really work?

In time, they built fifty-two homes in the newly founded Sycamore Village—named after the tree of Zacchaeus.

---

7 *Gacaca* (pronounced gah-chah-chah) means grass and refers to a grassy area where an entire community could sit down to talk. By some estimates, around twelve thousand *gacaca* courts have been held throughout Rwanda since 2004.

8 In one story we heard, a widow heard the confession of the young man who had killed her only son. She said, "You took from me the only son I had. I have no one to take care of me, and you don't have a home. So now that you are out of prison, you will come and live with me, and you will be my son."

A Glorious New Way

Near the end of our conversation Frederick said, "Please tell the world two things: first, that this genocide really happened, and second, that this village really exists."

"Yes," said Jacquline, "And I want you to know something else." As she spoke, she looked up, as if to heaven. "When you drove up here, you saw children playing, and you didn't know whose children were whose. We are not just neighbors here—we are family, and we are raising our children together."

As Jacquline said these words, her face radiated with an exaltation I had never seen before. To this day, I am moved to tears whenever I remember her face—the face of a person who was deeply satisfied with *glory*. I believe she *knew* that she was part of a miracle. She knew that the glory of God had been given to her community. And I think she knew that there is nothing greater that the human being could ever hope to attain.

Right as she said these words, the woman sitting in the corner finished her basket. She held it up, examining her work, and the words flashed across my mind: "For we are his handiwork, created inside of Christ Jesus for good works, which God prepared ahead of time that we should walk in them" (Eph 2:10).[9]

Jesus has taken the hand of each and made one new humanity inside of himself. He has taken threads from every people under heaven and brought them together in a relational beauty beyond imagining "so that, through the church, the multicolored wisdom of God might now be made known to the Powers and Principalities in the heavenly places" (Eph 3:10).[10]

He has done it! And now, the glory given to him by the Father is given to us—that we would be one even as he and the Father are one—so that the world would see his glory, and so that we would be satisfied in our Beloved.

Jacquline had shown up to the Feast, even though it meant taking a seat beside her enemies; she had tasted and seen that the Lord is good. Because she accepted the invitation of the cross, her longing for glory had been met in a way that few of us will experience on this side of the grave.

The mystery of evil is profound, and its depths are limitless. But the mystery of Christ's gospel of peace is greater still.

---

9 Kristin's translation.

10 Kristin's translation.

Werner: ## Frederic's Story and My Story

Frederic sat close beside me in that little home in Reconciliation Village. "I was one of the perpetrators," Frederic said to us. After the genocide, "I was arrested by the new government. I was put in prison, like so many other Hutu men." Frederick spared us the details about the crimes he committed. What he wanted us to know is that while in prison, he became honest about his crimes and was released.

Frederic finished this first part of his story. Then, a momentary silence.

I asked, "You two men who were perpetrators, do you ever look back and think of yourselves as victims?"

"Yes, in part, we are also victims. We had bad leadership. Every day, we were told lies about the Tutsi. 'They are cockroaches, not real humans; they should die.'"

I wondered aloud, "What would I have done? If I had lived in Rwanda with all the propaganda every day about killing enemies, would I have done differently?"

Sharing from My Family Story

From this tiny home in a Rwandan village my thoughts traveled back to my parents and their World War II experience as Germans. I thought about Germany's responsibility for *its genocide,* the Holocaust.

Sitting closely beside Frederic, I wanted him to know that he and I had something in common, and something in contrast.

I said, "My parents were from Germany. The German government drafted my father into Hitler's army. Near the end of the war, the Allied Forces captured my father, and he became a prisoner of war for four years in Poland. After he was released, my grandfather took his family with three sons, and they all came to America. My grandfather wanted to go far away from the Russians. My German father and mother married in America, so I was born there."

I paused. I was heading toward the subject of the genocide in Germany—the Holocaust. Then Kristin asked, "Werner, we see here the openness and honesty of this community; is this openness possibly different from how you grew up? Is their honesty touching you in an unexpected way?"

This touched a nerve. Suddenly, a new topic was in front of us: *Open, authentic talking about painful, even shameful, things.*

"Good question, Kristin."

Genocide in Other Lands, Too

As a teenager, I learned about the Holocaust in Germany in World War II. I asked my parents about it. They didn't want to discuss it. They rarely if ever acknowledged to me the horrors of Germany's pogrom to systematically kill six million Jews—and multitudes of others deemed "life unworthy of life."

So, as we talked together in that little home in Reconciliation Village, I said: "You know there have been genocides in other lands, right?" They nodded yes.

"Have you heard of the concentration camp called Auschwitz?" I asked. "At Auschwitz, the Germans killed 20,000 people a day through gas chambers and burning. Rwanda is not the only country with genocide in its history."

I told our little group I had questions about my grandfather's participation in Germany's system of brutality. He was a businessman selling fuel. Did my grandfather sell fuel to the German army, which helped them do evil? A mysterious stigma remains.

I revealed another stigma about my extended family: "My father and one uncle suffered from mental illnesses. Was it because they could not talk openly about the painful, shameful things they witnessed or suffered?" It was a rhetorical question.

"Do you have any questions for us?" I asked the four Rwandan villagers.

"I have a question," said Frederic. "You shared about your family and grandfather. Do you still have pains in your heart about what your grandfather may have done? If so, has this time with us been helpful to you?" Frederic's question surprised me.

"Yes, I have been helped. Your honesty and openness are different from how I grew up with family secrets. You are willing to talk about painful things with forgiveness. For many years, I had a shadow of shame over the questions about my German family and my father's mental illness. But in recent years, I have been learning that Jesus does not just forgive our guilt. He also covers our shame."

Frederic thanked us. He said I was just the second visitor to their village in eighteen years who, after hearing the stories of the victims and perpetrators, also openly shared from his heart. I felt a surprising closeness to Frederic, however brief it was. There was comfort in being together with these men and women in the Village of Reconciliation, Nyamata,

Rwanda. Frederic and his co-villagers were honest and vulnerable. We briefly joined them with a bit of our own vulnerability. It was like a cleansing fresh breeze.

If reconciliation is possible here, it is possible anywhere.

> Let the one who is thirsty come; let the one who desires
> take the water of life without price. (Rev 22:17)

BEING HUMAN: Horror and Beauty

Our visit to Rwanda was dramatic, disturbing, unforgettable. On the one hand, we gained a sobering awareness of humanity's ever-present potential for horrific violence fueled by collective identity dynamics and state-sponsored propoganda. Rwanda became a stage for the Ethical Paradox of Group Loyalty; the nation became a cauldron for "unethical behavior toward an out-group" magnified to the *nth* degree through unrestrained violence and bloodshed. Moreover, we began to grapple with the church's complicity with violence.

On the other hand, in Rwanda we engaged with humanity's capacity for the beautiful grace of Jesus and his gospel of peace—reconciliation with God *plus* reconciliation socially with hostile "others," indeed, with enemies toward whom hatred was justified. A reconciliation had occurred. It was forged through intense fires, the most profound losses and painful, humiliating trials.

Next up is chapter 10: "Pax Romana versus Pax Christi: Contrasts in Peace." We will examine the historical roots of Christianity's merge with imperial power and violence. We will explore and grapple: To what degree is Christianity's *partnership with empire* a deviation from Christ's gospel of peace?

CHAPTER 9 SUMMARY

- The 1994 Rwandan genocide was rooted in colonial "divide-and-conquer" policies. The hostility between rival peoples was driven by "ethnicity," "class," and "ideology."
- Although over 90 percent of Rwandans identified as Christian, in April 1994, violence erupted and hundreds of thousands of people were killed in the span of about 100 days.
- Rwanda shared some similar dynamics with Nazi Germany: Violence was fueled by government propaganda and ideology. As loyalty to the dominant in-group increased, the unethical, indeed murderous, behavior toward the out-group also increased.
- Christian institutions, though prominent in the land, were impotent in halting the violence.
- Embodying a reconciling gospel of peace (not mere preaching) was fundamental to Rwanda's recovery and rebuilding as a nation.

FOR FURTHER REFLECTION

- In this chapter, we placed the Rwandan genocide and Jesus's crucifixion—two epic evils—side by side in the same story. How does one help us grapple with the other?
- Jew and gentile reconciliation through Christ is the prototype for any hostile groups reconciled—"through the cross … killing the hostility" (Eph 2:16). How does this "rhyme" with the dramatic reconciliation of enemies in Rwanda?
- In what ways does Rwanda serve as a warning, a cautionary tale?

Chapter 10

PAX ROMANA VERSUS *PAX CHRISTI*: CONTRASTS IN PEACE

Augustus, "who has brought war to an end and has ordained peace ... for the world, the birthday of the god [Augustus] means the beginning of his tidings of peace."

"Pax Romana—a golden age or a peace with bloodshed?" –Klaus Wengst

"For he himself is our peace, ... that he might create in himself one new humanity in place of the two, so making peace ... And he came and preached the gospel of peace ... "
—Ephesians 2:14–15, 17 (our translation)

IN THIS CHAPTER

- *Pax Romana* (peace of Rome) was a Latin term idealizing the Roman Empire, in which Ephesus was a major city. This chapter compares *Pax Romana* to *Pax Christi* (peace of Christ).
- In Ephesians 2, Christ is our peace; Christ makes peace; Christ preaches peace (Eph 2:14–15, 17).
- We examine how violence in the name of Christ began under Constantine, first Christian emperor of the Roman Empire.

Werner: ### Augustus, "the Great One"

"In those days a decree went out from Caesar Augustus that all the world should be registered" (Luke 2:1). Luke tells us Jesus was born during the reign of the renowned Caesar Augustus, first emperor of the Roman Empire. Who was Augustus? He was born Caius Octavian on September 23, 63 BC, the son of a wealthy man who died when Octavian was five.

It was most fortuitous for Octavian that Julius Caesar had become his substitute father. Since Caesar had no son by marriage, thus no rightful heir, it was a golden opportunity for Octavian.

Young Octavian won the admiration of Caesar through his drive, oratory, political skill, and extreme loyalty. He was "tenacious, cunning, and brave."[1] Octavian was also physically attractive. In time, Octavian's charisma, loyalty, and intense ambition were greatly rewarded.

---
1 Strauss, *Ten Caesars*, 10.

That time came in 44 BC. In one of the most significant events of ancient history, Octavian's adoptive father Julius Caesar was assassinated by stabbing—twenty-three stab wounds to be exact. A group of about forty Roman senators did the deed on March 15, 44 BC. It was the "Ides of March," the annual deadline for settling debts in Rome.

Following the bloody end of Julius Caesar, Octavian, just nineteen years old, was named heir to Caesar. Less than two years later, "Octavian had maneuvered his way through politics and war, outfoxed his competitors, and become one of the three most powerful men in the Roman Empire—all by the age of twenty."[2]

To consolidate his power, Octavian avenged the death of his adoptive father, Julius Caesar. A purge of some two thousand of Rome's most elite, powerful, property-owning men commenced. Octavian kept rising.

The Son of a God

On January 1, 42 BC, Octavian took his devotion to his father's memory up a notch and had the Senate declare Caesar a god, which allowed Octavian to declare himself the son of a god. A law was passed to build a temple and institute the worship of Julius Caesar.

Four years later, in 38 BC, Octavian was acclaimed by his troops as imperator, or victorious general. He now became known as "the victorious general Caesar son of a god."[3]

Fifteen years later, Octavian needed to stabilize Rome. He had recruited armies, organized and led to victory armies on land and at sea. What now? Caesar decided to magnify his name. It was a strategy to amplify one's title, one's ascribed honor. He chose the name Augustus, which means majestic, great, venerable. Octavian's Roman Senate legislated a formal name-change for their exalted leader. On January 16, 27 BC, the senators voted that henceforth, Octavian would be called Augustus—Caesar Augustus.

> Soon Augustus would be everywhere. You couldn't cross the street, go to a dinner party, enter a temple, or handle a coin without hearing his name or seeing his face, or that of his beautiful wife or his adorable children. He had been a man; now Augustus was a brand.[4]

---

2 Strauss, 17.

3 Strauss, 17–18.

4 Strauss, 25. Augustus was a master of propaganda. The Roman army was brutally efficient and used the latest technology. But Rome also functioned based on honor and grandeur—using words, architecture, and the arts to advance the power of Rome.

Augustus: the majestic one, son of a god, venerated by all, the most powerful brand in the empire. Caesar Augustus becomes the prototype emperor.[5] His intelligence, oratory, and political skill ... his brilliance as an administrator, his ways of conquest, cunning and cruelty ... his brutality and military victories all in the name of peace, and his Greco-Roman lust for glory and veneration—these attributes of Caesar Augustus cast a long shadow over the future history of the Roman Empire and its emperors.

The Roman Empire: Social Context of Ephesus (and Entire New Testament)

The "glory of Rome" was marked by advances in technology, architecture, culture and widespread political stability. But the empire was also marked by cruelty from the top down. As Terry Jones put it:

> We've all been sold a false history of Rome that has twisted our entire understanding of our own history—glorifying (and glossing over) a long era of ruthless imperial power, ... and wildly distorting our view of the so-called 'Middle Ages' and of the peoples whom Rome crushed and who were then blamed for its fall.[6]

The cruelty and degradation of Rome came to a high point during the reign of Nero, nearly five decades after the death of Caesar Augustus. It is likely that many of the New Testament's books were written during Nero's reign.

Nero becomes emperor when he is only sixteen. He is no less cruel than the Caesars before him. Nero is an entertainer. He loves to sing, to put on a show.[7] Historian Barry Strauss tells this story about Nero that occurred in 62.

> A new Praetorian prefect was appointed and encouraged Nero's worst impulses. ... Soon Nero would be sending a prominent man into exile merely for recognizing one of Caesar's murderers in his family tree. Nero was far less tolerant of people who wrote or said anything critical of him. He brought back the charge of treason that he had promised not to use. In 62, for the first time, he executed his enemies in the Senate. When the prefect convinced Nero to order the execution of two men of noble lineage, the emperor is supposed to have joked as each man's head was brought to him. One, he said, was prematurely gray. When he saw the other's head, he said, "Why, Nero, did you fear a man with such a big nose?"[8]

---

5 See chapter 1, "Augustus, The Founder," in Strauss, *Ten Caesars*, 7–45.
6 Ereira and Jones, *Terry Jones' Barbarians*, 7.
7 See chapter 3, "Nero: The Entertainer," in Strauss, *Ten Caesars*, 78–107.
8 Strauss, 96–97.

Then, in July 64, a horrible event occurs for which Nero is much remembered. A devastating five-day fire sweeps through the city of Rome. Not long after, Nero makes a king-size land-grab in the burnt center of Rome where many poor had lived. Nero wants to build himself a massive new palace—"the never-completed Domus Aurea (or Golden House)."[9]

This angers many. Nero's popularity falls. He has an idea: *Another show to entertain the Romans to halt their complaining.* "So after the fire, he put on another bizarre and ghastly show that turned prisoners into human torches"[10]—a better show for the citizens. Among the "prisoners turned human torches" were Christians. The Roman historian Tacitus (d. 117), not a Christian, describes Nero's "entertainment" as follows.

> First, Nero had self-acknowledged Christians arrested. Then, on their information, large numbers of others were condemned— not so much for incendiarism as for their anti-social tendencies *[lit.: because of their hatred of mankind]*. Their deaths were made farcical. Dressed in wild animals' skins, they were torn to pieces by dogs, or crucified, or made into torches to be ignited after dark as substitutes for daylight. Nero provided his Gardens for the spectacle and exhibited displays in the Circus, at which he mingled with the crowd—or stood in a chariot, dressed as a charioteer. Despite their guilt as Christians and the ruthless punishment it deserved, the victims were pitied. For it was felt that they were being sacrificed to one man's brutality rather than to the national interest.[11]

Pax Romana as Propaganda

The glory of Rome was celebrated through propaganda, best signified by the *Pax Romana* (Peace of Rome). *Pax Romana* originates with Caesar Augustus in *Res Gestae* ("Achievements of the Deified Augustus"). It's an honorific list of his achievements. In paragraph twelve, Augustus writes,

> When I returned from Spain and Gaul, ... after successful operations in those provinces, the Senate voted in honor of my return the consecration of an altar to *Pax Augusta* in the Campus Martius, and on this altar it ordered the magistrates and priests and Vestal Virgins to make annual sacrifice.[12]

---

9 Cahill, *Desire of the Everlasting Hills,* 164.
10 Strauss, 81.
11 Tacitus (55–117), *Annals* 15, 44.
12 Augustus, *Res Gestae,* paragraph 12.

Augustus wants to be recognized as divine. Is this hype? Propaganda? Or simply Augustus giving the people what they want?

"Much recent scholarship is appreciating that the early Christians lived in a world dominated by the Roman imperial cult."[13] Public enthusiasm for honoring the emperor as a god-like figure was widespread. This was reflected "in local architecture and artwork devoted to the emperor" which "dominated the cities' public visual-arts culture."[14] To a large degree, Augustus *was* giving the people what they wanted.

But to think of Augustus as merely doing what the people wanted—a kind of political populism—would be anachronistic. We would be reading modern attitudes back into the ancient world.

For the ancients, paying homage to the gods was not in a category separate from civic life. Separation of church and state was unthinkable. To be a loyal citizen of Rome required acknowledging and giving allegiance to Rome's pantheon of gods—in order the keep peace with the gods. Nijay Gupta helpfully explains:

> The gods were divine magistrates ruling over human life. Romans conceived of the social universe as a big pyramid. On the top were the Olympians, especially Jupiter as "Best and Greatest." Then there were other powerful gods of myth and legend. Below them stood demigods and special human figures like the Roman emperors. Then came the human elites, like men of the senatorial and equestrian classes, and, below them, commoners and freed slaves. Finally, at the bottom were slaves, criminals, and immigrants.... *Humans paid homage to keep the peace and inspire exchange.* Religion, as understood by the Romans, was meant to keep the peace with the gods, the *pax deorum*.[15]

So it is more likely that Augustus really believed[16] in the patronage of the gods—just like all Roman citizens. Thus, celebrating Augustus by changing the calendar to begin with his birthday (imagine the sheer arrogance of it all!) was probably not considered strange, but rather, a fitting and appropriate honor. A stone inscription found near Ephesus in a city called Priene celebrates Augustus "as the ruler given by providence, 'who has brought

---

13 Perrin, "The Imperial Cult," 124.

14 Perrin, 131–32

15 Gupta, *Strange Religion*, 20; emphasis in original.

16 The word *believed* here does not refer to the way that Christians normally think of *personal belief* in God. "For the Romans, religion was not a belief, a feeling ... it was purely utilitarian practice." See Gupta, 29–30.

war to an end and has ordained peace.'" The inscription pronounces the birth of Augustus as "the beginnings of his tidings of peace."[17]

Caesar Augustus started a trend. Inspired by Augustus, the philosopher Seneca (5 BC to AD 65) was the first to use the term *"Pax Romana"* to label the empire.[18] The term took hold. But how peaceful was the "Roman Peace?"

Classical scholar Adrian Goldsworthy writes, "The Latin verb *pacare* had the same root as pax and meant 'to pacify', and was often used to describe aggressive warfare against a foreign people. *Pax Romana* came from Roman victory and conquest."[19]

Historian Thomas Cahill describes the ancients as pragmatic about violence and conquest. "The emperor had created peace without end, *Pax Romana* (which in fact would last a very long two hundred years). That he had done so by merciless policies would not have given ancient readers pause. After all, how else could you create peace save by unswerving military imposition?"[20]

The traditional view is, "For periods of a century or more, large swathes of the empire were entirely free of warfare."[21] Goldsworthy adds, "let us just say that the truth is a good deal more complicated than this sweeping summary. Yet there can be no doubt about the enduring power of Rome, or that its domination did mean that large parts of the empire experienced no major military activity, let alone open warfare for long periods of time."[22]

But the Roman historian Tacitus quotes a British leader named Calgacus concerning Rome's conquest of Britain in AD 60.

> Robbers of the world, having by their universal plunder exhausted the land, they rifle the deep. If the enemy be rich, they are rapacious; if he be poor, they lust for dominion; neither the east nor the west has been able to satisfy them. Alone among men they covet with equal eagerness poverty and riches. To robbery, slaughter, plunder, they give the lying name of empire; they make a solitude [wilderness] and call it peace.[23]

---

17 Wengst, *Pax Romana*, 9.
18 Wengst, 9–10.
19 Goldsworthy, *Pax Romana*, 13.
20 Cahill, *Desire of the Everlasting Hills*, 62.
21 Goldsworthy, *Pax Romana*, 11.
22 Goldsworthy, 11
23 Newton, ed., "Tacitus, Agricola," paragraph 30.

"Robbers of the world …" The ones being invaded (in this case, the British), had for good reasons a negative perspective toward the so-called "glory of Rome." To them, the Romans were an army of murderers and robbers. Wright and Bird state, "The Roman Empire was, as empires have tended to be, built on a system of plunder, enslavement, and exploitation… . The great Roman peace was a peace that was created and sustained by merciless violence."[24]

"Empire" and Paul

The brutality of Rome is *suggested* in Ephesians as Paul identifies himself as a prisoner three times without specifically mentioning the empire (it was obvious to his readers).

> For this reason I, Paul, a prisoner of Christ Jesus on behalf of you Gentiles. (3:1)
>
> I therefore, a prisoner for the Lord, urge you to walk in a manner worthy of the calling to which you have been called. (4:1)
>
> … and also for me, that words may be given to me in opening my mouth boldly to proclaim the mystery of the gospel, for which I am an ambassador in chains, that I may declare it boldly, as I ought to speak. (6:19-20)

In Acts 28:17 Paul says to local Jewish leaders: "yet I was delivered as a prisoner from Jerusalem into the hands of the Romans." N. T. Wright describes it this way:

> Imagine Paul in prison in Ephesus. He is probably malnourished and short of sleep. He may well have suffered horrible illness; he will certainly have been beaten up by guards and perhaps by other prisoners. He feels helpless and alone in the dark and damp, with the smell of rot, excrement, and death all around him.[25]

Paul's dark prison cell serves as a foil for the brilliance and boldness of Paul's vision of King Jesus. *The Christ* is the crucified One now resurrected and enthroned at the right hand of God (Eph 1:20). *The Christ* is the head of the church, the fullness of him who fills all in all (Eph 1:20). *The Christ* preaches a gospel of peace, offering all persons, peoples, and nations a whole new way of being human (Eph 2:13-17).

---

24 Wright and Bird, *Jesus and the Powers*, 17.
25 Wright and Bird, *The New Testament World*, 450.

Kristin: **Pax Christi**

The Jesus-movement began during the "Roman Peace." Jesus says, "Peace I leave you, my peace I give to you. Not as the world gives do I give to you. Let not your hearts be troubled, neither let them be afraid." For Christians, it was not Augustus, but Christ who had "ordained peace" and proclaimed its glad tidings to the world. Christians claimed a crucified peasant as their King, who said that the last would be first, and the first would be last (Matt 20:16).

Christians were said to "turn the world upside down" by proclaiming that there is another King—Jesus (Acts 17:6-7). But Jesus is not a *rival* King vying for power among the many Powers. His kingdom is not of this world. If it were, his servants would have been fighting (John 18:36) and winning peace through bloodshed as every other kingdom had done. But they never did.

According to scholar George Kalantzis, the first three hundred years of church history show no evidence of early Christian approval for bloodshed whatsoever.[26] Prior to Emperor Constantine's adoption of Christianity in 312, Christian writings rejected both violence *and* involvement with state power maintained through violence. The early Christians clearly saw links between violence, idolatry, injustice, and demonic power.

Lactantius (ca. AD 250-325) articulates this view. "If God alone were worshiped," he says, "there would not be dissensions and wars, since people would know that they are the children of one God; and, therefore, among those who were connected by the sacred and inviolable bond of divine relationship."[27]

As we learned in chapter 7, in Greco-Roman thought, the people of a city were related to their gods. The obligations of religious and civic life were tied to their shared lineage with the god(dess) of the city in which they lived, and to which they made oaths of allegiance. But the Lord has come to redeem people from every nation. In this way, he ratifies a peace treaty with all peoples and conquers all gods.

We are now obligated to peace with one another because our Father holds us to the treaty. The "sacred and inviolable bond of divine relationship" says that we are brothers and sisters because of what Jesus has done. As Tertullian (ca. AD 160-225) put it, "Christ, in disarming Peter, disarmed every soldier."[28] Dionysius of Alexandria (d. AD 264) further says that Jesus "seized the weapons from their hands, and rent from them every occupation that relies upon them."

---

26 Kalantzis, lecture.
27 Lactantius, "Divine Institutes, Book V (Of Justice)."
28 Porterfield, *100 Early Christian Quotes*, 9.

For many early Christians, "every occupation that relies upon them" included not only military service, but also positions of state power. Some will argue that the only reason the early church had such a strong commitment to nonviolence was that they didn't have state power.

However, even in those days, magistrates and military men would sometimes convert to Christianity. And the expectation was that they would commit to nonviolence and *give up* state power. The Egyptian Church Order (along with several other sources) gives the following instructions for those already soldiers and magistrates, and those who aspire to become them:

> The soldier who is of inferior rank shall not kill anyone. If ordered to, he shall not carry out the order, nor shall he take the oath. If he does not accept this, let him be dismissed. Anyone who has the power of the sword or the magistrate of a city who wears the purple, let him give it up or be dismissed. The catechumen or believer who wish to become soldiers shall be dismissed, because they have despised God.[29]

They have despised God. To be a Christian and choose involvement with the sword was a contradiction dishonoring the God of peace. "Soldiers of inferior rank" were usually unable to leave military service. But still, they had to refuse orders to kill and refuse to take oaths, even if this should cost them their lives.

For political leaders—or any who maintain power through threat of violence—the only option was to renounce their position. Even if they do not kill human beings directly, they are "the magistrates of the Roman Empire who are stained in wars and have shed innocent blood" (from the *Didascalia Apostolorum,* written ca. AD 230). This was not only because of the idolatry of the imperial court. It was also because violence was seen as inherently incompatible with Jesus.

As Tertullian (AD 160–240) puts it,

> I think we must first inquire whether warfare is proper at all for Christians.... Shall it be held lawful to make an occupation of the sword, when the Lord proclaims that he who uses the sword shall perish by the sword? And shall the son of peace take part in the battle when it does not become him even to sue at law? ... And shall he diligently protect by night those whom in the day-time he has put to flight by his exorcisms, leaning and resting on the spear the while with which Christ's side was pierced?[30]

---

29 Porterfield, 19, 22.

30 Tertullian, *De Corona (The Chaplet),* chapter 11.

The early Christian Clement of Alexandria (ca. AD 150–215) writes that "Above all, Christians are not allowed to correct sinful wrongdoings by violence." Tertullian further adds, "If one were to make an exception for the Christian as soldier ... one would overturn the essence of Baptism."[31]

Lactantius says, "No exception at all ought to be made to the rule that it is always wrong to kill a man, whom God has wished to be a sacrosanct creature."[32] He further says that "God has commanded that enmities are never to be contracted by us, but are always to be removed, so that we may soothe those who are our enemies by reminding them of their relationship to us." He further adds that justice cannot bear the "tearing asunder" of the human family for any cause whatsoever. "Wherever arms have glittered," he says, "[justice] must be banished and exterminated."[33]

Aristides of Athens (died ca. AD 134) says, "It is the Christians, O Emperor, who have sought and found the truth, for they acknowledge God ... They speak gently to those who oppress them, and in this way they make them their friends. It has become their passion to do good to their enemies."[34]

"Many gain glory from the valor they show in battle," says St. Basil the Great. "They go so far as to boast of the murder of their brothers. Indeed, military courage and the triumphal arches erected by a general or the community exist only through the magnitude of the murder."[35]

As Tertullian said, "Shall we carry a flag? It is a rival to Christ." And St. John Chrysostom said, "I am a Christian. He who answers thus has declared everything at once—his country, profession, family; the believer belongs to no city on earth but to the heavenly Jerusalem."

Is it possible, then, to embrace both *Pax Romana* and *Pax Christi* without contradiction? Can Rome baptize the sword?[36]

---

31 Porterfield, *100 Early Christian Quotes on Not Killing*, 7.
32 Porterfield, 16.
33 Porterfield, 17.
34 Porterfield, 8.
35 Porterfield, 21.
36 Considering the church's prohibition against violence in the first three centuries, one wonders whether *theologically sanctioned church-and-state-violence* was an extra-biblical "accretion" similar to papal infallibility, the assumption of Mary, icon veneration, tradition equal in authority to Scripture, etc. As we emphasize in this volume Christ's teachings, his example of enemy-love, and his gospel of peace, could it be we are arguing for nonviolence as one aspect of what Gavin Ortlund calls "Protestant retrieval" of apostolic faith and practice? See Ortlund's excellent discussion in *What It Means To Be Protestant*, 135–58.

First Roman Emperor Claiming to be Christian

In October of AD 312, Constantine faced a defining battle over the future of the Roman Empire, and his own future as sole emperor. Facing civil wars between Rome's competing emperors, Constantine was desperate. According to the historian Eusebius,[37] God gave Constantine a vision.

The first vision was in the sky—"a solar halo, or ring around the sun." Christian bishops assured Constantine it was a sign, "not from the sun god, but from Christ ... 'the light of the world.'"[38] Eusebius writes: "At this sight he [Constantine] himself was struck with amazement, and his whole army also, which followed him on this expedition, and witnessed the miracle."[39]

Soon, Constantine had a clarifying dream. "Then in his sleep the Christ of God appeared to [Constantine] with the same sign which he had seen in the heavens, and commanded him to make a likeness of that sign which he had seen in the heavens, and to use it as a safeguard in all engagements with his enemies." The message was "Conquer by This"—to conquer by "Chi-Rho," the sign of Christ.[40]

Constantine and his army won the decisive battle. It is known as the Battle of Milvian Bridge. Twelve years later, in 324, Constantine was the sole ruler of the Roman Empire and the first Christian emperor.

Jesus Christ became the so-called guarantor of Constantine's military battles on behalf of the empire. Whereas earlier Christian writings do not allow a Christian even to serve as a local magistrate, Constantine now baptizes the sword and weds Christianity with the empire. Whereas the *Didascalia Apostolorum* admonishes leaders not to accept money from magistrates because of their part in an empire stained by war, the emperor himself now fills church coffers.

---

37 Eusebius (d. 339) was a bishop, historian, and an apologist for Constantine as Rome's first Christian emperor. Eusebius's "On the Holy Sepulchre" was proclaimed in 335 in Jerusalem in front of Emperor Constantine. The occasion was the dedication of the recently constructed Church of the Holy Sepulchre which was funded by the emperor's benefactions to the church. Eusebius said that in God's providence, the rule of Constantine represents the merging of two great powers—the gospel of Christ, and the Roman Empire. According to Donaldson, "had Eusebius lived to see the internecine conflicts among Constantine's successors during the next quarter century, he might have been more inclined to put clearer theological daylight between the dominion of the Christ and the dominion of the Caesar." Donaldson, *Gentile Christian Identity*, 1–7.

38 Strauss, *Ten Caesars*, 294.

39 Eusebius of Caesarea, *The Life of Emperor Constantine*.

40 Constantine "put a well-known early Christian symbol on (or above) his personal banner: the Greek letters *chi* and *rho*, the equivalent in Latin *CHR* for Christ." Strauss, *Ten Caesars*, 294–95.

For many Christians, this was an unbearable contradiction. Without being radically distinct from the society around them many believers no longer knew how to follow Jesus the crucified. For them, Christianity's "alliance with empire" made no sense. So tens of thousands fled to the wilderness to seek God in solitude with the Scriptures and learn what it meant to be believers in this new context.

This movement would become known as monasticism. The early monks and nuns of the desert had no official role within the emerging church hierarchy—and yet, they would be sought by thousands of ordinary people for their wisdom and spiritual insight. Often, they would raise a prophetic voice, especially to the churches of the cities, with whom they were often in conflict.

Over time, the monastic movement would also become embroiled in politics, money, and intrigue. Still, figures like St. Francis of Assisi emerged with calls back to commitments of poverty, prophetic proclamation, and service of the poor and vulnerable.

Martin Luther was disgusted by the opulence and corruption of the Roman Church and monasticism in the late Middle Ages.[41] But Luther himself was no stranger to political power, violence, or money. Calvin, Zwingli, and other leaders in the Reformation similarly made alliances with state rulers,[42] supported wars and fought in them,[43] and excused violent professions on the basis that the "public person" and his job was separate from the "private person" and his faith. Luther taught that "the kingdom of the world" was established by God and should be obeyed. Violence in carrying out official duties could thus be sanctioned, even though the same actions would be condemned if done by the "private person."[44]

And yet, even during this time there were those who held to peace. The Anabaptists believed the Reformers had not committed radically enough to Scripture's original ideals. Like the early Christians, they refused to take oaths to state governments or to fight in wars. They believed that believers' baptism was an oath to God's kingdom, which must override all others. Many of them chose death instead, at the hands of Catholics and Protestants alike.[45] Throughout history, nonviolent movements have

---

[41] Luther's disgust is most plain in his treatise *The Babylonian Captivity of the Church.*
[42] Orta, "How Martin Luther Started a Religious Revolution."
[43] Mark, "Two Accounts of Zwingli's Death."
[44] Althaus, "The Ethics of Martin Luther."
[45] Loganbill, "A Theology of Suffering: Suffering and Martyrdom in Sixteenth-Century Anabaptist Hymnody."

persisted within Christian faith; key evangelical figures like D. L. Moody, Charles Spurgeon, and Jim Elliot have also been among the ranks of total pacifists.[46]

Werner: ## Peace through Bloodshed—Two Kinds

Above we have seen that *Pax Romana*—peace propaganda of the Roman Empire—was a peace achieved with bloodshed.

With *Pax Christi*, we also have peace through bloodshed. But the peace is altogether different, both in its means and its ends. Gorman says it this way: "Christ has 'pacified' both the people of God and the gentiles, the nations, not by the shedding of their blood—as the Romans often did—but by the shedding of his own blood."[47] The contrast is clear. Keep in mind the early hearers of this letter to the Ephesians, living as they were amid the violence and cruelty of the empire. The way to an *in-my-home-and-community* peace between formerly hostile peoples was through the crucified God, Christ the Messiah-King. Gorman elaborates:

> Moreover, by simultaneously delivering us from "the power of the air" (2:2, referring to Satan's sphere of influence on humanity), Christ's death "allows the church to be established as a political space or realm that recognizes Christ's dominion." Thus the mission of God, and of Paul, the Ephesians, and all Christians, is to bring people from the realm of sin, death, and alienation governed by anti-God powers into the realm of forgiveness, resurrection life, and peace ruled by Jesus the Messiah and Lord.[48]

Christ's dominion is a profound contrast to the empire's dominion. Christ's dominion rules not by force of weapons. The gospel of peace forged through the blood of Christ was utterly new and innovative, fresh and alive. Christ-followers embodied the reconciliation and compassion of Jesus in the Roman Empire. But this gospel of peace was anticipated centuries prior in the writings of Isaiah, to which we now briefly turn.

Christ's Gospel of Peace Refers to Isaiah

The letter to the Ephesians draws significantly from Isaiah's poetry and vision. Isaiah offers a vision of God's servant, the Prince of Peace, reconciling those far and near ("the far" is the world of non-Jewish peoples; "the near" is God's people, the Jews). It is a vision of One who

---

46 Sider, "Christian Nonviolence and Church History."

47 Gorman, *Becoming the Gospel*, 191.

48 Gorman, 191. He quotes Fowl, *Ephesians*, 74.

proclaims good news of peace. Shouldn't the gospel of peace in Ephesians therefore be understood as a vital part of the biblical narrative, indeed, core to the gospel?

Quoting Stuhlmacher:

> On the basis of the catchword *eirēnē* [in Eph 2:13–17] it combines three passages of Scripture, Isa 57:19 (vv. 13 and 17), Isa 9:5–6 (v. 14) and Isa 52:7 (v. 17). The way the passages are connected is thoroughly Jewish in form. The "peace" announced to the far and the near in Isa 57:19 is brought about by the Messiah who is called the "prince of peace" (Isa 9:5–6) and that in such a way that the Messiah, in accord with Isa 52:7, appears as the proclaimer of peace for the far and near.[49]

ISAIAH		EPHESIANS	
57:19	to the far and to the near	2:13	you who once were far off have been brought near
9:5–6	v. 6: unto us a son is given…Prince of Peace v. 5: every boot of the tramping warrior in battle tumult and every garment rolled in blood will be burned as fuel for the fire	2:14	For he himself is our peace, who has made us both one and has broken down in his flesh the dividing wall of hostility
52:7	How beautiful upon the mountains are the feet of him who brings good news [gospel], who publishes peace	2:17	And he came and preached [the gospel of] peace
57:19	Peace, peace, to the far and to the near	2:17	preached peace to you were far off and peace to those who were near

Figure 10.1: Isaiah's vision of peace echoed in Ephesians 2

In writing to the Ephesians, Paul is drawing heavily from Isaiah in describing Jesus as the Christ, the Messiah-King, the reconciler, peacemaker, and Savior. The Isaiah connections to Ephesians 2:13–18 are linked to other New Testament passages. In Romans 10:15, Paul famously quotes Isaiah 52:7, "As it is written, 'How beautiful are the feet of those who preach the good news!'" In the Greek, "preach the good news" is one word—the verb form of gospel (εὐαγγελίζω, *euangelizō*). It is used in Ephesians 2:17. It is used in Isaiah 52:7 in the Septuagint (Greek version of the Old Testament).

---

49 Stuhlmacher, *Reconciliation, Law and Righteousness*, 200–201.

Consider also Peter's visit in Joppa to the Roman centurion Cornelius, a visit orchestrated by visions given by God to both men (Acts 10:1–16). Jennings imagines the drama of Peter in the home of Cornelius:

> Peter enters the home of Cornelius. Cornelius falls at his feet in worship of him. Peter picks him up and says, "Stand up; I am only a mortal." (v. 26). Together they talked and moved toward a room where Cornelius's family and close friends were waiting. The stage is set. How do you change the world? How do you turn it right side up if not by turning it upside down? Now God will transgress border and boundary in the best place for such transgression. It will be done in the intimate spaces of family and close friends and in a clandestine illicit meeting of those who should not be together.[50]

As Peter begins preaching, he immediately references Isaiah 52:7. "As for the word that he sent to Israel, preaching good news of peace through Jesus Christ (he is Lord of all)" (Acts 10:36).[51] Here also the verb form of gospel is used. The phrase in Greek is *euangelizomenos eirēnēn* it means "gospeling peace," or "preaching the gospel of peace." In the home of Cornelius, Peter embodies and preaches the good news of peace—bringing together with God those near and far. This peace is so much more than an individual private reality. Peter is gospeling a peace that is *personal* with God and simultaneously *social* with "others."

Peter embodies *shalom*.

Shalom (שָׁלוֹם) is the Hebrew word for peace in Isaiah. This word *shalom* is used in Isaiah 9:6, 52:7, and 57:19. In writing Ephesians 2:13–17, Paul quotes and interprets Isaiah.

- The Prince of Peace (Isa 9:6) is Jesus the Christ who proclaimed good news (εὐαγγελίζω, *euangelizō*) of peace (Eph 2:17; Isa 52:7).

- Christ has "broken down in his flesh the dividing wall of hostility" (Eph 2:14); this *breaking hostility* is pictured in Isaiah 9:5—"every boot of the tramping warrior in battle tumult and every garment rolled in blood will be burned as fuel for the fire." Through the cross, Christ is "killing the hostility" (Eph 2:16).

- Christ has proclaimed good news of peace to those far away, the gentiles—and peace to those who are near, the Jews (Eph 2:17; Isa 57:19).

---

50 Jennings, *Acts: A Theological Commentary*, 108.

51 "The references to the good news of peace and to Christ being Lord of all echo Isa. 52:7 and 57:19: the gospel is for all people, including Cornelius and his fellow Gentiles." *ESV Study Bible*.

These links in Acts 10 and Ephesians 2 to Isaiah's *shalom* have big implications.

In American Christian tradition, biblical peace normally refers to an individual's private spiritual peace with God. Consider Billy Graham's famous book *Peace With God,* first published in 1953.[52] It rightly emphasizes the necessity of individual reconciliation with God. The book "points the way, the *only* way, to authentic personal peace in a world in crisis."[53] The phrase "authentic personal peace" is noteworthy. Graham makes no mention of the robust theology of Ephesians 2 presenting a peace with God that also includes peace with distant or hostile "others" through Christ.

In *Peace With God,* Graham does mention Ephesians 2:12–13, along with a comment about God drawing us near to him in individual reconciliation.[54] But he *excludes* the verses about Christ making peace *socially*—verses like these: "For he [Christ] himself is our peace, who has made us both one and has broken down in his flesh the dividing wall of hostility … that he might create in himself one new man in place of the two, so making peace, and might reconcile us both to God in one body through the cross, thereby killing the hostility. And he [Jesus] came and preached peace to you who were far off and peace to you who were near" (2:14–17).

A Tragic Exclusion

Here's the tragedy: In our world of growing polarization, millions of Christians believe that peace with God through the cross excludes a social-horizontal dimension. Reconciliation with lower-status, racial, ethnic, or national "others" in the church? *That's nonessential. It's an option, a secondary part of the discipleship journey.* So the thinking goes.

Graham's book was ideal for persons who want personal peace with God but prefer to avoid reconciliation with Christians of another race, social class, ethnic group, or tribe. There's nothing unusual about this perspective in the American, or other, Christian traditions. American history shows that Christians have often ignored the social implications of Christ's crucifixion as revealed in Ephesians 2. It is therefore no surprise that in America and elsewhere in the global church, many pastors feel impotent in addressing—through the gospel—hostility and violence proceeding from group-identity conflict (like racism, tribalism, nationalism, casteism, or fascism).

---

52 Graham, *Peace With God.*
53 Graham, x; emphasis in original.
54 Graham, 120.

Ephesians 2:13–17 is routinely excluded from the preaching on the cross. Why? This text is routinely excluded from doctrine, namely, the doctrine of the cross and atonement.[55] But consider the density of cross-and-gospel content in this text: "brought near by the blood" (2:13), "has broken down in his flesh the wall of hostility" (2:14), "reconcile us both to God" (2:16), "through the cross, thereby killing the hostility" (2:16), "and he [Christ] came and proclaimed [gospeled] peace to you" (2:17).

Consider also the history of polarizing divisions in the church, our nation, and the present hostilities and threats around our world. We the church desperately need our cross-and-atonement doctrine to undergird gospel preaching that asserts the individual-personal *and* social-corporate reality of *Christ is our peace; Christ makes peace; Christ preaches peace* (Eph 2:14–15, 17). For an exploration on how Ephesians 2:13–17 may be incorporated into atonement doctrine, see Brad Vaughn's article in this volume, Appendix 1.

Now, getting back to our question: How does peace in Ephesians 2 connect to the Hebrew concept of peace (*shalom*)? What does *shalom* mean? "In the Bible, the word *shalom* is most commonly used to refer to a state of affairs, one of well-being, tranquility, prosperity, and security, circumstances unblemished by any sort of defect. Shalom is a blessing, a manifestation of divine grace."[56]

Biblical peace (*shalom*) is wholistic—harmony with God, harmony within our communities, harmony with creation. It is a vision of glory. "Nothing broken, nothing missing."[57]

Paul's mind was saturated with the Hebrew Scriptures. So we can readily see why for him, the work of Christ and the gospel of peace is wholistic and multidimensional. We therefore contend that for Paul, the dynamic of peace (*eirēnē*) as used in Ephesians was *in continuity with* and in fulfillment of Isaiah's *shalom*—with God, neighbor, and creation—a wholistic peace according to the Hebrew Scriptures.

The gospel of peace (offering vertical and horizontal reconciliation) is no outlier to the good news. This is core to the good news—the gospel of Christ. Unfortunately, the gospel of peace (vertical and horizontal) is rarely included in how pastors preach and Christians think about the gospel.

---

55 For example, see chapter 27, "Atonement," in Grudem, *Systematic Theology*, 1093–162. Grudem is conventional in excluding Eph 2:13–17 from atonement theology. Grudem gives ample attention to Eph 2:13–17 in *Christian Ethics*; this begs the question: On what basis does this text qualify for *ethics* but not *systematic theology*?

56 Ravitsky, "Shalom: Peace in Hebrew."

57 IsraelU, "What Does Shalom Mean?"

Christianity: Of Peace or of Empire?

Under Emperor Constantine the Great (272–337) the church adopted a practice of centralized power which embraced many features of Rome. This was first made possible when, in February AD 313, the Edict of Milan gave official toleration to Christianity. This formally ended ten years of brutal persecution of Christians ordered by Diocletian in 303.[58]

Scholars point to some positive developments of Christianity's partnership with the Roman Empire.[59] Women and mothers were given unprecedented legal rights. Marriage became protected and divorce restricted, contributing to family health and social stability. Infanticide, widely practiced by the ancients, was outlawed.[60] Constantine also famously funded the construction of churches. And to unify a much-divided church, he convened the Council of Nicaea in 325 out of which came the Nicene Creed. Constantine discovered that "the surest way to join a people as one was to unite them not in common ritual but in common belief."[61]

But there were also negatives. Wes Howard-Brook's *Empire Baptized: How the Church Embraced What Jesus Rejected* describes the complexity of Constantine and his times. Citing a wide range of scholars, he shows that Constantine established Christianity as the "religion of empire."[62] Broadly speaking, this had the effect of fusing Christianity with the empire's coercive (and corrupting) power, violence, and wealth while domesticating the teachings of Jesus.

How can we make sense of Christianity's transition in the Roman Empire—from persecuted minority faith to imperial religion? Here's an important piece of the puzzle: the tradition of *patronage*. In the Roman

---

58 In chapter 1 of his treatise, "Of the Manner in Which the Persecutors Died," Lactantius writes of Constantine and his times, "For God has raised up princes to rescind the impious and sanguinary edicts of the tyrants and provide for the welfare of mankind; so that now the cloud of past times is dispelled, and peace and serenity gladden all hearts. And after the furious whirlwind and black tempest, the heavens are now become calm, and the wished-for light has shone forth; and now God, the hearer of prayer, by His divine aid has lifted His prostrate and afflicted servants from the ground, has brought to an end the united devices of the wicked, and wiped off the tears from the faces of those who mourned."

59 For a brief overview of the positive and negative features of Christianity under Emperor Constantine, see Veith, "The Good, the Bad, and the Ugly."

60 Holland, *Dominion*, 125. Holland's historical work compellingly argues that the modern secular world, in broadly assuming values such as equal rights under the law, human dignity, compassion for the vulnerable, and freedom of conscience, owes much to Christ and Christianity, the many moral failures of Christendom notwithstanding.

61 Holland, 114–15.

62 Howard-Brook, *Empire Baptized*, 186–210.

tradition, an emperor was often both considered a god and had the gods as his patrons, his backers. "In other words, being a god [remember, it was normal for the emperor to be considered a god] expressed the maximum possible *human* honor. Having a divine patron expressed the maximum possible *divine* honor."[63] Constantine knew that in claiming the Christian God as a divine patron, he was assured a political constituency—a large network of Christians across the Roman Empire.[64]

Here's how Constantine's biographer, Eusebius, describes it in *The Life of the Blessed Emperor Constantine:*

> The victorious emperor himself long afterwards declared it to the writer of this history. ... He said that about mid-day, when the sun was beginning to decline, he saw with his own eyes the trophy of a cross of light in the heavens, above the sun, and bearing the inscription, CONQUER BY THIS. At this sight he himself was struck with amazement, and his whole army also, which happened to be following him on some expedition, and witnessed the miracle.[65]

Constantine's patron-god has told him—*Conquer by This*. What did it mean? If it was truly Jesus Christ giving the vision, Howard-Brook cleverly suggests Constantine could have interpreted the vision as "Abdicate the throne and become a true follower of Jesus," or, "Become a new kind of leader, one who rules as Jesus might, giving up war and status."[66]

The Question of Constantine's Vision

So, how *did* Constantine interpret the vision? Bishop Eusebius, Constantine's mythmaker,[67] writes in the next chapter of his biography of Constantine[68] these words about the vision:

> And while [Constantine] continued to ponder and reason on its meaning, night suddenly came on; then in his sleep the Christ of God appeared to him with the same sign which he had seen in

---

63 Howard-Brook, 188; emphasis in original.
64 James Carroll, *Constantine's Sword: The Church and the Jews: A History*, 172-77, 182.
65 Eusebius, The *Life of the Blessed Emperor Constantine*, ch. 28.
66 Howard-Brook, *Empire Baptized*, 193. This would be a straw man argument were it not for the life and teachings of Jesus and nearly three centuries of early Christian witness and writings rejecting violence and killing (as previously argued).
67 Carroll, *Constantine's Sword*, 178. Eusebius exaggerates about Constantine, e.g., "For no one was comparable to him for grace or beauty of person, or height or stature."
68 Carroll says that Eusebius's *Life of Constantine* "is a celebration of the divinely ordained union of the Church and the empire—Constantine as Moses—and not in any way an objective work of biography." *Constantine's Sword*, 173.

the heavens, and commanded him to make a likeness of that sign which he had seen in the heavens, and to use it as a safeguard in all engagements with his enemies.[69]

Constantine interpreted the vision as the way and validation for military conquest. Of course he did. As Howard-Brook describes it: "Use the symbol as a magic talisman that will guarantee military success." This had "earth-shaking consequences." ... It "reduced 'Christianity' to a label that could be placed on top of all the existing imperial structures and practices. It firmly established 'Christianity' as the 'religion of empire.'"[70]

How could Eusebius justify this theological turn away from the ways of Jesus toward the way of empire?[71] Did he see biblical precedence of God-as-patron serving the king-and-empire in the record of King Solomon?[72]

A traditional positive narrative about Constantine may be stated as follows: Constantine, prior to a most challenging battle against his rival emperor Maxentius, has a vision of Christ's cross with the saying, "Conquer By This" ... Constantine puts his faith in Christ ... Constantine achieves a surprising victory at Milvian Bridge defeating Maxentius who drowns in the Tiber River ... Constantine receives his military victory as

---

69 Eusebius, *Life*, ch. 29.

70 Howard-Brook, *Empire Baptized*, 193.

71 See Eusebius, *Life*, for his view of Constantine and why he believed the church is a legitimate partner to imperial Rome with its power, wealth, and military might.

72 In *The Prophetic Imagination*, Brueggemann explains the negative features of the God-as-patron dynamic under King Solomon. Chapter 2, "Royal Consciousness: Countering the Counterculture" (21–38), describes how the people of God under Moses had centuries later become the wealthy, powerful, and satiated kingdom of Israel. It was no longer a countercultural society critiquing the empire (as under Moses) by "the freedom of God." Rather, Solomon had gained imperial power and status by which his royal regime could domesticate God's laws and presence to his own interests, thereby "countering the counterculture." Citing numerous texts in 1 Kings, Brueggemann says Solomon's kingdom was characterized by three elements: (1) Economics of Affluence (1 Kgs 4:20–23); (2) Oppressive Social Policy (1 Kgs 5:13–18; 9:15–22); and (3) Static Religion or Religion of Immanence (1 Kgs 8:12–13). It is this third element about which Brueggemann writes, "So the third foundational element I suggest is the establishment of a controlled, static religion in which God and his temple have become part of the royal landscape, in which the sovereignty of God is fully subordinated to the purpose of the king. In Jerusalem in this period there is a radical revision in the character of God. Now God is fully accessible to the king who is his patron, and the freedom of God is completely overcome" (Brueggemann, *Prophetic Imagination*, 28). This begs the question: Could it be this self-interested theology of *God-as-our-national-patron* was at work in Solomon's regime, in the regime of Constantine, and is at work today in the Christian nationalism and dominionism embraced by a significant minority of America's Christian community? Is this a proof of the stability of human nature to "use God" to gain or maintain political power while avoiding divine critique?

the blessing of Christ ... Constantine serves the Christian God the rest of his days ... Christendom, with all its virtues, is launched.

We join Wes Howard-Brook, James Carroll, and Terrence Donaldson to say this traditional narrative is problematic.

Carroll writes, "Constantine was no underdog. He knew that Maxentius, whose army had been decimated in an earlier battle in Verona, had no chance... . The battle at the Tiber River was a predictable rout." The narrative constructed by Constantine and Eusebius can be seen as "infinitely shrewd."[73] Constantine was trying to consolidate his power and unify disparate peoples whose loyalties had been stretched across three power-sharing emperors. He knew Christians had been severely persecuted under the prior emperor Diocletian; he knew Christians were seeking relief. Constantine needed a political constituency—a power base among the people. In the Christian population of the empire, Constantine found that power base.[74]

Defending Constantine?

Peter Leithart's *Defending Constantine* adds nuance to this conversation. Leithart examines Constantine's legacy, his writings, and the likelihood of Constantine (over decades) becoming a genuine Christian. Leithart argues that Constantine changed the course of history by laying the foundation for Christendom. And Constantine's biggest contribution? Leithart argues that Constantine's signature legacy is that he ended pagan sacrifice to Greco-Roman gods. Thus, "Rome was baptized" into the Christian faith:

> Through Constantine, Rome was baptized, and sacrifice in all these senses either came to an end or began to. Constantine stopped the slaughter of Christians. He refused to sacrifice at the Capitol during his triumph in 312. He ended sacrifice for officers of his empire, thus opening imperial administration to Christians, and eventually outlawed sacrifice entirely. He closed a few temples where sacrifices were being offered. ... He stopped the gladiatorial combats. ... With Constantine, the Roman Empire became officially a desacrificial polity.[75]

Continuing with the baptism analogy for Rome, Leithart argues that "every baptism is an infant baptism," and although the change was not

---

73 Carroll, *Constantine's Sword*, 181–82.

74 Carroll, 181, citing Barnes, *Constantine and Eusebius*, 376. Constantine identifying with the Christian constituency of the Roman Empire rhymes with American presidential candidates courting the evangelical Christian voting block ever since Ronald Reagan.

75 Leithart, *Defending Constantine*, 328.

immediate, a new trajectory began.[76] Leithart argues this change had a long-term positive impact on Western civilization. At the same time, he plainly acknowledges Constantine's brutality. Constantine was a Roman imperial military man well-acquainted with strategy, conquest, and ruthless bloodshed—following in the footsteps of Roman emperors before him. Killing, whether for conquest or defense, was the way of an emperor. Constantine's targets included family members:

> By the time his life ended, [Constantine] was (indirectly in every case, so far as we know) responsible for the deaths of his father-in-law Maximian, his brother-in-law Maxentius, another brother-in-law Licinius along with his son, his wife Fausta and his son Crispus, and a few other relatives. Some or all of these executions may have been just acts of punishing rivals and rebels. Some or all of them may have been acts of a paranoid emperor eager to maintain his hard-won power. We know too little to be sure.[77]

But Leithart's defense of Constantine retains a problem. Yes, the church was welcomed into the center of the empire, but Roman imperial violence did not end. Not even close. If we grant that Roman sacrifice to the pagan gods ended under Constantine, a vexing question remains. What shall we make of the long history of Western Christianity's complicity with violence and conquest?[78] Could it be that under Constantine and the many kings who followed him, the dark spiritual Powers of violence, greed, and idolatry stayed put? Nilay Saiya says as much: "Before the fourth century, Christianity was marked by a radically countercultural spirit. Once Christianity became coopted by the powers, however, it quickly began to conform itself to the logic of the world, compromise its holy character, and lose its prophetic witness."[79] Could it be that the violent influence of the Powers over the various lands and peoples of the Roman Empire simply continued even though the cult practices largely ceased?[80]

---

76 Leithart, 341.

77 Leithart, 304.

78 Readers may conduct their own internet searches or other explorations about "Christianity and violence." Key word searches may include—Christian violence, Christian terrorism, Just War, Holy War, Inquisition, Christianity and slavery, Doctrine of Discovery, Christian colonial conquest, Christian genocide of native peoples, Crusades, Christian antisemitism, Christian lynching, Thirty-Years' War.

79 Saiya, *The Global Politics of Jesus*, 241.

80 Referencing Eph 1:20–21, 2:2, 3:10, 6:12, and 1 Cor 2:6–8, Heiser writes that Paul incorporated terms rooted in the Old Testament that describe "geographical domain rulership" of cosmic Powers. "Paul often interchanged these terms with others that are

Pax Romana Versus Pax Christi: Contrasts in Peace 159

Kingdom of the World versus Kingdom of the Cross

Indeed, Nilay Saiya contributes much to this conversation. He examines the stark contrasts between worldly kingdoms and Christ's kingdom in his book *The Global Politics of Jesus*. He compares "the kingdom of the world" with Christ's "kingdom of the cross." I made the comparison chart below (Figure 10.2) based largely on Saiya's analysis.[81]

	KINGDOM OF THE WORLD	KINGDOM OF THE CROSS
Power	• Power is coercive through threat of violence. • Authority is for gaining and maintaining status and control.	• Power is noncoercive; it is strength through humility, by obeying God, being filled with the Holy Spirit. • Authority is for serving; it is gained by serving.
Violence	• Violence is normative. • Use and threat of violence shapes social behavior and restrains evil.	• Nonviolence is normative. • Self-giving love, including enemy-love, is the standard for virtue and morality.
Social Boundaries	• More exclusive; boundaries essential. • Inclusion is based on nationality, tribe, ethnicity, status, etc. • Reinforcing social boundaries is normative.	• More inclusive; boundaries optional; open to all regardless of nationality, tribe, ethnicity, status. • Faith in King Jesus as basis of inclusion. • Crossing social boundaries is normative.
Goal	• Survival of the state. • Leaders justified in selfish, aggressive behavior.	• Redemption of the world. • Blessing all peoples through self-sacrificial living.

Figure 10.2: Kingdom of the world versus Christ's kingdom of the cross

Saiya critically evaluates Constantine as the first Christian emperor, for by Constantine the church gained immense privilege and power at the

---

familiar to most Bible students: "principalities" (*archē*); "powers"/"authorities" (*exousia*); "powers" (*dynamis*); "dominions"/" lords" (*kyrios*); "thrones" (*thronos*). These terms have something in common—they were used in both the New Testament and other Greek literature for geographical domain rulership. This is the divine dominion concept of Deut 32:8–9. At times these terms are used of humans, but several instances demonstrate that Paul had spiritual beings in mind." See Heiser, *Unseen Realm*, 120, ch. 15, "Cosmic Geography" (116–22). If this is true, could this help explain why violence prevailed in Christendom and among many so-called Christian kings and emperors? The murderous Powers, *staying put* even after Constantine ended the sacrificial system, still wielded influence despite the increasing numbers of Christians in the Roman Empire and subsequently in Christendom.

81 Saiya, *The Global Politics of Jesus*, 19–33.

center of the Roman Empire. Saiya says that for "the first three centuries of the church's existence, Christians were virtually unanimous in their rejection of the sword."

> But when they began to receive preferential treatment from the very empire that had previously persecuted them, they also began to rethink this political theology of pacifism and eventually came to embrace a radically different doctrine of dual allegiances to both God and the state. This revolution in thinking paved the way for Christian involvement in and support for political violence. The theology of dual allegiances naturally led Christians to conflate the violence of the state with the cause of God.[82]

It is this conflation "of the state with the cause of God" that we find disturbing. When the state privileges the church, Saiya points to a troubling contradiction; he calls it "the paradox of privilege."[83] *When the state privileges the church, it is neither good for the church nor good for the state.* And Constantine (and his descendants in Christendom) epitomized the unholy marriage of church and state.[84]

Of course, looking back to Constantine and the fourth century we see dimly, and we readily admit to conjecture about dark Powers "staying put" geographically while continuing their violent influence. Nevertheless, we do know enough of the Bible, the life and teachings of Jesus, the early church, and human history to grapple with difficult questions:

- Following Constantine, to what extent did Christianity's rise as the "religion of empire" coincide with a broad decline in the authentic way of Jesus and his gospel of peace?

- In what ways might Christians still be uncritically living under the long shadow of the empire's marriage of the Christian faith and the sword?

---

82 Saiya, 76.

83 "The paradox of privilege is that when the church allows itself to be co-opted by the state or defines itself on the basis of prevailing political, cultural, or economic ideologies, it blurs the distinction between its holy calling and the purpose of the state, fails to mark out a distinctive culture and politics of its own, becomes complicit in the evils of the state, and eventually fades into irrelevancy. On the other hand, the church contributes the most to the wellbeing of the world when it refuses to rule, rebuffs identity politics and nationalism, shuns violence, operates through the power of the truth, and remains committed to the contrarian way of the cross. ... As church and state move closer together, countries experience higher rates of religious hostilities and abuses of human rights. Christian privilege also has implications for the strength of Christianity itself. Paradoxically, it corresponds to the decline rather than the growth of Christianity." Saiya, 258.

84 For a brief overview of the extent to which, over the centuries, the church departed from the ethics of Jesus, including its use of state-sponsored brutality and violence, see Ortlund, *What It Means to Be Protestant*, 39–56.

- To what degree have we Christians been anesthetized by theology or tradition to the life and teachings of Jesus?

Grapple, we must.

Conversion Coercion

Latin American missiologist Samuel Escobar says the biggest change that began under Constantine was about the nature of Christian conversion.[85] Prior to Constantine, conversion meant voluntarily shifting one's allegiance from Caesar to Christ as Lord[86]—despite possible persecution.

Escobar points to the major change occurring in the year 381 when the Edict of Thessalonica proclaimed Catholic Christianity the official religion of the empire. "As for the others, since, in our judgment they are foolish madmen, we decree that they shall be branded with the ignominious name of heretics" (excerpt from the edict). Note the severe language in describing "others" as "foolish madmen" (curiously, the "heretics" are mainly Arian Christians). The decree concludes with a foreboding threat: "They will suffer in the first place the chastisement of the divine condemnation and in the second the punishment of our authority which in accordance with the will of Heaven we shall decide to inflict."[87]

Christian conversion *shifts*—from voluntarily choosing to give allegiance to King Jesus—to becoming a Christian via coercion—by force, legal decree, social pressure, or cultural accommodation.

Jesus says, "My kingdom is not of this world" (John 18:36). Jesus told Peter, "All who take the sword will perish by the sword" (Matt 26:52). But under Constantine and subsequent rulers, coercion wins the day. Voluntary allegiance to Christ declines, the peacemaking way of Jesus is marginalized, the gospel of peace is subverted, the Christian faith is wed to imperial force.

In the "Christian empire," the Christian hero shifts from martyr absorbing and subverting violence—to avenger employing violence.[88]

---

85 Escobar, *The New Global Mission*, 40–42.
86 See Mischke, "I pledge allegiance to 'the Christ.'"
87 Lyons, "The Edict of Thessalonica."
88 See Digeser, "The Violent Legacy of Constantine's Militant Piety," 228–48. Digeser examines Lactantius's *Divine Institutes*. Lactantius describes Constantine as a monarch who embodies the warrior-Christ (interpreted literally) of Rev 19. According to Digeser, Lactantius sees Constantine as a "militant soldier-emperor avenging injustice with violence." He does this by "fusing Constantine's image with that of Revelation's divine warrior." Thus, the Christian hero shifts from martyr—to a triumphant warrior-king, avenging idolaters and persecutors; this became a model for Christian monarchs for centuries to come.

This same "militant piety" persists in our day, and dangerously so, in political movements like dominionism and Christian nationalism.[89] One concerned pastor writes that nationalism has the same idolatrous dynamic as the tower of Babel, and is "inherently demonic." Nationalism "is the greatest religious rival to the Christian gospel that vies for the worship of the people whom I love and serve in my congregation, my broader community, and increasingly, my nation."[90]

The overlap between white Christian nationalism and the validity of violence is palpable. In 2023, an annual survey of Americans by Public Religion Research Institute (PRRI) found: "About 31% of white evangelical Protestants thought violence may be needed to 'save the country,' compared to 24% of black Protestants and 21% of Hispanic Catholics."[91]

This should give Christians pause, to say the least. Whenever Muslims (or Hindus, Buddhists, or other religious groups) use violence in *their* "militant piety," Christians rightfully condemn it. But shouldn't we first take the log out of our own eye?

Evangelicalism and the Empire Mindset

Karen Swallow Prior's book *The Evangelical Imagination* includes a chapter on the agreeable relationship between evangelicalism and empire. She points out that evangelicalism's rise coincided with the British Empire at its peak.[92] Karen Prior argues that *imperialism*—empire and domination—is bred into American evangelical attitudes:

> Because evangelicalism was so connected to the British Empire, imperialistic practices and attitudes are seldom far from the evangelical imagination. Names of events, organizations, and movements, such as the Salvation Army, Pioneers, the Billy Graham crusades, Campus Crusade for Christ (now called Cru), the original crusades (of course), theonomy,[93] Christian nationalism, and all forms of dominionism reflect the spirit of empire building within evangelicalism.[94]

---

89 Gorski and Perry, *The Flag and the Cross*; Neumann, *Kingdom of Rage*; Ritchie, *Why Do the Nations Rage*; and Whitehead and Perry, *Taking America Back for God*.
90 Ritchie, *Why Do the Nations Rage?*, 6.
91 Contreras, "Support for Political Violence Jumps in US"
92 Prior, *The Evangelical Imagination*, 197–99.
93 Theonomy is the belief that divine law, particularly the judical laws of the Old Testament, should be observed by modern societies.
94 Prior, *The Evangelical Imagination*, 201.

What is imperialism? What is colonialism? "Imperialism" is the mindset and practice of domination by a political-economic regime, ruling over a distant territory and its people. "Colonialism" derives from imperialism and means installing communities on distant lands for the purpose of controlling its assets or extracting its wealth.[95]

According to Jason Hickel, the British Empire was responsible for the death by starvation of some thirty million people in India between 1876 and 1902.

> The Indian famines of the late 19th century were not a natural disaster, as the British insisted at the time. They were the predictable consequence of imposing a foreign market logic that saw fit to eliminate basic human food security and sacrifice tens of millions of people in the service of profit. The famines had nothing to do with endogenous economic problems; rather, they were caused by India's incorporation into the emerging capitalist world system.[96]

Some may object: *Wasn't India poor before British rule?* According to Hickel, the opposite is true: "India, once self-sufficient and famous for its exports, was remade into 'the greatest captive market in world history'. The economic transformation was dramatic. Before the British arrived, India commanded 27 per cent of the world economy.... By the time they left, India's share had shrunk to just 3 per cent."[97]

Whatever injustices are hidden from us, God sees all, and he sees from beginning to end, across time, spanning all empires. In the overall biblical narrative, the empire—with Babel and Babylon as bookends—is continuously present, always oppressive and idolatrous, never celebrated. Preston Sprinkle says it well:

> Babylon. It's a city, a nation, and a concept. The ancient city lies in ruins in modern-day Iraq, but the concept of Babylon lives on. Throughout the Bible, Babylon symbolizes arrogant attempts to rule the world without God through power and oppression.[98]

In Revelation 17–19, John boldly exposes the sins of "Babylon," code word for the Roman Empire (just as Daniel, centuries before,

---

95 This definition is adapted from Said, *Culture and Imperialism*, 9.
96 Hickel, *The Divide*, 86–88.
97 Hickel, 90. Hickel references Davis, *Late Victorian Holocausts*, 298.
98 Sprinkle, *Exiles*, 38.

exposed the idolatries of Babylon by his faithful life).[99] John's Revelation describes symbolically how Christ will bring to a decisive end the dehumanizing idolatry and violence of the empire.[100]

Revelation is as magnificent in symbolism as in its exaltation of Jesus the Lamb of God. John writes as a kind of "double dissident."[101] On the one hand, John is protesting an unjust, oppressive empire; on the other hand, he is protesting about morally compromised churches. John is warning Christians across the empire: they were being influenced by the indulgent, immoral spirit of "Babylon" (Rev 2–3; 17–18). Many scholars recognize "Babylon" as John's code word for the Roman Empire of his day.[102] Tellingly, Peter uses the name Babylon as a code name for Rome (1 Pet 5:13).[103]

Klaus Wengst observes the text of Revelation has "not a single positive statement, nor even a neutral one; Rome and its actions are painted in the darkest of colours."[104] "The work is 'underground literature.'"[105]

---

99 The whole book of Daniel represents a call to God's people to resist the empire's idolatries while remaining faithful to the living God. "The idea that believers could give their allegiance to both God and Babylon doesn't exist in the book of Daniel." Sprinkle, *Exiles*, 47.

100 For nuanced critiques of empire see also Escobar, *The New Global Mission*, and Sanneh, *Translating the Message*. In Escobar, see chapter 2, "Mud and Glory," 28–53. Escobar describes "the ambiguity of the relationship between mission and empire"; he overviews imperial Christianity and its often-forced conversions accompanied by violent conquest—from Constantine and Charlemagne to the Iberian colonization of the Americas, as well as the British Empire. Escobar says British colonizers were sometimes at odds with British missionaries, referencing William Carey's experience in India. Escobar's chapter has a strong anti-imperial tone; he nevertheless recognizes that in "empire and mission" there are extensive dark episodes ("mud"), but also some bright exceptions ("glory").

Sanneh's work challenges the notion of "missionaries as colonial agents." He examines how widespread Bible translation in Africa contributed to the rise of a multitude of indigenous and national movements; these movements ultimately undercut the forces of empire. Biblical literacy in one's mother tongue, multiplied, gave rise to tribal and cultural dignity *en masse*. In turn, protests by African Christians against unjust imperial overlords eventually led to the formation of independent African nation-states. "The seeds of mission undercutting colonialism were sown with the translation enterprise. The idea of the church rooted in African soil, which is self-propagating, self-reliant, and furthermore, reared in the vernacular Scriptures, must diverge sharply from the idea of a local Christian society sustained by Western cultural transfusion" (p. 149).

101 Matchett and McKnight, *Revelation*, 19.

102 Wright and Bird, *The New Testament in Its World*, 809.

103 "The letter is written from Rome, for that is what 'Babulōn' [Babylon] means in 5:13." McKnight, *The Second Testament*, 261.

104 Wengst, *Pax Romana*, 118.

105 Wengst, 132.

As McKnight and Hatchett show, Revelation is not written so Christians can figure out the timing of future events. Revelation is a call for followers of Jesus—in whatever time or empire they live—to resist Babylon's seductions and violence, giving allegiance to Christ alone.[106] Revelation calls Christians to resist an empire mindset. I like the probing question of N. T. Wright and Michael Bird: "How do we build for the kingdom in the face of menacing empires while resisting the inevitable seduction to create an empire of our own?"[107]

What about the Roman Centurions Who Believed?

Some may contend that the Bible has texts and stories that *indirectly* endorse Roman imperial power. For example, in Acts 10, Peter visits the home of Cornelius, a centurion of "the Italian Cohort"; remarkably, Cornelius and his entire household believe in Christ (Acts 10). Consider also Matthew, Mark, and Luke; each writer has the story of Jesus both curing a Roman Centurion's daughter and commending his faith.[108] Do these stories either endorse or critique Roman imperial oppression or colonialism? Vaughn helpfully explains: "Notably, Jesus does not rebuke the centurion for his role within the Roman Empire but commends his faith. He even states that it surpasses that found in Israel." Vaughn continues:

> This interaction does not endorse colonialism. Instead, this account underscores Jesus's recognition of the centurion's humanity and faith. Christ's power to [form] Christian identity transcends sociopolitical boundaries. It illustrates the principle that God's grace and mercy extend even to those within oppressive systems, calling them toward a higher standard of love and service.[109]

So, although the New Testament records both Jesus and Peter each engaging with a Roman centurion, this obviously should not be viewed as sanctioning imperial power and violence. Rather, Jesus and Peter are examples to us of seeing the glory and faith-capacity of all persons—in this case the socially-*other* Roman centurions, whose position came with great power and status. These examples serve the biblical vision of peace,

---

106 See chapter 22, "A Manifesto for Dissident Disciples," in Matchett and McKnight, *Revelation*.

107 Wright and Bird, *Jesus and the Powers*, 9.

108 Matt 8:5–13; Mark 1:40–44; Luke 4:38–41. These Gospel writers likewise include the story of Jesus addressing the issue about paying taxes to Rome: "Render to Caesar the things that are Caesar's" (Matt 22:15–22; Mark 12:13–27; Luke 20:20–38). See also, e.g., McKnight and Modica, eds., *Jesus Is Lord, Caesar Is Not*.

109 Vaughn, "Jesus Loved Colonialists. Do We?"

for one of the building blocks for peace between persons and peoples is the practice of recognizing the Original Glory of every human being.

BEING HUMAN: Lusting for Power

We are grappling with the question: To what extent should the church be "counter-empire or partners in empire"? Donaldson imagines whether Christianity could have had a different relationship to empire than the *partners-in-empire* model that began with Constantine. He considers the Jews' enduring presence as a minority people in multiple empires:

> The Assyrians, the Babylonians, the Persians, the Greeks, the Romans—they [the Jews] had experienced them all, and through it all, they had learned to maintain their separate identity even as they adapted to changing circumstances.[110]

Donaldson is referring not to a Jewish state, but rather the Jewish diaspora, that "they did not envision themselves as occupying the center (at least in this age) but were content with a diaspora existence. While they were prepared to seek the welfare of the city (cf. Jer 29:7), they did not aspire (as it were) to obtain the keys to city hall."[111]

We lament this contradiction: Indifferent to the actual ways of Jesus and the gospel of peace—the name of Christ has been repeatedly and wrongly co-opted by persons and groups calling themselves Christian— on behalf of illicit armed force, colonial conquest, private militias, state power, or other forms of violence.

The contradiction casts a long shadow over the church, the gospel, and our world. We believe this lament calls us to imagine: What could be? What should be?

> *There is a wolf who is ranting / All of the sheep, they are clapping*
> *Promising power and protection / Claiming the Christ who was killed*
> *Killed by a common consensus / Everyone screaming "Barabbas"*
> *Trading their God for a hero / Forfeiting Heaven for Rome*
>
> *Coming to you 'cause I'm angry / Coming to you 'cause I'm guilty*
> *Coming to you 'cause you promised / To leave the flock for the one ...*
>
> "Citizens" by Jon Guerra

---

110 Donaldson, *Gentile Christian Identity,* 480.
111 Donaldson, 480.

CHAPTER 10 SUMMARY

- Understanding the prevailing violence of the New Testament in its world helps us grasp and grapple with the countervailing peace of the gospel.
- *Pax Romana* represents false peace—through violence *imposed* on others; *Pax Christi* represents true peace—through violence *absorbed* and *subverted*—offering an end to the cycle of violence.
- No record exists of Christians arguing in defense of violence or killing prior to the 300s.
- In Ephesians 2:17, Jesus "preached peace" (literally gospeled peace); this echoes Isaiah's prophecy, "How beautiful upon the mountains are the feet of him who brings good news, who publishes peace" (Isa 52:7).
- Christ is our peace; Christ makes peace; Christ preaches peace (Eph 2:14–15, 17).

FOR FURTHER REFLECTION

- What does it look like for the church to be partners with a worldly empire?
- The sayings of Jesus relative to "the sword" are paradoxical. As Jesus is arrested, he says to Peter, "Put your sword back into its place. For all who take the sword will perish by the sword" (Matt 26:52; cf. John 18:10–11). But in Matthew 10:34 and Luke 22:36, Jesus seems okay with "a sword." What complexities does this suggest?
- Christ is our peace; Christ makes peace; Christ preaches peace (Eph 2:14–15, 17). Try making this personal; put it into your own words or tell a story that makes it "come alive."

Chapter 11

PERFECTION IN WEAKNESS: CONTRASTS IN POWER

I have a heart full of questions / Quieting all my suggestions
What is the meaning of Christian / In this American life?
I'm feeling awfully foolish / Spending my life on a message
I look around and I wonder / Ever if I heard it right

Coming to you 'cause I'm confused / Coming to you 'cause I feel used
Coming to weep while I'm waiting / Tell me you won't make me go.

–*"Citizens" by Jon Guerra*

For the sake of Christ, then, I am content with weaknesses, insults, hardships, persecutions, and calamities. For when I am weak, then I am strong.

—2 Corinthians 12:10

Blessed are you when others revile you and persecute you and utter all kinds of evil against you falsely on my account. Rejoice and be glad, for your reward is great in heaven, for so they persecuted the prophets who were before you. You are the salt of the earth, but if salt has lost its taste, how shall its saltiness be restored? It is no longer good for anything except to be thrown out and trampled under people's feet.

—Matthew 5:11–13

IN THIS CHAPTER

- *Pax Christiana* is a term representing the so-called "peace of Christianity" and its long "partnership with empire."
- History shows *Pax Christiana* has been—and often continues to be—complicit with violence, greed, and idolatry, contra *Pax Christi*.
- Many in the early church embodied Christ's simplicity and his gospel of peace, subverting worldly pursuits of power, wealth, and status. What about us?

Werner:

On January 6, 2021, a violent mob attacked the United States Capitol. The mob's intent was to overturn the 2020 presidential election. US senators and representatives narrowly escaped as rioters entered by force and vandalized the building for several hours. Many feared for their lives. Five people were killed. Of the many injured, 138 were police officers.

Many in the mob claimed to be Christian. I have collected numerous news articles describing the prominent presence of Christians in the crowd. How can it be—Americans confessing to be Christian supported this attack?

Matthew Taylor's *The Violent Take It by Force* meticulously documents how a loose but formidable network of charismatic Christians played a major role in fomenting the events of January 6th. That loose network is known as the New Apostolic Reformation or NAR. Taylor investigates more than fifty people of the NAR who were at the Capitol on January 6th. He also examines "the theological ideas that kindled the Capitol Riot."[1] Those ideas include engaging in "spiritual violence" based on Matthew 11:12.[2] Taylor soberly writes, "What had been subtext became text. What had been innuendo became a riot. The forcible discourse of spiritual violence tipped over into actual violence before our very eyes."[3] As this volume shows, Christians co-opting the name of Jesus on behalf of violence, conquest, or the pursuit of political power is nothing new.

In my view, the Capitol Riot was a form of tribal violence incited by Donald Trump to overturn the election. Despite all the evidence, he was defiant. He would not accept defeat. He would keep telling "the big lie."[4]

The morning of January 6th, I wept at my office. I wept for shame as the name of Christ was dishonored through group-based conflict on behalf of a man who refused to concede. The long American tradition of the peaceful transfer of power was nearly broken.

---

1 Taylor, *The Violent Take It by Force*, 2. Taylor identifies "more than fifty charismatic Christian leaders to Washington, DC, on January 6" (p. 3).

2 Matt 11:12 (cf. Luke 16:16) is widely recognized by Bible scholars as notoriously difficult to translate. "From the days of John the Baptist until now the kingdom of heaven has suffered violence, and the violent take it by force." Taylor includes social media posts from January 6 as examples showing that this verse was "one of the most repeated biblical citations" (11).

3 Taylor, *The Violent Take It by Force*, 14.

4 Remnick and Raskin, *The January 6th Report*, chapter 1, "The Big Lie," 374–481. While the official government account of January 6th is disputed, it remains indisputable that thousands of Christians responded to Trump's call to attend the rally which eventually led to the violence.

Kristin:

On January 6th, a friend came to find me at our church building in a panic. He asked if I saw what was happening at the Capitol. As we watched live streamed videos, he thought it was the beginning of a civil war. I wasn't so sure. But as I thought about the millions watching from around the world, I felt like I was witnessing the beginning of the end of the American empire, and certainly of American democracy as we knew it.

Later that day, I watched footage of a march leading up to the insurrection and heard the crowd sing "How Great Is Our God." I heard about the people who prayed after breaking in. I felt my stomach drop, and yet I wasn't surprised. All the controversy about "what really happened" notwithstanding, I saw that what happened aligned with what I had heard preached, discussed, and lauded by many evangelicals over the previous five years. I had always felt that if people took some of those ideas to their logical conclusions, something like January 6th could happen.

Since then, I've seen dozens of profiles, clips, and videos of people from the crowd on that day. I've read the alleged charges and some of the apparent confessions. I've seen those claiming that it was nonviolent, and those who expressed regret over not helping Capitol Police officers who were being attacked. As I revisit many of those testimonies today, in 2023, I'm moved for these people. I see human beings whose legitimate desire to be seen, heard, and known has been turned to illegitimate ends. I see people who have been exploited for a bad copy of the glory they were made for.

Today I also listened to the first rally for Trump's new campaign. I heard him praise the January 6th rioters and play a recording of imprisoned rioters singing in the "J6 Prison Choir." I think of the words of the song: "The splendor of the King, clothed in majesty—let all the earth rejoice ... how great is our God! And all will see how great, how great is our God." But what greatness, of what God, were those crowds extolling? What was it that the world saw on that day?

Was it the greatness of the Spirit of love, joy, peace, truth, and gentleness?

Or was it the greatness of America? Was it *their own* greatness they extolled?

Could these possibly be the same thing? To be truly *great*, to be truly *glorious*—this is the legitimate inheritance of every human being. But how easily we settle for lesser things!

Werner: **"Empire" and John's Revelation**

The Roman Empire also had visions of glory defined by figures like Augustus, "the Great One." The early church proclaimed *its kingdom* amid the *Pax Romana* and was often persecuted.

Although much more could be said, we have made a case for two things. First, the New Testament's political context is the violent but politically stable Empire of Rome. "Though not its dominant theme, violence provides a backdrop for much of the New Testament narrative."[5] Second, this violent context of the empire serves as a magnificent stage for Christ's nonviolence and peace. Christ absorbs and subverts the violence and shame of Roman crucifixion. Christ rises from death to life. Christ ascends to be enthroned at the right hand of God. Christ proclaims the gospel of peace (Eph 2:17).

That said, we must also acknowledge the Jesus of judgment in Revelation 19:11–16. The rider on a white horse is *the Christ*. From his mouth comes a sharp sword with which to strike down the nations. He rules with a rod of iron. He is making war against the injustice and abominations of Babylon. Jesus is the true King of kings, Emperor of emperors, Lord of lords.

In Revelation, Christ the Rider wages war in judgment. In contrast are the Gospels and Paul, revealing the nonviolent "Christ crucified," absorbing violence to bring an end to the cycle of violence. Are these visions opposed? Miroslav Volf offers valuable insights: Christ the crucified represents the theology of the cross, absorbing violence in selfless love. Christ the Rider represents the theology of judgment as he wages war against evil. Neither of these theologies "underwrite violence but offer important resources for living peacefully in a violent world."[6] Both theologies are necessary for the ultimate eradication of violence.

Volf offers an extensive analysis,[7] from which we are here only gleaning bits. For example, Volf asks about "those who suffer violence at the hand of the Rider? They are the people drunk with the blood of the innocent (Rev 17:6) who make war against the Lamb and those who adorned themselves with righteous deeds." God's justice is against those who refuse the selfless love of the Crucified One. Volf emphasizes that Revelation unveils God's judgment against the systemic evil, exploitation, and oppression of imperial Babylon (Rev 17–19).

---

5 Volf, *Exclusion and Embrace*, 285.

6 Volf, 270.

7 Volf; see especially chapter 7, "Violence and Peace."

Without such judgment, there can be no world of peace, of truth, and of justice: terror (the "beast" that devours) and propaganda (the "false prophet" that deceives) must be overcome, evil must be separated from good, and darkness from light. These are the causes of violence, and they must be removed, if a world of peace is to be established.[8]

Scripture lays out two different ways of being human, two different kingdoms and two different worlds, with two different visions of glory and of power. So what are the implications of the old and new humanity for power? Below, we begin to explore some possibilities for how to *rethink power* in light of the good news of peace and the biblical vision of glory as found in Jesus.

Kristin: ## Power Games and Glory

God's glory is *holy*. This means that it is radically distinct. It is not holy because it is the greatest power among powers. It's holy because it exists in a category all its own. There's no competition because God's glory can't even fit on the same playing field. It fills heaven, earth, and beyond so that the unceasing song of the seraphim is *holy, holy, holy*—heaven and earth are full of your glory! (Isa 6:6). His glory cannot be compared with anything that goes by the same name. "To whom will you liken me and make me equal, and compare me, that we may be alike" (Isa 46:5)?

Jesus said,

> You know that those who are considered rulers of the Gentiles lord it over them, and their great ones exercise authority over them. But it shall not be so among you. But whoever would be great among you must be your servant. (Mark 10:42–43)

Of these verses, David Fitch writes:

> There are two powers, worldly power and godly power, and whenever the two powers are blurred, and God's people take up worldly power in God's name, abuse and destruction are not far behind. Jesus's words now become all the more pronounced when He describes worldly power in terms of the way the Gentiles "lord it over them." But for Jesus, "it shall not be so among you." (Mark 10:43)[9]

To the desire for *power over*, Jesus simply says: "Not so among you." Is there a stronger critique of Christianity seeking worldly political dominion?

---

8 Volf, 291.

9 Fitch, *Reckoning with Power*, 55.

God's Power—A Paradox

From the perspective of the playing fields of the world, the power of God is a paradox. It looks like foolishness, weakness, or even cowardice. You simply don't become first by being last! And you can't become strong by being weak (2 Cor 12:10) or wise by being foolish. But in Jesus, we see that God's power has nothing to do with competition. As we pointed out in chapter 9, "Status Games," the Scriptures refute the idea that the world is based on competition. After all we've learned over the course of this project, the only conclusion I can come to is this: *self-proclaimed followers of Jesus make a deadly error when they follow the world in believing that God's good ends will be attained when the "right" people have power over the "wrong" people.* As Paul says,

> For the word of the cross is folly to those who are perishing, but to us who are being saved it is the power of God. For it is written,
>
> "I will destroy the wisdom of the wise, and the discernment of the discerning I will thwart."
>
> Where is the one who is wise? Where is the scribe? Where is the debater of this age? Has not God made foolish the wisdom of the world? For since, in the wisdom of God, the world did not know God through wisdom, it pleased God through the folly of what we preach to save those who believe. For Jews demand signs and Greeks seek wisdom, but we preach Christ crucified, a stumbling block to Jews and folly to Gentiles, but to those who are called, both Jews and Greeks, Christ the power of God and the wisdom of God. For the foolishness of God is wiser than men, and the weakness of God is stronger than men. (1 Cor 1:18–25)

But this does not absolve us from the use or possession of power. And it certainly does not give us an excuse for cowardice or inaction, when we find that good is in our hands to do. All of us have power, and all of us exercise power daily. We were born on the playing field. We must move within it, and our movements will impact the games. But that doesn't mean we need to play the games. And we never seek the same prize. So, what might this look like when it comes to power and its derivatives, status and money?

Power without Ownership

Power is defined by the types of relationships we have and how they function. Some are physically stronger in relation to others, and some are intellectually stronger. Some possess power through influence or respect. Power extends to relationships with nonhuman creatures as well, through control of resources. The way power is used will determine how it is maintained, lost, or furthered.

One way to put it is that *power is made within the framework of glory.* Our framework for glory defines our relationships, and our relationships define the power we understand ourselves to possess.

The biblical vision of glory—and by extension, of power—is founded on belonging, but not exclusion. It's about inheritance, but not ownership. It is about strength, but not competition. Belonging and power are defined first by relationship with the Giver of All and then by relationships with what he gives. This includes the gift of our own lives, our communities, and the "daily bread" which sustains us.

When God's glory is the standard, we can hold power without ownership. The true power which comes from God frees us from the need to hold power over others or take anything that God gave to them. We no longer need to compete in the world's power games.

St. Basil the Great offers a helpful framework in his discussion on wealth. While he speaks on the topic of money in particular, it can apply to all forms of power. Like most early Christians, Basil did not believe in hoarding wealth. He famously said, "The bread in your cupboard belongs to the hungry ... the money which you hoard up belongs to the poor."[10]

To many Christians today, this sounds radical and even seditious. But it wasn't radical at all up until the time of Basil (AD 330–379). It was only as the impacts of Constantinianism[11] began to take hold that this first became a contested idea, then finally a marginal one.

According to Duchatalez, "Basil simply swept aside such objections as 'To whom am I unjust when I keep what is mine?'" Basil replies,

> Tell me, which things are yours? Where did you get them from at the beginning of your life? It is like someone who has a seat in the theater, and who objects when others also take their places. He claims that he owns what is for the common use of all. So too with

---

10 Gilbert, "St. Basil on Stealing from the Poor."

11 By Constantinianism, we mean the merging of empire—its political power, military power, and wealth—with Christianity, which began under Emperor Constantine.

the rich. They claim in advance that which is common property and make themselves the owners of it. Moreover, if everyone acquires what they need and leave the excess over for the destitute, then there will be no rich and no poor. Did you not come naked out of your mother's womb? Are you not going to return naked to the earth? Where did you get your present possessions from? If you say "from fate," then that makes you an atheist who neither acknowledges your Creator nor gives thanks to your Benefactor. If you acknowledge that they came from God, then tell me the reason why He gave them to you. Is God unjust that He gives the things of life to people unequally? Why are you rich while another is poor?[12]

Within the American individualist narrative, we say that the reason for the inequality is "hard work." *Some work harder than others and therefore deserve more than others.* But this raises some questions: First, is this true? Have we earned a right to the earth's goods through some merit entirely of our own? Or are there any more complex, historical factors? Are we truly self-made people, or do we owe more than we realize to our community, history, and accidents of birth? Second, even if it is true, does anyone deserve to be deprived of life's essentials? And if the right to live is based on merit, then how can any of us say we have a right to it? On what merit did we cause ourselves to be born? The answer, of course, is none. We exist purely because the love of God willed for us to exist. Life itself is the gift of God. Third, *even if* we could say that we exist on our own merits, or that we deserve the world's goods because of them, doesn't the cross contradict this? Jesus gave us his very self and saw it as just to die even for those who could earn nothing. Can we say that the same God who fully revealed his glory and justice on the cross, has now determined that the church should function by another standard of justice in the here and now?

And what about those who are unable to work? What about the disabled, the elderly, or the mentally ill?

Is Wealth Earned?

Basil argues that the earth was given by God as the common property of all. If some have more while others lack, it is not because God ordained it this way. It can only be because of theft—the taking of what is not rightfully ours.[13]

---

12 Duchatelez, "The Social Doctrine of St. Basil the Great."

13 I want to acknowledge that this classical Christian view is also the traditional view of indigenous cultures around the world, including among native peoples in the United States.

Even if we inherited our wealth, if we have more while others suffer, it is only because our fathers took from others what God gave to them. In either case, the gift of God overrides everything for Basil. If it is not God's will that some starve while others have more than enough, then this is robbery—not only of human beings but of God himself. Basil goes on:

> Who is the plunderer? The one who takes that which belongs to all. ... The one who steals clothes off someone's back is called a thief. Why should we refer to the one who does not clothe the naked, while having the means to do so, as anything else? The bread that you have belongs to the hungry ... the money that you have buried belongs to the destitute. And so you commit injustice to so many when you could have helped them.[14]

St. John Chrysostom and others make similar arguments. At the same time, for both Basil and Chrysostom, God is working redemption even within the unjust distribution of wealth and power. They argue that each lot in life provides opportunity for greater glory than wealth can offer. Basil says that those who are born into wealth are meant *to steward it,* not by seeking to increase it, but by giving it away to those in need. In this way, they can find God's "true, resplendent kind [of status] that would conduct you into the kingdom of heaven. But," he adds, "what you love is simply to possess wealth, even if you derive no help from it."[15]

The Rich for the Poor, the Poor for the Rich

Stewardship for Basil was not about good budgeting. It was about giving our excess to those who have need and so fulfilling the law of Christ (Gal 6:2). And the poor—through patience in suffering and the willingness to help one another—also find a way to glory. As Chrysostom says, "The rich exist for the sake of the poor. And the poor exist for the deliverance of the rich."

John says that true love compels us to give the world's goods to those in need (1 John 3:17). If the greatest commandments to love God and love one's neighbor with all of one's might and all of one's power were truly followed, says Chrysostom,

---

14 Duchatelez, "The Social Doctrine of St. Basil the Great."
15 Duchow-Pressley, "St. Basil the Great's Sermon to the Rich."

there would be neither slave nor free, neither ruler nor ruled... . There would be no poverty, no unbounded wealth if there were love, but only the good parts that come from each. From the one we should reap its abundance, and from the other its freedom from care and should neither have to undergo the anxieties of riches nor the dread of poverty.

Chrysostom says, "the rule of the most perfect Christian life is seeking those things that are for the common advantage.... For nothing can so make a man an imitator of Christ as caring for his neighbor."[16] These arguments could be applied equally to all forms of power. God's gift of glory means we are all worthy to live by the earth's goods. But we fall short of true glory when we take those goods from others. To deny the glory of others—their inherent worthiness—is to deny our own and to deny our Maker's.

For the early church, God's gifts are for our daily bread—our true needs—not for excess of luxury. The pursuit of further wealth was seen as both unjust and dangerous for the soul. And yet, since we live in a world where some of us have vastly more than others, we are to find our path to glory through using our wealth in ways that affirm God's glory in ourselves, and others.

Power with Responsibility

We cannot simply say that all human life is precious—we must also use our resources accordingly. Only then will we live into the fullness of our own glory. As Basil points out, "Where your treasure is, there your heart will be also ... when you bury your treasure, you bury your heart."[17] This also means that *we cannot avoid power*. We are each born with power in our hands, whether we asked for it or not.

In *The Lord of the Rings* by J. R. R. Tolkien, Frodo the hobbit must bear the Ring of Power. In ages past, rings of power were created for elves, dwarves, and men, containing the glory and power of each race. But one Ring was made in secret by Sauron, who put enough of his own power into it to control the other rings. Only the elves were able to hide their rings from Sauron. And there was a reason for this. Ages before, the elves had succumbed to the seduction of Sauron in wars which culminated in elves committing genocide against other elves.

---

16 Jones, "St. John Chrysostom and the Problem of Wealth."
17 Duchow-Pressley, "St. Basil the Great's Sermon to the Rich."

They know by experience that the Ring cannot be used against its maker and cannot be used for good. They know that the only way for good to be preserved is for the Ring to be destroyed. But it can only be destroyed in the same fires where it was created. This forces Frodo to pass through many dangers to Mt. Doom in the heart of the enemy's land.

At one point in the film version by Peter Jackson, Frodo is overwhelmed by the power of the Ring and the weight of his task, so he offers it to Gandalf. Frodo doesn't know it, but Gandalf secretly holds one of the eleven rings. "Don't tempt me Frodo!" Gandalf replies. "I would use this Ring from a desire to do good. But through me, it would wield a power too great and terrible to imagine." A ring of power is a cross to carry and brings with it a deep loneliness. "To bear a ring of power is to be lonely," says Galadriel.

Hobbits are not gatherers of power and this is a virtue. But in the end, it is a hobbit who is tasked with the much harder task of carrying the Ring and refusing to give himself away by using it. It is his cross and he must never lay it down and never use it against another. We must all do the same. We must hold onto power, without thinking that we can or should own it.

The Problem of *Pax Christiana*

The church is called to carry the cross of Jesus. The cross, like the Ring, is an instrument of imperial power and terror. But when the weight of that power is borne to the end, instead of being used against others, it becomes the power, wisdom, and glory of God.

What if Frodo *had* given the Ring to Gandalf? What if they had tried to wed the power of the Ring with the power of good? Frodo's intention would be to escape a task that seemed too great. Gandalf's intention would be to gain power for the purpose of doing good. But this is not possible.

Likewise, the church can never surrender the weight of the cross with its weakness and suffering—nor take up the cross and use it against others, thinking to do good.

This begs the question—can *Pax Christi* ever reconcile itself to *Pax Romana*? Constantine attempted to do this by creating the *Pax Romana Christiana*. He asked for the church's power and promised worldly benefits in return. Many gave it to him eagerly. Eusebius allowed and encouraged him to take the cross and make it a sign of a war. Maybe the opportunity was too great to pass up. And the church did gain worldly power—but what did it give away? Is *Pax Christiana* the same as *Pax Christi*?

I believe there are many ways to give away our cross. There are many ways of abdicating our own responsibility, or of lending the cross's true power to someone else's agenda.

It can look like addiction or idleness, to escape the responsibility of discovering and using our gifts or to avoid facing our demons. It can look like sexual immorality, which buys and sells the sacred (Heb 12:16) and joins what should belong to God to idols (1 Cor 6:15–17). It can look like burying our talent out of fear (Matt 25:22–27).

It can look like refusing to address injustice or make peace, either because of indifference, or despair. It can look like passing to the other side like the Levite and the Pharisee in the good Samaritan story. It can be to prefer "order" over justice, and the absence of tension to the presence of true Peace. It is the lukewarm acceptance of "truth," more bewildering than outright rejection.[18]

BEING HUMAN: Power Seduces

There is the glory of Babel,[19] Babylon, and Rome; this glory brings a peace built around one language, one empire, and one central power, and overwhelming ownership—"they make a desert and call it peace."

The logic of Roman glory makes sense to us. It can feel "natural," even inevitable. How can we begin to imagine a different way when this one seems so strong, so unstoppable, so real? *But the other glory ... the other glory is different and strange.* Its King has no lasting city here; his people seek the city above. He has no military because his kingdom is not of this world, and so his servants do not fight (John 18:36). His people have no country, for the whole earth belongs to the meek. He has no palace, for his dwelling is among humankind, and his kingdom is within us (Luke 17:21). His power is perfected in weakness (2 Cor 12:9). His wisdom is made known not in conformity, but in the diversity of what he creates.

The old way of being human creates standards for glory and worth according to the "course of this world." It is a way that can seem right, but whose end is death (Prov 14:12).

---

18 King Jr., "Letter from a Birmingham Jail."

19 "The Tower of Babel episode ... shows that God isn't on the side of one kind of people— one nation, one empire, one ethnic group. He is for the nations. And he is particularly opposed to civilizations that glory in their efforts to make a name for themselves. Celebrating the greatness of one nation is a dangerous business, especially if the greatness of that nation was built on the backs of an oppressed—indeed, enslaved— people." Sprinkle, *Exiles,* 40.

The church is meant to be a display of the alternative peace of Christ (Eph 2:14-15, 17) and the wisdom of God (Eph 3:10). But too often, Christianity has ridden the coattails of imperial violence. It has not offered One New Humanity, but rather the same old, tired way of power, dominionism, and desert-like "peace." It has offered a form of godliness but denied its power, perhaps in favor of the world's (2 Tim 3:5).

> Not many of you were wise according to worldly standards, not many were powerful, not many were of noble birth. But God chose what is foolish in the world to shame the wise; God chose what is weak in the world to shame the strong; God chose what is low and despised in the world, even things that are not, to bring to nothing things that are, so that no human being might boast in the presence of God. And because of him you are in Christ Jesus, who became to us wisdom from God, righteousness and sanctification and redemption. (1 Cor 1:26–30)

BEING HUMAN: Foolish in Christ

You are *in Christ Jesus*. His new humanity makes no sense to the empire or to religion. And yet, God chose what is weak in the world to *shame* the strong by a glory far greater and more magnificent. He chose what is foolish in the world to *shame* the wise. He suffered the worst degradations of empire and religion, and the worst collusion of God's people with state power. He overcame them with the power of God—but that power didn't look anything like we were expecting.

God chooses those of us who are nothing in this world—those who are not wise, who are not of noble birth or money or power. He chooses not the scribe with his education nor the debater with lofty speech.

So why do we so often choose the "wise," the rich, the educated, and the violent? Why do we attempt to climb the very ladders Christ has descended? Why do we come with swords when true glory lay in a manger? Why are we enslaved to status games—within our places of work, within our homes, within our national politics? Why do we grasp and strive for glory, when the greatest of all is already so freely and richly given?

We have explored in this chapter the profound differences between *Pax Romana, Pax Christiana,* and *Pax Christi*. Just ahead is chapter 11: "The Homogenous Unit Principle: What Peace?" Perhaps you are well-acquainted with the HUP—a "principle" widely used in both local and global church ministry. Perhaps you're completely new to it. Either way, readers will find our discussion about the HUP in chapter 11 to be fairly extensive. We attempt to offer a few fresh insights, building on and integrating material from previous chapters.

CHAPTER 11 SUMMARY

- John's Revelation is not for Christians to figure out the date when Jesus returns.
- John wrote Revelation as a "double dissident." John is protesting: (1) an unjust, oppressive, idolatrous empire opposed to Christ's kingdom, and (2) churches and Christians who have compromised with the violence, greed, and idolatry of the empire.
- *Pax Romana* represents the "peace" of the empire with its violence, dominance, and idolatry. *Pax Christiana* represents the empire's "peace" with its violence, dominance, and idolatry wedded to Christian religion. *Pax Christi* represents Christ's peace subverting violence—halting the cycle of violence.
- Chrysostom said, "The rich exist for the sake of the poor. And the poor exist for the deliverance of the rich."
- The *Jesus-Christ-way* of being human makes no sense to the empire or to religion.

FOR FURTHER REFLECTION

- What's the difference between *Pax Romana*, *Pax Christiana*, and *Pax Christi*? (See Appendix 3.) Describe the differences in power—who, what, where, why?
- What is an example of a Christian group's desire for power turning foul?
- What values underlie Chrysostom's proverb, "The rich exist for the sake of the poor. And the poor exist for the deliverance of the rich."

Chapter 12

THE HOMOGENOUS UNIT PRINCIPLE: WHAT PEACE?

IN THIS CHAPTER

- Since the 1970s, the Homogenous Unit Principle (HUP) has been at the crux of two global movements—Church Growth and Unreached Peoples.
- We examine the HUP through the Law of Group Polarization and the Ethical Paradox of Group Loyalty (introduced in chapter 8).
- The HUP can be seen as theologizing or reinforcing social division and racial inequality—contrary to Christ's gospel of peace.
- We propose a missiology of every people group *recognized, relativized,* and *reconciled*.

Werner: ### The Homogenous Unit Principle: An Often-Hidden Influence

Since the mid-1970s, a single social observation has had an unusually far-reaching influence in evangelicalism. This observation became a principle which has helped fuel church growth in North America and beyond. It also fueled movements to "reach the unreached" throughout the world.

It's a simple observation: *people like to be with their own kind.* As the saying goes, "birds of a feather flock together." Missionary and missiologist Donald A. McGavran (1897–1990) gave it a name: the "homogeneous unit principle" (HUP).[1] He applied the "principle" to evangelism, church growth, and ministry to hidden (or unreached) peoples.[2]

Dr. McGavran's well-known statement is that people "like to become Christians without crossing racial, linguistic or class barriers." That is, the barriers to the acceptance of the gospel are often more sociological than

---

[1] McGavran used the word "homogeneous"; in this article we are mostly using the shorter word "homogenous" which has the same meaning.

[2] The phrase Homogenous Unit Principle (HUP) has an unwarranted connotation of moral goodness linked to the word "principle." Consider the phrase "Principle Centered Leadership" in which "Principle" refers to transcendent moral values. However, the HUP is based on a morally neutral observation, namely, that human beings have the tendency to want to be with people like themselves. That tendency *can* be morally good. But this tendency can likewise be ethically problematic, for when it is taken to extremes (as shown in ch. 8) the "principle" has been observed to be morally bad, ethically wrong—incompatible with the ways of Jesus.

theological; people reject the gospel not because they think it is false but because it strikes them as alien. They imagine that in order to become Christians they must renounce their own culture, lose their own identity, and betray their own people.[3]

One sociologist looking broadly at America's unhealthy divisions saw the Homogenous Unit Principle reflected in America's rise of megachurches. The HUP method

> worked so well that now these techniques for creating group cohesion through like-mindedness are employed in most churches. And the same power of building communities with "people like us" is used in subdivision development, advertising, college dormitories, volunteer groups, and political campaigns. It's the way we live today.[4]

McGavran grew up in India and saw few people convert to Christianity. But he also heard about movements in India in which many turned to follow Christ, including whole tribes.[5] For McGavran, this was a revelation that altered the trajectory of his life.

McGavran wanted conversion movements to succeed through homegrown evangelists. He argued that the gospel should be "contextualized in such a way that it communicates with them; [and] the church into which they are invited must itself belong to their culture sufficiently for them to feel at home in it."[6]

We (the authors) sympathize with McGavran's dictum that Christians of all cultures should be honored and should have indigenous leadership. Nelson Searcy, the founding pastor of a network of churches in New York City, says he owes a great deal to McGavran. In a biography of McGavran, Searcy writes in the foreword:

> Donald McGavran is the single most influential thinker on how we do ministry today. His life's work is the foundation of what you and I know about growing healthy, impactful churches.... If you have worked to grow a ministry and impact people for Jesus, you have been influenced by McGavran. Without his dedication to identifying

---

3 Lausanne Occasional Paper: "The Pasadena Consultation: Homogeneous Unit Principle."

4 Bishop, *The Big Sort*, 160.

5 McGavran was profoundly influenced by J. Wascom Pickett, a Methodist missionary who served 46 years in India. Pickett conducted a research study of ten mass movements to Christ. "Pickett's study sought to find out how effective mass movements really were at winning and maturing new Christian believers. The results of Pickett's study were published in Christian Mass Movement in India (1933)." Of this book, McGavran wrote in 1935, "Here is the most significant missionary book of the twentieth century." Later in his life, McGavran would say, "I lit my candle at Pickett's fire." See McIntosh, *Donald McGavran*, 88–90.

6 Lausanne: "The Pasadena Consultation: Homogeneous Unit Principle."

and overcoming the barriers that stand in the way of Christian conversion, you and I wouldn't be leading our churches the way we do.... Arguably, we wouldn't be reaching the world for Christ nearly as effectively as we are able to today.[7]

Rick Warren, founding pastor of Saddleback Community Church, also credits McGavran for the key strategy that propelled his church to become one of the largest in America.[8]

McGavran wanted to know: "Why do some churches grow rapidly while others don't grow at all?"[9] He set out to learn everything he could about overcoming obstacles to faith in Christ. Influenced much by missionary-missiologist Roland Allen,[10] McGavran discovered the huge contrast between "individual decision-making" and the faster, more movement-based "interdependent decision-making" in evangelism and church growth.

McGavran was hired in 1965 by Fuller Seminary to lead its School of World Mission (SWM).[11] McGavran's book *Understanding Church Growth*, published in 1970, was his *magnum opus*. The impact of this book in both church growth and world missions cannot be overstated, and yet the HUP was controversial from the beginning.

Since then, conferences have been held[12] and an abundance of articles[13] and books—both advocating[14] and critiquing[15]—have been

---

7 From Nelson Searcy's foreword in McIntosh, *Donald A. McGavran*, 7.

8 Rick Warren first learned of McGavran's ideas in an article in *HIS* magazine approximately subtitled, "Why Is This Man Dangerous?" Warren credits McGavran for the principles that helped grow Saddleback Community Church. See Warren, *Purpose Driven Church*, 29–30.

9 McIntosh, *McGavran*, 9.

10 Allen, *Missionary Methods: St Paul's or Ours?*; also, *The Spontaneous Expansion of the Church*.

11 Fuller Seminary's School of World Mission was the largest missions training institution in the world. The school was formed in 1965 when Dr. Donald McGavran brought his Institute for Church Growth to Fuller Seminary. The school later changed its name to the School of Intercultural Studies. The School of Intercultural Studies and the School of Theology at Fuller Seminary merged to form the School of Mission and Theology (SMT) on July 1, 2021.

12 The first conference addressing the HUP was May 31–June 2, 1977. It was hosted by Fuller Seminary in Pasadena, CA. See Lausanne: "The Pasadena Consultation: Homogeneous Unit Principle."

13 At the website of *International Journal of Frontier Missiology*, the search term "homogenous unit" yielded 107 results. At the website for *Missiology: An International Review* (Sage Journals) the term yielded 1,762 results.

14 Advocating for the Homogenous Unit Principle: McGavran, *Understanding Church Growth*; Wagner, *Our Kind of People*; Warren, *Purpose Driven Church*. The whole corpus of books by McGavran and many by Wagner can be understood as advocating for the HUP.

15 Critiquing and raising questions about the Homogenous Unit Principle: Conn, ed., *Theological Perspectives on Church Growth*; Costas, *The Church and Its Mission*; Shenk, ed., *The Challenge of Church Growth*. Another important book is Shenk, ed., *Exploring Church Growth*.

written.¹⁶ Relative to the "importance of the HUP to the church growth movement," missiologist Scott Moreau stated in 2002 that the HUP "has been an area that has been loudly criticized and just as loudly defended for over twenty years."¹⁷

The HUP helped shape two global movements in particular—Church Growth and Unreached Peoples, as illustrated below.

Three Key Ideas

With figure 12.1, we illustrate three key ideas.

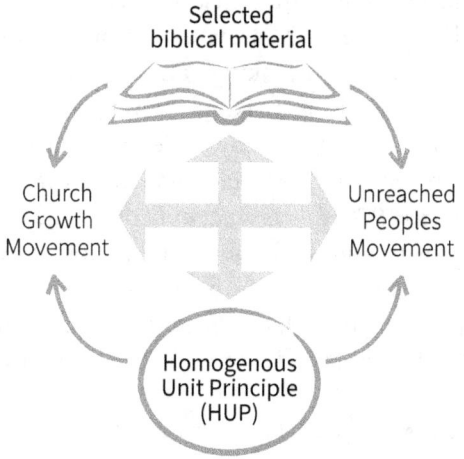

Figure 12.1: The Homogenous Unit Principle—large factor in global Christianity's growth since the 1970s

First, note the Bible graphic at the top of the diagram and the words "Homogenous Unit Principle (HUP)" at bottom; a vertical double-arrow connects them. This illustrates that the Bible and the HUP are "in conversation." Biblical material in dialog with the HUP—this is where the discussion/debate among practitioners and scholars occurs.

Second, note the words "Selected biblical material." HUP proponents select some Scriptures to support their view and give little or no attention to others. In this book, we ourselves use "selected biblical material" by focusing on the significance of Ephesians 2. All authors and preachers emphasize some texts over others.

Indeed, the HUP is based on "selected biblical material." On the one hand, McGavran says, "Nothing in the Bible, for instance, requires

---

16 An accessible and balanced review of the HUP is the series by Williams, "Reflections on the Homogenous Unit Principle."

17 Moreau, "The Homogenous Unit Principle."

that in becoming a Christian a believer must cross linguistic, racial, and class barriers,"[18] and he cites various examples from Scripture. Elsewhere he wrote, "The theologian finds the homogeneous unit principle firmly embedded in the Bible."[19] On the other hand, a variety of significant leaders point to additional "selected biblical material" and conflicting interpretations that dispute the biblical validity of the HUP.[20] For example, Ecuadorian theologian-missiologist René Padilla (1932–2021) wrote,

> Throughout the entire New Testament the oneness of the people of God as a oneness that transcends all outward distinctions is taken for granted. The thought is that with the coming of Jesus Christ, all the barriers that divide humankind have been broken down and a new humanity is now taking shape in and through the church.[21]

Like McGavran, Padilla cites numerous biblical texts.

Third, and finally, the diagram illustrates that the HUP has helped fuel both the Church Growth Movement and the Unreached People Group movement.

The Unreached Peoples Movement: A Very Brief History

The Unreached Peoples Movement was catalyzed in 1974 in Lausanne, Switzerland, at the International Congress on World Evangelization (ICOWE).[22] In a plenary presentation, missiologist Ralph D. Winter focused on "hidden peoples" (later named "unreached peoples"). He defined hidden peoples as: "Those cultural and linguistic sub-groups, urban or rural, for whom there is as yet no indigenous community of believing Christians able to evangelize their own people."[23] What was the *most* influential principle at the crux of Winter's presentation? "Most important among these ... was the homogeneous unit principle, which emphasized the human tendency to prefer association with others of similar affinities."[24]

---

18 McGavran, *Understanding Church Growth*, Kindle loc 2109–10.
19 McGavran, "The Homogeneous Unit in Mission Theory."
20 See especially Shenk, ed., *Exploring Church Growth*. The compendium includes articles by renowned missiologists David Bosch and René Padilla. For a view promoting multiethnic church planting see Hyatt, "From Homogeneous to a Heterogeneous Unit Principle."
21 Padilla, "The Unity of the Church, and the Homogenous Unit Principle," in Shenck, ed., *Exploring*.
22 The historical roots of the Unreached People Group movement in missiology are summarized in Datema and Bartlotti: "The People Group Approach."
23 Datema and Bartlotti, "The People Group Approach." The authors cite Ralph D. Winter, "Frontier Mission Perspectives," in Starling, ed., *Seeds of Promise*, 61.
24 Datema and Bartlotti, "The People Group Approach," 8.

For his Lausanne '74 presentation, Winter and his team gathered both biblical and statistical data in their research. From the Bible, they argued that the diversity of peoples had to do with ethnic and language groups, not geopolitical countries. They saw homogeneous units in the Bible identified as kinship groups, tribes, tongues, peoples, and nations (Gen 12:3; Matt 28:18–20; Rev 5:9; 7:9). The cultural and statistical data was also linked to the HUP. They wanted to know: *How many hidden peoples are there? How many distinct tribes, languages, or peoples had no Christian presence among them?* Based on collaborative research between three agencies, a printed directory was distributed at the 1974 conference. It listed 413 "hidden peoples."[25] For most conference participants, "it was surely the first time they had ever seen a list of unreached peoples. It defined a people group as a homogeneous unit."[26]

For the people gathered at Lausanne '74, Winter's conclusions were ground-shaking. For some years, many had considered "the mission" significantly complete. Nearly every geopolitical nation had churches and Christian converts. But the data about "hidden peoples" without a gospel witness showed massive gaps. The task of making Christ known among all peoples was not nearly complete. Not even close.

This people group concept has had staying power in the evangelical world. "Still today, the people group remains the unit of analysis most people think of when contemplating world evangelization."[27] Since 1974, the practice of defining, classifying, and numbering the peoples has expanded, to say the least. One of the most respected lists is compiled by Joshua Project, which offers these statistics:[28]

People Groups by Country	17,267	Population	8.08 Billion
Unreached Groups	7,188	Popl in Unreached	3.43 Billion
% Unreached Groups	41.6%	% Popl in Unreached	42.4%

Figure 12.2: General statistics about Unreached People Groups, January 2025

The increase in the number of identified and unreached people groups is dizzying. Scribner's helpful historical overview about "people group lists" helps explain this increase.[29] The Joshua Project website

---

25 Datema and Bartlotti, 9.
26 Datema and Bartlotti, 9.
27 Datema and Bartlotti, 11.
28 Joshua Project, "Seeking God's Glory Among All Peoples."
29 Scribner, "The Making of Lists."

gives special emphasis to "Frontier People Groups" (FPGs). The data is sobering. Comprising over two billion people, these unreached peoples have "virtually no followers of Jesus ... no known movements to Jesus ... still needing pioneer cross-cultural workers." One-fourth of the world lives in these FPGs and has almost no chance of hearing about Jesus from someone in their own people group. About *half* the population of all FPGs live in just 37 groups, each over ten million in population.[30]

Biblical Basis for People Groups

Steve Hawthorne shows how humanity's variety of peoples is woven into the biblical narrative.

- The diversity of the peoples comes from God the Creator (Gen 10–11).
- Abraham's family is called to bless every family or kinship group on earth (Gen 12:1–3).
- God calls into existence "one people of many tribes" (Gen 48:4)—template for a future people.
- God is forming "one people of many peoples" (the church)—and this is affirmed by the apostles (Acts 15).
- The salvation of "every tribe (*phule*), language (*glossa*), people (*laos*), and nation (*ethnos*) have been purchased 'for God' to become priests, or worship-servants, 'to our God' (Rev 5:9–10)."
- Jesus, in his earthly ministry, confirms the promise made by Isaiah that God's temple was created for the worship of all nations (Mark 11:15–18; Isa 56:3–8).
- The glory of the peoples is embodied in their worship: "The blood of the Lamb was shed to purchase men, women and children so that He would receive whole-life, culturally-enriched worship from every people" (Rev 21:24–26).[31]

We agree with Hawthorne that people groups are not mere social constructs. Peoples are grouped in various ways throughout Scripture and are part of God's *telos* or ultimate purpose.[32]

---

30 Joshua Project, "Frontier Unreached Peoples."
31 Hawthorne, "A Biblical Understanding of People Groups."
32 For various viewpoints about people group theory, see *Mission Frontiers* magazine, Sept/Oct 2024. https://www.missionfrontiers.org/issue/archive/people-group-theory, accessed Sept 6, 2024.

All the Peoples Recognized

McGavran's 1972 paper, "The Homogeneous Unit in Mission Theory," critiques Western mission imperialism while recognizing the value of each homogenous unit, tribe, or social caste:

> The old European imperialist dream of smashing tribal consciousness in Africa and caste consciousness in India is clearly not going to come true in this generation, and probably not in the next either. Both for reasons of justice, and to preserve the richness of the many patterns, the Church should seek not to erase variations in indigenous patterns but to enshrine them.[33]

McGavran wants Christian church-planting efforts to recognize and preserve the distinct cultural treasures of the world's many thousands of tribes. He is against churches that follow "the conglomerate mongrel"[34] model in which minority persons and peoples are swallowed into a dominant, larger community. McGavran also addresses the biblical unity of the church across social boundaries, as described in Pauline texts (Gal 3:28; Eph 2:11–3:19). He acknowledges that the text "strongly supports the conviction that the Church is one new race."

> [But] in what sense do the races and tongues and cultural units "become one" in Christ? My thesis is that they become one in a sense which still allows for considerable ethnic diversity. I maintain that as the Church spreads to thousands of homogeneous units, each unit becomes part of the great Unity while maintaining considerable cultural and ethnic diversity.[35]

This principle of ministering to the uniqueness of a people group is vividly emphasized by Bud Houston:

> The Zaza are an ethnolinguistic community within the larger Kurdish peoples of Turkey. They were mostly unrecognized for decades due to Turkey's assimilationist policies. Their Zazaki language and culture were suppressed. However, as the Zaza have asserted their unique identity in recent years, the Global Church has taken notice. Missionaries were assigned. Scripture translation efforts began. Prayer movements were launched. By God's grace, Zaza communities have responded to the gospel with new believers baptized and churches

---

33 McGavran, "The Homogeneous Unit in Mission Theory," 412.
34 McGavran, 412.
35 McGavran, 412–13.

formed. The once-overlooked Zaza are now recognized as a distinct people for whom Christ died and is calling into His Kingdom.[36]

Our point is simple: Ministry that preserves, treasures, and builds on people-group uniqueness is in keeping with Scripture. All the peoples are recognized in the biblical narrative. The biblical ideal is no people group excluded from God's blessing, none domineering over others, every people *honored*.

Ephesians 2 and People Groups

"And he came and preached peace to you who were far off and peace to those who were near" (Eph 2:17). Let's consider whether the concept of those "far off" rhymes with the notion of unreached people groups—first, in Ephesians 2:11–22, and second, how this text relates to the overall biblical narrative.

In Ephesians 2:11, Paul is plainly addressing gentiles (Gk. *ethnē*, root word, *ethnos*); in this context the word refers not to particular ethnic groups but to the monolithic outsider status of gentiles. As we have already described in chapters 6 and 7, Paul is making status distinctions between two groups of people—Jews and non-Jews (or, the people of God and the not-yet people of God). "The circumcision" represents the insider-Jews and "the uncircumcision" represents the outsider-gentiles. In the context of Ephesians 2 and 3,[37] "gentiles" does not refer to particular people groups.

Figure 12.3 (on the following page) is an attempt to clarify how the word "gentiles" is used in the New Testament. I refer to circle "G" for "gentiles" (left) as this monolithic group of gentiles/non-Jews. We can think of "G" as the *container* called gentiles.

Circle "G-1" (right) refers to another way *ethnos* is used in the Bible—to represent the *particularity* of gentiles as many peoples and ethnic groups. Indeed, it is hard to deny the particularity of people groups in the overarching story of the Bible.[38] Following through on the container analogy, if "G" is the *container*, "G-1" refers to *what's in the container*. Here's the thing to remember: sometimes the Bible uses the same word for the container and for what's in the container.

---

36 Mischke and Houston, "Recognized, Relativized, Reconciled," 29.

37 The same root word, *ethnos*, is translated "Gentiles" in Eph 3:1, 6, 8.

38 In response to the article by Lee and Park, "Beyond People Group Thinking," see Datema, "The Universal Particularism of *panta ta ethne*," and Hawthorne, "A Biblical Understanding of People Groups." Datema and Hawthorne defend the biblical basis for the particularism of peoples and hence the strategy of unreached people groups (UPGs) in missiology.

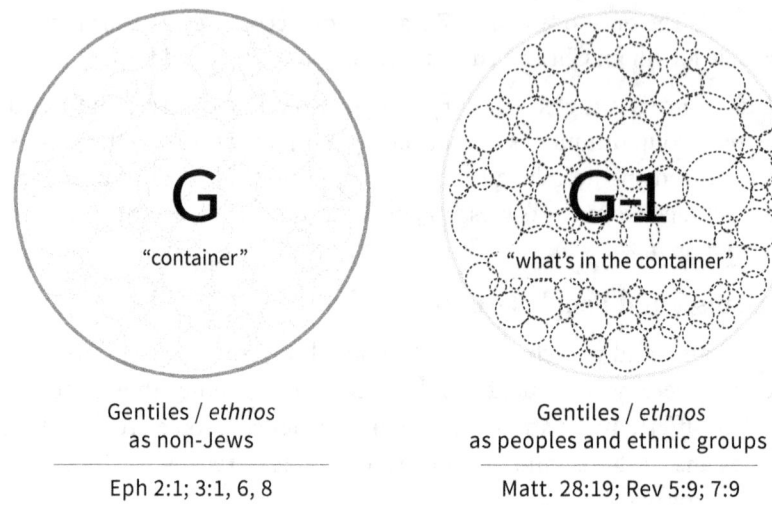

Figure 12.3: Two uses of "gentiles" / *ethnos* in the New Testament

The root word *ethnos* is translated "nations" in Matthew 28:19—"make disciples of all nations."[39] And in Revelation 5:9 and 7:9, the wording—every tribe, language, people, and "nation" (root word *ethnos*)—unmistakably portrays the particularity of people groups. This fulfills God's ancient promise to Abraham that he would bless all the families of the earth (Gen 12:3). We believe this all-peoples worship is at the crux of God's purpose for human history.

Now, consider again Ephesians 2:17: "And he [Jesus] came and preached peace to you who were far off and peace to those who were near." Recall from chapter 10 that this phrase, "peace to you who were far off and peace to you who were near," fulfills the promises of Isaiah 52:7 and 55:19. Certainly, "you who are far off" refers to the gentiles. But does this refer to the monolithic group of gentiles/non-Jews ("G")? Or does it refer to "G-1"—the particularity of many peoples and nations?

We propose that the answer is not either-or but both-and. In the immediate context of Ephesians 2 and 3, "you who are far off" refers to the gentiles as the monolithic group of non-Jews. But in the context of the overall biblical narrative, "you who were far off" also refers to the particularity of the peoples.

We affirm the biblical significance of the particular peoples who are "far off." Regardless of their distance from God, they are all inside God's

---

[39] Datema offers five reasons why *panta to ethne* in Matt 28:19 refers to particular peoples. "If Matthew 28:19 serves as a mission statement, a precise directive telling the disciples what it is they should do, Revelation 5:9 and 7:9 are more of a vision statement." Datema, "The Universal Particularism of *panta ta ethne*," 9.

ultimate purpose or *telos*. Participating with Christ includes gospeling peace to these "far off" peoples. The global church pursues reaching all the *ethne*/gentiles—all the peoples. This is our destiny—being unified in God's one new humanity in Christ while retaining all the magnificent diversity of the peoples. This mysterious beauty displays God's manifold wisdom "to the rulers and authorities in the heavenly places" (Eph 3:8–10).

"You Who Are Far Off"—Who Are They?

Researchers identify those groups most distant from Jesus as Frontier People Groups (FPG)—"an Unreached People Group (UPG) with virtually no followers of Jesus, and no known movements to Jesus, still needing pioneer cross-cultural workers."[40] One prayer guide prioritizes thirty-one FPGs of at least "10 million people with virtually no progress of the gospel. They have no known indigenous movements to Jesus and less than or equal to 0.1% Christian of any kind living among them."[41]

Immense challenges remain for the church to fulfill this mission. But since 1974, the growth in the number of previously unreached peoples who now have movements in them has been astounding. Researcher R. W. Lewis and her colleagues have plotted this growth, naming it "50 Unbelievable Years."[42] Briefly:

- In 1974, 60 percent of the world's four billion people were in Frontier People Groups. For every one believer, there were twelve people in FPGs.

- In 2024, 25 percent of the world's eight billion people are in Frontier People Groups—the percentage of people among the unreached has shrunk dramatically. For every one believer, there were two people in FPGs.

- In just fifty years, followers of Jesus have increased by 800 million while the population of FPGs has decreased by 400 million.

This is not just about more individuals following Jesus. It is also about people group movements to Christ as the Holy Spirit moves through the obedience of God's people.[43] As the global church gives witness near and far to the transforming life of Jesus—"from everywhere to everyone"— the momentum continues toward every people recognized, every people blessed and honored.

---

40 Joshua Project, "Frontier Unreached Peoples."
41 See Go31.org: "The Thirty-One Largest Frontier People Groups."
42 Lewis and Butler, "The Great Progress of the Gospel," 2–3.
43 See Farah, *Motus Dei*.

All the Peoples Relativized

In the biblical grand narrative, all the people groups are recognized—and also *relativized*. Psalm 96 gets us started down the road of all the peoples relativized.[44]

> ³ Declare his glory among the nations,
> his marvelous works among all the peoples!
>
> ⁴ For great is the Lord, and greatly to be praised;
> he is to be feared above all gods.
>
> ⁵ For all the gods of the peoples are worthless idols,
> but the Lord made the heavens.... .
>
> ¹⁰ Say among the nations, "The Lord reigns!
> Yes, the world is established; it shall never be moved;
> he will judge the peoples with equity."
>
> ¹¹ Let the heavens be glad, and let the earth rejoice;
> let the sea roar, and all that fills it;
>
> ¹² let the field exult, and everything in it!
> Then shall all the trees of the forest sing for joy
>
> ¹³ before the Lord, for he comes,
> for he comes to judge the earth.
>
> ¹⁴ He will judge the world in righteousness,
> and the peoples in his faithfulness.

"For all the gods of the peoples are worthless idols" (v. 5). "He will judge the peoples with equity" (v. 10). "He will judge … the peoples in his faithfulness" (v. 14). In Psalm 96, God's glory and righteous judgment relativize all peoples. God is drawing the nations to worship him,[45] and in so doing, God exposes their sin and judges all people group idolatry.

It's *because of sin* that people groups are under God's judgment. Isn't it also because of sin that massive numbers of peoples often migrate to distant lands? Natural and manmade disasters compel people to flee destitution, war, violence, and oppression in their homelands. Fleeing

---

44 The concept of every people relativized was first developed in Mischke and Houston, "Recognized, Relativized, Reconciled: Nuancing the People Groups Conversation." Excerpts used by permission.

45 Psalm 96 is the first key text in Hawthorne's influential article, "The Story of His Glory" (and basis for Lesson 2 in the course, *Perspectives on the World Christian Movement*). The key principle: God reveals glory to all nations in order to receive glory from all peoples through worship.

The Homogenous Unit Principle: What Peace? 195

destitution in Moab, Ruth the Moabite follows Naomi to join God's people in another land (Ruth 1–4). Fleeing persecution, the church comprised of Jewish believers is scattered to other lands; some interact with gentile peoples of whom many turn to the Lord (Acts 11:18–21). Consider this contemporary example.

> Dag, a new Kurdish believer from an Iraqi village, gathered with believers in Nashville, his eyes bright with hope for true equality between all peoples. His journey has been fraught. He was expelled from religious instruction for questioning teachings that divided humanity into classes. Later, he was rejected for baptism by ancient Christian groups wary of Muslim converts. But Dag was driven by a revelation he found in the Bible: God shows no partiality between people. "Love your enemies and pray for those who persecute you, so that you may be children of your Father in heaven," one verse reads. Dag ached for this reality in his homeland, where deep divisions run along ethnic and religious lines.
>
> Undeterred, Dag traveled far to find a church to baptize and welcome him as an equal brother in Christ. On that journey, he had a dream warning of tragedy, which he heeded to save his friends' lives. This sign convinced him that God was blessing his path. That day, Dag was baptized into the family of believers bound not by ethnicity but by faith in Jesus.[46]

We live in a world on the move—of globalization, urbanization, and migration.[47] We adapt to new cultures, history-changing events, and ever-fresh technologies. Plus, God intervenes. We see this in our own families, in the Bible, in early Christianity, and around the world. Virtually all people group identities are on a spectrum between "fixed and fluid."[48]

Can we soberly acknowledge that all-peoples-under-God's-judgment refers not merely to the unreached or other peoples, but to the people groups to which we ourselves belong? It is healthy for Christians in every land to examine their own idolatries and inhumanities. This may be especially fitting for American Christians.[49] Here's why: Could it be that in

---

46 Mischke and Houston, "Recognized, Relativized, Reconciled," 30.
47 Nguyen, "Globalization, Urbanization, Migration," 33–35.
48 Buell, *Why This New Race*.
49 What idolatries might we identify as part of America? One is abortion. "Since the Supreme Court invented a constitutional right to abortion in Roe v. Wade in 1973, abortion has killed more than sixty-five million of our youngest neighbors, a staggering loss" (Anderson and DeSanctis, *Tearing Us Apart*, 3). America's other idols might be sex

the long shadow America casts across the global church—of theological training, financial support, and cultural influence—some of our American idolatries have also been exported?[50]

A People Group Relativized in the Life of Paul

Paul relativizes group identity as he describes himself in Philippians 3. After listing his various sources of ascribed and achieved honors, including his tribal and national-religious identity (v. 5–6), Paul stuns his audience:

> But whatever gain I had, I counted as loss for the sake of Christ. Indeed, I count everything as loss because of the surpassing worth of knowing Christ Jesus my Lord. For his sake I have suffered the loss of all things and count them as rubbish, in order that I may gain Christ. (Phil 3:5–6)[51]

For Paul, knowing and serving "the Christ" is so magnificent that—by comparison—race, tribe, nationality, education, and other measures of social worth are irrelevant. They are "as rubbish." Were I to apply this to myself ... Being white, middle-class American—having German ancestry—having an honorary degree ... all are "rubbish" compared to knowing Christ.

This is why tribal, national, or people group identity can be brought into balance. God recognizes all peoples, thus honoring them; God judges all people and nations, thus relativizing them. We observe this dynamic in Revelation; chapters 5 and 7 point to every people relativized. How? By the overwhelming, awe-inspiring, beauty and glory of Christ.

---

trafficking, pornography, racism, homelessness, poverty, nationalism, or gun violence. More subtle forms of idolatry may be consumerism, individualism, greed, fitness, or entertainment. If idolatry is understood through the lens of oppression, recognizing the idol-and-its-oppression may depend on one's point of view or social location. For the multitudes in chronic need or homelessness, is *poverty itself* an American idolatry? (Desmond, *Poverty, by America*). A native American might say America's primary idolatry is genocidal conquest (Charles and Rah, *Unsettling Truths*); an African-American might say it's racial hatred and white supremacy (Cone, *The Cross and the Lynching Tree*).

50 For example, could it be America's idolatry of consumerism morphed into the "Prosperity Gospel?" Also called the "health and wealth gospel," it is widely embraced in the global church. See Hinn, "The Prosperity Gospel: A Global Epidemic."

51 "Paul's passion for reaching all peoples hinges on his own people group relativized. We propose a dual truth: The surpassing worth of knowing Christ relativizes Paul's relationship with his own people group, and this is exemplary for all believers; simultaneously, Paul's passion for Christ being worshiped among all people groups (Rom 15:18–21) is also exemplary. This continues to inspire believers globally toward reaching all the peoples. Christ is all in all." See Mischke and Houston, "Recognized, Relativized, Reconciled."

People Groups Relativized by the Glory of Christ

I recall an insight from a presentation by Steve Hawthorne about the epic shout of Revelation 7:10. The startling emphasis is not, *We got saved!* but, *Salvation belongs to our God ... and to the Lamb!* This insight rhymes with the concept of every people relativized. Here's how:

Consider Revelation 5 and 7. Observe first—all the peoples recognized: "you ransomed people for God from every tribe and tongue and people and nation" (5:9); "and behold, a great multitude, that no one could number, from every nation, from all tribes and peoples, and languages, standing before the throne and before the Lamb" (7:9). What a picture of all the various human groups recognized as they worship Jesus the Lamb of God.

However, with a careful reading of Revelation 5 and 7, we also see the nations *relativized*. In Revelation 5:1-4, John envisions a strong angel asking with a loud voice, "Who is worthy to open the seals and to break its seals?" John weeps when "no one in heaven or on earth or under the earth [is] able to open the scroll." But "one of the elders says to John, 'Weep no more: behold, the Lion of the tribe of Judah, the Root of David, has conquered, so that he can open the scroll and the seven seals.'"

John further unveils "the four living creatures and the twenty-four elders fell down before the Lamb ... and they sang a new song, saying, 'Worthy are you to take the scroll and to open its seals, for you were slain, and by your blood you ransomed [people] for God from every tribe and language and people and nation'" (Rev 5:8-9). The focus is on the Lamb! Worthy is the Lamb!

Again, in Revelation 5:11-12, observe the overwhelming emphasis is on the worthiness of the Lamb. Here the particular peoples are not mentioned. What is unveiled is "the voice of many angels, numbering myriads of myriads and thousands of thousands, saying with a loud voice, 'Worthy is the Lamb who was slain, to receive power and wealth and wisdom and might and honor and glory and blessing!'"

And John isn't done. In verse 13, John "heard every creature in heaven and on earth and under the earth and in the sea, and all that is in them, saying, "To him who sits on the throne and to the Lamb be blessing and honor and glory and might forever and ever!'" Again, no mention of the peoples. Rather, every creature gives rapt attention and adoration—honor and glory to the Lamb.[52]

---

52 Rev 5 may be considered a template for Rev 7:9-17. The peoples are recognized in Rev 7:9, but the chapter's focus is on the glory and honor of the Lamb of God.

King Jesus, Lamb of God, in his love, humility, majesty, glory, and wisdom so captivates us that our longing for glory is more than satiated in our worship. Our hunger for belonging as a collective identity is fully satisfied as we are a "kingdom of priests to our God" (Rev 5:10). Keener rightly says, "loyalty to Christ entails loyalty to one another as God's family, above all ethnic, cultural, and earthly kinship connections."[53] We observe that Christ honors but also relativizes all the people groups. Which leads us to our next topic: Why does God's purpose also include all the peoples *reconciled*?

All the Peoples Reconciled

The Bible gives witness to all people groups recognized, relativized, and *reconciled*. The Bible's storyline has all peoples, all nations, all things, indeed, the whole cosmos reconciled in Jesus.[54]

Here's a contemporary example of a *peacemaker as church planter* whose ministry of reconciliation extends across people groups:

> Yeva is an Armenian believer. She has devoted her life to seeing Christ reconcile the divided peoples of the Caucasus. Despite her family's past suffering at the hands of Turks and Kurds, an encounter with the Prince of Peace transformed Yeva's heart. "Christ has torn down the dividing walls of hostility." Now, Yeva plants churches among Turks, Kurds from Turkey, and Armenians. She trusts that in Christ's gospel of peace, their united fellowship will overcome ethnic barriers. As fractured groups gather in one spiritual family, Christ's reconciliation is melting centuries-long hostilities. Yeva believes these new churches, whether integrated or parallel, will end age-old hatreds.[55]

Christ inaugurates a new social way of being human. It's reconciliation beginning *now*. Peace in Christ with formerly hostile peoples *now*. Ephesians 1:10 offers the brilliant vision about God's purpose in Christ in "the fullness of time, to unite all things in him, things in heaven and things on earth"; this does not represent a distant utopia disconnected from our present world. It's already begun:

- Eph 2:13, "But *now* in Christ Jesus you [gentiles] who once were far off have been brought near by the blood of Christ."

---

53 Keener, "One New Temple in Christ," 92.

54 Rom 8:19–21; Eph 1:10; 2:13–16; Col 1:19–20; Rev 22:1–3. See Behr, *Becoming Human*; Sweet, *Jesus Human*.

55 Mischke and Houston, "Recognized, Relativized, Reconciled," 33.

- Eph 2:19, "So then you are [present active tense—*now*] no longer strangers and aliens, but you are [present active tense—*now*] fellow citizens with the saints and members of the household of God."
- Eph 3:6, "This mystery is that the Gentiles are [present active tense—*now*] fellow heirs, members of the same body, and partakers of the promise in Christ Jesus through the gospel."
- Eph 3:10, "so that through the church the manifold wisdom of God might *now* be made known to the rulers and authorities in the heavenly places."

N. T. Wright calls this "a crescendo of 'now.'"[56] Persons and peoples "brought near by the blood" are reconciled to God. Jews and gentiles, whose hostility toward one another was well-known, are now reconciled to each other into same-temple fellowship (Eph 2:19–22). Craig Keener writes, "Paul's image of a temple uniting Jew and gentile challenged the ethnically segregated reality of the temple standing in his own day."[57] World-renowned missiologist Andrew Walls writes of this text that it represents a fellowship of unity-in-diversity that is *same-temple* and *same-table*:

> It is usual to see the great celebration of Ephesians 2 in terms of the reconciliation of two races, Jew and Gentile; and the words have in modern times spoken powerfully to situations of racial division. But in their own time these also stood for two cultures; and, in the church, they stood for two contrasting Christian lifestyles. Two lifestyles met at the institution that had once symbolized the ethnic and cultural division: the meal table.[58]

This triggers us to savor again the biblical vision of the Great Feast with King Jesus as host, everyone unified and honored at his table. It is an altogether new way of being together as humans. It's being truly human together across social, class, racial, caste, and ethnic boundaries, united by the love of Christ. When Christ who is our peace (Eph 2:14) makes peace (2:15) between hostile peoples "through the cross" (2:16), he is doing nothing short of creating a new sociology otherwise called the local church. Walter Brueggemann writes, "Our sociology is predictably derived from, legitimated by, and reflective of our theology."[59] In Ephesians 2,

---

56 Wright, *Paul and the Faithfulness of God*, 556–57.
57 Keener, "One New Temple in Christ," 76.
58 Walls, "The Ephesian Moment," 77.
59 Brueggemann, *The Prophetic Imagination*, 8. In the afterword of this volume, Niringiye writes, "sociologies are theologies, just as theologies are sociologies."

Paul is revealing a *new-humanity sociology* deriving from a through-the-cross, new-creation-in-Christ *theology*. Reconciliation is now, vertical and horizontal "through the cross ... killing the hostility" (Eph 2:13–16).

It begs the question: How would I describe the sociology of my local church, and what does this reflect about our theology as a community? Jew-and-gentile-reconciliation through Christ is the prototype for all people groups reconciled through Christ. Indeed, Christ is our peace; Christ makes peace; Christ preaches peace (Eph 2:14–15, 17). King Jesus is *now* risen from the dead. New creation has begun as one new humanity—all the peoples *recognized, relativized,* and *reconciled.*

Critiquing HUP with Social Science and Ephesians 2

We now turn to explore the HUP through the grid of the social science material we previously explored in this book and in conversation with Scripture.

The Law of Group Polarization

We begin with the Law of Group Polarization:[60] When groups of like-minded persons deliberate about an issue (e.g., social issues, politics, doctrine), they consistently move toward a more extreme position in the direction of where they began talking about it. This applies to the group as well as the individuals in the group. (See diagrams in chapter 8, above.)

Figure 12.4 on the following page illustrates how politically homogenous units may contribute to polarization. The diagram shows two groups on each end of a spectrum. Members of group 1 (on the left) all agree on their view. On the right, members of group 2 hold a contrary view. To the degree that each group excludes voices with other perspectives, they will very likely reinforce their views and move further in the direction of their leanings. As stated in chapter 8, the more homogenous and like-minded a group is, the smaller the "argument pool." A small argument pool simply means that there is a narrow range of perspectives from which to draw knowledge and insight. It therefore can lead to conclusions and behaviors which may be nearsighted at best, or foolishly destructive at worst.

---

60 Sunstein, "The Law of Group Polarization."

The Homogenous Unit Principle: What Peace?

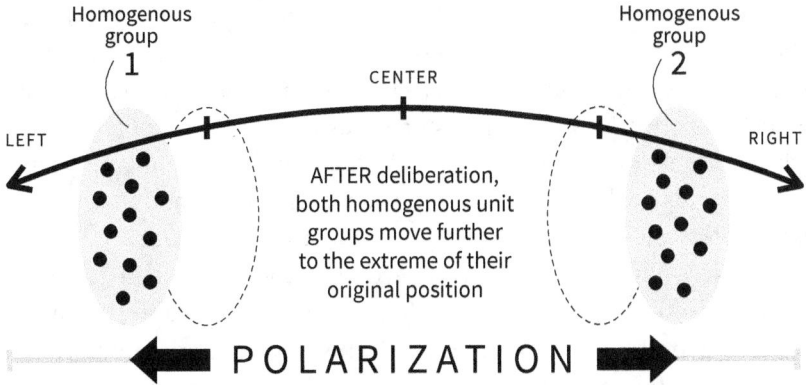

Figure 12.4: The HUP contributes to polarization

Figure 12.4 indicates politically homogenous units—where each of the two units (left and right) represents a group united by political views. While political polarization is increasing in churches, many churches are even more racially and ethnically divided than politically.

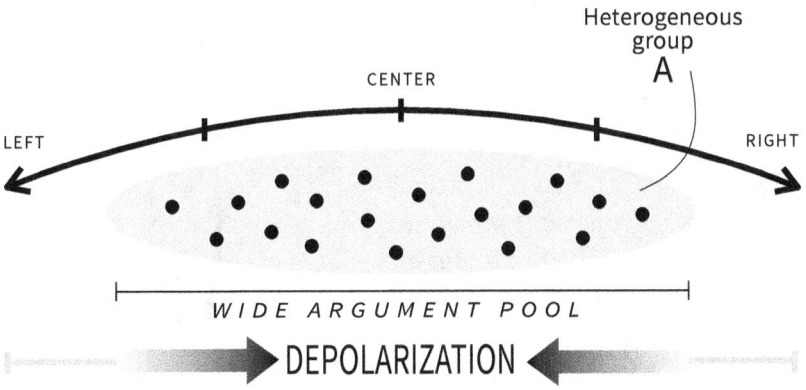

Figure 12.5: Heterogeneous groups offer varied perspectives from a "wide argument pool" thus tending toward depolarization

Figure 12.5 illustrates what can happen with a "wide argument pool." Instead of two homogenous groups, there is one heterogeneous group (A). Members of this group listen and gather insights from diverse voices. If this is conducted with empathic listening, the result is not polarization but depolarization. It ideally leads to healthy compromise.

What is one implication? In the United States, many churches still struggle with the nation's increasing diversity, whether around politics, race, or class. Churches and denominations long organized around the HUP can unintentionally reinforce segregated faith communities.

Relative to racially homogenous churches, Emerson and Smith conclude, "The basic workings of American religion promote more ingroup friends, marriages, and acquaintances. Thus, religion ... both helps to create racially distinctive networks and, in using them as the basis for congregational and denominational growth, helps maintain and justify them."[61] Since religion tends to heighten the importance of "racial boundaries, and reduce interracial ties, it necessarily reproduces racial inequality."[62]

For fifty-plus years, church growth methods rooted in the HUP have apparently perpetuated this side effect: racial inequality. As church growth advocates and cross-cultural mission trainers promote the HUP for its effectiveness, the HUP's side effects of polarization, racial inequality, or segregation may go unacknowledged.

The Ethical Paradox of Group Loyalty

We now look at the HUP in light of the Ethical Paradox of Group Loyalty.

Racially exclusive identities and congregations necessitate bias. We might call this the ethical paradox of group loyalty. The paradox is that even if made up of loving, unselfish individuals, the group transmutes individual unselfishness into group selfishness.[63]

As presented in chapter 8, figure 12.6 expresses the paradox: *As loyalty to one's in-group increases—the potential of unethical behavior toward an out-group likewise increases.* The greater the unselfishness or loyalty toward one's in-group (e.g., family, church, tribe, race or ethnic group, people, nation), the greater the potential selfishness toward the out-group (e.g., other family, other church, other tribe, other race or ethnic group, other people, other nation).

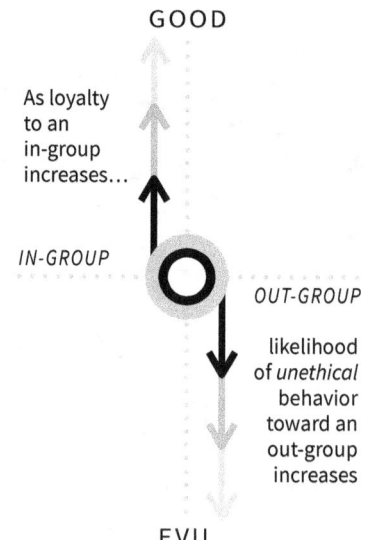

Figure 12.6: The Ethical Paradox of Group Loyalty

---

61 Emerson and Smith, *Divided by Faith*, 161. (We, the authors, recognize that in discussing politically homogenous units first and then referring to racially homogenous units we may be generalizing to a fault.)

62 Emerson and Smith, 161.

63 Emerson and Smith, 158.

When Niebuhr's book on the subject came out, some didn't like it because it was too negative about human nature. Plus, it challenged the optimism of many elites (like John Dewey) who believed that secular reason, science, and education would save humanity. But the book gained broad acceptance as the rise of fascism in the 1930s and 1940s was seen as predicted by Niebuhr.

As World War II progressed, German propaganda proliferated, and German loyalty to their in-group grew in intensity. German pastors were not excluded from the demand for loyalty to Germany's Führer. In 1934, this gave rise to a protest by some evangelical Christian leaders against the overreach of the German state. This protest was embodied in a document[64] called The Barmen Declaration, its principal author being Karl Barth.[65]

Today pastors all over the world struggle to speak to their congregants about social, political, national, or tribal loyalties that compromise the ways of Jesus and the word of God. For example, in America, Christian nationalism currently represents a vexing question for many pastors. Where does the good of patriotism end—and the idolatry of nationalism begin?

One of the most troubling aspects of the rise of Hitler is that he was a (nominal) Christian. Moreover, he understood the vital importance of

---

64 Evangelische Kirche in Deutschland (EKD), "The Barmen Declaration." Barmen's six declarations, summarized, are: (1) John 14:6; 10:1, 9. The church's authority derives solely from God's Word, not from any "other events, powers, historic figures and truths." (2) 1 Cor 1:30. Barmen rejects the doctrine that there are "areas of our life in which we would not belong to Jesus Christ but to other lords." (3) Eph 4:15–16. Christians are to ignore the loyalty demands of any "special leader" outside of the church as someone with ultimate ruling authority. (4) Matt 20:25–26. Barmen identifies the totalizing claim of the German Reich in ordering the life and loyalty of its people as a false claim. Jesus Christ is Lord over all. (5) 1 Pet 2:17. The State exists by divine appointment for the purpose of "justice and peace," and is accountable to God. The church should never "become an organ of the state." (6) Matt 28:20; 2 Tim 2:9. The church has its commission from God to preach the free grace of God. "We reject the doctrine" that "could place the Word and work of the Lord in the service of self-chosen desires, purposes and plans."

Modeled after Barmen is Evangelical Confession 2024: Titled "Our Confession of Evangelical Conviction," it offers the American evangelical community seven confessional declarations. Summarized: "In this moment of social conflict and political division, we confess the following Christian convictions: (1) We give our allegiance to Jesus Christ alone. ... (2) We will lead with love, not fear. ... (3) We submit to the truth of Scripture. ... (4) We believe the Gospel heals every worldly division. ... (5) We are committed to the prophetic mission of the Church. ... (6) We value every person as created in God's image. ... (7) We recognize godly leaders by their character." Like Barmen, each affirmation ("We affirm") is matched with a rejection ("We reject").

65 McKnight and Matchett, *Revelation*, 233–35. In chapter 22, "A Manifesto for Dissident Disciples," they discuss Barmen as Barth's courageous work as a dissident disciple of Christ. "Those who surrender to the Word of God become disciples who are dissidents in Babylon" (p. 37).

Christianity to Germany's people and cultural identity. Hitler attracted the support of the majority of Christians because he consistently made positive overtures toward Christianity.

> Article 24 of the [Nazi] party program had demanded "liberty for all religious denominations in the State so far as they are not a danger to ... the moral feelings of the German race. The party stands for positive Christianity." In his speech of March 23, 1933, Hitler paid tribute to the Christian faiths as "essential elements for safeguarding the soul of the German people," promised to respect their rights, declared that his government's "ambition is a peaceful accord between Church and State" and added—with an eye to the votes of the Catholic Center Party, which he received—that "we hope to improve our friendly relations with the Holy See."[66]

The degree to which Christian leaders—Catholic and Protestant—became loyal to Hitler and Naziism is breathtaking. Although hundreds of Christian leaders were dissidents—they resisted giving allegiance to Hitler—these dissidents were but a small minority among Germany's 45 million Protestants. The vast majority "submitted in the face of Nazi terror."[67]

In the face of polarization and political hostility, to what extent does your church lean into civil dialog, enemy-love, kindness, and empathy? Will you, out of loyalty to Christ, resist unethical in-group loyalties that may lead to hostility and violence?

Loyalty to Your In-Group or Loyalty to Christ Jesus

The Ethical Paradox of Group Loyalty has proven to be horribly verifiable: Extreme loyalty to one's family or bloodline, to one's racial or ethnic identity, to one's tribe or nation, far too easily leads to unethical division, bloodshed, violence.

There is an alternative—loyalty to Jesus. Let's consider figure 12.7 (on the next page). The diagram illustrates the contrast between (A) "Loyalty to an in-group," and (B) "Loyalty to Christ Jesus." At stake is whether behavior toward an out-group will be unethical or ethical. In contrast to (A), we propose the following (B):

---

66 Shirer, *Rise and Fall*, 234.
67 Shirer, 239. See "The Persecution of the Christian Churches," in *Rise and Fall*, 234–40.

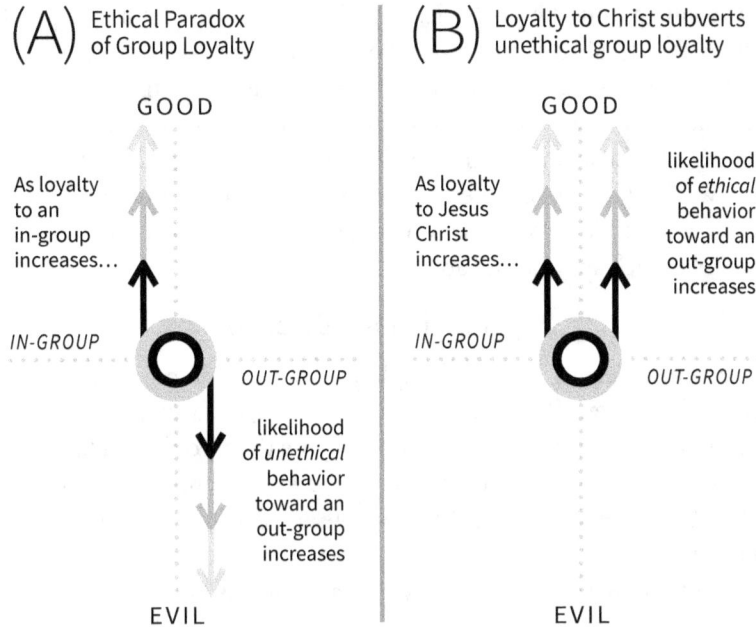

Figure 12.7: Loyalty to an in-group relative to an out-group vs. loyalty to Christ relative to an out-group

As loyalty to Christ Jesus increases—the potential for ethical behavior toward an out-group likewise increases.

Is this proposal rooted in the witness of Scripture? Let's briefly consider the life and teachings of Christ.

The good Samaritan. A lawyer asks, "And who is my neighbor?" In this parable (Luke 10:29–37), Jesus has the religious elites ignoring an outsider who has been attacked "by robbers, leaving him half dead." To add to the drama, a Samaritan (considered an enemy-outsider to many Jews), does everything necessary to love the one who needs help. "Which of these three, do you think, proved to be a neighbor to the man who fell among the robbers?" He said, "The one who showed him mercy." And Jesus said to him, "You go, and do likewise" (Luke 10:36–37). Jesus subverts insider status and in-group loyalty.

Enemy love. In Matthew 5:43–45, Jesus says, "You have heard that it was said, 'You shall love your neighbor and hate your enemy.' But I say to you, 'Love your enemies and pray for those who persecute you, so that you may be sons of your Father who is in heaven.'" Jesus makes the stunning claim that loving one's enemies is linked with the core identity of being a child of God.

The sheep and the goats. Jesus teaches about the final judgment in Matthew 25:31–46. It is the separation of the sheep and the goats. Jesus identifies with persons most vulnerable: the hungry, thirsty, strangers, naked, sick, and in prison. Jesus rewards those who serve the vulnerable, the outsiders, those unable to contribute to your own social status.

As we discussed in chapter 2, the Gospels include numerous accounts of Jesus's interactions with persons from out-groups, people considered vulnerable, unclean, untouchable.

Depolarizing the Disciples

Consider also Jesus's twelve disciples. Jesus calls Simon (later named Peter) and Andrew (Mark 1:16–20). Socially, they are Jewish peasants. From their earnings as fishermen, we imagine they would grudgingly pay taxes to Rome. Not only because they need every penny to support their families, but because their land and people are forced to exist under pagan Roman rule.

Then there is Levi (or Matthew), a tax collector. Jesus calls him, too, to join his band of disciples (Matt 9:9–10). Matthew collects taxes from his own Jewish community to support the Roman state. To faithful Jews Matthew is a traitor. Luke tells us that Matthew made for Jesus "a great feast in his home, and there was a large company of tax collectors and others reclining at table with them" (Luke 5:29). Matthew was wealthy, upper class. We wonder: how surprised, how offended, were Simon and Andrew when they learned Jesus chose a traitor, a hated tax collector, to join their in-group?

At the other end of the spectrum is Simon the Zealot.[68] The name "Zealot" could have meant he was a member of an underground resistance group fighting for independence from Rome. If so, it is possible that Simon the Zealot might have wanted to kill Matthew the tax collector for Matthew's complicity with unclean idolatrous Rome. Al Tizon comments, "No one dared to bring together fisherman, whom the state heavily taxed, and Matthew, who collected those taxes on behalf of the state. And to add fuel to the fire, Jesus invited Simon the Zealot, someone bent on overthrowing the Roman state, to join the group."[69]

Finally, we add faithful women to Jesus's group, likely of various social classes. These women provided for Jesus and the disciples "out of their means" (Luke 8:1–3). Women supporting Jesus and his (male) disciples? It's a shocking inversion of traditional gender roles.

---

[68] Matt 10:4; Luke 6:15; Mark 3:18; Acts 1:18.

[69] Tizon, *Christ Among the Classes*, 17.

Luke is hinting at the subversive nature of Jesus's unusual community. What matters is this: *Jesus holds the group together.* Jesus himself depolarizes and unites diverse persons and perspectives among his followers, as figure 12.8 illustrates. Allegiance to Christ as sovereign Lord and truest human being relativizes lesser loyalties, lesser allegiances, lesser glories.

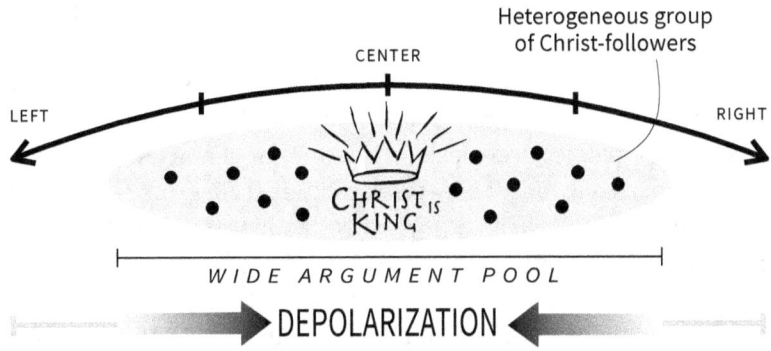

Figure 12.8: Depolarization through allegiance to Christ the King

Jesus is not merely open to the "other." Jesus is desiring, pursuing, embracing, saving, healing, setting free, dignifying—revealing himself as grace and truth—to the other. Christ the King, the True Human, embodies depolarization for all human beings. He is calling persons and peoples to be centered on himself in a vocation of learning, reconciliation, and peacemaking.

So, although group identity is often a potent source of polarization, when our identity is primarily in King Jesus, he is the depolarizing source of our unity in diversity. "Identity can be used to divide, but it can and has also been used to integrate."[70]

This begs the question: To what degree does your local church offer this asset—*the ministry of depolarization*—to the world? Is this not an under-leveraged ministry of the church of our Lord Jesus Christ?

Is this diversity-loving Jesus an outlier, a "woke" part of God, who happens to be a lot nicer than some bigger, truer, holier God? I jest. Obviously not. This is Jesus revealing the true God. Jesus said, "I and the Father are one" (John 10:30). "Whoever has seen me has seen the Father" (John 14:9). God really is like Jesus, who loves, forgives, and transforms human enemies. Jesus brings persons and peoples together across social boundaries. "He is the radiance of the glory of God and the exact imprint of his nature" (Heb 1:3).

---

70 Fukuyama, *Identity,* loc 2552.

Depolarization in Ephesians 2

We see this same Jesus-centered reconciliation and depolarization in Ephesians 2:11–22. When Paul writes to the early Christian communities in and around Ephesus, he is advocating for local churches to embody the "one new man" (Gk., *anthrōpos*, humanity).

Paul is the former super-zealous Pharisee (Phil 3:5–6); in his prior life he was committed to separation from all-things-gentile. Now Paul is a slave of Christ and apostle to the gentiles. He zealously advocates for a reconciled Jew-and-gentile assembly (Gal 2:11–14; Eph 2:11–22), a fellowship of peoples previously in conflict for centuries. This miracle of peace happens only one Way—through mutual allegiance to Christ the King whose body was crucified, and whose blood was shed to break down "the dividing wall of hostility" (Eph 2:13–16).

Why am I emphasizing this aspect of Christ? The HUP has silently and broadly shaped the American evangelical community. "It was a missional principle, and when it came to the US, it became a marketing principle: how to gather more people like us.... mission morphed into marketing."[71] For too long evangelicals have settled for homogenous units as a standard framework for gaining converts, starting churches, sustaining churches, and building community.

But in our increasingly diverse cities, many workplaces, the military, and other communities, this doesn't look like Jesus. And the world knows it. "Whereas the world recognizes that segregation is a kind of moral failure, in the evangelical church it is basically a go-to strategy. Instead of seeking to be unified in our diversity, we segregate into communities that look alike, make similar amounts of money, appreciate the same kinds of music, and share the same social status."[72]

In our broken world of social divisions and polarization, of political tribalism, bullying, and unprecedented demographic shifts, of wars born of imperial or tribal jealousies, of social media shouting matches, of mass migrations and 100 million forcibly displaced persons[73]—what *does* it mean to follow Jesus?

In America, white Protestant Christians have lost the political dominance and majority status they once enjoyed.[74] Since the early 1990s, "the country has, for the first time in our history, moved from being a

---

71 Quote from Fuller Seminary professor Eddie Gibbs in Bishop, *The Big Sort*, 181.
72 Goggin and Strobel, *The Way of the Dragon or the Way of the Lamb*, 203.
73 UNHCR, "More than 100 Million People Are Forcibly Displaced."
74 Jones, *The End of White Christian America*.

majority-white Christian nation, demographically speaking, to one in which there is no ethno-religious cultural majority."[75] Among white Protestant Christ-followers, it's popular to complain about this loss and wish for the way it used to be. Is this the best way forward?

How does the HUP fit into this intercultural local-and-global mix? What can homogeneous churches do to increase their welcome to, desire for, and acceptance of outsiders?

HUP—In Continuity with Christianity's Racist History?

Western Christianity, including evangelicalism, has a long history of racism and white supremacy. Below we will attempt to hit some high points concerning the role of theologized racism or segregation—in the Doctrine of Discovery, in Reconstruction and Dispensationalism, and in the HUP. We examine below the ways in which the HUP is *in continuity* and in *discontinuity* with the Doctrine of Discovery and Dispensationalism.

The Doctrine of Discovery

In the year 1452, the age of European colonial expansion was well underway.[76] A papal bull (a public decree from the pope) was issued. The edict had one purpose: To combine European interests of empire-building, including the African slave trade, with Christian mission. The edict explicitly granted King Alfonso V of Portugal an unbelievable expanse of rights and powers:

> To invade, search out, capture, vanquish, and subdue all Saracens [Muslims] and pagans whatsoever, and other enemies of Christ wheresoever placed, and the kingdoms, dukedoms, principalities, dominions, possessions, and all movable and immovable goods whatsoever held and possessed by them and to reduce their persons to perpetual slavery.[77]

This papal bull, and others after it, became known as the Doctrine of Discovery.[78] "The papal decree elevated what had been accepted practice into official church doctrine and international law."[79] The use of violence in conquering lands and peoples—along with confiscating their wealth and resources—was given official legal and Christian sanction. The great vices of injustice, greed, bloodshed, conquest, and slavery were given moral cover in the name of Christ.

---

75 Jones, *The Hidden Roots of White Supremacy*, 4.
76 I am indebted to key ideas in this section to Jones, *Hidden Roots*, 15.
77 Doctrine of Discovery Project, "Papal Bull Dum Diversas 18 June, 1452."
78 See also Charles and Rah, *Unsettling Truths*.
79 Jones, *Hidden Roots*, 15.

In 1493 (one year after Columbus landed) the papal bull Inter Caetera was decreed by another pope—Alexander VI. The edict ratified Spain's rights of ownership over previously "undiscovered" lands in the Americas. Here's the opening paragraph:

> Among other works pleasing the divine majesty and close to our heart, this indeed stands out the most: elevating the Catholic faith and the Christian religion, especially in [these] our times, as well as extending and spreading it everywhere, securing the salvation of souls and subduing the barbarous nations and bringing them back to the faith itself.[80]

With its theologized racism,[81] the practice of "subduing the barbarous nations" is again given moral cover in the name of Christian mission. In hindsight we see this papal decree giving precedent to the Pilgrims who first came to America:[82] Like the holy land promised by God to the wandering Hebrews, America is the promised land given to God's chosen Christians coming from England. This became the foundation for what we know today as American exceptionalism.[83]

This myth of exceptionalism has one key idea: America is a land promised by God to white European Christians. Many millions of Christians believe this. They like the ideas of Christian nationalism. According to authors Charles and Rah, "This assumption of exceptionalism hinders the work of reconciliation as a dysfunctional imagination of white supremacy, and exceptionalism continues unabated in the US church and US society." [84]

Both American exceptionalism and Christian nationalism are biblically problematic. Most concerning, it doesn't look like Jesus, but his name is used anyway to give it moral credibility.

Was Reconstruction the Runway for Dispensationalism?

The horrors of the American Civil War could have presented many occasions to question American exceptionalism. But the idea persisted, and even gained strength, during the period of Reconstruction. How might this have happened?

---

80 Modrow and Smith, "The Papal Bull Inter Caetera of May 4, 1493."
81 The racialized nature of European imperial conquest and the theological foundations created to support racial hierarchies, including the slave trade, are deeply and disturbingly examined in Jennings, *The Christian Imagination: Theology and the Origins of Race*.
82 Jones, *Hidden Roots*, 15.
83 Charles and Rah, *Unsettling Truths*, 69–81.
84 Charles and Rah, 81.

In the mid-1800s, American Christianity was greatly influenced by John Nelson Darby. The Irish-born Darby developed a system of interpreting the Bible focused much on the "end times" that would later be called Dispensationalism. America's most famous evangelical of the nineteenth century was Dwight L. Moody (1837–1899), a successful businessman turned revivalist. During his lifetime, Moody had to reckon with the wounds of the Civil War—its trauma, loss, unrest, and division. Reconstruction began at the end of the war but only lasted until about 1877.[85] The environment was ripe for a leader who could help white Americans unify—both from the North and South. As he grappled with these challenges, Moody adopted dispensationalist ideas.

Dispensationalism is a way of interpreting the entire biblical narrative by dividing history into several ages—or "dispensations." Depending on the dispensation, God acts with his chosen people in different ways. Dispensationalism is known for the following:

- The theology was originally constructed by John Nelson Darby (1800–1882), an Irish clergyman. He made lengthy visits across America to promote his ideas.

- Darby's theology spawned a host of conferences in America and England. His teachings had a huge impact on Christian fundamentalism, and later, evangelicalism.

- Dispensationalism features the distinct difference between the Jewish people and the church.[86]

- Dispensationalism emphasized robust doctrines of the "end times"—especially the pretribulation rapture of the church—and would later come to attach particular biblical prophecies to the secular government of the state of Israel.

- At the same time, Dispensationalism deemphasized the ethical teachings of Jesus for the church. The Scofield Reference Bible (1909) contributed widely to the spread of dispensational theology as its

---

85 Reconstruction went from the end of the Civil War until about 1877. In this brief twelve-year span, African Americans in the South gained a significant political voice. blacks gaining power meant whites lost some of their power, which was anathema to Southern whites. The long-term result of the so-called Compromise of 1877 was that by 1905 "most black people were effectively disenfranchised in every Southern state." Wikipedia Contributors, "Compromise of 1877."

86 Many believe this is contrary to Romans 11, which teaches that gentile believers are "grafted in" as a branch to the olive tree (Israel); moreover, Eph 2:11–22 reveals a similar truth—that Jewish and gentile Christ-followers are one new people of God. See Mathison, "What Is Dispensationalism?"

notes were written from a dispensational perspective. Astonishingly, the *Scofield Reference Bible* domesticates the ethical teachings of Jesus: "The Sermon on the Mount in its primary application gives neither the privilege nor the duty of the church."[87] The Scofield Bible became the Bible of choice for millions of American Christians in the twentieth century.

- Dispensationalism was the underlying theology in a whole host of conferences, books, and films about the end times, such as Hal Lindsey's *The Late Great Planet Earth*,[88] and the *Left Behind* book series by Tim LaHaye and Jeremy B. Jenkins. Book sales were "more than 65 million copies."[89] Combined with the *Left Behind* film series, they had a towering impact on evangelical popular culture and theology. These works still cast a long shadow across American evangelicalism.

Critiquing Moody, Critiquing Ourselves

Moody was not a trained theologian, but he embraced much of Darby's theological system. Hummel writes:

> In the aftermath of the war, Moody idealized sectional reconciliation.[90] During Reconstruction he minimized the political issues and moral stakes of the conflict and instead called for overcoming division

---

[87] Concerning Jesus's Sermon on the Mount, one of Scofield's notes includes this stunning comment: "In this sense the Sermon on the Mount is pure law, and transfers the offense from the overt act to the motive (Mt. 5. 21, 22, 27, 28). ... For these reasons, the Sermon on the Mount in its primary application gives neither the privilege nor the duty of the church. These are found in the Epistles." According to Scofield, no "duty of the church" is contained in the "primary application" of Jesus's Sermon on the Mount; thus, the Christian and the church are given license to water down if not ignore Jesus's teachings and commands in Matt 5–7. However, in the Sermon's closing Jesus says, "Everyone then who hears these words of mine and does them will be like a wise man who built his house on the rock." Evidently, for Scofield, Jesus only meant "everyone" at the time of that dispensation which was prior to our own. The early Christians had no such rigid theological system by which to domesticate Jesus's teachings and commands. See Scofield, ed., *The Scofield Reference Bible*, p. 1000.

[88] "*The Late Great Planet Earth* was the best-selling nonfiction book of the 1970s: Ten million copies were in circulation by the end of the decade. It sold more than 28 million copies by 1990, an estimated 35 million by 1999, and was translated into more than 50 languages." See Smith, "The Late Great Planet Earth Made the Apocalypse a Popular Concern."

[89] Wilkerson, "The 'Left Behind' Series Was Just the Latest Way America Prepared for the Rapture."

[90] Sectional reconciliation was "a process that greatly assisted the United States' emergence as a great power by reducing persistant and divisive internal tensions after the carnage of th Civil War." See Cook, "The Quarrel Forgotten? Toward a Clearer Understanding of Sectional Reconciliation."

> through forgiveness and common religion. The reconciliation he spearheaded after the war cannot be separated from his repudiation of the radical goals of social reform proposed by victorious Republicans. For Moody ... this historical moment made interdenominational networking on the basis of separating churchly from political issues—race and Reconstruction in particular—deeply appealing.[91]

I find these words significant: "radical goals of social reform" and "separating churchly from political issues—race and Reconstruction in particular."

> Moody's goal was to turn the country's Christians away from the past and the world, and toward the future and heaven. In practical terms, Moody encouraged Americans to abandon political analysis of the country, which in the mid-1870s meant dropping the polarizing issues of blame for the war and black civil rights.[92]

What's the assumption here? Black civil rights are merely a worldly, political matter disconnected from what truly matters—heavenly things, world missions, souls saved. I wonder: Did Moody ever ask a black pastor if the mob practice of lynching[93] was worthy of biblical comment and pastoral, spiritual consideration?

A contemporary of Moody was Ida B. Wells. A passionate and articulate Christian, Wells spearheaded America's anti-lynching crusade by writing and speaking. According to Cone:

> Wells was especially critical of evangelist Dwight Moody, who segregated his revivals to appease whites in the South. "Our American Christians are too busy saving the souls of white Christians from burning in hellfire to save the lives of black ones from present burning in fires kindled by white Christians."[94]

Did Moody ever discuss with American missionaries serving in Africa whether America's history of slavery and racial violence was an obstacle to Africans becoming Christians? This is more than a

---

91 Hummel, *Rise and Fall of Dispensationalism*, 86–87.
92 Hummel, 89.
93 "During the period between the Civil War and World War II, thousands of African Americans were lynched in the United States. Lynchings were violent and public acts of torture that traumatized black people throughout the country and were largely tolerated by state and federal officials. These lynchings were terrorism." Equal Justice Initiative, *Lynching in America*, 3.
94 Cone, *The Cross and the Lynching Tree*, 182–83, citing Giddings, *Ida*, 153; Wells, *Crusade for Justice*, 154–55.

theoretical question. Note the concern of American missionary statesman A. T. Pierson (1837–1911): "The Christian missionary makes slow progress in Africa because he can offer the negro no true brotherhood except in another world."[95]

Half a century later, American missiologist Eugene Nida, in his classic volume *Customs and Cultures*, insisted that his readers "understand racial prejudice better, especially as it may affect the work of Christian missions." ... "The Protestant church, especially in its more theologically conservative branches, is the most racially prejudiced institution in American life."[96] Even though America's Civil Rights movement has, across decades, led to significant progress in curtailing systemic racism, few would argue that there is still much work to do in the church.

Aloof to Genocide?

Mark Noll wrote that the focus on "the end times" in Dispensationalism tends to make American Christians aloof to pressing social problems.[97] Meanwhile, racism and hostility toward "the other" persist in the church, political violence in America is fermenting, and Christians are in the mix.

In addition to struggles with living up to equality here at home, many American Christians (both dispensationalists and others) give unconditional support to the state of Israel's policies, no matter what they mean for Palestinians. While we may not justify the violent conquest of non-European peoples in theory, on the ground Palestinians are being ethnically cleansed from their historic homeland, with widespread Christian justification.

---

95 Pierson, *Evangelistic Work in Principle*, 219; cited in Hummel, *Rise and Fall*, 124.

96 Nida, *Customs and Cultures*, 65–66; later Nida says, "White supremacy and superiority have been assumed by many and even defended as biblical," 255. See also: Worthen, "Missions and the Color Line," 135–38; McAlister, "The Fatherhood of God and the Brotherhood of Man: Racism as a Missionary Problem," 17–29.

97 Noll offers a chapter-long critique of Dispensationalism, namely, that Dispensationalism's focus on the study of the Bible's "prophetic literature" tends to make Christians aloof to the issues, needs, and concerns of the present world. Noll points to leading dispensational theologian Lewis Sperry Chafer, who wrote that the attentive Christian "is little concerned with ... the transitory now." See Noll, "The Intellectual Disaster of Fundamentalism," in *The Scandal of the Evangelical Mind*, 161, citing Chafer, *Systematic Theology*, 1:xxxiii–xxxiv. Refusing to grapple with the uncomfortable, complex, difficult challenges of this world (like racism and lynching) was integral to Dispensationalism; it was not a bug, but a feature.

For many, it does not seem possible to condemn both the war crimes committed by Hamas, and the crimes against humanity committed by the state of Israel in Gaza and the West Bank. In Gaza, a genocide is being carried out, and in the West Bank the amount of land being illegally seized from Palestinians has accelerated rapidly since October 7, 2023. The duplicity of this status quo is only further revealed by our ignorance (and sometimes avoidance) of the plight of our Palestinian Christian brothers and sisters, who trace their history back to the time of Jesus, and whose genetic lineage shows connections to the ancient Hebrew people and Jesus's first disciples. This community is currently facing extinction in the land of Jesus for the first time since his earthly ministry there.

This justification reveals a continued legacy of anti-Arab racism which gives license to crimes against humanity carried out against Muslims and Christians alike. Meanwhile—against incredible odds, and in the face of great brutality—Palestinian Christians have maintained a strong nonviolent, peacemaking ethic, from the days of Jesus himself, until now. In Jesus's name they cross divides with Israeli Jews, Muslims, and others for the sake of peace and security for all. They continue to strive for peace as they fight for their survival, often without Western Christian support.

Social Impacts of Theology and Missiology

Before reading Hummel's book on Dispensationalism, it never occurred to me: Dispensational theology, with its focus on heavenly things and the end times, permeated much of my own white American evangelical experience. Could it be that Dispensationalism in America has been a theological diversion that sanctions the church's gaze away from the unjust social realities of impoverished brothers and sisters in our land?

The Doctrine of Discovery was explicit and direct. Violent conquest and racial hierarchies were theologized in the name of Christian mission for empire-building. It justified a gaze away from the ways of Jesus.

Dispensationalism was more implicit and indirect. It concentrated our gaze on individual piety, heavenly things, the end times, and the modern secular state of Israel. It justified turning our attention away from the social and relational ways of Jesus. Dispensationalism says, *No need to gaze at or follow the social ways of Jesus in light of our own social world—because Jesus's world was of a dispensation different from our own.*

The HUP is both beneficial and problematic. On the one hand, the HUP has been a major part of the "operating system" of missions since 1974—contributing to a dramatic rise in reaching unreached peoples and catalyzing church planting movements among them. On the other hand, we believe the HUP has also reinforced or even sacralized group division in the name of church growth or reaching the unreached. And like the Doctrine of Discovery and Dispensationalism, HUP missiology sidelines the horizontally reconciling gospel of peace (Eph 2:13–17; 6:15).

Figure 12.9 reflects some of the comparisons stated above. We contend that the HUP is both *in continuity* and *in discontinuity* with the Doctrine of Discovery and Dispensationalism.

IMPACT	DOCTRINE OF DISCOVERY	DISPEN-SATIONALISM	HOMOGENOUS UNIT PRINCIPLE (HUP)
Served the expansion of Christianity	✓	✓	✓
Justifies violent conquest of non-European peoples and their lands in the name of Jesus Christ	✓	✓	
Marginalizes the social ways and teachings of Jesus	✓	✓	
Directly or indirectly reinforces racial inequality	✓	✓	✓
Values every people in the global purpose of God in Christ			✓
Undergirds indigenous church planting movements for all peoples			✓
Sidelines Christ's horizontally reconciling gospel of peace (Eph 2:13–17; 6:15)	✓	✓	✓

Figure 12.9: Comparing impacts—Doctrine of Discovery, Dispensationalism, HUP

BEING HUMAN: Honor for All Peoples

In concluding this chapter on the Homogenous Unit Principle, we are proposing a threefold people groups missiology.

1. We serve the biblical end-goal of all the peoples glorified; they are blessed, transformed, *recognized* in the worship of the living God through Christ. Every people's ultimate glory and honor are located in King Jesus, Lamb of God.
2. We live under a sober reality: all the people groups including our own are *relativized* under God's judgment and by the glory of Christ.
3. We are peacemakers with Christ to *reconcile* formerly hostile people groups as the One New Humanity, envisioned in Ephesians 2.

Can we imagine a three-part missiology of people groups recognized, relativized, and reconciled, centered in King Jesus and rooted in the story of God's glory? Figure 12.10 (on the following page) offers additional initial thoughts on this three-part approach to people groups.

Next up is chapter 13, "Being Human, and the Gospel," where we begin to summarize our investigations and explorations. We will be digging deep into the truth that Jesus as Son of Man is True Human Being. Could it be that following Jesus means to pursue becoming truly human?

A Three-Part People Group Missiology

Initial ideas

1. All the peoples **RECOGNIZED**
2. All the peoples **RELATIVIZED**
3. All the peoples **RECONCILED**

All the Peoples	1) RECOGNIZED	2) RELATIVIZED	3) RECONCILED
Biblical key idea	Every people is honored in Christ's kingdom—to glorify God.	Every people in Christ's kingdom is critiqued (judged)—to transform and glorify them.	Every people in Christ's kingdom is brought into harmony with other peoples, ending hostility.
Centrality of Jesus as King	God desires and honors the worship of every people. In love Christ gave his life for the redemption and transformation of every tribe and people—for the beauty of every people and for the glory of God.	God critiques and judges the inhumanity and idolatry of every people. Christ opposes the dishonoring of God, the oppression that derives from false worship, and idolatry's dehumanization.	God in Christ has already begun to reconcile all things, including all peoples, all tribes, all language groups, all nations. Reconciling Jews and gentiles through Christ's gospel of peace is a prototype for reconciling all peoples in conflict.
Witness of humanity	As persons and peoples experience salvation and the honor of knowing Christ, they gain an honor-surplus, which: (1) Allows for critique and examination of themselves, their people and idolatry, by which their group is relativized and transformed. (2) Love for King Jesus opens doors of desire to evangelize, to serve, to be reconciled with "other" persons and peoples.	As persons and peoples experience the effects of sin and its dehumanizing oppressions within their own families, tribes, and nations, they hunger for freedom from sin, for true humanity, for human flourishing. Amid their sin and shame (individual or collective) their longing for forgiveness and the glory for which they were created, is fulfilled through salvation and allegiance to King Jesus.	We live in a world of increasing globalization, urbanization, and migration. Social and national borders have blurred. Conflicts abound globally around identity: culture, race, status, people, tribe. This fuels anxiety, hostility, violence: "Diversity + Proximity = War." Amid a hunger for peace, for ending violence, for recognizing the honor and dignity of all persons and peoples—Christ is our peace; Christ makes peace; Christ preaches peace.

Figure 12.10: A three-part people group missiology—initial ideas

CHAPTER 12 SUMMARY

- The Homogenous Unit Principle (HUP) derives from a simple observation: people like to be with their own kind. While the HUP can be seen as consistent with selected biblical material, it can also be seen as inconsistent with Ephesians 2 and related biblical material.
- The HUP helped shape two global movements—Church Growth and Unreached Peoples.
- People groups are not mere social constructs. Peoples are grouped in various ways throughout Scripture and are part of God's ultimate purpose.
- This is an ethical paradox: Loyalty to one's in-group is considered ethical, but as loyalty to one's ingroup increases the potential for unethical behavior to an out-group also increases.
- Loyalty to Jesus and his ways increases the potential for ethical behavior toward out-groups.
- The Bible envisions all people groups as recognized, relativized, and reconciled.

FOR FURTHER REFLECTION

- How have you seen the HUP used as a default for ministry in your local church, mission organization, or elsewhere?
- The idea that in the Bible all the people groups are relativized may be seen as controversial. What might be the various viewpoints?
- What might be the key ideas from Ephesians 2:11–22 that comprise a depolarizing message of unity for your church?

Chapter 13

BEING HUMAN, AND THE GOSPEL

IN THIS CHAPTER

- Jesus is the True Human Being. What if our aim in being human is Jesus himself? What if discipleship included enemy-love and peacemaking?
- What if Christ Jesus preaches the gospel of peace? What if the gospel is primarily not about going to heaven, but about being truly human with King Jesus—for his kingdom on earth as it is in heaven?

Werner:

Jesus embodied what he taught and is our example: Daily intimacy with the Father ... loving enemies ... washing the disciples' feet ... self-giving love for one lost sheep ... living and dying to glorify God's name ... extreme generosity ... speaking truth resulting in one's own hurt ... concern for all, especially outsiders ... dignifying the poor, powerless, and vulnerable ... relinquishing glory and status in love for the world ... crossing social boundaries compassionately for others ... enduring shame and persecution ... taking up his cross ... passion for God's glory.

The (Radical?) Didache

As we saw in chapter 10, the early Christians did not consider the ways and teachings of Christ impractical or extreme. For them, the Sermon on the Mount *did* contain "the privilege and duty of the church."[1] One of the earliest Christian writings sums it up well. The Didache (pronounced *did-ah-KAY*), probably written in the first or second century, was a compact set of instructions for persons leaving paganism to become Christ-followers. Here are the first three verses:

1. There are two Ways, one of Life and one of Death, and there is a great difference between the two Ways.
2. The Way of Life is this: "First, thou shalt love the God who made thee, secondly, thy neighbour as thyself; and whatsoever thou wouldst not have done to thyself, do not thou to another."

---

1 See footnote 80 on page 158.

3. Now, the teaching of these words is this: "Bless those that curse you, and pray for your enemies, and fast for those that persecute you. For what credit is it to you if you love those that love you? Do not even the heathen do the same?" But, for your part, "love those that hate you," and you will have no enemy.[2]

The first two verses are introductory. There are two ways of living—one leads to life and the other to death. The foundation for the way of life is first loving God, plus loving your neighbor as yourself, and the Golden Rule—treat others the way you want to be treated.

Then, recalling Jesus's commands, verse three: Bless those who curse you, and pray for your enemies. Indeed, *love those that hate you*. This is the first behavior to distinguish Christians. And it's practical: this is how "you will have no enemy." *Imagine:* one of the first instructions concerning what it means to join the Christian community is … enemy-love. This is one of many examples in The Didache making the teachings and ways of Jesus essential for what it means to be a Christian.

Martin Luther King Jr. represents a famous example of enemy-love in American history. On January 27, 1956, King was threatened to leave town, or his house would be bombed. King's fear was paralyzing. Three evenings later while away at a meeting, King's house was bombed. Fortunately, his wife, daughter, and a family friend escaped injury. How did King respond? *Jesus says, Love your enemies.* According to James Cone,

> As King saw it, the most powerful religious authority for black Christians was Jesus Christ, and Jesus's teachings on love and nonviolence became his primary focus: "Jesus still cries out in words that echo across the centuries: 'Love your enemies; bless them that curse you; pray for them that despitefully use you.' This is what we must live by."[3]

In King's life, enemy-love was practical in subverting white supremacy and racial hatred. But King's enemy-love while pursuing racial justice did not prevent his enemies from killing him.[4]

In his book *The Patient Ferment of the Early Church*, Alan Kreider tells the story of how Cyprian (d. 258) became a Christian.[5] Cyprian was

---

2 Anonymous, *The Didache*, 27.
3 Cone, *The Cross and the Lynching Tree*, 119, citing King Jr., *Stride toward Freedom*, 135–38.
4 See also King's sermon, "Love Your Enemies."
5 Kreider, *Patient Ferment of the Early Church*, 137.

an aristocrat from Carthage, North Africa, a major city in the Roman Empire. He was well-born and trained in rhetoric. His *habitus* (his learned practice) was formed by the default cultural values of the Roman Empire. This included the *cursus honorum*—the relentless competition for honor and glory among peers and in posterity.⁶

Is the Christian life even accessible to someone as worldly as Cyprian? Cyprian is aware of the Christians. He sees their manner of life—their *habitus*—of loving God and neighbor, of enemy-love, of moral and sexual purity, of living patiently and generously in community. The peaceable *Jesus-way-of-life* is so different. Cyprian is attracted to this life. He gains a friend and mentor, Caecilianus, and under his guidance, Cyprian finally becomes a Christian. Cyprian is baptized. His transformation begins:

> But after that, by the help of the water of new birth, the stain of former years had been washed away, and a light from above, serene and pure, had been infused into my reconciled heart,—after that, by the agency of the Spirit breathed from heaven, a second birth had restored me to a new man;—then, in a wondrous manner, doubtful things at once began to assure themselves to me, hidden things to be revealed, dark things to be enlightened, what before had seemed difficult began to suggest a means of accomplishment, what had been thought impossible, to be capable of being achieved.⁷

Indeed, the Christian life *was* accessible to Cyprian. He becomes a presbyter and later, Bishop of Carthage. And among his writings is a letter giving instruction to guide the next generation of Christians in the *habitus* of knowing and following Jesus.

In his closing for the Sermon on the Mount, Jesus said, "Everyone then who hears these words of mine and does them will be like a wise man who built his house on the rock" (Matt 7:24). In keeping with Jesus's teachings, Cyprian wrote in 256,

> Beloved brethren, [we] are philosophers not in words but in deeds; we exhibit our wisdom not by our dress, but by truth; we know virtues by their practice rather than through boasting of them; we do not speak great things but we live them.⁸

It is clear from the early Christians: the teachings and ways of Jesus are not mere suggestions. Jesus is the way to live. Through Jesus, we do not

---

6 See Hellerman, *Reconstructing Honor in Roman Philippi*, Kindle loc 483.
7 Cyprian, "The Epistles of Cyprian, Epistle 1: To Donatus," paragraph 4.
8 Kreider, 13. Citing Cyprian, *Pat.* 3, trans. G. E. Conway, FC 36 (1958), 265.

speak great things, but we live them. *Jesus is God's way of being human and our way of being truly human.* We are to be Jesus for the world.

C. S. Lewis said it this way: "The Church exists for nothing else but to draw [people] into Christ, to make them little Christs.... God became Man for no other purpose."[9]

True Human Being

Researching for this book, I came upon these startling words: *Jesus is the True Human Being.* How does this relate to the gospel of peace? First, let's consider some key texts from Scripture concerning the phrase "son of man." We begin with Daniel 7:13–14.

> I saw in the night visions, and behold, with the clouds of heaven there came one like a son of man, and he came to the Ancient of Days and was presented before him. And to him was given dominion and glory and a kingdom, that all peoples, nations, and languages should serve him; his dominion is an everlasting dominion, which shall not pass away, and his kingdom one that shall not be destroyed.

Who is this "one like a son of man"?

In Mark 14, Jesus is arrested and interrogated. Jerusalem's high priest questions Jesus, "Are you the Christ, the Son of the Blessed?" Jesus replies, "I am, and you will see the Son of Man seated at the right hand of Power, and coming in the clouds of heaven" (14:61–62). *Jesus* is "Son of Man." He uses this title for himself more than any other—seventy-eight times in the Gospels.

What does Son of Man mean? Leonard Sweet's book *Jesus Human* gets us going in the right direction.

> Jesus is Truth. Yes, the truth about God, but also the truth of what it means to be fully human. Jesus is how we discover how to be human. Jesus is our best shot at being human. Biblical scholar Walter Wink (d. 2012) calls Jesus "the archetype of the Human Being," or "the archetype of humanness." Jesus's favorite phrase for himself was "Son of Man," which more literally translates as "The Human Being" or "The Human One."[10]

Jesus as the ideal human being? I found this strange but encouraging, especially in this time when many evangelicals have "decentered Jesus."[11]

---

9 Lewis, *Mere Christianity*, 199.
10 Sweet, *Jesus Human*, 22. Sweet references Wink, *The Powers That Be*, 11.
11 French, "Evangelicals Decenter Jesus."

According to a 2022 theological survey, "In the evangelical sphere, doctrines including the deity and exclusivity of Jesus Christ, as well as the inspiration and authority of the Bible, are increasingly being rejected."[12]

It is no wonder that, as one Christian ethics textbook says, "the teachings and practices of Jesus—especially the largest block of his teachings, the Sermon on the Mount—are routinely ignored or misinterpreted in the preaching and teaching ministry of the churches and in Christian scholarship and ethics."[13]

In John's Gospel, Jesus stands up at the close of a feast. He cries out to the crowd, "If anyone thirsts, let him come to me and drink. Whoever believes in me, as the Scripture has said, 'Out of his heart will flow rivers of living water'" (John 7:37–38). Jesus is talking about being fully alive. "For whoever would save his life will lose it, but whoever loses his life for my sake will find it" (Matt 16:25). The most flourishing, valuable life we'll ever find is in Jesus. "What if the highest human is the 'Christ-in-me' human, and the highest humanity is the 'Christ-in-us' humanity?"[14]

Jesus Humanizes, Idolatry Dehumanizes

Appendix 2 offers a word study comparing *Son of Man* with *first Adam, last Adam, man (humanity)*, and *new humanity* (1 Cor 15:45; Eph 2:15; 4:24). The comparison points out that Jesus's designation for himself as "Son of Man" overlaps significantly with "Adam" and "humanity" in the Greek. Jesus is the "genuine human being," says N. T. Wright. Here's how he puts the pieces together:

> Jesus, completely in line with the hope of Israel, was to be seen as the genuine human being, the "true Adam", the ultimate image-bearer, doing for Adam what Adam could not do for himself, reversing the "fall" and reinscribing the notion that image-bearing humans were to be set in authority over God's creation.[15]

Later in the same book, Wright says that Jesus "is the human being in whom YHWH, Israel's one and only God, has acted within cosmic history, human history and Israel's history to do for Israel, humanity and the world what they could not do for themselves."[16] And what

---

12 Ligonier and Lifeway, "The State of Theology."
13 Gushee and Stassen, *Kingdom Ethics*, xvi.
14 Sweet, *Jesus Human*, 33.
15 Wright, *Paul and the Faithfulness of God*, 908.
16 Wright, 683.

about the *opposite* of humanness? Wright says that Paul's view of idolatry is dehumanizing. What is the cure to the dehumanizing, defiling forces of idolatry? *The ideal human: Christ,* "the image of the invisible God" (Col 1:15).

> Paul's typically Jewish reaction against the dehumanization that results directly from idolatry was only heightened by his belief that there had come at last a *truly human being,* "the image of the invisible God," whose aim was precisely to *rehumanize other humans,* to rescue them from the corruption brought on by idolatry and to re-establish them as what they were supposed to be.[17]

To rehumanize other humans ... It is tantalizing to think about following Christ as the way of rehumanizing persons and peoples. Commenting on Romans 8:18–30 and the transforming life of Christ, Wright says "we are called to be fully human in a way most of us have scarcely begun to imagine."[18]

Son of Man: True Human Being

The title "True Human Being" appears frequently in the *First Nations Version: An Indigenous Translation of the New Testament.* The phrase "Son of Man" is translated as "True Human Being."

> He answered the man, "The foxes live in their holes, the winged ones who fly above us live in their nests, but the True Human Being has no place to lay his head." (Matt 8:20)[19]

> For the True Human Being has come to find the lost ones and set them free. (Matt 18:11)[20]

> In the same way, the True Human Being did not come to be served by others, but to offer his life in the place of many lives, to set them free. (Matt 20:28)[21]

Carmen Joy Imes, in her book *Being God's Image,* says, "Jesus is the ultimate human who models for us how God intends for us to live as humans."[22] She expands on this in a chapter called, "Jesus, the Human."

---

17 Wright, 377; emphasis mine.
18 Wright, *Into the Heart of Romans,* 102.
19 Wildman, *First Nations Version,* 13–14.
20 Wildman, 35.
21 Wildman, 39.
22 Imes, *Being God's Image,* 5–6.

For many of us, it goes without saying that Jesus is the image of God. After all, he is God! But if we view his status as God's image primarily as a feature of his deity, we will be missing the point. Jesus is not the image of God because he is God. Jesus is the image of God because he is human. His entry into human history is not plan B but the culmination of plan A. Jesus is and does what humans were meant to be and do. He surrenders his own life for the sake of others.[23]

Jesus as the ideal human? Some might object. For one thing, he was a single male. Don't most men aspire to be married? Others might ask how a woman can model her life after a male?[24] Another challenge—the Bible says Jesus relinquished the status of divine glory in heaven and made himself vulnerable as a human on earth. Who willingly endures such humiliation?

Is Jesus really the best life to follow?

Myth of the Marlboro Man

Some think the ideal human is a virile, middle-aged, outdoors-loving, independent male. Which reminds me:

In earlier decades of my life, the "Marlboro Man" ad campaign was visible everywhere across America to advertise Marlboro cigarettes. "The campaign featured rugged, masculine men, often depicted riding horses or engaged in other outdoor activities, and was designed to appeal to men who valued independence and self-sufficiency."[25]

"Come to Marlboro country"—the slogan was everywhere—in magazines, on billboards, on TV. It was advertising as mythmaking: the American West with its frontier-independence, outdoor adventure, and fresh air ... it was all (symbolically) yours if you smoked Marlboros.

One of the male models featured as the Marlboro Man was Wayne McLaren. In 1992 he was diagnosed with lung cancer and (briefly) became an anti-smoking advocate. McLaren died later that year at age fifty-one.[26] What a tragedy; what an irony.[27]

---

23 Imes, 109.
24 Imes addresses questions about gender and Jesus in *Being God's* Image in chapter 7, "Jesus, the Human."
25 Mohindroo, "The Tragic Story of the Marlboro Man."
26 Mohindroo, "The Tragic Story of the Marlboro Man."
27 Related myths about the ideal man are likewise toxic and tragic. See Du Mez, *Jesus and John Wayne*. The author chronicles the "militant masculinity" that has for decades influenced American evangelicalism.

Launched in 1954, the ad campaign's success is legendary. In one year, Marlboro sales grew by three thousand percent to $5 billion.[28] Three thousand percent! The iconic Marlboro Man myth was incredibly potent in selling cigarettes. The campaign in the US finally ended in 1999, but not because the advertising wasn't working. It was working too well.

Because smoking was causing cancer in so many Americans, cigarette advertising on TV and radio was outlawed in the US in 1970. In 1999, more than 3,000 billboards in America featuring the Marlboro Man were removed as part of a $206 billion lawsuit. But the mythic, iconic dream of the rugged American individual remains. No wonder Frank Sinatra's 1969 hit song "My Way" remains popular.[29] It's a hymn idolizing a masculinity of unbridled autonomy, an *I-don't-need-God* individualism.

The rugged, powerful, freedom-loving, autonomous individual—is this the ideal human?

Alexander, "Ideal Man" of the Ancient Near East

Jesus was born into the Roman Empire under Caesar Augustus (as discussed in chapter 10). But we haven't discussed the extent to which Alexander the Great was considered the ideal human at the time of Jesus.

> The accomplishments of Alexander, fueled by his incomparable daring, inspired ancient writers. Where modern historians count the casualties and detect cruelty, and inhumanity, the ancients saw only glory. Public action, that is, by war and conquest was the most dangerous, and, in consequence, the most noble of all human endeavors. Alexander was, therefore, "The Great," the greatest man who had ever lived. If Plato was the measure of all subsequent philosophy, ... Alexander was the measure of man himself.... Indeed, down the whole course of history, the invincible warrior, with raised sword has been an archetypal hero of many societies and cultures.[30]

Alexander never lost a military battle. He identified himself as Son of God and King of Kings.[31] Claiming divine favor (if not divinity) was conventional. It's what you do—as a pharaoh, a conqueror, a ruler. Likewise, three centuries later, Caesar Augustus was not being radical when he pronounced Julius Caesar, his adoptive father, a god—thereby

---

28 Shirk, "The Real Marlboro Man."
29 Frank Sinatra, C. Francois, Revaux, and Paul Anka, "My Way" (1967).
30 Cahill, *Desire of the Everlasting Hills*, 23.
31 Cahill, 17–18.

hinting in no uncertain terms that he, himself, was the son of a god. Indeed, the violent warrior-king as prototypical human continues to inspire multitudes to this day. Human history has been written in blood ever since Cain killed Abel. Being human means violence is inescapably part of the story—often heroically so.

Then ... Jesus. "In the fullness of times, God sent his Son" (Gal 4:4).

Through humility, Jesus redefines what it means to be human according to the standards of Original Glory. Instead of inflicting violence, Jesus absorbs violence in self-giving love. Jesus reframes the meaning of life and death, glory and immortality. The full humanity of Jesus includes "frailty, weakness, and dependence" without Jesus "losing an inch of his status or dignity."[32] The character of God is revealed in Jesus as he dignifies all who embrace him. Jesus lives in affectionate union with God the Father. Jesus humbly serves. Jesus compassionately heals. Jesus confidently teaches because his words are God's. He fearlessly speaks truth to power. And vulnerably suffers for the glory of God (John 12:27–28).

Truest humanity looks like Jesus. In a chapter titled, "We Become Human," Johannes Metz writes:

> Christ showed us how to really become human beings. In him we see the unimagined heights and depths of our human lot. He is the prototype of human existence, the "first-born of all creation" (Col. 1:15), the "son of earth." In him we find out what it means to be human; in him we find the kernel and the acme of our existence.[33]

Behold, the Human

In John's Gospel, chapters 18 and 19 describe the arrest, flogging, interrogation, and crucifixion of Jesus. In 19:1–4, Pilate had Jesus flogged; the Roman soldiers, experts in mockery, placed on Jesus a crown of thorns and a purple robe; then "they struck him with their hands." I imagine Jesus's back and legs were shredded from the flogging, and he could barely stand. His head and face bloody and disfigured, he is a shocking gory mess.

Then Jesus came out to the crowd.

Pilate says, "Behold the man." ... Behold the Anthropos.[34]

Behold, the Human.

---

32 Imes, *Being God's Image*, 110.
33 Metz, *Poverty of Spirit*, 19.
34 In Greek, "man" is *anthrōpos*.

What is Pilate thinking? Is this all about mocking Jesus? Is he secretly amazed at the ways of Jesus? While Jesus stands beside Pilate in front of the hostile crowd, could it be Pilate unwittingly proclaims an eternal truth?—*Jesus is the human ideal.* As Len Sweet says, "What if Pilate got Jesus right as the paradigmatic human when he looked at the man in purple robes and a crown of thorns standing in front of him and said, 'Behold the Human?'"[35]

Behold ... Humanity?

Imagine you are there in Jerusalem. You are among the crowd. You see Pilate standing outside on the empire's civic court platform. You know he is entirely comfortable with deadly violence to maintain order (after all, this is his job). Pilate has spoken, "Behold, the man." That man is hunched over—a broken, bloody, shameful figure. Submerged in the mob, you join the chant: "Crucify him!"

Suddenly, breathless, you are lifted into the sky. You are transfixed, peering and pondering from fifty meters above. You come to your senses. Your eyes are opened.

You see Jesus, the innocent Son of Man, condemned by the Powers. You detect self-giving love. Underneath a bloodied purple robe and crown of thorns is an already broken body, thrashed by the empire's scourges. Jesus reveals the extreme vulnerability of his humanity while suppressing his divine power. You wonder: *How can this be?*

The Powers have conspired—the empire and its soldiers, the religion and its ruling elites, the mob and its angry mass, the satan and its demons. To the Powers, Jesus is a problem. He has unmasked the status quo, the Old Way of being human. But the Old Way must be defended at any cost. Violence is the default solution.

Behold, humanity.
Behold, the human condition.

You are seeing humanity's standard: addressing problems through dehumanizing-violence-bloodshed-shame. What is this violence, except ... *being human?* Whether verbal violence, sexual violence, economic violence, physical violence, military violence, or ecological violence, you see it for what it is—mysteriously, typically *human*. You soon see Rome's crucifixion of Jesus: *humanity denied to the ultimate Human.* You want to look away. You are repulsed. You have witnessed the slow, gruesome violence-unto-death. It is intentionally, utterly dehumanizing.

---

35 Sweet, *Jesus Human*, 32.

The hours pass into darkness… .

The excruciating drama is not over. Two mornings later, somehow Jesus has conquered death! Just as he said. Another mystery: this violence against Jesus becomes a shift of death to life and shame to glory, pulsing with hope. A New Way to be human is launched in the cosmos. Humanity's violence-as-default is being subverted by King Jesus, Son of Man, True Human Being … *"through the cross, killing the hostility."*

Origen of Alexandria (d. 254) wondered how Christ, "the Wisdom of God can have entered the womb of a woman, and have been born an infant, and have uttered wailings like the cries of little children! And that afterwards it should be related that He was greatly troubled in death, saying, as He Himself declared, 'My soul is sorrowful even unto death.'" Origen's wonderment continues:

> Since, then, we see in Him some things so human that they appear to differ in no respect from the common frailty of mortals, and some things so divine that they can appropriately belong to nothing else than to the primal and ineffable nature of Deity, the narrowness of human understanding can find no outlet; but, overcome with the amazement of a mighty admiration, knows not whither to withdraw, or what to take hold of, or whither to turn.[36]

The first Adam failed in fulfilling God's purpose for humanity because of sin; but Jesus, the last Adam (1 Cor 15:45; Rom 5:12–17), fulfills God's purpose for humanity to redeem, reconcile, and restore.

What does this mean for us? It means joining Jesus in his glory-drenched, humanity-reconciling and peacemaking vocation—*for the world.*[37]

Our Vocation in Christ

According to N. T. Wright, "God has promised in Scripture (not least in Isaiah and the Psalms) to put the whole world right. Through the gospel (the events concerning Jesus, and their announcement in the power of the Holy Spirit) he puts humans right—so that they can be part of his putting-right project for the world."

I love this: *being part of his putting-right project for the world.* In a similar vein, Haley Goranson Jacob writes: "As those with the unique image-bearing vocation, humans share in the glory of God as they rule over his good creation."[38] Jacob concludes that Christians, "once participants in

---

36 Origen, *On First Principles* 2.6.2.
37 Wright, *Into the Heart of Romans*, 15.
38 Jacob, *Conformed to the Image of His Son*, 76.

the Adamic submission to the powers of sin and death, now participate in the reign of the new Adam over creation. Mankind's position on earth as God's vicegerents to his creation is now restored, though now through the image of the Son of God."[39]

We turn again to Carmen Joy Imes, who makes a parallel argument in *Being God's Image*.

> This created world is an integral part of our human vocation—now and for eternity.[40]

> From the beginning, our human vocation had to do with the cultivation and care of creation, making the rest of the earth like Eden.[41]

> ... Being saved is so much more than avoiding an eternity without God. It is a declaration of allegiance to the true king that results in the actualization of human potential. In short, we cannot become all we were meant to be without the victory of Jesus over sin and death and our participation in his reign on earth.[42]

What does it mean to be human? This matter represents no small opportunity for the global church. The gospel of peace offers a profound hope-filled answer to this question—to which we now turn.

Being Truly Human Is Being in Christ, For the World, Far and Near

Ephesians 2:17 is the key text: "And he came and preached peace to you who were far off and peace to those who were near."

As discussed in chapter 10, we believe that in this verse, Paul is identifying King Jesus as the servant of Isaiah 52:7: "How beautiful upon the mountains are the feet of him who brings good news, who publishes peace, who brings good news of happiness, who publishes salvation, who says to Zion, 'Your God reigns.'" Moreover, Paul combines Isaiah 52:17 with Isaiah 57:19: "Peace, peace, to the far and to the near."

And speaking of feet: "As shoes for your feet put on whatever will make you ready to proclaim the gospel of peace" (Eph 6:15 NRSV). Gospeling peace to those who are "far off" and those who are "near" (Isa 57:19; Eph 2:17)—this is part of our vocation with Christ.

---

39 Jacob, 226.

40 Imes, *Being God's Image*, 7.

41 Imes, 36.

42 Imes, 170.

The True Human Is Never Inhumane

As our society grows more addicted to the virtual world of screens and social media, author Sarah Kendzior sees a damaging decline in our humanity. "Humanity has been stripped from the virtual world: deliberately, maliciously. The goal is to make humans less human. Less imaginative and more callous; more desperate and less kind. ... Memes and mantras replace contemplation and compassion, rendering humans indistinguishable from bots."[43] Journalist David Brooks says that in our dehumanizing world, barbarism is on the rise. "The causes of this rising culture of dehumanization are almost too many to count: tribalism, racism, ideological dogmatism, social media."[44] So, before we move to this chapter's concluding thoughts, I offer a warning in consideration of our "rising culture of dehumanization."

We have presented three key ideas in this chapter: (1) Jesus Christ is the True Human Being. (2) Idolatry is often dehumanizing. (3) Following Jesus—being Christian—leads toward being fully human.

Here's the warning: Christians can take these ideas to reinforce their in-group loyalty, leading them down a twisted road of logic that ends with this highly toxic attitude: *People of non-Christian religions, different points of view or lifestyle, opposite political parties, or contrary beliefs are less human or less deserving of dignity than our nation, our tribe, our church, our people.* This attitude violates the way of King Jesus.

> Under no circumstances does King Jesus permit us
> to treat persons or peoples different from our community, group,
> or lifestyle—in a way that is dehumanizing.

Every human being is the image of God, worthy of dignity and respect. We see this plainly in the Gospels as Jesus relates to "others." His way of relating is consistently uplifting, dignifying, humanizing. Even when he speaks truth to power, he is pointing people toward God, away from evil and brokenness. "Every human being, regardless of income or class, is the image of God, possessing inherent dignity. Our job is to ensure the flourishing of those around us."[45]

It is never acceptable to use derogatory epithets. We should never demean others, even if our enemies do so. Jesus admonishes us, "whoever says 'You fool!' will be liable to the hell of fire" (Matt 5:22). The True

---

43 Kendzior, "It's a Tough Time for the Truth."
44 Brooks, "A Humanist Manifesto."
45 Imes, *Being God's Image*, 57.

Human is never inhumane. As persons who follow Christ, we refuse to be inhumane toward other humans. If our world becomes more divisive, inhumane, violent, even barbaric—our humanity and kindness toward "others" will surely point more people to Jesus, True Human Being.

Dreams of What If

What if the gospel of peace—that is, the good news about reconciling persons and peoples to God *and one another!*—was understood as one simultaneous reality?

What if the story of his glory is one and the same as the story of our glory?

What if the gospel of peace ("through the cross, killing the hostility") were an evangelistic entry point for persons and peoples (many unreached) struggling with hostility and violence?

What if Paul's vision of starting churches among unreached peoples is implicit in Romans 15:8–21? And what if this vision is also implicit in Ephesians 2:17, gospeling "peace to you who were far off and peace to those who were near"?

What if the gospel of peace to those far off and those near requires a local and global mindset? What if that includes nearby communities that are distant by culture or social status, as well as geographically distant communities that are in some way near?

What if the gospel of peace (creating one new humanity) is the most depolarizing dynamic in the world, preserving cultural distinctions while overcoming group hostilities through common allegiance to King Jesus, True Human Being?

What if our climate-change-world leads to more mass migrations as many scientists expect? What if the question *To whom do we belong?*—concerning citizenship, immigration, and identity—will only become more urgent? Does the gospel of peace offer hope? Will the church and our gospel adapt?

What if Jesus as True Human Being is the answer to one of the questions of our time: *What does it mean to be human?* What if living the gospel is the most rehumanizing dynamic in the world?

What if we were *for* humanity, *for* the world, far and near?

Being Truly Human—Through the Gospel

A six-point gospel narrative:

1. **Original Glory.** Our story begins with Creator God who makes the heavens and the earth, the skies and the land. God's last and crowning finish to creation is Adam and Eve—he makes them his image. Creator gives man and woman a royal vocation: *Represent God* in stewardship ("dominion") over the earth under Creator's good limitations (Gen 1:26–28). The psalmist says the Lord made humanity "crowned with glory and honor" (Ps 8:5–8). This is humanity's Original Glory—stewarding the earth for relational beauty, harmony, and flourishing. As Bates says, "Humans are made in God's image for the purpose of ruling creation on his behalf."[46] Humanity's "good road" begins with God, with glory.

2. **Fall from Original Glory.** Man and Woman "walk the good road" with Creator,[47] but then they are seduced by a cunning serpent to be like God. They fall from their high place of glory. They trade their glorious God-given human vocation and status (Rom 1:23; Gen 1:26–28; Ps 8:5–8) for shameful, dehumanizing idols. They exchange *relationship with the Creator* for *creatures and idols* (Rom 1:23–24). Humanity's fall (Gen 3) is more serious than a descent from innocence to guilt. It is a descent from regal glory under God to the shameful dishonoring of God through idolatry (Rom 1:23–32; 2:23–24; 3:23). Death enters the cosmos. The cosmos is broken and corrupted, humanity is defiled by sin and idolatry. The cosmos begins to await being "set free from its bondage to corruption [to] obtain the freedom of the glory of the children of God" (Rom 8:21). "Glory-loss is the foundational problem solved by the gospel."[48]

3. **The True Human.** Jesus is born to the Virgin Mary. The Christ enters the cosmos. He shows the completed meaning of the Torah by first remaking humanity, and then all things. Where the *first Adam fails*, Jesus the Son of Man loves God and loves humans perfectly: *Jesus succeeds*. He is the True Human Being. Jesus manifests God's "name" (John 17:3), revealing God's glory through his extraordinarily beautiful life and teachings. God in Christ condemns sin (Rom 8:3), dies an

---

46 Bates, *Why the Gospel?*, 62.

47 "Walk the good road" is a frequent phrase used in Wildman, *First Nations Version*, e.g., "Creator's blessing rests on you when you are hated and rejected, looked down on and treated as worthless, all because you have chosen to walk the good road with the True Human Being" (Luke 6:22).

48 Bates, *Why the Gospel?*, 68.

atoning death, absorbs and cures humanity's guilt and shame, exposes the dehumanizing idolatry of empire, overcomes Principalities and Powers, rises in victory over death, and is enthroned at the right hand of God. In self-giving love, in grace and truth, the Christ—King Jesus—reveals the glory of God in human form to rehumanize persons, peoples, and nations.

4. **New creation, new humanity now.** Christ is the Creator of a new way of being human. Jesus is King of the cosmos and of a new humanity (Eph 2:15; 4:24; 2 Cor 5:17). With Christ's beautiful life, with his resurrection and ascension, new creation begins. This new creation / new humanity is not a distant future dispensation. "After the opening statement of [Eph] 1:10 ... ('the fullness of times'), we find a crescendo of 'now' moments: *now*, in the Messiah Jesus, the gentiles have been brought near to the God of Israel; *now* the mystery of full gentile inclusion has been revealed; *now* the age-old mystery can be made known to the rulers and authorities in the heavenly places" (Eph 2:13; 3:6, 10).[49] Persons and peoples of every social status, ethnicity, and nation are offered salvation, unity, and peace by their allegiance to King Jesus. Our loyalty to Jesus relativizes all other human loyalties and puts them into balance for human flourishing. The True Human Being has created a new social way of being human. As Christ-followers, we celebrate the new humanity; we begin the Great Feast now in our local communities of believers.

5. **Saved for the world for God's glory.** In our new-humanity-through-Christ, we are conformed to his image and regain our glorified status (Rom 8:29–30). We give allegiance to King Jesus and thereby become children of God to participate with him in the gift of eternal life—for us and for the world—for human flourishing. "Salvation is not simply God's gift to his people, it is God's gift through his people—to the wider world."[50] God calls us to make known his glorious humanizing gospel for all peoples in all the world—regardless how opposed the empire, how distant the people, how different the culture. It's all about recovering glory. Bates rightly says, "*When God begins to restore human glory through the gospel, a cycle of glory recovery ensues for all creation—and this simultaneously restores God's own glory.*"[51]

---

49 Wright, *Paul and the Faithfulness of God*, 556–57; emphasis in original.
50 Wright, *Heart of Romans*, 163.
51 Bates, *Why the Gospel?*, 58; emphasis in original.

6. **Gospeling peace, our vocation with King Jesus.** Christ is our peace; Christ makes peace; Christ preaches peace (Eph 2:14-15, 17). By his blood, through the cross, in his flesh, King Jesus reconciles persons and peoples to God (Eph 2:13) and to each other (2:13-16). Echoing Isaiah's prophecy, King Jesus is the servant who has "gospeled peace" (Eph 2:17), whose feet are "beautiful," who "brings good news, who publishes peace" (Isa 52:7)—peace to those far off and peace to those who are near (Isa 57:19; Eph 2:17). And if Christ's feet are beautiful, so also are ours: "As shoes for your feet put on whatever will make you ready to proclaim the gospel of peace" (Eph 6:15 NRSV). This is our vocation.

Gospeling peace to those who are "far off" and those who are "near" is a vital part of our vocation with Christ.

CHAPTER 13 SUMMARY

- The early Christians did not consider the ways and teachings of Christ, including enemy-love, impractical or extreme. It was discipleship.
- Jesus Christ, Son of Man, is the one and only True Human Being.
- Alexander the Great is an example of the myth of the invincible, violent warrior-conqueror—the prototypical hero to this day in many societies and cultures.
- Jesus subverts the myth of *manhood as violent conqueror;* he absorbs human violence through love of his human enemies for God's glory, thereby conquering humanity's greatest enemies—death, sin, and the Powers of darkness. Christ is the new humanity.
- We are saved not to escape the world. We are saved *for the world,* that the world is transformed for human flourishing by the glory of Christ, True Human Being.
- Gospeling peace with Christ far and near is our Christian vocation.

FOR FURTHER REFLECTION

- Describe in your own words the *relational* ways of Jesus, the True Human Being.
- What if living in Christ, in the ways of Jesus, offers both the greatest test of courage and the greatest rest from striving? How might this be true?
- How does *gospel as a verb* (as in Isa 52:7 and Eph 2:17) expand our understanding of the gospel?

Chapter 14

GOSPELING PEACE WITH KING JESUS

I feel the tremors, the rumors of war
Upon the surface of my door ...
I don't have the tools to deal with this
I don't have the drugs
And I've got no place to call my country
I've got no place to have my love anymore
Yeah, when the bomb went off
We were dancing in the kitchen with a neon cross
–"No Country" by John Mark McMillan

IN THIS CHAPTER

- The choice between 1) power and privilege, and 2) the Jesus way of enemy-love and gospeling peace: Are we in a "Bonhoeffer moment?"
- The most powerful force at work in the universe is pushing toward Peace.
- Kristin offers four principles and four provocations for a way forward.
- Werner reflects on the article by missiologist Andrew Walls: "The Ephesian Moment."

Kristin: A "Bonhoeffer Moment"?

I am going to speak about some heavy, uncomfortable, and shameful things in this chapter. I'm doing this because I feel a sense of urgency about what is happening in the church and in our world. It's time for Western Christians to find freedom from the sin which so easily entangles our culture. We can do this through asking Jesus to walk alongside us as we tell our stories of shame with as much honesty as we can. With him yoked up beside us, we can have courage to face these things, knowing that he always has a marvelous plan for transformation, and for us to be better than we were. The purpose of this is never to condemn, nor simply to make people feel bad. The purpose of naming shame is so that it can be transformed by the Good News of Christ our Peace. In more ways than one, many Americans sense we are at a pivotal moment, and a moment of crisis.[1]

---

1 Manchester, "Analyst Says US Is Most Divided Since Civil War."

Dietrich Bonhoeffer also found himself in a moment of crisis and increasing tension with the rise of Naziism in Germany. He was one of the few German pastors who stood against the Nazi agenda. He and others formed what was called "The Confessing Church." In 1943, Bonhoeffer was arrested and imprisoned in Tegel Prison. Eighteen months later he was transferred to Flössenberg Concentration Camp, and on April 9, 1945—but not (as is commonly believed) for taking part in the plot to assassinate Adolf Hitler. Rather, as Mark Nation argues, Bonhoeffer was hanged mainly for helping to rescue Jews, for his written and spoken words, for challenging the idolatries and inhumanities of the German state—all in light of the gospel of Jesus Christ.[2]

Some Christian leaders say that we are in "a Bonhoeffer moment"—a time to decide if we will speak with consistent moral clarity, even when many fellow Christians are promoting dehumanization, extremism, and dominionism, or simply being silent on the grave injustices and complicity of the church with violence.

"Can I Be Your Friend?"

A few weeks ago, I sat on a bench enjoying the Mediterranean breeze in Bethlehem, the place of Jesus's birth. An eleven-year-old girl came up to me and asked, "Can I be your friend?" We spent a couple of hours together, helping her practice for the spelling bee, and singing a duet with a Billie Eilish song. She was the friend I needed that day.

Later that day, I learned that this sweet girl's aunt and uncle had been bombed by the state of Israel while sheltering in St. Porphyrius Church in Gaza.[3] Her aunt perished under the rubble, and her uncle died shortly thereafter due to lack of medical care. Another relative (eighty-three years old) had her hip crushed and underwent a total hip replacement without anesthesia. I would hear that day about the anguish of my friend's mother in walking her children through this. Her other daughter was in an exchange program in rural Montana at the time, where she heard classmates and fellow Christians cheering over the destruction of Gaza.

When I told this little girl that she could be my friend, I didn't fully realize what that meant. But to be her friend means that I committed to

---

[2] See Nation, *Discipleship in a World Full of Nazis*, Chapter 1: "Toward Retreiving the True Legacy of Dietrich Bonhoeffer," 22–46.

[3] Sadly, the vast majority of Western Christians are unaware that the Palestinian Christian community has existed in Palestine (including Gaza) since the time of the early church. For Palestinian Christian perspectives, see, e.g., Isaac, *The Other Side of the Wall*, and Raheb, *Faith in the Face of Empire*.

stand *with* and *for* her humanity. I committed to love her as myself, and to wish for her every good thing I could wish for myself. I committed to standing by Jesus's intentions for her Palestinian life—both to her and to others.

I know that someday, my new friend will be old enough to grasp the horrific reality that what happened to her family in Gaza and what continues to happen to her people in the West Bank, happened with the support of Christians in the United States. She will realize that many of them don't know she exists, others don't care, and that others only care because she is a Christian and not a Muslim.

Still others will say that what happened to her family is sad, but not condemnable, because Hamas fighters were probably hiding underneath them when the church was bombed. They will talk as though the "higher cause" of eliminating Hamas was worth the sacrifice of this church and of the human beings sheltering inside. They will take it for granted that sometimes we have to make such cut-throat ethical calculations, even if it means children are dismembered by American weapons, even if bombs are "signed" by American Christian politicians,[4] and even if it means that the Christian community in Gaza is wiped out for the first time since Jesus walked those shores.[5] Many cheer as these things are done in Jesus's name.

I think of the words from Billie Eilish which my friend sang with so much feeling:

I used to float, now I just fall down
I used to know, but I'm not sure now
What I was made for

What was I made for?

Taking a drive, I was an ideal
Looked so alive, turns out I'm not real
Just something you paid for

What was I made for?
I don't know how to feel
But someday I might
Someday I might …

---

4 Kattab, "Mike Pence Writes Messages on Bombs Meant for Lebanon."
5 Khalil Sayegh, "This Easter, Gaza's Christian Community Is on the Brink of Extinction," *The New Arab*, March 28, 2024, https://www.newarab.com/opinion/easter-gazas-christian-community-faces-extinction.

> *Think I forgot how to be happy*
> *Something I'm not, but something I can be*
> *Something I wait for*
> *Something I'm made for ...*[6]

I don't think we have to wonder how things like the transatlantic slave trade or the rise of the Third Reich happened. We can see similar dynamics unfolding right now.

On the other hand, some Israeli Jews have also chosen to fight for my friend and for her right to equality, justice, and security, including even those who lost family members during the Hamas attack on October 7, 2023. Consider the story of Maoz:

> Through his own pain and loss, Maoz Inon fights so that others will not have to keep experiencing the same loss in Gaza, Lebanon, and elswhere. He points to the reality that the only real "sides" here are those who are willing to make peace, and those who are not. As a Christian I would say that Jesus is always on the side of the widow and the orphan and the oppressed, and always on the side of the peacemaker. Maoz says, "I won so many brothers and sisters in the last year. That started with losing my parents. But I won so many brothers and sisters, Palestinian, Israelis, from the international community. And my brothers and sisters, they are not giving me hope; we are making hope together."[7]

How much more should we as believers in Jesus be willing to do the same! How much more so should we be willing to stand in the gap, to stand against "our people" and to stand with God's beloved ones!

I write these things because I am obligated to speak on what I have seen, especially for Palestinian Christian brothers and sisters who are suffering persecution and genocide funded by my tax dollars and in the name of my God. I have to speak also because I love my fellow Americans and my Israeli friends, and because this situation threatens all of us with decades of war to follow. I do believe we are in a Bonhoeffer moment in more ways than one, and that the watchmen need to raise alarm bells (Ezek 33:1–6).

At the same time, I know these topics are overwhelming. It can feel like yet one more burden is being heaped upon us if we seriously

---

6 Billie Eilish O'Connell and Finneas Baird O'Connell, "What Was I Made For?" Lyrics © Kobalt Music Publishing Ltd., Universal Music Publishing Group.

7 Democracy Now, "Israeli Peace Activist Maoz Inon Lost His Parents on October 7."

consider Palestinians or the Congo or the role of the US government in destabilizing nations and fueling violent "blowback" around the world.[8] Many of us already carry heavy burdens. And the emotional burdens heaped on us by media outlets add to the strain. When it's time to act, we may find ourselves out of energy and out of hope. It can seem like the tide of evil in the world is unstoppable, and the cycles of violence unbreakable.

It had to feel like this for Jesus's first disciples too, especially on the Friday when they watched their teacher be condemned, tortured, and then killed. "We had hoped," they said, "that he was the one to redeem Israel" (Luke 24:21). And the Friday story is still being told in every moment of crisis.

The church is at a moment of crisis. American society is at a moment of crisis. Our youth are in crisis. Time to save our land and our ability to live upon it from economic and environmental degradation is quickly running out.

These big crises are marked by smaller moments of crisis along the way: addiction, estrangement of family and loved ones, crises of faith and meaning, realizing that integrity could mean losing everything … each of these is a crisis to itself.

And during any crisis, we see the Friday story:

Like the crowds, there are those who shout "hosanna!" and then turn to condemn. There are the wolves who run to the smell of blood, ready to take advantage of the crisis for their own gain.

Like the disciples, there are many who try to run and hide. They don't know what to do, so they just try not to look. Or, they look on from afar but fail to act.

Like Peter, some are disloyal, even to the ones they love the most.

Like the women, it's often those with the least power who remain loyal anyway. They will stay present in the agony, in the tension of not knowing.

Like the centurion who proclaims Jesus as the Son of God (Mark 15:39), the most unexpected people see with the greatest clarity.

---

8 Johnson, *Blowback*. "Blowback is another way of saying that a nation reaps what it sows. Although individuals usually know what they have sown, they rarely have the same knowledge on a national level, especially since so much of what the managers of the American empire have sown has been kept secret. As a concept, blowback is obviously most easily grasped in its straightforward manifestations. The unintended consequences of American policies and acts in country X lead to a bomb at an American embassy in country Y or a dead American in country Z." Kindle loc 94.

The politicians try to simply appease the masses, doing whatever they think is politically expedient. And the religious authorities? They will do anything they can to maintain the status quo they find comfortable and safe. They will excuse the wrongdoing, and even support it. They will create sanctimonious rationales and theology for moral evils.

But it is not possible for the inhuman to hold him.

Right in the middle of the worst moment, death itself is undone by death. If only we knew the hour of our visitation! If only we knew what is being offered *right in the middle of the crisis.*

In the moment of crisis, he extends the invitation to forsake all and follow him, to leave everything and join the Feast. It can be the moment of revelation, as it was for the centurion. It can be the moment of repentance, as it was for Peter. It can be the moment of choosing weakness and loyalty to him above all else, like it was for the women.

Maybe you've wondered what you would have been doing in Germany in the 1920s and '30s—or perhaps, what you would have done while Jesus was being tried and crucified. I think it's possible that we're all doing it now.

But death is not the end of the story.

And it wasn't the beginning either.

God created a universe full to the brim with Original Glory (Isa 6:3), patterned after his own goodness. Jesus is the true Logic of the Universe. It was built for his harmonious Way, and he is fully committed to the "plan for the fullness of time to unite all things in him" (Eph 1:10).

He also promised that he would not leave us as orphans, but that the Helper and the Comforter would come to us. He is "the Spirit of Truth Who is everywhere present and fills all things, the Treasury of Blessings and the Giver of Life." He is the Guarantor of our inheritance in glory. This means that there is a tidal force at work in the Universe—from its beginning to its end—which is relentlessly committed to bringing his glory to all.

Evil has never been the true foundation or the greatest Power. The most powerful force at work in the universe is pushing toward Peace. And if that is the case, then the only reason we are not seeing that Peace, is because we are actively resisting him, actively swimming *against* the true current of the Universe. So is it any wonder that we often experience such deep exhaustion, "kicking against the goads" (Acts 26:14)? We are going to find this resistance incredibly difficult. As Curt Thompson puts it,

> God sees us not as problems to be solved or broken objects to be repaired but as beauty on the way to being formed. Sin, then, is what keeps us in a posture of resisting God's desire for creating beauty in, with, and through us. His desire is for us to join him in creating

and adding to the beauty we are becoming, which transforms the world around us into much the same. But shame, mediated by our traumas both large and small, has a way of shearing off our capacity to imagine this. As such we often remain mired in telling our stories mostly through the lens of sin and pathology.[9]

But the moment we stop resisting him, and come together, he will do it.

> Come to me all who labor and are heavy laden, and I will give you rest. Take my yoke upon you, and learn from me, for I am gentle and lowly in heart, and you will find rest for your souls. For my yoke is easy, and my burden is light. (Matt 11:28–30)

This is no guarantee that there will not be trouble. As we were reminded in chapter 7, the making of peace will be at least as costly as the making of war. Jesus promised that in the world we will have troubles (John 16:33). But he also promised that he would give us his own peace (John 14:27).

Sociology tells us that the principles we've discussed in this book can work. But we have an even surer hope! Scripture tells us that if we obey him, the Holy Spirit will meet our efforts with his own, unstoppable power and might. On our way to the Feast, we are not alone.

> For this reason I bow my knees before the Father, from whom every family in heaven and on earth is named, that according to the riches of his glory he may grant you to be strengthened with power through his Spirit in your inner being, so that Christ may dwell in your hearts through faith—that you, being rooted and grounded in love, may have strength to comprehend with all the saints what is the breadth and length and height and depth, and to know the love of Christ that surpasses knowledge, that you may be filled with all the fullness of God.
>
> Now to him who is able to do far more abundantly than all that we ask or think, according to the power at work within us, to him be glory in the church and in Christ Jesus throughout all generations, forever and ever. Amen. (Eph 3:14–21)

> The Spirit and the Bride say, "Come." And let the one who hears say, "Come." And let the one who is thirsty come; let the one who desires take the water of life without price. (Rev 22:16–17)

---

9 Thompson, *The Soul of Desire*, 46.

What Can We Do?

Bonhoeffer was in a moment of crisis. The problems he faced and the battles he fought were urgent. In that critical moment, what did Bonhoeffer do? Yes, he spoke out, and yes, he proclaimed the true gospel. But in that urgency, Bonhoeffer dedicated much of his time to *building an alternative community*. Of all his books, *Life Together* is one of the most famous; it outlines the principles and rule of life in his underground Confessing Church seminary.

Jesus was also born into a world in crisis. He knew with prophetic foresight that Judea was facing an imminent destruction in AD 70. And how did Jesus respond? He also spoke out and proclaimed his true Way. But he didn't give all his efforts to spreading his message and mobilizing the masses. Instead, he spent time building an alternative community, to live under the reign of another King, with another citizenship, and a new humanity.

I think that both Jesus and Bonhoeffer recognized that the crises they were facing were not primarily crises of ideology or of thought. They were not even crises of political power. They were *crises of glory*, and therefore, crises of community and belonging.

The foundational crisis of Nazi Germany was not opinions. It was actually "life together" and how it was being lived. It was *life together* that created the soil in which Naziism took root.

Jesus knew that only people living life together in a radically different way stand any chance of making change, of holding integrity for the long haul, and of remaining loyal to the end. Bonhoeffer knew this too, that we need to find our glory in Jesus alone, and that we must practice new habits of thought and life. They knew that we need others to remind us why we resist evil—and to start living as citizens of God's household now. They knew we need to confront our own shame narratives, and the idols to which we so often turn for salvation.

Bonhoeffer embodied Jesus's model. Bonhoeffer understood that we can only do this if we know we belong more radically to the Beloved Son than to anything else. This is about allegiance to another King.

What Can I Do?

As I've shared these things with people in many places, I am often asked, "What can I do?" Usually, my response has been something like this: "I don't really know! I don't think this is something that 'you' can do, or that 'I' can do. It has to be something that *we* do. I only have one part of the puzzle, and you have one part. I don't know your community or your situation. But I can share with you a few of the things I've learned from others. And I think it's going to take a gathering, an *ecclesia,* to come together." I am not "the gathering" or the church. I am not the body of Christ. I do not, individually, put on the full armor of God to withstand the evil one.

Often, I hear people say, "Well you know there's a lot of bad things happening, and I can't do it all." And I'm starting to respond by saying, "No, you can't! It's not possible for me alone to show up for Palestinians, and the Congo, and the unhoused, and the addicted, and the immigrant, and the environment, and so on. But *we* as the church *can.*" And this is how we must begin to think and reimagine our lives in the new humanity.

So, I'm going to share four principles, and four provocations, that I think can help us in the task.

Four Principles

1. Imagination beyond individualism

The first guiding principle is growing our imaginations beyond individualism.

In some cultures, thinking communally is natural. But even then, theology has often been dominated by individualistic cultural lenses from the West. This means that all of us can find it difficult to think *theologically* about the structures of our communities.

In individualistic cultures, this task is harder. Not only do we think about theology and our "walk" with God as an individual task, but we think of nearly everything this way—education, finances, career, health, and the like.

We talk about how to build personal structures to further our spiritual growth and keep us from sin: "If you struggle with alcohol, don't go to a bar!" We also talk about setting aside times for prayer and devotions. We talk about the need to forgive. We talk about how the way we spend our time and money is an indicator of our true priorities. We will say that we need to "look at the fruit" of a person to see how the tree is doing.

But how often do we talk about how to structure our *shared* lives, and build *corporate* habits to further spiritual growth? Do we step back and think about why we gather the way we do, why we spend money on what we do? How often do we look at the fruit of our entire community?

In the places where reconciliation has begun in Rwanda, this was only possible because people chose to think and move forward *together*—as a whole community. Yes, individuals were held accountable—but this could not happen outside the context of the village. This opened the opportunity to be reintegrated rather than simply eliminated or cast out. It allowed shame to move in a direction of transformation and restored glory.

If John Braithwaite and Te-Li Lau are right (see chapter 5), then many of our communities, especially in the United States, are not set up to make this possible. We are not living in the communitarian, interdependent way that the early Christians lived—or that most of our ancestors did. We are isolated and fragmented, and continue to address problems in a highly individualistic manner.

So before we get to the question of *how* to make change, we need to ask *who?* Who do I need to bring along first? What relationships do I need to take time to cultivate, before I jump toward goals? Whose voice is missing? Who have we overlooked? While there are always urgent needs, we need to also slow down to spend time honoring and cultivating life together, so that we can have the sustainable help we need to accomplish things *together*. As I like to put it, we can plant lettuce seeds and fruit trees on the same day. Lettuce seeds will sprout with edible greens in a matter of days or weeks. Fruit trees won't produce for years. We must act both for the urgency of the moment and for five to ten years from now. And we will only be as sustainable as the strength of our relationships.

Addressing the walk of a whole community is not easy, because by myself, I don't have everything we need. It requires that I first enter deep relationships with others which are characterized by interconnection, interdependence, and trust. This was what Bonhoeffer did with his underground seminary during the Third Reich.

2. Focus on the tangible and local

Again and again, we see that those who share tangible, local work form the strongest bonds of friendship and discipleship. And those who focus on neighbor love find ways to overcome barriers that otherwise might keep them apart from others.

In one small town in eastern Washington, the four churches (Presbyterian, Lutheran, Methodist, and Catholic) formed a joint deacon board with its own nonprofit to address community needs. While their denominational structures and differing beliefs prevent certain kinds of "unity," nothing was there to stop their deacons from coming together. As a result, they also began holding gathered worship in the park every July, with each pastor taking their turn to preach on a different Sunday of the month.

In another small town in Oregon, a community church addresses tangible needs for the vulnerable. They are able to unite with other churches and even secular organizations to serve the community. They have built a reservoir of trust by building relationships. Though modest in size, this church has become mighty in its local reputation.

Through these acts of obedience to the commands of the New Testament to love our neighbors (Luke 10:25–29), to remember the poor (Gal 2:10), and to practice true religion (James 1:27), God has enabled these churches to be known by their love (John 13:35) and to show the world who Jesus is (John 17:22).

This was also what Bonhoeffer did. It wasn't enough that the Christians of the Confessing Church shared the same ideas. They shared *life* together.

3. Learning to tell our shame narratives

Shame is often why things stay broken. But it doesn't have to be that way. Shame can also be a starting point for healing and transformation. If Braithwaite is right, shame can only move toward restoration in certain types of communities. So what do we do if we don't live in that type of community?

A first step will be to tell the stories of shame we carry as individuals, families, communities, churches, organizations, cultures, etc. Kingdom Rice in San Francisco uses a "global lens" to help people understand how narratives of shame impact their view of themselves, God, and others.[10] Here's what this does:

Reverses Shame: Shame-reversal is seen throughout the Bible where God consistently meets people in their state of brokenness, weakness, emptiness, rejection, loss, and brings them to a place of honor. This is the essence of the cross and the resurrection.

Centers Vulnerability: Counter to the Western lens that emphasizes personal strength, power and victory, the gospel centers those who perceive their insufficiency: "Blessed are the poor in spirit."

Heals Communities Holistically: When Jesus heals, he restores bodies and hearts, renews minds, and reintegrates individuals into communities where they become vital contributors.

---

10 See https://kingdomrice.org.

Where do we see shame in our lives? Can we discern where questions about our identity and belonging are shaping the way we live and treat others? These are not easy questions. Often, we cannot gain perspective on them without "help from the outside." This proved to be true in the life of Bonhoeffer as well, which leads to our fourth principle.

4. Seeking help from outside

When shame cycles become too deep, we cannot escape without help from the outside. Jesus arrives as God's help from the outside, and he often shows a preference for working through others who are also outsiders, strangers, and outcasts to us. When we care for the vulnerable and the outcast, it is as if we had done it *for him*—but we also find that we must often receive his good news from someone socially "other" to us.

While Bonhoeffer was a student at Union Theological Seminary in New York City (1930-31), he attended Abyssinian Baptist Church in Harlem where he also taught Sunday school.[11] His experience there was life-changing. To understand the critical importance of Bonhoeffer's experience in this black church, it's vital to first know some of Bonhoeffer's prior perspective about the German *Volk* (people) and how that shaped his Christianity.

According to Bonhoeffer scholar Reggie Williams, prior to his time in Harlem, Bonhoeffer had blended his Christian faith with German nationalism. In December 1928, Bonhoeffer gave a lecture series to a congregation of German expatriates in Barcelona. Williams writes:

> Bonhoeffer's third lecture, entitled "Basic Questions of a Christian Ethic," emphasized German patriotic discipleship, with Bonhoeffer's emphasis on loyalty to the superior German peoples, or *Völker*: "[*Völker*] are like individuals. At first they are immature and need guidance. Then they grow into the blossom of youth, mature into adults, and they die.... Growth requires expansion; an increase in strength involves pushing aside other individuals. In that respect the life of an individual person is no different than that of a people [Volk].... Strength also comes from God and power and victory for God creates youth in individuals as well as in nations.... Should not a Volk experiencing God's call on its own life in its own youth and in its own strength, should not such a people be allowed to follow that call, even if it disregards the lives of other people? God is the Lord of history."[12]

---

11 Metaxas, *Bonhoeffer*, 107-11.

12 Williams, *Bonhoeffer's Black Jesus*, 11-12, citing *Dietrich Bonhoeffer Works*, 10:373n34, 339-42.

For people who consider Bonhoeffer a hero of Christian courage and virtue, these words from the German martyr may be shocking. Williams writes, "The *Volk*ish German Christian was the result of theology shaped by an early longing for empire and triumph, rather than by what Bonhoeffer would later value: the recognition of suffering."[13]

In New York, Bonhoeffer's life began to take a different turn. He reported that though he had been a pastor and a preacher before, until his time in Harlem, he had not yet truly become a Christian.[14] Bonhoeffer needed the "help from the outside" that the black people of Harlem and others had to offer him, so that he could finally begin to fall in love with a Jesus who wanted to save him from sin—including poisonous ideologies.

Similarly, we have much to learn from our local and global neighbors. In our own polarized and violent society, we can learn from Palestinian Christian peacemakers and the bridges that have been built with Israeli Jews, Muslims, and others. We can learn from their radical commitment to the ethics of Jesus.

Diversity is God's antidote to the Law of Group Polarization (chapter 8). Diversity can unveil our blind spots. Diversity helps us recognize our shame stories and how they impact us. If we want to more fully see his glory, we need relationships with those who are different.

Imagining beyond individualism and focusing on tangible action will move us to reach out and build relationships with people we would not have thought of before. Our dinner tables will look different. Our humility and vulnerability will grow. And so will the strength of our true identity in Christ.

Four Provocations

Let's take the principles we've discussed a little further into practical applications, especially for Western Christians. These are statements made not to judge—and certainly not to condemn. Rather, they are to push and provoke our thinking a little further.

1. Instead of aiming to be "incredible," aim to be credible.

Churches often seek an *incredible* "Sunday morning experience." They want an incredible small group ministry. They want to be incredible for

---

13 Williams, 12.

14 "Bonhoeffer later recalled his pre–New York career and wrote, 'I had not yet become a Christian but, wildly and undisciplined, was my own master. I know that at that time I took personal advantage of the cause of Christ and served my own vanity.'" Williams, 15.

their diversity, theology, or impact. Some of them may even succeed. But they can still lack *credibility*.

Many times, we seek to be "incredible" by the standards of the world around us—or more often, by the standards of other Christians. We're concerned with what other churches and pastors will think. We're concerned with how to meet the expectations of "church." We want our main event to showcase our best. That main event is usually Sunday morning, for which we spend the better part of the week preparing, and in which we will expend the majority of our volunteer help.

This is so normal, that few of us will ever pause to ask if it's really accomplishing our truest priorities—to meet human needs and make disciples in the peace of Jesus. And leaders rarely stop to ask if it's even meeting their needs. This leads to my second provocation:

2. People don't need more information or better teaching.

One of the main reasons we've lost credibility is that our teaching is not reflected in what our communities look like. We continue with a model of "church" developed to meet the needs of another time. Modernity taught that with more education, people would become better. So, Protestant churches replaced the standard ten-to-twenty-minute homilies with sermons of forty-five minutes or more. Perhaps this made sense in a time with limited literacy, where people still lived in tight-knit communities.

I believe in preaching and teaching. But how well are our churches meeting the gravest spiritual, emotional, social, and physical needs of people *today*? "When words are many, transgressions are not lacking" (Prov 10:19). Our transgression has been that in spite of unparalleled access to Scripture, our lives often do not align with it. And so the words we speak do not distinguish themselves from the unrelenting barrage of propaganda presented through social media and news in the Information Age. Sermons can easily sound like one more sales pitch among many.

If what people are most desperately in need of are communities of peace and discipleship, how can we align our structures with those needs and goals, and nurture our own spiritual, mental, and social health?

3. We need to take an honest look at how well our actual use of time and resources aligns with our priorities.

Should all the accoutrements of Sunday be a main priority when the majority of people now have 24/7 access to thousands of hours of preaching in their pockets? Meanwhile, nearly everyone suffers from loneliness, isolation, addiction, and/or mental illness. And often, it is our pastors and leaders who suffer the most, as the pressure to juggle so many priorities and respond to so many needs continually piles up.

The Lord never asked us to maintain buildings, or to make sure enough money is coming in for them. He never asked us to be event planners or show-stopping preachers. He never asked us to build a brand. Furthermore, even the things he has called us to, he has not called us to do alone, in spite of what leaders (or their congregations) might think. "Imagination Beyond Individualism" can help us to stop running on the hamster wheel of what we can achieve on our own and allow us to empower others who can run in their gifts.

Hear me Christian leaders—*the Feast is for you too!* But it still requires checking everything at the door. Too often, leaders have become the weakest by trying to carry the most. And they have borne the most shame by being held up on a pedestal—and struggling to stay up.

4. Consider buying an apartment complex instead of a church building.

Or doing something just as radical! People involved in a new church plant usually work toward the day when they will have enough money for their own building; instead, what if they dreamed of the day when some of them could move in together in a co-housing community? They could have a big kitchen for shared dinners. They could create common areas for gardens and fellowship, and make life together the first priority.

Through sharing resources, the community of Jesus has more to give. They could house an elderly widow on a fixed income, so she can spend her "evening years" surrounded by the laughter of children without her gifts going to waste. They could invite others who need food or are lonely to shared dinners. Rather than raising children essentially alone, as most American parents do, people could have a true village. This might also make them more ready to adopt. Discipleship and spiritual formation could happen in the day-to-day, as people are able to truly share burdens. The possibilities are endless.

In the Boston area, one church community bought a tri-level house. They know that it's hard for people and communities to change without secure housing. People from the church live together in the tri-level. A single dad gets out of prison and gets back full custody of his kids. He lives with an older widow on the second-floor unit who can provide support while he gets on his feet and learns to parent. The church also has gained use of adjoining city land. They cultivate it into a park and community garden with shady places for passersby to sit and enjoy.

Does your church open its buildings for other churches and groups in the community? Could you begin dreaming about how your building and your people could better weave themselves into the larger community? Maybe you convert part of your lawn into a community garden. Maybe a retired teacher offers English classes once a week for incoming refugees and immigrants.

Every context and community is different. But in every context and community, the same Spirit is present, desiring and empowering a new humanity.

A Time for Radical Experimentation

In the 1940s, Clarence Jordan wrote:

> From populous city and desolate wilderness has gone up the universal cry of lonely hearts for fellowship. We have sought for it in amusement places; we have pursued it through the halls of learning. We have organized it into clubs, lodges, fraternities, and "fellowships." We have given it thousands of banquets—interracial, international, intereverything. Committees, leagues, and councils have spared the social order in quest of it. And at times we have gone wistfully and hopefully to church, feeling that we would catch a glimpse there of this elusive pearl of great price.
>
> Perhaps we haven't really known what we were searching for. And in our desperate hunger, we have been willing to accept any cheap substitute which offered a measure of relief. These substitutes have been delightful to the taste, but give no nourishment.[15]

Jordan urged Christians to begin "some rather bold experimentation" in seeking true Christian fellowship. In so many ways, we are even lonelier today than we were then, and even further from true *koinonia,* true life together. Jordan calls it a "pearl of great price" for a reason—to have it, we must be prepared to sell everything we own. We must be prepared for profound and unexpected difficulty, as we seek life together in ways that are radically different and often opposed to this world's systems, power, and logic.

I'm saying this because I have been broken on the rocks of these efforts, and there is a real cost to be counted. But there is also everything to be gained. "He who did not spare his own Son but gave him up for us all, how will he not also with him graciously give us all things?" (Rom 8:32).

---

15 Jordan, *The Inconvenient Gospel,* 5.

A few friends and I are starting to talk about what this kind of "bold experimentation" could look like for us. Often, people try to create a Jesus community around the concept of "church" with all the baggage and expectations it carries. And then, we hope we can meet the needs in our community. But we haven't asked if all the structures we expect from "church" are really meeting those needs, or if in some cases they hinder them.

So what if instead, we start with the needs themselves, with a holistic view of the glory of the human being—spiritual, emotional, social, and physical? What if, instead of trying to call people from "church" to the gates of hell, we go to the gates first?

In Phoenix, our police department was just declared the worst in the country by the Department of Justice. When I saw this news, it struck me that the churches of Phoenix have far more resources than the police departments. I wondered what would happen if the church started showing up in the places the police show up the most? What if we started a group with this goal—showing up to meet human needs, to advocate, to be agents of peace, and to let people know that they are seen? This could include under-resourced neighborhoods, but it could also include political rallies and other large events. What if we began by simply trying to be present "in the name of Jesus" as Jesus is in the world?

And then, what if we went back to plan, organize, and read Scripture, but all in the context of taking action in Jesus's name? What if we went to Scripture not simply to learn, but to get what we need to walk out a life of obedience to Christ's commands with feet shod in the Good News of Peace (Eph 6:15)?

Our world barrages us with ideas, propaganda, and entertainment. It shapes a habit of engaging with ideas and stories which are *not meant to inform the way we actually live*. When we talk about doing a worthwhile thing, we experience satisfaction and approval from others without having actually done the thing. In fact, there is evidence to suggest that talking about things can make it harder to follow through in real life.[16] Our shoes of the Good News of Peace are often ornamental—they haven't always hit the trail to walk out the peace they carry.

Of course, false theology has also made it easier to divorce faith from action. But I think the bigger hindrance is not lack of access to truth, but that we have been unwilling to obey the truth we do have.

---

16 Huberman, "Controlling Your Dopamine."

The "Love in Action" group would study Scripture in the context of being as Jesus in the world. We would invite those who are hurting, broken by religion, thirsty for something new, to come and see the kinds of things the Living Lord does, and the difference he makes in those who obey him. We would invite them to come and read Job with the homeless and addicted. We would invite them to consider Matthew 10 in the context of advocacy and confronting the works of the devil in our community. We would represent the unseen in our community at city council meetings, churches, and elsewhere.

I find that in these contexts, it is quite natural to pray with people, to tell them about the love of God and the glory they are made for. It has never felt forced or like selling something. Instead, sharing the *evangel* feels like sharing really good news—of dignity, purpose, and deliverance from sin and death. It is letting people know, in the whole of their being, that God's glory is greater than sin.

Complex, but not Complicated

The Good News of Peace is complex in its implications. But it isn't *complicated*. It is only the schemes of human beings which have complicated it, to excuse violence and division, and even to commit acts of violence in Jesus's name. Søren Kierkegaard put it well:

> The matter is quite simple. The Bible is very easy to understand. But we Christians are a bunch of scheming swindlers. We pretend to be unable to understand it because we know very well that the minute we understand, we are obliged to act accordingly. Take any words in the New Testament and forget everything except pledging yourself to act accordingly. *My God,* you will say, *if I do that my whole life will be ruined. How would I ever get on in the world?* Herein lies the real place of Christian scholarship. Christian scholarship is the Church's prodigious invention to defend itself against the Bible, to ensure that we can continue to be good Christians without the Bible coming too close. Oh, priceless scholarship, what would we do without you? Dreadful it is to fall into the hands of the living God. Yes, it is even dreadful to be alone with the New Testament.[17]

Last week, I was talking with a friend who has no background in religion. The parable of the prodigal son came up (Luke 15:11–32). She had never heard the story before and was visibly amazed as I told it. Later, she said, "When I heard that, I was thinking, 'Who am I in

---

17 Kierkegaard, *Provocations,* 193; emphasis added.

this story?' Of course I would want to be like the Father, forgiving and seeking restoration. But I don't know if I always am." The story made her think about her own relationships differently.

In the same week, I heard two different Christian leaders interpreting the same story. Both compared themselves to the Father, and someone else to the prodigal. Both concluded that the other person needed to show humility and repent first. By their reading, it was not up to them to reach out, own up to their own faults, or extend forgiveness first. They missed that the parable is also about the older brother, who doesn't think that the prodigal deserves to come home because he hasn't done anything to earn it. They missed how the Father sees his son "from a long way off" and runs to him.

I think my nonreligious friend found herself more "alone with the New Testament" than either ministry leader. Just as the Levite and the priest passed by the wounded man, these two religious leaders used their theology to pass by their brothers and sisters. Strangely enough, it was the Samaritan—a foreigner to the faith and a heretic—who saw and chose to be a neighbor to the one who had offended her. Now, I'm not saying to overlook theology. And Jesus wasn't saying this either. But perhaps the Samaritan became a law unto himself (Rom 2:14) where the religious leaders who had "right" theology failed. This is profoundly challenging.

I'm also not saying that God's acceptance is dependent on our good works. That's also far from the heart of the Father. However, I think we can miss out on the party the Father is throwing. I also think that our interpretation of Scripture will always be emaciated if it doesn't happen in the context of radical obedience, which is the way that we meet Jesus where he's at work in the world. It is the way we come to join his Feast.

At a certain point, there is no satisfactory intellectual explanation or answer for violence, and all the atrocities being committed every hour by the human race, often in God's name. There is only the mystery of evil, and the mystery of the good news which reaches even there.

And so come points of crisis, decision, and loyalty. We can no longer wait to figure it all out. We must simply follow our Jesus into the dark of the wind and the waves and walk it out (Matt 14:24–33). There comes a point where our questions will leave us on the shore if we let them (Matt 8:18–22). And if we do decide to get in the boat with him, we must do so without knowing where we are going (Heb 11:8). In the end, he himself is our Peace, and the only answer to truly meet the longing of our hearts.

Werner:

Kristin is advocating a radical Jesus-shaped love-in-action *locally*, for those near. Allegiance to King Jesus includes gospeling peace with him, locally and sometimes publicly. Kristin is all about showing up in the name of Jesus among hurting people and communities nearby. We may refer to this as a "theology of locality."[18] To continue our concluding chapter, we'll segue from Kristin's principles and provocations to engage with world Christian historian Andrew Walls.

An "Ephesian Moment"

British historian Andrew Walls (1928–2021) made major contributions to the study of World Christianity. His article "The Ephesian Moment" (published in 2002) resonates with much of our material in this volume.[19] I summarize Walls's article below and offer comments along the way.

Let's imagine ourselves in the time that Ephesians was written. Jewish believers comprise most of the church, but gentiles are joining fast. The writer of Ephesians calls for Christ-centered unity in diversity. This means that even though Jews and gentiles share a long history of hostility and division, through Christ they are called to *same-temple* and *same-table* fellowship (2:14–16). Why? Andrew Walls points to the vision of Ephesians 4:13. The local body of believers is to experience together as much as possible "the measure of the stature of the fullness of Christ." In other words, diversity in the body is not for diversity's sake. *Diversity is for the purpose of knowing more of the fullness of Christ.*

Writing to the Ephesian churches, Paul didn't want culturally distinct local churches in Ephesus. After all, every member is a valuable part of the body of Christ. It's one temple (2:21) forged by one Holy Spirit—one body, one faith, one Lord, one God and Father of all (4:4–6). It was the first "Ephesian moment" in history: Jew-and-gentile cultural diversity forming the One New Humanity in Christ through his cross and resurrection. But that first "Ephesian moment" was short-lived. When Rome destroyed Jerusalem and the Jewish state in AD 70, all Jews including Jewish followers of Jesus were dispersed. Soon, the gentile church—now absent Jewish-background Christians—became culturally monolithic.

---

18 Vaughn, "A Theology of Locality."
19 Walls, "The Ephesian Moment," 72–82.

The Current Ephesian Moment

Fast forward two millennia. "The global church today is at another 'Ephesian moment,'" Walls writes,

> which brings a church more culturally diverse than it has ever been before; potentially, therefore, nearer to that "full stature of Christ" that belongs to his summing up of humanity. The Ephesian moment also announces a church of the poor. Christianity will be mainly the religion of rather poor and very poor peoples, with few gifts to bring except the gospel itself, and the heartlands of the church will include some of the poorest countries on earth.[20]

The center of gravity of the global church has shifted in a massive way. From middle-class white European-background Christianity to a predominantly non-white Christianity of the poor in the Global South.[21] (Supplementing this emphasis on the poorest is the 2024 report by Lausanne indicating a global rise in the middle class—also reflected in the global church.[22]) Walls continues with a sobering prediction.

> A developed world in which Christians become less prominent will seek to protect its position against the rest.[23]

By "developed world," could it be Walls mostly means America because the developed world is so broadly influenced by the United States economically, culturally, and militarily? Is Walls giving a prophetic snapshot of Western Christians protecting their position and status in the global church? Will leaders from the minority-but-wealthy Western segment of the global church engage in honor competition and the tactics of "power-over" (Mark 10:43)?

> The Ephesian question at the Ephesian moment is whether or not the church in all its diversity will demonstrate its unity by the interactive participation of all its culture-specific segments, the interactive participation that is to be expected in a functioning body.[24]

---

20 Walls, 82.

21 Jenkins, *The Next Christendom*.

22 "In 2018, for the first time in history, half of the global population was middle class or higher. Income inequality remains a challenge, and many continue in poverty, but the last half century has witnessed a transformation in the distribution of global wealth." See Lausanne, "New Middle Class."

23 Walls, "The Ephesian Moment," 82.

24 Walls, 82.

The challenge from Walls for Christian leaders may be posed by a set of questions: To what extent can we diversify our local churches?[25] To what degree can we facilitate the interactive participation of all its culture-specific segments? Can we better reflect the cultural diversity of the cities, communities, and neighborhoods we serve? Will we allow ourselves to expand the range of theological voices to which we listen? In pursuit of the full stature of Christ, will we serve with and listen to persons and peoples from diverse social classes and communities? And for those engaged in reaching the least evangelized, can *all-the-peoples-reconciled* be an entry point for evangelism, as proposed in chapter 12?

It is no small challenge for a monocultural local church to become a multicultural church. I offer this suggestion: *Focus relentlessly on Jesus.* Recenter everything in Christ—his life and teachings, his grace and truth, his saving death and resurrection, and his relational ways of courageous compassion. Be centered in Christ. (A classic resource centering on Jesus is Bonhoeffer's *The Cost of Discipleship*. Two newer resources, also excellent, are Mark Baker's *Centered Set Church*[26] and Matthew Bates's *Why the Gospel?*[27])

Finally, Walls points to various non-European diaspora communities in America and the opportunity this represents for the church.

> Will the body of Christ be realized or fractured in this new Ephesian moment? ... Perhaps the African and Asian and Hispanic Christian diasporas in the West have a special significance in the posing of the Ephesian question, and the United States, with its large community of indigenous believers and growing Christian communities of the diasporas, may be crucial for the answer that will be given to it.[28]

Most large cities have immense and vibrant cultural diversity, along with a host of social and cultural collisions. There we are—the Bride of

---

25 Following McGavran, this would be a "mongrel" church—implying the negative connotation of "mixed breed" (McGavran, "The Homogeneous Unit in Mission Theory," 412). Contra McGavran, and following Walls, this is a church that more closely represents the full stature of Christ (Eph 4:31)—a positive view.

26 Baker, *Centered-Set Church: Discipleship and Community Without Judgmentalism.* Referencing Hiebert, Missiological Reflections, 107–36, Baker proposes a shift for the local church from "bounded-set" to "centered-set"—centered in Christ in ways that are fresh, practical, and biblically sound. See centeredsetchurch.com.

27 Bates's *Why the Gospel: Living the Good News of King Jesus on Purpose* is a compact book that demonstrates why the New Testament is relentlessly focused on the gospel of the kingdom and the saving life and work of King Jesus.

28 Walls, "The Ephesian Moment," 82.

Christ, his beloved—in the midst of it all. The migration of peoples around the world will continue into the foreseeable future. International hostilities and group hatreds are part of the human condition. Dynamics fueling the migration of peoples include economic desperation, educational need, cultural clashes, climate change emergencies, civil wars and other kinds of hot wars—or simply the hope for a fresh start in another land.

The need for reconciliation between hostile groups through Christ has never been greater. Can the church make a dent in the hostility of our world by proclaiming Christ's gospel of peace? Do we even want to do this? Will we grasp the opportunity of this "Ephesian moment"?

BEING HUMAN: Gospeling Peace Far and Near

For the glory of God ... for the world God loves, all persons, all peoples, all creation ... for the church's witness to the rulers and authorities (Eph 3:10) ... for the blessing of unreached peoples ... for the poor and oppressed ... for the credibility of the church claiming Jesus is Lord ... for the sake of displaying our humanity as we imitate Jesus, True Human Being: We believe we can recover the horizontal dimension of the gospel of Christ by whom hostile persons and peoples are reconciled—"through the cross, thereby killing the hostility" (Eph 2:16). Will we join Jesus in living and proclaiming the gospel of peace, far and near?

Ephesians 2:13-19

[13] *But now in Christ Jesus you who once were far off have been brought near by the blood of Christ.*

> Persons and peoples far-off and loved by God—the gentiles—whom we might consider outsiders, enemies, and least reached—are now brought near to God and near-to-one-another in same-table-fellowship. Christ's bloodshed, absorbing shame and violence, is the bloodshed of reconciliation. We share a common allegiance to King Jesus and his reconciling cross.

[14] *For he himself is our peace, who has made us both one and has broken down in his flesh the dividing wall of hostility,*

> With King Jesus as our peace, former walls that divide are broken down. Strangers or former enemies are now friends joining hands in a journey of life and hope for the world. We're on a wholeness journey together to recover our humanity.[29]

---

29 I'm indebted to Dave Dicken for the phrase, "We're on a wholeness journey together."

¹⁵ *by abolishing the law of commandments expressed in ordinances, that he might create in himself one new man in place of the two, thus making peace,*

King Jesus has forged in his blood a peace treaty with us and for us. There's now a brand-new way of being human together. It goes by various names: new creation, one new humanity, unity in diversity, the beloved community. Christ transforms us in his glory.

¹⁶ *and might reconcile both to God in one body through the cross, thereby killing the hostility.*

Killing death by death, the risen King is killing hostility between persons and peoples. The Lamb of God has absorbed and subverted violence. Violence no longer has the final say. With death and hostility defeated, we open ourselves to unlikely new friends in the beloved community.

¹⁷ *And he came and preached peace to you who were far off and peace to those who were near.*

King Jesus embodies the ancient prophecy proclaiming God's reign of grace and truth. Good news! A new kingdom, a new regime has dawned. The King is gospeling peace to everyone, those far off and those near. Those far off—who are they? They are peoples and persons yet to worship Jesus as the Christ, their Savior, Redeemer, Lord. They are those who have never heard the story of Jesus in their language. They have no churches in their context, no access to the gospel. They have yet to receive God's blessing—having sins forgiven, worshiping the living God, set free from evil oppression, joining God in his global-glory-story. Those who are near—who are they? They are persons and peoples with access to the good news but have yet to join God in the story of his glory.

¹⁸ *For through him we both have access in one Spirit to the Father.*

Through King Jesus, with undivided and unrestricted access, we worship in one Spirit the one true God. Our Father unites us in our worship of Christ Jesus, True Human Being. With access to God, we give our allegiance to Christ; we are in his story and join him in gospeling, serving, and peacemaking.

¹⁹ *So then, you are no longer strangers and aliens, but you are fellow citizens with the saints and members of the household of God.*

Outsiders to God's family? That's all behind us now. Jesus has made us insiders and given us himself—he is now our source of life and honor. With our allegiance to King Jesus, our citizenship is in God's kingdom. We share in the same household of God, members in God's family, with the status of God's children. King Jesus is at the head of the table where we feast together. We are at last fully human and uniquely ourselves while reflecting Christ's beauty. Jesus is our glory and honor.

Worthy, worthy, worthy is the Lamb!

CHAPTER 14 SUMMARY

- A "Bonhoeffer moment" represents a time when we must decide if we will speak with consistent moral clarity—when refusing to be silent requires uncommon courage.
- Being part of an alternative community centered in Jesus is essential for living in times of moral uncertainty or upheaval.
- The world shapes a habit of engaging with ideas and stories which are not meant to inform the way we actually live.
- An "Ephesian moment" represents an opportune time in the global purpose of God—when circumstances emerge for the church to know more of the "full stature of Christ"—through believers from diverse cultural backgrounds being in *same-temple* and *same-table* fellowship.
- One goal of Christian discipleship, including world missions, is to be conformed to the full stature of Christ—to become truly, fully, gloriously human.

FOR FURTHER REFLECTION

- How does your faith community help you imitate the social ways of Jesus? How is your faith community embodying Christ's One New Humanity?
- If you were to put on the shoes of the gospel of peace (Eph 6:15), where would you go? And with whom?
- To what degree might your church be resisting or embracing an "Ephesian moment?"

AFTERWORD

By D. Zac Niringiye

When Werner Mischke introduced the Ephesian 2 Gospel Project on a call in July 2022, I was glad to be invited to the table as a conversation partner on the book project he and Kristin Caynor had begun. Serendipitously, they were grappling with similar questions as I was, about the good news in Jesus of Nazareth and its imperative for those who live by the gospel in a world in which injustice and violence have been normalized, not least by Christianity.

I joyfully welcomed the opportunity to journey together—reading each other's work, making time to discuss, giving candid feedback. "As iron sharpens iron," we plowed over our writings and reflections. This conviction unites us: Jesus of Nazareth—who he was and is, what he proclaimed and embodied—is good news for all humanity and creation.

We became friends as we sat together over coffees and lunches in Phoenix, freely sharing our stories—highs and lows, joys and trials, hopes and fears. This freedom and joy created the space to own and name our different social locations that shape our perspectives. It is uncommon to have a conversation in which this is regularly named and interrogated. I have a lot I could write in appreciation for the gift of our conversations and the broadening of my horizons. I am delighted to offer this afterword.

One New Humanity is more than I hoped and longed for: a fruit of deep, wide, and long conversations. It should also be read in conversation. It models inter- and multicultural disciplinary and generational discourse. Moreover, lines are artificial because our stories as the human family are connected; disciplines are interrelated and interconnected; and sociologies are theologies, just as theologies are sociologies. We do not read or see what we are looking at or hear what is being said or sung; it is with what we read, see, or hear. As Mark Labberton has put it:

> Seeing is important and reliable in many ways, but it is neither neutral nor comprehensive. Sight is not just what we see but how we see – and that is a function of our values, experiences, relationships, associations, beliefs, culture, race, gender and age. This means that everything we see passes through invisible lenses of perception that take a lot of the information the eye receives and the brain sorts, and places it within the framework of our experience or understanding or plausibility. [1]

---

[1] Labberton, *The Dangerous Act of Loving Your Neighbor*, 74.

Meaning is assigned by social location; it is always contextual; what we make of the past and geography (place) matter.

One New Humanity considers many angles and perspectives. It not only quotes from a diversity of sources but also locates them. Like all good conversations, it is not just the people conversing but the nuances, perspectives, and honesty in grappling with big questions of faith and life. But it also leaves one pondering who else, and what else, could or should have been in the conversation.

Gratefully, *One New Humanity* is a living work; it invites us to join the conversation. Although its primary audience is Christians, theologians, and church and mission leaders in America, the critical issues, questions, and ideas they grapple with are relevant in other lands, especially where Christianity is the dominant religion.

There are passages in the Bible that capture the contours of the biblical narrative comprehensively. Ephesians 2 is one such text. The chapter bridges chapters 1 and 3 which emphasize the multifaceted glory of God. Ephesians 2 is a lens for making sense of God's revelation and reconciling purpose in Christ. "Glory" as a grand narrative of Scripture is intriguing and refreshing. Yes! It is all about glory: the glory of the One who, in the beginning, created "the heavens and the earth" (Gen 1:1), reflected in all humanity and all creation; indeed, creation was by Glory, in Glory, for Glory.

Glory is the context. Glory is also a hermeneutic—a lens through which to interpret the rest of the Story. Glory is a way of making sense of humanity—who we were meant to be; what we became due to "violence"; and what we are becoming together in Christ.

The motif of "glory" relocates and realigns us to a bigger, greater, more majestic and compelling vision and imagination of what we are about as a people "in Christ, in the world." Werner and Kristin's conversation about glory enables us to better understand "sinful" humanity-and-world, manifested in the triad of shame, violence, and trauma. In naming attitudes, events, epochs, and personal experiences that show how this triad works, they challenge us to do the same.

I confess that I was eager to hear more in this work about how honor-shame status games, undergirded by ideologies and theologies, justify social hierarchies and generate monstrous atrocities, such as apartheid, ethnic cleansing, and genocide. Violence in the name of "God of the Bible" remains with us today. How critical it is that we distinguish Christianity from the gospel! Kristin and Werner have presented a compelling exposition of the good news, the gospel of peace: Jesus in his death on the cross is the Person and the place where "the powers" of shame, violence, and trauma were disarmed and conquered by Glory, and manifested in Christ's resurrection.

What glory, that saved us, saves us, and will save us from besetting shame, violence, and trauma that linger within us and we live with, each moment, each place! What a weight and joy of glory is ours who live by that Story—embodying, seeking, proclaiming, and pursuing the good news of shalom, toward the "one new humanity" that is now and not yet, in Christ!

When I joined Werner and Kristin in the conversation, I had concluded that another triad—shame, guilt, and fear—would explain why Christianity has often portrayed *Pax Romana* rather than *Pax Christi* (chapter 10). Christianity has, past and present, cohabited with violence. But it was also deeply complicit with historical injustices, exploitation, and violent conflicts such as the transatlantic slave trade, European imperialism, colonial conquest, apartheid in South Africa. Even in the 1994 Rwandan genocide, churches were not merely silent but intimately associated.[2]

Now, in conversation with the triad of shame, violence, and trauma, I wonder whether violence and trauma are less causal factors and more symptoms or even the hardware for ensuring dominance in honor-shame rivalry games. I surmise that guilt and fear produce and reinforce shame, creating hate and violence. In contrast, Glory is the ethos, pathos, and logic of shalom. Glory subverts narratives and patterns of power that justify and reinforce shame, guilt, and fear.

What is at the heart of the problem of religion in general and Christianity in particular? I believe it is captivity to narratives of shame, guilt, and fear of "the other" that creates "the barrier, the dividing wall of hostility" (Eph 2:14). It is not an overstatement to suggest that one of evangelical Christianity's distinctives is its bondedness to doctrines and perspectives of guilt and fear. The gospel of shalom challenges and subverts sociologies and theologies that justify and perpetrate shame, guilt, and fear, irrespective of their pretensions to offer some good. I am eager to converse with Werner and Kristin, on how "reintegrative" shame works for entire peoples and histories of "being shamed" and marginalized based on long-held readings of the Scriptures.

As I have already remarked, sociologies are theologies, just as theologies are sociologies. *One New Humanity* challenges us to reexamine our readings of Scripture, our theologies, our sociologies. This work asks

---

2 Katongole, *A Future for Africa*, 95.

us anew whether the "gospel" we profess and embody is consistent with the good news of shalom in Jesus Christ.

In shining the searchlight of glory on some of the "gospels" embodied and proclaimed in various Christian eras and traditions, many are found wanting; they are truncated versions of the gospel. The overall picture painted by Christianity of these traditions and eras (*Pax Christiana*) does not point to *Pax Christi* but to *Pax Romana* (chapter 11). Should we not be bold and declare some of these not mere aberrations but counterfeit and antagonistic to the story of Jesus of Nazareth?

The prophetic word from Werner and Kristin to the churches in America (and indeed to the churches in the Western World) is clear, echoing the message of apostle John, to "the seven churches in the province of Asia" (Rev 1:4). Indeed, the story of the churches in Rwanda should act as a mirror, as Katongole rightly observed that "the crisis of Western Christianity is reflected back in the broken bodies of Rwanda. Western Christians cannot look into this mirror without coming face-to-face with betrayal, idolatry, and death." I hope those of us who hail from churches in other lands, where *Pax Christiana* is a performance of *Pax Romana* will write our version of *One New Humanity*.

The vision and imagination of the "one new humanity" in Christ is glorious; it is living glory, hallowing God's name, God's kingdom come, and God's will be done "on earth as it is in heaven" (Matt 6:9–10). Werner and Kristin have given us glimpses of glory on earth, communities seeking paths toward breaking the barriers and dividing walls of hostility in Jesus's name, and subverting narratives of shame, violence, and trauma.

We need more; the world needs more. Where are the communities challenging today's imperial power centers and modeling *Pax Christi* in the management of public power? We have too many examples of *Pax Christiana* in collusion with *Pax Romana*; we need new stories of communities of followers of Jesus subverting *Pax Romana*. Let us write them, not just in another volume but in places and spaces where we live.

Appendix 1
RECONCILING ATONEMENT IN EPHESIANS 2

An Exegetical Study by Brad Vaughn, PhD

I. Overlooking Atonement in Ephesians[1]

How does Christ's atonement inform Paul's message in Ephesians? Surprisingly, this question has received scant attention from theologians and biblical commentators. Systematic theologies explain Christ's atoning work extensively yet with only passing reference to Ephesians.[2] More specialized texts only fare marginally better.[3] Authors mention ways that Ephesians contributes to our understanding of the atonement, yet few offer sustained treatments on the subject.[4]

Certain exceptions are nevertheless problematic. A few authors typify the ways that countless interpreters explain Ephesians 2. Although the chapter emphasizes horizontal enmity between people, Leon Morris only mentions it to underscore the point that Christ mends humanity's vertical relationship to God.[5] Likewise, John Stott cites Ephesians 2:13 as evidence of Christ's reconciling an individual's relationship to God when in fact the context primarily stresses the horizontal reconciliation of gentiles to God's people.[6] With these comments, I don't wish to overdramatize the problem. Scholars have long proclaimed the rich message of salvation found in Ephesians.

Still, we should consider how interpreters overlook or minimize several aspects of Paul's letter in Ephesians. While his message at times is nuanced, it has practical significance for the church historically and globally. Therefore, this essay explores the explicit and implicit

---

1 All Scripture quotations in this appendix are from the NRSV.

2 For examples, see Grudem, *Systematic Theology*; Erickson, *Christian Theology*; Berkhof, *Systematic Theology*; McGrath, *Christian Theology*; Frame, *Systematic Theology*.

3 For instance, one finds no mention of Ephesians 2:13-16 in Boersma, *Violence, Hospitality, and the Cross*. By contrast, Torrance periodically highlights Ephesians in Torrance, *Atonement: The Person and Work of Christ*.

4 E.g., McNall, *The Mosaic of Atonement*; Hill, "Atonement in the Old and New Testaments," in *The Glory of the Atonement*, ed. Hill and James III, 23-34.

5 Morris, *The Cross in the New Testament*, 249-50.

6 Stott, *The Cross of Christ*, 198-99.

atonement theology of Ephesians. One reason for this study is to discern the relationship between Christ's atoning work and the horizontal reconciliation discussed in Ephesians 2. Our observations will both contribute to and contrast many popular atonement theologies. We will find that a robust, biblical theology of atonement necessarily entails an understanding of how God in Christ reconciles the nations to form a new humanity in keeping with his covenant promises to Israel.

The following sections survey Paul's view of the atonement as seen in Ephesians. I lay particular stress on Ephesians 2 for reasons that will soon become clear. We first consider what constitutes an atonement theology. After reflecting on John Driver's emphasis on Ephesians 2, we examine the context of Paul's letter in order to interpret its message. How does Ephesians present the effects and mechanics of Christ's atoning work? Finally, we will identify several theological and practical implications of Paul's letter to Ephesus.

Methodologically, this study seeks to use a more exegetical approach characteristic of biblical theology. This strategy differs from thematic readings that mark systematic theology. Certainly, the two fields are inseparable and interdependent. Nevertheless, in theory, they have different starting points. Biblical theologians attempt to begin with the questions and concerns raised by the original authors. The original literary, historical, and cultural contexts are prioritized. Systematic theologians typically begin with questions pertinent to their contemporary readers. Such writers synthesize various (often unrelated) passages to distill the Bible's teaching on a particular subject (e.g., soteriology, Christology, ecclesiology).

When reading scholars from both disciplines, one finds that they usually discuss the atonement in quite different ways. For instance, works produced by systematic theologians typically center on a handful of popular atonement theories (e.g., penal substitution, Christus Victor). Such theories are contextualizations proposed by theologians across church history. None of these formulations is explicitly found in Scripture, even if they accurately reflect the Bible's teaching. By contrast, biblical scholars usually limit the scope of their study to specific books or passages (e.g., Leviticus). Their publications outline the logic of particular texts in light of their ancient cultural and literary contexts. They rarely attempt to construct entire doctrines that explain the meaning and significance of the atonement across the whole of Scripture.

II. What Is a Theology of Atonement?

Not everyone agrees about what a theology of atonement should consist of. In fact, theologians often answer entirely different questions. For example, popular atonement theories fall into two general types. Some offer theories that explain what is achieved by atonement. Examples include recapitulation theory and Christus Victor. By contrast, a second set of theories suggest how Christ secures atonement. Ransom theory, satisfaction theory, and penal substitution belong to this group. In truth, a robust theology of atonement includes both aspects. Why this divide among theologians? Put simply, people have different questions and theological methods. Differing questions and assumptions produce diverging (but not necessarily contradictory) trajectories.

What is atonement? Broad descriptions abound. For the sake of this essay, the atonement broadly refers to the reconciling work of God through Christ. It is what secures our salvation and "at-one-ment" with God. While such sweeping descriptions are helpful, they lack sufficient precision to assist us in interpreting the Bible. Countless ideas and concepts might fall within the category of God's reconciling work in Christ.

Key biblical terms that speak of atonement are *kpr* and *exilaskomai*. In the Old Testament, Greenberg explains, *kpr* is "to repair or create a new protective connection" between the worshiper and the Lord. It "reflects [the Lord's] acceptance of the priestly offering."[7] In the Septuagint (LXX), the Greek translation of the Old Testament, *kpr* is translated as *exilaskomai*. Some translators render it "atone" or "propitiate." However, "entreat" is a simpler, more consistent translation.[8]

Biblical writers use three primary metaphors to describe atonement—purity, payment, and load bearing. In other words, atonement solves the problems of impurity, debt, and burden.[9] A few examples will suffice. Leviticus 14:19–20 connects atonement with purification: "The priest shall offer the reconciliation offering, to make atonement for the one to be cleansed from his uncleanness. Afterward he shall slaughter the burnt offering; and the priest shall offer the burnt offering and the grain offering on the altar. Thus the priest shall make atonement on his behalf and he shall be clean."[10] Likewise, "bearing" entails atonement in Leviticus 10:17,

---

7 Greenberg, *A New Look at Atonement in Leviticus*, 45, 48.

8 Many interpreters suppose that "propitiate" implies anger on the part of the Lord (i.e., the one receiving propitiation). While this is possible, it more generally refers to one's gaining of favor or making peace with another party. See Vaughn, *The Cross in Context*, 72–74.

9 Vaughn, *The Cross in Context*.

10 Cf. Lev 12:6–7; 16:30; Num 8:21.

where Moses asks, "Why have you not eaten the reconciliation offering in the place of the sanctuary, since it is a thing most holy and has been given to you that you *may bear* [*nāśā'*] the iniquity of the congregation, to *make atonement for them* before the Lord"? Finally, atonement comes by way of compensation or reparation in Leviticus 5:14–16, which says,

> The Lord spoke to Moses, saying, "If anyone commits a breach of faith and sins unintentionally in any of the holy things of the Lord, he shall bring to the Lord as his *compensation* [*asham*], a ram without blemish out of the flock, valued in silver shekels, according to the shekel of the sanctuary, for a *reparation offering* [*asham*]. He shall also *make restitution* [*shlm*] for what he has done amiss in the holy thing and shall add a fifth to it and give it to the priest. And the priest shall *make atonement* [*kpr*] for him with the ram of the *reparation offering* [*asham*], and he shall be forgiven."

Elsewhere, I summarize the meaning of atonement in this way:

> Atonement refers to the biblical process of making things right. It is how people seek God's favor.... biblical writers highlight three primary metaphors of atonement. It cleanses, ransoms, and removes a burden. These metaphors are entwined. Atonement saves people from impurity and the burden of debt that ensues. It entreats God's favor. The end result is reconciliation.[11]

This review of the Old Testament's theology of atonement is not a diversion from our main task of interpreting Ephesians. Instead, understanding the Bible's presentation of atonement is critical for two reasons. First, it alerts us to potential ways that Paul might allude to Christ's atoning work in his letters. Second, it guards readers against eisegesis, wherein one imposes ideas into the Bible that are otherwise foreign to its meaning.

A few other points are noteworthy before turning our attention to Ephesians. It is commonly believed that people are the primary objects receiving atonement. This impression is mistaken. In the Old Testament, atonement is made on behalf of people. Nevertheless, Levitical priests make atonement for sacred objects and space. In this way, atonement creates or restores a proper relationship between people and sacred things.

Furthermore, the work of atonement effects two types of transformation. On the one hand, it makes an unclean object become clean.[12] On the other hand, atonement transforms a clean object into

---

11 Vaughn, *The Cross in Context*, 74.
12 Lev 12:7–8; 14:18–20, 29, 31, 53; 15:30; 16:16, 30; Num 8:21; Ezek 43:26.

something holy (cf. Exod 29:33-37; Lev 16:19-20). This process, in essence, is one of consecration or sanctification. Numbers 8 illustrates how the atonement brings about both the cleansing and consecration of the Levites. As we'll see, this Old Testament background serves as the backdrop for Paul's thinking. These observations will prove critical for discerning Paul's atonement theology in Ephesians.

III. Atonement and Identity in Ephesians 2

We noted how writers often overlook or underemphasize aspects of Paul's teaching on the atonement in Ephesians. An important exception is John Driver. In *Understanding the Atonement for the Mission of the Church*, he surveys ten principal biblical images used for the atonement.[13] Driver ultimately concludes, "all ten of these motifs are present in one way or another in the key passage of Ephesians 2:11-22"; thus, "we can point to Ephesians 2:11-22 as the key and high point of Ephesians and as a fundamental capstone to Pauline reflection on the meaning of the saving work of Christ."[14] Interestingly, few commentators have seriously engaged Driver's stunning assertion. This lack of engagement is surprising and so is a catalyst for this essay.

What does Driver draw from his study? A key conclusion is summarized:

> The peace between Jews and Gentiles is the realm in which the reality of peace with God may be experienced—rather than being a possible secondary and derivative consequence of a solely transcendent peace with God. Traditionally, theories of atonement have tended to focus on the ways in which barriers have been removed between humanity and God. This Pauline summary, however, focuses on the fact that Christ's death served to remove social barriers and thus make peace among human enemies, as well as making possible their common access to God.[15]

At first glance, this insight might seem mundane. However, this reading of Ephesians significantly expands on conventional interpretations.

For Driver, the atonement of Christ accomplishes more than saving individual sinners. He contends that the atonement is collectivist in nature. That is, it fundamentally aims to create a new community and social order. He says,

---

13 Driver, *Understanding the Atonement for the Mission of the Church*.
14 Driver, 213. He cites Markus Barth, *Ephesians*, 275.
15 Driver, 228.

> If we take our clue from Ephesians 2:11–22, it is possible to affirm that the New Israel of God, this messianic community of peace, is the point at which all of the principal New Testament images for understanding the work of Christ converge. Peoplehood under God's reign is the organizing center around which all of those images rotate. ... Extracted from this covenant-community context, the death and resurrection of Christ cannot really be understood in their fullest biblical meaning.[16]

Because of Christ, both Jew and gentile "come into a share of salvation history. The history of God's ancient covenant people becomes our history." [17]

At points, one could accuse Driver of overstating his case. For example, he contends, "The implication of this creation of 'one new man' out of the two is that neither of the two can enjoy salvation, peace, and life without the other. People need each other if they are to be saved at all."[18] He adds, "Just as Christ's reconciling of Jews and gentiles in 'one new man' is essential to their continuing access to God, so also every person's worship must be preceded by reconciliation with hostile brothers and sisters."[19]

These comments might claim too much and therefore need qualification. First, by their nature, salvation, peace, and life (as Paul explains them) are inherently communal and social. In this respect, the former quote is correct. This clarification is necessary because of what Driver says in the latter quotation, which could be (mis)understood as saying that horizontal reconciliation is a precondition for reconciliation with God.

The word *essential* creates difficulty in interpreting what Driver means. The key text is Ephesians 2:15–16:

> He has abolished the law with its commandments and ordinances, that [ἵνα] he might create in himself one new humanity in place of the two, thus making peace, and might reconcile both groups to God in one body through the cross, thus putting to death that hostility through it.

The word ἵνα ("so that") modifies the main clause (2:15a), introducing two purpose clauses in 2:15b, 16a. These purpose statements appear to be two facets of the same reality, which Paul also highlights in 2:14, 17, 19. Accordingly, becoming "one new man" is not a precondition to being reconciled with God. By analogy, a child is not adopted and *only then* gains new siblings. Rather, the very act of adoption *is the precise moment*

---

16 Driver, 222.
17 Driver, 227.
18 Driver, 226.
19 Driver, 227.

she gets new brothers and sisters. Thus, becoming one new man is essential to gaining access to God in the sense that they must occur simultaneously, being different aspects of the same reality.

Driver pulls the phrase "access to God" from 2:18 and 3:12. In each case, Paul's remarks are a matter of fact, not conditioned upon people being wholly reconciled with hostile brothers and sisters. To be clear, I don't think Driver actually asserts this conditional access to God. However, he draws a flawed analogy that could be misinterpreted as though horizontal reconciliation (among social groups) were a precondition for vertical reconciliation (God with humanity).

We can read Driver sympathetically by clarifying his logic in the following way. Reconciliation with God necessarily creates one new humanity in Christ (ontologically speaking). Therefore, any perspective that minimizes or denies our being "one new humanity" misunderstands or misrepresents Christ's reconciling us to the Father.

Brian Bantum contextualizes and even reframes the discussion about atonement in ways that reinforce Driver's stress on the social features of salvation in Ephesians. He suggests,

> The doctrine of atonement seeks to address a fundamental question, "Who are we?" ... The atonement concerns identity insofar as it attempts to narrate the particularities of the relationship between God and humanity and thus articulate who humanity is. In this respect the claim concerning atonement is not only about humanity's relationship with God, but about an identity with God that echoes and becomes present within human interrelationships.[20]

Accordingly, if Christ dies to reconcile the world (not merely Israel) to God, then our doctrine of atonement needs to account for the bringing together of Jews and gentiles. This is precisely what we see in Ephesians 2:11–22. Christ's atonement is not an ahistorical reality; it arises from a particular historical and cultural milieu. Bantum reminds us, "The atonement is an act that works from within a particular relationship and the parameters of that relationship that have been established within the covenant. [Furthermore,] the Day of Atonement expresses Israel's identity as belonging to YHWH, as subject to a particular mode of life with one another and with the world because of this identity."[21] In this respect, "it hardened the boundaries between Jewish and gentile identity."[22] As we'll

---

20 Bantum, "To Those Who Were Distant," 128.

21 Bantum, 139.

22 Bantum, 140.

see, these reflections on the significance of atonement in ancient Israel magnify the contrast found in Ephesians 2, where Christ's atonement brings Jew and gentile together.

IV. The Context of Ephesians 2

We now turn to the context of Ephesians, giving special attention to Paul's message in Ephesians 2:11–22. Noel Schoonmaker contends, "Eph 2:11–18 concerns atonement from start to finish" and observes, "Eph 2:14–18 contains the only explicit reference to 'the cross' in Ephesians."[23] Markus Barth considers Ephesians 2:11–22 "the key and high point" of Paul's letter.[24] Likewise, Rader calls it "the theological center" of Ephesians.[25] In what follows, we begin to evaluate these claims.

Paul's letter is written for a largely gentile audience. Ephesians 2:11–22 directly addresses non-Jewish readers. Accordingly, we would not anticipate Paul to appeal explicitly to the logic of Leviticus. As a Jewish teacher however, Paul draws from a Hebrew understanding of atonement, and so we would expect to find more subtlety when he discusses the atonement. In other words, it would be surprising to see him sending an elaborate exposition of Leviticus to gentile Ephesians.

Nevertheless, Paul does not present an abstract theology. The historical particularity of Paul's conception of atonement means that he relates Jews and gentiles in a distinct way. Bantun explains,

> The condition of the Gentiles described by Paul is fundamentally related to the covenantal identity of Israel, but Paul's description of their atonement renders their position within this redemptive process in a particular way. "Dead according to transgressions" is not the same as being "without God in the world." These two related but distinct ways of describing humanity's condition in need of Christ's atoning work begin to highlight how in Christ human particularity becomes present in Christ and reconstituted through his life and thus within the church.[26]

Paul does not speak of atonement in ahistorical terms. His view stems from the larger narrative of God's promises to bless the world through one nation, Israel. Therefore, contemporary readers must be alert not to suppose an individualized conception of the atonement that does not account for the election of ancient Israel.

---

23 Noel Schoonmaker, "Preaching Ethnic Atonement," 113–14.
24 Barth, *Ephesians*, 275.
25 Rader, *The Church and Racial Hostility*, 246.
26 Bantum, "To Those Who are Distant," 138.

Where might we get a glimpse of Paul's atonement theology as expressed in Ephesians? As we've noted, payment (e.g., debt-imagery, redemption) is a primary atonement metaphor in the Old Testament. In Paul's letter, he directly speaks of redemption three times.

> In him we have *redemption through his blood,* the forgiveness of our trespasses, according to the riches of his grace. (1:7)

> This is the pledge of our inheritance toward redemption as God's own people, to the praise of his glory. (1:14)

> And do not grieve the Holy Spirit of God, with which you were marked with a seal for the day of redemption. (4:30)

Furthermore, a couple of texts describe Christ effecting purification and making his people holy. As we've seen, these are two fundamental functions of atonement.

> Just as he chose us in Christ before the foundation of the world *to be holy and blameless* before him in love. (1:4)

> Husbands, love your wives, just as Christ loved the church and gave himself up for her, in order to *make her holy by cleansing her with the washing of water by the word,* so as to present the church to himself in splendor, *without a spot or wrinkle or anything of the kind*—yes, so that she *may be holy and without blemish.* (5:25–27)

Ephesians 5:2 is an overt reference to the Levitical system and requires more reflection.

> And live in love, as Christ loved us and gave himself up for us, a *fragrant offering and sacrifice to God* [προσφορὰν καὶ θυσίαν τῷ θεῷ εἰς ὀσμὴν εὐωδίας]. (5:2)

A more subtle allusion comes when Paul identifies God's people with his temple.

> So then you are no longer strangers and aliens, but you are citizens with the saints and also members of the household of God, built upon the foundation of the apostles and prophets, with Christ Jesus himself as the cornerstone. In him the whole structure is joined together and *grows into a holy temple in the Lord;* in whom you also are built together spiritually into a dwelling place for God. (2:19–22)

Finally, Ephesians 2:13–18 is dense with language describing Christ's work of atonement.

> ... by the blood of Christ (2:13)
> ... in his flesh (2:14)

He has abolished the law with its commandments and ordinances, that he might create in himself one new humanity in place of the two, thus making peace (2:15)

... in one body through the cross (2:16)
... for through him both of us have access in one Spirit to the Father" (2:18)

Schoonmaker notes, "Eph 2:14–18 contains the only explicit reference to 'the cross' in Ephesians," an intriguing feature of the letter.[27]

The focus of this essay concerns Ephesians 2:11–22. The range of texts above will inform our reading of this compact passage. Paul's meaning will remain opaque to us unless we interpret these verses in light of the atonement theology found in the Old Testament.

What is Paul's argument in Ephesians 2:11–22? Discourse analysis clarifies his main idea, reiterated in different ways in 2:13–16, 19. The contrast in 2:11–13 leads to the point: "you who once were far off have been brought near" (13b). He elaborates slightly in 2:14, "he has made both groups into one." The purpose clauses in 2:15b–16a provide more specificity: "that he might create in himself one new humanity in place of the two and [that] might reconcile both groups to God." Finally, Paul couches the point when he says, "you are no longer strangers and aliens, but you are citizens with the saints and also members of the household of God" (2:19). In short, Paul proclaims a fundamentally new reality wrought by Christ's atonement.

We must not miss how significant it is that Paul stresses this horizontal reconciliation. Paul's entire reason he exposits Christ's work in this passage is to emphasize the union between Jew and gentile in Christ. One new humanity now exists. Harmony in the church is no mere byproduct among others of the atonement. The creation of one from two is an overt purpose of Christ's atoning ministry. Although Paul obviously cares about our reconciliation with God (cf. 2:16a), that point is manifestly not the primary thread that weaves throughout Paul's message in 2:11–22.

Therefore, we must consider the nature of the hostility that stands in contrast to the peace achieved in Christ. One could easily overlook the fact that Paul does not talk about the reconciliation of social groups in general; rather, he specifically speaks to the unity of Jewish and non-Jewish followers of Christ. Ephesians 2 concerns ethnic unity within the church. It does not exhort readers to bring about harmony in society at

---

27 Noel Schoonmaker, "Preaching Ethnic Atonement," 113.

large as though such unity were not a supernatural reality among God's people secured by the atonement. We'll return to this idea later; for now, it's necessary to acknowledge the point lest we overlook the historical particularity of Paul's letter (and his theology).

V. Atonement in Ephesians

How do we make sense of these seemingly vague and disparate references to Christ's atoning work? Ephesians 2:19–22 is a fitting entry point into the discussion because it aptly reflects a critical function of atonement in the Old Testament. In ancient Israel, the most common objects that received atonement were the Holy Place, the altar, and the tent of meeting (cf. Lev 16:20; Ezek 43:20, 26).

> Contrary to popular belief, the primary object of atonement is not people. Although atonement is made on behalf of people, the priests make atonement for sacred objects and space. When impurity threatens to defile the temple, atonement cleanses the sacred space by removing the uncleanness that belongs to people. In so doing, unclean people are protected from God's anger that would otherwise fall upon them. Even land receives atonement. Moses says of the Lord, "He will repay those who hate him and cleanse [*kpr*] the land for his people" (Deuteronomy 32:43). In this sense, *kpr* bestows honor upon the land or altar. In short, *atonement restores a proper relationship between the sacred object and people.*[28]

On this point, the New Testament makes an important modification. In Ephesians, as in other letters, Paul likens Christ's people to God's temple (cf. 1 Cor 3; 6; 2 Cor 6).[29] What constitutes the Lord's holy temple or tabernacle? It is the place where God's Spirit dwells among his people.[30] This innovation helps us discern how a procedure not applied to people in the Old Testament suddenly can apply to people in the New Testament.

Why do sacred places and objects receive atonement? What's involved in this process? They represent God's presence and unique honor. They are purified and set apart for God's special use. This purity and holiness are achieved through atonement.[31] Therefore, it's only natural that Paul

---

28 Vaughn, *The Cross in Context*, 74. Italics are original.

29 McMurry says, "potential implicit temple references occur in Ephesians 2:14, 18; 3:16–18; 4:8–16, and 29" in "The Temple of God and the Temple of Artemis," 231.

30 Thus, Romans 8 also presents God's people as a holy dwelling place.

31 Vaughn, *The Cross in Context*, 77–83. We saw above that atonement both transitions an object from being unclean and changes an object from a state of being clean to being holy.

notes that Christ cleanses his people, making them holy and blameless (1:4; 5:25–27). Such cleansing and sanctifying are prerequisites for making the temple to be the place where God dwells with his people.

Consistent with these observations, Ephesians 5:2 presents Christ as "a fragrant offering and sacrifice to God" (5:2). This dense description opens a way for us to explore the doctrine of atonement more deeply. In several essays, Christian Eberhart underscores an often-unnoticed detail.[32] He asks why the Levitical sacrifices routinely lay stress on the burning of the offering. He finds a consistent pattern in the biblical text: atonement is achieved shortly after burning. The pronouncement of forgiveness and that atonement has been made does not follow the shedding of blood but the burning at the altar.[33] Burning acts as the mechanism whereby worshipers send their offerings to God. The smoke rises from the fire, carrying fat or incense upward to God. Greenberg adds, "burning flesh seems to reflect a dedication, or relationship confirmation, between the offerer and YHWH, for example, the burnt offering."[34]

Max Botner builds on this dynamic. Referencing Ephesians 5:2, he writes that

> ritual burning is about the transformation of sacrificial material into an appropriate and pleasing substance—ὀσμὴ εὐωδίας—for the deity; "the moment when God accepts the sacrifices brought by humans." Likewise, for the writer of Ephesians, the telos of the Christ-gift is not the cross but the enthronement; the cosmic moment when God receives his messiah and commissions him to rule at his right hand. Hence, an apt analogue: *as sacrificial material would be burned upon the altar and thus transformed into an appropriate gift for God, so the resurrected messiah ascends to heaven where he is received by his Father as an acceptable and pleasing sacrifice.*[35]

Botner "seeks to relocate the referent of the sacrificial metaphor in Eph 5:2 from Christ's crucifixion to his enthronement—that is, from the fragrance of death to the fragrance of life."[36] While there is no space

---

32 E.g., Eberhart, "A Neglected Feature of Sacrifice in the Hebrew Bible," 491; "The Lamb of God That Takes Away the Sin of the World."

33 E.g., Lev 4:20, 26, 31, 35; 5:12–23; 8:32, 34; 16:24–25, 27; Num 15:24–25, 28. Outside the Pentateuch, note Isaiah 6:6–7.

34 Greenberg, *A New Look at Atonement in Leviticus*, 74.

35 Botner, "The Fragrance of Life: Reconsidering the Sacrificial Logic of Ephesians 5:2," 77–78. Italics added. He quotes Eberhart, "To Atone or Not to Atone," 215 [197–231].

36 Botner, "The Fragrance of Life," 70.

here to trace out his argument in full, his thesis is not unprecedented. Similar and far more extensive scholarship has been completed by David Moffitt.[37] In summary, these authors suggest that the goal of Jesus's death was his ascension to heaven as a royal priest, whose blood purifies us, whose entire life is a pleasing gift to God, and who intercedes forever on our behalf. The death of the animal is incidental to the efficacious ritual application of the blood and body.

If we take this scholarship seriously, what would we expect to see in Ephesians? How might Paul reinforce this view of atonement? Presumably, his letter would have significant stress on the resurrection. Indeed, it does (Eph 1:20–21; 2:5–6; 5:14; cf. 4:8–10). Salvation is explicitly portrayed in terms of resurrection such that he "made us alive together with Christ" (2:5).

Resurrection and atonement are also linked via the theme of enthronement. On the one hand, Paul says, "God put this power to work in Christ when he raised him from the dead and seated him at his right hand in the heavenly places, far above all rule and authority and power and dominion, and above every name that is named, not only in this age but also in the age to come" (Eph 1:20–21). On the other hand, scholars have long recognized that "mercy seat" serves as a symbolic throne for God.[38] This word for "mercy seat" (*kapporath; hilastērion* [LXX]) refers to the cover atop the ark, which sat in the innermost room of the tabernacle. From these connections, we can draw certain conclusions. Still, these observations deserve further study and contribute to a more robust understanding of Paul's theology of atonement in Ephesians.

Finally, Zechariah provides additional Old Testament background that connects several parts of Ephesians.[39] In Zechariah 6:12–14, the prophet says,

> Thus says the Lord of hosts: Here is a man whose name is Branch: for he shall branch out in his place, and he shall build *the temple of the Lord*. It is *he that shall build the temple of the Lord*; he shall bear *royal honor*, and shall sit and rule on his throne. *There shall be a priest by his throne*, with peaceful understanding between the two of them. And the crown shall be in the care of Heldai, Tobijah, Jedaiah, and Josiah

---

37 See David M. Moffitt, *Atonement and the Logic of Resurrection in the Epistle to the Hebrews*; "Atonement at the Right Hand," 549–68.

38 Some think it signifies the footstool of God's throne. See Gallusz, *The Throne Motif in the Book of Revelation*, 21–23; Luther calls it the "throne of grace" in *The Complete Works of Martin Luther*. Cf. Vaughn, *The Cross in Context*, 33–35.

39 Mark Stirling, "Transformed Walking and Missional Temple Building," 80–95.

son of Zephaniah, as a memorial in the temple of the Lord. *Those who are far off* shall come and *help to build the temple of the Lord;* and you shall know that the Lord of hosts has sent me to you. This will happen if you diligently obey the voice of the Lord your God.[40]

Multiple literary hyperlinks connect this passage with Ephesians. A royal figure, who is also a priest, constructs the Lord's temple. He will bring people to his people, who have suffered in exile. Also, those who are "far off" come near and somehow contribute to the temple's building (cf. Eph 2:13, 17).

VI. The Law and Hostility

Ephesians 2:11–22 does not elaborate extensively concerning the precise way that Christ secures atonement. Interpreters must debate what Paul implies with phrases like "by the blood of Christ," "in his flesh," and "in one body through the cross." Verse 15 explicitly speaks to how Christ brings about reconciliation: "He has abolished the law with its commandments and ordinances, that he might create in himself one new humanity in place of the two, thus making peace." The gospel of peace, which is proclaimed to those "far off" and those "near" (2:17), is the same gospel foretold in Isaiah 52:7, where the prophet exclaims, "How beautiful upon the mountains are the feet of the messenger who announces peace, who brings *good news* [= gospel], who announces salvation, who says to Zion, 'Your God reigns.'" Peace thus comes with the announcement of a kingdom secured through atonement on a cross. Christ in death redeems fallen notions of dominion and reconciles those who fear the former or lust for the latter.

Paul's comment has long puzzled interpreters. In what sense does Christ "abolish the law"? And how does it break down the dividing wall and end hostility? Some readers try to resolve a seeming contradiction between Ephesians 2:15 and other New Testament texts (e.g., Matt 5:17). This concern, however, is unnecessary. Peter O'Brien explains,

> This word can mean to "make ineffective, or powerless, nullify", and it is employed figuratively with reference to nullifying the faithfulness

---

[40] Cf. Zech 8:20–23, "Thus says the Lord of hosts: Peoples shall yet come, the inhabitants of many cities; the inhabitants of one city shall go to another, saying, "Come, let us go to entreat the favor of the Lord, and to seek the Lord of hosts; I myself am going." Many peoples and strong nations shall come to seek the Lord of hosts in Jerusalem, and to entreat the favor of the Lord. Thus says the Lord of hosts: In those days ten men from nations of every language shall take hold of a Jew, grasping his garment and saying, 'Let us go with you, for we have heard that God is with you.'" In 8:22, "entreat the favor" translates חלה (MT) which the LXX renders ἐξιλάσκομαι ("to atone").

of God (Rom. 3:3), of making God's promise ineffective (Gal. 3:17), or of nullifying the things that exist (1 Cor. 1:28). Here in Ephesians 2:15 the verb signifies that Christ by his death made the law of no effect. He nullified it, so that it is no longer binding. He "abolished" the enmity by nullifying the law.[41]

Similarly, we could add 2 Corinthians 3:6–15, where Paul uses this verb when stating that the Old Covenant and its glory are "set aside." Likewise, he says "we are discharged from the law" (Rom 7:2, 6).

By setting aside the law or making it ineffective, Christ tears down the dividing wall and destroys hostility. What does Paul mean? We first need to understand what is accomplished by the law's being made ineffective. Then we will consider the meaning of "making peace" (15b).

Observe how "that" [ἵνα] in 2:15 introduces the purpose for nullifying the law. Paul explicitly states the intended effect ("create in himself one new humanity in place of the two, thus making peace," 2:15b). Accordingly, nullifying the law here does not speak about *salvation in general,* in which case the law is not presented here as a universal encumbrance to being saved from sin. Instead, Paul's comments particularly concern the law's acting as a source of division between Jews and gentiles. Furthermore, the phrase "thus making peace" makes clear the nature of the peace spoken of back in verse 14. It's not primarily peace with God here. That aspect is discussed in 2:16.

What is it about the Mosaic law that gets set aside? Several scholars address this question. For example, Balla concludes, "I suggest from the closer context that the law may be thought of as a part of the privileges the Jews had and which the gentile Christians are reminded of as among the things they had missed before they came to accept Jesus Christ (v. 12)."[42] Different interpreters argue the point in different ways but draw a similar conclusion. Thus, Bruce says, "the law in that sense is done away with, the barrier between Jews and gentiles is removed; Jewish particularism and gentile exclusion are things of the past."[43] The definitive treatment on the subject might be Tet-Lim Yee's *Jews, Gentiles and Ethnic Reconciliation.*[44] He states,

---

41 O'Brien, *The Letter to the Ephesians,* 196–97. Cf. Peter Balla, "Is the Law Abolished According to Eph. 2:15?," 14.

42 Balla, "Is the Law Abolished," 14.

43 Bruce, *The Epistle to the Ephesians,* 298–99.

44 Yee, *Jews, Gentiles and Ethnic Reconciliation,* esp. 144–83.

> [O]ne can conclude firmly that the author of Ephesians does not single out the law (Torah) as the sole obstacle that stands between Jew and Gentile, nor does he speak of the law without reservation ... rather, he speaks of the law in correlative terms, signaling to his Gentile readers that the law to which the Jews rallied has marked out the Jews (i.e., the "circumcision") as the elect of God and united them in their ethnically based "body politic", but has in turn become a boundary marker, aiding the Jews to distance themselves from the Gentiles.
>
> In short, the author has spoken critically of the law, but this by no means amounts to a personal attack on the law. Rather, he is speaking from an insider's perspective on the law which Jews have deemed significant but used as an instrument of division in order to reinforce their distinctive identity (e.g., the "circumcision" and the "uncircumcision") and the "body politic" as based on a particular *ethnos*. This, the enmity between Jew and Gentile, lies not in the Torah *per se* but with the human attitude that perverted the gifts of God into signs of separation and exclusiveness.[45]

Yee's study does not reduce the law merely to its social function. However, he underlines several features of the text that suggest that Paul, here in Ephesians 2:11–22, zeros in on this facet of the law. Besides what we've already discussed, we also note Paul's stress on a specific expression of the law—circumcision (2:11). His parallel statement in 2:12 immediately teases out the significance of (un)circumcision. The law, as epitomized in ordinances like circumcision, forged a wedge between Jews and gentiles. Christ removes this deleterious effect.

To this, we can add a more subtle observation. Paul's reasoning in Ephesians (especially 2:14–18) mirrors that found in Romans 3:28–30, Galatians 3:20, and 1 Timothy 2:5. Each text directly ties the unity within the faith to oneness. In Romans 3:28–30, the justification of both Jews and gentiles is grounded in the oneness of God. Likewise, Paul in Galatians 3:20 speaks of one God when discussing the insufficiency of the Mosaic covenant. First Timothy 2:5 appeals to "one God" and "one mediator" to explain both the breadth and exclusivity of salvation. Similarly, why does Paul say that both Jews and gentiles be reconciled? According to Ephesians 2:18, both have the same Father via the same Spirit. Also, per Ephesians 2:16, we are reconciled to God via one body (i.e., Christ).

---

45 Yee, 160–61.

VII. What Kind of Unity?

Our reflections thus far suggest an important application. Put simply, Ephesians 2:11–22 concerns ethnic and social reconciliation within the church; it does not address unity or harmony among social groups at large (i.e., outside the church). This point does not imply that the church should not care about seeking peace among communities within society in general. However, two implications follow. First, Paul does not write Ephesians 2:11–22 to spur the church's efforts to pursue peace among various factions outside the church. Second, his explicit concern is the unity of social groups within the church, particularly since such unity testifies to the oneness of God and his plan in Christ. Therefore, while Christians do well to seek peace among groups in general, the immediate application of this text for the church lies elsewhere. Paul's priority in this passage concerns church unity.

Notice Paul's lone imperative—"remember" (2:11). The passage speaks about a reality in which to live; 2:11–22 is not an exhortation to live up to something. Furthermore, as contemporary readers, we must guard ourselves against the temptation to map ourselves on the place of the Jews (within Eph 2:11–22). We are not ancient Jews; they are not us. Most readers today are gentiles and do well to remember that they are reckoned among God's people by a grace that neither Paul nor other ancient Jews anticipated. Having such an expectation would seemingly ignore the specific nature of redemptive history to that point in time. Indeed, New Testament writers do feel compelled to explain this "mystery," namely, that "the Gentiles have become fellow heirs, members of the same body, and sharers in the promise in Christ Jesus through the gospel" (Eph 3:6).[46]

The historical circumstances of redemptive history are such that Christ needed to account for the Mosaic law (2:15). In other words, Ephesians 2:11–22 from beginning to end does not generalize to any two social groups chosen at random. Paul does not suggest that Christ abolish the Mosaic law so that Chinese and Cushite people might be reconciled (though I don't doubt Paul could have wished for such a thing). Paul's exposition of the atonement in Ephesians is rooted in a particular historical understanding of redemption. We need to "remember" this fact because perspective is practical.

Let's put a sharper point on this idea. Ephesians 2 specifically speaks to ethnic unity *within* the church; thus, Paul does not exhort his audience to bring about social harmony in general *as though such unity were not a*

---

46 Cf. Ephesians 1:9; 3:3–5, 9; 6:19.

supernatural reality brought about by the atonement. He calls on readers to remember true reality. The atonement has accomplished this unity between Jew and gentile, regardless of whether we live up to it. We mustn't confuse the true state of things and right behavior. For example, I am married, thus one with my wife, regardless of whether we are at peace or in conflict.

Contemporary readers can sometimes assume that applications stemming from Scripture are the church's ministry to the world. In fact, the practical import of Ephesians 2 is for the church. Accordingly, a legitimate application of this passage would concern divisions within the body of Christ. In America, teachers might seek to mend the fissure between Christian Democrats and Christian Republicans. In the 1990s, churches could have applied Ephesians 2 to the division between Serb and Croat Christians. Within a local setting, various social, economic, and ethnic lines split congregations. Ephesians 2 calls us to "remember" that Christ even relativizes what had been the most fundamental social divide in human history—between Jews and gentiles. If Christ does not achieve this essential unity, gentiles remain "aliens from the commonwealth of Israel, and strangers to the covenants of promise, having no hope and without God in the world," even if hostility ceases between specific gentile groups.

Christ's atonement aims to bring a particular community into existence. This "peculiar people" is called to embody an alternative body politic.[47] Ephesians 2 attests to a new way of being in the world. It first challenges the presumption that faith is individualized or private. Second, it discredits assertions that social change happens merely when people are converted as individuals as if untethered to their cultural and social identity.

Where then does Paul envision the removal of social hostility? Among Christ's followers. In the church. Why? Because there can be no peace apart from allegiance to Jesus, and allegiance to Christ supersedes all other group allegiances.

VIII. The Atonement Changes Identity

For many scholars, the atonement merely concerns a transaction that changes an individual's eternal state. As Brian Bantum explains, it involves so much more. He says, "salvation or atonement is fundamentally a mode of personhood, an identity. That is, in Christ's identification with humanity, with his presence among Jews and his ministry to gentiles, Jesus *creates* from those who abide within his body."[48] Bantum rightly highlights two oft-neglected aspects of atonement theology—union with Christ and collective identity.

---

47 See Hauerwas and Willimon, *Resident Aliens*.
48 Bantum, "To Those Who Were Distant," 140.

First, union-with-Christ language pervades Paul's letter to the Ephesians.[49] Phrases like "in Christ Jesus," "in him," and "through him" are just a few ways that he speaks of the union that exists between Christ and his followers. How does this relate to the atonement? Bantum explains, "The atonement is Christ's identification with humanity such that humanity's identity is irrevocably tied to Jesus's body, not only to his body but to his people. In his body two are made one."[50] Accordingly, Paul's stress on union imagery reinforces the point made above that the reconciliation envisioned by Ephesians 2:11–22 occurs among those who are "in Christ."

This *union with Christ* motif naturally leads to the second point—collective identity. Paul's theology does not lead to a vague individualism that doesn't see culture or color; instead, he sees people as inherently cultural beings who, nevertheless, are not fundamentally identified by ethnic, economic, or gender categories. Salvation does not eradicate a person's social nature, nor does the atonement rescue people to God from social belonging. Instead, Christ's salvation transforms us *from* having one social identity to belonging to a fundamentally different community. In short, allegiance to Christ relativizes all other allegiances. For many ancient people, salvation and group membership were interlinked. Modern readers can easily miss Paul's collectivist perspective that vertical and horizontal reconciliation are logically inseparable. Hence, Bantum concludes, "Identity in Christ in this way suggests a personhood that is both bound to God but also is bound to a people who were understood to be radically other."[51]

IX. Implications

What are some practical implications that stem from Paul's teaching in Ephesians 2? Let's begin with Paul's central claim that Christ removed the dividing wall by nullifying the law on the cross. This point articulates a significant aspect of atonement.

> Atonement removes whatever obstacle impedes one's having a right relationship with another. Intentional sin is not the only thing that destroys friendships. What else gets in the way of fostering good relationships? Lack of awareness. Disparities in social status. Accidents of the past. Misinformation and suspicions inherited from one's family also undermine social harmony.

---

49 One study exploring this theme is Jipp, "Sharing in the Heavenly Rule," 251–79.
50 Bantum, "To Those Who Were Distant," 142.
51 Bantum, 140.

A person can feel neither prejudice nor hatred towards another person yet feel separation between them. Once that invisible wall becomes visible, however, one is responsible to tear it down. Otherwise, that person effectively approves of its existence. They reinforce the barrier.[52]

The Mosaic law was a divine blessing to the world. God's people rejoiced in the law. Still, a good thing can become a detrimental force when used improperly (cf. Rom 7:16; 1 Tim 1:8). How often it is that people can use God's blessings to sow disorder in relationships. Even well-intended comments, said at the wrong time and circumstance, can offend or harm another person.

Not everything that causes relational separation is itself sin. For example, in the Old Testament, people become unclean for a variety of causes. Some are moral by nature; others are not. As a result, they were required to fix the problem. A person needed to make atonement lest they remain unclean. Otherwise, neglecting to do so would dishonor God and incite his wrath. However, God's willingness to punish those individuals does not suggest that God feels wrath toward any and all unclean people (even before they make atonement). God pours out wrath on those who disregard or reject the opportunity he gives them for making atonement.

What does this mean for us? In part, we're called to discern any barriers that get in the way of healthy relationships. Christ's followers should seek out the deepest roots of surface tensions. When finding a potential source of division, we could be tempted to respond in counterproductive ways. Perhaps, we will claim innocence or ignorance. Maybe other people are overreacting or dramatizing an issue (so we think). Of course, we might be correct; we also could be mistaken. Whatever the case, who's right and wrong or good and bad is not the primary concern for Christ's people. Reconciliation is. Unity *in Christ* is the priority.

Christ suffered injustice in order to make peace between Jews and gentiles. Although he was not the cause of their hostility, he bore humanity's animosity against him so that both groups would be reconciled in him. The Mosaic law was not sinful or evil, yet Christ removed it as a source for division.

How might we restore relationships when we bring harm to others? Again, we should consider how atonement works in the Old Testament. Recall that Christ is described as "a fragrant offering and sacrifice to God," reminiscent of the Levitical offerings that effect atonement. Several sacrifices functionally serve as restitution payments.[53] This is because they fulfill a

---

52 Vaughn, *The Cross in Context*, 74.

53 For more on this, see Vaughn, *The Cross in Context*, 139–40.

debt or obligation on the part of worshipers to make right what kept them from God (e.g., uncleanness). Thus, restitution is a means of restoration. God's sacrificial means of making atonement becomes a model for his people to effect horizontal reconciliation. Numbers 5:5–10 illustrates this point.

> The Lord spoke to Moses, saying: Speak to the Israelites: When a man or a woman wrongs another, breaking faith with the Lord, that person incurs guilt and shall confess the sin that has been committed. The person shall make *restitution* [*asham*] for the wrong, adding one-fifth to it, and giving it to the one who was wronged. If the injured party has no next of kin to whom *restitution* [*asham*] may be made for the wrong, the *restitution* [*asham*] for wrong shall go to the Lord for the priest, in addition to the ram of atonement with which atonement is made for the guilty party. Among all the sacred donations of the Israelites, every gift that they bring to the priest shall be his. The sacred donations of all are their own; whatever anyone gives to the priest shall be his.

Observe how the writer interlinks wronging another and breaking faith with the Lord. Also, God requires that the offender make restitution. Similar statutes are found in Exodus 21:28–22:6.

Another application stems from Paul's repeated emphasis on peace. In a Roman metropolis like Ephesus, his words would likely remind people of the imperial claims of *Pax Romana* ("Roman Peace"). In proclaiming *Pax Romana*, Rome did not suggest that they had rid the world of conflict; far from it. Instead, the slogan drew a contrast from the pre-imperial period that had plagued the region with war. In actual fact, so-called "peace" within the empire itself required violence or the threat of it. Revolts were suppressed and conquest stretched the imperial borders. Woolf underlines the illusory nature of *Pax Romana*:

> What the continued war on the frontiers and the repeated disturbances of the Roman peace within the empire show is that the Roman empire was characterized not by the absence of violence but by a carefully balanced economy of it. If war is organized societal violence, then the Roman peace qualifies as war, as the opening quotation from Foucault suggests it might. The emperors ruled not by abolishing violence but by channeling it, using and perpetuating rivalries between cities, between soldiers and civilians, between social classes and within the élite, to ensure a dynamic equilibrium which they controlled and which necessitated their participation.[54]

---

54 Woolf, "Roman Peace," 191.

To this, we add the words of Tacitus, an ardent apologist of Rome. He sobers those drunk on Roman propaganda when he says, "To robbery, slaughter, plunder, [Romans] give the lying name of empire; *they make a wasteland and call it peace.*"[49]

Accordingly, we encounter a fundamentally different brand of peace in Ephesians 2. Paul's gospel of peace does not privilege any group according to common cultural categories. Peace is made possible within and between people of varied ethnic or national identities. To accomplish this peace, Christ does not inflict violence; he endures it. He does so for the sake of those who are hostile toward him. What's more, Jesus usurps death so that even the fear of dying loses its power to divide people. The peace of Christ is possible because he reconciles us to the same Father and grants us the same Spirit. Thus, his people are not united by economic, biological ancestry, or social ideologies; they belong to the same human family. When preaching the gospel of peace, we should underscore its social implications within the Christian community. In so doing, both believers and nonbelievers would discern not only the importance of belief but also of belonging. Our pursuit of reconciliation becomes a practical manifestation of repentance.

Theologically, we discern another practical implication for the church. One must first note a striking similarity in Ephesians 2 between the gentiles and Christ. The gentiles are reckoned "aliens" and "strangers" (2:12). They were "far off" and treated as though cut off from God's covenant people. In the same way, this is how Jesus's contemporaries regarded him as he hung on the cross. He was put to death to end hostility (of a political nature). Jesus had set himself against Israel's false leaders, many of whom did not want to provoke a confrontation with Rome because an itinerant preacher from Nazareth went about announcing another kingdom. And so, they cast him outside the city gates to endure the curse of forsakenness.

His crucifixion reflects the manner of his ministry. Time and again, Jesus touched and healed the unclean. He transgressed social conventions, many of which were based on typical readings of the law. His embracing of cultural outsiders increasingly isolated Jesus in the eyes of community leaders. From the perspective of his enemies, Jesus behaved little better than a gentile. Nevertheless, Jesus became an outcast to make sons and daughters out of strangers.

---

49 Tacitus, *Agricola*, 30.

In Ephesians and other letters, Paul invites the church to embrace this approach to ministry. Thus, he exhorts, "be imitators of God, as beloved children, and live in love, *as Christ loved us and gave himself up for us, a fragrant offering and sacrifice to God*" (5:1–2). Paul calls on his audience to live in contrast to the norms of their former identity. Though speaking *to gentiles*, Paul nevertheless says, "Now this I say and testify in the Lord, that you must no longer walk as the gentiles do, in the futility of their minds" (4:17). Rather than vying for elevated social status, Christ's followers should be known for their mutual submission to one another (5:21). They advance their cause with humble service and prayer rather than military armor (6:14–18). How strange it is (and will always be) for God's people to behave in such countercultural ways! Even so, the Christian path to reconciliation is marked by weakness, not worldly strength.

By now, another application should be obvious from what's been said. In addition to *being* a distinctly diverse people, the church should speak against racism, tribalism, casteism, nationalism, etc. Schoonmaker underlines the atonement's social dimension saying,

> If becoming one with people of different races is part of becoming one with God, we must preach about race if we are to bring listeners closer to God. Preaching racial reconciliation is not only a social responsibility; *it is a theological necessity.* Popular American Christianity, which focuses too much on the individual, often highlights one's "personal relationship with God." Eph 2:14–18 reminds us that our personal relationship with God is interpersonal, and even interracial. *Interracial hostility is a significant part of the hostility between God and humanity.*[56]

Rejecting racism is more than a mere corollary to the command to "love your neighbor." It flows naturally from Christ's atoning work, as expressed in Ephesians 2:11–22. Paul eviscerates any cultural "Christianity" that separates vertical from horizon reconciliation.

X. Conclusion

We began this study pondering the extraordinary comments of John Driver, who suggests that Ephesians 2 is "a fundamental capstone to Pauline reflection on the meaning of the saving work of Christ." On this point, our study certainly validates his claim. Paul unpacks the meaning of the atonement in a rich and robust fashion. Driver's contribution is noteworthy

---

56 Noel Schoonmaker, "Preaching Ethnic Atonement," 118. Italics added.

precisely because he directs our attention to this reality: "that Christ's death served to remove social barriers and thus make peace among human enemies, as well as making possible their common access to God."[57]

With respect to the mechanism of atonement, Driver's argument is more modest. In this way, our discussion buttresses his main conclusions by adding exegetical reflections on Ephesians 2:11–22 in context.[58] Although less explicit, some details from Ephesians do suggest how atonement is accomplished. Accordingly, Paul's message concerning the meaning and mechanism of Christ's atonement not only exposes a lacuna in popular theologies; it can inform the church's mission practice in the world.

Bibliography to Appendix 1

Balla, Peter. "Is the Law Abolished According to Eph. 2:15?" *EurJTh* 3, no. 1 (1994): 9–16.

Bantum, Brian. "'To Those Who Were Distant and Those Who Were Near': Atonement, Identity, and Identification." *Ex Auditu* 26 (2010): 128–44.

Barth, Markus. *Ephesians: Introduction, Translation and Commentary on Chapters 1–3*. Anchor Bible. Doubleday, 1974.

Berkhof, Louis. *Systematic Theology*. Eerdmans, 1996.

Boersma, Hans. *Violence, Hospitality, and the Cross: Reappropriating the Atonement Tradition*. Baker Academic, 2006.

Botner, Max. "The Fragrance of Life: Reconsidering the Sacrificial Logic of Ephesians 5:2." *BBR* 64 (2019), 67–82.

Bruce, F. F. *The Epistle to the Ephesians*. Pickering & Inglis, 1973.

Driver, John. *Understanding the Atonement for the Mission of the Church*. Herald Press, 1986.

Eberhart, Christian. "To Atone or Not to Atone: Remarks on the Day of Atonement Rituals According to Leviticus 16 and the Meaning of Atonement." In *Sacrifice, Cult, and Atonement in Early Judaism and Christianity: Constituents and Critique*, ed. Henrietta L. Wileys and Christian A. Eberhart. RBS 85. Atlanta: Society of Biblical Literature, 2017.

Eberhart, Christian. "The Lamb of God That Takes Away the Sin of the World." *Touchstone* 31, no. 2 (June 2013).

---

57 Driver, *Understanding the Atonement*, 228.

58 We have avoided the speculative theories that typically surround atonement debates. Instead, we have grounded our interpretation on the letter's immediate context and its Old Testament background.

Eberhart, Christian. "A Neglected Feature of Sacrifice in the Hebrew Bible." *HTR* 97, no. 4 (2004): 491.

Erickson, Millard. *Christian Theology*. 2nd ed. Baker, 2002.

Frame, John M. *Systematic Theology: An Introduction to Christian Belief*. P&R Publishing, 2013.

Gallusz, Laszlo. *The Throne Motif in the Book of Revelation*. Bloomsbury, 2013.

Greenberg, James. *A New Look at Atonement in Leviticus: The Meaning and Purpose of Kipper Revisited*. Bulletin for Biblical Research Supplements. Eisenbrauns, 2019.

Grudem, Wayne A. *Systematic Theology: An Introduction to Biblical Doctrine*. Zondervan, 2020.

Hauerwas, Stanley, and William H. Willimon. *Resident Aliens: Life in the Christian Colony*. Abingdon Press, 1989.

Hill, Charles. "Atonement in the Old and New Testaments." In *The Glory of the Atonement: Biblical, Theological & Practical Perspectives,* edited by Charles E. Hill and Frank A. James III. IVP Academic, 2004.

Jipp, Joshua W. "Sharing in the Heavenly Rule of Christ the King: Paul's Royal Participatory Language in Ephesians." In *"In Christ" in Paul: Explorations in Paul's Theology of Union and Participation*, edited by Michael J. Thate, Kevin J. Vanhoozer, and Constantine R. Campbell. Wissenschaftliche Untersuchungen Zum Neuen Testament. Mohr Siebeck, 2014.

Luther, Martin. *The Complete Works of Martin Luther, Vol. 6*. Delmarva, 2015.

McGrath, Alister E. *Christian Theology: An Introduction*. 4th ed. Blackwell, 2007.

McMurry, Howard Christopher. "The Temple of God and the Temple of Artemis: Exploring the Building/Temple Image in Ephesians." PhD diss., Southwestern Baptist Theological Seminary, 2019.

McNall, Joshua M. *The Mosaic of Atonement*: An Integrated Approach to Christ's Work. Zondervan, 2019.

Moffitt, David M. *Atonement and the Logic of Resurrection in the Epistle to the Hebrews*. Brill, 2011.

Moffitt, David M. "Atonement at the Right Hand: The Sacrificial Significance of Jesus's Exaltation in Acts." NTS 62, no. 4 (2016), 549–68.

Morris, Leon. *The Cross in the New Testament*. Eerdmans, 1965.

O'Brien, Peter. *The Letter to the Ephesians*. PNTC. Eerdmans, 1999.

Rader, William. *The Church and Racial Hostility: A History of Interpretation of Ephesians 2:11–22*. Mohr, 1978.

Schoonmaker, Noel. "Preaching Ethnic Atonement: A Homiletic Study of Ephesians 2:11–18." Paper presented at annual meeting of the Academy of Homiletics, 2006, West Palm Beach, Florida, 113–14.

Stirling, Mark. "Transformed Walking and Missional Temple Building: Discipleship in Ephesians." *Presbyterion* 45, no. 2 (2019): 80–95.

Stott, John R. W. *The Cross of Christ*. IVP, 2006.

Tacitus. *Agricola*, 30. https://www.thelatinlibrary.com/imperialism/readings/agricola.html. Accessed 11 June 2024.

Torrance, Thomas F. Atonement: *The Person and Work of Christ*. IVP Academic, 2009.

Vaughn, Brad. *The Cross in Context: Reconsidering Biblical Metaphors for Atonement*. IVP Academic, 2022.

Woolf, Greg. "Roman Peace." In *War and Society in the Roman World*, edited by John Rich and Graham Shipley, 171–94. Leicester-Nottingham Studies in Ancient Society. Routledge, 1993.

Yee, Tet-Lim N. *Jews, Gentiles and Ethnic Reconciliation: Paul's Jewish Identity and Ephesians*, Society for New Testament Studies Monograph Series. Cambridge University Press, 2005.

APPENDIX 2

Figure A.2: Word study: Son of Man, first Adam, last Adam, humanity

Gospel texts (78 occurrences)	1 Cor 15:45	1 Cor 15:45	Eph 2:15	Eph 4:24
"Son of Man"	"first man Adam"	"last Adam"	"might create one new man"	"put on the new self"
υἱὸν τοῦ ἀνθρώπου	πρῶτος ἄνθρωπος Ἀδάμ	ἔσχατος Ἀδάμ	ἐνδύσασθαι καινὸν ἄνθρωπον	ἐνδύσασθαι καινὸν ἄνθρωπον
huion tou anthrōpou		eschatos Adam	ktisē en autō eis hena kainon anthrōpon	endysasthai kainon anthrōpon
son the man; the human one		last (state of) Adam	create in himself a unified, brand-new kind of humanity	to put on (clothe ourselves) with the brand-new kind of humanity
Jesus is the True Human, the Human One, fulfilling Daniel's ancient prophecy.	Adam is the human prototype who fails.	Jesus is the True Human—the final prototype succeeds, fulfilling God's will and design where the first Adam failed.	Jesus the True Human creates a brand-new way of being human together, "through the cross killing the hostility"—reconciling persons and peoples to God and one another.	As members of the body of Christ we "put on" a brand-new kind of being human: the unity-in-diversity of reconciled persons and peoples in Christ's life and peace.

APPENDIX 3

Comparison Exercise: *Pax Romana, Pax Christiana, Pax Christi*

The chart on the following page offers an exercise for readers to identify differences between three different approaches to social peace.

- *Pax Romana* represents peace primarily through allegiance to the empire: state force, violence, and fear of violence.
- *Pax Christiana* represents peace primarily through Christian laws wedded to imperial or state powers—enforced through punishment and the fear of punishment.
- *Pax Christi* represents peace primarily through voluntary allegiance to Christ. Christ is our peace; Christ makes peace; Christ preaches peace (Eph 2:14–15, 17).

	Pax Romana	Pax Christiana	Pax Christi
Jesus			
Church			
Power			
The Cross			
Culture			
Law			
Diversity			

BIBLIOGRAPHY

Alberta, Tim. *The Kingdom, the Power, and the Glory: American Evangelicals in an Age of Extremism.* Harper, 2023.

Allen, Roland. *Missionary Methods: St. Paul's or Ours?* Eerdmans, 1962. Kindle.

Allen, Roland. *The Spontaneous Expansion of the Church.* Wipf and Stock, 1997. Kindle.

Alter, Robert. *The Hebrew Bible: A Translation with Commentary (Vol. 2 Three-Volume Set).* W. W. Norton, 2018. Kindle.

Althaus, Paul. "The Ethics of Martin Luther." Elca.org. *Evangelical Lutheran Church in America*, December 1, 2001. https://www.elca.org/JLE/Articles/1039.

Anastasis Center, The. "Christian Restorative Justice: A Study Guide." Accessed June 14, 2024. https://www.anastasiscenter.org/study-guide-restorative-justice.

Anderson, Ryan T., and Alexandra DeSanctus. *Tearing Us Apart: How Abortion Harms Everything and Solves Nothing.* Regnery, 2022.

Anonymous. *The Didache: The Original Greek Text with Four English Translations.* Amazon Kindle, 2011.

Appelbaum, Anne. *Autocracy, Inc.: The Dictators Who Want to Run the World.* Doubleday, 2024

Augustus. "Augustus, Res Gestae." Livius.org, 2007. Accessed June 14, 2024. https://www.livius.org/sources/content/augustus-res-gestae/.

Baker, Mark D. *Centered-Set Church: Discipleship and Community Without Judgmentalism.* IVP Academic, 2021.

Barna Group. "Most Americans Take Well-Known Bible Stories at Face Value." *Barna Group*, October 21, 2007. https://www.barna.com/research/most-americans-take-well-known-bible-stories-at-face-value/.

Barna Group. "Pastors Share Top Reasons They've Considered Quitting Ministry in the Past Year." Barna Group, April 27, 2022. https://www.barna.com/research/pastors-quitting-ministry/.

Barnes, Timothy D. *Constantine and Eusebius.* Harvard University Press, 1981.

Bateman, Tom. "Ex-Officials Say Gaza Policy Has Put US at Risk." *BBC News*, July 2, 2024, https://www.bbc.com/news/articles/c725wxky293o.

Bates, Matthew W. *Salvation by Allegiance Alone.* Baker Academic, 2017. Kindle.

Bates, Matthew W. *Why the Gospel? Living the Good News of King Jesus with Purpose.* Eerdmans, 2023.

Behr, John. *Becoming Human: Meditations on Christian Anthropology in Word and Image.* St. Vladimir's Seminary Press, 2013.

Berrigan, Daniel. *No Bars to Manhood*. Wipf and Stock, 2007. https://en.wikiquote.org/wiki/Daniel_Berrigan.

Biddle, Mark E. *Missing the Mark: Sin and Its Consequences in Biblical Theology*. Abingdon Press, 2005.

Bishop, Bill. *The Big Sort: Why the Clustering of Like-Minded America Is Tearing Us Apart*. Houghton-Mifflin, 2008.

BMJ. "'Diseases of Despair' Have Soared Over the Past Decade in US." *Science Daily*, November 9, 2020. https://www.sciencedaily.com/releases/2020/11/201109184933.htm.

Bonhoeffer, Dietrich. *The Cost of Discipleship*. Touchstone/Simon & Schuster, 2012. Kindle.

Bonhoeffer, Dietrich. *Dietrich Bonhoeffer Works*. Fortress, 2008.

Braithwaite, John. *Crime, Shame, and Reintegration*. Cambridge University Press, 1989.

Brooks, David. "A Humanist Manifesto." *The Atlantic*, October 24, 2023. https://www.theatlantic.com/ideas/archive/2023/10/humanism-skills-for-better-society-world/675745/.

Brooks, David. "The Dissenters Trying to Save Evangelicalism from Itself." *New York Times*, February 4, 2022. https://www.nytimes.com/2022/02/04/opinion/evangelicalism-division-renewal.html.

Brueggemann, Walter. *Ancient Echoes: Refusing the Fear-Filled, Greed-Driven Toxicity of the Far Right*. Fortress, 2023.

Brueggemann, Walter. *The Prophetic Imagination: 40th Anniversary Edition*. Fortress, 2018.

Buell, Denise Kimber. *Why This New Race: Ethnic Reasoning in Early Christianity*. Columbia University Press, 2008.

Cahill, Thomas. *Desire of the Everlasting Hills: The World before and after Jesus*. Anchor, 2010.

Carmen Joy Imes. *Being God's Image: Why Creation Still Matters*. IVP, 2023.

Carney, J. J. *Rwanda before the Genocide: Catholic Politics and Ethnic Discourse in the Late Colonial Era*. Oxford University Press, 2016.

Carothers, Thomas, and Andrew O'Donohue. "How to Understand the Global Spread of Political Polarization." *Carnegie Endowment for International Peace*, October 1, 2019. https://carnegieendowment.org/2019/10/01/how-to-understand-global-spread-of-political-polarization-pub-79893.

Carroll, James. *Constantine's Sword: The Church and the Jews: A History*. Houghton-Mifflin, 2001.

Chappell, Timothy. "Knowledge of Persons." *European Journal for Philosophy of Religion 5*, no. 4 (2013): 3–28.

Charles, Mark, and Soong-Chan Rah. *Unsettling Truths: The Ongoing, Dehumanizing Legacy of the Doctrine of Discovery*. IVP, 2019.

Chrysostom, St. John. "Church Fathers: Homily 5 on Ephesians." New Advent. Accessed April 5, 2024. https://www.newadvent.org/fathers/230105.htm.

Cohen, Dov. "The American National Conversation about (Everything but) Shame." *Social Research: An International Quarterly* 70, no. 4 (December 2003): 1075–108. https://doi.org/10.1353/sor.2003.0026.

Cohick, Lynn H. *The Letter to the Ephesians*. New International Commentary on the New Testament. Eerdmans, 2020. Kindle.

Cone, James H. *The Cross and the Lynching Tree*. Orbis, 2011. Kindle.

Contreras, Russell. "Support for Political Violence Jumps in US, Survey Says." *Axios*, October 25, 2023. https://www.axios.com/2023/10/25/support-us-political-violence-prri-brookings-survey.

Conn, Harvie M., ed. *Theological Perspectives on Church Growth*. P&R Publishing, 1976.

Cook, Robert. "The Quarrel Forgotten? Toward a Clearer Understanding of Sectional Reconciliation." *The Journal of the Civil War Era* 6, no. 3 (2016): 413–36. https://doi.org/10.1353/cwe.2016.0052.

Cooper, Michael T. *Ephesiology: A Study of the Ephesian Movement*. William Carey Publishing, 2020.

Costas, Orlando E. *The Church and Its Mission: A Shattering Critique from the Third World*. Tyndale House, 1974.

Cox, Harvey. "The Market as God." *The Atlantic*, March 1999. https://www.theatlantic.com/magazine/archive/1999/03/the-market-as-god/306397/.

Cyprian. "The Epistles of Cyprian, Epistle 1: To Donatus." Andrews.edu. *Andrews University*, 2024. https://www.andrews.edu/~toews/classes/sources/early/Cyprian%20Epistles.htm#.

Damaj, Yara M. "Fatal Attraction: The Islamic State's Politics of Sentimentality." *Global-e* 10, no. 63 (September 28, 2017). https://globaljournal.org/global-e/september-2017/fatal-attraction-islamic-states-politics-sentimentality.

Datema, David E., and Leonard N. Bartlotti. "The People Group Approach: A Historical Perspective." *Evangelical Missions Quarterly* 56, no. 4 (October 2020): 8–11.

Davis, Mike. *Late Victorian Holocausts*. Verso, 2001.

DeSilver, Drew. "The Polarization in Today's Congress Has Roots That Go Back Decades." *Pew Research Center*, March 10, 2022. https://www.pewresearch.org/short-reads/2022/03/10/the-polarization-in-todays-congress-has-roots-that-go-back-decades/.

Desmond, Matthew. *Poverty, by America.* Crown, 2023.

Digeser, Elizabeth DePalma. "The Violent Legacy of Constantine's Militant Piety." In *Religious Violence in the Ancient World*, edited by Jitse H. F. Dijkstra and Christian R. Raschle, 228–48. Cambridge University Press, 2020.

Doctrine of Discovery Project. "Papal Bull *Dum Diversas* 18 June, 1452." *Indigenous Values*, July 23, 2018. https://doctrineofdiscovery.org/dum-diversas/.

Donaldson, Terence L. *Gentile Christian Identity from Cornelius to Constantine: The Nations, the Parting of the Ways, and Roman Imperial Ideology.* Eerdmans, 2020.

Doxsee, Catrina, Seth G. Jones, Jared Thompson, and Grace Hwang. "Pushed to Extremes: Domestic Terrorism amid Polarization and Protest." CSIS.org, May 17, 2022. https://www.csis.org/analysis/pushed-extremes-domestic-terrorism-amid-polarization-and-protest.

Du Mez, Kristin Kobes. *Jesus and John Wayne: How White Evangelicals Corrupted a Faith and Fractured a Nation.* Liveright, 2020.

Duchatelez, Kamiel. "The Social Doctrine of St. Basil the Great." *In Communion*, November 24, 2010. https://incommunion.org/2010/11/24/the-social-doctrine-of-st-basil-the-great/.

Duchow-Pressley, Deacon Innocent. "St. Basil the Great's Sermon to the Rich." St. John the Baptist Greek Orthodox Church, August 21, 2015. https://stjohngoc.org/st-basil-the-greats-sermon-to-the-rich/.

Dunlap, David. "The Origins of the Scofield Reference Bible | Plymouth Brethren Writings." Plymouthbrethren.org. Accessed April 6, 2024. https://plymouthbrethren.org/article/426.

Eastman, Susan Grove. *Paul and the Person: Reframing Paul's Anthropology.* Eerdmans, 2017.

Emerson, Michael O., and Christian Smith. *Divided by Faith: Evangelical Religion and the Problem of Race in America.* Oxford University Press, 2000.

Equal Justice Initiative. *Lynching in America: Confronting the Legacy of Racial Terror, Third Edition.* Equal Justice Initiative, 2017.

Ereira, Alan, and Terry Jones. *Terry Jones' Barbarians.* Random House, 2009. Kindle.

Escobar, Samuel. *The New Global Mission: The Gospel from Everywhere to Everyone.* IVP, 2003.

Eusebius of Caesarea. "The Life of the Blessed Emperor Constantine." Edited by Ernest Cushing Richardson. *Fordham.edu*, 2020. https://sourcebooks.fordham.edu/basis/vita-constantine.asp.

Evangelische Kirche in Deutschland (EKD). "The Barmen Declaration." www.ekd.de, n.d. https://www.ekd.de/en/The-Barmen-Declaration-303.htm.

Evangelical Confession 2024. www.evangelicalconfession2024.com. Accessed October 7, 2024.

Farah, Warrick, ed. *Motus Dei: The Movement of God to Disciple the Nations.* William Carey Publishing, 2021.

Fattal, Isabel. "Is Politics Filling the Void of Religion?" *The Atlantic*, August 19, 2022. https://www.theatlantic.com/newsletters/archive/2022/08/is-politics-filling-the-void-of-religion-helen-lewis-interview/671198/.

Fitch, David E. *Reckoning with Power: Why the Church Fails When It's on the Wrong Side of Power.* Baker, 2024. Kindle.

Flanders, Christopher L. *About Face: Rethinking Face for 21st Century Mission.* Wipf and Stock, 2011.

Flanders, Christopher L., and Werner Mischke. *Honor, Shame, and the Gospel: Reframing Our Message and Ministry.* William Carey Publishing, 2020.

Folsom, Marty. *Karl Barth's Church Dogmatics for Everyone, Volume 1—the Doctrine of the Word of God: A Step-By-Step Guide for Beginners and Pros.* HarperCollins Christian Publishing, 2022. Kindle.

Fowl, Stephen E. *Ephesians: A Commentary.* Westminster John Knox Press, 2012.

Frank, Sinatra, C. Francois, J. Revaux, and Paul Anka. *My Way.* Vocal Popular Sheet Music Collection. Score 3598, 1967.

French, David. *Divided We Fall: America's Secession Threat and How to Restore Our Nation.* St. Martin's Press, 2020.

French, David. "Evangelicals Decenter Jesus." *The Atlantic*, September 23, 2022. https://www.theatlantic.com/newsletters/archive/2022/09/us-evangelical-christian-republican/676553/.

Fredriksen, Paula. "Power, Politics, and God: Religion in the Roman Empire." Conference presentation, February 6, 2022. https://www.youtube.com/watch?v=Gan8Ik30q88.

Fukuyama, Francis. *The End of History and the Last Man.* Free Press, 1992. Kindle.

Fukuyama, Francis. *Identity: The Demand for Dignity and the Politics of Resentment.* Farrar, Straus and Giroux, 2019. Kindle.

Gerodimos, Roman. "Humiliation, Shame, and Violence: Honor, Trauma, and Political Extremism before and after the 2009 Crisis in Greece." *International Forum of Psychoanalysis* 31, no. 1 (October 22, 2018): 1–12. https://doi.org/10.1080/0803706x.2018.1523558.

Giddings, Paula. *Ida: A Sword Among Lions: Ida B. Wells and the Campaign Against Lynching.* HarperCollins, 2009.

Gilbert, Peter. "St. Basil on Stealing from the Poor." *De unione ecclesiarum*, October 8, 2009. https://bekkos.wordpress.com/2009/10/08/st-basil-on-stealing-from-the-poor/.

Gilligan, James. *Violence: Reflections on a National Epidemic.* Vintage Books, 1997.

Girard, René. *The Girard Reader.* Herder & Herder, 1996.

Godfrey, W. Robert. "Bebbington's Four Points of Evangelicalism." *Ligonier Ministries,* August 29, 2020. https://www.ligonier.org/posts/bebbingtons-four-points-evangelicalism.

Goggin, Jamin, and Kyle Strobel. *The Way of the Dragon or the Way of the Lamb: Searching for Jesus's Path of Power in a Church That Has Abandoned It.* Thomas Nelson, 2021.

Goldsworthy, Adrian Keith. *Pax Romana: War, Peace, and Conquest in the Roman World.* Yale University Press, 2016. Kindle.

Gorman, Michael J. *Becoming the Gospel: Paul, Participation, and Mission.* Eerdmans, 2015. Kindle.

Gorman, Michael J. *Reading Revelation Responsibly: Uncivil Worship and Witness: Following the Lamb into the New Creation.* Cascade Books, 2011. Kindle.

Gorski, Philip S., and Samuel L. Perry. *The Flag and the Cross: White Christian Nationalism and the Threat to Democracy.* Oxford, 2022.

Graham, Billy. *Peace with God: The Secret of Happiness.* W Publishing Group, a division of Thomas Nelson, 1984.

Graham, Carol. "America's Crisis of Despair: A Federal Task Force for Economic Recovery and Societal Well-Being." *Brookings,* January 21, 2021. https://www.brookings.edu/research/americas-crisis-of-despair-a-federal-task-force-for-economic-recovery-and-societal-well-being.

Green, Joel B., and Lee Martin McDonald. *The World of the New Testament: Cultural, Social, and Historical Contexts.* Baker Academic, 2013.

Grudem, Wayne. *Systematic Theology: An Introduction to Biblical Doctrine.* 2nd ed. Zondervan Academic, 2020. Kindle.

Grudem, Wayne. *Christian Ethics: An Introduction to Biblical Moral Reasoning.* Crossway, 2018.

Gupta, Nijay K. *Strange Religion: How the First Christians Were Weird, Dangerous, and Compelling.* Brazos Press, 2024. Kindle.

Gushee, David P., and Glen H. Stassen. *Kingdom Ethics: Following Jesus in Contemporary Context.* 2nd ed. Eerdmans, 2016.

Hamid, Shadi. "America without God." *The Atlantic,* April 2021.

Hatina, Thomas R. "Rome and Its Provinces." In *The World of the New Testament: Cultural, Social, and Historical Contexts,* edited by Joel B. Green and Lee Martin McDonald, 557–70. Baker Academic, 2013.

Hawthorne, Steven C. "A Biblical Understanding of People Groups." *Evangelical Missions Quarterly* 56, no. 4 (October 2020): 4–7.

Hawthorne, Steven C. "The Story of His Glory." In *Perspectives on the World Christian Movement: A Reader*, edited by Ralph D. Winter and Steven C. Hawthorne, 36–48. 4th ed. William Carey Publishing, 2009.

Hayes, Adam. "What Is Redlining? Definition, Legality, and Effects." *Investopedia*, February 20, 2024. https://www.investopedia.com/terms/r/redlining.asp.

Haynes, Trevor. "Dopamine, Smartphones & You: A Battle for Your Time." Science in the News. *Harvard University*, May 1, 2018. https://sitn.hms.harvard.edu/flash/2018/dopamine-smartphones-battle-time/.

Hellerman, Joseph H. *Reconstructing Honor in Roman Philippi: Carmen Christi as Cursus Pudorum*. Cambridge University Press, 2005. Kindle.

Heiser, Michael S. *Demons: What the Bible Really Says about the Powers of Darkness*. Lexham, 2020. Kindle.

Heiser, Michael S. *The Unseen Realm: Recovering the Supernatural Worldview of the Bible*. Lexham, 2019.

Hiebert, Paul G. *Anthropological Reflections on Missiological Issues*. Baker, 1994

Heschel, Susannah. *The Aryan Jesus: Christian Theologians and the Bible in Nazi Germany*. Princeton University Press, 2008.

Hickel, Jason. *The Divide: A Brief Guide to Global Inequality and Its Solutions*. Windmill Books, 2017.

Hinn, Costi. "The Prosperity Gospel: A Global Epidemic." *For The Gospel*. Accessed August 11, 2024. https://www.forthegospel.org/read/the-prosperity-gospel-a-global-epidemic.

Hirsch, Alan, and Mark Nelson. *Reframation: Seeing God, People, and Mission through Reenchanted Frames*. 100 Movements Publishing, 2019.

Holland, Tom. *Dominion: The Making of the Western Mind*. Little, Brown Book Group, 2019.

Howard-Brook, Wes. *"Come Out My People!" God's Call Out of Empire in the Bible and Beyond*. Orbis, 2010.

Howard-Brook, Wes. *Empire Baptized: How the Church Embraced What Jesus Rejected (Second to Fifth Centuries)*. Orbis, 2016.

Huberman, Andrew. "Controlling Your Dopamine for Motivation, Focus & Satisfaction." *Huberman Lab*, September 27, 2021. https://hubermanlab.com/controlling-your-dopamine-for-motivation-focus-and-satisfaction/.

Hummel, Daniel G. *The Rise and Fall of Dispensationalism: How the Evangelical Battle over the end times Shaped a Nation*. Eerdmans, 2023.

Hyatt, Erik. "From Homogeneous to a Heterogeneous Unit Principle." *Missio Nexus*, April 1, 2014. https://missionexus.org/from-homogeneous-to-a-heterogeneous-unit-principle/.

International Journal of Frontier Missiology. "IJFM Home Page." ijfm.org. Accessed September 2, 2023. https://ijfm.org.

IsraelU. "What Does Shalom Mean? | Hebrew Words Every Christian Should Know." YouTube. Accessed April 6, 2024. https://www.youtube.com/watch?v=avj4aBeMQsY.

Isaac, Munther. *The Other Side of the Wall: A Palestinian Christian Narrative of Lament and Hope.* IVP, 2020. Kindle.

Jacob, Haley Goranson. *Conformed to the Image of His Son: Reconsidering Paul's Theology of Glory in Romans.* IVP Academic, 2018. Kindle.

Jenkins, Philip. *The Next Christendom: The Coming of Global Christianity.* Oxford, 2002.

Jennings, Willie James. *The Christian Imagination: Theology and the Origins of Race.* Yale University Press, 2010.

Jennings, Willie James. *Acts: A Theological Commentary on the Bible.* Westminster John Knox Press, 2017. Kindle.

Johnson, Chalmers. *Blowback: The Costs and Consequences of American Empire.* 2nd ed. Henry Holt, 2007. Kindle.

Jones, John D. "St. John Chrysostom and the Problem of Wealth." *In Communion.* Accessed April 5, 2024. https://incommunion.org/2007/05/09/st-john-chrysostom-and-the-problem-of-wealth/.

Jones, Robert P. *The End of White Christian America.* Simon & Schuster, 2017.

Jones, Robert P. *The Hidden Roots of White Supremacy: And the Path to a Shared American Future.* Simon & Schuster, 2023. Kindle.

Jones, Robert P. *White Too Long: The Legacy of White Supremacy in American Christianity.* Simon & Schuster, 2020. Kindle.

Jordan, Clarence. "Christian Fellowship Isn't Just Being Nice." *Plough,* October 19, 2022. https://www.plough.com/en/topics/community/christian-fellowship-isnt-just-being-nice.

Jordan, Clarence. *The Inconvenient Gospel: A Southern Prophet Tackles War, Wealth, Race, and Religion.* Plough Publishing, 2022. Kindle.

Joshua Project. "Seeking God's Glory among All Peoples." n.d. https://joshuaproject.net.

Kalantzis, George. *Caesar and the Lamb: Early Christian Attitudes on War and Military Service.* Wipf and Stock, 2012. Kindle.

Kalantzis, George. "There Will (Not!) Be Blood! Early Christian Attitudes toward War and Military Service." Lecture, Emory University. September 19, 2012.

Katongole, Emmanuel. *A Future for Africa: Critical Essays in Christian Social Imagination.* The University of Scranton Press, 2005.

Katongole, Emmanuel. *Who Are My People? Love, Violence, and Christianity in Sub-Saharan Africa*. University of Notre Dame Press, 2022.

Kattab, Daoud. "Mike Pence Writes Messages on Bombs Meant for Lebanon. Would Jesus Do That?" *Religion News Service*, January 8, 2024. https://religionnews.com/2024/01/08/mike-pence-writes-messages-on-bombs-meant-for-lebanon-would-jesus-do-that/.

Keener, Craig S. "One New Temple in Christ (Ephesians 2:11–22; Acts 21:27–29; Mark 11:17; John 4:20–24." *Asian Journal of Pentecostal Studies* 12, no. 1 (2009): 75–92.

Kendzior, Sarah. "It's a Tough Time for the Truth." *Substack*, October 17, 2024. https://open.substack.com/pub/sarahkendzior/p/its-a-tough-time-for-the-truth?selection=231ba89c-2c6a-4b03-94c5-176a157f54c5&r=8cavf&utm_medium=ios.

Kiyomi, Wendy. "The Stranger in My House." *Plough Quarterly* 34. December 19, 2022. https://www.plough.com/en/topics/life/parenting/the-stranger-in-my-house.

Kierkegaard, Søren. *Provocations: Spiritual Writings of Kierkegaard*. Plough Publishing, 1999.

Kimball, Jill. "US Is Polarizing Faster than Other Democracies, Study Finds." *Brown University*, January 21, 2020. https://www.brown.edu/news/2020-01-21/polarization.

King, L. W. "The Avalon Project: The Code of Hammurabi." Yale.edu. *Lillian Goldman Law Library*, 2008. https://avalon.law.yale.edu/ancient/hamframe.asp.

King, Margaret J. "Deep Culture." *The Journal of Popular Culture* 45, no. 4 (July 26, 2012): 687–94. https://doi.org/10.1111/j.1540-5931.2012.00952.x.

King, Martin Luther, Jr. "Letter from Birmingham Jail, by Dr. Martin Luther King, Jr." Letterfromjail.com, April 16, 1963. https://letterfromjail.com/.

King, Martin Luther, Jr. "Loving Your Enemies." Sermon Delivered at Dexter Avenue Baptist Church." The Martin Luther King Jr. Research and Education Institute, Stanford University. Accessed August 12, 2024. https://kinginstitute.stanford.edu/king-papers/documents/loving-your-enemies-sermon-delivered-dexter-avenue-baptist-church.

King, Martin Luther, Jr. *Stride Toward Freedom: The Montgomery Story (King Legacy)*. Beacon Press, 2010.

Klein, Ezra. *Why We're Polarized*. Simon & Schuster, 2020.

Kreider, Alan. *The Patient Ferment of the Early Church: The Improbable Rise of Christianity in the Roman Empire*. Baker Academic, 2016. Kindle.

Krepinevich, Andrew F. "Is Putin a Rational Actor? How and Why the Kremlin Might Use the Bomb." *Foreign Affairs*, November 22, 2022. https://www.foreignaffairs.com/russian-federation/putin-rational-actor-nuclear-weapons.

Krug, Etienne G., L. L. Dahlberg, J. A. Mercy, A. B. Zwi, and R. Lozano, eds. *World Report on Violence and Health*. Geneva: World Health Organization, 2002. http://apps.who.int/iris/bitstream/10665/42495/1/9241545615_eng.pdf.

Kurtzleben, Danielle. "Why Trump's Authoritarian Language about 'Vermin' Matters." *NPR*, November 17, 2023. https://www.npr.org/2023/11/17/1213746885/trump-vermin-hitler-immigration-authoritarian-republican-primary.

Labberton, Mark. *The Dangerous Act of Loving Your Neighbor*. IVP, 2010.

Lactantius. "Divine Institutes, Book v (Lactantius)." Edited by Kevin Knight. *New Advent*. Accessed April 5, 2024. https://www.newadvent.org/fathers/07015.htm.

Lau, Te-Li. *Defending Shame: Its Formative Power in Paul's Letters*. Baker Academic, 2020.

Lausanne. "New Middle Class: Global Middle Class 1950–2030." https://lausanne.org/report/demographics/statistics-new-middle-class

Lausanne Committee for World Evangelization. "The Pasadena Consultation: Homogeneous Unit Principle." *Lausanne Movement*, 1978. https://lausanne.org/content/lop/lop-1.

Lee, Bandy X. *Violence: An Interdisciplinary Approach to Causes, Consequences, and Cures*. Wiley-Blackwell, 2019.

Lee, Peter T., and James Sung-Hwan Park. "Beyond People Group Thinking: A Critical Reevaluation of Unreached People Groups." *Missiology* 46, no. 3 (May 2018): 212–25.

Leithart, Peter J. *Defending Constantine: The Twilight of an Empire and the Dawn of Christendom*. IVP Academic, 2010. Kindle.

Lewis, C. S. *Mere Christianity*. HarperCollins, 2009. Kindle.

Lewis, R. W., and R. Butler. "The Great Progress of the Gospel." Accessed August 8, 2024. https://joshuaproject.net/GreatProgress.

Ligonier Ministries, and Lifeway. "The State of Theology." *The State of Theology*, 2022. https://thestateoftheology.com/.

Lindahl, Julie. *The Pendulum: A Granddaughter's Search for Her Family's Forbidden Nazi Past*. Rowman & Littlefield, 2018.

Lindsey, Hal, and Carole C. Carlson. *The Late Great Planet Earth*. Zondervan, 1971.

Loganbill, Alec. "A Theology of Suffering: Suffering and Martyrdom in Sixteenth-Century Anabaptist Hymnody." *Anabaptist Historians*, February 4, 2021. https://anabaptisthistorians.org/2021/02/04/a-theology-of-suffering-suffering-and-martyrdom-in-sixteenth-century-anabaptist-hymnody/.

Longman, Timothy. *Christianity and Genocide in Rwanda*. Cambridge University Press, 2010.

Lorch, Donatella. "Thousands of Rwanda Dead Wash Down to Lake Victoria." *New York Times*, May 21, 1994. https://www.nytimes.com/1994/05/21/world/thousands-of-rwanda-dead-wash-down-to-lake-victoria.html.

Lyons, Mathew. "The Edict of Thessalonica | History Today." www.historytoday.com, February 2, 2021. https://www.historytoday.com/archive/months-past/edict-thessalonica.

Manchester, Julia. "Analyst Says US Is Most Divided Since Civil War." *The Hill*, October 3, 2018. https://thehill.com/hilltv/what-americas-thinking/409718-analyst-says-the-us-is-the-most-divided-since-the-civl-war/.

Marantz, Andrew. *Antisocial: Online Extremists, Techno-Utopians, and the Hijacking of the American Conversation.* Viking, 2019.

Marion, Jean-Luc. *God Without Being: Hors-Texte 2nd ed. Religion and Postmodernism.* University of Chicago Press, 2012.

Mark, Joshua J. "Two Accounts of Zwingli's Death." *World History Encyclopedia*, January 19, 2022. https://www.worldhistory.org/article/1928/two-accounts-of-zwinglis-death/.

Marmot, Michael. *The Status Syndrome (How Social Standing Affects Our Health and Longevity).* Henry Holt, 2013. Kindle.

Mathison, Keith. "What Is Dispensationalism?" *Ligonier Ministries*, February 2, 2022. https://www.ligonier.org/learn/articles/Dispensationalism.

McAlister, Melani. *The Kingdom of God Has No Borders: A Global History of American Evangelicals.* Oxford University Press, 2018.

McGavran, Donald. "The Homogeneous Unit in Mission Theory." *Papers*, January 1, 2018. https://place.asburyseminary.edu/firstfruitspapers/140/.

McGavran, Donald A., and C. Peter Wagner. *Understanding Church Growth.* Eerdmans, 1974.

Mcintosh, Gary. *Donald A. McGavran: A Biography of the Twentieth Century's Premier Missiologist.* Church Leader Insights, 2015. Kindle.

McKnight, Scot. "Gospeling the Gospel in Acts." *Scriptura* 103 (2013): 30. doi:10.7833/103-0-586.

McKnight, Scot. *The King Jesus Gospel: The Original Good News Revisited.* Zondervan, 2016. Kindle.

McKnight, Scot. *The Second Testament.* IVP, 2023. Kindle.

McKnight, Scot, and Cody Matchett. *Revelation for the Rest of Us.* Zondervan, 2023.

McKnight, Scot, and Joseph B. Modica, eds. *Jesus Is Lord, Caesar Is Not: Evaluating Empire in New Testament Studies.* IVP, 2013. Kindle.

McNall, Joshua M. *The Mosaic of Atonement: An Integrated Approach to Christ's Work.* Zondervan Academic, 2019.

Metaxas, Eric. *Bonhoeffer: Pastor, Martyr, Prophet, Spy*. Thomas Nelson, 2010.

Milbank, John. *Theology and Social Theory: Beyond Secular Reason*. Blackwell Publishing, 1990.

Metz, Johannes Baptist. *Poverty of Spirit*. Paulist Press, 1998.

Mischke, Werner. "The Baseball Try-Out That Forged in Me a Shadow of Shame." *Culture Learner* (blog), June 12, 2012. https://wernermischke.org/2012/06/12/the-baseball-try-out-that-forged-in-me-a-shadow-of-shame.

Mischke, Werner. *The Global Gospel: Achieving Missional Impact in Our Multicultural World*. Mission One, 2015.

Mischke, Werner. "An Honor-Bearing Gospel for Shame-Fueled Crises." *Missio Dei Journal*, March 27, 2021. https://missiodeijournal.com/issues/md-11/authors/md-11-mischke.

Mischke, Werner. "I Pledge Allegiance to 'the Christ:' Conclusion." *Culture Learner* (blog), May 28, 2020. https://wernermischke.org/2020/05/28/i-pledge-allegiance-to-the-christ-conclusion/.

Mischke, Werner. "'Sin' / 'Sins' / 'Sinned' / 'Sinning' in the New Testament (ESV)—an Analysis." December 2, 2022. https://mission1.org/wp-content/uploads/2022/12/Sin-verse-analysis.pdf.

Mischke, Werner, and Bud Houston. "Recognized, Relativized, Reconciled: Nuancing the People Groups Conversation." *Mission Frontiers*, Sept/Oct 2024: 29–33.

Mischke, Werner, and Kristin Caynor. "Ephesians 2 Gospel Project—Does the Atonement Speak to Collective Identity Conflict?" HBI & College Webinar Series. Accessed October 6, 2024. https://www.youtube.com/watch?v=Ozt_Odg92V8&t=2510s.

Modrow, Sebastian, and Melissa Smith. "The Papal Bull Inter Caetera of May 4, 1493." *Doctrine of Discovery*. Accessed September 22, 2023. https://doctrineofdiscovery.org/assets/pdfs/Inter_Caetera_Modrow&Smith.pdf.

Mohindroo, Sanjay K. "The Tragic Story of the Marlboro Man: From Iconic Ad Campaign to Anti-Smoking Advocate." *Medium*, May 14, 2023. https://medium.com/@sanjay.mohindroo66/the-tragic-story-of-the-marlboro-man-from-iconic-ad-campaign-to-anti-smoking-advocate-757ecd56c0c1.

Moreau, Scott. "The Homogeneous Unit Principle." *Academia.edu*, January 1, 2002. https://www.academia.edu/64352099/The_Homogeneous_Unit_Principle.

Nagasawa, Mako A. *Abortion Policy and Christian Social Ethics in the United States*. Wipf & Stock, 2021.

Naím, Moisés. "The Other Deadly Pandemic." *El País* English Edition, February 22, 2023. https://english.elpais.com/opinion/the-global-observer/2023-02-22/the-other-deadly-pandemic.html.

National Institutes of Health. "Will Stress During Pregnancy Affect My Baby?" *US Department of Health and Human Services*. Accessed January 14, 2023. https://www.nichd.nih.gov/health/topics/preconceptioncare/conditioninfo/stress.

Nation, Mark Thiessen. *Discipleship in a World Full of Nazis: Recovering the True Legacy of Dietrich Bonhoeffer*. Wipf and Stock, 2022. Kindle.

Neal, Jeff. "'There Was No Promise Not to Enlarge NATO.'" *Harvard Law Today*. March 16, 2022. https://hls.harvard.edu/today/there-was-no-promise-not-to-enlarge-nato/

Nelson, Caleb. "Millennials & Gen Z Are Leaving Church. What Can We Do?" *Word by Word*, May 27, 2021. https://www.logos.com/grow/millennials-gen-z-leaving-church/.

Neumann, Elizabeth. *Kingdom of Rage: The Rise of Christian Extremism and the Path Back to Peace*. Worthy/Hatchett Book Group, 2024.

Newport, Frank. "Fewer in US Now See Bible as Literal Word of God." *Gallup.com*, July 6, 2022. https://news.gallup.com/poll/394262/fewer-bible-literal-word-god.aspx.

Newton, Michael, ed. "Tacitus, Agricola." *Exploring Celtic Civilizations*. Accessed April 18, 2023. https://exploringcelticciv.web.unc.edu/tacitus-agricola/.

Neyrey, Jerome H. *Honor and Shame in the Gospel of Matthew*. Westminster John Knox Press, 1998.

Nguyen, Minh Ha "Globalization, Urbanization, Migration, and Rethinking the People Group Concept." *EMQ* 56, no. 4 (October–December 2000): 32–35.

Nida, Eugene A. *Customs and Cultures: The Communication of the Christian Faith*. Rev. ed. William Carey Publishing, 1975.

Norris, Richard A. *Gregory of Nyssa Homilies on the Song of Songs*. SBL Press, 2012.

Numbeo. "Crime Comparison between Vancouver and Seattle, WA." *Numbeo.com*, March 23, 2023. https://www.numbeo.com/crime/compare_cities.

On, Keen. "Scott Galloway: Tech Companies Should Be Broken Up." *Literary Hub*, October 11, 2019. https://lithub.com/scott-galloway-tech-companies-should-be-broken-up.

Origen. "Church Fathers: De Principiis, Book II (Origen)." Newadvent.org. *New Advent*. Accessed April 6, 2024. https://www.newadvent.org/fathers/04122.htm.

Orta, Josep Palau. "How Martin Luther Started a Religious Revolution 500 Years Ago." *History*, October 12, 2017. https://www.nationalgeographic.com/history/history-magazine/article/history-martin-luther-religious-revolution.

Ortlund, Gavin. *What It Means to be Protestant: The Case for an Always Reforming Church*. Zondervan, 2024.

Perrin, Nicholas. "The Imperial Cult." In *The World of the New Testament*, edited by Joel B. Green and Lee Martin McDonald, 124–34. Baker Academic, 2013.

Peters, Senator Gary. "The Rising Threat of Domestic Terrorism: A Review of the Federal Response to Domestic Terrorism and the Spread of Extremist Content on Social Media." *A HSGAC Majority Staff Report*, November 2022. https://www.hsgac.senate.gov/wp-content/uploads/imo/media/doc/221116_HSGACMajorityReport_DomesticTerrorism&SocialMedia.pdf.

Pierson, Arthur Tappan. *Evangelistic Work in Principle and Practice*. Baker & Taylor, 1887.

Porterfield, Jason. *100 Early Christian Quotes on Not Killing*. JasonPorterfield.com, n.d. https://jasonporterfield.com/wp-content/uploads/2022/07/100ECQ-Web-Optimized.pdf.

Prior, Karen Swallow. *The Evangelical Imagination: How Stories, Images & Metaphors Created a Culture in Crisis*. Baker Books, 2023.

Raheb, Mitri. *Faith in the Face of Empire: The Bible through Palestinian Eyes*. Orbis, 2014. Kindle.

Rao, Pallavi. "Which Countries Are the Most Polarized?" *Visual Capitalist*, January 18, 2023. https://www.visualcapitalist.com/polarization-across-28-countries/.

Ravitsky, Aviezer. "Shalom: Peace in Hebrew." *My Jewish Learning*. Accessed April 6, 2024. https://www.myjewishlearning.com/article/shalom.

Remnick, David, and Jamie Raskin. *The January 6th Report*. Celadon Books, 2022. Kindle.

Richards, E. Randolph, and Richard James. *Misreading Scripture with Individualist Eyes*. IVP, 2020. Kindle.

Ritchie, David A. *Why Do the Nations Rage: The Demonic Origin of Nationalism*. Wipf & Stock, 2022.

Roberts, Mark D. *Ephesians*. Zondervan, 2016.

Sachs, Jeffrey. "Jeffrey Sachs: The Untold History of the Cold War, CIA Coups Around the World, and COVID's Origin." Interview by Tucker Carlson. *The Tucker Podcast*, May 28, 2024. Audio 0:00–21:04. https://podcasts.apple.com/us/podcast/the-tucker-carlson-show/id1719657632?i=1000657058513.

Said, Edward W. *Culture and Imperialism*. Vintage, 2007. Kindle.

Saiya, Nilay. *The Global Politics of Jesus: A Christian Case for Church-State Separation*. Oxford University Press, 2022. Kindle.

Sanneh, Lamin. *Translating the Message: The Missionary Impact on Culture*. Rev. ed. Orbis, 2009.

Sayegh, Khalil. "This Easter, Gaza's Christian Community Is on the Brink of Extinction." *The New Arab*, March 28, 2024. https://www.newarab.com/opinion/easter-gazas-christian-community-faces-extinction.

Scheff, Thomas, G. Reginald Daniel, and Joseph Sterphone. "Shame and a Theory of War and Violence." *Aggression and Violent Behavior* 39 (March 2018): 109–15. https://doi.org/10.1016/j.avb.2018.02.006.

Scheff, Thomas. "The Ubiquity of Hidden Shame in Modernity." *Cultural Sociology* 8, no. 2 (February 17, 2014): 129–41. https://doi.org/10.1177/1749975513507244.

Sciolino, Anthony J. *The Holocaust, the Church, and the Law of Unintended Consequences: How Christian Anti-Judaism Spawned Nazi Anti-Semitism.* Iuniverse, 2014. Kindle.

Scofield, Cyrus Ingerson, ed. *The Scofield Reference Bible.* Oxford University Press, 1945.

Scribner, Dan. "The Making of Lists." *Evangelical Missions Quarterly* 56, no. 4 (October 2020): 39–42.

Shenk, Wilbert R. *The Challenge of Church Growth.* Institute of Mennonite Studies, 1973.

Shenk, Wilbert R., ed. *Exploring Church Growth.* Wipf and Stock, 2010.

Sherman, Franklin. "Dietrich Bonhoeffer, German Theologian." *Britannica.* April 5, 2024. https://www.britannica.com/biography/Dietrich-Bonhoeffer.

Shirer, William L. *The Rise and Fall of the Third Reich: A History of Nazi Germany (50th Anniversary Edition).* Simon & Schuster, 2011.

Shirk, Adrian. "The Real Marlboro Man." *The Atlantic*, February 17, 2015. https://www.theatlantic.com/business/archive/2015/02/the-real-marlboro-man/385447/.

Sider, Ronald J. "Christian Nonviolence and Church History." *Plough*, March 25, 2020. https://www.plough.com/en/topics/justice/nonviolence/christian-nonviolence-and-church-history.

Smith, Erin A. "The Late Great Planet Earth Made the Apocalypse a Popular Concern." *National Endowment for the Humanities (NEH)*, 2017. https://www.neh.gov/humanities/2017/winter/feature/the-late-great-planet-earth-made-the-apocalypse-popular-concern.

Sommers, Tamler. *Why Honor Matters.* Basic Books, 2018.

Sprinkle, Preston. Exiles: *The Church in the Shadows of Empire.* David C Cook, 2024.

St. Augustine. *The Confessions of Saint Augustine.* Translated by Rex Warner. New American Library, 1963.

St. Cyril of Alexandria. *Commentary on the Twelve Prophets, Vol. 3.* Trans. Robert C. Hill. Catholic University of America Press, 2012.

St. Ignatius. "Church Fathers: Epistle to the Smyrnaeans." www.newadvent.org. *New Advent.* Based on Roberts and Donaldson, *Ante-Nicene Fathers, Vol. 1.* Edited by Alexander Roberts, James Donaldson, and A. Cleveland Coxe. Christian Literature Publishing Co., 1885. Accessed April 5, 2024. https://www.newadvent.org/fathers/0109.htm.

St. Irenaeus, Bishop of Lyon. "The Demonstration of the Apostolic Preaching." *Documenta Catholica Omnia*, March 15, 2021. https://www.documentacatholicaomnia.eu/03d/0130-0202,_Iraeneus,_Demonstration_Of_The_Apostolic_Preaching,_EN.pdf.

Stanford Graduate School of Business. "Chamath Palihapitiya, Founder and CEO Social Capital, on Money as an Instrument of Change." YouTube Video, November 13, 2017. https://www.youtube.com/watch?v=PMotykw0SIk.

Stonestreet, John, and Maria Baer. "Is Genesis Just One of the Many Creation Myths?" Breakpoint. January 31, 2023. https://breakpoint.org/is-genesis-just-one-of-the-many-creation-myths/.

Storr, Will. *Status Game: On Social Position and How We Use It*. HarperCollins, 2021.

Strauss, Barry. *Ten Caesars: Roman Emperors from Augustus to Constantine*. Simon & Schuster, 2019.

Stuhlmacher, Peter. *Reconciliation, Law & Righteousness: Essays in Biblical Theology*. Translated by John Vriend. Fortress, 1986.

Sunstein, Cass R. "The Law of Group Polarization." *Journal of Political Philosophy* 10, no. 2 (June 2002): 175–95.

Sweet, Leonard. *Jesus Human: Primer for a Common Humanity*. Salish Sea Press, 2023. Kindle.

Tacitus. "Annals 15, 44." Prof. K. Dickson, Romans on Christians. *Purdue University*, 2024. https://web.ics.purdue.edu/~kdickson/christians.html.

Taylor, Matthew D. *The Violent Take It by Force: The Christian Movement That Is Threatening Our Democracy*. Fortress, 2024. Kindle.

Taylor, Terry F. "The Influence of Shame on Posttrauma Disorders: Have We Failed to See the Obvious?" *European Journal of Psychotraumatology* 6, no. 6 (September 22, 2015). https://doi.org/10.3402/ejpt.v6.28847.

Ten Elshof, Gregg A. *For Shame: Rediscovering the Virtues of a Maligned Emotion*. Zondervan, 2021.

Tertullian. *De Corona (The Chaplet) in The Complete Works of Tertullian*. Amazon Kindle, 2016.

Thacker, Jason. "Discipled by Algorithms: Where Is 'Big Tech' Leading You?" *Desiring God*, January 7, 2022. https://www.desiringgod.org/articles/discipled-by-algorithms.

The *ESV Study Bible, English Standard Version*. Crossway Bibles, 2008.

Thompson, Curt. "Beauty from Darkness with Curt Thompson." Interview by Cherie Harder. *Trinity Forum Conversations*, December 22, 2022. https://podcasts.apple.com/us/podcast/trinity-forum-conversations/id1554038962?i=1000589980753.

Thompson, Curt. *The Soul of Desire: Discovering the Neuroscience of Longing, Beauty, and Community*. IVP, 2021.

Thurman, Howard. *Jesus and the Disinherited*. Beacon Press, 1976.

Tisby, Jemar. *The Color of Compromise: The Truth about the American Church's Complicity in Racism*. Zondervan, 2019.

Tizon, Al. *Christ among the Classes: The Rich, the Poor, and the Mission of the Church*. Orbis Books, 2023.

UNHCR. "100 Million People Forcibly Displaced." *UNHCR Refugee Statistics*, 2023. https://www.unhcr.org/refugee-statistics/insights/explainers/100-million-forcibly-displaced.html.

United Nations. "A New Era of Conflict and Violence." *United Nations*, 2020. https://www.un.org/en/un75/new-era-conflict-and-violence.

Vaughn, Brad. "Jesus Loved Colonialists. Do We?" *Saving God's Face* (blog), May 14, 2024. https://www.patheos.com/blogs/jacksonwu/2024/06/25/jesus-loved-colonialists-do-we/.

Vaughn, Brad. *One Gospel for All Nations*. William Carey Publishing, 2015.

Vaughn, Brad. *Reading Romans with Eastern Eyes: Honor and Shame in Paul's Message and Mission*. IVP, 2019.

Vaughn, Brad. "A Theology of Locality Embraces the Call to be Present." *Saving God's Face* (blog), July 16, 2024. https://www.patheos.com/blogs/jacksonwu/2024/07/16/a-theology-of-locality-embraces-the-call-to-be-present/.

Veith, Gene Edward. "The Good, the Bad, and the Ugly by Gene Edward Veith." *Ligonier Ministries*, August 1, 2004. https://www.ligonier.org/learn/articles/good-bad-and-ugly.

Volf, Miroslav. *Exclusion and Embrace: A Theological Exploration of Identity, Otherness, and Reconciliation*. Abingdon Press, 2008. Kindle.

Wagner, C. Peter. *Our Kind of People: The Ethical Dimension of Church Growth in America*. John Knox Press, 1978.

Walls, Andrew F. "The Ephesian Moment: At a Crossroads in Christian History." In *The Cross-Cultural Process in Christian History: Studies in the Transmission and Appropriation of Faith*, 72–82. Orbis, 2002.

Ward, Antonia. "ISIS's Social Media Use Poses a Threat to Stability in the Middle East and Africa." *Rand.org*, December 11, 2018. https://www.rand.org/blog/2018/12/isiss-use-of-social-media-still-poses-a-threat-to-stability.html.

Warren, Rick. *The Purpose Driven Church: Growth without Compromising Your Message and Mission*. Zondervan, 2007.

Watkin, Christopher. *Biblical Critical Theory: How the Bible's Unfolding Story Makes Sense of Modern Life and Culture*. Zondervan Academic, 2022.

Wells, Ida. *Crusade for Justice: The Autobiography of Ida B. Wells.* 2nd ed. University of Chicago Press, 2009.

Wengst, Klaus. *Pax Romana and the Peace of Jesus Christ.* SCM Press, 1987.

Whitehead, Andrew L., and Samuel L. Perry. *Taking America Back for God: Christian Nationalism in the United States.* Oxford, 2020.

Wikipedia Contributors. "Compromise of 1877." Wikipedia. Wikimedia Foundation, June 17, 2019. https://en.wikipedia.org/wiki/Compromise_of_1877.

Wildman, Terry M. *First Nations Version: An Indigenous Translation of the New Testament.* IVP, 2021.

Wilkerson, Alissa. "The 'Left Behind' Series Was Just the Latest Way America Prepared for the Rapture." *Washington Post*, July 13, 2016. https://www.washingtonpost.com/news/act-four/wp/2016/07/13/the-left-behind-series-was-just-the-latest-way-america-prepared-for-the-rapture/.

Wilkerson, Isabel. *Caste: The Origins of Our Discontents.* Random House, 2020.

Willard, Dallas. *The Divine Conspiracy: Rediscovering Our Hidden Life in God.* Harper, 2018.

Williams, David. "Reflections on the Homogeneous Unit Principle: Part 2 of 4." *Church Missionary Society*, July 26, 2021. https://www.cms.org.au/reflections-on-the-homogeneous-unit-principle-part-2-of-4/.

Williams, Reggie L. *Bonhoeffer's Black Jesus: Harlem Renaissance Theology and an Ethic of Resistance.* Baylor University Press, 2021. Kindle.

Wink, Walter. *Engaging the Powers, 25th Anniversary Edition.* Fortress, 2017. Kindle.

Wink, Walter. *The Powers That Be: Theology for a New Millennium.* Galilee, 1999.

Winter, Ralph D., and Steven C. Hawthorne. *Perspectives on the World Christian Movement: A Reader.* 4th ed. William Carey Publishing, 2009.

Winter, Ralph W. "Frontier Mission Perspectives." In *Seeds of Promise: World Consultation on Frontier Missions, Edinburgh '80*, edited by Allan Starling. William Carey Library, 1981.

World Population Review. "Prison Population by State 2020." *WorldPopulationReview.com*, 2021. https://worldpopulationreview.com/state-rankings/prison-population-by-state.

Worthen, Molly. *Apostles of Reason: The Crisis of Authority in American Evangelicalism.* Oxford University Press, 2014.

Wright, N. T. *Into the Heart of Romans: A Deep Dive into Paul's Greatest Letter.* Zondervan Academic, 2023. Kindle.

Wright, N. T. *Paul and the Faithfulness of God.* Book II. Parts III and IV. Fortress, 2013. Kindle.

Wright, N. T., and Michael F. Bird. *Jesus and the Powers: Christian Political Witness in an Age of Totalitarian Terror and Dysfunctional Democracies*. Zondervan, 2024.

Wright, N. T., and Michael F. Bird. *The New Testament in Its World: An Introduction to the History, Literature, and Theology of the First Christians*. Zondervan Academic, 2019.

Yee, Tet-Lim N. *Jews, Gentiles and Ethnic Reconciliation: Paul's Jewish Identity and Ephesians*. Cambridge University Press, 2005.

Zank, Michael. "Enuma Elish and Genesis." *Michael Zank, Professor of Religion, Boston University* (blog), September 17, 2017. https://blogs.bu.edu/mzank/2017/09/14/enuma-elish-and-genesis/.

Ziegler, Dominic (a.k.a. Banyan). "India's Caste System Remains Entrenched, 75 years after Independence." *Economist*, September 11, 2021. https://www.economist.com/asia/2021/09/11/indias-caste-system-remains-entrenched-75-years-after-independence.

SCRIPTURE INDEX

Genesis
1:26–28	10, 17, 235
2:23	21
2:25	21
3:11	21
4:5	22
5:3	8
9:6	22
10–11	189
12:1–3	9, 16, 189
31:1	5
37–50	97
38:2	35
38:9–10	35
48:4	189
49:6	5

Exodus
1–15	97
9:13–16	38
15:14–15	38
16:10	5
24:16	5
33:19	5
33:20–23	6
34:29–30	6
34:34	6
40:34	6

Leviticus
18	13
19:28	13
21:4–5	13

Numbers
6:27	70
19:11–16	13

Deuteronomy
4:11	5
5:24	5
15:11–15	12
16:11–12	12
17:18–20	35
17:19	70
24:17–22	12
32:8	70

1 Samuel
8:5	35
8:11–18	35
13	34
17:26	99
23:39	32

2 Samuel
9:11	85
9:13	xxiv
11	33
11:1–4	31
11:6–14	31
11–12	39
11:27	31
12:1	31
12:5	31
12:7	31
12:11	32
12:13	31
12:14	32

1 Kings
2	34
4:20–23	156
5:13–18	156
8:10–11	6
8:12–13	156
8:16	70
9:15–22	156
16:26	35
22:52	35

2 Kings
3:3	35
13:11	35

1 Chronicles
17:7	44
22:10	70

Esther
1–10	97

Job
1–42	97
29:11–16	12
40:10	5

Psalms
2:6–7	70
7:5	5
8:5	5
8:5–8	235
8:6	xxvii
21:5	5
22:23	5
30:12	5
34:5	6
51	32
51:4	33
57:7–11	10
57:8	10
68:18	72
72:4	12
79:9	5
82:1–2	87
82:1, 6	70
86:8–9	70
86:12	5

96:3–14	194	42:16	xxiv	**Amos**	
96:5	194	43:7	5	5:11	12
96:10, 14	194	46:4	xxiv	**Micah**	
115:8	79	46:5	173	4:3–4	85
Proverbs		48:9–11	5	**Habakkuk**	
8:30–31	87	52:1–15	77	2:14	5
10:19	252	52:6	77	2.16	19
14:12	180	52:7	72, 77, 83, 150–51,	**Haggai**	
14:21, 32	12		167, 192, 237, 238	2:7–9	89
17:5	12	52:17	232	2:9	89
19:17	12	55:1–3	79	**Matthew**	
21:13	12	55:19	192	3:7	15
22:9, 16	12	56:3–8	189	4:8	15
28:27	12	57:19	xxiv, 150–51,	4:15–16	16
29:7	12		232, 237	5:2–12	12
31:20	12	58:6–7	12	5:8	14
Isaiah		59:1–21	77	5:11–13	169
3:14–15	12	59:14–17	77	5:21–22	78
4:2	5	60:1–5	89	5:22	233
6:3	6, 244	61:1–2	11	5:43–45	205
6:6	173	62:2	xxiv, 5	8:5–13	165
6:8	77	**Jeremiah**		8:18–22	257
9:5	151	13:16	5	8:19–22	14
9:5–6	150	29:7	166	8:28	13
9:6	151	30:17	xxiv	8:28–34	13
17:4–6	5	48:17–18	5	9:9–10	206
25:3	5	**Ezekiel**		9:11–13	12
25:6	16, 85	1:15–26	6	10:4	206
25:7	67	1:28	6	10:34	167
25:7–8	89	16:49	12	11:12	170
25:8	86, 89	33:1–6	242	11:19	12
35:1–3	5	**Daniel**		11:28–30	245
40:4	97	1–3	97	12:18–21	16
40:11	xxiv	4:1–37	97	13:3–9	88
42:3	88	5:1–31	97	14:24–33	257
42:8	5	7:9–10	55	16:24	97
42:12–13	5	7:13–14	224	16:25	225
		10:13, 20	70		

Scripture Index

17:9	15	**Luke**		19:10	43
20:11–12	xxiv	1:3	34	19:41–44	43
20:16	144	1:51–53	14	20:16–19	15
20:28	226	1:52	97	20:17	97
23:13–29	15	2:32	16	20:19	15
24:4–5	xxiv	2:52	85	22:36	167
25:22–27	180	4:16–21	11	24:21	243
25:31	6	4:38–41	165	24:26	97
25:31–46	206	5:13	12	**John**	
25:40	12	5:14	15	1:1–2	88
26:3–4	15	5:29	206	1:1–3, 8	18
26:52	161, 167	6:15	206	1:14	xxx, 47
28:19	192	6:22	235	2:11	16
Mark		7:3	xxiv	3:13	68
1:16–20	206	7:22	11	3:16	xxiii
1:40–44	165	7:28	97	5:17–19	43
3:18	206	7:39	xxiv, 12	5:41	15
5:1–13	12	8:26–39	13	6:15	15
5:1–20	13, 18, 47	8:27	13	6:55–57	79
5:3–4	13	8:41	13	6:60	15
5:5	13	8:56	15	6:66	15
5:19–20	48	9:26	6	7:37–38	225
7:26	16	9:48	97	8:44	45
7:36	15	10:25–29	249	8:50	15
8:30	15	10:29–37	205	10:10	85
9:35	102	10:36–37	205	10:30	207
10:29–30	xxv	13:30	97	12:27–28	229
10:30	6	14:11	97	13:35	249
10:42–43	173	14:12–24	100	14:9	207
10:43	102	14:16–24	xxiii	14:27	245
11:15–18	189	15:11–32	97, 256	15:4	77
11:17	16	15:28–30	xxiv	16:33	245
12:13	15	16:16	170	17:3	235
14:61–62	224	17:21	181	17:22	xxiv, 7, 9, 16, 249
15:39	243	17:33	97	17:22–23	7
		18:13	38	18:10–11	167
		18:14	97	18–19	229

18:36	161, 180	7:16–18, 20	54	**Galatians**	
19:1–4	229	8:3	235	2:10	249
20:3	34	8:14–17	102	2:11–14	208
20:21	48, 97	8:18	4	2:19–20	54
21:25	34	8:19–21	198	2:20	97
Acts		8:19–23	8	2:23	67
1:18	206	8:21	235	3:22	67
2:8	60	8:29–30	236	3:28	98, 190
4:32–37	61	8:32	254	4:4–5	68
4:34	60	9:33	12	4:8	67
10:1–16	151	10:15	150	5:15–23	80
10:1–48	152, 165	11:1–36	211	6:15	73, 75
10:36	151	15:18–21	196	**Ephesians**	
15:1–41	189	**1 Corinthians**		1–2	xxvii, xxviii
17	8	1:18–25	174	1:10	198, 236, 244
17:6–7	144	1:18–30	181	1:17–18	68
17:29	8	1:25–31	14	1:20–23	69
26:14	244	1:28–30	11	1:21	xxviii, 66
Romans		5:6	63	1:22	72
1:18	8	5:20	102	1:22–23	70
1:20	8	6:15–17	180	1:23	9
1:22	22	6:16–20	49	2	xvii–xviii, xxi, xxviii, xxix, 7
1:23	8, 11, 44, 235	8:5–6	67	2:1	75–76
1:23–24	235	12:19	74	2:1–3	76
1:23–32	235	12:26	49	2:1–6	104
2:7	4, 8	15:34	63	2:1–7	98
2:14	257	15:45	225, 231	2:1–22	71, 98, 104
2:23	44	**2 Corinthians**		2:2	xxviii, 66–67, 70, 83, 149
2:23–24	33, 235	2:5–11	61	2:2–3	71
3:9	67	3:17–18	7	2:3	75
3:13–17	114	3:18	xxx	2:6	8–9, 70, 75–76
3:23	8, 22, 44, 235	4:17	4, 5	2:6	98
5:5	102	5:16	xxiv, 73	2:10	71, 132
5:6–8	11, 47	5:17	75, 236	2:11	98–99, 191
5:8	11	5:18–19	48	2:11–3:19	190
5:12–17	231	12:9	180	2:11–12	9
6:3–5	97	12:10	169, 174		
6:5	76				

2\11–12	75	
2:11–12, 19	98, 102–104	
2:11–16	74–75	
2:11–20	100	
2:11–22	xvii, xxiii, xxix, 75, 121, 191, 208, 211, 219	
2:12	12	
2:12–13	152	
2:12–14	76	
2:13	150, 153, 198, 236–37, 261	
2:13–16	xvii, xxix, 102, 113, 198, 200, 208, 237	
2:13–17	56, 83, 143, 151, 153, 192, 216	
2:13–18	150	
2:13–19	261	
2:14	76, 83, 101, 150, 153, 261	
2:14–15	75	
2:14, 15, 17	xxi, xxviii, 137, 153, 167, 237	
2:14–16	258	
2:14–17	152	
2:15	xxiv, 17, 71, 73, 75, 100, 225, 236, 262	
2:15; 4:24	83	
2:16	136, 151, 153, 261–62	
2:17	xxiii, 72, 77, 150–151, 153, 167, 172, 191–92, 232, 234, 237–38, 262	
2:18	75, 262	
2:19	85, 98, 100, 199, 262	
2:19–20	100	
2:19–22	199	
2:21	258	
2:21–22	75
2:22	75
3:1	143
3:1–3, 13	74
3:1, 6, 8	191
3:6	199
3:6, 10	236
3:8–10	73, 83, 193
3:10	xxviii, 12, 21, 66, 181, 199
3:14	72
3:14–15	21
3:14–19	21
3:14–21	245
3:15	44
3:16	21
3:16–19	21
3:17	77
3:18–19	77
4:1	143
4:2–3	74
4:4–6	258
4:8	72
4:8–10	69
4:9–10	11
4:10	68
4:13	258
4:17–19	76
4:22–24	75
4:24	225, 236
4:25	76
4:28–31	76
4:31	83
5:20	76
6:11	76
6:11–12	77
6:11–17	77

6:12	xxviii, 43, 65–66
6:15	xxiii, 77, 216, 232, 237, 255, 264
6:19–20	143

Philippians

1:11	8
2:5–11	97
2:6–8	68
2:6–11	11
2:9–10	69
3:4–8	102
3:5–6	196, 208
3:8	101
3:9	98

Colossians

1:15	7, 229
1:19–20	198
1:27	9
2:14	79
2:14–15	56
2:20–3:1	73
3:9	75
3:9–12	73

1 Thessalonians

2:12	8

1 Timothy

5:8	117

2 Timothy

3:5	181

Hebrews

1:2–3	70
1:3	7, 18, 207
2:9	4
4:15	43
4:16	100
11:8	257

12:16	180	3:8	13, 39, 43	18:4–5	39
James		4:17	76	19:7	16
1:27	249	**Revelation**		19:9	85
1 Peter		2–3	164	19:11–16	172
2:7	100	3:12	xxiv	20:13–15	38
2:9	16	5, 7	196	21:24–26	189
3:18–19	130	5:9	16, 192	22:1–2	85
5:13	164	5:9–10	189	22:1–3	198
2 Peter		5:10	198	22:16–17	245
1:4	7	7:9	192	22:17	135
2:4	39	17:6	172		
1 John		17–18	164		
3:2	7	17–19	163, 172		

TOPIC INDEX

A

addiction *See* social science concepts
Alberta, Tim   162
Alexander the Great,
  as human ideal   228
allegiance
  oaths of, to gods   144
  pledged to Christ   161
  shifting, from Caesar to Christ   161
  to another King   246
  to Christ   9, 165, 207, 262, 286
  to Christ, relativizes other
    allegiances   287
  to Hitler   204
  to King Jesus   103, 161, 208, 232,
                          234, 236, 261, 263
  transfer of   80
  voluntary vs. coercive   161
Alter, Robert   31, 34
America(n)
  an Ephesian moment?   260
  Christian nationalism
    See Christian nationalism
  decline of religion in   114
  decline of white majority   208
  Dispensationalism   215
  domestic extremists in   113
  exceptionalism   210
  idolatries in   195
  its greatness, how measured?   125
  January 6th, 2021   170
  lynching in   213
  manhood myth of the
    Marlboro Man   227
  political domination in   106
  political violence   214
  poverty in   92
  racial division in   115
  redlining in   92
  rugged individualism   228
  shadow cast across global
    church   196
  shame, silence around   51
  slavery and racism   213–14
  unhealthy divisions in   184
  white evangelicalism in   72
Anabaptist(s)   148
Augustus Caesar.
  See Roman Caesar or Emperor

B

Babylon   6, 38–39, 51, 163–165,
                              172, 180, 203
Barmen Declaration   203
Barth, Karl   12, 203
Bartlotti, Leonard N.   187
Bates, Matthew W   12, 55
Bates, Matthew W.   80, 235, 236
being human
  engaging the powers   82
  foolish in Christ   181
  glory for all peoples   217
  gospeling peace far and near   261
  horror and beauty   135
  in community   62
  lusting for power   166
  Original Glory   17
  seeking glory   8
  sin and shame   26
  status-driven   103
  the group's magnetic pull   120
  under the complexity of sin   45
Berrigan, Daniel   80
Biddle, Mark   34
Bird, Michael F.   143, 165
Bonhoeffer, Dietrich   239, 242,
                246, 248–51, 264, 313, 316

Braithwaite, John   57, 59, 248–49
Brueggemann, Walter   156, 199
Buell, Denise Kimber   71

C

Cahill, Thomas   142, 228
Carroll, James   157
caste   93
Charles, Mark   196, 210
Christ in me, Christ in us
    "in his own image" (imago Dei)   10
Christian nationalism   162, 203, 210
Civil War   211
Coggin, Jamin   208
Cohick, Lynn   98
Cone, James H.   196, 213, 222
Constantine
    See Roman Caesar or Emperor
Cox, Harvey   88

D

Datema, David E.   187, 191–92
David, King
    and Bathsheba   35
    and Goliath   99
    longing for glory   10
    rejected God's glory   44
demonic, the   11, 13, 43, 144, 147, 162
Descartes, René   39
Diocletian
    See Roman Caesar *or* Emperor
Dispensationalism
    and Doctrine of Discovery   209
    John Nelson Darby   211
    Scofield Reference Bible   211
Doctrine of Discovery   210, 215
Donaldson, Terrence L.   147, 157, 166
Driver, John   273, 275, 291

E

Early Christian writings
    Aristides of Athens   146
    Augustine   17, 313
    Basil the Great   146, 175–77
    Clement of Alexandria   146
    Cyprian   222–23
    Cyril of Alexandria   89
    Didascalia Apostolorum   145
    Egyptian Church Order   145
    Eusebius   147, 155–57, 179
    Gregory of Nyssa   7, 17
    Irenaeus of Lyons   72
    John Chrysostom   74, 130, 146, 177, 182
    Justin Martyr   72
    Lactantius   144, 146, 154, 161
    Origen of Alexandria   231
    Tertullian   55, 144–46
    The Didache   221–22
Emerson, Michael O   72, 115, 202
Enuma Elish   87
Escobar, Samuel   161, 164
Evangelical Confession 2024   203

F

Fair Housing Act of 1968   92
Fitch, David   173
Folsom, Marty   12
French, David   224
Fukuyama, Francis   93, 207

G

Germany
    Bonhoeffer *See* Bonhoeffer, Dietrich
    Christianity of, recognized
      by Hitler   204
    German Christian Movement   119
    Hitler *See* Hitler, Adolf

Holocaust, The	42	hiding from	22
like other lands	134	hope of	11–12, 14, 18
Nazi		humanity, crowned with	235
blood and honor	119	in community	21
case history of life together	246	in the Hebrew Scriptures	6
loyalty demanded	203	in the New Testament	8
similar to Rwanda	136	Jesus, our	9, 18
the Holocaust *See* Holocaust, the		longing for	3–4, 10, 26, 78–79, 110, 132, 198
theologizing violence	119	made for	10, 17
Gilligan, James	52, 58	of being human	17
Girard, René	79	of community	61–62
glory	171	of God	3, 6–7, 27, 42, 66, 68, 70, 101, 132, 173, 179, 194, 207, 229
and belonging	110–11, 121	of humanity	21
and peace	3	of Israel	89
and power games	176	of Jesus Christ	xxx, 6, 16, 43, 47, 79, 173, 196, 217, 231
and righteousness	8	of military conquest	146, 228
and shalom	153	of resurrection	231
and shame	62	of Rome	139–140, 143, 172, 180
and status	5, 15, 18, 89–90	of salvation	10
and suffering	4, 74	of the cross	179
and unity	3	of the Father	3, 68
and violence	10, 19, 22, 25, 63	of the Great Feast	86
and wealth	177–78	of the idol	79
as God's offspring	8	of the Lord	xxx, 5, 7
as regal identity	9	of the peoples	189
as relational beauty	3, 5, 19–20, 27	of the Son	6
as status	104	of the world	15, 180
broken by sin	21	original *See* Original Glory	
cloud of	6	ours, in Christ	9, 74, 80, 99, 234
competing for	223	ours, in unity	7–8, 16
degraded	3, 17, 19, 45, 53, 78	restored	98, 236
exchanging God's	11	seeking	4, 8, 15, 66, 76, 78, 101
fallen short of	8, 22, 44	story of his	5, 16, 18, 217, 262
false	76	structures of	67
given us by God	7, 16, 132, 178	to God	7–8
Gk. *doxa*	6		
Heb. *chabod*	5		

Gorman, Michael J. 149
Gorski, Philip S. 162
gospel of peace and gospeling peace
   (Eph 2:17) 151, 167, 234
   and mass violence xxiii
   and our need for status 104
   and the ways of Jesus 166
   as depolarizing dynamic 234
   as evangelistic entry point 234
   as Jesus, True Human Being 231
   as shoes for your feet (Eph 6:15) 232, 237, 264
   Christ's, the mystery of 132
   contra Homogenous Unit Principle 183, 216
   contra 'religion of empire' 160
   core to the gospel 150
   demands sacrifice 80
   eirēnē and *shalom* 153
   euēngelisato eirēnē means "gospeled peace" in Eph 2:17 72
   foretold in Isaiah 149
   for the far off and the near 234
   fulfilling Isaiah's shalom 153
   ignored 56
   ignored in preaching 153
   in early Christianity 169
   In Rwanda, embodied 136
   of King Jesus 93
   preached by Jesus 137, 143, 151, 153, 167, 172, 221
   proclaiming with King Jesus 261
   subverted by empire 161
   the key to being human 232
   utterly new 149
   vertical and horizontal 153, 234
Graham, Billy 55, 152, 162
Great Feast xxiii, 16, 19, 79, 86, 88, 100, 104, 199, 236, 253
Grudem, Wayne 37, 153
Gupta, Nijay 67, 141
Gushee, David P. 225

H

Hawthorne, Steven 3, 5, 16, 189, 194
Heiser, Michael S. 66, 70, 158
Hickel, Jason 163
Hirsch, Alan 37
Hitler, Adolf 119, 133, 203–04
Holocaust, The 42, 126, 133–34
Homogenous Unit Principle 190
honor-status reversal 98
Howard-Brook, Wes 38, 86, 154–157
humanity
   all, under God's judgment 39
   and Adam *See* Appendix 2 295
   and status games 85
   as Christian vocation being for humanity, for the world 234
   as longing for glory 10
   complexity of sin 45
   crowned with glory 235
   enemies of, final judgment 38
   Gk. *anthropos* *See* Appendix 2 295
   great variety of peoples 191
   Gregory of Nyssa, on Christ's humanity 7
   having humanity for 234
   highest form of 225
   inhumanity
      idolatry and oppression 194
      the ancients' cruelty as glory 228
   Jesus
      as True Human Being 231
      fulfilling God's purpose 231
      weakness and dependence 229
Jesus, the new 76

Topic Index

new humanity
  and the full stature of Christ 259
  and the Great Feast 236
  a new divine way of being human 101
  as a wholeness journey together 261
  as depolarization 208
  as foolishness 181
  as God's manifold wisdom 83
  as new sociology 200
  as sidelined truth 56
  Christ in us 98
  contra imperial violence, dominionism 181
  created by Jesus 17
  from new creation 200
  Gk. *kainon anthropon* 75
  healing the pathology of violence 120
  in both Eph 2:15 and 4:24 75
  Jews and gentiles together 101
  new birth and new creation 73
  New Testament people of God 187
  new way of being human xxiv
  now 236
  our united destiny in Christ 193
  relinquishing swords 81
  under another King 246
old humanity 73
  as living in flesh 76
  as living in the world 76
  a way of relating 76
  glory degraded 19
old vs new humanity 76
our Original Glory
  See Original Glory
propensity for group hostility 105
transcendent dignity 43
under Satan's influence 149
violence of, root of 21
Hummel, Daniel G. 212, 215

I

Imes, Carmen Joy 226–27, 232
individualism and collectivism 51
ISIS 94
Israel 211

J

Jenkins, Philip 259
Jennings, Willie James 100, 151
Jesus 193
  King *See* King Jesus
  Lamb of God 16, 72, 85, 164, 172, 189, 198, 262–63
  redefines moral standard 43
  Savior 55, 150, 191, 262
  self-giving love for humanity 42
  Sermon on the Mount 212
  Son of Man 14, 42–43, 224–25
  True Human Being 11, 221, 224, 226, 231, 233–36, 238, 261
John Nelson Darby
  See Dispensationalism
Johnson, Chalmers 243
Jones, Robert P. 208–09
Joshua Project 188, 193
Julius Caesar
  See Roman Caesar or Emperor

K

Kalantzis, George 72, 144
Keener, Craig S. 198, 199
Kierkegaard, Søren 256
King Jesus
  allegiance to, voluntary 161
  and his gospel of peace 234
  gospeling peace 83

gospel of 237
in, new source of honor 104
joining, in his reconciling vocation 231
loyalty to, for shame resilience 101
our host for Great Feast 199
our primary identity in 207
Paul's bold vision of 143
proclaiming a peace treaty 83
ratifies peace between nations 71
satisfies our longing for glory 198
Servant in Isa 52:7 232
subverting violence 231
through, access to God's family 100
under, unity of all peoples 73
ways in violation of 233
with, being truly human 221
King, Martin Luther 222
Kreider, Alan 222

L

Lausanne, 1974 187
Lau, Te-Li 57, 60–61, 248
Lee, Bandy X. 21, 36
Lewis, C. S. 19–20, 26, 65
Lewis, R. W. 193
Lindsey, Hal 212
Luther, Martin 148, 281

M

Marboro Man, the 227
Marion, Jean-Luc 79
Marmot, Michael 90
Matchett, Cody 164–165, 203
McGavran, Donald A. 187, 190
McKnight, Scot 38, 55, 165, 203
Metz, Johannes 229
Milbank, John 86
Moody, D. L. 149, 211, 213, 214
Moses 5–7, 155, 272, 279, 289

N

Nero *See* Roman Caesar or Emperor
Neyrey, Jerome 88, 93, 115
Nida, Eugene 214
Niebuhr, Reinhold 118, 203
Noll, Mark 214

O

Original Glory 17, 19–20, 22, 52, 58, 229, 235, 244
Original Sin 19

P

Padilla, René 187
Pax Christi 146, 167, 179, 182, 267, 268
Pax Christiana xiii, 169, 179, 182, 268, 297
Pax Romana 137, 182, 289
Pax Romana vs. *Pax Christi*: 166
peacemaking 62, 161, 231
peoples
all, at the Great Feast 16
all, recognized 193
all, reconciled 200
all, relativized 198
all, under God's judgment 194
arrogant, brought low 97
biblical basis for 189
conquered, colonialized 209
critiqued by God 46
depolarized 208
desire for recognition 95
far-off and near (Eph 2) 192
gentiles, as many 191–92
gentiles, as monololithic, non-Jews 191
gentile superiority, critiqued 100
gods of the 71
Hittites 33

honor equally available	100	of darkness	43, 47
hostility between	136, 149	of sin under which we live	46
idolatry of	196	of violence, greed, idolatry	158
migration of	261	revealing God's wisdom to	73
mutually exclusive attitudes, destroyed	89	sacrifices to	78
		Son of Man condemned by	230
non-Jewish	149	subverted by Jesus	79, 238
peace treaty, the Lord's	144	with Christ above	71
playing the status game	91	wrestling against	77
sinfulness of	67, 71	Prior, Karen Swallow	162
to all, gospeling peace	237	prison	23–24, 52, 57, 59, 131, 143, 171, 240, 316
unity of, under King Jesus	73		
unreached		Prosperity Gospel	196

R

People Groups (UPGs)	189, 193	
Frontier (FPGs)	193	Rah, Soong-Chan	196, 210
violence of	83	reconciliation	
Perry, Samuel L.	162	across racial divide	152
Pierson, A. T.	214	after genocide	135
Powers and Principalities	82	and repentance	290
and ethnicity	71	by the blood of Christ	261, 282
and the divine council	87	centered in Jesus	207, 208
are anti-God	149	hindered by exceptionalism	210
as understood in ancient world	66	in Christ	287
captives freed from	70	individual and social	153
Christ, seated above	66	in Rwanda	248
deemphasized in the West	66	Jew and gentile	136, 199–200
enslavement to	67	ministry of	48
four texts in Eph		ministry of Jesus	149
1:21	66	new way of being human	198
2:2	70	offering, by the priest	271
3:10	73	of formerly hostile	
6:12	77	groups	83, 121, 127, 136, 261
geographical domain rulership	158	brothers and sisters	274
God's wisdom revealed to	132	personal/vertical	56, 152
hostile, yet nothing	67	racial, a theological necessity	291
in complexity of sin	41	sectional, after Civil War	212
Jesus a problem to	230	social/horizontal	56, 270, 274–75, 278, 285, 289
Jesus overcomes	236		

the Christian path	291	shame	
through atonement	272	being ashamed of shame	53
vertical and horizontal	291	blocks imagination	245
vertical and horizontal, inseparable	287	Cain and Abel	22, 27
		collective	25, 63
reductionism	36–38, 62	cycle of	22, 25, 27, 47–48, 250
retributive vs. restorative justice	57	cycle of, in social systems	47
Richards, Randall	48	David's	44
Ritchie, David A.	162	debilitating, healed by Jesus	13
Roman Caesar or Emperor		defending	56
Augustus	139–40, 142, 144, 228	definition	19
Constantine	144, 147, 157, 175, 179	disintegrative vs reintegrative	57, 63
Diocletian	154, 157	healing of, in community	62
Julius Caesar	137, 228	healthy and appropriate	57
Nero	139	in hiding	21
Roman Empire	149	language of Paul	60–61
Rwanda	80–82, 105, 125, 268	naked and without	21

S

Said, Edward W.	163	narratives	246, 249, 251, 267
Sanneh, Lamin	164	natural, even healthy	19
shame	19	of crucifixion	172
Adam and Eve	22	of God's people	12
and crime	58	of prison system	58
and depression	58	origin of	20
and glory	3, 20	ours, absorbed by Christ	261
and guilt	53, 57, 236, 267	reintegrative	59
and honor	35, 44, 47, 51, 55, 85, 94, 97, 266	resilience	101
		reversal	96
and individualism	48, 56	rooted in glory	20
and Jesus	12, 14, 61, 221	seeking salvation from	78
and sin	26, 44	shaming the strong	181
and social media	59, 111	shaming the wise	14, 181
and stigma	59	telling our stories of	239
and the shameless	63	to glory	231, 248
and violence, trauma	3, 10, 19, 27, 44–45, 47, 230, 266, 267	toxic, in prison system	52
		Shirer, William L.	204
as greatest pain	20	Sider, Ronald J.	149
as symptom of social pathology	56		
asymmetry thesis	57		

sin
- as dehumanizing 43
- complexity of 31, 39, 42
- cosmic and social 42
- David and Bathsheba 35, 46
- definitions 44
- individual 38
- intergenerational 35
- of angels 39
- of Babylon 39
- of empires 38
- of human groups 39
- revealed in narrative 39
- structures of 43
- supernatural 39
- systemic 39, 42

Sinatra, Frank, My Way 228
Smith, Christian 72, 115, 202
social science concepts
- addiction 25, 49, 111, 114, 180, 253
- Ethical Paradox of Group Loyalty 121, 183, 202
- Homogenous Unit Principle 189
- identity and recognition 95, 207
- Law of Group Polarization 111, 200
- Reintegrative Shaming Theory (RST) 61
- trauma 25, 63, 213, 247
  - *See also* violence

Solomon, King 6
Sommers, Tamler 58
Stassen, Glen H. 225
status
- and caste 91
- and health 90
- and identity 59
- and Jesus 15, 18, 221
- and property 61
- and redlining 92
- and social class 89
- and the Great Feast 85
- and vocation, God-given 235
- and wealth 174, 177
- anxiety, hidden power of 92
- as honor 96
- collective 94
- competition 95
- contest, David and Goliath 99
- definition 89
- desire for, and violence 82
- desire for recognition 93
- dominant-group, anxiety 93
- fear of losing it 92
- game, the 15, 90, 181
- Gk. *isothymia*, demanding equal respect 93
- Gk. *megalothymia*, desiring superiority 93
- Gk. *thymos*, craving recognition 93
- glorified, regained 236
- honor, of gentile community 99
- honor, of Jewish community 98
- in deriding others 76
- insider, in Christ 100
- insiders and outsiders 100, 191, 205
- love of, drives humans 93
- majority white 208
- of God's children 263
- of Jesus 227, 229
- of kingship 17
- of nations 93
- of the ministry 78
- of things 89
- of violence—a religion 51
- ours, in Christ 98
- quo, unmasked by Jesus 230
- rearranged by Jesus 14

relativized, by Paul 99
relinquished 80
relinquished by Jesus 227
reversal, Bible motif 95–96, 104
reversal, in Eph 2 98
reversal, of Jesus Christ 97
reversal, personal and social, in Christ 98
reversals, other biblical figures 97
reversal, U-shaped 97
Roman obsession with 100
social 100, 206, 208
source of identity 9
traditional forms, subverted 101
true, with the Father 72
walls, via zoning restrictions 92
we need it 85, 90–91, 104
status of kingship 7
Storr, Will 15, 90
Strauss, Barry 137, 139, 147
Strobel, Kyle 208
subverting
  gospel of peace 161
  insider status 205
  Pax Romana 268
  power and wealth 169
  power narratives 267
  sociologies of shame 267
  traditional beliefs 101
  violence 120, 161, 167, 182, 231, 228, 262
  violence and shame 172
  white supremacy 222
Sunstein, Cass 108, 200
Sweet, Leonard 224–25, 230

T

Ten Elshof, Gregg 57
Thompson, Curt 13, 21, 24, 244
Tisby, Jemar 72
Tolkien, J. R. R. 178
trauma *See* social science concepts

V

Vaughn, Brad xxix, 44, 153, 165, 258
violence
  and shame 48
  Cain and Abel 22, 229
  cycle of 25, 63, 115, 167, 172, 183
  spiritual violence 170
  trauma 26
Volf, Miroslav 42, 118, 172

W

Walls, Andrew 199, 261
Warren, Rick 185
Watkin, Christopher 87
Wells, Ida B 213
Wengst, Klaus 137, 142, 164
Western bias 39, 46, 49, 62
Whitehead, Andrew L. 162
white supremacy 196, 209
Wilkerson, Isabel 91
Williams, Reggie 250
Wink, Walter 38, 51, 86, 224
Winter, Ralph D. 187
Wright, N. T. 43, 143, 165, 199, 225–26, 231
Wright, N. T. and Michael F. Bird 143, 164–65

Y

Yee, Tet-Lim 98

visit us at missionbooks.org

Honor, Shame, and the Gospel:
Reframing Our Message and Ministry

Christopher Flanders and Werner Mischke, editors

This book, with over a dozen practitioners and scholars, highlights the ongoing conversation around the theological and missiological implications of an honorific gospel. Eight illuminating case studies explore ways to make disciples in a diversity of social contexts—for example, East Asian rural, Middle Eastern refugee, African tribal, and Western secular urban.

One Gospel for All Nations:
A Practical Approach to Biblical Contextualization

Brad Vaughn

When the biblical writers explain the gospel, they consistently use a pattern that is both firm and flexible. Vaughn builds on this insight to demonstrate a model of contextualization that starts with interpretation and can be applied in any culture. In the process, he explains practically why we must not choose between the Bible and culture. Contextualization should be practical, not pragmatic; theological, not theoretical.

Unity through Repentance:
The Journey to Wittenberg 2017

Thomas Cogdell

Unity through Repentance is the story of God interrupting the lives and plans of an ordinary couple to invite them into the adventure of a lifetime, gathering all the major streams of Jesus-followers in Wittenberg on the 500th anniversary of the Reformation. As he tells his story, Cogdell emphasizes spiritual formation and conflict resolution underscoring the importance of unity in the body of Christ.

www.ingramcontent.com/pod-product-compliance
Lightning Source LLC
Chambersburg PA
CBHW052131070526
44585CB00017B/1779